D1431733

THE ANNALS
OF
AMERICA

THE ANNALS OF AMERICA

Volume 9

1858 - 1865

The Crisis of the Union

William Benton, *Publisher*

ENCYCLOPÆDIA BRITANNICA, INC.

Chicago London Toronto Geneva Sydney Tokyo Manila

The editors wish to express their gratitude for permission to reprint
material from the following sources:

The Arthur H. Clark Company for Selections 10, 106,
126, 153, from *A Documentary History of American
Industrial Society*, ed. by John R. Commons *et al.*

International Publishers for Selection 131, from *Letters
to Americans 1848-1895*, by Karl Marx and Frederick
Engels, Copyright 1953 by International Publishers.

The Jewish Publication Society of America for Selection 84, from *Three Years in America 1859-1862*, by I.
J. Benjamin, tr. by Charles Reznikoff, Vol. I.

The Macmillan Company for Selection 9, from *The
Diary of George Templeton Strong*, ed. by Allan Nevins
and Milton Halsey Thomas, Vol. II, Copyright 1952
by the Macmillan Company.

Random House, Inc. for Selection 147, from *Great Issues in American History*, ed. by Richard Hofstadter,
Vol. II, © Copyright 1958 by Richard Hofstadter.

The University of Minnesota Press for Selection 79,
from *Land of Their Choice: The Immigrants Write
Home*, ed. by Theodore C. Blegen, Minneapolis: The
University of Minnesota Press, © Copyright 1955 by
the University of Minnesota.

CODED SOURCES IN THIS VOLUME

Ainsworth
[United States War Department] *The War of the Rebellion: A Compilation of the Official Records of the Union and Confederate Armies.* In 4 series. Edited by Fred C. Ainsworth, George B. Davis, Joseph W. Kirkley, Henry M. Lazelle, Leslie J. Perry, and Robert N. Scott. Washington, 1880-1901.

Blegen
Land of Their Choice. Edited by Theodore C. Blegen. Minneapolis, 1955.

Commons
A Documentary History of American Industrial Society. Edited by John R. Commons *et al.* In 10 vols. Cleveland, 1910-1911.

Globe
Congressional Globe. A record of the proceedings of Congress from 1833 to 1873, arranged by number of Congress and by session. In 46 vols. Washington, 1834-1873.

McPherson
The Political History of the United States of America, During the Great Rebellion, From November 6, 1860, to July 4, 1864; etc., etc. Edited by Edward McPherson. Washington, 1864.

Moore
The Rebellion Record: A Diary of American Events, with Documents, Narratives, Illustrative Incidents, Poetry, etc., etc. Edited by Frank Moore. In 11 vols. New York, 1861-1868. Supplement, Volume 1, 1864.

Nicolay-Hay
Complete Works of Abraham Lincoln. Edited by John G. Nicolay and John Hay. New and enlarged edition in 12 vols. New York, 1905.

PRFA
[United States Department of State] *Papers Relating to Foreign Affairs.* Compiled annually since 1861 except for 1869 with supplements issued periodically. Title changed to *Papers Relating to Foreign Relations of the United States* in 1870 and to *Foreign Relations of the United States* in 1947. Washington, 1862 *et seq.*

Richardson
A Compilation of the Messages and Papers of the Presidents 1789-1897. Edited by James D. Richardson. In 10 vols. Washington, 1896-1899.

Statutes
The Public Statutes at Large of the United States of America from the Organization of the Government in 1789, etc., etc. In 79 vols. as of August 1966. 1845 *et seq.* Vols. 12, 13 edited by George P. Sanger. Boston, 1865, 1866.

Contents

1861 - 1864

1862

1863

1864

1865

Index of Authors, 640

THE CRISIS OF THE UNION

In Pictures

Pre-War Promise 111-120

Behind the political debate and maneuver in Washington and elsewhere, the country was occupied with the usual business of getting on. Recent economic improvement, considered by itself, seemed to foster an optimism about the future. Individuals conducted their lives, not on the basis of impending doom, but on the assumption that the world would continue as always.

Irrepressible Conflict 177-186

In contrast with the well-being that seemed to be implied in mansion houses and baseball games, political events rapidly outpaced the politicians' ability to compromise.
It became increasingly clear that the election of 1860 would decide the question of union or disunion.

The War, 1861-1863 283-294

With the election of Lincoln, and the South's belief that it had no choice left but secession, the long-standing conflict entered its military phase. The first engagements, tentative and inconclusive, were primarily useful in identifying the competent military leaders.

The Home Front 349-362

The Civil War was a "total war," involving the entire populations
and economic resources of the belligerents fully as much as the
soldiers. As a result, the success of the war effort depended in
large degree on the support and sacrifice of the people at home.

A Slow Death 443-454

With huge losses on both sides, the war dragged on through 1864.
The South was openly on the defensive, and the costly campaigns
in Georgia and Virginia effectively destroyed the Confederacy's
ability to continue. In April 1865 it ended at Appomattox.

Wartime Politics 503-516

The political conduct of the war was often more difficult than
the military, for the political leaders often had more enemies.
Lincoln was surrounded by intriguers and ambitious men in his
Cabinet and in Congress. Davis had to contend with a political
structure totally unsuited to efficient mobilization.

The Union Restored 583-592

The end of the war was not the end of the problems of North-South
political relationships; indeed, it inaugurated a host of new problems.
The loss of Lincoln was truly a loss to the entire nation, for both
his moderating influence and his understanding of the deep issues
at stake were largely lacking in his rivals and successors.

Introduction

The American Civil War began at 4:30 A.M. on April 12, 1861, when Confederate guns in Charleston Harbor began to fire on Fort Sumter, and ended (for all intents and purposes) at about 1:30 P.M. on April 9, 1865, when Generals Grant and Lee met in a home in Appomattox Court House and agreed to terms for the surrender of the Army of Northern Virginia. Thus the war lasted almost exactly four years. But preparations had been making for it during eight decades before 1861, as even the most casual reader of the earlier volumes of the *Annals* will have long since seen. And the echoes of the war were heard for a century after, as the reader who peruses the following volumes will also discover.

In one sense, indeed, all of American history led up to the Civil War, just as most of our history since 1865 followed from it — or at least was affected by it. Since this is true it is impossible in this place to "sum up" the war, to state its causes exhaustively or to trace all of its effects. Nor is it desirable, perhaps, to single out one event or series of events as having special meaning or relevance for an understanding of the conflict. From one point of view, the Civil War cannot be fully understood any more than can any fraternal struggle. Why do brothers fight? An adequate answer would involve no less than a full scale theory of human nature. From another point of view, there is no problem at all. There were thirty-four states, and eleven of them seceded. The remaining twenty-three were not going to let that happen, and they did not.

One could almost stop there, except that there is one truth about the Civil War that is sometimes obscured nowadays by our modern insistence on the "hard facts" of history. The Civil War was a potent producer of myths, which is one reason why our memories of the conflict are on the one hand so full of nostalgia, and on the other hand so full of bitterness. Above all, the war produced far more than its share of American heroes and villains — quasimythological figures that, already larger than life, seem to loom even larger as the years go by.

Generals, politicians, sailors, poets, women — one could make a long list in each category, and then find other categories, too. Men on both sides served and fought with sincere devotion. Men on both sides cheated their governments and betrayed their friends. Battles were brilliantly won — and fumblingly lost. Terrible mistakes were made by leaders — and by followers. There was much cruelty, as there always is in war, and there was much love and sacrifice, as is also true of all wars. There were many, many stories, and not even a quarter of the good ones have yet been told. There were many figures whom we do not want to forget.

Let us remember three. John Brown was born near Torrington, Connecticut, in 1800. By the 1850s, like many of his neighbors in western New England, he was a staunch Abolitionist. Unlike them, Brown was also mad. He was deeply involved in antislavery agitation in Kansas in 1856, and at two curiously named Kansas towns, Pottawatomie and Osawatomie, he gained a reputation as an extremist of the first rank. He next conceived a plan for a new state in the mountains of western Virginia as a refuge for free Negroes and as a base from which to organize a general slave uprising. He received financial support from Northern Abolitionists who probably did not know what he was about and, having gathered a small troop that included several of his sons and five Negroes, seized the government arsenal at Harpers Ferry, Virginia (now West Virginia), on the night of October 16-17, 1859. He was overpowered by a government force commanded by Colonel Robert E. Lee, imprisoned, and tried for treason. He was convicted, of course, and was hanged on December 2, 1859. (For selections by or about Brown, see numbers 23-25.)

The affair terrified and outraged the South, which had long feared slave insurrections and now asserted that the madman Brown was typical of all Northern Abolitionists. Northern official opinion was also horrified. But Emerson called him "that new saint, than whom nothing purer or more brave was ever led by love of men into conflict and death." Thoreau, referring in his fervent *Plea for Captain John Brown* to his subject's lack of formal education, epitomized him in a ringing sentence: "He would have left a Greek accent standing the wrong way, and righted up a falling man." And the ordinary soldiers of the Union immortalized him, singing slowly and softly as they marched to and from battle:

> John Brown's body lies a-mould'ring in his grave,
> But his soul goes marching on.

Robert E. Lee was born in 1807, the scion of one of Virginia's oldest and most distinguished families. He graduated from West Point in 1829 (he was its superintendent in 1852) and remained in the Army, serving on various frontiers, in the Mexican War, and in Texas, and was in 1861 probably the most capable U.S. officer. Indeed, he was offered the command of the Union Army, but he refused it. His decision, like that of many other Americans, was made only with great difficulty.

He wrote to one of his sons in January 1861. "Secession," he said, "is nothing but revolution." He pointed out that the framers would not have devoted so much care to the formation of the Constitution if it was intended to be broken "by any member of the Confederacy at will." And he went on: "In 1808, when New England states resisted Mr. Jefferson's embargo law, and the Hartford Convention assembled, secession was termed treason by Virginian statesmen; what can it be now?"

These were strong arguments for loyalty, and with Lee, if not with others, they almost won the day. But there were arguments on the other side, too. Lee summed them up in the same letter: "Still, a Union that can only be maintained by swords and bayonets, and in which strife and civil war are to take the place of brotherly love and kindness, has no charm for me. If the Union is dissolved, the government disrupted, I shall return to my native state and share the miseries of my people. Save in her defense, I will draw my sword no more."

He chose Virginia, in other words, and not the United States, and became probably the most distinguished soldier of the war — a statement that no Union general, certainly not his great adversary, Grant, would have disputed. After the war Grant was elected President of the United States; Lee was made president of Washington College, which changed its name to Washington and Lee, and devoted himself to persuading his fellow Virginians to accept the Union. These efforts were largely in vain. He died in 1870. "He was a Caesar," said a eulogist, "without his ambition, a Frederick without his tyranny, a Napoleon without his selfishness, and a Washington without his reward." (For selections by or about Lee, see numbers 51, 99, 140-141, and 150.)

Abraham Lincoln was born in Kentucky in 1809, went to Illinois with his family while still a child, served in the Illinois legislature and in Congress, practised law with some but not notable success, and was elected President of the United States in 1860. Southerners had warned that his election would lead to the disruption of the Union, and they were as good as their word; Lincoln refused to accept secession, and the war began.

Lincoln was of course far from being unknown, even in the East, else he could not have been nominated; but almost nobody except his closest friends knew what a candidate had been chosen, or what a leader their man would be. It is possible, indeed, that Lincoln did not know it himself. He rose to occasion after occasion, always surprising his associates by his intelligence, his political skill, his strength of purpose, and — many people said it — the beauty of his character.

Alone, these would probably not have been enough. Lincoln also brought to his task a rhetorical gift — in the highest sense of the term — that, in the end, had no less an effect than the reforging of the American Union. Over and over Lincoln found the right words — the words that said what millions felt, but what they could not say themselves. We tend to understand the Civil War as Lincoln understood it, because of the things he said about it; and we often forget that its meaning might now be much different, as it might have been much different then, if it had not been for his shaping intellect. A case in point is his insistence throughout the conflict that it was a war primarily about the Union, and not about slavery. Even so, Lincoln could be seemingly inconsistent, and recognize, sooner and more fully than anyone else did, that the Emancipation Proclamation — though in fact it freed no slaves — would have an effect that a dozen victories could not have had: that is, of enlisting the sympathy of European liberal and humanitarian opinion on the side of the North.

There was more to his vision, of course, than mere expediency. The political idea of the Union, and the moral idea of emancipation from slavery, added up to more, for Lincoln, than they did for most of his contemporaries. In this case, two plus two, to take a homely example, was somehow, magically, even mystically, more than four. What it added up to, no one has ever expressed so well as Lincoln himself, in the ten sentences that he delivered at the dedication of the Union cemetery at Gettysburg, on November 19, 1863. It was he, and he almost alone before he said it, who realized that the Civil War was ultimately a test not of the power of industrial organization, not of the efficacy of the federal system, not of the legitimacy or illegitimacy of a society based on slavery, but instead of the viability of democracy — of government, as he put it, of the people, by the people, for the people. Victory in the war, he claimed, would insure that such a government would endure. Defeat would mean the end of democracy, not only in America but also in the world.

Lincoln was assassinated by John Wilkes Booth at Ford's Theatre in Washington on the evening of April 14, 1865 — Good Friday; he died the next morning. Gideon Welles, the secretary of the navy, was present and described the event in his *Diary.* "I went after breakfast to the Executive Mansion," Welles wrote. "There was a cheerless cold rain and everything seemed gloomy. On the Avenue in front of the White House were several hundred colored people, mostly women and children, weeping and wailing their loss. This crowd did not appear to diminish through the whole of that cold, wet day; they seemed not to know what was to be their fate since their great benefactor was dead, and their hopeless grief affected me more than almost anything else, although strong and brave men wept when I met them." (For selections by or about Lincoln, see numbers 1-2, 20, 30, 49-50, 53, 58, 67, 75-76, 87-88, 90, 98, 103, 107, 110, 114, 128, 131, 136, and 142-143.)

This volume of the *Annals* contains more selections — 159 — than any other, and since the volume covers a period of only eight years it shows forth the richness and diversity of American life in that period with considerable effectiveness. The topics with which the selections deal are very numerous, but half a dozen or so demand special mention here.

First and foremost, of course, is the war itself — the actual fighting, the talk about it, the attempts, before 1861, to avoid it, and the attempts, after April 1865, to bind up the wounds it had inflicted. Altogether, some seventy-five selections in the volume deal with the desperate, frustrating efforts to produce still another compromise after the Dred Scott decision had invalidated that of 1820, and the Kansas question that of 1850; with the onset of the war, which began almost as a lark but soon settled down to the bitter, bloody conflict that endured so much longer than anyone expected; and with the efforts during and after the war, efforts that were almost as frustrating as those before it, to restore the Union and to reconstruct the South. Many of these last selections are referred to in the Introduction to Volume 10 and so need no reference here. But the reader should take special note of many of the others.

Selections 1 and 2, for example, show Lincoln at his best as a master of political oratory. Selection 2, which includes a number of passages from the famous series of debates between him and Senator Douglas, is particularly notable in this regard. Their subject, essentially, was the Union, and the essential question was how to save it. Lincoln addressed himself to the same question in many later speeches, among them the great Address at Cooper Union (Selection 30) and the First Inaugural Address (Selection 49). But others, too, were almost equally anxious to save the Union, for example Senator John J. Crittenden of Kentucky (see Selections 40 and 48) and Alexander H. Stephens of Georgia (see Selection 37). Both men, significantly, were Southerners; Stephens later served as vice-president of the Confederacy.

There were many, however, who either wanted to destroy the Union or did not care whether it was saved or not. In the former class belonged those Southerners who advocated the secession of their states (see especially Selections 37-38 and 44-46), but it should not be forgotten that some Northerners, too, urged secession (see Selections 18 and 43), while others agreed with the sentiments expressed by General Winfield Scott in a letter to Secretary of State William H. Seward: "Say to the seceded states, 'Wayward sisters, depart in peace.'"

The war came, bringing with it trouble and death, and the destruction of the South's way of life. It was perhaps the last that had been least expected; the bafflement of many in the South is well expressed in the *Diary* of Mary Boykin Chesnut, passages from which, extending over several years of the war, are reprinted as Selection 62. There were not only bafflement and confusion but also spies (see Selection 68), and economic problems (see Selections 70, 82, 105, 111, and 115), and censorship (see Selections 91 and 92), and a general abridgment of civil rights in both North and South (see Selections 57, 94, and 119). And then there were the cries of the wounded and the groans of the dying (see Selections 99, 121, and 123).

Some of the war's results were less somber than these. The nation as a whole, but especially the North, found itself surging forward, as the country always has done during wartime, along the road of technical progress, and the volume contains a number of selections (see numbers 4, 13, 16, 21, 33, 61, 104, and 155) that reflect, in one way or another, the changes that new inventions were bringing about. The greatest change of all — the change in the North from a primarily agricultural to a primarily industrial economy — is not much mentioned, partly because it did not occur all at once, and partly because people at the time were not really aware of it. But Senator John Sherman of Ohio gives some hint, in Selection 154, of how they felt about what was going on.

One of the best, and most memorable, things to come out of the war was the flood of poetry and songs. Poets with established reputations produced important new work — for example, Longfellow (see Selections 29 and 116) and Whittier (see Selections 78 and 159). Whitman had published the first edition of *Leaves of Grass* in 1855, but the war can be said to have made him a great poet, if it did not make him a poet in the first place. (See, for example, Selection 138, one of a series of touching vignettes that he produced during the war years.) In addition, the war seems to have made at least three poets almost out of whole cloth. Herman Melville (see Selection 35) never came to much in the poetical line — his genius was in prose — and Henry Timrod (see Selections 46 and 124) was hindered by his entire devotion to a single section, the South. But a strange little recluse in Amherst, Massachusetts, Emily Dickinson (see Selection 85), read all the papers and was inspired to produce a vast number of unforgettable lyrics that are among the nation's richest literary treasures. She is not merely America's greatest woman poet; she is one of its greatest poets, period.

Finally, this volume of the *Annals* contains no less than fifteen songs, most of them dealing with the war and its events (see Selections 25-26, 54, 57, 60, 64, 73, 80, 89, 113, 120, 122, and 135). Some of them are cheery and patriotic, some are mournful and sad, some are irreverent and cynical about military glory, some express the all but inexpressible joy of the Negro with his new freedom. One, however, seemed to sum up the feelings of a great part of the country better than any other. Julia Ward Howe wrote it very early one morning in January 1862. Everyone knows the first verse, which went like this:

> Mine eyes have seen the glory of the coming of the Lord;
> He is trampling out the vintage where the grapes of wrath are stored;
> He hath loosed the fateful lightning of His terrible swift sword:
> > His truth is marching on.

Chronology: 1858-1865

1858

Feb. 2. President Buchanan supports the Lecompton constitution and recommends in submitting it to Congress that Kansas be admitted as a slave state. **Feb. 3.** Stephen A. Douglas leads revolt of Northern Democrats against Buchanan. **March 23.** In spite of Douglas, Senate votes to admit Kansas under constitution, but House does not. **April 23.** Compromise measure sponsored by the administration is submitted to Congress; it gives Kansas a choice of accepting the constitution and becoming a state or rejecting it and remaining a territory. **May 4.** The measure is passed over Douglas' opposition. Kansas argument has given Republicans a strong campaign issue and left the Democratic split unhealed; Buchanan has lost the support of the North, and Douglas has lost the South.

May 11. Minnesota is admitted to the Union as thirty-second state and seventeenth free state. Its population is about 150,000, many of these settlers having arrived since completion of railroads to Mississippi River.

June 16. Abraham Lincoln makes "House Divided" speech at Illinois Republican state convention that nominates him for U.S. senator; the "house divided" idea from St. Mark has already been used several times in connection with U.S. controversy over slavery.

July 24. Lincoln challenges Stephen A. Douglas, Democratic candidate, to public debates as part of campaign for election to U.S. Senate. **Aug. 21-Oct. 15.** Debates are held in seven Illinois cities; they are concerned with slavery and its moral, legal, political, and governmental aspects; although locally held, they draw attention of entire U.S. In the election, Lincoln wins a majority of the popular vote, but because of inequities of districting Douglas is reelected by the state legislature.

Oct. 25. Senator William H. Seward of New York, leading Republican presidential aspirant, pronounces the slavery issue an "irrepressible conflict" in speech at Rochester. The remark is ultimately fatal to Seward's presidential ambitions, since it marks him as an antislavery radical.

October-November. In autumn elections, Republicans carry all Northern states except Indiana and Illinois and gain 18 seats in Congress; new House of Representatives has a majority of Republicans and Democrats who are opposed to President Buchanan's Kansas policy.

Business depression that has continued since financial panic of 1857 is over by end of the year, when a period of prosperity begins.

Macy's department store is established in New York City. Its successful use on a large scale of a fixed-price policy, developed in smaller New York stores since 1840, establishes an American retail sales custom.

Oliver Wendell Holmes publishes his witty, conversational volume *The Autocrat of the Breakfast-Table*, followed in later years by *The Professor at the Breakfast-Table* and *The Poet at the Breakfast-Table*; initially, all appeared as serials. Henry Wadsworth Longfellow publishes *The Courtship of Miles Standish*, a long narrative poem in the same meter as *Evangeline*; it is a love story based on a traditional Pilgrim triangle.

1858 - 1859

1858. Rush of gold seekers to Colorado starts when gold is discovered near present-day Denver, although amount of gold is small; slogan of the time is "Pikes Peak or bust!" **May 6, 1859.** Rush increases when first gold-bearing vein is found in Colorado. **June.** Comstock Lode is discovered in Virginia City, Nevada; one of the world's richest deposits, it yields $300 million of gold and silver in following 20 years.

1859

Feb. 14. Oregon is admitted to the Union as the thirty-third state, and eighteenth free state; population is about 50,000.

May 9-19. Southern Commercial Convention at Vicksburg, Mississippi, advocates repeal of U.S. laws prohibiting importation of slaves.

Aug. 27. Edwin L. Drake, drilling with steam-operated rig, finds oil near Titusville, Pennsylvania, marking beginning of large-scale petroleum industry. Petroleum rapidly replaces whale oil as a lamp fuel.

Oct. 16. Abolitionist John Brown,

hoping to inspire a general slave insurrection and backed by six prominent Northerners, leads 18 of his 21 men, including 5 Negroes, in seizure of U.S. arsenal at Harpers Ferry, Virginia; he takes about 60 hostages and is able to hold off local militia, but no Negroes arrive to support him. **Oct. 18.** He surrenders to small force of U.S. Marines under Colonel Robert E. Lee; Brown is wounded, and 10 men, including 2 of his sons, are dead. **Dec. 2.** Brown is hanged after trial and conviction on charges of treason and conspiring with slaves to commit murder. Six of his men are hanged later. The raid spreads alarm throughout the South, and Ralph Waldo Emerson says: "He will make the gallows as glorious as the cross."

Dec. 19. President Buchanan's message to Congress affirms U.S. commitment to enforce slave importation laws, but administration also provides for protection of U.S. merchant ships from search, which allows foreign ships illegally flying U.S. flag to avoid British antislavery patrol of African coast.

Cooper Union, institute mainly for adult education, is established in New York City by Peter Cooper, pioneer industrialist and inventor, "for the advancement of science and art."

1860

Feb. 22. Strike of 20,000 New England shoe-industry workers, including many women, wins higher wages and demonstrates power of industry-wide protest.

Feb. 27. Abraham Lincoln speaks at Cooper Union in New York City, his first important appearance in the East; he appeals for understanding between North and South and criticizes extremists of both sections.

May 9. Constitutional Union Party, made up of combination of remnants of Whig and Know-Nothing parties, nominates John Bell of Tennessee for President and Edward Everett of Massachusetts for Vice-President; platform criticizes sectionalism and calls for "enforcement of the laws" of the Constitution. May 18. Abraham Lincoln of Illinois, regarded as a moderate on the slavery question, is nominated by the Republicans at Chicago convention; Hannibal Hamlin of Maine is nominated for Vice-President. Well-written platform is planned to win radicals as well as conservatives of West and East; it supports principles of Wilmot Proviso, domestic improvements, liberal immigration laws, and industrial development.

June 18. Democrats nominate Stephen A. Douglas for President on platform that supports territorial right to choose slavery without intervention by Congress. June 28. Radical delegates from eight Southern states bolt the party and nominate John C. Breckinridge of Kentucky; their platform supports territorial slavery.

Nov. 6. Abraham Lincoln is elected sixteenth President of the United States with 1,866,000 votes to 1,383,000 for Douglas, 848,000 for Breckinridge, and 593,000 for Bell. Vote is almost completely sectional: electoral vote is Lincoln, 180 (18 free states); Breckinridge, 72 (11 slave states); Bell, 39 (3 border slave states); and Douglas, 12 (Missouri and 3 New Jersey votes). Hannibal Hamlin is elected Vice-President.

Nov. 10. On receiving news of Lincoln's election, South Carolina legislature calls special state convention to meet at Columbia on December 20.

Dec. 3. President Buchanan in his State of the Union message decries disruption of the Union but declares, after consultation with the attorney general, that the federal government has no legal power to prevent it by force.

Dec. 18. Senator John J. Crittenden of Kentucky offers resolution in attempt to conciliate South; it calls for recognition of slavery everywhere south of 36°30′ parallel. Dec. 31. Senate committee, urged by President-elect Lincoln, rejects resolution on the ground that its principle has been repudiated in the recent election.

Dec. 20. South Carolina secedes from the Union by unanimous vote at special convention. Dec. 24. Convention issues "Declaration of Immediate Causes," which affirms right of state sovereignty, condemns the North's attack on slavery, and refuses to be governed by a President who is hostile to slavery.

Oliver F. Winchester of New Haven, Connecticut, patents lever-action repeating rifle, first of many Winchesters; with superior manufacturing capacity of North, weapon gives important arms advantage in ensuing war.

1860 - 1861

April 3, 1860. Pony Express begins fast overland mail service from St. Joseph, Missouri, to Sacramento, California, a distance of more than 1,900 miles. Ten-day service to Sacramento is frequently achieved by riders changing horses at 157 stations 7 to 20 miles apart; fastest time under emergency circumstances is seven days, seven hours. Oct. 24, 1861. Pony Express is discontinued with completion of transcontinental telegraph. A financial failure, it has proved valuable at critical period in informing West Coast of news from Washington.

Dec. 30, 1860-Feb. 16, 1861. Federal arsenals and forts are seized by Southern state troops in South Carolina, Georgia, Alabama, Florida, Louisiana, Arkansas, and Texas. All these states eventually secede; most occupy federal property before formal secession occurs.

1861

Jan. 9. President Buchanan attempts to send reinforcements and provisions to federal garrison at Fort Sumter in Charleston Harbor, South Carolina. Unarmed supply vessel is repelled by cannonade from South Carolina batteries.

Jan. 9-Feb. 1. Six more Southern states secede from the Union: Mississippi, Florida, Alabama, Georgia, Louisiana, and Texas; all cite interference of North with their "institutions" as reason; secessionists are jubilant, but feeling in Alabama and Georgia is moderate and vote on measure almost fails to pass. Virginia, Arkansas, Tennessee, and North Carolina do not secede at this time but warn against federal interference with any state.

Jan. 29. Kansas is admitted to the Union as thirty-fourth state and nineteenth free state; its population is 107,000.

Feb. 4-23. Twenty-one Northern, Border, and Southern states send representatives to Washington, D.C., peace conference called by Virginia. Proposal agreed on is almost the same as Crittenden Compromise. President-elect Lincoln, still in Springfield, Illinois, advises against measure; Senate committee rejects it on eve of inauguration.

Feb. 4-March 11. Seven seceded states, aware of necessity for central government, send delegates to Montgomery, Alabama, to form new Southern union. **Feb. 8.** Provisional government is set up for Confederate States of America. **Feb. 9.** Jefferson Davis of Mississippi is elected President and Alexander H. Stephens of Georgia (who has three months earlier publicly opposed secession) Vice-President for six-year terms.

February. Henry Timrod of South Carolina publishes his ode "Ethnogenesis," which expresses hope for a Southern civilization and, with later passionate war poems, earns him the title of "the laureate of the Confederacy."

March 2. Congress reestablishes protection of U.S. industry by enacting Morrill Tariff, with duties on specific import items instead of on the value of imported goods, at the same time raising duties to 10 percent. Policy continues, with a gradual rise in duties to 47 percent average, until 1870.

March 4. Abraham Lincoln is inaugurated President of the U.S. His inaugural address asserts that the Union is indestructible, urges reconciliation of North and South, denies any intention of using force anywhere except to occupy government property, and reminds South that without an aggressor there can be no conflict.

March 5. President Lincoln discovers that garrison at Fort Sumter will be starved out if not provisioned. **April 6.** After long hesitation, and faced with the dilemma of risking civil war or conceding weakness of the federal government, Lincoln decides (after advising South Carolina governor that no arms are involved) to send an unsupported supply expedition. **April 12.** Without waiting for arrival of expedition, Confederates open fire on the fort, which is forced to surrender on April 14.

March 11. Permanent constitution of the Confederate States of America is adopted; it resembles U.S. Constitution but forbids enactment by Congress of a protective tariff or measures for internal improvements and requires a two-thirds vote of the House of

Representatives for any appropriation. African slave trade is prohibited (to appease France and Britain), but no "law denying or impairing the right of property in Negro slaves" is allowed.

April 15. President Lincoln, in effort to minimize Fort Sumter attack, calls for 75,000 militia to suppress "insurrection." **April 17-May 20.** Free states respond, but move provokes remaining Southern states — Virginia, Arkansas, Tennessee, and North Carolina — to secede and join the Confederacy. **May 21.** Richmond, Virginia, is chosen as capital of the Confederacy. Some of the ablest officers of the U.S. Army resign, including Robert E. Lee of Virginia, who previously has been offered the post of commander of the Union Army.

April 19. President Lincoln proclaims blockade of Southern ports; the Union has few effective naval ships but possesses the industrial capacity to build more, and the Confederacy has few major ports to be closed. Dependent on the North and Europe for manufactured goods, the Confederacy is gradually strangled by the increasingly effective blockade and eventual capture of its ports by Union armies. In the first year of the blockade, less than one-seventh as many ships reach Southern ports as in 1860.

May 3. The President calls for 42,000 volunteers to serve three-year enlistments and 40,000 additional men for regular Army and Navy.

May-July. Power of the President to suspend habeas corpus privilege or delegate this power to military commanders is challenged early in war. In the *Ex parte Merryman* case, a civilian Maryland secessionist protesting his arrest by Union military forces, Chief Justice Roger B. Taney, sitting as judge of a federal circuit court, holds that

the power to suspend constitutional rights belongs only to Congress, even in wartime. **July.** President Lincoln justifies action of his administration in a message to Congress, which votes approval. Power of military agencies over civilians, both near the fighting and in the interior of the Union, is questioned throughout the war and Reconstruction era.

June 11. Western counties of Virginia, in bitter conflict with eastern areas from colonial times, form provisional state government loyal to the Union shortly after Virginia secedes. **Nov.-Feb. 1862.** Constitution is prepared, changing proposed state name Kanawha (place of white stone) to West Virginia.

July 21. First Battle of Bull Run, at Manassas Junction, Virginia, appears at first to be Union victory, but Confederate reinforcements beat back Union troops in a disorganized retreat to Washington. Confederate General Thomas J. Jackson makes a gallant stand, earning the nickname "Stonewall." As Confederate success exposes Washington to threat of capture, the North realizes that war effort must be serious and may be protracted. **July 24.** President Lincoln replaces General Irvin McDowell with Major General George B. McClellan, who is later made general in chief of the Union Army. Armies in the East on both sides are mostly inactive for months afterward, devoting themselves to organization, equipment, and training.

Aug. 5. First federal income tax of 3 percent on incomes over $800 is enacted; increased in following years, it supplies about one-fifth of federal government revenues by 1865, but the war is financed chiefly by loans and currency issues.

Oct. 24. First transcontinental telegraph begins operation. Continuation of existing line that reaches from East Coast to Missouri has been authorized by Congress in June 1860; in 16 months, with enormous difficulty, linemen have strung wire to San Francisco; making a total of 3,500 miles of telegraph line, open for use at both ends.

Nov. 8. Confederate agents James M. Mason and John Slidell, on the way to seek diplomatic recognition from England and France, are removed from British mail steamer *Trent* by order of U.S. naval vessel. Incident produces strong popular and official disapproval in Britain, where it is called a "violation of neutral right." War talk in Britain is calmed by the tactful joint efforts of Prince Consort Albert and President Lincoln. **Dec. 26.** Secretary of State Seward finally placates British by ordering release of the two Confederates.

Dec. 20. Congress appoints a Joint Committee on the Conduct of the War, dominated by radical Republicans who urge immediate emancipation of slaves, demand action by the almost idle Union armies, and protest Lincoln's assumption of extensive emergency powers.

At outset of the war, 11 Confederate states oppose 23 Union states (including California and Oregon, which are too far away to take part in hostilities). Population of the Confederacy is 9 million, including 3,500,000 slaves; population of the Union is 22 million. Small U.S. Army, except for one-third of the officers, is on the Union side, as is entire Navy. The South has been dependent on the North for virtually all products except food. But the Union must carry attack to the South, which is thinly populated and lacks roads and railroads, making long supply lines necessary. Both sides must build armies, and, in doing so, the Confederacy has advantage of a majority of the best officers from the U.S. Army who have resigned when their states seceded; Southern men, accustomed to outdoor life, are more easily trained as soldiers than Northerners (except for those from the West); Northerners are mostly city men and foreign immigrants. Equipping armies is a problem to both sides, but the Union is vastly superior in materials and manufacturing ability.

Dakota Territory is formed from parts of Minnesota and Nebraska territories; Colorado Territory from parts of territories of Utah, New Mexico, Kansas, and Nebraska; and Nevada Territory from part of Utah Territory.

U.S. mails begin for first time to carry merchandise as well as letters.

Yale University awards first Ph.D. degree in U.S.; graduate school has been established in 1847. Vassar Female College opens at Poughkeepsie, New York; it is nonsectarian and endowed by Matthew Vassar.

1861 - 1862

Jan. 3, 1861-March 8, 1862. Border slave states remain loyal to Union — Delaware unanimously, Maryland and Kentucky after failure of efforts to remain neutral, and Missouri only after a year-long intrastate civil war in which Union forces are victorious.

1861 - 1863

May 13, 1861. Great Britain declares neutrality; recognizes belligerent status but not independence of Confederacy; other European states soon do the same. British sentiment is divided, with the working class and most of the middle class favoring the free democratic North, while the upper classes, with some notable exceptions, tend to favor the "aristocratic" South. British commercial interests, affected by U.S. tariffs and the prospect of free trade with an independent South, tend to favor the Confederacy; on the other hand, Britain is concerned about the prospect of a Union invasion of Canada if Britain offers any real aid. The South believes that Britain and France depend on Southern cotton exports, and that it will be only a short time before these countries are forced to both recognize and help the Confederacy. Actually, Britain has large surplus of cotton from previous year and need for Northern food grains affects British policy to a much greater extent. British government waits for decisive Confederate military successes before venturing beyond formal neutrality; such successes never come. Meanwhile, British sentiment favors Union increasingly, and decisively after Emancipation Proclamation of January 1, 1863.

Aug. 11. The *New York Daily News* loses postal privileges and is suspended for 18 months for such open hostility to the war effort that it is considered aid to the enemy. Five other Northern papers are seized or suspended for the same reason from 1861 to 1863, but President Lincoln is firm in prohibiting interference with publications unless "they are working palpable injury to the military."

1861 - 1865

Popular songs of the period are chiefly war songs. The North sings "John Brown's Body" and, later, Julia Ward Howe's "Battle Hymn of the Republic" to the same tune; "We Are Coming Father Abraham" is written in response to the President's appeal for 300,000 more soldiers; "Tramp! Tramp! Tramp!" and "Marching Through Georgia" are written near the end of the war. "Tenting on the Old Camp Ground" and "When Johnny Comes Marching Home" originate in the North but are soon taken up by the South as well. Most popular Southern songs are "Dixie" and "The Bonnie Blue Flag."

1862

In effort to secure the Mississippi River and thus split the Confederacy, Union forces in the West commanded by General Henry W. Halleck aim at Fort Henry on the Tennessee River and Fort Donelson on the Cumberland. **Feb. 6.** General Ulysses S. Grant takes Fort Henry with help of Union gunboats. **Feb. 16.** Grant takes Fort Donelson, defended by 15,000 Confederate troops. **Feb. 24.** General Don Carlos Buell occupies Nashville, Tennessee, which has been abandoned by Confederate troops on news of Fort Donelson defeat. General Albert S. Johnston, commander of Confederate forces in West, is forced to withdraw to railroad center of Corinth, Mississippi. South has lost Kentucky and half of Tennessee.

Feb. 25. Congress authorizes first U.S. legal tender bank notes; by 1865 more than $400 million in "greenbacks" has been issued. At first these stimulate business activity, but by end of the war they have depreciated to 39 cents gold equivalent per dollar.

March 6-8. Union forces defeat Confederates at Pea Ridge, Arkansas; this almost ends hostilities west of the Mississippi River and secures Missouri, to the north, for the Union.

March 8. Ironclad vessel *Virginia* (originally sunken federal ship *Merrimack* that has been raised by the Confederates and armored with iron plates) sinks two Northern ships at Hampton Roads. **March 9.** Northern ironclad *Monitor*, just arrived, engages *Virginia;* battle is inconclusive, but continued presence of *Virginia* at mouth of James

River prevents General George B. McClellan, commander of Army of the Potomac, from using river as a route for attack on Richmond, as planned.

March-April. General McClellan's forces land on Virginia peninsula. **April 5.** Yorktown is laid under siege lasting until May 5. McClellan has expected to take Yorktown quickly with help from Navy and from troops under General Irvin McDowell, but Navy is blocked by the *Virginia,* and President Lincoln has held McDowell to protect Washington, D.C.

April 6. Grant and his force reach Pittsburg Landing, Tennessee, 30 miles north of Corinth, where Buell is to join him; Confederate Generals Johnston and Pierre Beauregard attack before Buell arrives, nearly defeating Grant. **April 7.** Buell's troops having come during night, Grant forces Confederates back to Corinth with huge losses on both sides; 13,000 Union casualties and 11,000 Confederate, including General Johnston, killed on first day.

April 11. General Halleck joins Grant and Buell, and they proceed down Mississippi River. **May 30.** Beauregard evacuates Corinth. **June 3.** Memphis is taken.

April 16. No longer able to rely on enlistments, Confederacy passes Conscription Act, making all white males from 18 to 35 years old liable to three-year draft administered by central government. Exemptions because of occupation, privilege of paying substitutes, fraud, and evasions cause wide discontent, especially among the poor. Desertions during war amount to about 10 percent of army.

April 24-25. Flag Officer David G. Farragut with U.S. Gulf Squadron sails past forts guarding New Orleans at mouth of Mississippi River. Abandoned by its garrison, New Orleans surrenders. **May 1.** City is occupied by General Benjamin F. Butler; South's largest city is thereafter held by the North until end of the war.

April. Union spy James J. Andrews and 20 men capture railroad engine behind Confederate lines in Georgia, run it toward Chattanooga, Tennessee, destroying telegraph lines as they go. Chased and captured by Confederate troops in second engine, Andrews and seven of his men are hanged.

May 15. U.S. Department of Agriculture established; department has been agricultural branch of the Patent Office. Commissioner is not given Cabinet rank until 1889.

May 16. McClellan arrives within striking distance of Richmond, the Confederate capital, and awaits reinforcements, but Confederate command has sent General "Stonewall" Jackson along Shenandoah Valley toward Washington in effort to hold Union reinforcements back. **May 31.** Confederate General Joseph E. Johnston attacks McClellan. In two-day battle, Johnston is at first successful but then retires toward Richmond; he is wounded, and General Robert E. Lee takes over command.

May 20. Homestead Act grants free family-size parcels of public land to actual settlers after five years' residence. Encouragement of agricultural expansion results in crops able to meet Union demands as well as those of Europe, where harvests have been small. England requires Northern wheat as much as Southern cotton.

May. Thaddeus Lowe, balloonist, is first to make aerial photographs for military purposes when he records entire Richmond area for the Union in 64 overlapping photographs; Lowe is also first to carry telegraphic transmitter aloft to direct artillery fire and troop movements.

June 12-15. Confederate General James E. B. ("Jeb") Stuart, called the "eyes" of Lee's army, leads daring cavalry raid, traveling around entire Union Army in three days with loss of only one man; raid briefly threatens Washington from North, gains information about Union troop movements, and improves Southern morale.

June 25. McClellan, four miles from Richmond, telegraphs President Lincoln that he is about to attack, but he is too late; Lee's army, reinforced by Jackson's, numbers 85,000. **June 26-July 1.** Lee attacks McClellan in first of series of battles called The Seven Days. Battles are inconclusive, but McClellan, feeling hopelessly outnumbered (although his forces are actually superior), retreats to the James River.

July 2. Morrill Land Grant Act authorizes sales of public land in each state loyal to the Union for endowment of state agricultural education. The act in effect creates the great state universities with income from sale of 17 million acres.

July 11. President Lincoln yields to political pressure and replaces McClellan with General Halleck, who has come to Washington from Western campaign. **July 25.** Halleck orders McClellan's army to northern Virginia to join with General John Pope's forces.

Aug. 25-27. General Lee, anxious to attack Pope before McClellan can reach him, sends Jackson on swing through Bull Run Mountains to attack from the rear at Manassas Junction. **Aug. 29-30.** Pope attacks Jackson but is unsuccessful and next day attacks Lee's newly arrived forces, which · sweep his army back toward Washington. **Sept. 3.** Beaten Union Army retires to protection of Washington fortifications.

Sept. 7. Lee, hoping to convince Europe of Confederate strength and win Maryland for the South by fighting on Union soil, invades Maryland, sending (Sept. 10) half his forces under Jackson to capture Harpers Ferry. On same day McClellan starts slow march toward Lee from Washington. **Sept. 13.** McClellan finds copy of Lee's orders and learns Confederate Army is split; Lee, discovering this, takes up position (Sept. 14) with his half of army at Sharpsburg, behind Antietam Creek. **Sept. 17.** McClellan, having waited too long before taking advantage of his knowledge, attacks Lee, who by this time has been reinforced. **Sept. 18.** Although Lee's army has remained firm through a bloody battle (12,000 Northern and 10,000 Southern casualties), his losses are so heavy that he is forced to retreat to Virginia. His stay in Maryland has not been long enough to impress either Europe or the citizens of Maryland.

Sept. 22. On the strength of the Antietam victory, President Lincoln issues preliminary Emancipation Proclamation, to take effect on January 1, 1863, in areas still in rebellion on that date. Previous acts of local military commanders have emancipated some slaves. Slavery has already been abolished, with compensation to owners, in District of Columbia on April 16, and, without compensation, in all territories on June 19. Act of Congress on August 6, 1861, has emancipated slaves used by the South against Union forces as labor or under arms; another act, on July 17, 1862, has freed slaves who are property of persons engaged in treason against the U.S. Proclamation actually frees no slaves, since it concerns only areas over which federal government has no jurisdiction.

Nov. 7. President Lincoln, impatient at McClellan's failure to press his advantage after Antietam, replaces him with General Ambrose E. Burnside, who plans to attack Lee at Fredericksburg, Virginia. **Dec. 13.** In

Battle of Fredericksburg Union forces attack Confederates at Marye's Heights, a line of well-fortified hills; 12,000 Union troops are killed or wounded, and Army retreats. Burnside is later relieved of his command at his own request.

Dec. 17. Radical Republicans in Senate fail in attempt to force President Lincoln to reorganize Cabinet by appointing radicals to all posts and replacing Secretary of State William H. Seward, the object of their wrath, with Secretary of the Treasury Salmon P. Chase, their favorite; Lincoln, supported by the entire Cabinet except Seward, persuades Republicans that no conflict exists in Cabinet and refuses to accept (though he pockets) resignations offered by both Seward and Chase.

Jay Cooke, Pennsylvania banker, is employed by U.S. Treasury Department to raise money by selling $500 million in bonds. By using 2,500 subagents and appealing to Northern patriotism, he raises $11 million more than authorized before he can stop machinery set in motion. Congress immediately authorizes extra amount.

Richard Jordan Gatling perfects machine gun he has worked on for past year; gun will fire 350 rounds per minute, but it is not adopted by Union authorities until war is almost over.

William Gannaway Brownlow, editor of the *Knoxville* (Tennessee) *Whig,* and Union sympathizer, publishes his *Sketches of the Rise, Progress, and Decline of Secession; with a Narrative of Personal Adventure Among the Rebels;* he has previously been arrested for treason in Tennessee because of pro-Union newspaper editorial and then released by Confederate authorities.

Photographer Mathew Brady receives official permission from President Lincoln and the Secret Service to establish complete photographic coverage of Civil War. Though he has photographed battles and events previously, he and his many photographic teams take more than 7,000 pictures of battles, individuals, camps, and devastated battlefields. Project ruins Brady financially; an enormously popular portrait photographer before the War, he spends $100,000, his entire fortune, on expenses.

Painter and illustrator Winslow Homer accompanies Union armies as artist-correspondent for *Harper's Weekly.*

1862 - 1863

Dec. 31, 1862-Jan. 2, 1863. General Braxton Bragg, who has replaced Beauregard and has dominated central Tennessee, is finally forced to withdraw after Battle of Murfreesboro (Stone River), in which each side sustains more than 9,000 casualties.

July 1, 1862. Pacific Railway Act authorizes Union Pacific Railroad to build line from Nebraska to Utah to meet Central Pacific, which is building eastward from California. **July 2, 1864.** Land grants of 10 alternate sections per mile given railroads to aid finances having proved inadequate, new act grants twice as much land. Union Pacific uses largely immigrant Irish labor; Central Pacific imports Chinese laborers.

1862 - 1864

Dislocation of foreign markets for cotton and efforts to become self-sufficient in food production result in drop in Southern cotton production from average of 4,500,000 bales per year to 1,600,000 in 1862 and a low of 300,000 in 1864.

1863

Jan. 1. President Lincoln issues Emancipation Proclamation, freeing "all slaves in areas still in rebellion," but actually most of these slaves continue to work productively for the South.

Feb. 3. French Emperor Napoleon III offers to mediate in American Civil War. **Feb. 6-March 3.** Secretary of State Seward and Congress, in resolution of both houses, promptly refuse offer, Congress criticizing it as "foreign intervention."

March 3. First Union conscription act makes all men 20 to 35, unmarried to 45 years old, liable to military service. Provisions are similar to those of Confederate draft act, making it easy to avoid actual service by paying $300 for a substitute to enlist for three years. This provision is especially objectionable to working-class men, for whom $300 is about two-thirds of annual income.

Confederate and Union armies spend most of winter facing each other across Rappahannock River in Virginia. By spring, Union Army, now commanded by General Joseph Hooker, numbers about 130,000 and Confederate Army, about 60,000. **April 30.** Hooker moves to hold Lee at Fredericksburg while sending force to attack his flank but hesitates and sets up position to the west at Chancellorsville. **May 2.** At Battle of Chancellorsville, Lee attacks Hooker from two directions. After a notable victory, General Jackson, riding around his lines, is shot accidentally by one of his men, and his left arm is amputated. Lee writes: "You are better off than I am, for while you have lost your left, I have lost my right arm." **May 5.** Hooker, badly beaten, although his forces are vastly superior, retreats across Rappahannock. **May 10.** Jackson dies of effects of amputation and pneumonia.

April. Having failed during winter to take key city of Vicksburg, Mississippi, from the north, Grant sends gunboats and supplies downriver at night to take positions south of the city, then sends army southward on west side of Mississippi River to cross to Union positions. **May 16-18.** Direct attacks having failed, Grant begins Siege of Vicksburg. **July 4.** Hopelessly cut off and having been under constant bombardment for seven weeks, Vicksburg surrenders. **July 9.** Port Hudson, Louisiana, is taken by Union forces, leaving North in control of Mississippi River. President Lincoln says, "The Father of Waters again goes unvexed to the sea."

June 3. Encouraged by Chancellorsville and hoping for further victories in order to win European recognition for the Confederacy, Lee starts up Shenandoah Valley toward Pennsylvania with Union General Hooker's Army of the Potomac following northward toward Gettysburg. Lee is unaware of Hooker's exact position as Jeb Stuart is away on a raid around Union Army. **June 15.** President Lincoln calls for 100,000 volunteers for six-month service; Confederate invasion of North stimulates response to this appeal. **June 28.** After numerous clashes between the Union command and the administration, President Lincoln accepts Hooker's resignation; General George G. Meade is appointed head of the Army of the Potomac in his stead. Meade realizes that a battle is probably imminent and works around the clock to prepare his forces. **June 30.** Confederate brigade searching for shoes in Gettysburg comes upon Union cavalry. Armies, now aware of each other's position, maneuver in attempt to gain advantage. **July 1.** Greatest battle of Civil War begins. Union forces are hard pressed by Confederates converging on Gettysburg from north and west, but by end of day have taken up position on Cemetery Ridge, southeast of town. **July 2.** Confederates attack flanks of Union position — Culp's Hill on north, Little Round Top on South — but Union line holds. Casualties on both sides are high. **July 3.** Lee, believing that Union center has been depleted in order to meet flank attacks of previous day, orders artillery barrage to be followed by attack on Cemetery Ridge by Pickett's Virginia division — 15,000 fresh men. Charge takes place at two o'clock in the afternoon; it is made in parade formation under withering artillery fire, and only a small number of Confederates reach the Union lines. Pickett withdraws after twenty minutes of fierce fighting within the Union position, his division destroyed. **July 4.** Having lost more than 20,000 men killed and wounded, Lee begins retreat into Virginia. Meade, his army exhausted — hardly anyone has slept for five days — does not follow up his advantage, and Confederates escape. However, battle is first major Union victory, and thereafter European recognition of the Confederacy is out of the question.

June 20. West Virginia, which has broken away from Virginia to support the Union, is admitted as the thirty-fifth state; its population is about 380,000, including 15,000 slaves.

June 20. Jay Cooke establishes first national bank in Philadelphia; it is chief agent for sale of U.S. bonds. By end of war, many state banks have become national banks, issuing national bank notes, which for the first time gives the country a uniform currency.

July 13-16. First draft drawings cause riots in New York City; rioters burn, loot, and kill, and Irish immigrant laborers, lowest paid of all, attack Negroes and lynch several of them. Rioting is put down by police, heavy rain, and arrival of regular Army troops brought from Gettysburg, Pennsylvania. Anti-Negro riots occur also in other Northern cities, notably Detroit.

Sept. 4. General William S. Rosecrans, with 55,000 men, advances on Chattanooga, Tennessee, occupied by General Braxton

Bragg. **Sept. 8.** Bragg retreats southward into Georgia to avoid being put out of action. Rosecrans, thinking he is in full retreat, pursues him, but Bragg has withdrawn only 25 miles and has received reinforcements from Virginia that increase his army to 70,000. **Sept. 19.** Bragg attacks fiercely. In two-day Battle of Chickamauga, Union forces are badly defeated and retreat to Chattanooga.

Although Britain favors the Union in Civil War, Confederate ships are still being built in Britain; British-built raiders have destroyed more than 250 Union ships. Charles Francis Adams, U.S. minister to Britain, warns British after Gettysburg and Vicksburg victories, that building of ironclads for Confederacy means war. **Oct.** British government takes over ships, and France follows suit, ordering vessels under construction in France to be sold to European governments. By end of year, the South has lost all hope of recognition from abroad.

Oct. 23. General Grant, now Western commander, reaches Chattanooga to join General Hooker, who has arrived from Virginia, and averts danger of starvation of besieged garrison by bringing in supplies. **Nov. 23.** Reinforced by General William T. Sherman and aware that Bragg's army has been weakened, Grant orders Sherman and Hooker to attack Confederate-held heights around Chattanooga. **Nov. 25.** Dramatic charge up heavily-fortified Missionary Ridge ends battle. Most of eastern Tennessee is now controlled by the Union, and from Chattanooga, Union armies can move into Georgia and Alabama.

Nov. 19. Statesman Edward Everett delivers oration as chief speaker at dedication of national cemetery at Gettysburg Battlefield; President Lincoln also makes brief 10-sentence address, after which Everett writes him, "I should be glad if I could flatter myself that I came as near to the central idea of the occasion in two hours as you did in two minutes."

Dec. 8. President Lincoln's plan of Reconstruction offers amnesty to Southerners taking loyalty oath and federal recognition of state governments in which 10 percent of 1860 voters have taken oath and state has agreed to free slaves.

Arizona Territory is formed from part of Territory of New Mexico; Territory of Idaho is formed from parts of Washington, Dakota, Utah, and Nebraska territories.

Congress grants 3 million acres of land to Atchison, Topeka and Santa Fe Railway in alternate sections in Kansas. Eventually line runs from Chicago to Los Angeles.

Congress authorizes, for the first time, free mail delivery service in certain cities for distribution of mail direct to destination.

1863 - 1865

Feb. 25. National Bank Act is passed; banks operating under this act must invest up to one-third of their reserves in U.S. securities, against which they may make extensive note issues to finance the war. Without a similar financial system, the Confederacy raises some money in taxes and foreign and domestic loans, but issue of more than $1 billion in paper money results in disastrous inflation.

1863 - 1867

Great Britain, Spain, and France have invaded Mexico in 1861 in effort to collect foreign debts after payments are suspended by nearly bankrupt country. Spain and Great Britain, learning that France, supported by Mexican conservatives, plans to

set up Catholic empire under French support, have withdrawn in 1862. **June 7, 1863.** French troops, reinforced by Napoleon III, attack and after heavy fighting take Mexico City. President Benito Juárez, head of liberal Mexican government, flees to northern Mexico. **April 10, 1864.** Archduke Maximilian of Austria is established by Napoleon as emperor of Mexico; but Mexican people and government continue to fight French, while U.S. continues to recognize Juárez. **March 12, 1867.** Napoleon III, convinced by U.S. protests over past years that U.S. may provide military aid to Mexico, withdraws support from Maximilian. **May 15.** Emperor surrenders to Mexicans, who execute him in following month.

1864

March 9. General Grant is appointed commander in chief of all Union forces and moves to Eastern arena to oppose Lee. His policy, and President Lincoln's, is to use superior manpower and industrial strength of North to destroy Confederate armies; although Union casualties will be heavy, it is assumed that the South cannot support comparable losses of men and equipment.

May 4. General Sherman starts from Chattanooga into Georgia. He is opposed by Confederate General Joseph E. Johnston, who, as Sherman advances toward Atlanta, fights series of defensive actions as he retreats southeastward. **July 17.** Union Army reaches within eight miles of Atlanta, and President Jefferson Davis, impatient with Johnston's tactics, replaces him with General John B. Hood.

May 5-6. In desolate area of northern Virginia known as the Wilderness, Grant, with 100,000 men, meets Lee's army of 60,000 in tangled forest. Indecisive battle rages for two days, but Union casualties are far greater than Confederate.

May 8-12. Ignoring his losses, Grant moves eastward toward Richmond and again meets Lee's army, at Spotsylvania Court House; in five days of bloody fighting in which neither side is victorious, Grant loses about 10,000 men. He doggedly wires Washington, "I propose to fight it out on this line if it takes all summer." War of attrition continues sporadically throughout April and May.

June 1-3. Having again moved to his left, Grant meets Lee at Cold Harbor, a few miles from Richmond. In another attempt to crush Lee's entrenched army, Grant loses about 7,000 men in only one hour of fighting. In a month, Grant has lost almost 60,000 men; finally realizing Lee's magnificent defensive skill, he is forced to change tactics.

June 7. Abraham Lincoln is nominated for reelection as President and Governor Andrew Johnson, Tennessee "War" Democrat, for Vice-President by Republican Party (using name "National Union Party"). **Aug. 29.** Democrats nominate General George B. McClellan for President and George H. Pendleton of Ohio for Vice-President. Democratic platform proposes immediate end of war, but McClellan repudiates it in campaign and demands preservation of the Union. Northern defeatist feeling and peace demands make Lincoln's chances for reelection seem slim.

June 12-18. Grant decides to try to capture railroad complex at Petersburg and cut supply lines to Richmond. He crosses the James River on a 2,000-foot pontoon bridge and almost achieves victory, but small Confederate force delays him until Lee's army arrives. Only alternative is to besiege Petersburg.

June 20. Union and Confederate armies start digging miles of trenches around Petersburg. They face each other for nine months, during which all Union attempts to break through Confederate lines fail.

July 2-13. Lee sends General Jubal A. Early through the Shenandoah Valley to raid Washington, D.C., hoping to divert some of Grant's troops from Petersburg. Traveling through Maryland, Early reaches within five miles of Washington by July 11. Two divisions of Union troops, hastily sent from Petersburg, drive Early back into Virginia.

July 4. Congress establishes Bureau of Immigration; contract labor law allows for admittance of immigrant laborers who agree to pay for their transportation out of wages earned for no more than one year after entry into U.S. Law is later repealed.

July 8. President Lincoln pocket-vetoes Wade-Davis Bill, congressional plan for postwar reconstruction of the South. Lincoln considers Bill's provisions too severe and issues statement of his reasons only after Congress adjourns; his leniency is heavily criticized by radical Republicans.

July 20 and 22. General Hood attacks Sherman near Atlanta but is forced to withdraw to the city and on September 1 to evacuate it; Sherman occupies it the next day. Capture of Atlanta lifts Union morale, which has sunk to new low over Grant's losses at Richmond, and improves President Lincoln's prospects for reelection.

Aug. 5. In effort to make blockade of South more effective, naval squadron commanded by Admiral Farragut sails into Mobile Bay, Alabama, although Farragut knows it bristles with mines, called torpedoes. ("Damn the torpedoes! Full steam ahead!") Mobile forts surrender by August 23, and port is closed to shipping, although Mobile is not occupied.

Sept. 19-Oct. 19. General Philip H. Sheridan, having become commander of the Army of the Shenandoah, defeats Early at Winchester, Fisher's Hill, and Cedar Creek, and devastates the Shenandoah Valley, which has become the grain-growing area supplying Richmond.

Oct. 31. Nevada is admitted to the Union as thirty-sixth state, although population does not meet requirements for state law. Action is hastened by Congress, anxious to acquire an additional free state to secure ratification of Thirteenth Amendment to the Constitution, prohibiting slavery; amendment is scheduled for submission to the states by next Congress, and ratification by 27 states is required.

Nov. 8. President Lincoln is reelected. National Union candidates carry all but three states, with electoral vote of 212 for Lincoln to 21 for McClellan (81 votes of Confederacy are not cast), but popular vote is only 2,200,000 for Lincoln to 1,800,000 for McClellan. Andrew Johnson is elected Vice-President.

Nov. 14. Leaving Atlanta in flames, Sherman begins march to Savannah, Georgia. His army of 60,000 men marches forward on 60-mile front, systematically destroying everything — buildings, roads, bridges, factories, cotton gins — that might be of use to the Confederacy. Sherman deliberately orders men to "forage," hoping total destruction will break will of the South. Looting soldiers strip everything in their path and destroy what they cannot use; Sherman later estimates that they have destroyed $100 million in Georgia property. **Dec. 10.** Army reaches Savannah, which surrenders on December 22.

Dec. 15-16. In two-day battle, Union Army takes Nashville after almost complete destruction of General Hood's army.

Montana Territory is formed from part of Idaho.

Although few strikes have been held during war, national labor groups have expanded; employers in Michigan and elsewhere set up associations of employers to counteract spread of labor unions.

First Bessemer-process steel plant starts operating at Wyandotte, Michigan; it produces chiefly steel railroad rails. Peter Cooper has previously used process experimentally in 1856 as first iron manufacturer in U.S. to use Bessemer converter. For some years more iron than steel rails are made.

First comfortable sleeping car is constructed by George Pullman; sleeping cars have been in use for almost 30 years, but builders have not been concerned with public comfort. Pullman's car has, in addition to well-constructed berths, more width, more height, and rubber-reinforced springs.

Clara Barton, who has organized nursing services for Union troops in Washington since beginning of war, works without payment or accreditation behind Union lines and on battlefields as superintendent of nurses. She later is responsible for establishment of American Red Cross.

George Perkins Marsh, lawyer, scholar, and minister to Italy, publishes *Man and Nature, or Physical Geography as Modified by Human Action*, a pioneer effort suggesting the importance of conservation, improvement of waste areas, and restoration of exhausted land.

1865

Jan.-April. General Sherman's army marches through South Carolina, then North Carolina, more destructively than through Georgia; it is only slightly slowed by Johnston's forces.

Feb. 3. Hampton Roads, Virginia, peace conference between President Lincoln and Confederate Vice-President and others fails when Confederates insist on recognition of Confederate independence as condition.

March 3. Freedmen's Bureau is established by Congress to assist emancipated Southern Negroes and to care for deserted Southern land.

March 4. President Lincoln, in Second Inaugural Address, stresses again his conviction that when peace comes, it must be peace "with malice toward none" if it is to achieve a true reunion of the states.

March 25. General Lee's attempt to break out of Petersburg fails before Grant's superior forces. **April 1.** Lee makes his last attack of the war but is again unsuccessful. **April 2-3.** He evacuates Petersburg and Richmond in attempt to move south to join General Johnston, who is opposing Sherman in North Carolina.

April 7. Surrounded by Union forces, and with only 30,000 men remaining. Lee receives Grant's message requesting surrender. **April 9.** They meet at Appomattox Court House to discuss terms. All Confederate soldiers are released to return home; all may keep private horses and mules; officers may keep sidearms, but all other equipment is surrendered. Union Army gives hungry Confederates 25,000 rations.

April 14. President Lincoln is shot by John Wilkes Booth while watching *Our American Cousin* in Ford's Theater, Washington; he is taken, unconscious, to rooming house nearby. Simultaneously, Secretary Seward, ill at home, is attacked and severely wounded by Lewis Powell, confederate

of Booth. Booth, having broken his leg in leap from theater box, escapes to Virginia. **April 15.** President Lincoln dies at 7:22 A.M., and Andrew Johnson becomes President. **April 26.** Booth, traced to barn near Bowling Green, Virginia, refuses to surrender; barn is set on fire, and Booth either shoots himself or is shot. **July 7.** Four of nine persons involved in assassination plot are hanged, including one woman; four are imprisoned; one is not convicted.

April 26. Johnston surrenders to Sherman, with final terms similar to those at Appomattox. **May 4.** All remaining Southern forces east of Mississippi surrender. **May 26.** Confederate forces west of Mississippi surrender near New Orleans in final capitulation of war.

May 29. President Johnson issues amnesty and reconstruction proclamation embodying principles of Lincoln's 1863 plan. During summer recess of Congress he recognizes provisional governments of Virginia, Louisiana, Arkansas, and Tennessee that Lincoln had set up and establishes such governments for other seven states. All states have abolished slavery, amended their constitutions, and repudiated their war debts by December, except Texas, which does so in following year.

July. *The Nation* is founded in New York; a weekly concerned with politics and the arts, it is edited by Edwin Lawrence Godkin and supported by Eastern intellectuals.

Nov. 18. *The Celebrated Jumping Frog of Calaveras County* by Mark Twain is published in *The Saturday Press*, New York; an immediate hit, it is reprinted in newspapers across the country.

Nov. 22-29. Mississippi enacts first "Black Code," attempting to control freed

Negroes by such means as vagrancy laws and apprenticeship regulations that tie Negroes to land. Other Southern states soon pass similar laws; some are severe, others more liberal.

Dec. 4. New Congress convenes and forms 15-member Joint Committee on Reconstruction, controlled by radical Republicans. **Dec. 6.** President Johnson's first message to Congress announces that Union is restored, but Congress refuses to seat representatives and senators elected under provisional Southern governments that are recognized by Johnson. Joint Committee denies that these state governments exist legally until recognized by Congress under such conditions as Congress, and only Congress, may prescribe. Senator Charles Sumner contends that former states have committed suicide: Representative Thaddeus Stevens calls them a conquered province. Stevens first dominates Committee and, eventually, House and entire Republican Party.

Dec. 18. Thirteenth Amendment to Constitution declared in effect, having been ratified by 27 states, including 8 formerly Confederate states. Amendment prohibits slavery in all states and territories. Fearing obstruction in Southern states, Congress for first time assumes power to enforce provisions of an amendment.

About 4 million men have served in the war, but many of these have been for three- and six-months' enlistments, and figure includes repeaters who have enlisted for a fee, deserted, and enlisted again. Union Negro forces have numbered 180,000, half of them from the South. Total casualties: Union, 359,000 dead, 275,000 wounded; Confed-

eracy, 258,000 dead, 100,000 wounded. War has cost Union $5 billion and Confederacy $3 billion. Most war costs having been financed by loans and paper money issues, the federal public debt reaches over $75 per capita, highest figure up to this time.

Union Stockyards open in Chicago; they become largest stockyards in the U.S., serving the cattle industry over a wide area.

Cornell University founded at Ithaca, New York, with endowments from private sources and with aid provided by the Morrill Act of 1862; Ezra Cornell, builder of telegraph system, is a major benefactor.

William Bullock develops first web press, using roll, or web, of paper instead of cut sheets; earliest models print 15,000 sheets per hour, both sides at once.

1865 - 1868

May 10, 1865. Jefferson Davis captured in Georgia; he spends two years in jail in Virginia, then is released on bond. **Dec. 25, 1868.** Treason charge against him is dropped.

Oct. 1865. Cheyenne and Arapaho Indians, at war with settlers and miners since 1861 in Colorado, are conquered following massacre of 450 Indians by militia in previous year. First Sioux War begins when U.S. starts building road from southern Wyoming to Montana; hostilities are intensified when miners and settlers invade Black Hills. War continues until 1868, when Indians consent to move to Dakota Territory reservation.

The Civil War and Slavery

The Civil War has been called the first modern war. It was fought on several fronts, simultaneously on both land and sea, with an unprecedented involvement of men and material. Maps 1-4 depict the general progress of the war, which began in the East, but soon settled down to a series of engagements in three theaters: eastern, middle (Tennessee), and western (along the Mississippi River). Victory for the North moved from West to East. After the Battle of Vicksburg opened the Mississippi and split the Confederacy, the North was gradually able to move into the Southern states and destroy their warmaking capacity, while increasing its own supplies of men and material. Grant's campaigns in Virginia and Sherman's "March to the Sea" effectively ended the South's ability to continue the war.

Map 5 depicts the slave trade in its two aspects: foreign and domestic. Importing slaves to the colonies began in 1619, although slaves had been brought to the Caribbean islands since early in the 16th century. The United States outlawed the foreign trade in slaves in 1808, but the domestic trade between the Southern states continued until the Civil War.

Map 6 indicates the percentages of slaves in the total population throughout the South on the eve of the Civil War and points out the various "branches" of the Underground Railroad by which some slaves escaped to freedom in Canada. This illegal "railroad" operated in numerous localities in defiance of the federal Fugitive Slave Law. But the Underground Railroad's notoriety and infamy in the South outweighed its actual usefulness in freeing significant numbers of slaves.

Maps prepared by Uni-Map Inc., Palatine, Ill.
for Encyclopaedia Britannica, Inc.

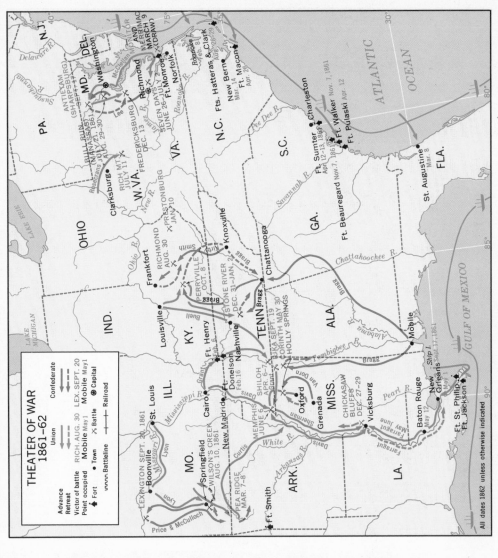

THEATER OF WAR
1861-62

Advance
Retreat
Victor of battle   RICH. AUG. 30   LEX. SEPT. 20
Point occupied   Mobile May 1   Mobile May 1
▲ Fort   • Town   ✕ Battle   ⊛ Capital
ⵏⵏⵏⵏ Battleline   ┼┼┼ Railroad

Union   Confederate

All dates 1862 unless otherwise indicated

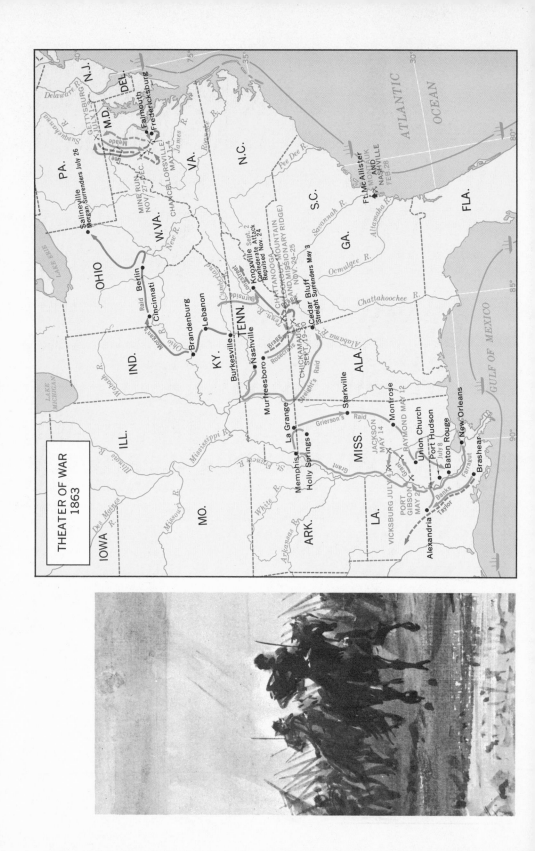

THEATER OF WAR
1863

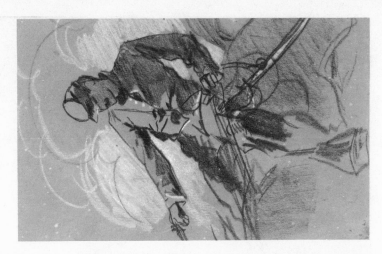

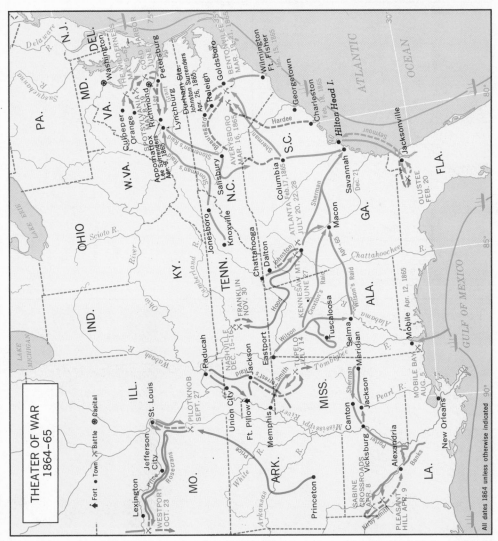

THEATER OF WAR
1864-65

♣ Fort ● Town ✕ Battle ⊛ Capital

All dates 1864 unless otherwise indicated

LAKE MICHIGAN

LAKE ERIE

Delaware R. N.J. DEL.

Susquehanna R.

PA.

MD.

Washington ⊛

VA.

W. VA.

THE WILDERNESS
MAY 5-6 COLD HARBOR
JUNE 3
SPOTSYLVANIA
MAY 8-21
Richmond ⊛ Petersburg
Culpeper
Orange
Appomattox
Lee Surrenders
Apr. 9, 1865
Lynchburg
Grant

OHIO

Scioto R.

River

Ohio

IND.

ILL.

St. Louis

Jefferson
City
Price
Lexington

MO.

WESTPORT
OCT. 23

Rosecrans

PILOT KNOB
SEPT. 27

Union City

White R.

Arkansas R.

ARK.

Princeton

Memphis
Ft. Pillow
Paducah

KY.

Cumberland R.

Wabash R.

Knoxville
Jonesboro

TENN.

Chattanooga
Dalton

NASHVILLE
DEC. 15-16
FRANKLIN
NOV. 30
Hood
Eastport

Jackson
Forrest's
Raid
Smith
TUPELO
JULY 14

MISS.

Sherman
Canton
Jackson
Meridian

Pearl R.

Tombigbee R.

Mississippi River

Vicksburg
Porter
Alexandria
Banks
SABINE
CROSSROADS
APR. 8
PLEASANT
HILL APR. 9
Kirby Smith

LA.

New Orleans

MOBILE BAY
AUG. 5
Mobile Apr. 12, 1865

Tuscaloosa
Selma
Wilson
Croxton's Raid
Wilson's Raid

ALA.

Alabama R.

Chattahoochee R.

ATLANTA
JULY 20, 22, 28
Johnston
KENNESAW MT.
JUNE 27

GA.

Macon
Apr. '65
Sherman
Savannah
Dec. 21

N.C.

Salisbury
Stoneman's Raid
Greensboro
Durham Sta.
Johnston Surrenders
Apr. 26, 1865
Raleigh
Goldsboro
AVERYSBORO
MAR. 16, 1865
BENTONVILLE
MAR. 19-21, 1865
Wilmington
Ft. Fisher
Jan. 15, 1865

S.C.

Columbia
Feb. 17, 1865
Hardee
Charleston
Feb. 18, 1865
Georgetown

Hilton Head I.

Seymour

FLA.

Jacksonville
OLUSTEE
FEB. 20

GULF OF MEXICO

ATLANTIC
OCEAN

90° 85° 80° 75° 30°

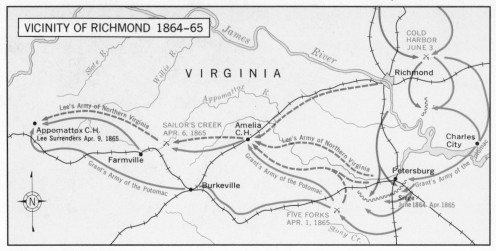

VICINITY OF RICHMOND 1864–65

COLD HARBOR JUNE 3

James River

Richmond

V I R G I N I A

State R.

Willis R.

Appomattox R.

Charles City

Lee's Army of Northern Virginia

Appomattox C.H.
Lee Surrenders Apr. 9, 1865

SAILOR'S CREEK APR. 6, 1865

Amelia C.H.

Lee's Army of Northern Virginia

Petersburg

Grant's Army of the Potomac

Farmville

Grant's Army of the Potomac

Grant's Army of the Potomac

Siege June 1864 - Apr. 1865

Burkeville

FIVE FORKS APR. 1, 1865

Stony Cr.

N

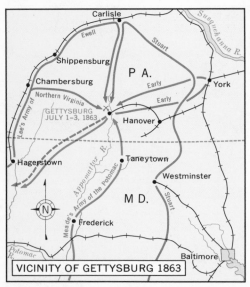

Carlisle

Susquehanna R.

Ewell

Stuart

Shippensburg

P A.

Chambersburg

Early

York

Lee's Army of Northern Virginia

Early

GETTYSBURG JULY 1–3, 1863

Hanover

Hagerstown

Appomattox R.

Taneytown

Westminster

Meade's Army of the Potomac

Stuart

M D.

Frederick

Potomac R.

Baltimore

VICINITY OF GETTYSBURG 1863

N

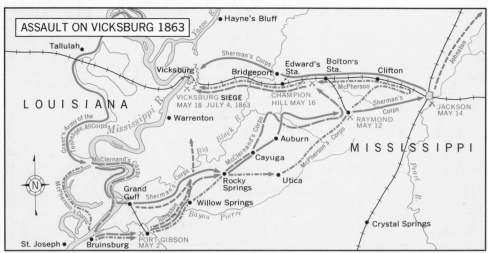

ASSAULT ON VICKSBURG 1863

Hayne's Bluff

Yazoo R.

Tallulah

Sherman's Corps

Vicksburg

Bridgeport

Edward's Sta.

Bolton's Sta.

Clifton

Johnston

L O U I S I A N A

VICKSBURG SIEGE MAY 18 JULY 4, 1863

CHAMPION HILL MAY 16

McPherson

JACKSON MAY 14

Grant's Army of the Tennessee. All Corps.

Mississippi R.

Warrenton

Black R.

Sherman's Corps

RAYMOND MAY 12

M I S S I S S I P P I

McClernand's Corps

Big Black R.

Auburn

McPherson's Corps

McClernand's Corps

Cayuga

McClernand's Corps

Grand Gulf

Sherman's

Rocky Springs

Utica

Pearl R.

McPherson's Corps

Willow Springs

Johnston

Bayou Pierre

Crystal Springs

St. Joseph

Bruinsburg

PORT GIBSON MAY 2

N

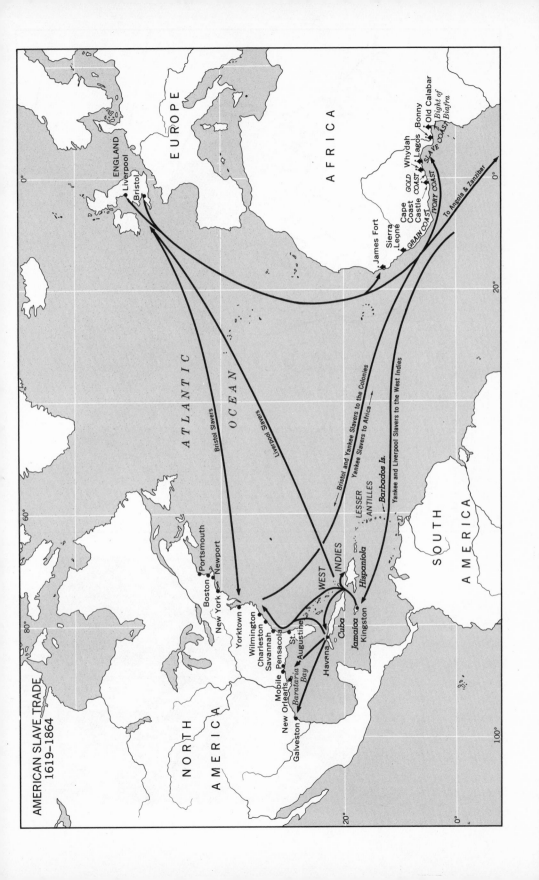

AMERICAN SLAVE TRADE
1619-1864

EUROPE

AFRICA

ENGLAND
Liverpool
Bristol

ATLANTIC

OCEAN

Bristol Slavers

Liverpool Slavers

James Fort

Sierra
Leone

Cape GOLD Whydah
Coast COAST Lagos
Castle COAST SLAVE COAST Bonny
GRAIN COAST IVORY COAST Old Calabar
Bight of
Biafra

To Angola & Zanzibar

Bristol and Yankee Slavers to the Colonies

Yankee Slavers to Africa

Yankee and Liverpool Slavers to the West Indies

LESSER
ANTILLES

Barbados Is.

SOUTH

AMERICA

WEST INDIES

Hispaniola

Cuba

Jamaica
Kingston

Havana

St.
Augustine

Barataria
Bay

Galveston

New Orleans

Mobile
Pensacola

Savannah
Charleston
Wilmington

Yorktown

New York

Boston Portsmouth
Newport

NORTH

AMERICA

0°

20°

0°

20°

60°

80°

100°

0°

20°

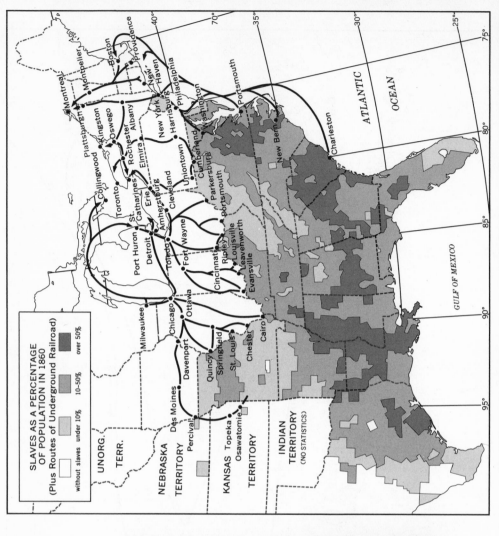

SLAVES AS A PERCENTAGE
OF POPULATION IN 1860
(Plus Routes of Underground Railroad)

without slaves   under 10%

10–50%   over 50%

"STAND UP A MAN!"

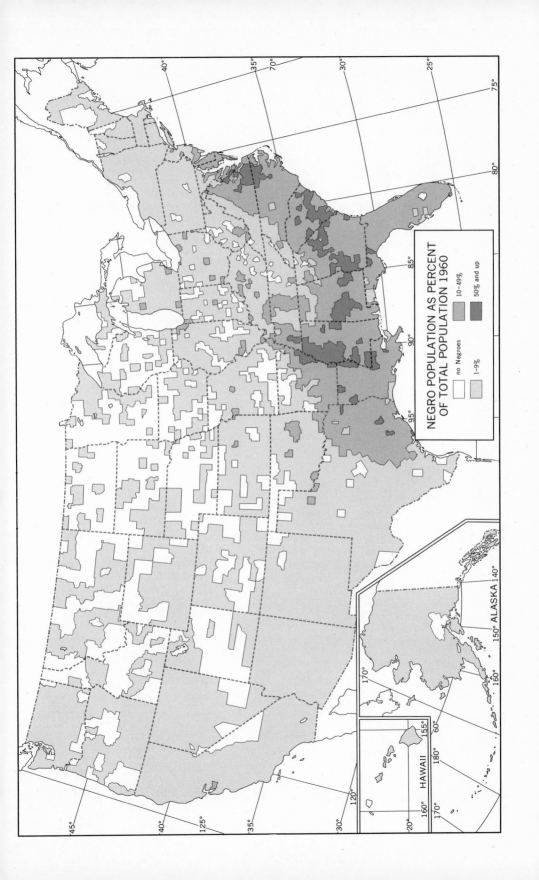

NEGRO POPULATION AS PERCENT
OF TOTAL POPULATION 1960

no Negroes

1-9%

10-49%

50% and up

ALASKA

HAWAII

1858

1.

The Union and Popular Sovereignty

The speech by Abraham Lincoln to the Republican State Convention at Springfield, Illinois, on June 16, 1858, launched his campaign for the U.S. Senate seat held by Stephen A. Douglas. Douglas replied less than a month later at Chicago, after which the two men sparred in their famous series of debates. Lincoln's speech was considered radical at the time and potentially dangerous. His former law partner, William H. Herndon, predicted, however, that the Republicans would eventually make him President. The challenge of Lincoln's "House Divided" speech was met by Douglas in his July 9 Chicago address, which began his campaign for reelection. Douglas was committed to the idea of "popular sovereignty" in opposition to the Republicans, who wished to exclude slavery from the territories. He also had to satisfy the Southern wing in his own Democratic Party, which wanted unlimited extension of slavery.

Source: *Political Speeches and Debates of Abraham Lincoln and Stephen A. Douglas 1854-1861*, Alonzo T. Jones, ed., Battle Creek, Mich., 1895, pp. 52-74.

I.

ABRAHAM LINCOLN:
A House Divided

Mr. President and Gentlemen of the Convention:

If we could first know where we are and whither we are tending, we could better judge what to do and how to do it. We are now far into the fifth year since a policy was initiated with the avowed object and confident promise of putting an end to slavery agitation. Under the operation of that policy, that agitation has not only not ceased but has constantly augmented. In my opinion, it will not cease until a crisis shall have been reached and passed. "A house divided against itself cannot stand." I believe this government cannot endure, permanently, half slave and half free. I do not expect the Union to be dissolved; I do not expect the house to fall; but I do expect it will cease to be divided. It will become all one thing, or all the other. Either the opponents of slavery will arrest the further spread of it and place it where the public mind shall rest in the belief that it is in the course of ultimate extinction, or its advocates will push it forward till it shall become alike lawful in all the states, old as well as new, North as well as South.

Have we no tendency to the latter condition?

Let anyone who doubts carefully contemplate that now almost complete legal combination — piece of machinery, so to speak — compounded of the Nebraska doctrine and the Dred Scott decision. Let him consider, not only what work the machinery is adapted to do, and how well adapted, but also let him study the history of its construction and trace, if he can, or rather fail, if he can, to trace the evidences of design and concert of action among its chief architects, from the beginning.

The new year of 1854 found slavery excluded from more than half the states by state constitutions and from most of the national territory by congressional prohibition. Four days later commenced the struggle which ended in repealing that congressional prohibition. This opened all the national territory to slavery and was the first point gained.

But, so far, Congress *only* had acted; and an endorsement by the people, real or apparent, was indispensable to save the point already gained and give chance for more.

This necessity had not been overlooked, but had been provided for, as well as might be, in the notable argument of "squatter sovereignty," otherwise called "sacred right of self-government," which latter phrase, though expressive of the only rightful basis of any government, was so perverted in this attempted use of it as to amount to just this: That if any *one* man choose to enslave *another*, no *third* man shall be allowed to object. That argument was incorporated into the Nebraska Bill itself, in the language which follows:

> It being the true intent and meaning of this act not to legislate slavery into any territory or state, nor to exclude it therefrom, but to leave the people thereof perfectly free to form and regulate their domestic institutions in their own way, subject only to the Constitution of the United States.

Then opened the roar of loose declamation in favor of "squatter sovereignty" and "sacred right of self-government." "But," said opposition members, "let us amend the bill so as to expressly declare that the people of the territory may exclude slavery." "Not we," said the friends of the measure; and down they voted the amendment.

While the Nebraska Bill was passing through Congress, a law case, involving the question of a Negro's freedom, by reason of his owner having voluntarily taken him first into a free state and then into a territory covered by the congressional prohibition, and held him as a slave for a long time in each, was passing through the United States Circuit Court for the district of Missouri; and both Nebraska Bill and lawsuit were brought to a decision in the same month of May 1854. The Negro's name was Dred Scott, which name now designates the decision finally made in the case. Before the then next presidential election, the law case came to, and was argued in, the Supreme Court of the United States; but the decision of it was deferred until after the election. Still, before the election, Senator Trumbull, on the floor of the Senate, requested the leading advocate of the Nebraska Bill to state his opinion whether the people of a territory can constitutionally exclude slavery from their limits; and the latter answers: "That is a question for the Supreme Court."

The election came. Mr. Buchanan was elected, and the endorsement, such as it was, secured. That was the second point gained. The endorsement, however, fell short of a clear popular majority by nearly 400,000 votes, and so, perhaps, was not overwhelmingly reliable and satisfactory. The outgoing President, in his last annual message, as impressively as possible echoed back upon the people the weight and authority of the endorsement. The Supreme Court met again, did not announce their decision, but ordered a reargument.

The presidential inauguration came, and still no decision of the Court; but the incoming President, in his inaugural address, fervently exhorted the people to abide by the forthcoming decision, whatever it might be. Then, in a few days, came the decision.

The reputed author of the Nebraska Bill finds an early occasion to make a speech at this capital endorsing the Dred Scott decision, and vehemently denouncing all opposition to it. The new President, too, seizes the early occasion of the Silliman letter to endorse and strongly construe that decision, and to express his astonishment that any different view had ever been entertained!

At length a squabble springs up between the President and the author of the Nebraska Bill, on the mere question of *fact*, whether the Lecompton constitution was or was not in any just sense made by the people of Kansas; and in that quarrel the latter declares that all he wants is a fair vote for the people, and that he cares not whether slavery be voted *down* or voted *up*. I do not understand his declaration, that he cares not whether slavery be voted down or voted up, to be intended by him other than as an apt definition of the policy he would impress upon the public mind — the principle for which he declares he has suffered so much and is ready to suffer to the end. And well may he cling to that principle! If he has any parental feeling, well may he cling to it. That principle is the only shred left of his original Nebraska doctrine.

Under the Dred Scott decision, "squatter sovereignty" squatted out of existence, tumbled down like temporary scaffolding; like the mold at the foundry, served through one blast and fell back into loose sand; helped to carry an election and then was kicked to the winds. His late joint struggle with the Republicans against the Lecompton constitution involves nothing of the original Nebraska doctrine. That struggle was made on a point — the right of a people to make their own constitution — upon which he and the Republicans have never differed.

The several points of the Dred Scott decision, in connection with Senator Douglas' "care not" policy, constitute the piece of machinery in its present state of advancement. This was the third point gained. The working points of that machinery are:

First, that no Negro slave, imported as such from Africa, and no descendant of such slave can ever be a citizen of any state in the sense of that term as used in the Constitution of the United States. This point is made in order to deprive the Negro, in every possible event, of the benefit of that provision of the United States Constitution which declares that "the citizens of each state shall be entitled to all the privileges and immunities of citizens in the several states."

Second, that, "subject to the Constitution of the United States," neither Congress nor a territorial legislature can exclude slavery from any United States territory. This point is made in order that individual men may fill up the territories with slaves, without danger of losing them as property, and thus enhance the chances of permanency to the institution through all the future.

Third, that whether the holding a Negro in actual slavery in a free state makes him free, as against the holder, the United States courts will not decide, but will leave to be decided by the courts of any slave state the Negro may be forced into by the master. This point is made, not to be pressed immediately but, if acquiesced in for awhile, and apparently endorsed by the people at an election, then to sustain the logical conclusion that what Dred Scott's master might lawfully do with Dred Scott in the free state of Illinois, every other master may lawfully do with any other one, or 1,000 slaves, in Illinois or in any other free state.

Auxiliary to all this, and working hand in

hand with it, the Nebraska doctrine, or what is left of it, is to educate and mold public opinion, at least Northern public opinion, not to care whether slavery is voted down or voted up. This shows exactly where we now are; and partially, also, whither we are tending.

It will throw additional light on the latter to go back and run the mind over the string of historical facts already stated. Several things will now appear less dark and mysterious than they did when they were transpiring. The people were to be left "perfectly free," "subject only to the Constitution." What the Constitution had to do with it, outsiders could not then see. Plainly enough, now, it was an exactly fitted niche for the Dred Scott decision to afterward come in and declare the perfect freedom of the people to be just no freedom at all.

Why was the amendment expressly declaring the right of the people voted down? Plainly enough, now, the adoption of it would have spoiled the niche for the Dred Scott decision. Why was the Court decision held up? Why even a senator's individual opinion withheld till after the presidential election? Plainly enough, now, the speaking out then would have damaged the "perfectly free" argument upon which the election was to be carried. Why the outgoing President's felicitation on the endorsement? Why the delay of a reargument? Why the incoming President's advance exhortation in favor of the decision? These things look like the cautious patting and petting of a spirited horse preparatory to mounting him when it is dreaded that he may give the rider a fall. And why the hasty after-endorsement of the decision by the President and others?

We cannot absolutely know that all these exact adaptations are the result of preconcert. But when we see a lot of framed timbers, different portions of which we know have been gotten out at different times and places and by different workmen — Stephen, Franklin, Roger, and James, for instance — and when we see these timbers joined together and see they exactly make the frame of a house or a mill, all the tenons and mortises exactly fitting, and all the lengths and proportions of the different pieces exactly adapted to their respective places, and not a piece too many or too few, not omitting even scaffolding, or, if a single piece be lacking, we see the place in the frame exactly fitted and prepared yet to bring such piece in — in such a case, we find it impossible not to believe that Stephen and Franklin and Roger and James all understood one another from the beginning, and all worked upon a common plan or draft drawn up before the first blow was struck.

II.

STEPHEN A. DOUGLAS:
Reply to Lincoln

I REGARD THE GREAT PRINCIPLE of popular sovereignty as having been vindicated and made triumphant in this land as a permanent rule of public policy in the organization of territories and the admission of new states. Illinois took her position upon this principle many years ago. . . .

The great principle is the right of every community to judge and decide for itself whether a thing is right or wrong, whether it would be good or evil for them to adopt it; and the right of free action, the right of free thought, the right of free judgment, upon the question is dearer to every true American than any other under a free government. My objection to the Lecompton contrivance was that it undertook to put a constitution on the people of Kansas against their own will, in opposition to their wishes, and thus violated the principle upon which all our institutions rest. It is no answer to this argument to say that slavery is an evil, and hence should not be tolerated.

You must allow the people to decide for themselves whether it is a good or an evil.

You allow them to decide for themselves whether they desire a Maine Liquor Law or not; you allow them to decide for themselves what kind of common schools they will have, what system of banking they will adopt, or whether they will adopt any at all; you allow them to decide for themselves the relations between husband and wife, parent and child, guardian and ward; in fact, you allow them to decide for themselves all other questions; and why not upon this question? Whenever you put a limitation upon the right of any people to decide what laws they want, you have destroyed the fundamental principle of self-government.

Mr. Lincoln made a speech before that Republican Convention which unanimously nominated him for the Senate — a speech evidently well prepared and carefully written in which he states the basis upon which he proposes to carry on the campaign during this summer. In it he lays down two distinct propositions which I shall notice, and upon which I shall take a direct and bold issue with him.

His first and main proposition I will give in his own language, Scripture quotations and all. [*Laughter.*] I give his exact language: " 'A house divided against itself cannot stand.' I believe this government cannot endure, permanently, half *slave* and half *free.* I do not expect the Union to be *dissolved;* I do not expect the house to *fall;* but I do expect it to cease to be divided. It will become *all* one thing, or *all* the other."

In other words, Mr. Lincoln asserts, as a fundamental principle of this government, that there must be uniformity in the local laws and domestic institutions of each and all the states of the Union; and he therefore invites all the nonslaveholding states to band together, organize as one body, and make war upon slavery in Kentucky, upon slavery in Virginia, upon the Carolinas, upon slavery in all of the slaveholding states in this Union, and to persevere in that war until it shall be exterminated.

He then notifies the slaveholding states to stand together as a unit and make an aggressive war upon the free states of this Union with a view of establishing slavery in them all; of forcing it upon Illinois, of forcing it upon New York, upon New England, and upon every other free state, and that they shall keep up the warfare until it has been formally established in them all.

In other words, Mr. Lincoln advocates boldly and clearly a war of sections, a war of the North against the South, of the free states against the slave states, a war of extermination to be continued relentlessly until the one or the other shall be subdued and all the states shall either become free or become slave.

Now, my friends, I must say to you frankly that I take bold, unqualified issue with him upon that principle. I assert that it is neither desirable nor possible that there should be uniformity in the local institutions and domestic regulations of the different states of this Union. . . .

The framers of the Constitution well understood that each locality, having separate and distinct interests, required separate and distinct laws, domestic institutions, and police regulations adapted to its own wants and its own condition; and they acted on the presumption, also, that these laws and institutions would be as diversified and as dissimilar as the states would be numerous and that no two would be precisely alike, because the interests of no two would be precisely the same. Hence, I assert that the great fundamental principle which underlies our complex system of state and federal governments contemplated diversity and dissimilarity in the local institutions and domestic affairs of each and every state then in the Union or thereafter to be admitted into the confederacy.

I therefore conceive that my friend Mr. Lincoln has totally misapprehended the great principles upon which our government rests. Uniformity in local and domestic affairs would be destructive of state rights, of state sovereignty, of personal liberty and personal freedom. Uniformity is the parent of despotism the world over, not only in politics but in religion. Wherever the doctrine of uniformity is proclaimed that all the states must be free or all slave, that all labor must be white or all black, that all the citizens of the different states must have the same privileges or be governed by the same regulations, you have destroyed the greatest safeguard which our institutions have thrown around the rights of the citizen.

How could this uniformity be accomplished if it was desirable and possible? There is but one mode in which it could be obtained, and that must be by abolishing the state legislatures, blotting out state sovereignty, merging the rights and sovereignty of the states in one consolidated empire, and vesting Congress with the plenary power to make all the police regulations, domestic and local laws, uniform throughout the limits of the republic. When you shall have done this, you will have uniformity. Then the states will all be slave or all be free; then Negroes will vote everywhere or nowhere; then you will have a Maine Liquor Law in every state or none; then you will have uniformity in all things, local or domestic, by the authority of the federal government. But, when you attain that uniformity, you will have converted these thirty-two sovereign, independent states into one consolidated empire, with the uniformity of disposition reigning triumphant throughout the length and breadth of the land.

From this view of the case, my friends, I am driven irresistibly to the conclusion that diversity, dissimilarity, variety in all our local and domestic institutions is the great safeguard of our liberties and that the framers of our institutions were wise, sagacious, and patriotic when they made this government a confederation of sovereign states, with a legislature for each, and conferred upon each legislature the power to make all local and domestic institutions to suit the people it represented, without interference from any other state or from the general Congress of the Union. If we expect to maintain our liberties, we must preserve the rights and sovereignty of the states; we must maintain and carry out that great principle of self-government incorporated in the compromise measures of 1850; endorsed by the Illinois legislature in 1851; emphatically embodied and carried out in the Kansas-Nebraska Bill, and vindicated this year by the refusal to bring Kansas into the Union with a constitution distasteful to her people.

The other proposition discussed by Mr. Lincoln in his speech consists in a crusade against the Supreme Court of the United States on account of the Dred Scott decision. On this question, also, I desire to say to you unequivocally that I take direct and distinct issue with him. I have no warfare to make on the Supreme Court of the United States, either on account of that or any other decision which they have pronounced from that bench. The Constitution of the United States has provided that the powers of government (and the constitution of each state has the same provision) shall be divided into three departments: executive, legislative, and judicial. The right and the province of expounding the Constitution and constructing the law is vested in the judiciary established by the Constitution. As a lawyer, I feel at liberty to appear before the Court and controvert any principle of law while the question is pending before the tribunal; but, when the decision is made, my private opinion, your opinion, all other opinions must yield to the majesty of that authoritative adjudication.

I wish you to bear in mind that this involves a great principle, upon which our rights, our liberty, and our property all depend. What security have you for your property, for your reputation, and for your personal rights if the courts are not upheld and their decisions respected when once fairly rendered by the highest tribunal known to the Constitution? I do not choose, therefore, to go into any argument with Mr. Lincoln in reviewing the various decisions which the Supreme Court has made, either upon the Dred Scott case or any other. I have no idea of appealing from the decision of the Supreme Court upon a constitutional question to the decisions of a tumultuous town meeting. . . .

Hence, I am opposed to this doctrine of Mr. Lincoln by which he proposes to take an appeal from the decision of the Supreme Court of the United States, upon this high constitutional question, to a Republican caucus sitting in the country. Yes, or any other caucus or town meeting, whether it be Republican, American, or Democratic. I respect the decisions of that august tribunal; I shall always bow in deference to them. I am a law-abiding man. I will sustain the Constitution of my country as our fathers have made it. I will yield obedience to the laws, whether I like them or not, as I find them on the statute book. I will sustain the judicial tribunals and constituted authorities in all matters within the pale of their jurisdiction as defined by the Constitution.

But I am equally free to say that the reason assigned by Mr. Lincoln for resisting the decision of the Supreme Court in the Dred Scott case does not in itself meet any approbation. He objects to it because that decision declared that a Negro descended from African parents, who were brought here and sold as slaves, is not, and cannot be, a citizen of the United States. He says it is wrong because it deprives the Negro of the benefits of that clause of the Constitution which says that citizens of one state shall enjoy all the privileges and immunities of citizens of the several states; in other words, he thinks it wrong because it deprives the Negro of the privileges, immunities, and rights of citizenship which pertain, according to that decision, only to the white man.

I am free to say to you that in my opinion this government of ours is founded on the white basis. It was made by the white man, for the benefit of the white man, to be administered by white men, in such manner as they should determine. It is also true that a Negro, an Indian, or any other man of inferior race to a white man should be permitted to enjoy, and humanity requires that he should have, all the rights, privileges, and immunities which he is capable of exercising consistent with the safety of society. I would give him every right and every privilege which his capacity would enable him to enjoy, consistent with the good of the society in which he lived.

But you may ask me: What are these rights and these privileges? My answer is that each state must decide for itself the nature and extent of these rights.

Illinois has decided for herself. We have decided that the Negro shall not be a slave, and we have at the same time decided that he shall not vote, or serve on juries, or enjoy political privileges. I am content with that system of policy which we have adopted for ourselves. I deny the right of any other state to complain of our policy in that respect, or to interfere with it, or to attempt to change it.

On the other hand, the state of Maine has decided that in that state a Negro man may vote on an equality with the white man. The sovereign power of Maine has the right to prescribe that rule for herself. Illinois has no right to complain of Maine for conferring the right of Negro suffrage, nor has Maine any right to interfere with or complain of Illinois because she has denied Negro suffrage. . . .

Thus you see, my fellow citizens, that the issues between Mr. Lincoln and myself . . . are direct, unequivocal, and irreconcilable. He goes for uniformity in our domestic institutions, for a war of sections, until one or the other shall be subdued. I go for the great principle of the Kansas-Nebraska Bill — the right of the people to decide for themselves.

2.

The Lincoln-Douglas Debates

The debates between Abraham Lincoln and Stephen A. Douglas for the U.S. Senate seat from Illinois in 1858 constitute one of the most famous political dialogues in American history. A man of great ability with a magnificent voice, Douglas had served in the Senate since 1847, and was generally regarded as a certain presidential candidate in 1860. Lincoln's voice was high-pitched; he tended to speak indifferently at first, but then to warm to his subject. Riding into town on a wagon, he played to the hilt the contrast with Douglas' splendid entourage, which included a private railroad car. In the end, Lincoln narrowly lost the election through inequitable apportionment, but acquired a national reputation.

Source: *Collections of the Illinois State Historical Library,* Vol. III, Lincoln Series, Vol. I: "The Lincoln-Douglas Debates of 1858," Edwin E. Sparks, ed., Springfield, 1908, pp. 86-364, 474-496.

I.

OTTAWA, August 21

Douglas' Speech

I APPEAR BEFORE YOU TODAY for the purpose of discussing the leading political topics which now agitate the public mind. By an arrangement between Mr. Lincoln and myself, we are present here today for the purpose of having a joint discussion, as the representatives of the two great political parties of the state and Union, upon the principles in issue between those parties, and this vast concourse of people shows the deep feeling which pervades the public mind in regard to the questions dividing us. . . .

Mr. Lincoln . . . says that this government cannot endure permanently in the same condition in which it was made by its framers — divided into free and slave states. He says that it has existed for about seventy years thus divided, and yet he tells you that it cannot endure permanently on the same principles and in the same relative condition in which our fathers made it.

Why can it not exist divided into free and slave states? Washington, Jefferson, Franklin, Madison, Hamilton, Jay, and the great men of that day made this government divided into free states and slave states, and left each state perfectly free to do as it pleased on the subject of slavery. Why can it not exist on the same principles on which our fathers made it?

They knew when they framed the Constitution that in a country as wide and broad as this, with such a variety of climate, production, and interest, the people necessarily required different laws and institutions in different localities. They knew that the laws and regulations which would suit the granite hills of New Hampshire would be unsuited to the rice plantations of South Carolina. And they therefore provided that each state should retain its own legislature and its own sovereignty, with the full and complete power to do as it pleased within its own limits, in all that was local and not national.

One of the reserved rights of the states was the right to regulate the relations between master and servant on the slavery question. At the time the Constitution was framed, there were thirteen states in the Union, twelve of which were slaveholding states and one a free state. Suppose this doctrine of uniformity preached by Mr. Lincoln, that the states should all be free or all be slave, had prevailed, and what would have been the result? Of course, the twelve slaveholding states would have overruled the one free state, and slavery would have been fastened by a constitutional provision on every inch of the American republic, instead of being left, as our fathers wisely left it, to each state to decide for itself.

Here I assert that uniformity in the local laws and institutions of the different states is neither possible or desirable. If uniformity had been adopted when the government was established, it must inevitably have been the uniformity of slavery everywhere, or else the uniformity of Negro citizenship and Negro equality everywhere.

We are told by Lincoln that he is utterly opposed to the Dred Scott decision and will not submit to it for the reason that he says it deprives the Negro of the rights and privileges of citizenship. That is the first and main reason which he assigns for his warfare on the Supreme Court of the United States and its decision. I ask you, are you in favor of conferring upon the Negro the rights and privileges of citizenship? Do you desire to strike out of our state constitution that clause which keeps slaves and free Negroes out of the state and allows the free Negroes to flow in and cover your prairies with black settlements? Do you desire to turn this beautiful state into a free Negro colony in order that, when Missouri abolishes slavery, she can send 100,000 emancipated slaves into Illinois to become citizens and voters, on an equality with yourselves?

If you desire Negro citizenship, if you desire to allow them to come into the state and settle with the white man, if you desire them to vote on an equality with yourselves and to make them eligible to office, to serve on juries, and to adjudge your rights, then support Mr. Lincoln and the Black Republican Party, who are in favor of the citizenship of the Negro.

For one, I am opposed to Negro citizenship in any and every form. I believe this government was made on the white basis. I believe it was made by white men, for the benefit of white men and their posterity forever, and I am in favor of confining citizenship to white men, men of European birth and descent, instead of conferring it upon Negroes, Indians, and other inferior races.

Mr. Lincoln, following the example and lead of all the little Abolition orators who go around and lecture in the basements of schools and churches, reads from the Declaration of Independence that all men were created equal, and then asks — How can you deprive a Negro of that equality which God and the Declaration of Independence award to him? He and they maintain that Negro equality is guaranteed by the laws of God and that it is asserted in the Declaration of Independence. If they think so, of course they have a right to say so, and so vote.

I do not question Mr. Lincoln's conscientious belief that the Negro was made his equal and hence is his brother. But for my own part, I do not regard the Negro as my equal, and positively deny that he is my brother or any kin to me whatever. Lincoln has evidently learned by heart Parson Lovejoy's catechism. He can repeat it as well as Farnsworth, and he is worthy of a medal from Father Giddings and Fred Douglass for his Abolitionism. He holds that the Ne-

Stephen A. Douglas; photographed before 1860

gro was born his equal and yours, and that he was endowed with equality by the Almighty, and that no human law can deprive him of these rights which were guaranteed to him by the Supreme Ruler of the Universe.

Now I do not believe that the Almighty ever intended the Negro to be the equal of the white man. If he did, he has been a long time demonstrating the fact. For thousands of years the Negro has been a race upon the earth, and during all that time, in all latitudes and climates, wherever he has wandered or been taken, he has been inferior to the race which he has there met. He belongs to an inferior race and must always occupy an inferior position.

I do not hold that because the Negro is our inferior that, therefore, he ought to be a slave. By no means can such a conclusion be drawn from what I have said. On the contrary, I hold that humanity and Christianity both require that the Negro shall have and enjoy every right, every privilege, and every immunity consistent with the safety of the society in which he lives. On that point, I presume, there can be no di-

versity of opinion. You and I are bound to extend to our inferior and dependent beings every right, every privilege, every facility and immunity consistent with the public good.

The question then arises — What rights and privileges are consistent with the public good? This is a question which each state and each territory must decide for itself. Illinois has decided it for herself. We have provided that the Negro shall not be a slave, and we have also provided that he shall not be a citizen, but protect him in his civil rights, in his life, his person, and his property, only depriving him of all political rights whatsoever and refusing to put him on an equality with the white man. That policy of Illinois is satisfactory to the Democratic Party and to me; and if it were to the Republicans, there would then be no question upon the subject.

But the Republicans say that he ought to be made a citizen, and when he becomes a citizen he becomes your equal, with all your rights and privileges. They assert the Dred Scott decision to be monstrous because it denies that the Negro is or can be a citizen under the Constitution. Now, I hold that Illinois had a right to abolish and prohibit slavery as she did, and I hold that Kentucky has the same right to continue and protect slavery that Illinois had to abolish it. I hold that New York had as much right to abolish slavery as Virginia has to continue it, and that each and every state of this Union is a sovereign power, with the right to do as it pleases upon this question of slavery and upon all its domestic institutions.

Slavery is not the only question which comes up in this controversy. There is a far more important one to you and that is — What shall be done with the free Negro? We have settled the slavery question as far as we are concerned; we have prohibited it in Illinois forever; and in doing so, I think we have done wisely. And there is no man in the state who would be more strenuous in his opposition to the introduction of slavery than I would. But when we settled it for ourselves, we exhausted all our power over that subject. We have done our whole duty and can do no more. We must leave each and every other state to decide for itself the same question.

In relation to the policy to be pursued toward the free Negroes, we have said that they shall not vote; while Maine, on the other hand, has said that they shall vote. Maine is a sovereign state and has the power to regulate the qualifications of voters within her limits. I would never consent to confer the right of voting and of citizenship upon a Negro; but still I am not going to quarrel with Maine for differing from me in opinion. Let Maine take care of her own Negroes and fix the qualifications of her own voters to suit herself without interfering with Illinois, and Illinois will not interfere with Maine.

So with the state of New York. She allows the Negro to vote, provided he owns $250 worth of property, but not otherwise. While I would not make any distinction whatever between a Negro who held property and one who did not; yet, if the sovereign state of New York chooses to make that distinction, it is her business and not mine, and I will not quarrel with her for it. She can do as she pleases on this question if she minds her own business, and we will do the same thing.

Now, my friends, if we will only act conscientiously and rigidly upon this great principle of popular sovereignty, which guarantees to each state and territory the right to do as it pleases on all things, local and domestic, instead of Congress interfering, we will continue at peace one with another. Why should Illinois be at war with Missouri, or Kentucky with Ohio, or Virginia with New York, merely because their institutions differ? Our fathers intended that our institutions should differ. They knew that the North and the South, having different climates, productions, and interests, required different institutions. This doctrine of Mr. Lincoln, of uniformity among the institutions of the different states, is a new doctrine, never dreamed of by Washington, Madison, or the framers of this government. Mr. Lincoln and the Republican Party set themselves up as wiser than these men who made this government, which has flourished for seventy years under the principle of popular sovereignty, recognizing the right of each state to do as it pleased.

Under that principle, we have grown from a nation of 3 or 4 million to a nation of about 30 million people; we have crossed the Allegheny Mountains and filled up the whole Northwest, turning the prairie into a garden, and building up churches and schools, thus spreading civilization and Christianity where before there was nothing but savage barbarism. Under that principle we have become, from a feeble nation, the most powerful on the face of the earth; and if we only adhere to that principle, we can go forward increasing in territory, in power, in strength, and in glory until the republic of America shall be the North Star that shall guide the friends of freedom throughout the civilized world.

Lincoln's Reply

I WILL SAY HERE . . . that I have no purpose, directly or indirectly, to interfere with the institution of slavery in the states where it exists. I believe I have no lawful right to do so, and I have no inclination to do so. I have no purpose to introduce political and social equality between the white and the black races. There is a physical difference between the two which, in my judgment, will probably forever forbid their living together upon the footing of perfect equality; and inasmuch as it becomes a necessity that there must be a difference, I, as well as Judge Douglas, am in favor of the race to which I belong having the superior position.

I have never said anything to the contrary, but I hold that, notwithstanding all this, there is no reason in the world why the Negro is not entitled to all the natural rights enumerated in the Declaration of Independence — the right to life, liberty, and the pursuit of happiness. I hold that he is as much entitled to these as the white man. I agree with Judge Douglas he is not my equal in many respects — certainly not in color, perhaps not in moral or intellectual endowment. But in the right to eat the bread, without the leave of anybody else, which his own hand earns, he is my equal, and the equal of Judge Douglas, and the equal of every living man. . . .

As I have not used up so much of my time as I had supposed, I will dwell a little longer upon one or two of these minor topics upon which the Judge has spoken. He has read from my speech in Springfield, in which I say "that a house divided against itself cannot stand." Does the Judge say it can stand? I don't know whether he does or not. The Judge does not seem to be attending to me just now, but I would like to know if it is his opinion that a house divided against itself can stand. If he does, then there is a question of veracity, not between him and me, but between the Judge and an authority of a somewhat higher character.

Now, my friends, I ask your attention to this matter for the purpose of saying something seriously. I know that the Judge may readily enough agree with me that the maxim which was put forth by the Savior is true, but he may allege that I misapply it; and the Judge has a right to urge that, in my application, I do misapply it, and then I have a right to show that I do *not* misapply it.

When he undertakes to say that because I think this nation, so far as the question of slavery is concerned, will all become one thing or all the other, I am in favor of bringing about a dead uniformity in the various states, in all their institutions, he argues erroneously. The great variety of the local institutions in the states, springing from differences in the soil, differences in the face of the country, and in the climate,

are bonds of union. They do not make "a house divided against itself" but they make a house united. If they produce in one section of the country what is called for by the wants of another section, and this other section can supply the wants of the first, they are not matters of discord but bonds of union, true bonds of union.

But can this question of slavery be considered as among *these* varieties in the institutions of the country? I leave it to you to say whether, in the history of our government, this institution of slavery has not always failed to be a bond of union, and, on the contrary, been an apple of discord and an element of division in the house. I ask you to consider whether, so long as the moral constitution of men's minds shall continue to be the same, after this generation and assemblage shall sink into the grave and another race shall arise, with the same moral and intellectual development we have, whether, if that institution is standing in the same irritating position in which it now is, it will not continue an element of division?

If so, then I have a right to say that, in regard to this question, the Union is a house divided against itself; and when the Judge reminds me that I have often said to him that the institution of slavery has existed for eighty years in some states, and yet it does not exist in some others, I agree to the fact, and I account for it by looking at the position in which our fathers originally placed it — restricting it from the new territories where it had not gone and legislating to cut off its source by the abrogation of the slave trade, thus putting the seal of legislation *against its spread.*

The public mind *did* rest in the belief that it was in the course of ultimate extinction. But lately, I think — and in this I charge nothing on the Judge's motives — lately, I think, that he, and those acting with him, have placed that institution on a new basis, which looks to the *perpetuity and nationalization of slavery.* And while it is placed upon this new basis, I say, and I have said that I believe we shall not have peace upon the question until the opponents of slavery arrest the further spread of it, and place it where the public mind shall rest in the belief that it is in the course of ultimate extinction; or, on the other hand, that its advocates will push it forward until it shall become alike lawful in all the states, old as well as new, North as well as South.

Now, I believe if we could arrest the spread and place it where Washington and Jefferson and Madison placed it, it would be in the course of ultimate extinction, and the public mind *would*, as for eighty years past, believe that it was in the course of ultimate extinction. The crises would be past, and the institution might be let alone for a hundred years, if it should live so long, in the states where it exists; yet it would be going out of existence in the way best for both the black and the white races.

Well, then, let us talk about popular sovereignty. What is popular sovereignty? Is it the right of the people to have slavery or not have it, as they see fit, in the territories? I will state — and I have an able man to watch me — my understanding is that popular sovereignty, as now applied to the question of slavery, does allow the people of a territory to have slavery if they want to, but does not allow them *not* to have it if they *do not* want it.

I do not mean that if this vast concourse of people were in a territory of the United States, any one of them would be obliged to have a slave if he did not want one; but I do say that, as I understand the Dred Scott decision, if any one man wants slaves, all the rest have no way of keeping that one man from holding them.

When I made my speech at Springfield, of which the Judge complains, and from which he quotes, I really was not thinking of the things which he ascribes to me at all. I had no thought in the world that I was doing anything to bring about a war between the free and slave states. I had no

Library of Congress

Abraham Lincoln; from a photograph made at Beardstown, Ill., during the 1858 debates

thought in the world that I was doing anything to bring about a political and social equality of the black and the white races. It never occurred to me that I was doing anything, or favoring anything to reduce to a dead uniformity all the local institutions of the various states. But I must say, in all fairness to him, if he thinks I am doing something which leads to these bad results, it is none the better that I did not mean it.

It is just as fatal to the country, if I have any influence in producing it, whether I intend it or not. But can it be true that placing this institution upon the original basis — the basis upon which our fathers placed it — can have any tendency to set the Northern and the Southern states at war with one another, or that it can have any tendency to make the people of Vermont raise sugarcane because they raise it in Louisiana; or that it can compel the people of Illinois to cut pine logs on the Grand Prairie, where they will not grow, because they cut pine logs in Maine, where they do grow?

The Judge says this is a new principle started in regard to this question. Does the

Judge claim that he is working on the plan of the founders of the government? I think he says in some of his speeches — indeed, I have one here now — that he saw evidence of a policy to allow slavery to be south of a certain line, while north of it, it should be excluded; and he saw an indisposition on the part of the country to stand upon that policy, and therefore he sat about studying the subject upon *original principles*, and upon *original principles* he got up the Nebraska Bill! I am fighting it upon these "original principles" — fighting it in the Jeffersonian, Washingtonian, and Madisonian fashion. . . .

I want to ask your attention to a portion of the Nebraska Bill which Judge Douglas has quoted: "It being the true intent and meaning of this act not to legislate slavery into any territory or state, nor to exclude it therefrom, but to leave the people thereof perfectly free to form and regulate their domestic institutions in their own way, subject only to the Constitution of the United States." Thereupon, Judge Douglas and others began to argue in favor of "popular sovereignty" — the right of the people to have slaves if they wanted them, and to exclude slavery if they did not want them. "But," said, in substance, a senator from Ohio (Mr. Chase, I believe), "We more than suspect that you do not mean to allow the people to exclude slavery if they wish to; and if you do mean it, accept an amendment, which I propose, expressly authorizing the people to exclude slavery."

I believe I have the amendment here before me which was offered, and under which the people of the territory, through their proper representatives, might, if they saw fit, prohibit the existence of slavery therein. And now I state it as a fact, to be taken back if there is any mistake about it, that Judge Douglas and those acting with him voted that amendment down. I now think that those men who voted it down had a *real reason* for doing so. They know what that reason was.

It looks to us, since we have seen the Dred Scott decision pronounced, holding that "under the Constitution," the people cannot exclude slavery — I say it looks to outsiders, poor, simple, "amiable, intelligent gentlemen" as though the niche was left as a place to put that Dred Scott decision in — a niche which would have been spoiled by adopting the amendment. And now, I say again, if *this* was not the reason, it will avail the Judge much more to calmly and good-humoredly point out to these people what that *other* reason was for voting the amendment down than, swelling himself up, to vociferate that he may be provoked to call somebody a liar. . . .

In the first place, what is necessary to make the institution national? Not war. There is no danger that the people of Kentucky will shoulder their muskets, and, with a young "nigger" stuck on every bayonet, march into Illinois and force them upon us. There is no danger of our going over there and making war upon them. Then what is necessary for the nationalization of slavery? It is simply the next Dred Scott decision. It is merely for the Supreme Court to decide that no state under the Constitution can exclude it, just as they have already decided that under the Constitution neither Congress nor the territorial legislature can do it. When that is decided and acquiesced in, the whole thing is done.

This being true, and this being the way, as I think, that slavery is to be made national, let us consider what Judge Douglas is doing every day to that end. In the first place, let us see what influence he is exerting on public sentiment. In this and like communities, public sentiment is everything. With public sentiment, nothing can fail; without it, nothing can succeed. Consequently, he who molds public sentiment goes deeper than he who enacts statutes or pronounces decisions. He makes statutes and decisions possible or impossible to be executed. This must be borne in mind, as also the additional fact that Judge Douglas is a man of vast influence, so great that it is enough for many men to profess to believe anything, when they once find out that Judge Douglas professes to believe it.

Consider also the attitude he occupies at the head of a large party — a party which he claims has a majority of all the voters of the country. This man sticks to a decision which forbids the people of a territory from excluding slavery; and he does so, not because he says it is right in itself — he does not give any opinion on that — but because it has been decided by the Court; and being decided by the Court, he is, and you are, bound to take it in your political action as law, not that he judges at all of its merits but because a decision of the Court is to him a "Thus saith the Lord." He places it on that ground alone; and you will bear in mind that thus committing himself unreservedly to this decision commits him to the next one just as firmly as to this. He did not commit himself on account of the merit or demerit of the decision, but it is a "Thus saith the Lord." The next decision, as much as this, will be a "Thus saith the Lord." . . .

Now, having spoken of the Dred Scott decision, one more word and I am done. Henry Clay, my *beau ideal* of a statesman — the man for whom I fought all my humble life — Henry Clay once said of a class of men who would repress all tendencies to liberty and ultimate emancipation that they must, if they would do this, go back to the era of our independence and muzzle the cannon which thunders its annual joyous return; they must blow out the moral lights around us; they must penetrate the human soul and eradicate there the love of liberty; and then, and not till then, could they perpetuate slavery in this country! To my thinking, Judge Douglas is, by his example and vast influence, doing that very thing in this community when he says that the Negro has nothing in the Declaration of Independence. Henry Clay plainly understood the contrary.

Judge Douglas is going back to the era of our Revolution, and, to the extent of his ability, muzzling the cannon which thunders its annual joyous return. When he invites any people, willing to have slavery, to establish it, he is blowing out the moral lights around us. When he says he "cares not whether slavery is voted down or voted up" — that it is a sacred right of self-government — he is, in my judgment, penetrating the human soul and eradicating the light of reason and the love of liberty in this American people.

And now I will only say that when, by all these means and appliances, Judge Douglas shall succeed in bringing public sentiment to an exact accordance with his own views; when these vast assemblages shall echo back all these sentiments; when they shall come to repeat his views and to avow his principles, and to say all that he says on these mighty questions, then it needs only the formality of the second Dred Scott decision, which he endorses in advance, to make slavery alike lawful in all the states, old as well as new, North as well as South.

II.

FREEPORT, August 27

Lincoln's Speech

I HAVE SUPPOSED MYSELF, since the organization of the Republican Party at Bloomington, in May 1856, bound as a party man by the platforms of the party, then and since. If in any interrogatories which I shall answer I go beyond the scope of what is within these platforms, it will be perceived that no one is responsible but myself.

Having said thus much, I will take up the Judge's interrogatories as I find them printed in the *Chicago Times*, and answer them *seriatim*. In order that there may be no mistake about it, I have copied the interrogatories in writing, and also my answers to it. The first one of these interrogatories is in these words:

Question 1. "I desire to know whether Lincoln today stands as he did in 1854 in favor of the unconditional repeal of the Fugitive Slave Law?"

Answer. I do not now, nor ever did, stand in favor of the unconditional repeal of the Fugitive Slave Law.

Q. 2. "I desire him to answer whether he stands pledged today as he did in 1854 against the admission of any more slave states into the Union, even if the people want them?"

A. I do not now, nor ever did, stand pledged against the admission of any more slave states into the Union.

Q. 3. "I want to know whether he stands pledged against the admission of a new state into the Union with such a constitution as the people of that state may see fit to make?"

A. I do not stand pledged against the admission of a new state into the Union with such a constitution as the people of that state may see fit to make.

Q. 4. "I want to know whether he stands today pledged to the abolition of slavery in the District of Columbia?"

A. I do not stand today pledged to the abolition of slavery in the District of Columbia.

Q. 5. "I desire him to answer whether he stands pledged to the prohibition of the slave trade between the different states?"

A. I do not stand pledged to the prohibition of the slave trade between the different states.

Q. 6. "I desire to know whether he stands pledged to prohibit slavery in all the territories of the United States, north as well as south of the Missouri Compromise line?"

A. I am impliedly, if not expressly, pledged to a belief in the *right* and *duty* of

Congress to prohibit slavery in all the United States territories.

Q. 7. "I desire him to answer whether he is opposed to the acquisition of any new territory unless slavery is first prohibited therein?"

A. I am not generally opposed to honest acquisition of territory; and, in any given case, I would or would not oppose such acquisition, accordingly as I might think such acquisition would or would not aggravate the slavery question among ourselves. . . .

Now, in all this the Judge has me, and he has me on the record. I suppose he had flattered himself that I was really entertaining one set of opinions for one place and another set for another place; that I was afraid to say at one place what I uttered at another. What I am saying here I suppose I say to a vast audience as strongly tending to Abolitionism as any audience in the state of Illinois, and I believe I am saying that which, if it would be offensive to any persons and render them enemies to myself, would be offensive to persons in this audience.

I now proceed to propound to the Judge the interrogatories, so far as I have framed them. I will bring forward a new installment when I get them ready. I will bring them forward now, only reaching to number four. . . .

Question 1. If the people of Kansas shall, by means entirely unobjectionable in all other respects, adopt a state constitution and ask admission into the Union under it, *before* they have the requisite number of inhabitants according to the English Bill — some 93,000 — will you vote to admit them?

Q. 2. Can the people of a United States territory, in any lawful way, against the wish of any citizen of the United States, exclude slavery from its limits prior to the formation of a state constitution?

Q. 3. If the Supreme Court of the

United States shall decree that states cannot exclude slavery from their limits, are you in favor of acquiescing in, adopting, and following such decision as a rule of political action?

Q. 4. Are you in favor of acquiring additional territory in disregard of how such acquisition may effect the nation on the slavery question?

Douglas' Reply

IN REFERENCE TO KANSAS, it is my opinion that as she has population enough to constitute a slave state, she has people enough for a free state. I will not make Kansas an exceptional case to the other states of the Union.

I hold it to be a sound rule, of universal application, to require a territory to contain the requisite population for a member of Congress before it is admitted as a state into the Union. I made that proposition in the Senate in 1856, and I renewed it during the last session in a bill providing that no territory of the United States should form a constitution and apply for admission until it had the requisite population.

On another occasion I proposed that neither Kansas nor any other territory should be admitted until it had the requisite population. Congress did not adopt any of my propositions containing this general rule, but did make an exception of Kansas. I will stand by that exception. Either Kansas must come in as a free state, with whatever population she may have, or the rule must be applied to all the other territories alike. I therefore answer at once that, it having been decided that Kansas has people enough for a slave state, I hold that she has enough for a free state. . . .

The next question propounded to me by Mr. Lincoln is: Can the people of a territory, in any lawful way, against the wishes of any citizen of the United States, exclude slavery from their limits prior to the formation of a state constitution? I answer emphatically, as Mr. Lincoln has heard me answer a hundred times from every stump in Illinois, that in my opinion the people of a territory can, by lawful means, exclude slavery from their limits prior to the formation of a state constitution. Mr. Lincoln knew that I had answered that question over and over again. He heard me argue the Nebraska Bill on that principle all over the state in 1854, in 1855, and in 1856, and he has no excuse for pretending to be in doubt as to my position on that question.

It matters not what way the Supreme Court may hereafter decide as to the abstract question whether slavery may or may not go into a territory under the Constitution; the people have the lawful means to introduce it or exclude it as they please, for the reason that slavery cannot exist a day or an hour anywhere unless it is supported by local police regulations. Those police regulations can only be established by the local legislature, and, if the people are opposed to slavery, they will elect representatives to that body who will by unfriendly legislation effectually prevent the introduction of it into their midst. If, on the contrary, they are for it, their legislation will favor its extension. Hence, no matter what the decision of the Supreme Court may be on that abstract question, still the right of the people to make a slave territory or a free territory is perfect and complete under the Nebraska Bill. I hope Mr. Lincoln deems my answer satisfactory on that point. . . .

The third question which Mr. Lincoln presented is: If the Supreme Court of the United States shall decree that a state of this Union cannot exclude slavery from its own limits, will I submit to it? I am amazed that Lincoln should ask such a question. . . . Mr. Lincoln's object is to cast an imputation upon the Supreme Court. He knows that there never was but one man in America, claiming any degree of intelligence or decency, who ever for a moment pretended such a thing.

It is true that the Washington *Union,* in an article published . . . last December, did put forth that doctrine, and I denounced the article on the floor of the Senate in a speech which Mr. Lincoln now pretends was against the President. The *Union* had claimed that slavery had a right to go into the free states and that any provision in the Constitution or laws of the free states to the contrary were null and void. I denounced it in the Senate, as I said before, and I was the first man who did. Lincoln's friends, Trumbull, and Seward, and Hale, and Wilson, and the whole Black Republican side of the Senate, were silent. They left it to me to denounce it.

And what was the reply made to me on that occasion? Mr. Toombs of Georgia got up and undertook to lecture me on the ground that I ought not to have deemed the article worthy of notice and ought not to have replied to it; that there was not one man, woman, or child south of the Potomac, in any slave state, who did not repudiate any such pretension. Mr. Lincoln knows that that reply was made on the spot, and yet now he asks this question. He might as well ask me — Suppose Mr. Lincoln should steal a horse, would I sanction it, and it would be as genteel in me to ask him, in the event he stole a horse, what ought to be done with him?

He casts an imputation upon the Supreme Court of the United States by supposing that they would violate the Constitution of the United States. I tell him that such a thing is not possible. It would be an act of moral treason that no man on the bench could ever descend to. Mr. Lincoln himself would never in his partisan feelings so far forget what was right as to be guilty of such an act.

The fourth question of Mr. Lincoln is:

Are you in favor of acquiring additional territory in disregard as to how such acquisition may affect the Union on the slavery question? This question is very ingeniously and cunningly put.

The Black Republican creed lays it down expressly that under no circumstances shall we acquire any more territory unless slavery is first prohibited in the country. I ask Mr. Lincoln whether he is in favor of that proposition. Are you [addressing Mr. Lincoln] opposed to the acquisition of any more territory, under any circumstances, unless slavery is prohibited in it? That he does not like to answer. When I ask him whether he stands up to that article in the platform of his party, he turns, Yankee-fashion, and, without answering it, asks me whether I am in favor of acquiring territory without regard to how it may affect the Union on the slavery question.

I answer that whenever it becomes necessary, in our growth and progress, to acquire more territory, that I am in favor of it, without reference to the question of slavery; and, when we have acquired it, I will leave the people free to do as they please, either to make it slave or free territory, as they prefer. It is idle to tell me or you that we have territory enough. Our fathers supposed that we had enough when our territory extended to the Mississippi River, but a few years' growth and expansion satisfied them that we needed more, and the Louisiana Territory, from the west branch of the Mississippi to the British possessions, was acquired. Then we acquired Oregon, then California and New Mexico. We have enough now for the present, but this is a young and a growing nation. It swarms as often as a hive of bees; and, as new swarms are turned out each year, there must be hives in which they can gather and make their honey.

In less than fifteen years, if the same progress that has distinguished this country for the last fifteen years continues, every foot of vacant land between this and the Pacific Ocean owned by the United States will be occupied. Will you not continue to increase at the end of fifteen years as well as now? I tell you, increase and multiply and expand is the law of this nation's existence. You cannot limit this great republic by mere boundary lines, saying, "Thus far shalt thou go and no farther." Any one of you gentlemen might as well say to a son twelve years old that he is big enough and must not grow any larger and, in order to prevent his growth, put a hoop around him to keep him to his present size. What would be the result? Either the hoop must burst and be rent asunder or the child must die.

So it would be with this great nation. With our natural increase, growing with a rapidity unknown in any other part of the globe, with the tide of emigration that is fleeing from despotism in the Old World to seek refuge in our own, there is a constant torrent pouring into this country that requires more land, more territory upon which to settle; and, just as far as our interests and our destiny require additional territory in the North, in the South, or on the islands of the ocean, I am for it; and, when we acquire it, will leave the people, according to the Nebraska Bill, free to do as they please on the subject of slavery and every other question.

III.

Jonesboro, September 15

Lincoln's Speech

I HOLD THAT THE PROPOSITION that slavery cannot enter a new country without police regulations is historically false. It is not true at all. I hold that the history of this country shows that the institution of slavery was originally planted upon this continent *without* these "police regulations" which the Judge now thinks necessary for the actual establishment of it. Not only so, but is there not another fact: How came this Dred Scott decision to be made? It was made upon the case of a Negro being taken and actually held in slavery in Minnesota Territory, claiming his freedom because the act of Congress prohibited his being so held there. *Will the Judge pretend that Dred Scott was not held there without police regulations?* There is at least one matter of record as to his having been held in slavery in the territory, not only without police regulations but in the teeth of congressional legislation supposed to be valid at the time. This shows that there is vigor enough in slavery to plant itself in a new country even against unfriendly legislation. It takes not only law but the *enforcement* of law to keep it out. That is the history of this country upon the subject.

I wish to ask one other question. It being understood that the Constitution of the United States guarantees property in slaves in the territories, if there is any infringement of the right of that property, would not the United States courts, organized for the government of the territory, apply such remedy as might be necessary in that case? It is a maxim held by the courts that there is no wrong without its remedy; and the courts have a remedy for whatever is acknowledged and treated as a wrong.

Again: I will ask you, my friends, if you were elected members of the legislature, what would be the first thing you would have to do before entering upon your duties? *Swear to support the Constitution of the United States.* Suppose you believe, as Judge Douglas does, that the Constitution of the United States guarantees to your neighbor the right to hold slaves in that territory, that they are his property; how can you clear your oaths unless you give him such legislation as is necessary to enable him to enjoy that property? What do you understand by supporting the constitution of a state or of the United States? Is it not to give such constitutional helps to the rights established by that Constitution as may be practically needed? Can you, if you swear to support the Constitution and believe that the Constitution establishes a right, clear your oath without giving it support?

Do you support the Constitution if, knowing or believing there is a right established under it which needs specific legislation, you withhold that legislation? Do you not violate and disregard your oath? I can conceive of nothing plainer in the world. There can be nothing in the words "support the Constitution" if you may run counter to it by refusing support to any right established under the Constitution. And what I say here will hold with still more force against the Judge's doctrine of "unfriendly legislation." How could you, having sworn to support the Constitution and believing it guaranteed the right to hold slaves in the territories, assist in legislation *intended to defeat that right?* That would be violating your own view of the Constitution. Not only so, but, if you were to do so, how long would it take the courts to hold your votes unconstitutional and void? Not a moment.

Lastly I would ask: Is not Congress itself under obligation to give legislative support to any right that is established under the United States Constitution? I repeat the question: Is not Congress itself bound to give legislative support to any right that is established in the United States Constitution? A member of Congress swears to support the Constitution of the United States, and if he sees a right established by that Constitution which needs specific legislative protection, can he clear his oath without giving that protection? Let me ask you why

many of us who are opposed to slavery upon principle give our acquiescence to a fugitive slave law? Why do we hold ourselves under obligations to pass such a law and abide by it when it is passed? Because the Constitution makes provision that the owners of slaves shall have the right to reclaim them. It gives the right to reclaim slaves and that right is, as Judge Douglas says, a barren right, unless there is legislation that will enforce it.

The mere declaration, "no person held to service or labor in one state under the laws thereof, escaping into another, shall in consequence of any law or regulation therein be discharged from such service or labor, but shall be delivered up on claim of the party to whom such service or labor may be due," is powerless without specific legislation to enforce it. Now, on what ground would a member of Congress who is opposed to slavery in the abstract vote for a fugitive slave law, as I would deem it my duty to do? Because there is a constitutional right which needs legislation to enforce it. And although it is distasteful to me, I have sworn to support the Constitution; and having so sworn, I cannot conceive that I do support it if I withhold from that right any necessary legislation to make it practical. And if that is true in regard to a fugitive slave law, is the right to have fugitive slaves reclaimed any better fixed in the Constitution than the right to hold slaves in the territories? For this decision is a just exposition of the Constitution, as Judge Douglas thinks.

Is the one right any better than the other? Is there any man who, while a member of Congress, would give support to the one any more than the other? If I wished to refuse to give legislative support to slave property in the territories, if a member of Congress, I could not do it, holding the view that the Constitution establishes that right. If I did it at all, it would be because I deny that this decision properly construes the Constitution. But if I acknowledge, with Judge Douglas, that this decision properly construes the Constitution, I cannot conceive that I would be less than a perjured man if I should refuse in Congress to give such protection to that property as in its nature it needed.

At the end of what I have said here I propose to give the Judge my fifth interrogatory which he may take and answer at his leisure. My fifth interrogatory is this:

If the slaveholding citizens of a United States territory should need and demand congressional legislation for the protection of their slave property in such territory, would you, as a member of Congress, vote for or against such legislation?

Douglas' Reply

MR. LINCOLN HAS FRAMED another question, propounded it to me, and desired my answer. As I have said before, I did not put a question to him that I did not first lay a foundation for by showing that it was a part of the platform of the party whose votes he is now seeking; adopted in a majority of the counties where he now hopes to get a majority; and supported by the candidates of his party now running in those counties.

But I will answer his question. It is as follows: "If the slaveholding citizens of a United States territory should need and demand congressional legislation for the protection of their slave property in such territory, would you, as a member of Congress, vote for or against such legislation?" I answer him that it is a fundamental article in the Democratic creed that there should be noninterference and nonintervention by Congress with slavery in the states or territories. Mr. Lincoln could have found an answer to his question in the Cincinnati platform if he had desired it. The Democratic

Party have always stood by that great principle of noninterference and nonintervention by Congress with slavery in the states and territories alike, and I stand on that platform now.

IV.

CHARLESTON, September 18

Lincoln's Speech

JUDGE DOUGLAS HAS SAID TO YOU that he has not been able to get from me an answer to the question whether I am in favor of Negro citizenship. So far as I know, the Judge never asked me the question before. He shall have no occasion to ever ask it again, for I tell him very frankly that I am not in favor of Negro citizenship.

This furnishes me an occasion for saying a few words upon the subject. I mentioned, in a certain speech of mine which has been printed, that the Supreme Court had decided that a Negro could not possibly be made a citizen; and without saying what was my ground of complaint in regard to that, or whether I had any ground of complaint, Judge Douglas has from that thing manufactured nearly everything that he ever says about my disposition to produce an equality between the Negroes and the white people. If any one will read my speech, he will find I mentioned that as one of the points decided in the course of the Supreme Court opinions, but I did not state what objection I had to it. But Judge Douglas tells the people what my objection was when I did not tell them myself.

Now, my opinion is that the different states have the power to make a Negro a citizen, under the Constitution of the United States, if they choose. The Dred Scott decision decides that they have not that power. If the state of Illinois had that power, I should be opposed to the exercise of it. That is all I have to say about it.

V.

GALESBURG, October 7

Douglas' Speech

WHAT DO YOU REPUBLICANS THINK of a political organization that will try to make an unholy and unnatural combination with its professed foes to beat a man merely because he has done right? You know that such is the fact with regard to your own party. You know that the axe of decapitation is suspended over every man in office in Illinois, and the terror of proscription is threatened every Democrat by the present administration, unless he supports the Republican ticket in preference to my Democratic associates and myself.

I could find an instance in the postmaster of the city of Galesburg and in every other postmaster in this vicinity, all of whom have been stricken down simply because they discharged the duties of their offices honestly and supported the regular Democratic ticket in this state in the right. The Republican Party is availing itself of every unworthy means in the present contest to carry the election, because its leaders know that if they let this chance slip they will never have another, and their hopes of making this a Republican state will be blasted forever.

Now, let me ask you whether the country has any interest in sustaining this organization known as the Republican Party. That party is unlike all other political organizations in this country. All other parties have been national in their character, have avowed their principles alike in the slave and free states — in Kentucky as well as Illinois, in Louisiana as well as in Massachusetts. Such was the case with the old Whig Party, and such was and is the case with the Democratic Party. Whigs and Democrats could proclaim their principles boldly and fearlessly in the North and in the South, in the East and in the West, wherever the Constitution ruled and the American flag waved over American soil.

But now you have a sectional organization, a party which appeals to the Northern section of the Union against the Southern, a party which appeals to Northern passion, Northern pride, Northern ambition, Northern prejudices, against Southern people, the Southern states, and Southern institutions. The leaders of that party hope that they will be able to unite the Northern states in one great sectional party; and, inasmuch as the North is the strongest section, that they will thus be enabled to outvote, conquer, govern, and control the South. Hence you find that they now make speeches advocating principles and measures which cannot be defended in any slaveholding state of this Union. . . .

Not only is this Republican Party unable to proclaim its principles alike in the North and in the South, in the free states and in the slave states, but it cannot even proclaim them in the same forms and give them the same strength and meaning in all parts of the same state. My friend Lincoln finds it extremely difficult to manage a debate in the center part of the state, where there is a mixture of men from the North and the South. In the extreme northern part of Illinois, he can proclaim as bold and radical Abolitionism as ever Giddings, Lovejoy, or Garrison enunciated; but when he gets down a little farther south, he claims that he is an Old Line Whig, a disciple of Henry Clay, and declares that he still adheres to the Old Line Whig creed, and has nothing whatever to do with Abolitionism, or Negro equality, or Negro citizenship. . . .

The signers of the Declaration of Independence never dreamed of the Negro when they were writing that document.

They referred to white men, to men of European birth and European descent, when they declared the equality of all men. I see a gentleman there in the crowd shaking his head. Let me remind him that when Thomas Jefferson wrote that document, he was the owner, and so continued until his death, of a large number of slaves. Did he intend to say in that Declaration that his Negro slaves, which he held and treated as property, were created his equals by Divine law and that he was violating the law of God every day of his life by holding them as slaves? It must be borne in mind that when that Declaration was put forth, every one of the thirteen colonies were slaveholding colonies, and every man who signed that instrument represented a slaveholding constituency. Recollect, also, that no one of them emancipated his slaves, much less put them on an equality with himself, after he signed the Declaration. On the contrary, they all continued to hold their Negroes as slaves during the Revolutionary War.

Now, do you believe — are you willing to have it said — that every man who signed the Declaration of Independence declared the Negro his equal and then was hypocrite enough to continue to hold him as a slave in violation of what he believed to be the Divine law? And yet, when you say that the Declaration of Independence includes the Negro, you charge the signers of it with hypocrisy.

I say to you frankly that in my opinion this government was made by our fathers on the white basis. It was made by white men for the benefit of white men and their posterity forever and was intended to be administered by white men in all time to come. But while I hold that under our Constitution and political system the Negro is not a citizen, cannot be a citizen, and ought not to be a citizen, it does not follow by any means that he should be a slave. On the contrary, it does follow that the Negro, as an inferior race, ought to possess every right, every privilege, every immunity which he can safely exercise consistent with the safety of the society in which he lives.

Humanity requires, and Christianity commands, that you shall extend to every inferior being, and every dependent being, all the privileges, immunities, and advantages which can be granted to them consistent with the safety of society. If you ask me the nature and extent of these privileges, I answer that that is a question which the people of each state must decide for themselves. Illinois has decided that question for herself. We have said that in this state the Negro shall not be a slave, nor shall he be a citizen. Kentucky holds a different doctrine. New York holds one different from either, and Maine one different from all. Virginia, in her policy of this question, differs in many respects from the others, and so on, until there are hardly two states whose policy is exactly alike in regard to the relation of the white man and the Negro. Nor can you reconcile them and make them alike. . . .

Lincoln's Reply

I HAVE NEVER MANIFESTED any impatience with the necessities that spring from the actual presence of black people among us and the actual existence of slavery among us where it does already exist; but I have insisted that, in legislating for new countries where it does not exist, there is no just rule other than that of moral and abstract right! With reference to those new countries, those maxims as to the right of people to "life, liberty, and the pursuit of happiness" were the just rules to be constantly referred to. There is no misunderstanding this, except by men interested to misunderstand it.

I take it that I have to address an intelligent and reading community who will peruse what I say, weigh it, and then judge whether I advance improper or unsound views, or whether I advance hypocritical and deceptive and contrary views in different portions of the country. I believe myself to be guilty of no such thing as the latter, though, of course, I cannot claim that I am entirely free from all error in the opinions I advance.

The Judge has also detained us awhile in regard to the distinction between his party and our party. His he assumes to be a national party; ours a sectional one. He does this in asking the question whether this country has any interest in the maintenance of the Republican Party. He assumes that our party is altogether sectional — that the party to which he adheres is national — and the argument is that no party can be a rightful party, can be based upon rightful principles, unless it can announce its principles everywhere.

I presume that Judge Douglas could not go into Russia and announce the doctrine of our national democracy; he could not denounce the doctrine of kings and emperors and monarchies in Russia; and it may be true of this country that in some places we may not be able to proclaim a doctrine as clearly as the truth of democracy, because there is a section so directly opposed to it that they will not tolerate us in doing so. Is it the true test of the soundness of a doctrine that in some places people won't let you proclaim it? Is that the way to test the truth of any doctrine? Why, I understood that at one time the people of Chicago would not let Judge Douglas preach a certain favorite doctrine of his. I commend to his consideration the question whether he takes that as a test of the unsoundness of what he wanted to preach.

There is another thing to which I wish to ask attention for a little while on this occasion. What has always been the evidence brought forward to prove that the Republican Party is a sectional party? The main one was that in the Southern portion of the Union the people did not let the Republicans proclaim their doctrines among them.

That has been the main evidence brought forward — that they had no supporters, or substantially none, in the slave states. The South have not taken hold of our principles as we announce them; nor does Judge Douglas now grapple with those principles.

We have a Republican state platform, laid down in Springfield in June last, stating our position all the way through the questions before the country. We are now far advanced in this canvass. Judge Douglas and I have made perhaps forty speeches apiece, and we have now for the fifth time met face to face in debate, and up to this day I have not found either Judge Douglas or any friend of his taking hold of the Republican platform, or laying his finger upon anything in it that is wrong.

I ask you to recollect that Judge Douglas turns away from the platform of principles to the fact that he can find people somewhere who will not allow us to announce those principles. If he had great confidence that our principles were wrong, he would take hold of them and demonstrate them to be wrong. But he does not do so. The only evidence he has of their being wrong is in the fact that there are people who won't allow us to preach them. I ask again, is that the way to test the soundness of a doctrine?

I ask his attention also to the fact that by the rule of nationality he is himself fast becoming sectional. I ask his attention to the fact that his speeches would not go as current now south of the Ohio River as they have formerly gone there. I ask his attention to the fact that he felicitates himself today that all the Democrats of the free states are agreeing with him, while he omits to tell us that the Democrats of any slave state agree with him. If he has not thought of this, I commend to his consideration the evidence in his own declaration, on this day, of his becoming sectional, too. I see it rapidly approaching. Whatever may be the result of this ephemeral contest between Judge Douglas and myself, I see the day rapidly approaching when his pill of sectionalism, which he has been thrusting down the throats of Republicans for years past, will be crowded down his own throat. . . .

The Judge tells us, in proceeding, that he is opposed to making any odious distinction between free and slave states. I am altogether unaware that the Republicans are in favor of making any odious distinctions between the free and slave states. But there is still a difference, I think, between Judge Douglas and the Republicans in this. I suppose that the real difference between Judge Douglas and his friends and the Republicans, on the contrary, is that the Judge is not in favor of making any difference between slavery and liberty; that he is in favor of eradicating, of pressing out of view the questions of preference in this country for free or slave institutions; and consequently every sentiment he utters discards the idea that there is any wrong in slavery.

Everything that emanates from him or his coadjutors in their course of policy carefully excludes the thought that there is anything wrong in slavery. All their arguments, if you will consider them, will be seen to exclude the thought that there is anything whatever wrong in slavery. If you will take the Judge's speeches and select the short and pointed sentences expressed by him — as his declaration that he "don't care whether slavery is voted up or down," you will see at once that this is perfectly logical, if you do not admit that slavery is wrong. If you do admit that it is wrong, Judge Douglas cannot logically say he don't care whether a wrong is voted up or down.

Judge Douglas declares that if any community want slavery, they have a right to have it. He can say that logically if he says that there is no wrong in slavery; but if you admit that there is a wrong in it, he cannot logically say that anybody has a right to do wrong. He insists that, upon the score of equality, the owners of slaves and owners of property — of horses and every other sort of property — should be alike and hold them alike in a new territory. That is perfectly logical if the two species of property are alike and are equally founded in right. But if you admit that one of them is wrong, you cannot institute any equality between right and wrong. And from this difference of sentiment — the belief on the part of one that the institution is wrong and a policy springing from that belief which looks to the arrest of the enlargement of that wrong; and this other sentiment, that it is no wrong, and a policy sprung from that sentiment, which will tolerate no idea of preventing the wrong from growing larger and looks to there never being an end of it through all the existence of things — arises the real difference between Judge Douglas and his friends on the one hand and the Republicans on the other.

Now, I confess myself as belonging to that class in the country who contemplate slavery as a moral, social, and political evil, having due regard for its actual existence among us and the difficulties of getting rid of it in any satisfactory way, and to all the constitutional obligations which have been thrown about it; but, nevertheless, desire a policy that looks to the prevention of it as a wrong, and looks hopefully to the time when as a wrong it may come to an end. . . .

I believe that the right of property in a slave *is not* distinctly and expressly affirmed in the Constitution, and Judge Douglas thinks it *is*. I believe that the Supreme Court and the advocates of that decision may search in vain for the place in the Constitution where the right of property in a slave is distinctly and expressly affirmed. I say, therefore, that I think one of the premises is not true in fact. But it is true with Judge Douglas. It is true with the Supreme Court, who pronounced it. They are estopped from denying it, and, being stopped from denying it, the conclusion follows that, the Constitution of the United States being the supreme law, no constitution or law can interfere with it. It being affirmed in the decision that the right of property in a slave is distinctly and expressly affirmed in the Constitution, the conclusion inevitably follows that no state law or constitution can destroy that right.

I then say to Judge Douglas and to all others that I think it will take a better answer than a sneer to show that those who have said that the right of property in a slave is distinctly and expressly affirmed in the Constitution are not prepared to show that no constitution or law can destroy that right. I say, I believe it will take a far better argument than a mere sneer to show to the minds of intelligent men that whoever has so said is not prepared, whenever public sentiment is so far advanced as to justify it, to say the other.

This is but an opinion, and the opinion of one very humble man; but it is my opinion that the Dred Scott decision, as it is, never would have been made in its present form if the party that made it had not been sustained previously by the elections. My own opinion is that the new Dred Scott decision, deciding against the right of the people of the states to exclude slavery, will never be made if that party is not sustained by the elections. I believe, further, that it is just as sure to be made as tomorrow is to come, if that party shall be sustained. . . .

VI.

ALTON, October 15

Lincoln's Speech

I SAID WE WERE NOW FAR into the fifth year since a policy was initiated with the avowed object and confident promise of putting an end to the slavery agitation. Is it not so? When that Nebraska Bill was brought for-

ward four years ago last January, was it not for the "avowed object" of putting an end to the slavery agitation? We were to have no more agitation in Congress; it was all to be banished to the territories. . . .

I have intimated that I thought the agitation would not cease until a crisis should have been reached and passed. I have stated in what way I thought it would be reached and passed. I have said that it might go one way or the other. We might, by arresting the further spread of it and placing it where the fathers originally placed it, put it where the public mind should rest in the belief that it was in the course of ultimate extinction. Thus the agitation may cease. It may be pushed forward until it shall become alike lawful in all the states, old as well as new, North as well as South. I have said, and I repeat, my wish is that the further spread of it may be arrested, and that it may be placed where the public mind shall rest in the belief that it is in the course of ultimate extinction. I have expressed that as my wish.

I entertain the opinion upon evidence sufficient to my mind that the fathers of this government placed that institution where the public mind *did* rest in the belief that it was in the course of ultimate extinction. Let me ask why they made provision that the source of slavery — the African slave trade — should be cut off at the end of twenty years? Why did they make provision that in all the new territory we owned at that time slavery should be forever inhibited? Why stop its spread in one direction and cut off its source in another if they did not look to its being placed in the course of ultimate extinction?

Again: The institution of slavery is only mentioned in the Constitution of the United States two or three times, and in neither of these cases does the word "slavery" or "Negro race" occur; but covert language is used each time, and for a purpose full of significance. What is the language in regard to the prohibition of the African slave trade? It runs in about this way: "The migration or importation of such persons as any of the states now existing shall think proper to admit shall not be prohibited by the Congress prior to the year 1808."

The next allusion in the Constitution to the question of slavery and the black race is on the subject of the basis of representation, and there the language used is:

> Representatives and direct taxes shall be apportioned among the several states which may be included within this Union according to their respective numbers, which shall be determined by adding to the whole number of free persons, including those bound to service for a term of years, and excluding Indians not taxed, three-fifths of all other persons.

It says "persons," not slaves, not Negroes; but this "three-fifths" can be applied to no other class among us than the Negroes.

Lastly, in the provision for the reclamation of fugitive slaves, it is said:

> No person held to service or labor in one state, under the laws thereof, escaping into another, shall in consequence of any law or regulation therein be discharged from such service or labor, but shall be delivered up, on claim of the party to whom such service or labor may be due.

There again, there is no mention of the word "Negro" or of slavery.

In all three of these places, being the only allusions to slavery in the instrument, covert language is used. Language is used not suggesting that slavery existed or that the black race were among us. And I understand the contemporaneous history of those times to be that covert language was used with a purpose, and that purpose was that in our Constitution, which it was hoped and is still hoped will endure forever — when it should be read by intelligent and patriotic men, after the institution of slavery had passed from among us — there should be

nothing on the face of the great charter of liberty suggesting that such a thing as Negro slavery had ever existed among us.

This is part of the evidence that the fathers of the government expected and intended the institution of slavery to come to an end. They expected and intended that it should be in the course of ultimate extinction. And when I say that I desire to see the further spread of it arrested, I only say I desire to see that done which the fathers have first done. When I say I desire to see it placed where the public mind will rest in the belief that it is in the course of ultimate extinction, I only say I desire to see it placed where they placed it. . . .

The Judge alludes very often in the course of his remarks to the exclusive right which the states have to decide the whole thing for themselves. I agree with him very readily that the different states have that right. He is but fighting a man of straw when he assumes that I am contending against the right of the states to do as they please about it. Our controversy with him is in regard to the new territories. We agree that when the states come in as states they have the right and the power to do as they please. We have no power as citizens of the free states, or in our federal capacity as members of the federal Union through the general government, to disturb slavery in the states where it exists.

We profess constantly that we have no more inclination than belief in the power of the government to disturb it; yet we are driven constantly to defend ourselves from the assumption that we are warring upon the rights of the *states*. What I insist upon is that the new territories shall be kept free from it while in the territorial condition. Judge Douglas assumes that we have no interest in them, that we have no right whatever to interfere. I think we have some interest. I think that as white men we have.

Do we not wish for an outlet for our surplus population, if I may so express myself?

Do we not feel an interest in getting to that outlet with such institutions as we would like to have prevail there? If *you* go to the territory opposed to slavery, and another man comes upon the same ground with his slaves, upon the assumption that the things are equal, it turns out that he has the equal right all his way, and you have no part of it your way. If he goes in and makes it a slave territory and, by consequence, a slave state, is it not time that those who desire to have it a free state were on equal ground?

Let me suggest it in a different way. How many Democrats are there about here who have left slave states and come into the free state of Illinois to get rid of the institution of slavery? I reckon there are a thousand and one. I will ask you, if the policy you are now advocating had prevailed when this country was in a territorial condition, where would you have gone to get rid of it? Where would you have found your free state or territory to go to? And when, hereafter, for any cause, the people in this place shall desire to find new homes, if they wish to be rid of the institution, where will they find the place to go to?

Now, irrespective of the moral aspect of this question as to whether there is a right or wrong in enslaving a Negro, I am still in favor of our new territories being in such a condition that white men may find a home — may find some spot where they can better their condition — where they can settle upon new soil and better their condition in life. I am in favor of this, not merely (I must say it here as I have elsewhere) for our own people who are born among us but as an outlet for *free white people everywhere*, the world over — in which Hans and Baptiste and Patrick, and all other men from all the world, may find new homes and better their condition in life.

I have stated upon former occasions, and I may as well state again, what I understand to be the real issue in this controversy

between Judge Douglas and myself. On the point of my wanting to make war between the free and the slave states, there has been no issue between us. So, too, when he assumes that I am in favor of introducing a perfect social and political equality between the white and black races. These are false issues upon which Judge Douglas has tried to force the controversy. There is no foundation in truth for the charge that I maintain either of these propositions.

The real issue in this controversy — the one pressing upon every mind — is the sentiment on the part of one class that looks upon the institution of slavery as a wrong and of another class that does not look upon it as a wrong. The sentiment that contemplates the institution of slavery in this country as a wrong is the sentiment of the Republican Party. It is the sentiment around which all their actions, all their arguments, circle — from which all their propositions radiate. They look upon it as being a moral, social, and political wrong; and, while they contemplate it as such, they nevertheless have due regard for its actual existence among us and the difficulties of getting rid of it in any satisfactory way and to all the constitutional obligations thrown about it. Yet, having a due regard for these, they desire a policy in regard to it that looks to its not creating any more danger. They insist that it should, as far as may be, *be treated* as a wrong, and one of the methods of treating it as a wrong is to *make provision that it shall grow no larger*. They also desire a policy that looks to a peaceful end of slavery at some time as being wrong. . . .

And if there be among you anybody who supposes that he, as a Democrat, can consider himself "as much opposed to slavery as anybody," I would like to reason with him. You never treat it as a wrong. What other thing that you consider as a wrong do you deal with as you deal with that? Perhaps, you *say* it is a wrong, *but your leader never does, and you quarrel with anybody who says it is wrong.* Although you pretend to say so yourself, you can find no fit place to deal with it as a wrong.

You must not say anything about it in the free states, *because it is not here.* You must not say anything about it in the slave states, *because it is there.* You must not say anything about it in the pulpit, because that is religion and has nothing to do with it. You must not say anything about it in politics, *because that will disturb the security of "my place."* There is no place to talk about it as being a wrong, although you say yourself it *is* wrong.

But, finally, you will screw yourself up to the belief that if the people of the slave states should adopt a system of gradual emancipation on the slavery question, you would be in favor of it. You would be in favor of it. You say that is getting it in the right place and you would be glad to see it succeed. But you are deceiving yourself.

You all know that Frank Blair and Gratz Brown, down there in St. Louis, undertook to introduce that system in Missouri. They fought as valiantly as they could for the system of gradual emancipation, which you pretend you would be glad to see succeed. Now, I will bring you to the test. After a hard fight they were beaten, and when the news came over here, you threw up your hats and *hurrahed for democracy.* More than that, take all the argument made in favor of the system you have proposed, and it carefully excludes the idea that there is anything wrong in the institution of slavery. The arguments to sustain that policy carefully exclude it.

Even here, today, you heard Judge Douglas quarrel with me because I uttered a wish that it might sometime come to an end. Although Henry Clay could say he wished every slave in the United States was in the country of his ancestors, I am de-

nounced by those pretending to respect Henry Clay for uttering a wish that it might sometime, in some peaceful way, come to an end. . . .

I was glad to express my gratitude at Quincy, and I reexpress it here to Judge Douglas — *that he looks to no end of the institution of slavery.* That will help the people to see where the struggle really is. It will hereafter place with us all men who really do wish the wrong may have an end. And whenever we can get rid of the fog which obscures the real question, when we can get Judge Douglas and his friends to avow a policy looking to its perpetuation, we can get them out from among that class of men and bring them to the side of those who treat it as a wrong. Then there will soon be an end of it, and that end will be its "ultimate extinction." Whenever the issue can be distinctly made and all extraneous matter thrown out so that men can fairly see the real difference between the parties, this controversy will soon be settled, and it will be done peaceably, too.

There will be no war, no violence. It will be placed again where the wisest and best men of the world placed it. Brooks of South Carolina once declared that when this Constitution was framed, its framers did not look to the institution existing until this day. When he said this, I think he stated a fact that is fully borne out by the history of the times. But he also said they were better and wiser men than the men of these days; yet the men of these days had experience which they had not, and, by the invention of the cotton gin, it became a necessity in this country that slavery should be perpetual.

I now say that, willingly or unwillingly, purposely or without purpose, Judge Douglas has been the most prominent instrument in changing the position of the institution of slavery which the fathers of the government expected to come to an end ere this

— and putting it upon Brook's cotton gin basis — placing it where he openly confesses he has no desire there shall ever be an end of it.

Douglas' Reply

MR. LINCOLN TRIES TO AVOID THE MAIN ISSUE by attacking the truth of my proposition, that our fathers made this government divided into free and slave states, recognizing the right of each to decide all its local questions for itself. Did they not thus make it? It is true that they did not establish slavery in any of the states or abolish it in any of them; but, finding thirteen states, twelve of which were slave and one free, they agreed to form a government uniting them together as they stood, divided into free and slave states, and to guarantee forever to each state the right to do as it pleased on the slavery question. Having thus made the government and conferred this right upon each state forever, I assert that this government can exist as they made it, divided into free and slave states, if any one state chooses to retain slavery.

He says that he looks forward to a time when slavery shall be abolished everywhere. I look forward to a time when each state shall be allowed to do as it pleases. If it chooses to keep slavery forever, it is not my business, but its own; if it chooses to abolish slavery, it is its own business, not mine. I care more for the great principle of self-government, the right of the people to rule, than I do for all the Negroes in Christendom. I would not endanger the perpetuity of this Union, I would not blot out the great inalienable rights of the white men for all the Negroes that ever existed. Hence, I say, let us maintain this government on the principles that our fathers made it, recognizing the right of each state to keep slavery as long as its people determine, or to abolish it when they please.

But Mr. Lincoln says that, when our fathers made this government, they did not look forward to the state of things now existing, and therefore he thinks the doctrine was wrong; and he quotes Brooks, of South Carolina, to prove that our fathers then thought that probably slavery would be abolished by each state acting for itself before this time. Suppose they did; suppose they did not foresee what has occurred — does that change the principles of our government? They did not probably foresee the telegraph that transmits intelligence by lightning, nor did they foresee the railroads that now form the bonds of union between the different states, or the thousand mechanical inventions that have elevated mankind. But do these things change the principles of the government? Our fathers, I say, made this government on the principle of the right of each state to do as it pleases in its own domestic affairs, subject to the Constitution, and allowed the people of each to apply to every new change of circumstances such remedy as they may see fit to improve their condition. This right they have for all time to come.

Mr. Lincoln went on to tell you that he does not at all desire to interfere with slavery in the states where it exists, nor does his party. I expected him to say that down here. Let me ask him, then, how he expects to put slavery in the course of ultimate extinction everywhere if he does not intend to interfere with it in the states where it exists? He says that he will prohibit it in all territories, and the inference is, then, that unless they make free states out of them, he will keep them out of the Union; for, mark you, he did not say whether or not he would vote to admit Kansas with slavery or not, as her people might apply (he forgot that, as usual, etc.); he did not say whether or not he was in favor of bringing the territories now in existence into the Union on the principle of Clay's Compromise Measures on the slavery question. I told you that he would not.

His idea is that he will prohibit slavery in all the territories and thus force them all to become free states, surrounding the slave states with a cordon of free states and hemming them in, keeping the slaves confined to their present limits while they go on multiplying, until the soil on which they live will no longer feed them; and he will thus be able to put slavery in a course of ultimate extinction by starvation. He will extinguish slavery in the Southern states as the French general exterminated the Algerines when he smoked them out. He is going to extinguish slavery by surrounding the slave states, hemming in the slaves and starving them out of existence, as you smoke a fox out of his hole.

He intends to do that in the name of humanity and Christianity in order that we may get rid of the terrible crime and sin entailed upon our fathers of holding slaves. Mr. Lincoln makes out that line of policy, and appeals to the moral sense of justice and to the Christian feeling of the community to sustain him. He says that any man who holds to the contrary doctrine is in the position of the king who claimed to govern by Divine right.

Let us examine for a moment and see what principle it was that overthrew the Divine right of George III to govern us. Did not these colonies rebel because the British Parliament had no right to pass laws concerning our property and domestic and private institutions without our consent? We demanded that the British government should not pass such laws unless they gave us representation in the body passing them; and this the British government insisting on doing. We went to war on the principle that the home government should not control and govern distant colonies without giving them a representation.

Now, Mr. Lincoln proposes to govern the territories without giving them a representation, and calls on Congress to pass laws controlling their property and domestic concerns without their consent and against their will. Thus he asserts for his party the identical principle asserted by George III and the Tories of the Revolution.

I ask you to look into these things and then tell me whether the Democracy or the Abolitionists are right. I hold that the people of a territory, like those of a state (I use the language of Mr. Buchanan in his letter of acceptance), have the right to decide for themselves whether slavery shall or shall not exist within their limits. The point upon which Chief Justice Taney expresses his opinion is simply this — that slaves, being property, stand on an equal footing with other property and, consequently, that the owner has the same right to carry that property into a territory that he has any other, subject to the same conditions. . . .

If you take Negroes to Kansas, as Col. Jefferson Davis said in his Bangor speech . . . you must take them there subject to the local law. If the people want the institution of slavery, they will protect and encourage it; but if they do not want it, they will withhold that protection, and the absence of local legislation protecting slavery excludes it as completely as a positive prohibition. You slaveholders of Missouri might as well understand what you know practically, that you cannot carry slavery where the people do not want it. All you have a right to ask is that the people shall do as they please. If they want slavery, let them have it; if they do not want it, allow them to refuse to encourage it.

My friends, if, as I have said before, we will only live up to this great fundamental principle, there will be peace between the North and the South. Mr. Lincoln admits that under the Constitution, on all domestic questions except slavery, we ought not to interfere with the people of each state. What right have we to interfere with slavery any more than we have to interfere with any other question? He says that this slavery question is now the bone of contention. Why? Simply because agitators have combined in all the free states to make war upon it. Suppose the agitators in the states should combine in one-half of the Union to make war upon the railroad system of the other half? They would thus be driven to the same sectional strife. Suppose one section makes war upon any other peculiar institution of the opposite section, and the same strife is produced. The only remedy and safety is that we shall stand by the Constitution as our fathers made it; obey the laws as they are passed, while they stand the proper test; and sustain the decisions of the Supreme Court and the constituted authorities.

3.

WILLIAM H. SEWARD: An Irrepressible Conflict

The political career of William H. Seward moved from the Anti-Masonic Party of the 1830s to the Whig Party and finally after 1854 into the new Republican Party. Formerly governor of New York, he was in 1858 the U.S. senator from that state. During most of his political life, Seward had been an ardent foe of slavery. As a presidential aspirant in the coming 1860 election, his radical antislavery views seemed to become more temperate. He found himself in growing agreement with some of Lincoln's sentiments, especially with the latter's famous "House Divided" speech. Seward had warned in 1850 that if slavery were not abolished "by gradual voluntary effort" the Union would dissolve, civil war would ensue, and slavery would crumble at the cost of devastating violence. Eight years later in a speech on October 25, 1858, in Rochester, New York, he warned that the nation was faced with the choice of becoming all slave or all free. Portions of this speech are reprinted below.

Source: *The Works of William H. Seward*, George E. Baker, New edition, Vol. IV, Boston, 1889, pp. 289-294, 300-302.

THE UNMISTAKABLE OUTBREAKS of zeal which occur all around me show that you are earnest men — and such a man am I. Let us, therefore, at least for a time, pass by all secondary and collateral questions, whether of a personal or of a general nature, and consider the main subject of the present canvass. The Democratic Party — or, to speak more accurately, the party which wears that attractive name — is in possession of the federal government. The Republicans propose to dislodge that party and dismiss it from its high trust. . . .

Our country is a theater which exhibits in full operation two radically different political systems; the one resting on the basis of servile or slave labor, the other on the basis of voluntary labor of freemen.

The laborers who are enslaved are all Negroes, or persons more or less purely of African derivation. But this is only accidental. The principle of the system is that labor in every society, by whomsoever performed, is necessarily unintellectual, groveling, and base; and that the laborer, equally for his own good and for the welfare of the state, ought to be enslaved. . . .

The slave system is one of constant danger, distrust, suspicion, and watchfulness. It debases those whose toil alone can produce wealth and resources for defense to the lowest degree of which human nature is capable, to guard against mutiny and insurrection, and thus wastes energies which otherwise might be employed in national development and aggrandizement. . . .

In states where the slave system prevails, the masters directly or indirectly secure all political power and constitute a ruling aristocracy. In states where the free-labor system prevails, universal suffrage necessarily obtains and the state inevitably becomes sooner or later a republic or democracy. . . .

The two systems are at once perceived to be incongruous. But they are more than incongruous — they are incompatible. They never have permanently existed together in one country, and they never can. It would be easy to demonstrate this impossibility from the irreconcilable contrast between their great principles and characteristics. But the experience of mankind has conclusively established it. . . . Indeed, so incompatible are the two systems that every new state which is organized within our ever extending domain makes its first political act a choice of the one and the exclusion of the other, even at the cost of civil war, if necessary. The slave states, without law, at the last national election successfully forbade, within their own limits, even the casting of votes for a candidate for President of the United States supposed to be favorable to the establishment of the free-labor system in new states.

Hitherto, the two systems have existed in different states, but side by side within the American Union. This has happened because the Union is a confederation of states. But in another aspect the United States constitute only one nation. Increase of population which is filling the states out to their very borders, together with a new and extended network of railroads and other avenues, and an internal commerce which daily becomes more intimate, is rapidly bringing the states into a higher and more perfect social unity or consolidation. Thus, these antagonistic systems are continually coming into closer contact, and collision results.

Shall I tell you what this collision means? They who think that it is accidental, unnecessary, the work of interested or fanatical agitators and therefore ephemeral, mistake the case altogether. It is an *irrepressible conflict* between opposing and enduring forces, and it means that the United States must and will, sooner or later, become either entirely a slaveholding nation or entirely a free-labor nation. Either the cotton and rice fields of South Carolina and the sugar plantations of Louisiana will ultimately be tilled by free labor, and Charleston and New Orleans become marts for legitimate merchandise alone, or else the rye fields and wheat fields of Massachusetts and New York must again be surrendered by their farmers to slave culture and to the production of slaves, and Boston and New York become once more markets for trade in the bodies and souls of men. It is the failure to apprehend this great truth that induces so many unsuccessful attempts at final compromise between the slave and free states, and it is the existence of this great fact that renders all such pretended compromises, when made, vain and ephemeral.

Startling as this saying may appear to you, fellow citizens, it is by no means an original or even a moderate one. Our forefathers knew it to be true, and unanimously acted upon it when they framed the Constitution of the United States. They regarded the existence of the servile system in so many of the states with sorrow and shame, which they openly confessed, and they looked upon the collision between them, which was then just revealing itself, and which we are now accustomed to deplore, with favor and hope. They knew that either the one or the other system must exclusively prevail.

Unlike too many of those who in modern time invoke their authority, they had a choice between the two. They preferred the system of free labor, and they determined to organize the government and so to direct its activity that that system should surely and certainly prevail. For this purpose, and no other, they based the whole structure of government broadly on the principle that all men are created equal, and therefore free — little dreaming that within the short period of one hundred years their descendants would bear to be told by any orator, however popular, that the utterance of that principle was merely a rhetorical rhapsody; or by any judge, however venerated, that it was attended by mental reservations which rendered it hypocritical and false.

By the Ordinance of 1787, they dedicated all of the national domain not yet polluted by slavery to free labor — immediately, thenceforth and forever — while, by the new Constitution and laws, they invited foreign free labor from all lands under the sun and interdicted the importation of African slave labor at all times, in all places, and under all circumstances whatsoever. It is true that they necessarily and wisely modified this policy of freedom by leaving it to the several states, affected as they were by differing circumstances, to abolish slavery in their own way and at their own pleasure instead of confiding that duty to Congress; and that they secured to the slave states, while yet retaining the system of slavery, a three-fifths representation of slaves in the federal government until they should find themselves able to relinquish it with safety.

But the very nature of these modifications fortifies my position that the fathers knew that the two systems could not endure within the Union, and expected that within a short period slavery would disappear forever. Moreover, in order that these modifications might not altogether defeat their grand design of a republic maintaining universal equality, they provided that two-thirds of the states might amend the Constitution.

It remains to say on this point only one word to guard against misapprehension. If these states are to again become universally slaveholding, I do not pretend to say with what violations of the Constitution that end shall be accomplished. On the other hand, while I do confidently believe and hope that my country will yet become a land of universal freedom, I do not expect that it will be made so otherwise than through the action of the several states cooperating with the federal government, and all acting in strict conformity with their respective constitutions.

The strife and contentions concerning slavery, which gently disposed persons so habitually deprecate, are nothing more than the ripening of the conflict which the fathers themselves not only thus regarded with favor but which they may be said to have instituted. . . .

I think, fellow citizens, that I have shown you that it is high time for the friends of freedom to rush to the rescue of the Constitution, and that their very first duty is to dismiss the Democratic Party from the administration of the government.

Why shall it not be done? All agree that it ought to be done. What, then, shall prevent its being done? Nothing but timidity or division of the opponents of the Democratic Party. . . .

The Democratic Party derived its strength originally from its adoption of the principles of equal and exact justice to all men. So long as it practised this principle faithfully, it was invulnerable. It became vulnerable when it renounced the principle, and since that time it has maintained itself not by virtue of its own strength, or even of its traditional merits, but because there as yet had appeared in the political field no other party that had the conscience and the courage to take up, and avow, and practise the life-inspiring principle which the Democratic Party had surrendered.

At last, the Republican Party has appeared. It avows now, as the Republican Party of 1800 did, in one word, its faith and its works, "Equal and exact justice to all men." . . . The secret of its assured success lies in that very characteristic, which in the mouth of scoffers constitutes its great and lasting imbecility and reproach. It lies in the fact that it is a party of one idea; but that idea is a noble one — an idea that-fills and expands all generous souls — the idea of equality — the equality of all men before human tribunals and human laws, as they all are equal before the divine tribunal and divine laws.

I know, and you know, that a revolution has begun. I know, and all the world knows, that revolutions never go backward. Twenty senators and a hundred representatives proclaim boldly in Congress today sentiments and opinions and principles of freedom which hardly so many men, even in this free state, dared to utter in their own homes twenty years ago. While the government of the United States, under the conduct of the Democratic Party, has been all that time surrendering one plain and castle after another to slavery, the people of the United States have been no less steadily and perseveringly gathering together the forces with which to recover back again all the fields and all the castles which have been lost, and to confound and overthrow, by one decisive blow, the betrayers of the Constitution and freedom forever.

4.

The Right of the United States to Rule Mexico

In spite of the sectional conflicts raging over slavery and the Dred Scott Decision, "manifest destiny" was by no means a dead letter in 1858. One political group that favored annexation of territory to the south was the Young America faction of the Democratic Party. The movement was strongly nationalistic in orientation: with such issues as free trade, foreign markets, and expansionism, it sought to minimize sectional conflicts. An 1858 issue of Democratic Review, *which frequently espoused the Young America positions, carried the following editorial, an early version of the call to bear "the white man's burden."*

Source: *United States Magazine and Democratic Review,* May 1858: "The Fate of Mexico."

IT TAKES NATIONS SOME TIME to find out the laws of their existence. They spring into being, and they often go to decay, ignorant alike of the causes which gave them birth or which conduct them to dissolution. Some nations are born in the throes of revolution; and in the absence of great founders to mold them, they bear volcanic traces through their brief history, and expire at last amidst the ashes of their own convulsions. They lead a feverish life and are buried in the craters which once glowed with their own fitful fires.

Such was the origin of the great Republic of Mexico; such has been her history; and such is the fate to which she is hastening.

We are accused by other nations of dealing too much with destiny; they say we are always talking about our manifest destiny. Well, we agree with them. We are guilty of these things; and we should be a most irreligious people if we did not warrant these accusations. Unfold the whole scroll of history and show us the nation which, from its cradle to its manhood, has bristled so ceaselessly at every step with the movements of the electric machinery of Divine Providence. Our history was borrowed from none of the stereotyped forms of national life in the elder world. It had no antetype in the past. It began alone — it exists alone.

The announcement of the American republic inaugurated an era in the world newer in government than Bacon's inductive system in philosophy. The statesmen of the Old World don't know what to do with us. We are a new fact to them. They don't know where to locate us. They can't define us. They are always misunderstanding us, misinterpreting us, misrepresenting us, prophesying falsely about us. And all for the simple reason that we are a new nation, differing in origin, progress, developments, and prospects — spirit, elements, combination, power, and mode of achievement — from all states that have hitherto existed under the sun.

We feel the ever present hand of Omnipotence on us as really if not as reverently today as did our fathers on Plymouth Rock or on the banks of James River. We mean by all this that the history of this republic has amazed mankind more than the history of any nation that ever had an existence. And so we can and will go on as before, to speak of the destiny of our country; and, perhaps, by the light of the past, we may forecast some portion of our history not yet unfolded.

We now propose to speak of Mexico and answer the question which the whole world is asking — What is to become of her?

We cannot enter into her history. It is too long, involved, intricate, varied, and yet familiar. We know enough about it from other sources for our general argument. We know that it is a vast country embracing a territory larger than the original thirteen colonies which made war against George III. We know that it is the garden of North America, the natural hothouse of our continent, that it is to become one day the central source of mineral wealth for the world.

We also know that this illimitable region, blushing under the purple light of the tropics, with all the splendors and blandishments of a genial and prolific clime, has for ages suffered under the sway of despotism or the curses of anarchy. . . .

Let us then for a moment glance at her history since she achieved her independence. The yoke of monarchy once broken, she became republican in form, copying closely after the great model of the United States. She was not prepared, however, for the institutions she adopted. . . . There are nations which do not know how to be free. Mexico is one of them . . . while there are other nations which have learned the lesson and no yoke can rest unbroken upon their necks. Of such are the . . . Anglo-Saxon-Norman race of the United States.

But we have never heard that the Spaniards *knew how to be free.* They never showed that knowledge at home; they never showed it when they were transplanted abroad. Among all the colonies with which Spain enriched and embellished the New World, we do not recall one which knew how to be free. All of them but Cuba, we believe, asserted their independence and became nominally free. That freedom was soon recognized by other nations, and ultimately by Spain herself. But how have they used their freedom? One of those colonies knew what to do with herself. Florida wished to be admitted to the Union and we received her. At a later day, California, then a fossil ruin, fell under the shadow of our eagle wing, and at once electric fire streamed through every vein as though she had been touched by the spear of Ithuriel.

But all the rest of those Spanish colonies! Where are they? No one of them enjoys even any moderate degree of prosperity, except Cuba, which alone has kept herself moored to the throne of Castile; and no thanks to her loyalty for this. Cuba was an island; and islands can be more easily kept in subjection than provinces on the mainland. Besides Cuba was nearer to Spain and offered higher inducements to individual ambition, patronage, power, and fascination than any of the other Spanish colonies of the West. It was the gem of the Antilles, the *Koh-i-noor* of the whole empire of Ferdinand and Isabella.

But to come back to poor but opulent and beautiful Mexico. What did she do?

She became free, and the world looked for another Washington republic in the West. Humboldt had traversed all her plains and climbed her highest mountains. He had made that immense region of the continent a household word to mankind. She started with every chance in her favor except one: *her people were not white men; they were not Caucasians;* they were numerous enough — twice as many as our revolutionary ancestors — but they were not *white men.* They were a bad mixture of Spaniards, Indians, and Negroes, making an aggregate containing few of the virtues of either, with most of the vices of all.

Such men did not know how to be free. They have not learned the lesson to this day, nor will they learn it till they are taken into the district school of American democracy, where the master will govern them till they learn how to govern themselves. They must pass their novitiate. There is no other

road they can travel that will bring them into the community of free states and leave them seated at the council board of nations.

The time has about come for us to see the beginning of the end. The problem is nearly solved; quite so to the eye of statesmanship. It will shortly be clear enough to everybody. Mexico cannot govern herself. She has tried it under nearly or quite as many administrations as she has seen years since she cut loose from her parent country. Not infrequently, she has tried a new experiment every few months, and sometimes she has shortened the period and abridged her Olympiads into days and hours.

She has experimented with emperors, dictators, presidents, councils, committees of safety, generals, citizens, and usurpers; but one and all these have only been little players on the stage, each for his brief hour, but all playing such high, fantastic tricks before high Heaven as make all democratic angels weep. So often does Mexico change her regime that she has become a perfect nuisance, even to the newsmongers. Why, the newsboys — those very daredevils on the outskirts of the literary world — don't think any longer of arresting attention by crying out as they once did, "Extra! Revolution in Mexico."

Everybody expects a revolution there by the next steamer. Even the newspapers themselves have at last come down to the proper standard, and they announce the latest revolution in Mexico in the same type as they do the weather-wise Merriam's repeated edicts about the wind. And the one announcement excites just about as much public interest as the other. One of the latest bulletins on this subject tells us that "Santa Anna having recently sold out his unrivaled collection of gamecocks, it is considered certain now that he will immediately return to Mexico and assume the dictatorship of the Republic."

Shade of Washington! What kind of a republic must that be? If this be not the dissolution of Mexico, what is it? If this be not mummery, what is mummery? In a word, is it not clear enough to everybody that Mexico *has played out?*

But while we have spoken of the dissolution of Mexico as her fate, there is nothing sad in this thought to her or us. It often happens in the moral as in the natural world that dissolution is life. We see this in the ever recurring miracle of the reviving spring, which brings resurrection to the dead things of a previous period. The presence of life banishes death. All vitality is borrowed fire! Mexico is in a state of suspended animation. She is in fact dead. She must have resurrection. She must be electrified, restored. This American republic is strong enough to do anything that requires strength. It is vital enough to inject life even into the dead. That she can do it to Mexico we believe, we know it. It was done to Florida and to California. These experiments, it is true, were on a small scale. So was the experiment with Texas (originally settled by Mexicans). But the principle will hold true on a large scale, for the moral influences which govern mind are not restricted to mechanical limits. A single grand thought has more than once revolutionized the earth. Outward pomp and circumstance do not control human fortunes half so much as regenerating truth.

Among the regenerating political powers of the world, the United States hold today the complete precedence. We, of all the nations, can show a history and example of progress, order, and power, without monarchy or hierarchy, which can impart emphasis and conviction to the theoretical lessons and preachings of freedom. We are not new at this business. Our republic was conceived only in the holy embrace of liberty. It was born amidst the jeers of monarchy. Only a few wise men from the East followed the star as it traveled toward the West, till it halted over the manger where the newborn babe lay. But those wise men paid their homage, and the new political dispensation has not disappointed their predictions. Our nation has grown till it can measure its strength with the mightiest powers of the earth; and the question now comes up: *Shall we not begin as a republic to emancipate nations, as monarchies have long been crushing republics?* . . .

Europe may call this *filibusterism.* But of what else is the history of nations made up? Has England forgotten Hengist and Horsa, or William of Hastings? Above all, has she forgotten the most stupendous record of filibusterism on earth as unfolded in her distant conquests, especially in India? That India where her crimes are now being punished by the righteous vengeance of the insulted Sepoys! Let her, at least, hold her peace, for on what part of the earth's surface has she not pillaged and robbed where she could? Is she not filibustering in China today, and does she not filibusterize every day and every year, and has she not done it throughout her history? And, moreover, has she not, as a secluded island, gone forth and spread her empire by violence so far that her boast is made that upon that empire the sun never sets? Our history furnishes no such records of violence as all this. We have acquired by legitimate purchase or friendly negotiation every foot of ground over which our flag waves today.

But suppose England does criticize our deeds. Is that her business, so long as we do not invade her rights? Who has clothed her with this censorship over us or our fortunes? Once she was our mistress, and she ruled us with an iron hand. But her scepter was broken by an act of independence, and she resigned it by treaty. Therefore it is time that we were done with any further notice of her opinions about our acts, which do not concern her. She may have been so long accustomed to this assumption of censorship that she may keep it up a little longer from habit. But she will soon give it up, and it is a matter of very little consequence whether she does or not.

We have our own national duty to do; our own national destiny to fulfill; and we shall march to its fulfillment under infallible guidance, and all obstacles to our progress in the future will melt away, as they have in the past.

The time has come when it is as imperatively our duty — made so by Providence — to take control of Mexico and wheel her into the train of the world's progress, as it ever was our duty to plant the Caucasian race on this soil and open its illimitable bosom to the sun. Pocahontas, and King Philip, and Red Jacket were not fulfilling God's designs with this continent. It had to change hands. So must Mexico; and, for that matter, sooner or later, the whole American-Spanish world. No race but our own can either cultivate or rule the Western Hemisphere. No other system of government exists on the earth that has vitality, power, elasticity, sagacity, adaptation, or even stability to do this Herculean work. It is preeminently our own work, and it is a work which the Almighty has given us to do.

What has been the matter with Mexico? Why has she got along no better? What has weighed her down? By answering these questions, we shall discover the remedy for her troubles and the secret of her restoration. She is the richest nation in the world in mineral resources; then develop them by intelligent and well-directed labor. She is hopelessly crushed by debt, whose interest she does not dream of paying; and yet she could pay that interest every year and extinguish the principal easily in ten. She is as favorably situated for commerce, perhaps more favorably, than any other country in the world, for she touches two oceans and a hundred islands, and stands midway between North and South America, from pole to pole, and midway between all the commerce of Asia and Europe.

She now lies under all the terrors of anarchy. Extend over her the broad, protecting shield of a powerful and free government, and from that instant you quadruple the wealth of her nation; yes, you add to it a hundredfold. She is now bent down under the deadly incubus of a bloated and beastly hierarchy, which enslaves and besots the people, and roots out or undermines every successive administration. Dissolve that connection between church and state at a touch! and then Mexico is free.

Spread the network of telegraphs and let the lightnings play over her bosom. Cut through railways from ocean to ocean. Get steam engines to playing in her gold and silver, and copper and quicksilver mines; redeem her from idleness, and set her 8 million pairs of human hands to work; throw open her seaports on both sides; break down all barriers between her frontiers and ours; and, before twelve months have gone by, one of the greatest things will have been done for the human race; in fact, a nation will literally have been born in a day!

This is the work that Mexico wants done, and this is the work we, of all the nations, can do.

Now, how shall we initiate it? In any one of twenty we might mention, we have already missed an excellent chance. Once we had all Mexico. Then we should have kept it. The mass of the Mexican people did not have any correct idea of us before the war of 1847. But their prejudices against us quickly gave way to facts, and the desire was almost universal at the close of the war to have General Scott remain with his army and keep possession of the country. Santa Anna and his creatures, with a portion of the priests, were about the only opponents to the plan. Then we should have finished the whole business all up in a single job. It would have been a boon of priceless value to Mexico.

And only lately, President Comonfort was driven from his country, and took refuge on our shores, as all her presidents and dictators have sooner or later. He asked our intervention. England, or any first-rate power at any time in the world's history, would have accepted the invitation, and by all the established principles of international law, the act would have been justified and even applauded by mankind.

We should object to the purchase of Mexico for any considerable sum of money, and on two grounds: first, the money would be squandered by the political adventurers who should happen to be in power there at the time, instead of being applied honestly to swell the revenues of the state; and second, we claim that by taking Mexico into this Union and guaranteeing her domestic tranquillity and progress, we should give her a fiftyfold equivalent for what she parted with; and we should object to paying any higher premium for the privilege of issuing a premium of security and protection to such a nation.

There are other arguments which press home upon us the policy for which we are contending. Mexico, as she has been and as she is still, is a disgrace to North America,

an opprobrium to the whole system of republicanism, and consequently a disgrace to the United States. She is our near neighbor. She is nominally a free commonwealth, and yet she has always, since her independence, been giving the lie to her professions. This thing should be stopped. No nation has a right in this manner to blaspheme the holy name of liberty. Our republic has suffered long enough by contact with such a sham concern. We must now redeem our own reputation, and in the act redeem Mexico herself.

But we limit our arguments for this policy entirely to the grounds we have based it on. We do not place it on any narrow basis. We do not covet Mexico for our sake, for it would be the easiest joke imaginable to take it in that case and say nothing about it. But we should absorb Mexico for her own sake, to emancipate her from the despotism and anarchy which are plunging her 8 million people into barbarism; and we should do it for the good of the world. The streams of our regenerating fire should be poured into her bosom. She should be dragged up from her degradation and raised into the constellation of free states. This is the work our republic has yet to do. It is the business of statesmanship to determine the manner of its accomplishment.

5.

Anonymous: On the Need for Physical Fitness

The Atlantic Monthly, *a magazine of literature, art, and politics, had started
publication in Boston in November 1857, under the editorship of James Russell Lowell.
The following article, from which excerpts are reprinted, appeared in the magazine
in March 1858 under the title "Saints, and Their Bodies." The author criticized
Americans for neglecting to develop their bodies and disputed the theory of religious
newspapers of that time that physical strength was a relic of a barbarous age.*

Source: *Atlantic Monthly,* March 1858.

PHYSICAL HEALTH is a necessary condition of all permanent success. To the American people it has a stupendous importance, because it is the only attribute of power in which they are losing ground. Guarantee us against physical degeneracy, and we can risk all other perils — financial crisis, slavery, Romanism, Mormonism, border ruffians, and New York assassins; "domestic malice, foreign levy, nothing" can daunt us. Guarantee us health, and Mrs. Stowe cannot frighten us with all the prophecies of Dred; but when her sister Catherine informs us that in all the vast female acquaintance of the Beecher family there are not a dozen healthy women, we confess ourselves a little tempted to despair of the republic.

The one drawback to satisfaction in our public school system is the physical weakness which it reveals and helps to perpetuate. One seldom notices a ruddy face in the schoolroom without tracing it back to a transatlantic origin. . . .

There are statistics to show that the average length of human life is increasing; but it is probable that this results from the diminution of epidemic diseases rather than from any general improvement in physique.

There are facts also to indicate an increase of size and strength with advancing civilization. It is known that two men of middle size were unable to find a suit of armor large enough among the sixty sets owned by Sir Samuel Meyrick. It is also known that the strongest American Indians cannot equal the average strength of wrist of Europeans, or rival them in ordinary athletic feats. Indeed, it is generally supposed that any physical deterioration is local, being peculiar to the United States. . . .

We cannot speak for England, but certainly no one can visit Canada without being struck with the spectacle of a more athletic race of people than our own. On every side one sees rosy female faces and noble manly figures. In the shop windows, in winter weather, hang snowshoes, "gentlemen's and ladies' sizes." The street corners inform you that the members of the "Curling Club" are to meet today at "Dolly's," and the "Montreal Foxhounds" at St. Lawrence Hall tomorrow. And next day comes off the annual steeplechase, at the "Mile-End Course," ridden by gentlemen of the city with their own horses; a scene, by the way, whose exciting interest can scarcely be conceived by those accustomed only to "trials of speed" at agricultural exhibitions. Everything indicates outdoor habits and athletic constitutions.

We are aware that we may be met with the distinction between a good idle constitution and a good working constitution, the latter of which often belongs to persons who make no show of physical powers. But this only means that there are different temperaments and types of physical organization, while, within the limits of each, the distinction between a healthy and a diseased condition still holds; and we insist on that alone.

Still more specious is the claim of the Fourth of July orators that, health or no health, it is the sallow Americans and not the robust English who are really leading the world. But this, again, is a question of temperaments. The Englishman concedes the greater intensity, but prefers a more solid and permanent power. It is the noble masonry and vast canals of Montreal against the Aladdin's palaces of Chicago. "I observe," admits the Englishman, "that an American can accomplish more, at a single effort, than any other man on earth; but I also observe that he exhausts himself in the achievement. Kane, a delicate invalid, astounds the world by his two Arctic winters, and then dies in tropical Cuba." The solution is simple; nervous energy is grand and so is muscular power; combine the two and you move the world.

We shall assume, as admitted, therefore, the deficiency of physical health in America, and the need of a great amendment. But into the general question of cause and cure we do not propose to enter. In view of the vast variety of special theories and the inadequacy of any one (or any dozen) we shall forbear. To our thinking, the best diagnosis of the universal American disease is to be found in Andral's famous description of the cholera: "Anatomical characteristics, insufficient; cause, mysterious; nature, hypotheti-

cal; symptoms, characteristic; diagnosis, easy; *treatment, very doubtful.*" . . .

A great physician has said, "I know not which is most indispensable for the support of the frame, food or exercise." But who in this community really takes exercise? Even the mechanic commonly confines himself to one set of muscles; the blacksmith acquires strength in his right arm and the dancing master in his left leg. But the professional or businessman, what muscles has he at all? The tradition that Pheidippides ran from Athens to Sparta, 120 miles, in two days, seems to us Americans as mythical as the Golden Fleece. Even to ride 60 miles in a day, to walk 30, to run 5, or to swim 1 would cost most men among us a fit of illness, and many their lives.

Let any man test his physical condition, we will not say by sawing his own cord of wood, but by an hour in the gymnasium or at cricket, and his enfeebled muscular apparatus will groan with rheumatism for a week. Or let him test the strength of his arms and chest by raising and lowering himself a few times upon a horizontal bar, or hanging by the arms to a rope, and he will probably agree with Galen in pronouncing it *robustum validumque laborem* [firm and strong effort]. Yet so manifestly are these things within the reach of common constitutions that a few weeks or months of judicious practice will renovate his whole system, and the most vigorous exercise will refresh him like a cold bath.

To a well-regulated frame, mere physical exertion, even for an uninteresting object, is a great enjoyment, which is, of course, enhanced by the excitement of games and sports. To almost every man there is joy in the memory of these things; they are the happiest associations of his boyhood. It does not occur to him that he also might be as happy as a boy if he lived more like one. What do most men know of the "wild joys of living," the daily zest and luxury of outdoor existence, in which every healthy boy beside them revels — skating, while the orange sky of sunset dies away over the delicate tracery of gray branches, and the throbbing feet pause in their tingling motion, and the frosty air is filled with the shrill sound of distant steel, the resounding of the ice, and the echoes up the hillsides — sailing, beating up against a stiff breeze, with the waves thumping under the bow, as if a dozen sea-gods had laid their heads together to resist it — climbing tall trees, where the higher foliage, closing around, cures the dizziness which began below, and one feels as if he had left a coward beneath and found a hero above — the joyous hour of crowded life in football or cricket — the gallant glories of riding, and the jubilee of swimming? . . .

We cling still to the belief that the Persian curriculum of studies — to ride, to shoot, and to speak the truth — is the better part of a boy's education. As the urchin is undoubtedly physically safer for having learned to turn a somersault and fire a gun, perilous though these feats appear to mothers, so his soul is made healthier, larger, freer, stronger by hours and days of manly exercise and copious drafts of open air, at whatever risk of idle habits and bad companions. Even if the balance is sometimes lost and play prevails, what matter? We rejoice to have been a schoolmate of him who wrote

The hours the idle schoolboy squandered
The man would die ere he'd forget.

Only keep in a boy a pure and generous heart, and, whether he work or play, his time can scarcely be wasted. . . .

Should it prove, however, that the cultivation of active exercises diminishes the proportion of time given by children to study, we can only view it as an added advantage. Every year confirms us in the conviction that our schools, public and private, systematically overtask the brains of the ris-

ing generation. We all complain that Young America grows to mental maturity too soon, and yet we all contribute our share to continue the evil. It is but a few weeks since we saw the warmest praises, in the New York newspapers, of a girl's school, in that city, where the appointed hours of study amounted to nine and a quarter daily, and the hours of exercise to a bare unit. Almost all the students' manuals assume that American students need stimulus instead of restraint, and urge them to multiply the hours of study and diminish those of outdoor amusements and of sleep, as if the great danger did not lie that way already. When will parents and teachers learn to regard mental precocity as a disaster to be shunned, instead of a glory to be coveted? We could count up a dozen young men who have graduated at Harvard College, during the last twenty years, with high honors, before the age of eighteen; and we suppose that nearly every one of them has lived to regret it. . . .

One invaluable merit of outdoor sports is to be found in this, that they afford the best cement for childish friendship. Their associations outlive all others. There is many a man, now perchance hard and worldly, whom we love to pass in the street simply because in meeting him we meet spring flowers and autumn chestnuts, skates and cricket balls, cherry birds and pickerel. There is an indescribable fascination in the gradual transference of these childish companionships into maturer relations. We love to encounter in the contests of manhood those whom we first met at football, and to follow the profound thoughts of those who always dived deeper, even in the river, than our efforts could attain. There is a certain governor of whom we personally can remember only that he found the Fresh Pond heronry, which we sought in vain; and in memory the august sheriff of a neighboring county still skates in victorious pursuit of us (fit emblem of swift-footed justice!) on the black ice of the same lovely lake. Our imagination crowns the Cambridge poet and the Cambridge sculptor, not with their later laurels but with the willows out of which they taught us to carve whistles, shriller than any trump of fame, in the happy days when Mount Auburn was sweet Auburn still.

Luckily, boy-nature is too strong for theory. And we admit, for the sake of truth, that physical education is not so entirely neglected among us as the absence of popular games would indicate. We suppose that, if the truth were told, this last fact proceeds partly from the greater freedom of field sports in this country. There are few New England boys who do not become familiar with the rod or gun in childhood. We take it that, in the mother country, the monopoly of land interferes with this, and that game laws, by a sort of spontaneous pun, tend to introduce games.

Again, the practice of match playing is opposed to our habits, both as a consumer of time and as partaking too much of gambling. Still, it is done in the case of "firemen's musters," which are, we believe, a wholly indigenous institution. We have known a very few cases where the young men of neighboring country parishes have challenged each other to games of baseball, as is common in England; and there was, if we mistake not, a recent match at football between the boys of the Fall River and the New Bedford high schools. And within a few years regattas and cricket matches have become common events. Still, these public exhibitions are far from being a full exponent of the athletic habits of our people; and there is really more going on among us than this meager "pentathlon" exhibits. . . .

But, so far as there is a deficiency in these respects among us, this generation must not shrink from the responsibility. It is unfair to charge it on the Puritans. They are not even answerable for Massachusetts;

for there is no doubt that athletic exercises, of some sort, were far more generally practised in this community before the Revolution than at present. A state of almost constant Indian warfare then created an obvious demand for muscle and agility. At present there is no such immediate necessity. And it has been supposed that a race of shopkeepers, brokers, and lawyers could live without bodies. Now that the terrible records of dyspepsia and paralysis are disproving this, we may hope for a reaction in favor of bodily exercises. And when we once begin the competition, there seems no reason why any other nation should surpass us.

The wide area of our country and its variety of surface and shore offer a corresponding range of physical training. Take our coasts and inland waters alone. It is one thing to steer a pleasure boat with a rudder and another to steer a dory with an oar; one thing to paddle a birch canoe and another to paddle a ducking float; in a Charles River clubboat, the post of honor is in the stern, in a Penobscot bateau, in the bow; and each of these experiences educates a different set of muscles. Add to this the constitutional American receptiveness, which welcomes new pursuits without distinction of origin, unites German gymnastics with English sports and sparring, and takes the red Indians for instructors in paddling and running. With these various aptitudes, we certainly ought to become a nation of athletes.

We have shown that, in one way or another, American schoolboys obtain active exercise. The same is true, in a very limited degree, even of girls. They are occasionally, in our larger cities, sent to gymnasiums, the more the better. Dancing schools are better than nothing, though all the attendant circumstances are usually unfavorable. A fashionable young lady is estimated to traverse her 300 miles a season on foot; and this needs training. But outdoor exercise for girls is terribly restricted — first, by their costume, and second, by the remarks of Mrs. Grundy. All young female animals unquestionably require as much motion as their brothers, and naturally make as much noise; but what mother would not be shocked, in the case of her girl of twelve, by one-tenth part the activity and uproar which are recognized as being the breath of life to her twin brother? Still, there is a change going on, which is tantamount to an admission that there is an evil to be remedied. Twenty years ago, if we mistake not, it was by no means considered "proper" for little girls to play with their hoops and balls on Boston Common; and swimming and skating have hardly been recognized as "ladylike" for half that period of time.

Still it is beyond question that far more outdoor exercise is habitually taken by the female population of almost all European countries than by our own. In the first place, the peasant women of all other countries (a class nonexistent here) are trained to active labor from childhood; and what traveler has not seen, on foreign mountain paths, long rows of maidens ascending and descending the difficult ways, bearing heavy burdens on their heads, and winning by the exercise such a superb symmetry and grace of figure as were a new wonder of the world to cisatlantic eyes? Among the higher classes, physical exercises take the place of these things. Miss Beecher glowingly describes a Russian female seminary in which 900 girls of the noblest families were being trained by Ling's system of calisthenics, and her informant declared that she never beheld such an array of girlish health and beauty.

Englishwomen, again, have horsemanship and pedestrianism, in which their ordinary feats appear to our healthy women incredible. Thus, Mary Lamb writes to Miss Wordsworth (both ladies being between fifty and sixty), "You say you can walk fifteen miles with ease; this is exactly my stint, and more fatigues me"; and then speaks pityingly of a delicate lady who could accomplish only "four or five miles every third or fourth day, keeping very quiet between." How few American ladies, in the fullness of their strength (if female strength among us has any fullness) can surpass this English invalid!

But even among American men, how few carry athletic habits into manhood! The great hindrance, no doubt, is absorption in business; and we observe that this winter's hard times and consequent leisure have given a great stimulus to outdoor sports. But in most places there is the further obstacle, that a certain stigma of boyishness goes with them. So early does this begin that we remember, in our teens, to have been slightly reproached with juvenility because, though a senior sophister, we still clung to football. Juvenility! We only wish we had the opportunity now. Full-grown men are, of course, intended to take not only as much but far more active exercise than boys. Some physiologists go so far as to demand six hours of outdoor life daily; and it is absurd in us to complain that we have not the healthy animal happiness of children while we forswear their simple sources of pleasure.

Most of the exercise habitually taken by men of sedentary pursuits is in the form of walking. We believe its merits to be greatly overrated. Walking is to real exercise what vegetable food is to animal; it satisfies the appetite, but the nourishment is not sufficiently concentrated to be invigorating. It takes a man outdoors and it uses his muscles, and therefore, of course, it is good; but it is not the best kind of good. Walking, for walking's sake, becomes tedious. We must not ignore the play impulse in human nature, which, according to Schiller, is the foundation of all art. In female boarding schools, teachers uniformly testify to the aversion of pupils to the prescribed walk. Give them a sled, or a pair of skates, or a rowboat, or put them on horseback, and they will protract the period of exercise till the teacher in turn grumbles. Put them into a gymnasium, with an efficient teacher, and they will soon require restraint instead of urging.

Gymnastic exercises have two disadvantages: one, in being commonly performed under cover (though this may sometimes prove an advantage as well); another, in requiring apparatus and, at first, a teacher. These apart, perhaps no other form of exercise is so universally invigorating. A teacher is required less for the sake of stimulus than of precaution. The tendency is almost always to dare too much; and there is also need of a daily moderation in commencing exercises; for the wise pupil will always prefer to supple his muscles by mild exercises and calisthenics before proceeding to harsher performances on the bars and ladders. With this precaution, strains are easily avoided; even with this, the hand will sometimes blister and the body ache, but perseverance will cure the one and Russia Salve the other; and the invigorated life in every limb will give a perpetual charm to those seemingly aimless leaps and somersaults. The feats once learned, a private gymnasium can easily be constructed of the simplest apparatus, and so daily used; though nothing can wholly supply the stimulus afforded by a class in a public institution, with a competent teacher. In summer, the whole thing can partially be dispensed with; but we are really unable to imagine how any person gets through the winter happily without a gymnasium.

For the favorite indoor exercise of dumbbells we have little to say; they are not an enlivening performance, nor do they task a variety of muscles, while they are apt to strain and fatigue them, if used with energy. Far better, for a solitary exercise, is the Indian club, a lineal descendant of that antique one in whose handle rare medicaments were fabled to be concealed. The modern one is simply a rounded club, weighing from four pounds upward, according to the strength of the pupil. Grasping a pair of these by the handles, he learns a variety of exercises, having always before him the feats of the marvelous Mr. Harrison, whose praise is in the "Spirit of the Times," and whose portrait adorns the back of Dr. Trall's *Gymnastics*. By the latest bulletins, that gentleman measured forty-two and a half inches round the chest and employed clubs weighing no less than forty-seven pounds.

It may seem to our nonresistant friends to be going rather far if we should indulge our saints in taking boxing lessons; yet it is not long since a New York clergyman saved his life in Broadway by the judicious administration of a "cross-counter" or a "flying crook," and we have not heard of his excommunication from the Church Militant. No doubt, a laudable aversion prevails in this country to the English practices of pugilism; yet it must be remembered that sparring is, by its very name, a "science of self-defense"; and if a gentleman wishes to know how to hold a rude antagonist at bay, in any emergency, and keep out of an undignified scuffle, the means are most easily afforded him by the art which Pythagoras founded. Apart from this, boxing exercises every muscle in the body and gives a wonderful quickness to eye and hand. These same remarks apply, though in a minor degree, to fencing also.

Billiards is a graceful game, and affords, in some respects, admirable training, but is hardly to be classed among athletic exercises. Tenpins afford, perhaps, the most popular form of exercise among us, and have become almost a national game, and a good one, too, so far as it goes. The English game of bowls is less entertaining, and is, indeed, rather a sluggish sport, though it has the merit of being played in the open air. The severer British sports, as tennis and rackets, are scarcely more than names to us Americans.

Passing now to outdoor exercises (and no

one should confine himself to indoor ones), we hold with the Thalesian school and rank water first. Vishnu Sarma gives, in his apologues, the characteristics of the fit place for a wise man to live in; and enumerates among its necessities first "a Rajah" and then "a river." Democrats as we are, we can dispense with the first, but not with the second. A square mile even of pond water is worth a year's schooling to any intelligent boy. A boat is a kingdom. We personally own one, a mere flat-bottomed "float," with a center board. It has seen service, it is eight years old, has spent two winters under the ice, and been fished in by boys every day for as many summers. It grew at last so hopelessly leaky that even the boys disdained it. It cost $7 originally, and we would not sell it today for $17. To own the poorest boat is better than hiring the best. It is a link to nature; without a boat, one is so much the less a man.

Sailing is, of course, delicious; it is as good as flying to steer anything with wings of canvas, whether one stand by the wheel of a clippership, or by the clumsy stern oar of a "gundalow" [gondola]. But rowing has also its charms; and the Indian noiselessness of the paddle, beneath the fringing branches of the assabeth or artichoke, puts one into Fairyland at once, and Hiawatha's *cheemaun* becomes a possible possession. Rowing is peculiarly graceful and appropriate as a feminine exercise, and any able-bodied girl can learn to handle one light oar at the first lesson, and two at the second; this, at least, we demand of our own pupils.

Swimming has also a birdlike charm of motion. The novel element, the free action, the abated drapery give a sense of personal contact with nature which nothing else so fully bestows. No later triumph of existence is so fascinating, perhaps, as that in which the boy first wins his panting way across the deep gulf that severs one green bank from another (ten yards, perhaps), and feels himself thenceforward lord of the watery world. The Athenian phrase for a man who knew nothing was that he could "neither read nor swim." Yet there is a vast amount of this ignorance; the majority of sailors, it is said, cannot swim a stroke; and in a late lake disaster, many able-bodied men perished by drowning in calm water only half a mile from shore. At our watering places, it is rare to see a swimmer venture out more than a rod or two, though this proceeds partly from the fear of sharks, as if sharks of the dangerous order were not far more afraid of the rocks than the swimmers of being eaten. But the fact of the timidity is unquestionable; and we were told by a certain clerical frequenter of a watering place, himself a robust swimmer, that he had never met but two companions who would venture boldly out with him, both being ministers, and one a distinguished ex-president of Brown University. We place this fact to the credit of the bodies of our saints. . . .

It is pleasant . . . to observe the . . . growth of our indigenous American game of baseball, whose briskness and unceasing activity are perhaps more congenial, after all, to our national character than the comparative deliberation of cricket. Football, bating its roughness, is the most glorious of all games to those whose animal life is sufficiently vigorous to enjoy it. Skating is just, at present, the fashion for ladies as well as gentlemen, and needs no apostle; the open weather of the current winter has been unusually favorable for its practice, and it is destined to become a permanent institution.

6.

Oliver Wendell Holmes: On Old Age

Oliver Wendell Holmes, who had given the Atlantic Monthly *magazine its name, also contributed a monthly column called "The Autocrat of the Breakfast-Table," which discussed topics of current interest in a conversational tone. These articles were later collected into a book of the same title. The following selection is taken from the May 1858 column and is an agreeable response on behalf of the elderly to a previous article, "Saints, and Their Bodies," which had appeared in March.*

Source: *Atlantic Monthly*, May 1858.

THE LAST BLOSSOM

Though young no more, we still would
    dream
Of beauty's dear deluding wiles;
The leagues of life to graybeards seem
    Shorter than boyhood's lingering miles.

Who knows a woman's wild caprice?
    It played with Goethe's silvered hair,
And many a Holy Father's "niece"
    Has softly smoothed the papal chair.

When sixty bids us sigh in vain
    To melt the heart of sweet sixteen,
We think upon those ladies twain
    Who loved so well the tough old
      Dean.

We see the Patriarch's wintry face,
    The maid of Egypt's dusky glow,
And dream that Youth and Age embrace,
    As April violets fill with snow.

Tranced in her Lord's Olympian smile
    His lotus-loving Memphian lies —
The musky daughter of the Nile,
    With plaited hair and almond eyes.

Might we but share one wild caress
    Ere life's autumnal blossoms fall,
And earth's brown, clinging lips impress
    The long cold kiss that waits us all!

My bosom heaves, remembering yet
    The morning of that blissful day
When Rose, the flower of spring, I met,
    And gave my raptured soul away.

Flung from her eyes of purest blue,
    A lasso, with its leaping chain,
Light as a loop of larkspurs, flew
    O'er sense and spirit, heart and brain.

Thou com'st to cheer my waning age,
    Sweet vision, waited for so long!
Dove that wouldst seek the poet's cage,
    Lured by the magic breath of song!

She blushes! Ah, reluctant maid,
    Love's *drapeau rouge* the truth has told!
O'er girlhood's yielding barricade
    Floats the great Leveler's crimson fold!

Come to my arms! — love heeds not
      years;
    No frost the bud of passion knows.
Ha! what is this my frenzy hears?
    A voice behind me uttered — Rose!

Sweet was her smile, but not for me;
    Alas, when woman looks *too* kind,
Just turn your foolish head and see,
    Some youth is walking close behind!

As to *giving up* because the almanac or the family Bible says that it is about time to do it, I have no intention of doing any such thing. I grant you that I burn less carbon than some years ago. I see people of my standing really good for nothing, decrepit, effete, *la lèvre inférieure déjà pendante* [the lower lip already hanging], with what little life they have left mainly concentrated in their epigastrium. But as the disease of old age is epidemic, endemic, and sporadic, and everybody that lives long enough is sure to catch it, I am going to say, for the encouragement of such as need it, how I treat the malady in my own case.

First, as I feel that, when I have anything to do, there is less time for it than when I was younger, I find that I give my attention more thoroughly and use my time more economically than ever before; so that I can learn anything twice as easily as in my earlier days. I am not, therefore, afraid to attack a new study. I took up a difficult language a very few years ago with good success, and think of mathematics and metaphysics by-and-by.

Second, I have opened my eyes to a good many neglected privileges and pleasures within my reach and requiring only a little courage to enjoy them. You may well suppose it pleased me to find that old Cato was thinking of learning to play the fiddle, when I had deliberately taken it up in my old age and satisfied myself that I could get much comfort, if not much music, out of it.

Third, I have found that some of those active exercises, which are commonly thought to belong to young folks only, may be enjoyed at a much later period.

A young friend has lately written an admirable article in one of the journals, entitled "Saints, and their Bodies." Approving of his general doctrines and grateful for his records of personal experience, I cannot refuse to add my own experimental confirmation of his eulogy of one particular form of active exercise and amusement, namely, *boating*. For the past nine years, I have rowed about, during a good part of the summer, on fresh or salt water. My present fleet on the River Charles consists of three rowboats: (1) a small, flat-bottomed skiff of the shape of a flatiron, kept mainly to lend to boys; (2) a fancy "dory" for two pairs of sculls, in which I sometimes go out with my young folks; (3) my own particular water sulky, a "skeleton" or "shell" race boat, twenty-two feet long, with huge outriggers, which boat I pull with ten-foot sculls, alone, of course, as it holds but one — and tips him out, if he doesn't mind what he is about.

In this I glide around the Back Bay, down the stream, up the Charles to Cambridge and Watertown, up the Mystic, round the wharves, in the wake of steamboats, which have a swell after them delightful to rock upon; I linger under the bridges, those "caterpillar bridges," as my brother professor so happily called them; rub against the black sides of old wood schooners; cool down under the overhanging stern of some tall Indiaman; stretch across to the Navy Yard, where the sentinel warns me off from the *Ohio*, just as if I should hurt her by lying in her shadow; then strike out into the harbor, where the water gets clear and the air smells of the ocean, till all at once I remember that, if a west wind blows up of a sudden, I shall drift along past the islands, out of sight of the dear old statehouse — plate, tumbler, knife, and fork all waiting at home, but no chair drawn up at the table — all the dear people waiting, waiting, waiting, while the boat is sliding, sliding, sliding into the great desert, where there is no tree and no fountain. As I don't want my wreck to be washed up on one of the beaches in company with devil's-aprons, bladderweeds, dead horseshoes, and bleached crab shells, I turn about and flap my long, narrow wings for home.

When the tide is running out swiftly, I have a splendid fight to get through the bridges, but always make it a rule to beat, though I have been jammed up into pretty tight places at times, and was caught once between a vessel swinging round and the pier, until our bones (the boat's, that is) cracked as if we had been in the jaws of Behemoth. Then back to my moorings at the foot of the Common, off with the rowing dress, dash under the green, translucent wave, return to the garb of civilization, walk through my garden, take a look at my elms on the Common, and, reaching my habitat, in consideration of my advanced period of life, indulge in the Elysian abandonment of a huge recumbent chair.

When I have established a pair of well-pronounced feathering calluses on my thumbs, when I am in training so that I can do my fifteen miles at a stretch without coming to grief in any way, when I can perform my mile in eight minutes or a little less, then I feel as if I had old Time's head in chancery, and could give it to him at my leisure.

I do not deny the attraction of walking. I have bored this ancient city through and through in my daily travels, until I know it as an old inhabitant of a Cheshire knows his cheese. Why, it was I who, in the course of these rambles, discovered that remarkable avenue called *Myrtle Street*, stretching in one long line from east of the reservoir to a precipitous and rudely paved cliff which looks down on the grim abode of science, and beyond it to the far hills; a promenade so delicious in its repose, so cheerfully varied with glimpses down the northern slope into busy Cambridge Street, with its iron river of the horse railroad, and wheeled barges gliding back and forward over it, so delightfully closing at its western extremity in sunny courts and passages where I know peace, and beauty, and virtue, and serene old age must be perpetual tenants, so alluring to all who desire to take their daily stroll, in the words of Dr. Watts, "Alike unknowing and unknown," that nothing but a sense of duty would have prompted me to reveal the secret of its existence. I concede, therefore, that walking is

an immeasurably fine invention, of which old age ought constantly to avail itself.

Saddle leather is in some respects even preferable to sole leather. The principal objection to it is of a financial character. But you may be sure that Bacon and Sydenham did not recommend it for nothing. One's *hepar*, or, in vulgar language, liver, a ponderous organ, weighing some three or four pounds, goes up and down like the dasher of a churn in the midst of the other vital arrangements at every step of a trotting horse. The brains also are shaken up like coppers in a moneybox. Riding is good for those that are born with a silver-mounted bridle in their hand, and can ride as much and as often as they like, without thinking all the time they hear that steady grinding sound as the horse's jaws triturate with calm lateral movement the bank bills and promises to pay upon which it is notorious that the profligate animal in question feeds day and night.

Instead, however, of considering these kinds of exercise in this empirical way, I will devote a brief space to an examination of them in a more scientific form.

The pleasure of exercise is due, first, to a purely physical impression and, second, to a sense of power in action. The first source of pleasure varies, of course, with our condition and the state of the surrounding circumstances; the second, with the amount and kind of power, and the extent and kind of action. In all forms of active exercise there are three powers simultaneously in action, the will, the muscles, and the intellect. Each of these predominates in different kinds of exercise. In walking, the will and muscles are so accustomed to work together and perform their task with so little expenditure of force that the intellect is left comparatively free. The mental pleasure in walking, as such, is in the sense of power over all our moving machinery.

But in riding, I have the additional pleasure of governing another will, and my muscles extend to the tips of the animal's ears and to his four hoofs, instead of stopping at my hands and feet. Now in this extension of my volition and my physical frame into another animal, my tyrannical instincts and my desire for heroic strength are at once gratified. When the horse ceases to have a will of his own and his muscles require no special attention on your part, then you may live on horseback as Wesley did, and write sermons or take naps, as you like. But you will observe that, in riding on horseback, you always have a feeling that, after all, it is not you that do the work but the animal, and this prevents the satisfaction from being complete.

Now let us look at the conditions of rowing. I won't suppose you to be disgracing yourself in one of those miserable tubs, tugging in which is to rowing the true boat what riding a cow is to bestriding an Arab. You know the Esquimo's kayak (if that is the name of it), don't you? Look at that model of one over my door. Sharp, rather? On the contrary, it is a lubber to the one you and I must have; a Dutch fishwife to Psyche, contrasted with what I will tell you about. Our boat, then, is something of the shape of a pickerel, as you look down upon his back, he lying in the sunshine just where the sharp edge of the water cuts in among the lily pads. It is a kind of a giant pod, as one may say, tight everywhere, except in a little place in the middle, where you sit. Its length is from seven to ten yards, and as it is only from sixteen to thirty inches wide in its widest part, you understand why you want those "outriggers," or projecting iron frames with the rowlocks in which the oars play. My rowlocks are five feet apart; double or more than double the greatest width of the boat.

Here you are, then, afloat with a body a rod and a half long, with arms, or wings, as you may choose to call them, stretching more than twenty feet from tip to tip; every volition of yours extending as perfectly

into them as if your spinal cord ran down the center strip of your boat, and the nerves of your arms tingled as far as the broad blades of your oars, oars of spruce, balanced, leathered, and ringed under your own special direction. This, in sober earnest, is the nearest approach to flying that man has ever made or perhaps ever will make. As the hawk sails without flapping his pinions, so you drift with the tide when you will, in the most luxurious form of locomotion indulged to an embodied spirit.

But if your blood wants rousing, turn round that stake in the river, which you see a mile from here; and when you come in, in sixteen minutes (if you do, for we are old boys and not champion scullers, you remember), then say if you begin to feel a little warmed up or not! You can row easily and gently all day, and you can row yourself blind and black in the face in ten minutes, just as you like. It has been long agreed that there is no way in which a man can accomplish so much labor with his muscles as in rowing. It is in the boat, then, that man finds the largest extension of his volitional and muscular existence; and yet he may tax both of them so slightly, in that most delicious of exercises, that he shall mentally write his sermon, or his poem, or recall the remarks he has made in company and put them in form for the public, as well as in his easy chair.

I dare not publicly name the rare joys, the infinite delights that intoxicate me on some sweet June morning, when the river and bay are smooth as a sheet of beryl-green silk, and I run along ripping it up with my knife-edged shell of a boat, the rent closing after me like those wounds of angels which Milton tells of, but the seam still shining for many a long rood behind me. To lie still over the Flats, where the waters are shallow, and see the crabs crawling and the sculpins gliding busily and silently beneath the boat, to rustle in through the long, harsh grass that leads up some tranquil creek, to take shelter from the sunbeams under one of the thousand-footed bridges, and look down its interminable colonnades, crusted with green and oozy growths, studded with minute barnacles, and belted with rings of dark muscles, while overhead streams and thunders that other river whose every wave is a human soul flowing to eternity as the river below flows to the ocean, lying there moored unseen, in loneliness so profound that the columns of Tadmor in the desert could not seem more remote from life, the cool breeze on one's forehead, the stream whispering against the half-sunken pillars. Why should I tell of these things, that I should live to see my beloved haunts invaded and the waves blackened with boats as with a swarm of water beetles? What a city of idiots we must be not to have covered this glorious bay with gondolas and wherries, as we have just learned to cover the ice in winter with skaters!

I am satisfied that such a set of black-coated, stiff-jointed, soft-muscled, paste-complexioned youth as we can boast in our Atlantic cities never before sprang from loins of Anglo-Saxon lineage. Of the females that are the mates of these males I do not here speak. I preached my sermon from the lay pulpit on this matter a good while ago. Of course, if you heard it, you know my belief is that the total climatic influences here are getting up a number of new patterns of humanity, some of which are not an improvement on the old model. Clipper-built, sharp in the bows, long in the spars, slender to look at, and fast to go, the ship, which is the great organ of our national life of relation, is but a reproduction of the typical form which the elements impress upon its builder. All this we cannot help; but we can make the best of these influences, such as they are. We have a few good boatmen, no good horsemen that I hear of, nothing remarkable, I believe, in cricketing, and as for any great athletic feat performed by a

gentleman in these latitudes, society would drop a man who should run round the Common in five minutes. Some of our amateur fencers, single-stick players, and boxers, we have no reason to be ashamed of. Boxing is rough play, but not too rough for a hearty young fellow. Anything is better than this white-blooded degeneration to which we all tend.

I dropped into a gentlemen's sparring exhibition only last evening. It did my heart good to see that there were a few young and youngish youths left who could take care of their own heads in case of emergency. It is a fine sight, that of a gentleman resolving himself into the primitive constituents of his humanity. Here is a delicate young man now, with an intellectual countenance, a slight figure, a sub-pallid complexion, a most unassuming deportment, a mild adolescent in fact, that any Hiram or Jonathan from between the ploughtails would of course expect to handle with perfect ease. Oh, he is taking off his gold-bowed spectacles! Ah, he is divesting himself of his cravat! Why, he is stripping off his coat! Well, here he is, sure enough, in a tight silk shirt, and with two things that look like batter puddings in place of his fists. Now see that other fellow with another pair of batter puddings, the big one with the broad shoulders; he will certainly knock the little man's head off, if he strikes him. Feinting, dodging, stopping, hitting, countering — little man's head not off yet. You might as well try to jump upon your own shadow as to hit the little man's intellectual features. He needn't have taken off the gold-bowed spectacles at all. Quick, cautious, shifty, nimble, cool, he catches all the fierce lunges or gets out of their reach, till his turn comes, and then, whack goes one of the batter puddings against the big one's ribs, and bang goes the other into the big one's face, and, staggering, shuffling, slipping, tripping, collapsing, sprawling, down goes the big one in a miscellaneous bundle.

If my young friend, whose excellent article I have referred to, could only introduce the manly art of self-defense among the clergy, I am satisfied that we should have better sermons and an infinitely less quarrelsome church-militant. A bout with the gloves would let off the ill-nature and cure the indigestion, which, united, have embroiled their subject in a bitter controversy. We should then often hear that a point of difference between an infallible and a heretic, instead of being vehemently discussed in a series of newspaper articles, had been settled by a friendly contest in several rounds, at the close of which the parties shook hands and appeared cordially reconciled.

But boxing you and I are too old for, I am afraid. I was for a moment tempted, by the contagion of muscular electricity last evening, to try the gloves with the Benicia Boy, who looked in as a friend to the noble art; but remembering that he had twice my weight and half my age, besides the advantage of his training, I sat still and said nothing.

There is one other delicate point I wish to speak of with reference to old age. I refer to the use of dioptric media which correct the diminished refracting power of the humors of the eye, in other words, spectacles. I don't use them. All I ask is a large, fair type, a strong daylight or gaslight, and one yard of focal distance, and my eyes are as good as ever. But if *your* eyes fail, I can tell you something encouraging. There is now living in New York State an old gentleman who, perceiving his sight to fail, immediately took to exercising it on the finest print, and in this way fairly bullied nature out of her foolish habit of taking liberties at five-and-forty, or thereabout. And now this old gentleman performs the most extraordinary feats with his pen, showing that his eyes must be a pair of microscopes. I should be afraid to say to you how much he writes in the compass of a half-dime, whether the Psalms or the Gospels, or the Psalms *and* the Gospels, I won't be positive.

But now let me tell you this. If the time comes when you must lay down the fiddle and the bow because your fingers are too stiff, and drop the ten-foot sculls because your arms are too weak, and, after dallying awhile with eyeglasses, come at last to the undisguised reality of spectacles, if the time comes when that fire of life we spoke of has burned so low that where its flames reverberated there is only the somber stain of regret, and where its coals glowed, only the white ashes that cover the embers of memory, don't let your heart grow cold, and you may carry cheerfulness and love with you into the teens of your second century, if you can last so long. As our friend the poet once said, in some of those old-fashioned heroics of his which he keeps for his private reading —

Call him not old, whose visionary brain
Holds o'er the past its undivided reign.
For him in vain the envious seasons roll
Who bears eternal summer in his soul.
If yet the minstrel's song, the poet's lay,
Spring with her birds, or children with
    their play,
Or maiden's smile, or heavenly dream of
    art
Stir the few life drops creeping round his
    heart;
Turn to the record where his years are
    told,
Count his gray hairs — they cannot make
    him old!

7.

Rufus Choate: American Nationality

Rufus Choate's life was his law profession. His contributions to the political life of his times were abundant, mainly as a private citizen but also, from time to time, in public office. He was considered one of the outstanding courtroom lawyers and platform orators of his day. In July 1858, on the anniversary of the Declaration of Independence, Choate delivered an address against the background of the intense sectional conflict that was rending the nation. As a Whig, his concern was that the Union be preserved, which accounts for his dislike of Republicans, who he felt constituted a purely sectional and divisive party; yet he also felt that no sovereign state could be compelled to remain in the Union by the federal government. Choate's death, in 1859, prevented him from witnessing the ascendancy of the Republican Party and the subsequent division of the nation. Portions of his Fourth of July oration are reprinted below.

Source: *Addresses and Orations of Rufus Choate,* 5th edition, Boston, 1887.

THE BIRTHDAY OF A NATION, old or young, and certainly if young, is a time to think of the means of keeping alive the nation. I do not mean to say, however, because I do not believe, that there is but one way to this, the direct and the didactic. For at last it is the spirit of the day which we would cherish. It is our great annual national love feast which we keep; and if we rise from it with hearts larger, beating fuller, with feeling purer and warmer for America, what signifies it how frugally, or how richly, or how it was spread; or whether it was a strain on the organ, the trumpet tones of the Declaration, the prayer of the good man, the sympathy of the hour, or what it was which wrought to that end?

I do not, therefore, say that such an anniversary is not a time for thanksgiving to God, for gratitude to men, the living and the dead, for tears and thoughts too deep for tears, for eulogy, for exultation, for all the memories and for all the contrasts which soften and lift up the general mind.

I do not say, for example, that to dwell on that one image of progress which is our history; that image so grand, so dazzling, so constant; that stream now flowing so far and swelling into so immense a flood, but which burst out a small, choked, uncertain spring from the ground at first; that transition from the Rock at Plymouth, from the unfortified peninsula at Jamestown, to this America which lays a hand on both the oceans . . . to trace the long series of causes which connected these two contrasted conditions, the providences which ordained and guided a growth so stupendous; the dominant race, sober, earnest, constructive — changed, but not degenerate here; the influx of other races, assimilating, eloquent, and brave; the fusion of all into a new one; the sweet stimulations of liberty; the removal by the whole width of oceans from the establishments of Europe, shaken, tyrannical, or burdened; the healthful virgin world; the universal progress of reason and art, universal as civilization; the aspect of revolutions on the human mind; the expansion of discovery and trade; the developing sentiment of independence; the needful baptism of wars; the brave men, the wise men; the Constitution, the Union; the national life and the feeling of union which have grown with our growth and strengthened with our strength — I do not say that meditations such as these might not teach or deepen the lesson of the day. All these things, so holy and beautiful, all things American, may afford certainly the means to keep America alive.

That vast panorama unrolled by our general history, or unrolling; that eulogy, so just, so fervent, so splendid, so approved; that electric, seasonable memory of Washington; that purchase and that dedication of the dwelling and the tomb, the work of woman and of the orator of the age; that record of his generals; that visit to battlefields; that reverent wiping away of dust from great urns; that speculation, that dream of her past, present, and future; every ship built on lake or ocean; every treaty concluded; every acre of territory annexed; every cannon cast; every machine invented; every mile of new railroad and telegraph undertaken; every dollar added to the aggregate of national or individual wealth — these all, as subjects of thought, as motives to pride and care, as teachers of wisdom, as agencies for probable good, may work, may insure that earthly immortality of love and glory for which this celebration was ordained.

My way, however, shall be less ambitious and less indirect. Think, then, for a moment, on *American nationality* itself; the outward national life and the inward national sentiment. Think on this: *its nature, and some of its conditions, and some of its ethics;* I would say, too, some of its dangers,

but there shall be no expression of evil omen in this stage of the discourse; and today, at least, the word is safety, or hope.

To know the nature of American nationality, examine it first by contrast, and then examine it in itself.

In some of the elemental characteristics of political opinion, the American people are one. These they can no more renounce for substance than the highest summit of the highest of the White Hills, than the peak of the Alleghenies, than the Rocky Mountains can bow and cast themselves into the sea. Through all their history . . . all have held and felt that every man was equal to every other man; that every man had a right to life, liberty, and the pursuit of happiness, and a conscience unfettered; that the people were the source of power; and the good of the people was the political object of society itself. This creed, so grand, so broad — in its general and duly qualified terms, so true — planted the colonies, led them through the desert and the sea of ante-revolutionary life, rallied them all together to resist the attacks of a king and a minister, sharpened and pointed the bayonets of all their battles, burst forth from a million lips, beamed in a million eyes, burned in a million bosoms, sounded out in their revolutionary eloquence of fire and in the Declaration, awoke the thunders and gleamed in the lightning of the deathless words of Otis, Henry, and Adams, was graved forever on the general mind by the pen of Jefferson and Paine, survived the excitements of war and the necessities of order, penetrated and tinged all our constitutional composition and policy, and all our party organizations and nomenclature, and stands today, radiant, defiant, jocund, tiptoe, on the summits of our greatness, one authoritative and louder proclamation to humanity by freedom, the guardian and the avenger.

But in some traits of our politics we are not one. In some traits we differ from one another, and we change from ourselves.

You may say these are subordinate, executory, instrumental traits. Let us not cavil about names, but find the essences of things. Our object is to know the nature of American nationality, and we are attempting to do so, first, by contrasting it with its antagonisms.

There are two great existences, then, in our civil life, which have this in common, though they have nothing else in common, that they may come in conflict with the nationality which I describe; one of them constant in its operation, constitutional, healthful, auxiliary, even; the other, rarer, illegitimate, abnormal, terrible; one of them a force under law; the other, a violence and a phenomenon above law and against law.

It is first the capital peculiarity of our system, now a commonplace in our politics, that the affections which we give to country we give to a divided object, the states in which we live and the Union by which we are enfolded. We serve two masters. Our hearts own two loves. We live in two countries at once and are commanded to be capacious of both. How easy it is to reconcile these duties in theory; how reciprocally more than compatible, how helpful and independent they are in theory; how in this respect our system's difference makes our system's peace, and from these blended colors, and this action and counteraction, how marvelous a beauty and how grand a harmony we draw out, you all know. Practically you know, too, the adjustment has not been quite so simple. How the Constitution attempts it is plain enough. There it is; *litera scripta manet* [the written letter remains], and heaven and earth shall pass before one jot or one tittle of that Scripture shall fail of fulfillment. So we all say, and yet how men have divided on it. How they divided in the great Convention itself, and in the very presence of Washington. How the people divided on it. How it has created parties, lost and given power, bestowed great reputations and taken them away, and

colored and shaken the universal course of our public life!

But have you ever considered that in the nature of things this must be so? Have you ever considered that it was a federative system we had to adopt, and that in such a system a conflict of head and members is in some form and to some extent a result of course? There the states were when we became a nation. There they have been for 150 years — for 170 years. Some power, it was agreed on all hands, we must delegate to the new government. Of some thunder, some insignia, some beams, some means of kindling pride, winning gratitude, attracting honor, love, obedience, friends, all men knew they must be bereaved, and they were so.

But when this was done, there were the states still. In the scheme of every statesman they remained a component part, unannihilated, indestructible. In the scheme of the Constitution, of compromise itself, they remained a component part, indestructible. In the theories of all publicists and all speculators they were retained, and they were valued for it, to hinder and to disarm that centralization which had been found to be the danger and the weakness of federal liberty. And then when you bear in mind that they are sovereignties, *quasi*, but sovereignties still; that one of the most dread and transcendent prerogatives of sovereignties, the prerogative to take life and liberty for crime, is theirs without dispute; that in the theories of some schools they may claim to be parties to the great compact, and as such may, and that any of them may, secede from that compact when by their corporate judgment they deem it to be broken fundamentally by the others, and that from such a judgment there is no appeal to a common peaceful umpire; that in the theories of some schools they may call out their young men and their old men under the pains of death to defy the sword point of the federal arm; that they can pour around even the gallows and the tomb of him who died for treason to the Union, honor, opinion, tears, and thus sustain the last untimely hour, and soothe the disembodied, complaining shade; that everyone, by name, by line of boundary, by jurisdiction, is distinct from every other, and everyone from the nation; that within their inviolate borders lie our farms, our homes, our meetinghouses, our graves; that their laws, their courts, their militia, their police, to so vast an extent protect our persons from violence and our houses from plunder; that their heaven ripens our harvests; their schools form our children's mental and moral nature; their charities or their taxes feed our poor; their hospitals cure or shelter our insane; that their image, their opinions, their literature, their morality are around us ever, a presence, a monument, an atmosphere — when you consider this, you feel how practical and how inevitable is that antagonism to a single national life, and how true it is that we "buy all our blessings at a price."

But there is another antagonism to such a national life, less constant, less legitimate, less compensated, more terrible, to which I must refer — not for reprobation, not for warning, not even for grief, but that we may know by contrast nationality itself — and that is, the element of sections. This, too, is old; older than the states, old as the colonies, old as the churches that planted them, old as Jamestown, old as Plymouth. A thousand forms disguise and express it, and in all of them it is hideous. *Candidum seu nigrum hoc tu Romane caveto.* Black or white, as you are Americans, dread it, shun it!

Springing from many causes and fed by many stimulations; springing from that diversity of climate, business, institutions, accomplishment, and morality which comes of our greatness, and compels and should constitute our order and our agreement, but which only makes their difficulty and their merit; from that self-love and self-preference which are their own standard, exclusive, intolerant, and censorious of what is wise and holy; from the fear of ignorance, the jealousy of ignorance, the narrowness of ignorance; from incapacity to abstract; combine, and grasp a complex and various object, and thus rise to the dignity of concession and forbearance and compromise; from the frame of our civil polity, the necessities of our public life, and the nature of our ambition, which forces all men not great men — the minister in his parish, the politician on the stump on election day, the editor of the party newspaper — to take his rise or his patronage from an intense local opinion, and therefore to do his best to create or reinforce it; from our federative government; from our good traits, bad traits, and foolish traits; from that vain and vulgar hankering for European reputation and respect for European opinion, which forgets that one may know Aristophanes, and geography, and the cosmical unity and telluric influences, and the smaller morals of life, and all the sounding pretensions of philanthropy, and yet not know America; from that philosophy, falsely so called, which boasts emptily of progress, renounces traditions, denies God and worships itself; from an arrogant and flashy literature which mistakes a new phrase for a new thought and old nonsense for new truth, and is glad to exchange for the fame of drawing rooms and parlor windows, and the side lights of a car in motion, the approval of time and the world; from philanthropy which is shortsighted, impatient, and spasmodic, and cannot be made to appreciate that its grandest and surest agent, in His eye whose lifetime is eternity, and whose periods are ages, is a nation and a sober public opinion, and a safe and silent advancement, reforming by time; from that spirit which would rule or ruin, and would reign in hell rather than serve in heaven — springing from these causes and stimulated thus, there is an element of regions antagonistic to nationality.

Rufus Choate, photograph by Alexander Gardner

Always, I have said, there was one; always there will be. It lifted its shriek sometimes even above the silver clarion tone that called millions to unite for independence. It resisted the nomination of Washington to command our armies; made his new levies hate one another; assisted the caballings of Gates and Conway; mocked his retreats, and threw its damp passing cloud for a moment over his exceeding glory; opposed the adoption of any constitution; and perverted by construction and denounced as a covenant with hell the actual Constitution when it was adopted; brought into our vocabulary and discussions the hateful and ill-omened words North and South, Atlantic and Western, which the grave warnings of the Farewell Address expose and rebuke; transformed the floor of Congress into a battlefield of contending local policy; convened its conventions at Abbeville and Hartford; rent asunder conferences and synods; turned stated assemblies of grave clergymen and grave laymen into shows of gladiators or of the beasts of gladiators; checked the holy effort of missions, and set back the shadow on the dial plate of a certain amelioration and ultimate probable emancipation many degrees. . . .

But now, by the side of this and all antagonisms, higher than they, stronger than they, there rises, colossal, the fine, sweet spirit of nationality, the nationality of America! . . .

But if you would contemplate nationality as an active virtue, look around you. Is not our own history one witness and one record of what it can do? This day and all which it stands for — did it not give us these? This glory of the fields of that war, this eloquence of that Revolution, this wide one sheet of flame which wrapped tyrant and tyranny and swept all that escaped from it away, forever and forever; the courage to fight, to retreat, to rally, to advance, to guard the young flag by the young arm and the young heart's blood, to hold up and hold on till the magnificent consummation crowned the work — were not all these imparted as inspired by this imperial sentiment? Has it not here begun the masterwork of man, the creation of a national life? Did it not call out that prodigious development of wisdom, the wisdom of constructiveness which illustrated the years after the war, and the framing and adopting of the Constitution? Has it not, in the general, contributed to the administering of that government wisely and well since? Look at it! It has kindled us to no aims of conquest. It has involved us in no entangling alliances. It has kept our neutrality dignified and just.

The victories of peace have been our prized victories. But the larger and truer grandeur of the nations, for which they are created and for which they must, one day, before some tribunal give account, what a measure of these it has enabled us already to fulfill! It has lifted us to the throne, and has set on our brow the name of the great republic. It has taught us to demand nothing wrong and to submit to nothing wrong; it has made our diplomacy sagacious, wary, and accomplished; it has opened the iron gate of the mountain and planted our ensign on the great, tranquil sea; it has made the desert to bud and blossom as the rose;

it has quickened to life the giant brood of useful arts; it has whitened lake and ocean with the sails of a daring, new, and lawful trade; it has extended to exiles, flying as clouds, the asylum of our better liberty; it has kept us at rest within all our borders; it has repressed without blood the intemperance of local insubordination; it has scattered the seeds of liberty, under law and under order, broadcast; it has seen and helped American feeling to swell into a fuller flood; from many a field and many a deck, though it seeks not war, makes not war, and fears not war, it has borne the radiant flag all unstained; it has opened our age of lettered glory; it has opened and honored the age of the industry of the people!

We have done with the nature of American nationality, with its contrasts, analysis, and fruits. I have less pleasure to remind you that it has conditions, also, and ethics. And what are some of these? This is our next consideration.

And the first of these is that this national existence is, to an extraordinary degree, not a growth but a production; that it has origin in the will and the reason, and that the will and the reason must keep it alive, or it can bear no life. I do not forget that a power above man's power, a wisdom above man's wisdom, a reason above man's reason, may be traced without the presumptuousness of fanaticism in the fortunes of America. I do not forget that God has been in our history. Beyond that dazzling progress of art, society, thought which is of His ordaining, although it may seem to a false philosophy a fatal and inevitable flow under law, beyond this I do not forget that there have been, and there may be again, interpositions, providential, exceptional, and direct, of that Supreme Agency without which no sparrow falleth. . . .

Have you ever considered, speculating on the mysteries of our national being, how providentially the colonial life itself, in one respect, qualified for Union, and how provi-dentially it came to pass that independence and nationality were born in one day? . . .

Did not that colonial life, in its nature — that long winter and lingering spring — discipline and prepare men for the future of their civil life, as an April snow enriches the earth it seems to bury? Did it not keep back the growths which might otherwise have shot up into impracticable ranknesses and diversities? Did it not divert men from themselves to one another — from Massachusetts and Virginia and New York, to the forming or the possible America? Instead of stunting and enfeebling, did it not enlarge and strengthen? And when all that host flocked together, to taste together the first waters of independent life, and one high, common, proud feeling pervaded their ranks, lifted up all hearts, softened all hearts at once — and a Rhode Island general was seen to fight at the Eutaws; and a New Yorker, or one well beloved of Massachusetts, at Saratoga; and a Virginian to guide the common war and a united army to win the victory for all — was not the transition, in a moment so sublime, more natural, less violent, more easy to the transcendent conception of nationality itself? . . .

I do not know that I need to say next that such a spirit of nationality reposing on will and reason, or, however produced, not spontaneous, and therefore to some extent artificial, demands a specific culture to develop it and to make it intense, sure, and constant. I need not say this, because it is so plain; but it is important as well as plain. There is a love of country which comes uncalled for, one knows not how. It comes in with the very air, the eye, the ear, the instincts, the first taste of the mother's milk, the first beatings of the heart. The faces of brothers and sisters, and the loved father and mother, the laugh of playmates, the old willow tree and well and schoolhouse, the bees at work in the spring, the note of the robin at evening, the lullaby, the cows coming home, the singing book, the catechism, the visits of neighbors, the general training

— all things which make childhood happy, begin it.

And then as the age of the passions and the age of the reason draw on, and love and the sense of home and security and property under law come to life; and as the story goes round, and as the book or the newspaper relates the less favored lots of other lands, and the public and the private sense of a man is forming and formed, there is a type of patriotism already. Thus they had imbibed it who stood that charge at Concord, and they who hung deadly on the retreat, and they who threw up the hasty and imperfect redoubt on Bunker Hill by night, set on it the blood-red provincial flag, and passed so calmly with Prescott and Putnam and Warren through the experiences of the first fire.

But now to direct this spontaneous sentiment of hearts to the Union, to raise it high, to make it broad and deep, to instruct it, to educate it, is in some things harder, some things easier, but it may be done; it must be done. She, too, has her spectacles; she, too, has her great names; she, too, has her food for patriotism, for childhood, for man. "Americans," said an orator of France, "begin with the infant in the cradle. Let the first word he lisps be Washington." Hang on his neck on that birthday, and that day of his death at Mount Vernon, the Medal of Congress, by its dark ribbon; tell him the story of the flag, as it passes glittering along the road; bid him listen to that plain, old-fashioned, stirring music of the Union; lead him when school is out at evening to the grave of his great-grandfather, the old soldier of the war; bid him, like Hannibal, at nine years old, lay the little hand on that Constitution and swear reverently to observe it; lift him up and lift yourselves up to the height of American feeling.

Open to him, and think for yourselves, on the relation of America to the states; show him upon the map the area to which she has extended herself; the climates that come into the number of her months; the silver paths of her trade, wide as the world; tell him of her contributions to humanity, and her protests for free government; keep with him the glad and solemn feasts of her appointment; bury her great names in his heart, and into your hearts; contemplate habitually, lovingly, intelligently, this grand abstraction, this vast reality of good; and such an institution may do somewhat to transform this surpassing beauty into a national life, which shall last while sun and moon endure.

But there is another condition of our nationality of which I must say something, and that is that it rests on compromise. America, the Constitution, practicable policy, all of it, are a compromise. Our public is possible — it can draw its breath for a day — only by compromise. . . . Our history is a record of compromises; and this freedom and this glory attest their wisdom and bear their fruits. But can these compromises stand the higher test of morality? Concessions for the sake of the nation; concessions for what the general opinion of America has pronounced concessions for America; concessions in measures; concessions in spirit for such an end — are they a virtue? . . .

When you consider how easy and how tempting it is to fall in with and float with the stream on which so many swim . . . what courage, what love of truth are demanded to dissent; how hard it is to rise to the vast and varied conception and to the one idea which grasps and adjusts all the ideas; how easy it is for the little man to become great, the shallow man to become profound; the coward, out of danger, to be brave; the free-state man to be an antislavery man, and to write tracts which his friends alone read; when you think that even the laughter of fools and children and madmen, little ministers, little editors, and little politicians, can inflict the mosquito bite, not deep, but stinging — who wonders that the serener and the calmer judgment allots "to patient continuance in well doing," to resistance of the parts, to contention for the whole, to counsels of moderation and concession, "glory, honor, and immortality"? . . .

We see our morality working itself clearer and clearer; one historical and conventional right or wrong after another falling peacefully and still; we hear the chain breaking, but there is no blood on it, none of his whom it bound, none of his who put it on him; we hear the swelling chorus of the free, but master and slave unite in that chorus, and there is no discordant shriek above the harmony; we see and we hail the blending of our own glory with the eternal light of God, but we see, too, shapes of love and beauty ascending and descending there as in the old vision! . . .

Do no evil that good may come. Perform your share, for you have a share, in the abolition of slavery; perform your share, for you have a share, in the noble and generous strife of the sections — but perform it by keeping, by transmitting, a united, loving, and Christian America.

8.

ELLIS LEWIS: *Mott v. Pennsylvania Railroad Company*

The issue in Mott v. Pennsylvania Railroad Company *turned on whether a state legislature could legislate away permanently any of its constitutional authority. The state of Pennsylvania had owned certain canal and rail transportation facilities, known as the Main Line of the Public Works, which were put for sale. A legislative act was passed to provide that if the Pennsylvania Railroad purchased the Main Line and paid an extra $7,500,000, the railroad would be forever discharged from payment of tonnage taxes and "all other taxes . . . except for school, city, county, borough, or township purposes." This was in effect to do away with the legislative power of raising revenue for all time to come in this particular area. Chief Justice Ellis Lewis delivered the unanimous opinion of the Pennsylvania Supreme Court, asserting in his decision that "government . . . has no more right to commit political suicide than an individual has to destroy the life given by his Creator." Chief Justice Lewis' opinion is reprinted here in part.*

Source: *Pennsylvania State Reports*, Joseph Casey, ed., Vol. XXX, Philadelphia, 1860, pp. 25-29.

THE ACT OF ASSEMBLY of May 16, 1857, makes provision for a public sale; and, for the purpose of inviting competition, directs that public notice of the time and place be given in one or more newspapers of extended circulation, published in the cities of Philadelphia, Pittsburgh, Washington, Boston, New York, and in the borough of Harrisburg. It authorizes "any person or persons, or railroad or canal company now incorporated, or which may hereafter be incorporated under the laws of this Commonwealth, to become the purchasers for any sum not less than $7,500,000." But there is a proviso in the 3rd Section which declares that "if the Pennsylvania Railroad Compa-

Ellis Lewis; miniature by an unidentified artist

ny shall become the purchasers, at the said public sale, or by assignment, they shall pay, in addition to the purchase money at which it may be struck down, the sum of $1,500,000, and *in consideration thereof,* the said railroad company and the Harrisburg, Mount Joy, and Lancaster Railroad Company shall be discharged by the commonwealth *forever* from the payment of all taxes upon tonnage, or freight carried over said railroads; and the said Pennsylvania Railroad Company shall also be released from the payment of all other taxes or duties on its capital stock, bonds, dividends, or property, except for school, city, county, borough, or township purposes."

The amount of taxes proposed to be released is beyond calculation. It can only be conjectured. It would be greatly increased by the tax which would of course be levied on the property about to be sold to the company. Judging from the increase during the last five years and the constant augmentation of commerce and travel along the route, it would seem reasonable to believe that in five years from this time it would be

double its present amount. But conceding that the tax to be released will hereafter amount to no more per annum than the sum paid in 1856, the amount, according to the admissions of the railroad company itself, would be $280,739.21 per annum forever. This sum is more than equal to the interest on $5,600,000, at 5 percent, the rate to be charged to the purchasers. In other words, the Act of Assembly proposes to give to the railroad company a consideration equal to $5,600,000 for $1,500,000, and thus to give that company an advantage equal to $4,100,000 over every other bidder at the sale!

By means of this privilege the Pennsylvania Railroad Company may drive from the field of competition all other bidders. It is essential to every fair public auction that all the bidders shall stand upon an equal footing. If the object had been to make a fair sale of this portion of the state revenue, it might have been evinced by a provision for the transfer of it to the highest bidder without any distinction in favor of anyone. But this was not done. The extraordinary proviso in favor of the Pennsylvania Railroad Company is partial, and entirely repugnant to the general intent of the act; and if allowed to stand, the sale under it will furnish one of the most magnificent exhibitions of a "mock auction" that the world has ever witnessed! We rejoice to say that the highly respectable and upright officers of the corporation disclaim in the most solemn manner, under oath, all agency in procuring the enactment in question.

But has the constitution conferred upon the legislature the authority to extinguish *forever,* by bargain and sale, the power to raise revenue for the support of government? All free governments are established by the people for their benefit, and the powers delegated are to be exercised for their common good and not, under any circumstances, to be sold or destroyed so long as the nations establishing them have the physical power to maintain their independence. Individuals cannot subsist without food. Deprive them of "the means whereby" they live and you destroy them as certainly as if you did it by shedding their blood. The necessities of governments are as great as those of individuals. No government can exist without revenues to defray its expenses and support its officers and agents. The revenue is the food indispensable to its existence. Deprive it of this and you strip it of all power to perform its duties, bring it into contempt by its uselessness and helplessness, and ultimately destroy it as effectually as if it were overturned by domestic violence or subjugated by the conquest of a foreign foe.

Government is but an aggregation of individual rights and powers. It has no more right to commit political suicide than an individual has to destroy the life given by his Creator. Contracting away the taxing power in perpetuity tends, as we have seen, inevitably to the destruction of the government. If $12 million or $20 million of taxable property may be released today, $100 million may be released tomorrow, and, the principle being established, the process might go on until all power to raise revenue was gone. If this did not destroy the government, it would result in something infinitely more dangerous to the liberties of the people. It would make it the servile dependent of the wealthy corporations or individuals to whom it contracted away its means of support.

Although the taxing power is but an incidental one to be exercised only as the necessary means of performing governmental duties, it is nevertheless a branch of the legislative power which always, in its nature, implies not only the power of making laws but of altering and repealing them as the exigencies of the state and circumstances of the times may require. . . . If one portion of the legislative power may be sold, another may be disposed of in the same way. If the power to raise revenue may be sold today, the power to punish for crimes may be sold tomorrow, and the power to pass laws for the redress of civil rights may be sold the next day. If the legislative power may be sold, the executive and judicial powers may be put in the market with equal propriety. The result to which the principle must inevitably lead proves that the sale of any portion of governmental power is utterly inconsistent with the nature of our free institutions and totally at variance with the object and general provisions of the constitution of the state.

It may be urged that we must confide in the fidelity of the legislature, and that there is every ground for hope that they would not carry such measures to an unreasonable length. This is no answer to the argument. It is a question of constitutional authority and not a case of confidence at all. Limitations of power, established by written constitutions, have their origin in a distrust of the infirmity of man. That distrust is fully justified by the history of the rise and fall of nations.

But, conceding that this practice will not be carried so far as to destroy the government, is there any warrant for it to the extent to which the Act of Assembly proposes to go in the present case? It was held by this court in Wood's Estate, 9 *Harris* 114, that "the duties of sovereign and subject are reciprocal, and any person who is protected by a government in his person or property may be compelled to pay for that protection. As taxes are to be assessed for the sole purpose of supporting the government, the propriety of exacting them, the persons and property to be made liable, and the rules for their assessment and collection are to be determined by its authority. It is, however, *a rule of the public law, founded on a principle of justice which no government can disregard without violating the rights of its citizens, that taxes shall be assessed in such manner that all the citizens may pay their quota in proportion*

*to their abilities, and the advantages they de-
rive from the society."* . . .

It is upon this principle that, when the
private property of the citizen is taken for
public use, just compensation is to be made
to him *out of the common fund* in order that
the contribution to the public interest may
fall in a just proportion upon all the citizens. . . .

As the legislature are necessarily the
judges of the method of assessing taxes, it is
to be presumed that they have regarded the
rule of contribution sanctioned by justice
and the equal rights of the citizens; and
their enactments are not always subject to
judicial review. Where they make appropriations to institutions of learning or charity,
or grant lands or pensions to persons who
have served in the defense of the nation, it
is presumed to be a compensation for the
good that has been done or is to be done to
the community. Where they grant to the
same institutions or individuals an exemption from taxation, such grants, for the same
reason, are not regarded as a violation of
the rules of justice and equity. So long as
there is no contract which may tie the
hands of succeeding legislatures against repealing such exemptions, and so long as
they are not repealed, they seem to have
been enforced as a legitimate exercise of
legislative power. . . .

But where there is no pretense of an intention to equalize the taxation among the
people, but an avowed purpose to sell to
one class of citizens an exemption from all
taxes forever and thus to throw all the public burdens upon the other for all time to
come, it is, to all intents and purposes, imposing a tax upon them without the consent
of their representatives, and is such a plain,
palpable, and open violation of the rights
and liberties of the people, such a clear case
of transcending the just limits of legislative
power that the judiciary is bound to pronounce such an act null and void.

No class of corporations stand more in
need of the protection of the government,
or occupy more of the time of the legislature and the courts of justice, or occasion
more expense to the government than railroad corporations. From the extensive nature of their operations, the power to take
private property for the construction of
their works, and their continual collision
with each other's interests and with the interests of individuals and municipal communities, they require the constant and the energetic protection of the strong arm of the
government. Withdraw that protection and
they would be left to the mercy of popular
outbreaks, manifesting themselves by opposition to their progress and the destruction
of their works whenever the location of
their roads, or their depots, or any of their
numerous and necessary operations came in
conflict with the interests of particular localities. These corporations should be the last
to consent that the government should be
enfeebled by the diminution of its revenues,
or to ask that it should be bound to exert
all its energies and incur large and constant
expenditures for their protection while they
are exempt from contributing their share.

These principles are not so infirm as to
stand in need of the staff of authority for
support. They are the result of that liberty
and equality which was established by the
revolutionary struggle of our ancestors.
They are perfectly understood by everyone
who has capacity to comprehend the nature
of our free institutions; they are deeply impressed on the hearts of the people; and
they are fully recognized by the history, the
objects, and the language of our state constitution.

9.

George Templeton Strong: The First Atlantic Cable

George Templeton Strong was one of the many Americans who were skeptical of Cyrus Field's attempt to lay the first transatlantic cable in 1857. On the first attempt the cable broke after several hundred miles had been laid westward from Valentia, Ireland. Three other futile attempts were made. Finally, in 1866, a cable was successfully laid linking Ireland to Newfoundland. The following excerpts are taken from Strong's diary from July 1 through September 29, 1858, in which he records the public's reaction to the great undertaking.

Source: *The Diary of George Templeton Strong,* Allan Nevins and Milton H. Thomas, eds., New York, 1952, Vol. II, pp. 406-416.

July 1. No news yet of Atlantic telegraph squadron. Much betting on the result; odds that it will be failure. . . .

July 21, Wednesday. Atlantic telegraph squadron has failed again and worse than last summer. Disastrous for Peter Cooper and Cyrus Field. . . .

August 5. All Wall Street stirred up into excitement this morning, in spite of the sultry weather, by the screeching newsboys with their extras. The *Niagara* has arrived at Trinity Bay with her end of the telegraph cable in perfect working order. But the *Agamemnon* has not yet linked her end at Valentia, and in this enterprise nothing whatever has been done while enough remains to do. The transmission of a single message from shore to shore will be memorable in the world's history; for, though I dare say this cable will give out before long, it will be the first successful experiment in binding the two continents together, and the communication will soon be permanently established. It seems to me that gutta-percha must undergo some change under the vast pressure of superincumbent water,

and that the wire will soon cease to be insulated.

August 10. Everybody all agog about the Atlantic Cable. Telegraph offices in Wall Street decorated with the flags of all nations and sundry fancy pennons beside, suspended across the street. Newspapers full of the theme, and of the demonstrations the event has produced from New Orleans to Portland. The *Agamemnon* has brought her end safe to Valentia, so the whole cable is now in position. Newspapers vie with each other in gas and grandiloquence. Yesterday's *Herald* said that the cable (or perhaps Cyrus W. Field, uncertain which) is undoubtedly the Angel in the Book of Revelation, with one foot on sea and one foot on land, proclaiming that Time shall be no longer. Moderate people merely say that this is the greatest human achievement in history. Possibly not the very greatest; some few things have surely been done in the old time before us that run the cable rather hard. Morse's first forty miles of telegraph wire included this, and much more that shall be hereafter (perhaps), and the first

Cyrus Field, promoter of the first Atlantic Cable

message between Washington and Baltimore was a grander event than this. Laying
this wire rope unbroken across the abysses
of the Atlantic was no light undertaking,
but success, with all the armories of modern
science in the service, is not so much to
brag of. Is it success after all? No message
has yet been transmitted, and we are not
told the reason why.

If no great revolution or cataclysm throw
mankind off the track they've been traveling
for the last half century, if the earth doesn't
blow up or get foul of a comet and be not
rebarbarized by Brigham Young or Red Republicanism, it will be a strange place in
1958, most unlike what it is now. The di-
verse races of men certainly seem tending
toward development into a living organic
unit, with railroads and steam packets for a
circulating system, telegraph wires for
nerves, and the London *Times* and New
York *Herald* for a brain. . . .

August 24. That day came news of the
Queen's message over the telegraph cable.
Church bells rang their loudest all the
morning, and when we returned that evening late, after a long drive to Tyringham
(a lovely valley, east of Stockbridge, with a
Shaker settlement), the one street of Bar-

rington was illuminated with multitudinous
tallow candles in every shop window, and a
big bonfire that reduced the blessed moon
to insignificance. The Grand Army of Bar-
rington, with one fife and a drum, followed
by a string of citizens at large carrying
torches, marched perseveringly up and
down, attaining the dignity of a prolonged
procession by executing maneuvers in Indian file, and finished the performances by a
grand fusillade in front of the Berkshire
House. Then one Emerson, the village jurist, delivered an allocution to the assembled multitude, and told them that war, revulsions, and other calamities were henceforth impossible, that the millennium had
been manufactured by electrogalvanism,
gutta-percha, copper wire, and Cyrus Field,
that "tomorrow the whisper of the Kremlin
and the song of the Persian dancing girl
would be heard in the hills of Berkshire,"
that "the homesteads of good old Mother
England" were now situated in Massachusetts, and other like startling propositions.

It's almost alarming to consider the
amount of impious brag which this cable
has generated all over the country. Has so
extensive, simultaneous, vociferous, and insolent a bray been emitted by puffed-up humanity on any previous occasion? Here in
New York the triumphant pyrotechnics
with which our city fathers celebrated this
final and complete subjugation by man of
all the powers of nature — space and time
included — set the City Hall on fire,
burned up its cupola and half its roof, and
came near destroying the county clerk's office and unsettling the titles to half the
property in the city. The Hall presents a
most draggled and crestfallen appearance, all
singed and reeky and shorn of its headpiece.

August 27. First news came over the Atlantic Cable yesterday. Peace with China.
Another dispatch followed. This looks like
successful reality.

The city is utterly dismal. I'm thinking of
a course of lager-beer saloons and low theaters. . . .

September 11, Saturday. The telegraph cable celebration on the 1st seems to have been a grand affair. The services in Trinity Church were impressive, they say. The Fields are very puffy with the adulation they've swallowed, and no wonder. But people begin to tire of hearing Cyrus called the Great, and parallels between him and Galileo, generally to the disadvantage of the latter. We are a little disgusted, moreover, with the humors of the wondrous cord itself, which has remained obstinately silent for the last ten days. Its managers assure the public that it's all right, but descend to no explanation. Should it be permanently paralyzed, it will be curious to see the general reaction from our late orgasm of glorification. Possibly Cyrus will be lynched. . . .

September 15, Wednesday. The oracle of the cable is still dumb, and we begin to revile our fetish. The grand Cyrus is making little sales of stock. . . .

September 29. The Atlantic Cable speechless still. Its high priests talk of defective insulation at some point, probably not less than 200 miles west of Valentia, and are quite confident the interruption is only temporary. Hard to conceive of a remedy! People begin to turn up their noses at the house of Field and at the grand Cyrus in particular. What can the precise difficulty be? Perhaps some weak point in the gutta-percha casing has been infiltrated under the pressure of a thousand fathoms of water. Perhaps some huge sting ray grubbing in the oozy bed of ocean for bivalve mollusca has closed his massive grinding dental plates on the cable, mistaking it for an overgrown scrupula, and given it a fatal crunch.

10.

On Supporting the Local Economy

Some Southern leaders argued that the South should make itself economically independent of the North by developing an industrial capability and ceasing to be strictly agricultural. The author of the following editorial, which appeared in the Atlanta Daily Intelligencer, *October 8, 1858, solicited the support of the people of Atlanta to improve local manufacturing and small business. Despite such efforts, by 1860, less than 10 percent of all American industrial production originated in the South.*

Source: *Atlanta Daily Intelligencer,* October 8, 1858 [Commons, II, pp. 354-356].

ATLANTA, PROBABLY MORE than any other city of our state, is dependent upon her mechanical population for everything that constitutes wealth and power. While other towns and villages with only a few mechanics could not flourish without them, our city has for its chief basis this class of worthy and useful citizens. Nothing is so indicative of prosperity in a town as the fact that there is employment sufficient to support her mechanics. Take away those in our midst who compose this useful class of our population and our city would soon dwindle into insignificance and decay. We should lose the very bone and sinew, the main source of our power and strength.

It is impossible to appreciate too highly, then, the importance to any community of this element. Wealth is created by their handwork, and hundreds and probably thousands supported alone by the means growing out of the arts which they practise. The influence, in this point of view, which the foundries, workshops, and rolling mills of Atlanta have upon the advancement of the city of Atlanta can't yet be estimated. The future alone will develop it, when our city shall be filled up with a population of 20,000, 30,000, or 40,000 in number. Then will the conviction force itself irresistibly on every mind that to the mechanic arts will our growth be chiefly indebted.

Let our citizens feel the truth of this statement now and act as they should in relationship to the mechanics of Atlanta. Let them foster, encourage, and support those worthy members of our community who are engaged in these avocations. Heretofore there has been a habit among many of our people of sending off to some other place, to some Northern town or to some smaller other Southern town, for articles

which they could easily obtain at home. We know this to be the fact of several merchants in Atlanta, as well as others. Such a policy, let us tell them, is not only directly opposed to the interests of the city but to their own interests, and the man who upon reflection will not abandon such a course doesn't deserve to receive the patronage of his fellow citizens.

If you will build up a substantial community, you will gradually increase in wealth and thus be better able to indulge in all comforts and luxuries, support and sustain your domestic manufacturers and mechanics. Whatever you can buy from your neighbor in your own town, don't send off somewhere else for it because you can obtain it a fraction cheaper. What will be gained in that way will be lost tenfold in the long run. The merchant who doesn't sustain the home mechanic should not receive in turn for his goods the hard-earned money of the mechanical population.

11.

Farmers' Platform

In the history of the United States there is no trace of any agrarian party that has ever acted effectively for any extended period of time. Although earlier attempts were made to unite farmers, it was not until after the Civil War that a definite agrarian political organization appeared. In 1858 the following plan for a union of farmers in the United States was circulated by the Illinois farmers.

Source: Jonathan Periam, *The Groundswell, A History of the Origin, Aims, and Progress of the Farmers' Movement, etc., etc.,* Cincinnati, 1874, pp. 204-206.

FARMERS' PLATFORM OF 1858

WE BELIEVE that the time has come when the producing classes should assert, not only their independence but their supremacy;

that nonproducers cannot be relied upon as guarantees of fairness; and that laws enacted and administered by lawyers are not a true standard of popular sentiment.

We believe that a general application to

commerce of the principle that the majority should rule would increase the income and diminish the outlay of producers, and, at the same time, elevate the standard of mercantile morality.

We believe that the producer of a commodity and the purchaser of it should, together, have more voice in fixing its price than he who simply carries it from one to the other.

We believe that the true method of guarding against commercial revulsions is to bring the producer and consumer as near together as possible, thus diminishing the alarming number and the more alarming power of nonproducers.

We believe that in union there is strength, and that in union alone can the necessarily isolated condition of farmers be so strengthened as to enable them to cope, on equal terms, with men whose callings are, in their very nature, a permanent and self-created combination of interests.

We believe that system of commerce to be the best which transacts the most business, with the least tax on production, and which, instead of being a master, is merely a servant.

We believe that good prices are as necessary to the prosperity of farmers as good crops, and, in order to create such a power as to insure as much uniformity in prices as in products, farmers must keep out of debt; and that, in order to keep out of debt, they must pay for what they buy and exact the same from others.

DECLARATION OF PRINCIPLES

THESE TRUTHS we hold to be self-evident: that as production both precedes barter and employs more labor and capital, it is more worthy the care and attention of governments and of individuals; that in the honor-

able transaction of a legitimate business there is no necessity for secret cost marks; that in all well-regulated communities there should be the smallest possible number of nonproducers that is necessary to the welfare of the human race; that labor and capital employed in agriculture should receive as much reward as labor and capital employed in any other pursuit; that as the exchanger is merely an agent between the producer and consumer, he should not have a chief voice in the establishment of prices; that the interests of agriculture and of commerce can only be considered as identical when each has an equal share in regulating barter; and that the principal road to honor and distinction, in this country, should lead through productive industry.

PLAN OF OPERATIONS

FIRST, THE FORMATION of Farmers' Clubs wherever practical, the object of which shall be to produce concert of action on all matters connected with their interests.

Second, the establishment, as far as possible, of the ready-pay system in all pecuniary transactions.

Third, the formation of wholesale purchasing and selling agencies in the great centers of commerce, so that producers may, in a great measure, have it in their power to save the profits of retailers.

Fourth, the organization of such power as to insure the creation of a national agricultural bureau, the main object of which shall be an annual or semi-annual census of all our national products, and the collection and dissemination of valuable seeds, plants, and facts.

Fifth, the election of producers to all places of public trust and honor the general rule, and the election of nonproducers the exception.

12.

Ralph Waldo Emerson: Farming

The Industrial Revolution brought the railroad to Concord, Massachusetts, leading to the development of dairying and fruit growing. Emerson himself owned a few acres that were farmed for him. At the Middlesex Cattle Show, on September 29, 1858, Emerson delivered a lecture on farming that became the basis for the following essay. Originally titled "The Man With the Hoe," Emerson's "Farming" was the first essay in the collection that he called Society and Solitude.

Source: *Society and Solitude*, Boston, 1870.

THE GLORY OF THE FARMER is that, in the division of labors, it is his part to create. All trade rests at last on his primitive activity. He stands close to nature; he obtains from the earth the bread and the meat. The food which was not, he causes to be. The first farmer was the first man, and all historic nobility rests on possession and use of land. Men do not like hard work, but every man has an exceptional respect for tillage, and a feeling that this is the original calling of his race, that he himself is only excused from it by some circumstance which made him delegate it for a time to other hands. If he have not some skill which recommends him to the farmer, some product for which the farmer will give him corn, he must himself return into his due place among the planters. And the profession has in all eyes its ancient charm as standing nearest to God, the first cause.

Then the beauty of nature, the tranquillity and innocence of the countryman, his independence and his pleasing arts — the care of bees, of poultry, of sheep, of cows, the dairy, the care of hay, of fruits, of orchards and forests, and the reaction of these on the workman, in giving him a strength and plain dignity like the face and manners of nature — all men acknowledge. All men keep the farm in reserve as an asylum where, in case of mischance, to hide their poverty — or a solitude, if they do not succeed in society. And who knows how many glances of remorse are turned this way from the bankrupts of trade, from mortified pleaders in courts and senates, or from the victims of idleness and pleasure? Poisoned by town life and town vices, the sufferer resolves: "Well, my children, whom I have injured, shall go back to the land, to be recruited and cured by that which should have been my nursery, and now shall be their hospital."

The farmer's office is precise and important, but you must not try to paint him in rose-color; you cannot make pretty compliments to fate and gravitation, whose minister he is. He represents the necessities. It is the beauty of the great economy of the world that makes his comeliness. He bends to the order of the seasons, weather, the soils and crops as the sails of a ship bend to the wind. He represents continuous hard labor, year in, year out, and small gains. He is a slow person, timed to nature and not to city watches. He takes the pace of seasons, plants, and chemistry. Nature never hurries: atom by atom, little by little, she achieves her work. The lesson one learns in fishing, yachting, hunting, or planting is the manners of nature — patience with the delays of wind and sun, delays of the seasons, bad weather, excess or lack of water; patience with the slowness of our feet, with the parsimony of our strength, with the largeness of sea and land we must traverse, etc.

The farmer times himself to nature, and acquires that livelong patience which belongs to her. Slow, narrow man, his rule is that the earth shall feed and clothe him; and he must wait for his crop to grow. His entertainments, his liberties, and his spending must be on a farmer's scale and not on a merchant's. It were as false for farmers to use a wholesale and massy expense as for states to use a minute economy. But if thus pinched on one side, he has compensatory advantages. He is permanent, clings to his land as the rocks do. In the town where I live, farms remain in the same families for seven and eight generations; and most of the first settlers (in 1635), should they reappear on the farms today, would find their own blood and names still in possession. And the like fact holds in the surrounding towns.

This hard work will always be done by one kind of man; not by scheming speculators, nor by soldiers, nor professors, nor readers of Tennyson but by men of endurance — deep-chested, long-winded, tough, slow and sure, and timely. The farmer has a great health, and the appetite of health, and means to his end; he has broad lands for his home, wood to burn great fires, plenty of plain food; his milk at least is unwatered; and for sleep, he has cheaper and better and more of it than citizens.

He has grave trusts confided to him. In the great household of nature, the farmer stands at the door of the bread room and weighs to each his loaf. It is for him to say whether men shall marry or not. Early marriages and the number of births are indissolubly connected with abundance of food; or, as Burke said, "Man breeds at the mouth." Then he is the Board of Quarantine. The farmer is a hoarded capital of health, as the farm is the capital of wealth; and it is from him that the health and power, moral and intellectual, of the cities came. The city is always recruited from the country. The men in cities who are the centers of energy, the driving wheels of trade, politics, or practical arts, and the women of beauty and genius are the children or grandchildren of farmers, and are spending the energies which their fathers' hardy, silent life accumulated in frosty furrows, in poverty, necessity, and darkness.

He is the continuous benefactor. He who digs a well, constructs a stone fountain, plants a grove of trees by the roadside, plants an orchard, builds a durable house, reclaims a swamp, or so much as puts a stone seat by the wayside makes the land so far lovely and desirable, makes a fortune which he cannot carry away with him, but which is useful to his country long afterward. The man that works at home helps society at large with somewhat more of certainty than he who devotes himself to charities. If it be true that not by votes of political parties but by the eternal laws of political economy slaves are driven out of a slave state as fast as it is surrounded by free states, then the true Abolitionist is the farmer who, heedless of laws and constitutions, stands all day in the field, investing his labor in the land, and making a product with which no forced labor can compete.

We commonly say that the rich man can speak the truth, can afford honesty, can afford independence of opinion and action — and that is the theory of nobility. But it is the rich man in a true sense, that is to say, not the man of large income and large expenditure but solely the man whose outlay is less than his income and is steadily kept so.

In English factories, the boy that watches the loom, to tie the thread when the wheel stops to indicate that a thread is broken, is called a minder. And in this great factory of our Copernican globe, shifting its slides, rotating its constellations, times, and tides, bringing now the day of planting, then of watering, then of weeding, then of reaping, then of curing and storing, the farmer is the minder. His machine is of colossal proportions; the diameter of the waterwheel, the arms of the levers, the power of the battery are out of all mechanic measure; and it takes him long to understand its parts and its working. This pump never "sucks"; these screws are never loose; this machine is never out of gear; the vat and piston, wheels and tires never wear out, but are self-repairing.

Who are the farmer's servants? Not the Irish, nor the coolies, but geology and chemistry, the quarry of the air, the water of the brook, the lightning of the cloud, the castings of the worm, the plow of the frost. Long before he was born, the sun of ages decomposed the rocks, mellowed his land, soaked it with light and heat, covered it with vegetable film, then with forests, and accumulated the sphagnum whose decays made the peat of his meadow.

Science has shown the great circles in which nature works; the manner in which marine plants balance the marine animals, as the land plants supply the oxygen which the animals consume, and the animals the carbon which the plants absorb. These activities are incessant. Nature works on a method of *all for each and each for all*. The strain that is made on one point bears on every arch and foundation of the structure. There is a perfect solidarity. You cannot detach an atom from its holdings, or strip off

from it the electricity, gravitation, chemic affinity, or the relation to light and heat and leave the atom bare. No, it brings with it its universal ties.

Nature, like a cautious testator, ties up her estate so as not to bestow it all on one generation, but has a forelooking tenderness and equal regard to the next and the next, and the fourth and the fortieth age. There lie the inexhaustible magazines [stores]. The eternal rocks, as we call them, have their oxygen or lime undiminished, entire, as it was. No particle of oxygen can rust or wear, but has the same energy as on the first morning. The good rocks, those patient waiters, say to him: "We have the sacred power as we received it. We have not failed of our trust, and now, when in our immense day the hour is at last struck, take the gas we have hoarded, mingle it with water, and let it be free to grow in plants and animals and obey the thought of man."

The earth works for him; the earth is a machine which yields almost gratuitous service to every application of intellect. Every plant is a manufacturer of soil. In the stomach of the plant development begins. The tree can draw on the whole air, the whole earth, on all the rolling main. The plant is all suction pipe — imbibing from the ground by its root, from the air by its leaves, with all its might.

The air works for him. The atmosphere, a sharp solvent, drinks the essence and spirit of every solid on the globe, a menstruum which melts the mountains into it. Air is matter subdued by heat. As the sea is the grand receptacle of all rivers, so the air is the receptacle from which all things spring, and into which they all return. The invisible and creeping air takes form and solid mass. Our senses are skeptics, and believe only the impression of the moment, and do not believe the chemical fact that these huge mountain chains are made up of gases and rolling wind.

But nature is as subtle as she is strong.

She turns her capital day by day; deals never with dead, but ever with quick subjects. All things are flowing, even those that seem immovable. The adamant is always passing into smoke. The plants imbibe the materials which they want from the air and the ground. They burn, that is, exhale and decompose their own bodies into the air and earth again. The animal burns, or undergoes the like perpetual consumption. The earth burns, the mountains burn and decompose, slower, but incessantly. It is almost inevitable to push the generalization up into higher parts of nature, rank over rank into sentient beings.

Nations burn with internal fire of thought and affection, which wastes while it works. We shall find finer combustion and finer fuel. Intellect is a fire: rash and pitiless, it melts this wonderful bone house which is called man. Genius even, as it is the greatest good, is the greatest harm. While all thus burns — the universe in a blaze kindled from the torch of the sun — it needs a perpetual tempering, a phlegm, a sleep, atmospheres of azote, deluges of water to check the fury of the conflagration, a hoarding to check the spending, a centripetence equal to the centrifugence; and this is invariably supplied.

The railroad dirt cars are good excavators, but there is no porter like gravitation, who will bring down any weights which man cannot carry, and if he wants aid, knows where to find his fellow laborers. Water works in masses and sets its irresistible shoulder to your mills or your ships, or transports vast boulders of rock in its iceberg a thousand miles. But its far greater power depends on its talent of becoming little and entering the smallest holes and pores. By this agency, carrying in solution elements needful to every plant, the vegetable world exists.

But as I said, we must not paint the farmer in rose-color. While these grand energies have wrought for him and made his task possible, he is habitually engaged in small economies and is taught the power that lurks in petty things. Great is the force of a few simple arrangements; for instance, the powers of a fence. On the prairie you wander a hundred miles and hardly find a stick or a stone. At rare intervals a thin oak-opening has been spared, and every such section has been long occupied. But the farmer manages to procure wood from far, puts up a rail fence, and at once the seeds sprout and the oaks rise. It was only browsing and fire which had kept them down. Plant fruit trees by the roadside and their fruit will never be allowed to ripen. Draw a pine fence about them, and for fifty years they mature for the owner their delicate fruit. There is a great deal of enchantment in a chestnut rail or picketed pine boards.

Nature suggests every economical expedient somewhere on a great scale. Set out a pine tree, and it dies in the first year, or lives a poor spindle. But nature drops a pinecone in Mariposa, and it lives fifteen centuries, grows 300 or 400 feet high, and 30 in diameter — grows in a grove of giants, like a colonnade of Thebes. Ask the tree how it was done. It did not grow on a ridge but in a basin, where it found deep soil, cold enough and dry enough for the pine; defended itself from the sun by growing in groves, and from the wind by the walls of the mountain. The roots that shot deepest, and the stems of happiest exposure, drew the nourishment from the rest, until the less thrifty perished and manured the soil for the stronger, and the mammoth sequoias rose to their enormous proportions.

The traveler who saw them remembered his orchard at home, where every year, in the destroying wind, his forlorn trees pined like suffering virtue. In September, when the pears hang heaviest and are taking from the sun their gay colors, comes usually a gusty day which shakes the whole garden and throws down the heaviest fruit in bruised heaps. The planter took the hint of the sequoias, built a high wall, or, better, surrounded the orchard with a nursery of birches and evergreens. Thus he had the mountain basin in miniature; and his pears grew to the size of melons, and the vines beneath them ran an eighth of a mile. But this shelter creates a new climate. The wall that keeps off the strong wind keeps off the cold wind. The high wall reflecting the heat back on the soil gives that acre a quadruple share of sunshine,

> Enclosing in the garden square
> A dead and standing pool of air,

and makes a little Cuba within it, while all without is Labrador.

The chemist comes to his aid every year by following out some new hint drawn from nature, and now affirms that this dreary space occupied by the farmer is needless; he will concentrate his kitchen garden into a box of one or two rods square, will take the roots into his laboratory; the vines and stalks and stems may go sprawling about in the fields outside, he will attend to the roots in his tub, gorge them with food that is good for them. The smaller his garden, the better he can feed it, and the larger the crop. As he nursed his Thanksgiving turkeys on bread and milk, so he will pamper his peaches and grapes on the viands they like best. If they have an appetite for potash, or salt, or iron, or ground bones, or even now and then for a dead hog, he will indulge them. They keep the secret well and never tell on your table whence they drew their sunset complexion or their delicate flavors.

See what the farmer accomplishes by a cartload of tiles: he alters the climate by letting off water, which kept the land cold through constant evaporation and allows the warm rain to bring down into the roots the temperature of the air and of the surface soil; and he deepens the soil, since the discharge of this standing water allows the roots of his plants to penetrate below the surface to the subsoil, and accelerates the ripening of the crop.

The town of Concord is one of the oldest towns in this country, far on now in its third century. The selectmen have once in every five years perambulated the boundaries, and yet, in this very year, a large quantity of land has been discovered and added to the town without a murmur of complaint from any quarter. By drainage we went down to a subsoil we did not know, and have found there is a Concord under old Concord, which we are now getting the best crops from; a Middlesex under Middlesex; and, in fine, that Massachusetts has a basement story more valuable and that promises to pay a better rent than all the superstructure.

But these tiles have acquired by association a new interest. These tiles are political economists, confuters of Malthus and Ricardo; they are so many Young Americans announcing a better era, more bread. They drain the land, make it sweet and friable; have made English chat moss a garden, and will now do as much for the Dismal Swamp. But beyond this benefit they are the text of better opinions and better auguries for mankind.

There has been a nightmare bred in England of indigestion and spleen among landlords and loomlords, namely, the dogma that men breed too fast for the powers of the soil; that men multiply in a geometrical ratio, while corn multiplies only in an arithmetical; and hence that the more prosperous we are, the faster we approach these frightful limits — nay, the plight of every new generation is worse than of the foregoing because the first comers take up the best lands; the next, the second best; and each succeeding wave of population is driven to poorer, so that the land is ever yielding less returns to enlarging hosts of eaters. Henry Carey of Philadelphia replied: "Not so, Mr. Malthus, but just the opposite of so if the fact."

The first planter, the savage, without helpers, without tools, looking chiefly to safety from his enemy, man or beast, takes poor land. The better lands are loaded with timber, which he cannot clear; they need drainage, which he cannot attempt. He cannot plow, or fell trees, or drain the rich swamp. He is a poor creature; he scratches with a sharp stick, lives in a cave or a hutch, has no road but the trail of the moose or bear; he lives on their flesh when he can kill one, on roots and fruits when he cannot. He falls, and is lame; he coughs, he has a stitch in his side, he has a fever and chills; when he is hungry, he cannot always kill and eat a bear — chances of war — sometimes the bear eats him. 'Tis long before he digs or plants at all, and then only a patch.

Later he learns that his planting is better than hunting; that the earth works faster for him than he can work for himself — works for him when he is asleep, when it rains, when heat overcomes him. The sunstroke which knocks him down brings his corn up. As his family thrives and other planters come up around him, he begins to fell trees and clear good land; and when, by and by, there is more skill and tools and roads, the new generations are strong enough to open the lowlands, where the wash of mountains has accumulated the best soil, which yield a hundredfold the former crops. The last lands are the best lands. It needs science and great numbers to cultivate the best lands, and in the best manner. Thus true political economy is not mean, but liberal, and on the pattern of the sun and sky. Population increases in the ratio of morality; credit exists in the ratio of morality.

Meantime we cannot enumerate the incidents and agents of the farm without reverting to their influence on the farmer. He carries out this cumulative preparation of means to their last effect. This crust of soil which ages have refined he refines again for the feeding of a civil and instructed people.

The great elements with which he deals cannot leave him unaffected or unconscious of his ministry; but their influence somewhat resembles that which the same nature has on the child — of subduing and silencing him. We see the farmer with pleasure and respect when we think what powers and utilities are so meekly worn. He knows every secret of labor; he changes the face of the landscape. Put him on a new planet and he would know where to begin; yet there is no arrogance in his bearing, but a perfect gentleness.

The farmer stands well on the world. Plain in manners as in dress, he would not shine in palaces; he is absolutely unknown and inadmissible therein; living or dying, he never shall be heard of in them; yet the drawing room heroes put down beside him would shrivel in his presence — he, solid and unexpressive; they, expressed to gold leaf. But he stands well on the world, as Adam did, as an Indian does, as Homer's heroes, Agamemnon or Achilles, do. He is a person whom a poet of any clime — Milton, Firdusi, or Cervantes — would appreciate as being really a piece of the old nature, comparable to sun and moon, rainbow and flood; because he is, as all natural persons are, representative of nature as much as these.

That uncorrupted behavior which we admire in animals and in young children belongs to him, to the hunter, the sailor — the man who lives in the presence of nature. Cities force growth and make men talkative and entertaining, but they make them artificial. What possesses interest for us is the *naturel* of each, his constitutional excellence. This is forever a surprise, engaging and lovely; we cannot be satiated with knowing it, and about it; and it is this which the conversation with nature cherishes and guards.

13.

Anonymous: A Plea for Scientific Agriculture

As late as 1850, many American farmers were still intensively farming their lands and exhausting the soil without any provision for its replenishment. Such methods did not particularly worry the pioneer farmer, since he could, and often did, abandon his land and move west. For those who stayed behind, the prospect of a rich soil becoming increasingly unfertile caused considerable concern. The anonymous writer of the following selection, which appeared in the August 1858 issue of De Bow's Review, *an influential Southern magazine, advocated scientific agriculture as a desirable alternative to the existing practice. His ideas reflected the current thinking about science and agriculture that prompted Congress in later years to create the Department of Agriculture and pass the Morrill Land Grant Act, assisting the states to establish agricultural colleges and training programs.*

Source: *De Bow's Review*, August 1858: "Necessity of Agricultural Reforms."

WE HAVE A NUMEROUS, increasing, and industrious farming population; we rejoice in a comparatively rich soil; our agricultural machinery and implements are eminently practical, time- and laborsaving ones. Let us add theoretical knowledge, science, system to skill, experience, and inventive mood, and we shall not only be safe but may reach the climax.

But while yet surrounded by favorable circumstances, while yet living in a country the area of which is blessed to a great extent with a most productive soil requiring comparatively little toil and skill to make it yield abundant crops, experience as well as scientific research do forewarn and admonish us not to trust too implicitly to this apparently most prosperous state of things, for rapid are the changes that may come over us while we are dreaming or boasting of our prodigious condition. The happiest, wealthiest land may become poor and miserable, and the most prolific soil exhausted in the lapse of time, "if not certain constituent elements are returned to it in proportion to the extent to which they have been carried away by successful crops."

The restitution of the continually disturbed equilibrium alone secures fertility *in infinitum* [forever]; and wherever nature does not supply means to that end, human industry and human skill must take its place. We have striking examples for either relation. Thus in China and certain parts of Europe, it is chiefly manure, and to a great extent artificial manure, by means of which the soil is kept productive; in Hungary and a few other regions, it is owing to the quick disintegration of peculiarly adapted subsoils or rocks that a constant supply of nourishment for certain crops is furnished; in the Nile Valley and certain river bottoms of the United States, the yearly inundations secure fertility; and in the Netherlands, the same result is chiefly due to a regular system of irrigation. But most of these examples do not form the rule, but rather the exception, and the majority of agricultural regions are wont to imitate China if the yield of their soils shall not gradually decrease.

That the latter course is not more generally and more timely adopted in the United States, that there some of the most fecund tracts have been suffered to be laid waste, is easily explained. The immense area of unoccupied and unimproved land in the great West, together with the many other inducements to a settlement in those splendid, rising regions, make part of our people indifferent to the fate of the Atlantic states, and dazzle others to such an extent that they see no danger in the exhaustion and final abandonment of their former homes; at last they see no danger for them, and that is about all they mean to care for. To look to posterity is none of their business, neither do they dream that retribution may ever visit them in their new abodes; and perhaps it will not during *their* lifetime.

But wherein does consist the gain, if the annexation of a new agricultural district is analogous to the exhaustion and partial desertion of another? What have Virginia, Massachusetts, New York, etc., gained by the access and development of new territories and states? Has the process of exhaustion been retarded or checked in consequence; the population, the fertility, produce, wealth, and general prosperity increased in the ratio of her original capability? Not at all. The acquisition and occupation of new territory have only tempted and enabled people to be the more regardless of the mother state, and to quit it at the first signs of its receding prosperity, or its slower progress.

We do not judge at random; the history of the old states corroborates our assertions — how has, for instance, the white population of Virginia increased? In 1790 that state occupied the first rank; in 1800, 1810, and 1820, the third rank; in 1830 and 1840, the fourth; in 1850, the sixth; and in 1860, it will occupy probably the ninth rank in this respect. With a due allowance to the smaller area, the same relation is extant in the New England states, or elsewhere on the Atlantic slope; thus North Carolina fell from the fifth to the twelfth, Maryland from the seventh to the sixteenth, Connecticut from the sixth to the eighteenth rank, between the years 1790 and 1850.

But it may be said that these states contain a sufficient number of inhabitants to the square mile. Let us make an inquiry into that point. The area of Hesse Darmstadt, in Germany, is 1,444 square miles less than that of Connecticut, yet the former contains twice the number of inhabitants. The area of the kingdom of Bavaria, with over 5 million inhabitants, is the same as the area of South Carolina with 700,000 souls. Industrial, thriving Belgium feeds 5 million men on the same territory where Maryland sustains 600,000, Virginia and New York have an equal area with the kingdom of Prussia; the two first named with 5 million inhabitants, Prussia with nearly 18 million. Yet it does not seem as if these just-cited foreign states were overburdened with men, as they do by no means encourage the emigration to other countries, except, perhaps, such individuals as are a burden to any country.

All these circumstances, relations, and facts should arouse our people to a proper sense and appreciation of their duties to themselves and to future generations. It would require a volume to dwell upon all these interesting points having a bearing on this great question of our future. . . .

It has been proved that the method of cultivation must vary with the geological condition of the subsoil, by the disintegration of which, together with the access and accumulation of vegetable mold, or humus, the surface soil is formed. Wherever, therefore, the geological character of a region changes, the arable soil likewise varies; and in order to produce adequate and satisfactory crops, it has to be ascertained by analysis of the subsoil which mineral, earthy, or alkaline substances are wanting; and by analysis of the surface soil what kind of manure is chiefly to be applied to this end.

"If then the necessary geological researches go hand in hand with analytical investigations, we shall soon be in the possession of the necessary conditions and materials to find the method of cultivation for any particular agricultural district."

If these scientific labors are further extended to the analysis of the ashes of plants, we will soon have ascertained beyond fault "which of the constituent elements of the plants are constant, and which are subject to changes, arriving thus at an exact knowledge of the sum of all the ingredients which we withdraw from the soil in the different crops," and which in return we must bring to each field in order to keep it fertile or to increase its productiveness. If these labors are uniformly pursued and continued long enough, we cannot fail to establish the *rational system of agriculture,* applicable to all parts of the country and to all kinds of soil.

But as long as farmers are trying experiments with seeds and cuttings, with manures and fallows, without being guided by truly scientific principles, their prospect of success is rather small, and large capital and much power are wasted in consequence.

> The method pointed out by *science* is a different one, and far more reliable; there is no danger of a failure, but, on the contrary, every possible guarantee of success. But if failure should ensue in a particular case, science devises not only the means to detect the cause — we mean to say the cause of a barrenness of the soil for one or more plants — but at the same time provides the remedy without any great search and difficulty. . . .

That our great Confederacy cannot, without serious, vital injury to its imposing and still growing agricultural, industrial, and commercial interests, long remain behind other countries in nursing that branch of the natural sciences which is the teacher, guide, and benefactor of almost every trade and craft requires no argumentation in this place; nor do we think to have failed to make it manifest that no species of human pursuit is more depending and more indebted to chemistry than the agriculture.

Chemistry does not only give instruction to the farmer on everything that there is but it teaches him what is wanting and how it can be got. It makes known unto him the constituents in the composition of the surface soil, its fertility in general, and its adaptability to certain plants. It makes him acquainted with the proportions in which certain constituent and fertilizing elements are contained in the soil; and with the extent to which they are withdrawn from it by each succeeding crop, when he subjects the ashes to an analytical inquiry. It tells him how far and in which time a subsoil can be made capable of replacing the withdrawn minerals, earths, and alkalies, and gives him the information whether this is to be effected by deep plowing, rotation, fallow, irrigation, manuring, or any other contrivances or applications. It gives him certain knowledge of the capability of a soil to absorb and to retain moisture, and discloses unto him its power of the capillary attraction. It points out to him all the sources from which fertilizers or manures can be drawn, and suggests the most practical and efficient modes as to the quantities, forms, and combinations in which such fertilizers have to be brought upon the field in order to restore it either to its former productivity or to increase the same, etc.

These are but a few of the advantages and benefits to be derived from an appeal to science, from an application of chemistry to the art of culture.

It is, therefore, much to be regretted that the most useful and most practical feature of the National Agricultural Bureau has not been worked out in the shape that had been wisely suggested in the original Senate bill of 1850. The establishment of *agricultural laboratories* is the great desideratum for any successful initial step toward material improvements in the state of our agriculture. Single, solitary investigations of soil and ashes and subsequent devices to turn them to account will benefit locally òr individually, and should be more frequently resorted to as heretofore; but the whole object, the national aim, cannot be attained by this means. To accomplish that desirable and great end, a perfect chemical survey is wanting.

If but a single series of such investigations would be undertaken on the part of the federal or a state government, we do not for one moment doubt but that its results would be looked at with astonishment and hailed with delight by either legislators, statesmen, and practical agriculturists.

We have had topographical, geological, meteorological, nautical, and other "surveys," but we . . . have had no chemical one of but a single state or county.

In Ohio a very practical plan was once suggested to that end, but unfortunately has never been carried out. The plan was this:

At an expense of but a few thousand dollars, a chemical laboratory would have been erected in the capital of the states; next, an assessment of $50 levied upon the agricultural society of each county, and then, with the funds furnished by the state legislature and those of the just-named societies, a sufficient number of chemical analyses and other researches instituted to furnish such a chemical survey of the whole arable area of the state, upon which a more uniform, advantageous, and less exhausting method of cultivation could have been based.

If, with such an arrangement, a "state farm," "muster farm," or "farmers' high school," upon the principle as one is about being founded in Pennsylvania, would be connected, every desirable end could not only be achieved but the practical results and benefits to the farming community at large would be such as to warrant and secure for any future task the cooperation and assistance of every well-wisher of his country.

14.

HENRY P. TAPPAN: A Call for a Secularized University

Henry Tappan, president of the University of Michigan from 1852 to 1863, was a pioneer in American higher education. Influenced by his admiration for the Prussian educational system, he was the first educator to voice the opinion that a state university should be a center for advanced study, not merely a place for vocational training. On June 22, 1858, he delivered a speech to the Christian Library Association in which he articulated his idea of a true university. The excerpt reprinted here reflects Tappan's ideas on academic freedom and secular education, and shows how he hoped to adapt European models to American needs.

Source: *The University: Its Constitution, and Its Relations, Political and Religious,* Ann Arbor, 1858.

IN INSTITUTIONS of our own country belonging to particular sects, their usefulness and prosperity have been in proportion to their liberality. Take Yale College as an example — an institution, with the exception of Harvard, more fully developed than any institution in our country. Yale College belongs to the Congregationalists; it has a theological faculty, and a chaplain and preacher of its own order; and yet there is no sectarian exclusiveness in the appointment of professors in departments outside of the theological, and no sectarian pressure in its interior discipline and management. It cannot be said of Yale it has been devoted to the interests of Congregationalism, or that it has tended to extend Congregationalism.

The country does not think of it as a sectarian institution. It attracts attention and is valued generally for its educational benefits. Let it but change its policy and become intensely sectarian, and its glory would depart. Now it is resorted to by youth of all denominations, from all political parties, and from every section of the country, North and South, East and West; and it presents the largest number of students of any college or university of the United States. Indeed, Yale College derives no benefit from being attached to a particular sect, save the privilege of establishing a theological faculty.

Every sect has the right of establishing its own institutions; but no such institution can arise to eminence or gain large success by making the promotion of sectarian interests its great aim. Let anyone carefully examine the institutions of our country and he will find the above assertion fully sustained. Hence we find the sectarian institutions, so called, tending more and more to a liberal policy. The genius of our country demands that, if sectarian in name, they should not be so in their educational organization and procedures.

One is led by the consideration of these facts to inquire why sectarian colleges or universities exist, at all, where no theological faculty is established? Their origin is very easily accounted for.

In England the universities proper of Oxford and Cambridge fell into disuse; and the colleges, which were private and special endowments, originally designed to furnish board and lodging to theological students, and eventually came to have teachers attached to them, supplanted the former as educational institutions. Thus, Oxford and Cambridge merged into collections of colleges under ecclesiastical control.

It was natural, therefore, that when a university was established at Cambridge, Massachusetts, it should begin with a college after the English form. This precedent was followed as other similar institutions came into being. Besides, all education in our country began under the patronage of religious sects, or of individuals belonging to these sects. Men who emigrated to this country from religious principles naturally connected all their institutions, both educational and political, with their peculiar church organization.

But it did not follow, because this connection was originally demanded or could not be avoided on account of the peculiar exigencies of the times, that it was to continue when these exigencies had passed away. Hence, in time, the church and state came to be separated; and education in the common schools, at least, came to be separated from the church also. This movement has proceeded farther and farther; and we now have not only common schools but also high schools and academies, normal schools, and even many colleges and universities, removed from particular ecclesiastical connections. Indeed, it is hard to perceive any necessity for such a connection in any instance, save where a sect desires to create a theological faculty.

If it be said that colleges and universities require to be under religious control, and this can be best secured by a particular denominational connection, the argument proves too much. For why is not the same demanded for common schools, union schools, high schools, academies, normal schools, and the various private institutions? Nay, the lower schools, and especially the common schools, would seem to demand the very highest conditions for religious influence, since, in *these*, pupils are received at the most impressible period of human life and when the strongest bent is given to character and habits. It is on this very ground that the Roman Catholics have claimed the control of the apportionment of school money falling to their children. They say, "We deem it essential to educate our children under those religious influences which our consciences approve of." Now, are we consistent if we deny the necessity of denominational control in our common schools, and, indeed, in many other schools below the college and the university, but, the moment we reach this highest grade of education, claim it as essential?

If the state is competent to establish and to provide for the management of common, union, and normal schools without denominational interference, why is it not competent to do the same with respect to colleges and universities? And if the religious interests of the former can be secured under state organization, why not of the latter?

Besides, as a matter of fact, we cannot perceive what peculiar religious discipline is exercised in denominational institutions which does not exist elsewhere, unless these institutions should take rigid measures for the inculcation of their peculiar tenets. In this case their pupils could be derived only from their own communions, and they would become exceedingly limited in their sphere of operation. This, we know, they do not generally attempt, but aiming to afford education in science and literature, leave the conscience unfettered and establish only a moral and religious discipline which shall commend itself to the community generally without distinction of sect. And this is the very discipline which is introduced into state institutions and into institutions generally which are not denominational.

We come now to consider the University of Michigan under its moral and religious aspects.

First, as to the appointment of professors. If the principle . . . that the appointment of professors to chairs of literature and science, to all chairs, at least outside of the theological, is to be made independently alike of political and religious tests and solely in reference to literary and scientific qualifications and aptitude to teach, and that too in institutions professedly attached to particular religious denominations; and if the example not only of Protestant Leyden but also of Roman Catholic Padua and Pisa is worthy of all commendation, and its wisdom attested by its brilliant success; then, when we come to the University of Michigan, established as a state institution on a fund provided by the general government for no other purpose than that of promoting science and literature and advancing education, and whose great object is declared to be, in the first ordinance of the state passed in reference to it and approved March 18, 1837, "to provide the inhabitants of the state with the means of acquiring a thorough knowledge of the various branches of literature, science, and the arts"; then, I say, when we come to this institution, the principle of regulating appointments by qualifications alone cannot fail us. Here, if anywhere, political and religious tests must be utterly abolished, nor even a shadow of them appear.

All sects and parties, every individual in the state, would probably agree to this general statement. But a plan has somehow sprung up, and in one or two instances been acted upon, which, on the one hand, by proclaiming the equal rights of all religious denominations in university appointments, seems to avoid exclusiveness; while, on the other hand, in the very attempt to adjust these rights, it involves us in all the evils of denominational tests. For, on this plan, wherever a chair is to be filled, instead of confining ourselves to the considerations of the literary and scientific qualifications of the candidates and their aptitude to teach, we must raise two additional inquiries: first, to which of the denominations does the appointment about to be made of right belong; and, second, which of the candidates possesses the requisite denominational qualifications? Now it is plain that in both these questions we depart from the true principle before vindicated; and that were this plan once adopted, every appointment afterward made to the university would be governed by some denominational test.

But this would not be the only evil we should have to encounter. There would be the evil of denominational jealousy and competition. How would it be possible to adjust these denominational rights? Which denomination shall have the largest number of professors? Shall it be determined by the numbers, the wealth, the political influence, or the educated intelligence of the sect? Or, shall the same number be distributed alike to all the sects?

But some professorships may be regarded as more influential than others; and the full professorship would generally be regarded as taking precedence of the assistant. Then how many assistant professorships shall be considered equivalent to one full professorship? Shall it be two or one and a half? How shall we determine the relative importance of the full professorships? Which sect shall have the right to nominate the president? Or shall it be given to all in rotation? And shall he be elected for a limited term of years?

Then, again, it must be determined how far the power of the sects shall extend. Shall they have the power to make all nominations; or shall the regents be required to elect the proper number from each sect? Or will each sect be satisfied with one representative and leave the regents to elect the remainder according to their pleasure? Or suppose the rights of some sects have hitherto been neglected, as, for example, the Roman Catholics, who have not at present a single professor in the university — indeed the same is true with respect to the Dutch Reformed, the Unitarian, Universalist, and it may be other denominations — and that one or all of these should come forward and claim their rights when the chairs are all filled — would this difficulty be removed by creating new chairs or by vacating some of the chairs already filled in order to make way for what may be demanded as an equitable adjustment?

When once we admit the principle of denominational representation, we can exclude no denomination. When once we allow denominational interference, every denomination has an equal right to interfere. We must hear all; we must attend to all; and we must enter upon the impracticable task of satisfying all. And then this impracticable and unproductive work of endeavoring to harmonize the conflicting claims of numerous sects, ever prone to become more and more inflamed by competition, and rendered more and more unreasonable, will absorb the attention and labors of the regents, instead of the practicable, legitimate, and noble work of securing for the university eminent professors, and providing them with the means of fulfilling their functions and carrying out the ends of public instruction.

And when these representatives of the different sects are introduced into the university, acknowledged and known in this capacity, then the question arises how they are to act out this representative capacity and to maintain the interests of the bodies which they represent. Shall they all remit the peculiarities of their respective sects and endeavor to stand upon certain principles in which they all agree? Then there will, in reality, be no representation of sects, and the ends of the whole arrangement become null and void. Shall each one assert his sectarian peculiarities? Then will the university be split into conflicting parties and the professors be found heading their respective clans; and instead of an institution "providing the inhabitants of the state with the means of acquiring a thorough knowledge of the various branches of literature, science, and the arts," we shall have a grand gymnasium where Catholics and Protestants, the orthodox and the heterodox, engaged in endless logomachies, shall renew Milton's chaos —

> A universal hubbub wild
> Of stunning sounds and voices all
>   confused.

Better, far better, than to run the hazard of such confusion and ruin would it be to consign the university to any one denomination, Catholic or Protestant, animated by the noble spirit of Padua, Pisa, or Leyden. One, alone, possessing it might be generous and enlightened; a number attempting to share its functions and divide its spoils would only rend it in pieces. But egregiously do those mistake the character and ends of this institution who imagine that, because it belongs to no sect or party in particular, it therefore belongs to all sects and parties conjointly and of equal right. It not only does not belong to any sect or party in particular; it belongs to no sect or party at all. It belongs to the people of this state simply as the people of the state. The deed of trust by which it was founded, the ordinance by which its objects are defined makes no allusion to Catholic or Protestant, to Presbyterian, Methodist, Episcopalian, Baptist, Congregationalist, Unitarian, Universalist, or any other religious denomination. It speaks not of political parties; it refers to no particular localities. It speaks only of the state of Michigan, or of the people of the state.

It is a purely literary and scientific institution; it is in no sense ecclesiastical. It is designed for a simple purpose, advancing knowledge and promoting education. Occupying a higher grade, it is as purely a popular and educational institution as the common school itself. It is as absurd to speak of the university as belonging to religious sects conjointly as it would be to speak of the asylum, the state prison, the legislature, or any public body, institution, or works as

Henry P. Tappan, first president of the University of Michigan

thus belonging. The state is not composed of religious sects but of the people. And the institutions of the state do not belong to the sects into which the people may chance to be divided by their religious opinions and practices; but to the people considered as the body politic, irrespective of all such divisions. . . .

Since I have been acquainted with the University of Michigan, there has been an entire harmony on religious subjects among both professors and students. Denominationalism and proselytism have not appeared among us, and yet much healthful religious influence has been exerted, as much, I believe, as in any other institution of learning; and with consequences no less marked and happy. As to myself, I may be permitted to say that I have conscientiously endeavored to make the daily religious services as effective as possible. Beyond this, at the Sabbath morning prayers, I have always given brief, practical remarks drawn from the passage read. And on Sabbath afternoon, I have generally given a lecture either on natural theology, or the evidences of Christianity, or morals, or on some point of practical Christianity. Attendance on this lecture has always been at the option of the students. This lecture has also been open to the public.

I have never learned that either the professors, the students, or the public have charged me with any appearance of sectarianism or proselytism. If in any religious efforts on the part of the professors or myself beyond what is prescribed by the university ordinance there have been any improprieties or excess, we are open to correction and restraint from the regents, the legal guardians of the university. But while we hold ourselves amenable to the regents, we claim exemption from the authority of all ecclesiastical bodies either as imposing on us duties, restraining our actions, or censuring our measures. Legally, such bodies have no right to extend their authority over us in any way. Morally, they have no power to aid us, from the very fact that what one attempts all have an equal right to attempt; and that therefore, as their advice or prescriptions would not be likely to harmonize, their interference would only serve to confuse and embarrass us.

One of the most effectual ways of promoting religion among the students is to afford every encouragement to their voluntary associations for religious purposes, such as the Student's Christian Association and the Christian Library Association. The latter is especially to be commended to Christians of all denominations and to all persons desirous of aiding the best interests of the institution. Give us religious books. Give us as freely as you please. Give us the noble works of the old English divines — of the Established Church and of the Dissenters. Give us the excellent works of our American divines of all schools. There the books will stand, open to the choice of the students. Each one can consult his own taste and peculiarities; and all can profit by the spirit of Christianity nobly diffused through so many channels. . . .

The university, as an institution of the state, open to all the people of the state, and affording to them the means of the highest education, is a symbol of essential union of all religious sects and of all political parties. We are all Christians, we are all American citizens. Whatever may be our differences, we have a common agreement, a common interest in the great subject of education. It is the part of wisdom to preserve the university intact from the questions on which we differ, and to maintain and foster it purely as an educational institution. The regents and faculty may have their own opinions on politics, their own attachments for the sects to which they severally belong, their own views on questions of moral reform. These, as men and as American citizens, they claim to entertain in perfect freedom, without any interference or any rebuke. But they would violate the trust reposed in them did they allow these to influence their measures in respect to the university.

A child's education should begin at least a hundred years before he is born.
OLIVER WENDELL HOLMES, *The Autocrat of the Breakfast Table*, 1858

15.

David Smith Terry and Stephen J. Field: On Sunday Closing Laws

The legal reforms of the Jacksonian period did not affect the laws in most of the states forbidding public entertainments, sports, buying and selling, and traveling on Sunday, in addition to the time-honored prohibition on unnecessary work. Restriction of public activities continued to be the subject of legislation, to facilitate opportunities for worship and keep the day holy. The constitutionality of such legislation has often been challenged in the United States on the grounds of the separation of church and state. In the California Supreme Court in 1858, three different opinions were delivered in the case ex parte Newman, which involved a Jewish merchant who had been arrested for selling clothes on Sunday. Reprinted here are the opinion of Chief Justice David Smith Terry and a portion of the dissent by his perennial antagonist, Stephen J. Field.

Source: *Reports of Cases Argued and Determined in the Supreme Court of the State of California, During January and April Terms, 1858,* Harvey Lee, ed., Vol. IX, Sacramento, 1858, pp. 502-529.

Chief Justice Terry: The petitioner was tried and convicted before a justice of the peace for a violation of the act of April 1858, entitled "An act for the better observance of the Sabbath," and, upon his failure to pay the fine imposed, was imprisoned.

The counsel for petitioner moves his discharge on the ground that the act under which these proceedings were had is in conflict with the 1st and 4th sections of the 1st Article of the state constitution, and therefore void.

The 1st Section declares, "All men are by nature free and independent and have certain inalienable rights, among which are those of enjoying and defending life and liberty; acquiring, possessing, and protecting property; and pursuing and obtaining safety and happiness."

The 4th Section declares, "The free exercise and enjoyment of religious profession and worship, without discrimination or preference, shall forever be allowed in this state."

The questions which arise in the consideration of the case are:

1. Does the act of the legislature make a discrimination or preference favorable to one religious profession, or is it a mere civil rule of conduct?

2. Has the legislature the power to enact a municipal regulation which enforces upon the citizen a compulsory abstinence from his ordinary lawful and peaceable avocations for one day in the week?

There is no expression in the act under consideration which can lead to the conclusion that it was intended as a civil rule, as contradistinguished from a law for the benefit of religion. It is entitled "An act for the better observance of the Sabbath," and the prohibitions in the body of the act are confined to the "Christian Sabbath."

It is, however, contended, on the authority of some of the decisions of other states, that notwithstanding the pointed language of the act, it may be construed into a civil rule of action, and that the result would be the same even if the language were essentially different.

The fault of this argument is that it is opposed to the universally admitted rule which requires a law to be construed according to the intention of the lawmaker, and this intention to be gathered from the language of the law according to its plain and common acceptation.

It is contended that a civil rule requiring the devotion of one-seventh of the time to repose is an absolute necessity, and the want of it has been dilated upon as a great evil to society. But have the legislature so considered it? Such an assumption is not warranted by anything contained in the Sunday law. On the contrary, the intention which pervades the whole act is to enforce as a *religious institution* the observance of a day held sacred by the followers of one faith and entirely disregarded by all the other denominations within the state. The whole scope of the act is expressive of an intention on the part of the legislature to require a periodical cessation from ordinary pursuits, not as a civil duty necessary for the repression of any existing evil but in furtherance of the interests and in aid of the devotions of those who profess the Christian religion.

Several authorities, affirming the validity of similar statutes, have been cited from the reports of other states. While we entertain a profound respect for the courts of our sister states, we do not feel called upon to yield our convictions of right to a blind adherence to precedent, especially when they are, in our opinion, opposed to principle, and the reasoning by which they are endeavored to be supported is by no means satisfactory or convincing. In *Bryan* v. *Berry* (6 Cal., 398), in reference to the decisions of other states, we said, "Decided cases are, in some sense, evidence of what the law is. We say in some sense because it is not so much the decision as it is the reasoning upon which the decision is based which makes it authority and requires it to be respected."

It will be unnecessary to examine all the cases cited by the district attorney. The two leading cases in which the question is more elaborately discussed than in the others are the cases of *Sepect* v. *The Commonwealth* (8 Barr, 313) and *The City Council* v. *Benjamin* (2 Schobart, 508), decided, respectively, by the supreme courts of Pennsylvania and South Carolina. These decisions are based upon the ground that the statutes requiring the observance of the Christian Sabbath established merely a civil rule and make no discrimination or preference in favor of any religion.

By an examination of these cases, it will be seen that the position taken rests in mere assertion, and that not a single argument is adduced to prove that a preference in favor of the Christian religion is not given by the law. In the case in 8 Barr, the court said: "It (the law) intermeddles not with the natural and indefeasible right of all men to worship Almighty God according to the dictates of their own consciences; it compels none to attend, erect, or support any place of worship, or to maintain any ministry, against his consent; it pretends not to control or interfere with the rights of conscience, and it establishes no preference for any religious establishment or mode of worship."

This is the substance of the arguments to show that these laws establish no preference. The last clause in the extract asserts the proposition broadly; but it is surely no legitimate conclusion from what precedes it, and must be taken as the plainest example of *petitio principii* [begging the question]. That which precedes it establishes that the law does not destroy religious toleration, but that is all.

Now, does our constitution, when it forbids discrimination or preference in religion, mean merely to guarantee toleration? For that, in effect, is all which the cases cited seem to award, as the right of a citizen. In a community composed of persons of various religious denominations, having different days of worship, each considering his own as sacred from secular employment, all being equally considered and protected under the constitution, a law is passed which in effect recognizes the sacred character of one of these days by compelling all others to abstain from secular employment, which is precisely one of the modes in which its observance is manifested and required by the creed of that sect to which it belongs as a Sabbath. Is not this a discrimination in favor of the one? Does it require more than an appeal to one's common sense to decide that this is a preference? And when the Jew or Seventh-Day Christian complains of this, is it any answer to say your conscience is not constrained, you are not compelled to worship or to perform religious rites on that day nor forbidden to keep holy the day which you esteem as a Sabbath? We think not, however high the authority which decides otherwise.

When our liberties were acquired, our republican form of government adopted, and our Constitution framed, we deemed that we had attained not only toleration but religious liberty in its largest sense — a complete separation between church and state, and a perfect equality without distinction between all religious sects. "Our government," said Mr. [Richard M.] Johnson, in his celebrated Sunday-mail report, "is a civil and not a religious institution; whatever may be the religious sentiments of citizens, and however variant, they are alike entitled to protection from the government, so long as they do not invade the rights of others." And again, dwelling upon the danger of applying the powers of government to the furtherance and support of sectarian objects, he remarks, in language which should not be forgotten, but which ought to be deeply impressed on the minds of all who desire to maintain the supremacy of our republican system:

> Extensive religious combinations to effect a political object were, in the opinion of the committee, always dangerous. The first effort of the kind calls for the establishment of a principle which would lay the foundation for dangerous innovation upon the spirit of the Constitution and upon the religious rights of the citizen. If admitted, it may be justly apprehended that the future measures of the government will be strangely marked, if not eventually controlled by the same influence. All religious despotism commences by combination and influence, and when that influence begins to operate upon the political institution of a country, the civil power soon bends under it and the catastrophe of other nations furnishes an awful warning of the consequences. . . .
>
> What other nations call religious toleration, we call religious rights; they were not exercised in virtue of governmental indulgence but as rights of which the government cannot deprive any portion of her citizens, however small. Despotic power may invade those rights, but justice still confirms them. Let the national legislature once perform an act which involves the decision of a religious controversy and it will have passed its legitimate bounds. The precedent will then be established and the foundation laid for that usurpation of the divine prerogative in this country, which has been the desolating scourge of the fairest portions of the Old World. Our Constitution recognizes no other power than that of persuasion for enforcing religious observances.

We come next to the question whether, considering the Sunday law as a civil regulation, it is in the power of the legislature to enforce a compulsory abstinence from lawful and ordinary occupation for a given period of time without some apparent civil necessity for such action; whether a pursuit which is not only peaceable and lawful but also praiseworthy and commendable for six days in the week can be arbitrarily converted into a penal offense or misdemeanor on the seventh. As a general rule, it will be admitted that men have a natural right to do anything which their inclinations may suggest, if it be not evil in itself and in no way impairs the rights of others. When societies are formed, each individual surrenders certain rights, and as an equivalent for that surrender has secured to him the enjoyment of certain others appertaining to his person and property without the protection of which society cannot exist. All legislation is a restraint on individuals, but it is a restraint which must be submitted to by all who would enjoy the benefits derived from the institutions of society.

It is necessary for the preservation of free institutions that there should be some general and easily recognized rule to determine the extent of governmental power, and establish a proper line of demarcation between such as are strictly legitimate and such as are usurpations which invade the reserved rights of the citizen and infringe upon his constitutional liberty. The true rule of distinction would seem to be that which allows to the legislature the right so to restrain each one in his freedom of conduct as to secure perfect protection to all others from every species of danger to person, health, and property; that each individual shall be required so to use his own as not to inflict injury upon his neighbor; and these, we think, are all the immunities which can be justly claimed by one portion of society from another, under a government of constitutional limitation. For these reasons, the law restrains the establishment of tanneries, slaughterhouses, gunpowder depots, the discharge of firearms, etc., in a city, the sale of drugs and poisons, and the practice of physic by incompetent persons, and makes a variety of other prohibitions, the reason and sense of which are obvious to the most common understanding.

Now, when we come to inquire what reason can be given for the claim of power to enact a Sunday law, we are told, looking at it in its purely civil aspect, that it is absolutely necessary for the benefit of his health and the restoration of his powers, and in aid of this great social necessity, the legislature may, for the general convenience, set apart a particular day of rest and require its observance by all.

This argument is founded on the assumption that mankind are in the habit of working too much and thereby entailing evil upon society, and that without compulsion they will not seek the necessary repose which their exhausted natures demand. This is to us a new theory and is contradicted by the history of the past and the observations of the present. We have heard, in all ages, of declamations and reproaches against the vice of indolence, but we have yet to learn that there has ever been any general complaint of an intemperate, vicious, unhealthy, or morbid industry. On the contrary, we know that mankind seek cessation from toil from the natural influences of self-preservation in the same manner and as certainly as they seek slumber, relief from pain, or food to appease their hunger.

Again, it may be well considered that the amount of rest which would be required by one-half of society may be widely disproportionate to that required by the other. It is a matter of which each individual must be permitted to judge for himself, according to his own instincts and necessities. As well might the legislature fix the days and hours for work and enforce their observance by an unbending rule which shall be visited alike upon the weak and strong. Whenever such attempts are made, the lawmaking power leaves its legitimate sphere and makes an incursion into the realms of physiology and its enactments, like the sumptuary laws of the ancients which prescribe the mode and texture of people's clothing, or similar laws which might prescribe and limit our food and drink, must be regarded as an invasion, without reason or necessity, of the natural rights of the citizen, which are guaranteed by the fundamental law.

The truth is, however much it may be disguised, that this one day of rest is a purely religious idea. Derived from the sabbatical institutions of the ancient Hebrew, it has been adopted into all the creeds of succeeding religious sects throughout the civilized world; and whether it be the Friday of the Mohammedan, the Saturday of the Israelite, or the Sunday of the Christian, it is alike fixed in the affections of its followers, beyond the power of eradication, and in most of the states of our confederacy, the aid of the law to enforce its observance has been given under the pretense of a civil, municipal, or police regulation.

But it has been argued that this is a question exclusively for the legislature; that the lawmaking power alone has the right to judge of the necessity and character of all police rules, and that there is no power in the judiciary to interfere with the exercise of this right.

One of the objects for which the Judicial Department is established is the protection of the constitutional rights of the citizen. The question presented in this case is not merely one of expediency or abuse of power; it is a question of usurpation of power. If the legislature have the authority to appoint a time of compulsory rest, we would have no right to interfere with it even if they required a cessation from toil for six days in the week instead of one. If they possess this power, it is without limit and may extend to the prohibition of all occupations at all times.

While we concede to the legislature all the supremacy to which it is entitled, we cannot yield to it the omnipotence which has been ascribed to the British Parliament so long as we have a constitution which limits its powers and places certain innate rights of the citizen beyond its control.

It is said that the 1st Section of Article I of the constitution is a commonplace assertion of a general principle and was not intended as a restriction upon the power of the legislature. This court has not so considered it.

In *Billings* v. *Hall* (7 Cal., 1) Chief Justice Murray says, in reference to this section of the constitution:

> This principle is as old as the Magna Carta. It lies at the foundation of every constitutional government and is necessary to the existence of civil liberty and free institutions. It was not lightly incorporated into the constitution of this state as one of those political dogmas designed to tickle the popular ear and conveying no substantial meaning or idea, but as one of those fundamental principles of enlightened government, without a rigorous observance of which there could be neither liberty nor safety to the citizen.

In the same case, Mr. Justice Burnett asserted the following principles, which bear directly upon the question:

> That among the inalienable rights declared by our constitution as belonging to each citizen, is a right of "acquiring, possessing, and protecting property." . . . "That for the constitution to declare a right inalienable, and at the same time leave the legislature unlimited power over it, would be a contradiction in terms, an idle provision, proving that a constitution was a mere parchment barrier, insufficient to protect the citizen, delusive and visionary, and the practical result of which would be to destroy, not conserve, the rights it vainly assumed to protect."

Upon this point, I dissent from the opinion of the court in *Billings* v. *Hall,* and if I considered the question an open one, I might yet doubt its correctness, but the doctrine announced in that opinion, having received the sanction of the majority of the court, has become the rule of decision, and it is the duty of the court to see it is uniformly enforced, and that its application is not confined to a particular class of cases.

It is the settled doctrine of this court to

enforce every provision of the constitution in favor of the rights reserved to the citizen against a usurpation of power in any question whatsoever; and, although in a doubtful case, we would yield to the authority of the legislature, yet upon the question before us, we are constrained to declare that, in our opinion, the act in question is in conflict with the 1st Section of Article I of the constitution, because, without necessity, it infringes upon the liberty of the citizen by restraining his right to acquire property. And that it is in conflict with the 4th Section of the same article because it was intended as, and is in effect, a discrimination in favor of one religious profession and gives it a preference over all others.

It follows that the petitioner was improperly convicted, and it is ordered that he be discharged from custody.

Justice Field: After a careful and repeated perusal of the opinions of my associates, I am unable to concur either in their reasoning or in their judgment. I cannot perceive any valid ground for declaring the act of 1858, for the better observance of the Sabbath, unconstitutional. In ordinary cases I should be content with refraining from a concurrence or expressing a simple dissent, but in the present case I feel compelled to state the reasons of my dissent, as the opinions of my associates appear to me to assert a power in the judiciary never contemplated by the constitution, and of dangerous consequences; and to adopt a construction of constitutional provisions which must deprive the legislature of all control over a great variety of subjects upon which its right to legislate, in the promotion of the public weal, has never been doubted.

The enactment in question is held to conflict with the 1st and 4th sections of the 1st Article of the constitution.

The 1st Section declares that "all men are by nature free and independent and have certain inalienable rights, among which are those of enjoying and defending life and liberty; acquiring, possessing, and protecting property; and pursuing and obtaining safety and happiness."

The 4th Section declares that "the free exercise and enjoyment of religious profession and worship, without discrimination or preference, shall forever be allowed in this state."

In examining the questions raised by the petitioner, I will first consider the 4th Section, and whether the statute is in any sense within its provisions. The statute is prohibitory in its character, and its constitutionality must be determined by the acts it forbids. The inquiry is as to the power of the legislature, not as to the motives which induced the enactment. That power is exhibited in the clause which provides that no person shall, on the Christian Sabbath, or Sunday, keep open any store, warehouse, mechanic shop, workshop, banking house, manufacturing establishment, or other business house for business purposes; or sell, or expose for sale, any goods, wares, or merchandise on that day, and fixes the penalty for the violation of the provision. If the exercise of this power is not prohibited to the legislature by the constitution, either in express terms or by necessary implication, it is our duty to uphold the statute. Of its wisdom or policy, it is not within our province to judge. In what manner it conflicts with the 4th Section, I am unable to perceive. What have the sale of merchandise, the construction of machines, the discount of notes, the drawing of bills of exchange, the purchase of gold, or the business of the artisan, mechanic, or manufacturer to do with religious profession or worship? There is no necessary connection between them.

The petitioner is an Israelite, engaged in the sale of clothing, and his complaint is not that his religious profession or worship is interfered with but that he is not permitted to dispose of his goods on Sunday; not that any religious observance is imposed upon him but that his secular business is closed on a day on which he does not think proper to rest. In other words, the law as a civil regulation, by the generality of its provisions, interrupts his acquisitions on a day which does not suit him. The law treats of business matters not religious duties. In fixing a day of rest, it establishes only a rule of civil conduct. In limiting its command to secular pursuits, it necessarily leaves religious profession and worship free. It is absurd to say that the sale of clothing or other goods on Sunday is an act of religion or worship; and it follows that the inhibition of such sale does not interfere with either.

Religious profession springs from matters of faith, and religious worship is the adoration of the soul. As to the forms in which that profession or worship shall be exhibited, the law is silent; it utters no command, and it imposes no restraint. It makes no discrimination or preference between the Hebrew and Gentile, the Mussulman and pagan, the Christian and infidel, but leaves to all the privilege of worshiping God, or of denying His existence, according to the conclusions of their own judgments or the dictates of their own consciences. *It does not even allude to the subject of religious profession or worship, in any of its provisions.* It establishes, as a civil regulation, a day of rest from secular pursuits, and that is its only scope and purpose. Its requirement is a cessation from labor. In its enactment, the legislature has given the sanction of law to a rule of conduct, which the entire civilized world recognizes as essential to the physical and moral well-being of society.

Upon no subject is there such a concurrence of opinion — among philosophers, moralists, and statesmen of all nations — as on the necessity of periodical cessations from labor. One day in seven is the rule, founded in experience and sustained by science. There is no nation, possessing any degree of civilization, where the rule is not observed, either from the sanctions of the law or the sanctions of religion. This fact has not escaped the observation of men of science and distinguished philosophers have

not hesitated to pronounce the rule founded upon a law of our race.

The legislature possesses the undoubted right to pass laws for the preservation of health and the promotion of good morals, and if it is of opinion that periodical cessation from labor will tend to both, and thinks proper to carry its opinion into a statutory enactment on the subject, there is no power, outside of its constituents, which can sit in judgment upon its action. It is not for the judiciary to assume a wisdom which it denies to the legislature, and exercise a supervision over the discretion of the latter. It is not the province of the judiciary to pass upon the wisdom and policy of legislation; and when it does so, it usurps a power never conferred by the constitution.

It is no answer to the requirements of the statute to say that mankind will seek cessation from labor by the natural influences of self-preservation. The position assumes that all men are independent and at liberty to work whenever they choose. Whether this be true or not in theory, it is false in fact; it is contradicted by every day's experience. The relations of superior and subordinate, master and servant, principal and clerk, always have and always will exist.

Labor is in a great degree dependent upon capital, and unless the exercise of the power which capital affords is restrained, those who are obliged to labor will not possess the freedom for rest which they would otherwise exercise. The necessities for food and raiment are imperious, and the exactions of avarice are not easily satisfied. It is idle to talk of a man's freedom to rest when his wife and children are looking to his daily labor for their daily support. The law steps in to restrain the power of capital. Its object is not to protect those who can rest at their pleasure but to afford rest to those who need it, and who, from the conditions of society, could not otherwise obtain it. Its aim is to prevent the physical and moral debility which springs from uninterrupted labor; and in this aspect it is a beneficent and merciful law. It gives one day to the poor and dependent, from the enjoyment of which no capital or power is permitted to deprive them. It is theirs for repose, for social intercourse, for moral culture, and, if they choose, for divine worship. Authority for the enactment I find in the great object of all government, which is protection. Labor is a necessity imposed by the condition of our race, and to protect labor is the highest office of our laws.

But [it] is urged that the intention of the law is to enforce the Sabbath as a religious institution. This position is assumed from the description of the day and the title of the act, but is not warranted by either. The terms "Christian Sabbath or Sunday" are used simply to designate the day selected by the legislature. The same construction would obtain and the same result follow if any other terms were employed, as "the Lord's day, commonly called Sunday," contained in the statute of Pennsylvania, or simply "the Sabbath day," or "the first day of the week," as in several statutes. The power of selection being in the legislature, there is no valid reason why Sunday should not be designated as well as any other day. Probably no day in the week could be taken which would not be subject to some objection. That the law operates with inconvenience to some is no argument against its constitutionality. Such inconvenience is an incident to all general laws. A civil regulation cannot be converted into a religious institution because it is enforced on a day which a particular religious sect regards as sacred.

The legislature has seen fit in different enactments to prohibit judicial and various kinds of official business on Sunday, and yet it has never been contended that these enactments establish any religious observances, or that the compulsory abstinence from judicial or official labor is a discrimination or preference in favor of any religious sect. The law requires notes, when the last day of grace falls on Sunday, to be presented to the maker on Saturday, in order to hold the endorser. Would the complaint of an Israelite that this was a discrimination in an important class of contracts in favor of the Christian be listened to for a moment? But why not? In the course of his business it often becomes important to his interest that he should take commercial paper, not given to him in the first instance, and when, therefore, it is not in his power to fix the day of payment; and if the opinion of my associates is law, I see no reason why he should be compelled to have the note presented on Saturday in order to hold the endorser. And why should he be denied the power of enforcing on that day, by legal process, contracts entered into with him? To be consistent, we ought to hold all this legislation as discriminating and giving a preference in favor of one religious sect, and therefore unconstitutional.

The answer consists in the simple fact that the legislation is not based upon any idea of enforcing a religious observance but of establishing, as a civil regulation, a day of rest from judicial and other official labor; and the constitution itself contains a recognition of Sunday as a day of rest in the clause which provides that a bill presented to the governor shall become a law in like manner as if he had signed it if not returned by him within ten days, *Sundays excepted,* unless the legislature, by adjournment, prevent such return. The word "Sundays," in the plural, is in the constitution on file in the office of the secretary of state, not "Sunday," in the singular, as found in the printed copy. (*Price* v. *Whitman. . . .*)

The fact that the civil regulation finds support in the religious opinions of a vast majority of the people of California is no argument against its establishment. It would be fortunate for society if all wise civil rules obtained a ready obedience from the citizen, not merely from the requirements of the law but from conscientious or religious convictions of their obligation. The law against homicide is not the less wise and necessary because the divine command is, "Thou shalt do no murder." The legislation against perjury is not the less useful and essential for the due administration of justice because the injunction comes from the Most High, "Thou shalt not bear false witness against thy neighbor." The establishment by law of Sunday as a day of rest from labor is nonetheless a beneficent and humane regulation, because it accords with the divine precept that upon that day "Thou shalt do no manner of work; thou, and thy son, and thy daughter, thy manservant and thy maidservant, thy cattle, and the stranger that is within thy gates." . . .

The law in question is free from all ambiguity. Its purview, or body, speaks a command which no one can mistake. Its title, therefore, is not a subject for consideration. The law would be equally obligatory if entitled "An act to promote the general health." The section of the constitution, being directory in its character, can operate only on the conscience of the lawmaker. Like the provision that the laws shall be published in Spanish, it creates a duty of imperfect obligation, which the judiciary cannot enforce.

But aside from these views, there is nothing in the title of the act open to criticism. It reads, "An act to provide for the better observance of the Sabbath," which means nothing more or less than an act to provide for the better observance of a day of the week called the Sabbath. It does not indicate the manner of observance; that is exhibited in the body of the act. It is there commanded to be by cessation from labor, not by religious worship.

With the motives which operated upon the legislature to pass the act, we have nothing to do. They may have been as varied as the different minds of its members. With some, religious convictions may have controlled; with others, a sense of the necessity of protecting labor; with some, a belief that it would be a popular law with their constituents; and with others, less worthy considerations. It is a question of power that we are determining, and whether that power was wise or unwisely exercised, or from pure or impure motives, is of no moment. If we admit that the law had its origin in the religious opinions of the members of the legislature, we advance nothing in favor of its constitutionality and concede nothing against it. It would be, indeed, singular if a wise and beneficent law were the subject of objection because suggested by the principles of a pure religion. Christianity is the prevailing faith of our people; it is the basis of our civilization; and that its spirit should infuse itself into and humanize our laws is as natural as that the national sentiment of liberty should find expression in the legislation of the country. . . .

In the present case, the question under consideration is one of power dependent upon the construction of sections of the constitution. The rules of construction are settled and possess all the certainty which can exist out of the exact sciences; they do not vary in different courts; they are the same now that they were a century ago; they are the same now that they will be a century hence; and a concurrence upon their application of the highest tribunals of every state where a Sunday law exists, in the same judgment, ought to inspire confidence in its soundness.

I pass to the consideration of the 1st Section of the constitution which places among the inalienable rights of men "those of enjoying and defending life and liberty; acquiring, possessing, and protecting property; and pursuing and obtaining safety and happiness." This section embodies great principles of inestimable value but was never intended to inhibit legislation upon the rights enumerated. Men have an inalienable right to enjoy and defend life and liberty, but the conditions of its enjoyment, the circumstances under which life may be forfeited or liberty restrained are the subjects of constant legislation. Men have an inalienable right to acquire, possess, and protect property, but the mode and manner of the acquisition, possession, and protection are matters upon which laws are passed at every session of the legislature. Men have an inalienable right of pursuing and obtaining safety and happiness but subject to such restrictions as the public good may require. The rights enumerated in the section are to be enjoyed in a constitutional government in subordination to the general laws of the state.

That the legislature possesses the power to legislate for the good order, the peace, welfare, and happiness of society is not denied. The means by which these ends are to be effected are left to its discretion. The existence of discretion implies a liability to abuse, but because the discretion of the legislature may be abused, its acts are not, for that reason, void. It is no argument against the existence of the power to establish a day of rest that it may be exerted to the prohibition of labor for six days in the week instead of one. There is no single power which may not be so exercised as to become intolerable. The only limitation upon the exercise of the taxing power is that the taxation must be equal and uniform. The extent of the tax is not controlled; that rests in the discretion of the legislature; it may amount to nearly the entire value of the property upon which it is laid. It is to be supposed that the members of the legislature will exercise some wisdom in its acts; if they do not, the remedy is with the people. Frequent elections by the people furnish the only protection, under the constitution, against the abuse of acknowledged legislative power.

All sorts of restrictions and regulations are placed upon the acquisition and disposition of property. What contracts are valid and what are invalid; when they must be in writing and when they can be made by parol; what is essential to transfer chattels and what to convey realty are matters of con-

stant legislation. Some modes of acquisition are subject to licenses and some are prohibited. The right to acquire property, like the use of it, must be considered in relation to other rights. It may be regulated for the public good, though thereby the facility of acquisition is lessened, as in the sale of gunpowder and drugs, and in the practice of different professions. Men have a right to the labor of their children or slaves, yet the legislature may fix reasonable periods of labor, as is done in regard to children in factories and in regard to slaves, in some instances. . . .

If it be admitted that the legislature possesses the right to restrain each one in his freedom of conduct only so far as is necessary to secure protection to all others, from every species of danger to person, health, and property, no inference can be drawn against the validity of the act under consideration. The character and mode of protection, and what is dangerous to the person, or to health and property, must necessarily be left to its determination, and in the 1st Section of the constitution no inhibition to the exercise of its power in this respect can be found. The prohibition of secular business on Sunday is advocated on the ground that by it the general welfare is advanced, labor protected, and the moral and physical well-being of society promoted. The legislature has so considered it, and the judiciary cannot say that the legislature was mistaken, and, therefore, the act is unconstitutional, without passing out of its legitimate sphere and assuming a right to supervise the exercise of legislative discretion in matters of mere expediency. Such right, as I have already observed, does not belong to the judiciary. Its assumption would be usurpation and well-calculated to lessen the just influence which the judiciary should possess in a constitutional government. . . .

I am of opinion that the "Act for the better observance of the Sabbath" is constitutional, and that the petitioner ought to be remanded.

1859

16.

ANONYMOUS: The Influence Abroad of American Inventiveness

Since colonial days, Americans have prided themselves on their practicality and inventiveness. Their technical ingenuity, epitomized by men like Franklin, seemed to be unequivocally superior to that of Europe. The author of the following article, which appeared in 1859, considered the mechanical skill of Americans more important than "conquest, shrines, and ancestry," which he felt were the main sources of pride in the Old World. He predicted that American inventiveness would eventually raise the United States to the forefront of the world's nations.

Source: *Scientific American*, March 5, 1859: "American Influence Abroad."

VIRGIL, IN HIS DAY, sang songs and lauded high arms and prowess, deeds of heroism and martial glory, and it has long been an established idea that the greatness and the glory of a nation which hand it down to posterity are deeds upon the battlefield and honors won by human bloodshed. This idea is false — a slander on mankind — a disgrace to the race. All the nations and cities of antiquity are preserved in our memories more by the works of their artisans and artists than by their conquests or heroes. Who but the deep student knows aught of Babylonish arms? But everyone is familiar with the "hanging gardens" of that famous city. The history of the early rulers of Egypt is shrouded in mystery; but the Lake of Meroe, the Pyramids, and her excavated sepulchers remain as testimonials of her greatness. Greece, Rome, and the early Germanic Empire have all left their mark upon succeeding ages by real work that was done in

them and the skill which their artificers possessed.

And so it is with *us*. The value of labor and its productions is daily becoming more felt and hourly receiving a wider acknowledgment. Though we have few conquests of arms to boast of and no graves of mighty dead to revere — save one, and that we have too little patriotism to buy at once — though we have no long line of ancestral greatness to look back to; yet we have educated labor to be proud of, and skilled work that is winning for America a name among the nations of the world of more value to real progress than conquest, shrines, or ancestry. Americans, by their mechanical skill, are contesting in the glorious field of the liberal arts and are gaining peaceful victories on the continent of Europe of more importance to the world than Austerlitz or Waterloo. Reaping machines are greater civilizers than swords and Yankee unpickable locks greater securities to property than jails or gallows. We are led to these observations by the number of patents which our countrymen are continually securing in foreign countries — a number which is daily on the increase; and a few important ones recently secured in England through the Scientific American Patent Agency, we will now proceed to notice.

Stephen D. Carpenter, of Madison, Wis., has patented an improvement in operating railway brakes by electromagnets. The mechanism employed is rendered very simple, and facility is afforded for graduating the pressure of the brakes upon the wheels. The brakes are attached to horizontal bars placed before and behind the wheels, and are suspended from centers above the wheels. Electromagnets are adapted to the brake bars by means of links and screw bolts, so as to admit of adjustment when required. The electromagnets are supported in a horizontal position by means of pendant springs or arms, which will allow them to move a sufficient distance in a horizontal direction to bring the brakes against the peripheries of the wheels. The electromagnets are connected by means of suitable wires with a battery, and when the circuit is closed, they will be attracted toward each other, and will then draw up the brakes against the wheels and retard the carriages.

William Clemson, of East Woburn, Mass., has patented an improved method of grinding circular saws. The object of this invention is to grind these articles to a uniform thickness, and with their faces perfectly even or free from the wavy appearance so frequently produced by some of the methods of grinding generally practised, and to finish them perfectly from the center or eye. One of the improvements consists in grinding one side of a saw at a time, while its opposite side is supported by a roll, which has a rotary motion at the requisite speed for the purpose of causing the saw to rotate at the speed desired.

Another improvement consists in the employment of a rotating clamp applied to the saw during the grinding process in such a manner, that it derives rotary motion from the saw through the agency of friction, and by the momentum acquired by such rotary motion is caused to control and render uniform, or nearly so, the velocity of the rotation of the saw, notwithstanding any differences of thickness of the sawplate, and consequent tendency to variation in the action of the feed roll or other feeding contrivance upon the thicker and thinner portions of the plate. The spindle which carries the saw is, together with the friction clamp, mounted in a movable or traveling frame, whereby the saw may be moved up to the grinding surface as the grinding operation proceeds. The saw is also arranged to rotate in and during the grinding process upon a flat pivot, which is of sufficient width in one direction to fill the eye of the saw and steady the saw as it rotates, and is thin enough in a transverse direction to permit the grindstone to operate over the whole surface of the saw. . . .

Martial Dimock, of Mansfield Center, Conn., has patented an improvement in sewing machines, relating especially to that class in which a needle with an eye near the point is used to carry a thread through the cloth to be sewed, whether one or two threads be employed. This part of the invention consists in the employment of a pair of elastic nippers applied on the opposite side of the cloth or material to that on which the needle enters it, and operating in combination with the needle to seize the thread as it is protruded through the cloth and draw it away from the needle in such a direction and to such a distance as to leave plenty of room for the passage, between it and the needle, of the looper, shuttle, or other contrivance operating in combination with the needle to effect the enchaining of the single thread or the interlacing of the two threads, thereby preventing the failure of the looper, shuttle, or equivalent to enter the loop, and the consequent missing or dropping of stitches. A second part of the invention consists in a looper, of novel description, operating in combination with a needle having an eye near the point to sew with a single thread in what is known as the chain and tambour stitch.

Messrs. Lindsay and Geddes, of Westville, Conn., have obtained a patent for some improvements in the machinery employed in the manufacture of paper. The invention is: In making the "lip" or basin which conducts the pulp from the vat to the endless wire apron of two parts, and in connecting these parts with the "deckles," which, as well as the "deckle straps," are by a novel mechanism rendered susceptible of lateral adjustment. The "deckles" determine the width of the pulp on the endless wire apron and consequently also that of the paper, and as the two parts of the "lip" or basin which conducts the pulp to the apron are connected to the "deckles," one to each, the said two parts of the "lip" or basin will be moved simultaneously with the "deckles," and consequently the "lip" or basin will expand or contract in width, so as to correspond with the width or space between the "deckles." The machine is also provided with a novel way of adjusting the usual gauge employed for the even distribution of the pulp on the endless wire apron.

Such inventions as these, useful and new, are the best means we can adopt to keep our place in the ranks of the nations; and we hope that our citizens will ever be sending their improvements across the sea.

17.

CARL SCHURZ: True Americanism

German-born Carl Schurz came to America in 1852 and within a very few years had become active in American politics, in which he had a long and notable career. By 1859 he had become a leading member of the Republican Party in the North and was called upon for frequent campaigning in its behalf. It was during a senatorial campaign in Massachusetts that Schurz gave one of his most famous speeches, "True Americanism," on April 18, 1859. The issue on which he spoke was a proposal before the state legislature to deny the ballot to foreign-born citizens until two years after naturalization. Schurz's speech, reprinted below, was instrumental in defeating the proposal.

Source: *Speeches, Correspondence and Political Papers of Carl Schurz,* Frederic Bancroft, ed., New York, 1913, Vol. I, pp. 48-72.

A FEW DAYS AGO I stood on the cupola of your Statehouse and overlooked for the first time this venerable city and the country surrounding it. Then the streets and hills and waters around me began to teem with the life of historical recollections, recollections dear to all mankind, and a feeling of pride arose in my heart, and I said to myself, I, too, am an American citizen. There was Bunker Hill; there Charlestown, Lexington, and Dorchester Heights not far off; there the harbor into which the British tea was sunk; there the place where the old liberty tree stood; there John Hancock's house; there Benjamin Franklin's birthplace. And now I stand in this grand old hall, which so often resounded with the noblest appeals that ever thrilled American hearts, and where I am almost afraid to hear the echo of my own feeble voice. Oh, sir, no man that loves liberty, wherever he may have first seen the light of day, can fail on this sacred spot to pay his tribute to Americanism. And here, with all these glorious memories crowding upon my heart, I will offer mine. I, born in a foreign land, pay my tribute to Americanism? Yes, for to me the word "Americanism," *true* "Americanism," comprehends the noblest ideas which ever swelled a human heart with noble pride.

It is one of the earliest recollections of my boyhood that one summer night our whole village was stirred up by an uncommon occurrence. I say our village, for I was born not far from that beautiful spot where the Rhine rolls his green waters out of the wonderful gate of the Seven Mountains and then meanders with majestic tranquillity through one of the most glorious valleys of the world. That night our neighbors were pressing around a few wagons covered with linen sheets and loaded with household utensils and boxes and trunks to their utmost capacity. One of our neighboring families was moving far away across a great water, and it was said that they would never again return. And I saw silent tears trickling down weather-beaten cheeks, and the hands of rough peasants firmly pressing each other, and some of the men and women hardly able to speak when they nodded to one another a last farewell. At last the train started into motion, they gave three cheers for *America*, and then in the first gray dawn of the morning I saw them wending their way over the hill until they disappeared in the shadow of the forest. And I heard many a man say how happy he would be if he could go with them to that great and free country where a man could be himself.

That was the first time that I heard of America, and my childish imagination took possession of a land covered partly with majestic trees, partly with flowery prairies, immeasurable to the eye, and intersected with large rivers and broad lakes — a land where everybody could do what he thought best, and where nobody need be poor because everybody was free.

And later, when I was old enough to read, and descriptions of this country and books on American history fell into my hands, the offspring of my imagination acquired the colors of reality and I began to exercise my brain with the thought of what man might be and become when left perfectly free to himself. And still later, when ripening into manhood, I looked up from my school books into the stir and bustle of the world, and the trumpet tones of struggling humanity struck my ear and thrilled my heart, and I saw my nation shake her chains in order to burst them, and I heard a gigantic, universal shout for liberty rising up to the skies; and, at last, after having struggled manfully and drenched the earth of fatherland with the blood of thousands of noble beings, I saw that nation crushed down again, not only by overwhelming armies but by the deadweight of customs and institutions and notions and prejudices which past centuries had heaped upon them, and which a moment of enthusiasm, however sublime, could not destroy; then I consoled an almost despondent heart with the idea of a youthful people and of original institutions clearing the way for an untrammeled development of the ideal nature of man. Then I turned my eyes instinctively across the Atlantic Ocean; and America and Americanism, as I fancied them, appeared to me as the last depositories of the hopes of all true friends of humanity.

I say all this, not as though I indulged in the presumptuous delusion that my personal feelings and experience would be of any interest to you but in order to show you what America is to the thousands of thinking men in the Old World who, disappointed in their fondest hopes and depressed by the saddest experience, cling with their last remnant of confidence in human nature to the last spot on earth where man is free to follow the road to attainable perfection, and where, unbiased by the disastrous influence of traditional notions, customs, and institutions, he acts on his own responsibility. They ask themselves: Was it but a wild delusion when we thought that man has the faculty to be free and to govern himself? Have we been fighting, were we ready to die for a mere phantom, for a mere product of a morbid imagination? This question downtrodden humanity cries out into the world, and from this country it expects an answer.

As its advocate I speak to you. I will speak of Americanism as the great representative of the reformatory age, as the great champion of the dignity of human nature, as the great repository of the last hopes of suffering mankind. I will speak of the ideal mission of this country and of this people. . . .

The Anglo-Saxon may justly be proud of the growth and development of this country, and if he ascribes most of it to the undaunted spirit of his race, we may not accuse him of overweening self-glorification. He possesses, in an eminent degree, the enviable talent of acting when others only think; of promptly executing his own ideas and of appropriating the ideas of other people to his own use. There is, perhaps, no other race that at so early a day would have founded the stern democracy of the Plymouth settlement; no other race that would have defied the trials and hardships of the original settler's life so victoriously. No other race, perhaps, possesses in so high a degree, not only the daring spirit of independent enterprise but at the same time the stubborn steadfastness necessary to the final execution of great designs. The Anglo-Saxon spirit has been the locomotive of

progress; but do not forget that this locomotive would be of little use to the world if it refused to draw its train over the iron highway and carry its valuable freight toward its destination. That train consists of the vigorous elements of all nations; that freight is the vital ideas of our age; that destination is universal freedom and the ideal development of man. That is the true greatness of the Anglo-Saxon race; that ought to be the source of Anglo-Saxon pride. I esteem the son who is proud of his father, if at the same time he is worthy of him.

Thus, I say, was founded the colony of free humanity on virgin soil. The youthful elements which constitute people of the New World cannot submit to rules which are not of their own making; they must throw off the fetters which bind them to an old, decrepit order of things. They resolve to enter the great family of nations as an independent member. And in the colony of free humanity, whose mother country is the world, they establish *the republic of equal rights, where the title of manhood is the title to citizenship.* My friends, if I had a thousand tongues and a voice strong as the thunder of heaven, they would not be sufficient to impress upon your minds forcibly enough the greatness of this idea, the overshadowing glory of this result. This was the dream of the truest friends of man from the beginning; for this the noblest blood of martyrs has been shed; for this has mankind waded through seas of blood and tears. There it is now; there it stands, the noble fabric in all the splendor of reality.

They speak of the greatness of the Roman Republic! Oh, sir, if I could call the proudest of Romans from his grave, I would take him by the hand and say to him, Look at this picture, and at this! The greatness of thy Roman Republic consisted in its despotic rule over the world; the greatness of the American Republic consists in the secured right of man to govern himself. The dignity of the Roman citizen consisted in his exclusive privileges; the dignity of the American citizen consists in his holding the natural rights of his neighbor just as sacred as his own. The Roman Republic recognized and protected the *rights of the citizen,* at the same time disregarding and leaving unprotected the *rights of man;* Roman citizenship was founded upon monopoly, not upon the claims of human nature. What the citizen of Rome claimed for himself, he did not respect in others; his own greatness was his only object; his own liberty, as he regarded it, gave him the privilege to oppress his fellow beings. His democracy, instead of elevating mankind to his own level, trampled the rights of man into the dust. The security of the Roman Republic, therefore, consisted in the power of the sword; the security of the American Republic rests in the equality of human rights! The Roman Republic perished by the sword; the American Republic will stand as long as the equality of human rights remains inviolate. Which of the two republics is the greater — the republic of the Roman or the republic of *man?*

Sir, I wish the words of the Declaration of Independence, "that all men are created free and equal, and are endowed with certain inalienable rights," were inscribed upon every gatepost within the limits of this republic. From this principle the revolutionary fathers derived their claim to independence; upon this they founded the institutions of this country; and the whole structure was to be the living incarnation of this idea. This principle contains the program of our political existence. It is the most progressive and at the same time the most conservative one; the most progressive, for it takes even the lowliest members of the human family out of their degradation and inspires them with the elevating consciousness of equal human dignity; the most conservative, for it makes a common cause of individual rights. From the equality of rights springs identity

of our highest interests; you cannot subvert your neighbor's rights without striking a dangerous blow at your own. And when the rights of one cannot be infringed without finding a ready defense in all others who defend their own rights in defending his, then and only then are the rights of all safe against the usurpations of governmental authority.

This general identity of interests is the only thing that can guarantee the stability of democratic institutions. Equality of rights, embodied in general self-government, is the great moral element of true democracy; it is the only reliable safety valve in the machinery of modern society. There is the solid foundation of our system of government; there is our mission; there is our greatness; there is our safety; there and nowhere else! This is true Americanism and to this I pay the tribute of my devotion.

Shall I point out to you the consequences of a deviation from this principle? Look at the slave states. There is a class of men who are deprived of their natural rights. But this is not the only deplorable feature of that peculiar organization of society. Equally deplorable is it that there is another class of men who keep the former in subjection. That there are slaves is bad; but almost worse is it that there are masters. Are not the masters freemen? No, sir! Where is their liberty of the press? Where is their liberty of speech? Where is the man among them who dares to advocate openly principles not in strict accordance with the ruling system? They speak of a republican form of government, they speak of democracy; but the despotic spirit of slavery and mastership combined pervades their whole political life like a liquid poison. They do not dare to be free lest the spirit of liberty become contagious. The system of slavery has enslaved them all, master as well as slave. What is the cause of all this? It is that you cannot deny one class of society the full measure of their natural rights without imposing restraints upon your own liberty. If you want to be free, there is but one way — it is to guarantee an equally full measure of liberty to all your neighbors. There is no other.

True, there are difficulties connected with an organization of society founded upon the basis of equal rights. Nobody denies it. A large number of those who come to you from foreign lands are not as capable of taking part in the administration of government as the man who was fortunate enough to drink the milk of liberty in his cradle. And certain religious denominations do, perhaps, nourish principles which are hardly in accordance with the doctrines of true democracy. There is a conglomeration on this continent of heterogeneous elements; there is a warfare of clashing interest and unruly aspirations; and, with all this, our democratic system gives rights to the ignorant and power to the inexperienced. And the billows of passion will lash the sides of the ship, and the storm of party warfare will bend its masts, and the pusillanimous will cry out — "Master, master, we perish!" But the genius of true democracy will arise from his slumber and rebuke the winds and the raging of the water, and say unto them — "Where is your faith?" Aye, where is the faith that led the fathers of this republic to invite the weary and burdened of all nations to the enjoyment of equal rights? Where is that broad and generous confidence in the efficiency of true democratic institutions? Has the present generation forgotten that true democracy bears in itself the remedy for all the difficulties that may grow out of it?

It is an old dodge of the advocates of despotism throughout the world that the people who are not experienced in self-government are not fit for the exercise of self-government and must first be educated under the rule of a superior authority. But at the same time the advocates of despotism will never offer them an opportunity to acquire experience in self-government lest they suddenly become fit for its independent exercise. To this treacherous sophistry the fathers of this republic opposed the noble doctrine that liberty is the best school for liberty, and that self-government cannot be learned but by practising it. This, sir, is a truly American idea; this is true Americanism; and to this I pay the tribute of my devotion.

You object that some people do not understand their own interests? There is nothing that, in the course of time, will make a man better understand his interests than the independent management of his own affairs on his own responsibility. You object that people are ignorant? There is no better schoolmaster in the world than self-government independently exercised. You object that people have no just idea of their duties as citizens? There is no other source from which they can derive a just notion of their duties than the enjoyment of the rights from which they arise. You object that people are misled by their religious prejudices and by the intrigues of the Roman hierarchy? Since when have the enlightened citizens of this republic lost their faith in the final invincibility of truth? Since when have they forgotten that if the Roman or any other church plants the seed of superstition, liberty sows broadcast the seed of enlightenment? Do they no longer believe in the invincible spirit of inquiry, which characterizes the reformatory age? If the struggle be fair, can the victory be doubtful?

As to religious fanaticism, it will prosper under oppression; it will feed on persecution; it will grow strong by proscription; but it is powerless against genuine democracy. It may indulge in short-lived freaks of passion or in wily intrigues, but it will die of itself, for its lungs are not adapted to breathe the atmosphere of liberty. It is like the shark of the sea: drag him into the air and the monster will perhaps struggle fearfully and frighten timid people with the powerful blows of his tail and the terrible array of his teeth; but leave him quietly to die and he will die. But engage with him in a hand-to-hand struggle even then, and the last of his convulsions may fatally punish your rash attempt. Against fanaticism, genuine democracy wields an irresistible weapon — it is *toleration*. Toleration will not strike down the fanatic but it will quietly and gently disarm him. But fight fanaticism *with* fanaticism and you will restore it to its own congenial element. It is like Antaeus, who gained strength when touching his native earth.

Whoever reads the history of this country calmly and thoroughly cannot but discover that religious liberty is slowly but steadily rooting out the elements of superstition, and even of prejudice. It has dissolved the war of sects, of which persecution was characteristic, into a contest of abstract opinions, which creates convictions without oppressing men. By recognizing perfect freedom of inquiry, it will engender among men of different belief that mutual respect of true convictions which makes inquiry earnest and discussion fair. It will recognize as supremely inviolable what Roger Williams, one of the most luminous stars of the American sky, called the sanctity of conscience. Read your history and add the thousands and thousands of Romanists and their offspring together who, from the first establishment of the colonies, gradually came to this country, and the sum will amount to many millions; compare that number with the number of Romanists who are now here and you will find that millions are missing.

Where are they? You did not kill them; you did not drive them away; they did not perish as the victims of persecution. But where are they? The peaceable working of the great principles which called this republic into existence has gradually and silently absorbed them. True Americanism, toleration, the equality of rights has absorbed

their prejudices and will peaceably absorb everything that is not consistent with the victorious spirit of our institutions.

Oh, sir, there is a wonderful vitality in true democracy founded upon the equality of rights. There is an inexhaustible power of resistance in that system of government which makes the protection of individual rights a matter of common interest. If preserved in its purity there is no warfare of opinions which can endanger it — there is no conspiracy of despotic aspirations that can destroy it. But if not preserved in its purity — there are dangers which only blindness cannot see and which only stubborn party prejudice will not see.

I have already called your attention to the despotic tendency of the slaveholding system. I need not enlarge upon it; I need not describe how the existence of slavery in the South affected and demoralized even the political life of the free states; how they attempted to press us, you and me, into the posse of the slave catcher by that abominable act which, worse than the Alien and Sedition Laws, still disgraces our statute book; how the ruling party, which has devoted itself to the service of that despotic interest, shrinks from no violation of good faith, from no adulteration of the constitutional compact, from no encroachment upon natural right, from no treacherous abandonment of fundamental principles. And I do not hesitate to prophesy that, if the theories engendered by the institution of slavery be suffered to outgrow the equalizing tendency of true democracy, the American Republic will, at no distant day, crumble down under the burden of the laws and measures which the ruling interest will demand for its protection, and its name will be added to the sad catalogue of the broken hopes of humanity.

But the mischief does not come from that side alone; it is in things of small beginnings, but fearful in their growth. One of these is the propensity of men *to lose sight of fundamental principles when passing abuses are to be corrected.*

Is it not wonderful how nations who have won their liberty by the severest struggles become so easily impatient of the small inconveniences and passing difficulties which are almost inseparably connected with the practical working of general self-government? How they so easily forget that rights may be abused and yet remain inalienable rights? Europe has witnessed many an attempt for the establishment of democratic institutions; some of them were at first successful and the people were free, but the abuses and inconveniences connected with liberty became at once apparent. Then the ruling classes of society, in order to get rid of the abuses, restricted liberty; they did, indeed, get rid of the abuses but they got rid of liberty at the same time. You heard liberal governments there speak of protecting and regulating the liberty of the press; and in order to prevent that liberty from being abused they adopted measures, apparently harmless at first, which ultimately resulted in an absolute censorship. Would it be much better if we, recognizing the right of man to the exercise of self-government, should, in order to protect the purity of the ballot box, restrict the right of suffrage?

Liberty, sir, is like a spirited housewife; she will have her whims, she will be somewhat unruly sometimes, and, like so many husbands, you cannot always have it all your own way. She may spoil your favorite dish sometimes; but will you, therefore, at once smash her china, break her kettles, and shut her out from the kitchen? Let her practise, let her try again and again, and even when she makes a mistake encourage her with a benignant smile and your broth will be right after a while. But meddle with her concerns, tease her, bore her, and your little squabbles, spirited as she is, will ulti-

mately result in a divorce. What then? It is one of Jefferson's wisest words that "he would much rather be exposed to the inconveniences arising from too much liberty than to those arising from too small a degree of it." It is a matter of historical experience that nothing that is wrong in principle can be right in practice. People are apt to delude themselves on that point; but the ultimate result will always prove the truth of the maxim. A violation of equal rights can never serve to maintain institutions which are founded upon equal rights. A contrary policy is not only pusillanimous and small but it is senseless. It reminds me of the soldier who, for fear of being shot in battle, committed suicide on the march; or of the man who would cut off his foot because he had a corn on his toe. It is that ridiculous policy of premature despair which commences to throw the freight overboard when there is a suspicious cloud in the sky.

Another danger for the safety of our institutions, and perhaps the most formidable one, arises from the general propensity of political parties and public men to act on a policy of mere expediency and to sacrifice principle to local and temporary success. And here, sir, let me address a solemn appeal to the consciences of those with whom I am proud to struggle side by side against human thralldom.

You hate kingcraft, and you would sacrifice your fortunes and your lives in order to prevent its establishment on the soil of this republic. But let me tell you that the rule of political parties which sacrifice principle to expediency is no less dangerous, no less disastrous, no less aggressive, of no less despotic a nature than the rule of monarchs. Do not indulge in the delusion that in order to make a government fair and liberal the only thing necessary is to make it elective. When a political party in power, however liberal their principles may be, have once adopted the policy of knocking down their opponents instead of voting them down, there is an end of justice and equal rights. . . .

Remember the shout of indignation that went all over the Northern states when we heard that the border ruffians of Kansas had crowded the free-state men away from the polls and had not allowed them to vote. That indignation was just, not only because the men thus terrorized were free-state men and friends of liberty but because they were deprived of their right of suffrage and because the government of that territory was placed on the basis of force instead of equal rights. Sir, if ever the party of liberty should use their local predominance for the purpose of disarming their opponents instead of convincing them, they will but follow the example set by the ruffians of Kansas, although legislative enactments may be a genteeler weapon than the revolver and Bowie knife. They may perhaps achieve some petty local success, they may gain some small, temporary advantage, but they will help to introduce a system of action into our politics which will gradually undermine the very foundations upon which our republican edifice rests.

Of all the dangers and difficulties that beset us, there is none more horrible than the hideous monster whose name is "Proscription for opinion's sake." I am an antislavery man, and I have a right to my opinion in South Carolina just as well as in Massachusetts. My neighbor is a pro-slavery man; I may be sorry for it, but I solemnly acknowledge his right to his opinion in Massachusetts as well as in South Carolina. You tell me that for my opinion they would mob me in South Carolina? Sir, there is the difference between South Carolina and Massachusetts. There is the difference between an antislavery man, who is a freeman, and a slaveholder, who is himself a slave.

Our present issues will pass away. The slavery question will be settled, liberty will be triumphant, and other matters of difference will divide the political parties of this country. What if we, in our struggle against slavery, had removed the solid basis of equal rights on which such new matters of difference may be peaceably settled? What if we had based the institutions of this country upon a difference of rights between different classes of people? What if, in destroying the generality of natural rights, we had resolved them into privileges? There is a thing which stands above the command of the most ingenious of politicians: *it is the logic of things and events*. It cannot be turned and twisted by artificial arrangements and delusive settlements; it will go its own way with the steady step of fate. It will force you, with uncompromising severity, to choose between two social organizations, one of which is founded upon privilege and the other upon the doctrine of equal rights.

Force instead of right, privilege instead of equality, expediency instead of principle being once the leading motives of your policy, you will have no power to stem the current. There will be new abuses to be corrected, new inconveniences to be remedied, new supposed dangers to be obviated, new equally exacting ends to be subserved; and your encroachments upon the natural rights of your opponents now will be used as welcome precedents for the mutual oppression of parties then. Having once knowingly disregarded the doctrine of equal rights, the ruling parties will soon accustom themselves to consult only their interests where fundamental principles are at stake. Those who lead us into this channel will be like the sorcerer who knew the art of making a giant snake. And when he had made it, he forgot the charmword that would destroy it again. And the giant snake threw its horrid coils around him, and the unfortunate man was choked by the monster of his own creation.

On the evening of Nov. 2, 1855, there

stood on this very platform a man known and loved by every true son of Massachusetts, who, unmoved by the whirlwind of proscriptive movement howling around him, spoke the following words:

It is proposed to attaint men for their religion and also for their birth. If this object can prevail, vain are the triumphs of civil freedom in its many hard-fought fields; vain is that religious toleration which we all profess. The fires of Smithfield, the tortures of the Inquisition, the proscription of the Nonconformists may all be revived. Slowly among the struggling sects was evolved the great idea of the equality of all men before the law, without regard to religious belief; nor can any party now organize a proscription merely for religious (and I may add political) belief without calling in question this unquestionable principle.

The man who said so was Charles Sumner. Then the day was not far off when suddenly the whole country was startled by the incredible news that his noble head had drooped under the murderous blows of a Southern fanatic and that his warm blood had covered the floor of the Senate chamber, the noblest sprinkling that ever fertilized a barren soil. And now I tell you, when he lay on the lounge of the antechamber, his anxious friends busy around him and his cowardly murderers slinking away like Cain — if at that solemn moment the first question addressed to his slowly returning senses had been — Shall those who support your dastardly assailants with their votes be deprived of their suffrage? — he would have raised his bleeding head and, with the fire of indignation kindling in his dim eye, he would have answered: "No! In the name of my country, no! For the honor of Massachusetts, no! For the sake of the principles for which my blood is flowing, no! Let them kill me, but let the rights of man be safe!"

Sir, if you want to bestow a high praise upon a man you are apt to say he is an old Roman. But I know a higher epithet of praise; it is — He is a true American! Aye, Charles Sumner is a true American; he is a representative of the truest Americanism, and to him I pay the tribute of my enthusiastic admiration.

Sir, I am coming to the close of my remarks. But I cannot refrain from alluding to a circumstance which concerns myself. I understand it has been said that in speaking a few words on the principles of Jeffersonian democracy a few evenings since, I had attempted to interfere with the home affairs of this state and to dictate to the Republicans their policy. Ah, sir, is there a man in Massachusetts, except he be a servant of the slave power, who cannot hear me advocate the equal rights of man without feeling serious pangs of conscience? Is there a son of this glorious old Commonwealth who cannot hear me draw logical conclusions from the Declaration of Independence, who cannot hear me speak of the natural right of men to the exercise of self-government without feeling a blush fluttering upon his cheeks? If so, sir, I am sorry for him; it is his fault, not mine.

Interfere with your local matters! How could I? What influence could I, a humble stranger among you, exercise on the action of Massachusetts? But one thing I must tell you. It ought never to be forgotten that this old Commonwealth occupies a representative position. Her history is familiar to the nation; even South Carolina knows it. The nation is so accustomed to admire her glorious deed for freedom that with this expectation their eyes are turned upon her. Massachusetts can do nothing in secret; Massachusetts can do nothing for herself alone; every one of her acts involves a hundredfold responsibility. What Massachusetts does is felt from the Atlantic to the Pacific. But Massachusetts need only be herself in order to be great. This is her position among the free states, recognized by all. Can there be a more honorable one? Sons of Massachusetts, you may be proud of it. Do not forget that from her greatness you cannot separate your responsibility.

No, I will not meddle with your home concerns. I will, however, say a word for the West. Strenuous advocate of individual rights and of local self-government as I am, if you ever hear of any movement in the West against the integrity of the fundamental principles underlying our system of government, I invite you, I entreat you, I conjure you, come one and all, and make our prairies resound and our forests shake and our ears ring and tingle with your appeals for the equal rights of man.

Sir, I was to speak on republicanism at the West, and so I did. This *is* Western republicanism. These are its principles, and I am proud to say its principles are its policy. These are the ideas which have rallied around the banner of liberty, not only the natives of the soil but an innumerable host of Germans, Scandinavians, Scotchmen, Frenchmen, and a goodly number of Irishmen, also. And here I tell you, those are mistaken who believe that the Irish heart is devoid of those noble impulses which will lead him to the side of justice, where he sees his own rights respected and unendangered.

Under this banner all the languages of civilized mankind are spoken, every creed is protected, every right is sacred. There stands every element of Western society, with enthusiasm for a great cause, with confidence in each other, with honor to themselves. This is the banner floating over the glorious valley which stretches from the western slope of the Alleghenies to the Rocky Mountains — that Valley of Jehoshaphat where the nations of the world assemble to celebrate the resurrection of human freedom. The inscription on that banner is not "Opposition to the Democratic Party for the sake of placing a new set of men into office"; for this battle cry of speculators our hearts have no response. Nor is it "restriction of slavery and restriction of the right of suffrage," for this — believe my words, I entreat you — this would be the signal of deserved, inevitable, and disgraceful defeat. But the inscription is "Liberty and equal rights, common to all as the air of heaven — liberty and equal rights, one and inseparable!"

With this banner we stand before the world. In this sign — in this sign alone, and no other — there is victory. And thus, sir, we mean to realize the great cosmopolitan idea upon which the existence of the American nation rests. Thus we mean to fulfill the great mission of true Americanism, thus we mean to answer the anxious question of downtrodden humanity: "Has *man* the faculty to be free and to govern himself?" The answer is a triumphant "Aye," thundering into the ears of the despots of the Old World that "a man is a man for all that"; proclaiming to the oppressed that they are held in subjection on false pretenses; cheering the hearts of the despondent friends of man with consolation and renewed confidence.

This is true Americanism, clasping mankind to its great heart. Under its banner we march; let the world follow.

I went to the store the other day to buy a bolt for our front door, for as I told the storekeeper, the governor was coming here. "Aye," said he, "and the legislature too." "Then I will take two bolts," said I. He said that there had been a steady demand for bolts and locks of late, for our protectors were coming.

HENRY DAVID THOREAU, *Journal*, Sept. 8, 1859

18.

Nullification in the North

The doctrines of states' rights and nullification were not confined to the South. During the 1850s there was widespread Northern hostility to the Fugitive Slave Law. State policies made enforcement of the law practically impossible, much to the consternation of the slaveholding states. One series of incidents brought Wisconsin to a position of extreme state sovereignty in 1859 that could, with little provocation, have led her to secede from the Union. Sherman M. Booth, editor of the Wisconsin Free Democrat, *was arrested in 1854 and charged with violating the Fugitive Slave Law. He was released by a judge of the state supreme court on a writ of habeas corpus on the ground that the federal law was "unconstitutional and void." Booth was then tried and convicted in a federal court, resulting in much unrest and agitation throughout the state. Again the state supreme court released him. But Chief Justice Roger B. Taney obtained jurisdiction in the case, and in 1859 the U.S. Supreme Court reversed the state court's decision and Booth was rearrested; he was finally pardoned in 1861 by President Buchanan. Out of those events came a personal liberty law in Wisconsin in 1857 and a resolution of protest by the legislature in defiance of the U.S. Supreme Court. The protest, adopted March 19, 1859, is reprinted below.*

Source: *General Laws Passed by the Legislature of Wisconsin, in the Year 1859,* Madison, 1859, pp. 247-248.

Joint resolution relative to the decision of the United States Supreme Court, reversing decision of the Supreme Court of Wisconsin.

Whereas, the Supreme Court of the United States has assumed appellate jurisdiction in the matter of the petition of Sherman M. Booth for a writ of habeas corpus, presented and prosecuted to final judgment in the Supreme Court of this state, and has, without process or any of the forms recognized by law, assumed the power to reverse that judgment in a matter involving the personal liberty of the citizen, asserted by and adjusted to him by the regular course of judicial proceedings upon the great writ of liberty secured to the people of each state by the Constitution of the United States;

And whereas, such assumption of power and authority by the Supreme Court of the United States to become the final arbiter of the liberty of the citizen and to override and nullify the judgments of the state courts, declaration thereof is in direct conflict with that provision of the Constitution of the United States which secures to the people the benefits of the writ of habeas corpus; therefore,

Resolved, the Senate concurring, that we regard the action of the Supreme Court of the United States, in assuming jurisdiction in the case before mentioned, as an arbitrary act of power, unauthorized by the Constitution, and virtually superseding the benefit of the writ of habeas corpus, and prostrating the rights and liberties of the people at the foot of unlimited power.

Resolved, that this assumption of jurisdiction by the federal judiciary in the said case, and without process, is an act of undelegated power, and therefore without authority, void, and of no force.

Resolved, that the government formed by the Constitution of the United States was not made the exclusive or final judge of the extent of the powers delegated to itself; but that, as in all other cases of compact among parties having no common judge, each party has an equal right to judge for itself, as well of infractions as of the mode and measure of redress.

Resolved, that the principle and construction contended for by the party which now rules in the councils of the nation, that the general government is the exclusive judge of the extent of the powers delegated to it, stop nothing short of despotism, since the *discretion* of those who administer the government and not the *Constitution* would be the measure of their powers; that the several states which formed that instrument, being sovereign and independent, have the unquestionable right to judge of its infraction; and that a *positive defiance* of those sovereignties, of all unauthorized acts done or attempted to be done under color of that instrument, is the rightful remedy.

19.

Louis Antoine Godey: How To Be the Perfect Housewife

Godey's Lady's Book, founded by Louis Antoine Godey in 1830, was the first American magazine for women. In a statement of editorial policy, the magazine promised that "no story shall ever be published in the book that may not be read aloud in the family circle. . . . In vain may you look . . . for an impure thought or a profane word. . . ." The magazine dealt with manners, fashion, and edifying pursuits for women in an age when propriety was as much a concern as morality. The following article appeared in an 1859 issue.

Source: *Godey's Lady's Book and Magazine,* March 1859.

HAVING BEFORE SUGGESTED what is or should be the position of a wife, let us next consider her province as a housewife. The honeymoon is over. The seaside has been bidden adieu; the wife enters the new home of which she is the *chatelaine* — the mistress. She has received her visits of ceremonious gratulation and is left, at length, to look around her dominion and frame the laws by which she intends to govern.

What is her first duty?

To ascertain her husband's income, its resources, its limits, the amount beyond which she cannot pass without entailing ruin upon him and misery on herself. She must satisfy herself upon this head accurately, that by no unwise expenditure she may be induced to exceed the sum he can afford for domestic purposes; for, by a wise direction, she may be enabled to make the means she can apply produce comforts and the semblance, if not the realities, of luxuries; but by a careless or ignorant extravagance, the inconveniences as well as the wretchedness of embarrassed circumstances must inevitably be the portion of both.

Having done this, knowing the sum she may claim exclusively for household purposes without endangering the future, the young wife will then proceed to apply those lessons in domestic economy which she may have received in the earlier portion of her life, fitting her for the duties of the station she now fills.

But, alas! she has had no direction — no counsel — no lessons in household economy; she is at a loss what to do, save that she has a cook and housemaid; the first knows very well how to send up the meals, the other to keep the house clean, make the beds, and wait at table — else why are they there? Very true; but it is no less essential that the mistress of the household should be also acquainted with their duties that she may be enabled to know whether they properly perform them and that they are not the vehicles of wasteful carelessness. It will not be here out of place to give a few directions upon the management of servants.

It is a certain fact that servants are like soldiers in a field of battle: upon them depend the success of well-ordered arrangements. It is useless to expect regularity or good management if the orders are not properly executed, and, therefore, it becomes important to exercise the utmost care in taking any person into the family as a domestic. The character should undergo a strict investigation, and none but those who bear a certificate of industry, cleanliness, capability of fulfilling their situation, and early rising — the last indispensable — should be retained.

The servants having been chosen, and well chosen, rather for their knowledge in the strict and economical performance of their duties — it will be understood that these remarks apply to one servant as to five, or ten, or more — the next thing will be to see that the kitchen is properly provided: while there should be enough, there should not be more than enough. Where two or three articles may be used for the same purpose, it is almost a temptation for carelessness and laziness in their employment, fostering dirt and breakage; therefore, have sufficient, and no more.

It may be expected that one week will occasionally exceed the expenditure of the preceding, as one day will that of another; but whenever this occurs, the following week must make it good, the balance must be restored, or there will be no possibility of preserving the limit at the close of the year. It must be a matter of understanding between the husband and wife that while he appropriates a sum of money for household expenditure which he does not desire to be exceeded, a sum which will not admit of prodigality but will insure comfort and rescue his table from an appearance of meanness, he must not burden it unfairly — he must not invite friends and companions and expect them to be as well treated as himself, and yet presume that it is all to come out of the housekeeping money. It cannot be done; he must, therefore, if he cannot do without company, so increase the income allotted by him to the management of the household as shall enable his lady to meet his views and leave her frugality unembarrassed.

The amount once in the possession of the young housewife, whether it be $10, $15, or $25 weekly, or $60 or $100 monthly, let her take every care of it and devote it *only* to the purpose for which it is given; let no inducement cause her to appropriate it to any other use, neither for private wants of her own nor the pecuniary embarrassments of others. If she can create a convertible balance, all well and good, but she must not, on any account, break into sums which must be held sacred for special purposes. It is, perhaps, the best plan to have, with the grocer, the baker, the butcher, the fishmonger, and poulterer, butter and cheesemonger, weekly bills to be paid every Monday morning without fail; for all other articles, ready money should be paid; it enables goods to be of the best kind, at reasonable rates; it gives satisfaction, it commands attention, and secures independence in dealing.

We have now fairly commenced with

you, gentle young housekeeper. We have advised you upon your income, in your choice of a servant, your kitchen furniture, and your expenditures; and now we shall proceed with you in the economy and the etiquette of your household.

You will know how you can afford to live by the amount of your income; you will know that your husband cannot expect to live beyond the amount which he has allowed you to keep his house with; but it must be your ambition to know how to make the best appearance; with small means to appear — without improper assumption — richer than you are, or at least quite as rich as you are, and this may be done by means very simple in themselves, but yet very telling in appearance — two or three extra side dishes upon the table, a good dinner, deliciously white table linen, brightly polished glass, and well-made knives and forks, with a neat little sideboard, upon which everything necessary may be seen, create an appearance of a superior income, if well managed; and while it is only proper that this style should be preserved, yet its advantages make it incumbent for it not to be overlooked; even at a *tête-à-tête* dinner with your husband, there is an air of clean comfort about it, while your own good looks, kind words, and tender smiles make him feel that he cannot by friendship or purchase obtain the felicity elsewhere he meets with at home.

It will be as well to observe that the greatest regularity and punctuality should be preserved; at the hour named, dinner should be upon the table. You will make your arrangements with your cook to that effect, and she must so lay out her time that, at the hour appointed, she should serve up the meal. There is something very agreeable in having the dinner on the table the moment it is expected; the union between good temper and a good dinner amounts to a proverb; the marring or the pleasure of an evening may frequently be traced to as simple a cause as this.

The direction of the table is especially the province of the lady, for it involves not only her judgment in expenditure, a respectability of appearance, but the comfort of her husband and those who may have a seat at her table. . . .

Should you, in presiding over the table, be called upon to carve, as you possibly will be, be provided with a carving knife, light, of middling size and fine edge. Strength is not required in its use, but a knowledge of your joint, and where to cut with ease, address, and satisfaction to those to be helped.

Thus, before a joint leaves the butcher, he should have strict orders to "joint it" effectually and well; this will enable you in carving neck, breast, or loin to do so neatly. The more fleshy joints, as fillet of veal, leg, or saddle of mutton, and beef, you should help in thin slices, neatly and smoothly cut. In the mutton and beef joints, let the knife pass down to the bone. Do not let your dish be too far from you; it makes your task more difficult and appears awkward. Help the best portions as fairly as you can. In helping fish, do not break the flakes, which in cod and fresh salmon are large and contribute much to the fineness of their appearance. A fish knife should be used, as it is blunt and divides it in a better fashion.

In carving wild fowl, duck, goose, or turkey for a party, if you cut the slices down from pinion to pinion without mauling, there will be more prime pieces.

In directing and arranging the meals, the economy of time, a very important consideration, is involved. An early breakfast is especially necessary, for, that being over and cleared away, time, always valuable in the morning, is obtained to design and perfect the day's arrangements.

All orders should be given as early as possible; time is allowed to execute them, and with plenty of this valuable commodity at command, they are performed with ease, while little or no excuse is afforded for not doing them well.

(Top) John Brown's wife and daughters; (bottom) Jefferson Davis' children

PREWAR PROMISE

During the last years before the Civil War, as the country recovered rapidly from the Panic of 1857, there was a general air of material well-being that contrasted sharply with the loud and violent politics of the time. This prosperity was reflected both in growing comfort and leisure and in pressure from labor for a more equitable share. The pattern of conflict between business, growing in power, and labor, growing in numbers and self-consciousness, was already in evidence in the late 1850s.

In the South, belief in the established way of life was firm. Efforts by moderates to demonstrate slavery's limited usefulness in the new territories was more than matched by the extremist's visions of a new Southern empire expanding into Mexico and beyond. War caught many confident planters with grand new mansions still half-finished.

The Olivier Plantation in 1861; painted by Adrian Pensac

The South had much reason for satisfaction in the 1850s. The Compromise of 1850 appeared to have made a permanent settlement of issues. Unionism defeated secessionism in 1851 in Alabama, South Carolina, and Mississippi. Georgia's Southern Rights Party (1850) accepted the compromise, and the "peculiar institution" seemed secure. The growth of Southern economy was chiefly in the "new South," especially Texas.

(Left) Statue of George Washington in Richmond, Va., designed by Thomas Crawford; photo 1858; (below) Wetumpka Bridge, Alabama

Negro quarters at Drayton's House, Hilton Head, South Carolina, 1862; photo by H. P. Moore

(Left) "Plantation Kitchen"; painted by Samuel B. Palmer, c. 1860; (below) farming in South Carolina

(Above) View on the Or-
ange and Alexandria Rail-
road in Virginia; photo by
Sullivan in 1862

(Right) Presbyterian circuit-
riding preacher in Tonica
Hills, Illinois; ambrotype
dated 1860; (below) horse-
drawn combine used for
harvesting crops in Michigan

The settled life in most parts of the country allowed for a variety of diversions and began to express itself in the images associated with the "good old days": a boy watching a train, the circus in town, a baseball game. In this context it was hard to imagine a cruel and protracted war. But for David Gilmour Blythe repeated failure had tarnished the golden image somewhat. His painted cartoons, done while living in Pittsburgh, show his fellow citizens in a more sardonic light.

Three paintings by David G. Blythe: (Top) "Dry Goods and Millinery"; (right) "Post Office"; (bottom) "Trial Scene"

A baseball match at the Elysian Fields, Hoboken, N.J., 1859; engraving from "Harper's Weekly"

(Above) "The Great Fight for the Championship" between Heenan and Sayers, 1860; (below) "The Celebrated Trotting Stallions, 'Ethan Allen' and 'George M. Patchen' "; Currier and Ives lithographs

Ambrotype of a couple on the Canadian side of Niagara Falls, c. 1860

(Left) Vacationers at the Tip Top House on the top of Mt. Washington; (below) Blondin crossing the Niagara River, 1859

"The Philosopher's Camp in the Adirondacks" (1857), shows members of the Adirondack Club, including Estes Howe, Louis Agassiz, Emerson, James Russell Lowell and E. R. Hoar, on an outing

Interior of the Boston Athenaeum; photograph by Southworth and Hawes, about 1855

Elephant "Hannibal" on Seneca, N.Y., street

(Above) Burning of the New York Crystal Palace, 1858; lithograph by Currier and Ives

(Left) The burning of Cyrus Field's warehouse in New York City, 1859; from a stereograph by Edward Anthony; (below) fire in a southern city, about 1860. One of the earliest photos showing a steam fire engine in operation

Labor had scored numerous gains by 1860. The bitter struggle for shorter hours had resulted in the ten-hour day for federal employees and in most of the Northern states. Fourierism and all the related associationisms had largely disappeared, and labor was fairly well convinced that its future lay in unionism. But such unions, for the first time assuming nationwide scope, were organized on a craft basis, and the unskilled were poorly organized. In 1860, for the first time, a general strike of the entire New England shoe industry, involving 20,000 workers, scored large successes.

(Top) Procession of women operatives participating in the shoemakers strike, Lynn, Mass., 1860; handbill calling on workers to resist a wage cut

NOTICE!

We, the operatives of the several mills of Westerly and vicinity, after mature consideration of the propositions of the employers of the said mills, to increase the *hours of labor*, without a proportionate increase of *wages*, which, if permitted to be consumated, will add one spark to the faintly glimmering hope of these employers, that the old barbarous, but to them, glorious system, of grinding the laboring man into the dust, commonly called days of

"Many Hours and few Pennies," may soon be re-established—do protest against any such measure, as being unjust, uncalled for and tyranical in the extreme—and therefore, as a body, are determined in every possible manner, to resist it at all hazards.

The sympathies and co-operation of all our fellow laborers is earnestly solicited to assist us in this work. Those looking for employment we sincerely hope, will stand aloof from these mills till this matter is settled, and the eleven hour system firmly established.   OPERATIVES.

Westerly, R. I., March 26, 1858.

UNION & FRATERNITY.

Nº 1821?

MECHANICS' UNION ASSOCIATION.

CERTIFICATE OF MEMBERSHIP.

This Certificate of Membership witnesseth, that the "Mechanics' Union Association," In Consideration of the sum of *Five &* 5⁰/100 DOLLARS, to them in hand paid by *Louisa M Mason* of *Cavendish* in the County of *Windsor* State of *Vermont* and of the Annual Payment of *Four* /100 DOLLARS, to be paid on or before the *27th* day of *February*, in every year, DO RECEIVE the said *L. McMason* as an Associate Member for Life

20.

Abraham Lincoln: Labor, Education, and the American Farmer

The Lincoln-Douglas debates of 1858 and the ensuing senatorial contest in Illinois thrust Lincoln into national prominence. By 1859 he was a presidential prospect. He toured several Midwestern states with a politician's eye for votes and for gathering party support from important uncommitted political blocs such as the farmers. On September 30, 1859, Lincoln delivered the following speech before the Wisconsin State Agricultural Society at Milwaukee.

Source: Nicolay-Hay, V: "Annual Address Before the Wisconsin State Agricultural Society, at Milwaukee, Wisconsin, September 30, 1859."

My FIRST SUGGESTION is an inquiry as to the effect of greater thoroughness in all the departments of agriculture than now prevails in the Northwest — perhaps I might say in America. To speak entirely within bounds, it is known that 50 bushels of wheat or 100 bushels of Indian corn can be produced from an acre. Less than a year ago, I saw it stated that a man, by extraordinary care and labor, had produced of wheat what was equal to 200 bushels from an acre. But take 50 of wheat and 100 of corn to be the possibility, and compare it with the actual crops of the country. Many years ago, I saw it stated, in a patent office report, that 18 bushels was the average crop throughout the United States; and this year an intelligent farmer of Illinois assures me that he did not believe the land harvested in that state this season had yielded more than an average of 8 bushels to the acre; much was cut and then abandoned as not worth threshing, and much was abandoned as not worth cutting.

As to Indian corn, and, indeed, most other crops, the case has not been much better.

For the last four years I do not believe the ground planted with corn in Illinois has produced an average of 20 bushels to the acre. It is true that heretofore we have had better crops with no better cultivation, but I believe it is also true that the soil has never been pushed up to one-half of its capacity.

What would be the effect upon the farming interest to push the soil up to something near its full capacity? Unquestionably it will take more labor to produce 50 bushels from an acre than it will to produce 10 bushels from the same acre; but will it take more labor to produce 50 bushels from 1 acre than from 5? Unquestionably, thorough cultivation will require more labor to the acre; but will it require more to the bushel? If it should require just as much to the bushel, there are some probable, and several certain, advantages in favor of the thorough practice. It is probable it would develop those unknown causes which of late years have cut down our crops below their former average.

It is almost certain, I think, that by deeper plowing, analysis of the soils, experiments with manures and varieties of seeds, observance of seasons, and the like, these causes would be discovered and remedied. It is certain that thorough cultivation would spare half, or more than half, the cost of land, simply because the same product would be got from half, or from less than half, the quantity of land. This proposition is self-evident, and can be made no plainer by repetitions or illustrations. The cost of land is a great item, even in new countries, and it constantly grows greater and greater, in comparison with other items, as the country grows older.

It also would spare the making and maintaining of enclosures for the same, whether these enclosures should be hedges, ditches, or fences. This again is a heavy item — heavy at first, and heavy in its continual demand for repairs. I remember once being greatly astonished by an apparently authentic exhibition of the proportion the cost of an enclosure bears to all the other expenses of the farmer, though I cannot remember exactly what that proportion was. Any farmer, if he will, can ascertain it in his own case for himself.

Again, a great amount of locomotion is spared by thorough cultivation. Take 50 bushels of wheat ready for harvest, standing upon a single acre, and it can be harvested in any of the known ways with less than half the labor which would be required if it were spread over 5 acres. This would be true if cut by the old hand sickle; true, to a greater extent, if by the scythe and cradle; and, to a still greater extent, if by the machines now in use. These machines are chiefly valuable as a means of substituting animal power for the power of men in this branch of farmwork. In the highest degree of perfection yet reached in applying the horsepower to harvesting, fully nine-tenths of the power is expended by the animal in carrying himself and dragging the machine over the field, leaving certainly not more than one-tenth to be applied directly to the only end of the whole operation — the gathering in of the grain and clipping of the straw.

When grain is very thin on the ground, it is always more or less intermingled with weeds, chess, and the like; and a large part of the power is expended in cutting these. It is plain that when the crop is very thick upon the ground, a larger proportion of the power is directly applied to gathering in and cutting it; and the smaller to that which is totally useless as an end. And what I have said of harvesting is true in a greater or less degree of mowing, plowing, gathering in of crops generally, and, indeed, of almost all farm work.

The effect of thorough cultivation upon the farmer's own mind, and in reaction through his mind back upon his business, is perhaps quite equal to any other of its effects. Every man is proud of what he does well, and no man is proud to that he does not well. With the former his heart is in his work, and he will do twice as much of it with less fatigue; the latter he performs a little imperfectly, looks at it in disgust, turns from it, and imagines himself exceedingly tired — the little he has done comes to nothing for want of finishing.

The man who produces a good, full crop will scarcely ever let any part of it go to waste; he will keep up the enclosure about it and allow neither man nor beast to trespass upon it; he will gather it in due season and store it in perfect security. Thus he labors with satisfaction and saves himself the whole fruit of his labor. The other, starting with no purpose for a full crop, labors less and with less satisfaction, allows his fences to fall and cattle to trespass, gathers not in due season, or not at all. Thus the labor he has performed is wasted away, little by little, till in the end he derives scarcely anything from it.

The ambition for broad acres leads to poor farming, even with men of energy. I scarcely ever knew a mammoth farm to sustain itself, much less to return a profit upon the outlay. I have more than once known a man to spend a respectable fortune upon one, fail, and leave it; and then some man of modest aim get a small fraction of the ground and makes a good living upon it. Mammoth farms are like tools or weapons which are too heavy to be handled; ere long they are thrown aside at a great loss.

The successful application of steam power to farm work is a desideratum — especially a steam plow. It is not enough that a machine operated by steam will really plow. To be successful, it must, all things considered, plow better than can be done with animal power. It must do all the work as well, and cheaper; or more rapidly, so as to get through more perfectly in season; or in some way afford an advantage over plowing with animals, else it is no success. I have never seen a machine intended for a steam plow. Much praise and admiration are bestowed upon some of them, and they may be, for aught I know, already successful; but I have not perceived the demonstration of it.

I have thought a good deal, in an abstract way, about a steam plow. That one which shall be so contrived as to apply the larger proportion of its power to the cutting and turning of the soil, and the smallest to the moving itself over the field, will be the best one. A very small stationary engine would draw a large gang of plows through the ground from a short distance to itself; but when it is not stationary, but has to move along like a horse, dragging the plows after it, it must have additional power to carry itself; and the difficulty grows by what is intended to overcome it; for what adds power also adds size and weight to the machine, thus increasing again the demand for power.

Suppose you construct the machine so as to cut a succession of short furrows, say a rod in length, transversely to the course the machine is locomoting, something like the shuttle in weaving. In such case the whole machine would move north only the width of a furrow, while in length the furrow would be a rod from east to west. In such case a very large proportion of the power would be applied to the actual plowing. But in this, too, there would be difficulty, which would be the getting of the plow into and out of the ground at the end of all these short furrows.

I believe, however, ingenious men will, if they have not already, overcome the difficulty I have suggested. But there is still another, about which I am less sanguine. It is the supply of fuel, and especially water, to make steam. Such supply is clearly practicable; but can the expense of it be borne? Steamboats live upon the water and find their fuel at stated places. Steam mills and other stationary steam machinery have their stationary supplies of fuel and water. Railroad locomotives have their regular wood and water stations. But the steam plow is less fortunate. It does not live upon the water, and if it be once at a water station, it will work away from it; and when it gets away cannot return without leaving its work, at a great expense of its time and strength. It will occur that a wagon-and-horse team might be employed to supply it with fuel and water; but this, too, is expensive; and the question recurs: "Can the expense be borne?" When this is added to all other expenses, will not plowing cost more than in the old way?

It is to be hoped that the steam plow will be finally successful, and if it shall be, "thorough cultivation" — putting the soil to the top of its capacity, producing the largest crop possible from a given quantity of ground — will be most favorable for it. Doing a large amount of work upon a small quantity of ground, it will be as nearly as possible stationary while working, and as free as possible from locomotion, thus expending its strength as much as possible upon its work and as little as possible in traveling.

Our thanks, and something more substantial than thanks, are due to every man engaged in the effort to produce a successful steam plow. Even the unsuccessful will bring something to light which, in the hands of others, will contribute to the final success. I have not pointed out difficulties in order to discourage but in order that, being seen, they may be the more readily overcome.

The world is agreed that labor is the source from which human wants are mainly supplied. There is no dispute upon this point. From this point, however, men immediately diverge. Much disputation is maintained as to the best way of applying and controlling the labor element. By some it is assumed that labor is available only in connection with capital — that nobody labors unless somebody else owning capital, somehow, by the use of it, induces him to do it. Having assumed this, they proceed to consider whether it is best that capital shall hire laborers and thus induce them to work by their own consent, or buy them and drive them to it without their consent.

Having proceeded so far, they naturally conclude that all laborers are naturally either hired laborers or slaves. They further assume that whoever is once a hired laborer is fatally fixed in that condition for life; and, thence again, that his condition is as bad as, or worse than, that of a slave. This is the "mudsill" theory.

But another class of reasoners hold the opinion that there is no such relation between capital and labor as assumed; that there is no such thing as a freeman being fatally fixed for life in the condition of a hired laborer; that both these assumptions are false and all inferences from them groundless. They hold that labor is prior to, and independent of, capital; that, in fact, capital is the fruit of labor and could never have existed if labor had not first existed; that labor can exist without capital, but that capital could never have existed without labor. Hence they hold that labor is the superior — greatly the superior — of capital.

They do not deny that there is, and probably always will be, a relation between labor and capital. The error, as they hold, is in assuming that the whole labor of the world exists within that relation. A few men own capital, and that few avoid labor themselves; and with their capital hire or buy another few to labor for them. A large majority belong to neither class — neither work for others nor have others working for them. Even in all our slave states, except South Carolina, a majority of the whole people of all colors are neither slaves nor masters. In these free states, a large majority are neither hirers nor hired.

Men, with their families — wives, sons, and daughters — work for themselves, on their farms, in their houses, and in their shops, taking the whole product to themselves and asking no favors of capital, on the one hand, nor of hirelings or slaves, on the other. It is not forgotten that a considerable number of persons mingle their own labor with capital — that is, labor with their own hands and also buy slaves or hire freemen to labor for them; but this is only a mixed, and not a distinct, class. No principle stated is disturbed by the existence of this mixed class.

Again, as has already been said, the opponents of the "mudsill" theory insist that there is not, of necessity, any such thing as the free hired laborer being fixed to that condition for life. There is demonstration for saying this. Many independent men in this assembly doubtless a few years ago were hired laborers. And their case is almost, if not quite, the general rule.

The prudent, penniless beginner in the world labors for wages awhile, saves a surplus with which to buy tools or land for himself, then labors on his own account another while, and at length hires another new beginner to help him. This, say its advocates, is free labor — the just, and generous, and prosperous system, which opens the way for all, gives hope to all, and energy, and progress, and improvement of condition to all. If any continue through life in the condition of the hired laborer, it is not the fault of the system, but because of either a dependent nature which prefers it, or improvidence, folly, or singular misfortune.

I have said this much about the elements of labor generally as introductory to the consideration of a new phase which that element is in process of assuming. The old general rule was that educated people did not perform manual labor. They managed to eat their bread, leaving the toil of producing it to the uneducated. This was not an insupportable evil to the working bees so long as the class of drones remained very small. But now, especially in these free states, nearly all are educated — quite too nearly all to leave the labor of the uneducated in anywise adequate to the support of the whole.

It follows from this that, henceforth, educated people must labor. Otherwise, education itself would become a positive and intolerable evil. No country can sustain in idleness more than a small percentage of its numbers. The great majority must labor at something productive. From these premises the problem springs — How can labor and education be the most satisfactorily combined?

By the "mudsill" theory, it is assumed that labor and education are incompatible and any practical combination of them impossible. According to that theory, a blind horse upon a treadmill is a perfect illustration of what a laborer should be — all the better for being blind that he could not kick understandingly. According to that theory, the education of laborers is not only useless but pernicious and dangerous. In fact, it is, in some sort, deemed a misfortune that laborers should have heads at all. Those same heads are regarded as explosive materials, only to be safely kept in damp places, as far as possible from that peculiar sort of fire which ignites them. A Yankee who could invent a strong-handed man without a head would receive the everlasting gratitude of the "mudsill" advocates.

But free labor says, "No." Free labor argues that as the Author of man makes every individual with one head and one pair of hands, it was probably intended that heads and hands should cooperate as friends, and that that particular head should direct and control that pair of hands. As each man has one mouth to be fed, and one pair of hands to furnish food, it was probably intended that that particular pair of hands should feed that particular mouth — that each head is the natural guardian, director, and protector of the hands and mouth inseparably connected with it; and that being so, every head should be cultivated and improved by whatever will add to its capacity for performing its charge. In one word, free labor insists on universal education.

I have so far stated the opposite theories of "mudsill" and "free labor" without declaring any preference of my own between them. On an occasion like this, I ought not to declare any. I suppose, however, I shall not be mistaken in assuming as a fact that the people of Wisconsin prefer free labor, with its natural companion, education.

This leads to the further reflection that no other human occupation opens so wide a field for the profitable and agreeable combination of labor with cultivated thought as agriculture. I know nothing so pleasant to the mind as the discovery of anything that is at once new and valuable — nothing that so lightens and sweetens toil as the hopeful pursuit of such discovery. And how vast and how varied a field is agriculture for such discovery! The mind, already trained to thought in the country school, or higher school, cannot fail to find there an exhaustless source of enjoyment.

Every blade of grass is a study; and to produce two where there was but one is both a profit and a pleasure. And not grass alone, but soils, seeds, and seasons; hedges, ditches, and fences; draining, drafts, and irrigation; plowing, hoeing, and harrowing; reaping, mowing, and threshing; saving crops, pests of crops, diseases of crops, and what will prevent or cure them; implements, utensils, and machines, their relative merits, and how to improve them; hogs, horses, and cattle; sheep, goats, and poultry; trees, shrubs, fruits, plants, and flowers — the thousand things of which these are specimens — each a world of study within itself.

In all this, book learning is available. A capacity and taste for reading gives access to whatever has already been discovered by others. It is the key, or one of the keys, to the already solved problems. And not only so: it gives a relish and facility for successfully pursuing the unsolved ones. The rudiments of science are available, and highly available. Some knowledge of botany assists in dealing with the vegetable world — with all growing crops. Chemistry assists in the analysis of soils, selection and application of manures, and in numerous other ways. The mechanical branches of natural philosophy are ready help in almost everything, but especially in reference to implements and machinery.

The thought recurs that education — cultivated thought — can best be combined with agricultural labor, or any labor, on the principle of thorough work; that careless, half-performed, slovenly work makes no place for such combination; and thorough work, again, renders sufficient the smallest quantity of ground to each man; and this, again, conforms to what must occur in a world less inclined to wars and more devoted to the arts of peace than heretofore. Population must increase rapidly, more rapidly than in former times, and ere long the most valuable of all arts will be the art of deriving a comfortable susbistence from the smallest area of soil. No community whose every member possesses this art can ever be the victim of oppression in any of its forms. Such community will be alike independent of crowned kings, money kings, and land kings. . . .

I will detain you but a moment longer. Some of you will be successful, and such will need but little philosophy to take them home in cheerful spirits; others will be disappointed — and will be in a less happy mood. To such let it be said, "Lay it not too much to heart." Let them adopt the maxim, "Better luck next time," and then, by renewed exertion, make that better luck for themselves.

And by the successful and unsuccessful let it be remembered that while occasions like the present bring their sober and durable benefits, the exultations and mortifications of them are but temporary; that the victor will soon be vanquished if he relax in his exertion; and that the vanquished this year may be victor the next, in spite of all competition.

It is said an Eastern monarch once charged his wise men to invent him a sentence to be ever in view, and which should be true and appropriate in all times and situations. They presented him the words, "And this, too, shall pass away." How much it expresses! How chastening in the hour of pride! How consoling in the depths of affliction! "And this, too, shall pass away." And yet, let us hope it is not quite true. Let us hope, rather, that by the best cultivation of the physical world beneath and around us, and the best intellectual and moral world within us, we shall secure an individual, social, and political prosperity and happiness, whose course shall be onward and upward, and which, while the earth endures, shall not pass away.

21.

Peter Cooper: The Cooper Union for the Advancement of Science and Art

Peter Cooper was a successful New York businessman who devoted much of his time and money to philanthropy. Between 1857 and 1859, he established the Cooper Union for the Advancement of Science and Art in New York City, which still occupies quarters in downtown Manhattan. The institution was unique in that it offered free education in the sciences, in social studies, and in the arts to adults and young people and provided the first free public library in New York. Since its founding, the Cooper Union has continued to expand its educational program and facilities while adhering to Cooper's vision. The following letter by Cooper accompanied the Deed of Trust and set forth his intentions.

Source: *Charter, Trust Deed, and By-Laws of the Cooper Union for the Advancement of Science and Art, etc., etc.,* New York, 1888, pp. 26-37.

It is to me a source of inexpressible pleasure, after so many years of continued effort, to place in your hands the title to all that piece and parcel of land bounded on the west by Fourth Avenue, and on the north by Astor Place, on the east by Third Avenue, and on the south by Seventh Street, with all the furniture, rents, and income of every name and nature, to be forever devoted to the advancement of science and art in their application to the varied and useful purposes of life.

The great object I desire to accomplish by the establishment of an institution devoted to the advancement of science and art is to open the volume of nature by the light of truth — so unveiling the laws and methods of Deity that the young may see the beauties of creation, enjoy its blessings, and learn to love the Being "from whom cometh every good and perfect gift."

My heart's desire is that the rising generation may become so thoroughly acquainted with the works of nature and the great *mystery of their own being that they may see, feel, understand, and know that there are immutable laws, designed in infinite wisdom, constantly operating for our good — so governing the destiny of worlds and men that it is our highest wisdom to live in strict conformity to these laws.*

My design is to establish this institution in the hope that unnumbered youth will here receive the inspiration of truth in all its native power and beauty, and find in it a source of perpetual pleasure to spread its transforming influence throughout the world.

Believing *in* and hoping *for* such results, I desire to make this institution contribute in every way to aid the efforts of youth to acquire useful knowledge, and to find and fill that place in the community where their capacity and talents can be usefully employed with the greatest possible advantage to themselves and the community in which they live.

In order most effectually to aid and encourage the efforts of youth to obtain useful knowledge, I have provided the main floor of the large hall on the third story for a reading room, literary exchange, and scientific collections — the walls around that floor to be arranged for the reception of books, maps, paintings, and other objects of interest. And when a sufficient collection of the works of art, science, and nature can be obtained, I propose that glass cases shall be arranged around the walls of the gallery of the said room, forming alcoves around the entire floor for the preservation of the same. In the window spaces I propose to arrange such cosmoramic and other views as will exhibit in the clearest and most forcible light the true philosophy of life.

This philosophy will always show, when rightly understood and wisely applied, an inseparable connection between a course of vice and the misery that must inevitably follow. It will always show that "wisdom's ways are ways of pleasantness, and all her paths are peace."

To manifest the deep interest and sympathy I feel in all that can advance the happiness and better the condition of the female portion of the community, and especially of those who are dependent on honest labor for support, I desire the trustees to appropriate $250 yearly to assist such pupils of the Female School of Design as shall, in their careful judgment, by their efforts and sacrifices in the performance of duty to parents or to those that Providence has made dependent on them for support, merit and require such aid. My reason for this requirement is not so much to reward as to encourage the exercise of heroic virtues that often shine in the midst of the greatest suffering and obscurity without so much as being noticed by the passing throng.

In order to better the condition of woman and to widen the sphere of female employment, I have provided seven rooms to be forever devoted to a Female School of Design, and I desire the trustees to appropriate out of the rents of the building $1,500 annually toward meeting the expenses of said school.

It is the ardent wish of my heart that this School of Design may be the means of raising to competence and comfort thousands of those that might otherwise struggle through a life of poverty and suffering.

It is also my desire that females belonging to the School of Design shall have the use of one of the rooms not otherwise appropriated, for the purpose of holding meetings for the consideration and application of the useful sciences and arts to any of the various purposes calculated to improve and better their condition.

My hope is to place this institution in the hands and under the control of men that will both know and feel the importance of forever devoting it, in the most effectual manner, to the moral, mental, and physical improvement of the rising generation.

Desiring, as I do, to use every means to render this institution useful through all coming time, and believing that editors of the public press have it in their power to exert a greater influence on the community for good than any other class of men of equal number, it is therefore my sincere desire that editors be earnestly invited to become members of the Society of Arts to be connected with this institution. It is my desire that editors may at all times have correct information in relation to all matters in any way connected with this institution, believing that they, as a body, will gladly contribute their mighty influence to guard the avenues of scientific knowledge from all that could mar or prevent its influence from elevating the minds and bettering the hearts of the youth of our common country. I indulge the hope that the trustees will use their utmost efforts to secure instructors for the institution of the highest moral worth, talents, and capacity, fitting them to communicate a knowledge of science in its most lovely and inviting forms.

It is my design that the general superintendent, under the direction of the trustees, shall take all needful care of the building and rent all unoccupied parts of the same.

The person to be appointed as a general superintendent should be a man of known devotion to the improvement of the young. It will be his duty, not only to take charge of the building but also to keep an office in the same where persons may apply from all parts of the country for the services of young men and women of known character and qualifications to fill the various situations that may be open. It will be his duty to give, in the most kind and affectionate manner, such advice and counsel to all that may apply as will most effectually promote their best interests through life.

Should any person ever be appointed a professor or superintendent who shall be found incompetent or unworthy of the trust, it is my earnest desire that such professor or superintendent shall be promptly removed.

It is my desire that students, on leaving the institution, shall receive a certificate setting forth their actual proficiency in any of the branches of science taught in the institution.

In order to encourage the young to improve and better their condition, I have provided for a continued course of lectures, discussions, and recitations in the most useful and practical sciences, to be open and free to all that can bring a certificate of good moral character from parents, guardians, or employers, and who will agree on their part to conform faithfully to all rules and regulations necessary to maintain the honor and usefulness of the institution.

Believing that instruction in the science and philosophy of a true republican government, formed, as it should be, of the people and for the people, in all its operations, is suited to the common wants of our nature, and absolutely necessary to preserve and secure the rights and liberties of all; that such a government, rightly understood and wisely administered, will most effectually stimulate industry and afford the best means possible to improve and elevate our race by giving security and value to all forms of human labor; that it is on the right understanding and application of this science, based as it is on the Golden Rule, that eternal principle of truth and justice that unites the individual, the community, the state, and the nation in one common purpose and interest, binding all to do unto others as they would that others should do unto them; thus deeply impressed with the great importance of instruction in this branch of science, I have provided that it shall be continually taught, as of preeminent importance to all the great interests of mankind.

My feelings, my desires, my hopes, embrace humanity throughout the world; and if it were in my power, I would bring all mankind to see and feel that there is an Almighty power and beauty in goodness. I would gladly show to all that goodness rises in every possible degree from the smallest act of kindness up to the infinite of all good. My earnest desire is to make this building and institution contribute in every way possible to unite all in one common effort to improve each and every human being, seeing that we are bound up in one common destiny and by the laws of our being are made dependent for our happiness on the continued acts of kindness we receive from each other.

I desire that the students of this institution may have the privilege to occupy one of the large halls once in every month for the purpose of a lecture to be delivered by one of their number to all students and such friends as they may think proper to invite.

The monthly lecturer shall be chosen

from the body of the students by a majority vote, or a committee of the students selected for that purpose. The votes shall be counted and the name of the person chosen to deliver the lecture shall be announced, and a record made in a book to be provided for that purpose, to be the property of the institution. I desire that a record be kept of the names of the president, secretary, and speaker; the subject treated; and the general course of remark. A president and secretary shall be chosen from the body of students by a majority vote, who shall preside at all meetings for lectures or other purposes, and whose term of service shall expire every three months, when another president and secretary shall be elected to take their places.

I require this frequent change as I believe it to be a very important part of the education of an American citizen to know how to preside with propriety over a deliberative assembly.

It is my desire, also, that the students shall have the use of one of the large rooms (to be assigned by the trustees) for the purpose of useful debate. I desire and deem it best to direct that all these lectures and debates shall be exclusive of theological and party questions, and shall have for their constant object the causes that operate around and within us, and the means necessary and most appropriate to remove the physical and moral evils that afflict our city, our country, and humanity.

I desire that these lectures and debates shall always be delivered under a deep and abiding sense of the obligation that rests on all — first, to improve themselves, and then to impart to others a correct knowledge of that believed to be most important and within man's power to communicate.

To aid the speakers and those that hear to profit by these lectures and debates, I hereby direct to have placed in the lecture room, in a suitable position, full-length likenesses of Washington, Franklin, and Lafayette, with an expression of my sincere and anxious desire that all that behold them may remember that, notwithstanding they are dead, they yet speak the language of truth and soberness.

Their lives and words of warning cannot be spurned and neglected without a terrible retribution on us and on our children — such a retribution as will cause their spirits to weep in sorrow over the crumbling ruins of all their brightest hopes for the improvement and renovation of the world.

Under a deep sense of the responsibility that rests on us, as a people, entrusted as we are with the greatest blessings that ever fell to the lot of man — the glorious yet fearful power of framing and carrying on the government of our choice — it becomes us to remember that this government will be good or evil in proportion as the people of our country become virtuous or vicious. We shall do well to cherish the precept that the righteous (or rightdoers) are recompensed in the earth, and much more the wicked and the sinner. It will be found that there is no possible escape from the correction of our Father who is in heaven, who "afflicts us not willingly but of necessity, for our profit; by His immutable law that rewards every man according to his works, whether they be good or whether they be evil."

Desiring, as I do, that the students of this institution may become preeminent examples in the practice of all the virtues, I have determined to give them an opportunity to distinguish themselves for their good judgment by annually recommending to the trustees for adoption such rules and regulations as they, on mature reflection, shall believe to be necessary and proper to preserve good morals and good order throughout their connection with this institution. It is my desire, and I hereby ordain, that a strict conformity to rules deliberately formed by a vote of the majority of the students, and approved by the trustees, shall forever be an indispensable requisite for continuing to enjoy the benefits of this institution.

I now most earnestly entreat each and every one of the students of this institution, through all coming time, to whom I have entrusted this great responsibility of framing laws for the regulation of their conduct in their connection with the institution, and by which any of the members may lose its privileges, to remember how frail we are, and how liable to err when we come to sit in judgment on the faults of others, and how much the circumstances of our birth, our education, and the society and country where we have been born and brought up have had to do in forming us and making us what we are. The power of these circumstances, when rightly understood, will be found to have formed the great lines of difference that mark the characters of the people of different countries and neighborhoods. And they constitute a good reason for the exercise of all our charity. It is these circumstances that our Creator has given us the power, in some measure, to control.

This is the great garden that we are called upon to keep, and to subdue, and have dominion over in order to find that everything in it *is very good;* that the right use and improvement of everything is a *virtue;* and the wrong or excessive use and perversion of everything, a *sin.* We should always remember that pride and selfishness have ever been the great enemies of mankind. Men, in all ages, have manifested a disposition to cover up their own faults, and to spread out and magnify the faults of others.

I trust that the students of this institution will do something to bear back the mighty torrent of evils now pressing on the world. I trust that here they will learn to overcome the evils of life with kindness and affection. I trust that here they will find that all true greatness consists in using all the powers they possess to do unto others as they would that others should do unto them; and in this way to become really great by becoming the servant of all.

These great blessings that have fallen to our lot as a people are entrusted to our care for ourselves and for our posterity, and for the encouragement of suffering humanity throughout the world.

Feeling this great responsibility, I desire, by all that I can say and by all that I can do, to awaken in the minds of the rising generation an undying thirst for knowledge and *virtue,* in order that they may be able, by wise and honorable measures, to preserve the liberties we enjoy. . . .

I require, by this instrument and expression of my will, that neither my own religious opinions nor the religious opinions of any sect or party *whatever* shall ever be *made* a *test* or *requirement,* in any *manner* or *form,* of or for *admission to,* or *continuance to enjoy,* the *benefits* of *this institution.*

———◆———

The value of a dollar is to buy just things; a dollar goes on increasing in value with all the genius and virtue of the world. A dollar in a university is worth more than a dollar in a jail; in a temperate, schooled, law-abiding community than in some sink of crime, where dice, knives and arsenic are in constant play.
RALPH WALDO EMERSON, "Wealth"

22.

Horace Greeley: Interview with Brigham Young

In 1859 Horace Greeley, editor of the New York Tribune, *journeyed overland with the purpose of finding interesting information about the new West for his readers. Of particular interest to him in his travels were the Mormons, about whom much public controversy had raged. Passing through Salt Lake City, Greeley seized the chance to interview Brigham Young. Greeley later commented that the Mormons were not so harmful as the public believed, and though he did not approve of their theology, he regarded their accomplishments highly. His interview of July 13 is reprinted below.*

Source: *An Overland Journey from New York to San Francisco in the Summer of 1859*, New York, 1860: "Two Hours with Brigham Young."

MY FRIEND DR. BERNHISEL, late delegate in Congress, took me this afternoon, by appointment, to meet Brigham Young, president of the Mormon Church, who had expressed a willingness to receive me at 2 P.M. We were very cordially welcomed at the door by the president, who led us into the second-story parlor of the largest of his houses (he has three), where I was introduced to Heber C. Kimball, General Wells, General Ferguson, Albert Carrington, Elias Smith, and several other leading men in the church, with two full-grown sons of the president.

After some unimportant conversation on general topics, I stated that I had come in quest of fuller knowledge respecting the doctrines and polity of the Mormon Church, and would like to ask some questions bearing directly on these, if there were no objection. President Young avowing his willingness to respond to all pertinent inquiries, the conversation proceeded substantially as follows:

H.G. — Am I to regard Mormonism (so-called) as a new religion, or as simply a new development of Christianity?

B.Y. — We hold that there can be no true Christian Church without a priesthood directly commissioned by, and in immediate communication with the Son of God and Savior of mankind. Such a church is that of the Latter-day Saints, called by their enemies Mormons; we know no other that even pretends to have present and direct revelations of God's will.

H.G. — Then I am to understand that you regard all other churches professing to be Christian as the Church of Rome regards all churches not in communion with itself — as schismatic, heretical, and out of the way of salvation?

B.Y. — Yes, substantially.

H.G. — Apart from this, in what respect do your doctrines differ essentially from those of our orthodox Protestant churches — the Baptist or Methodist, for example?

B.Y. — We hold the doctrines of Christianity, as revealed in the Old and New Testaments — also in the Book of Mormon, which teaches the same cardinal truths, and those only.

H.G. — Do you believe in the doctrine of the Trinity?

B.Y. — We do; but not exactly as it is held by other churches. We believe in the Father, the Son, and the Holy Ghost as equal, but not identical — not as one person [being]. We believe in all the Bible teaches on this subject.

H.G. — Do you believe in a personal devil — a distinct, conscious, spiritual being whose nature and acts are essentially malignant and evil?

B.Y. — We do.

H.G. — Do you hold the doctrine of eternal punishment?

B.Y. — We do; though perhaps not exactly as other churches do. We believe it as the Bible teaches it.

H.G. — I understand that you regard baptism by immersion as essential?

B.Y. — We do.

H.G. — Do you practise infant baptism?

B.Y. — No.

H.G. — Do you make removal to these valleys obligatory on your converts?

B.Y. — They would consider themselves greatly aggrieved if they were not invited hither. We hold to such a gathering together of God's people as the Bible foretells, and that this is the place and now is the time appointed for its consummation.

H.G. — The predictions to which you refer have usually, I think, been understood to indicate Jerusalem (or Judea) as the place of such gathering.

B.Y. — Yes, for the Jews; not for others.

H.G. — What is the position of your church with respect to slavery?

B.Y. — We consider it of divine institution and not to be abolished until the curse pronounced on Ham shall have been removed from his descendants.

H.G. — Are any slaves now held in this territory?

B.Y. — There are.

H.G. — Do your territorial laws uphold slavery?

B.Y. — Those laws are printed; you can

read for yourself. If slaves are brought here by those who owned them in the states, we do not favor their escape from the service of those owners.

H.G. — Am I to infer that Utah, if admitted as a member of the federal Union, will be a slave state?

B.Y. — No; she will be a free state. Slavery here would prove useless and unprofitable. I regard it generally as a curse to the masters. I myself hire many laborers and pay them fair wages; I could not afford to own them. I can do better than subject myself to an obligation to feed and clothe their families, to provide and care for them in sickness and health. Utah is not adapted to slave labor.

H.G. — Let me now be enlightened with regard more especially to your church polity. I understand that you require each member to pay over one-tenth of all he produces or earns to the church.

B.Y. — That is a requirement of our faith. There is no compulsion as to the payment. Each member acts in the premises according to his pleasure, under the dictates of his own conscience.

H.G. — What is done with the proceeds of this tithing?

B.Y. — Part of it is devoted to building temples and other places of worship; part to helping the poor and needy converts on their way to this country; and the largest portion to the support of the poor among the saints.

H.G. — Is none of it paid to bishops and other dignitaries of the church?

B.Y. — Not one penny. No bishop, no elder, no deacon, nor other church officer receives any compensation for his official services. A bishop is often required to put his hand into his own pocket and provide therefrom for the poor of his charge; but he never receives anything for his services.

H.G. — How, then, do your ministers live?

B.Y. — By the labor of their own hands, like the first apostles. Every bishop, every elder may be daily seen at work in the field or the shop, like his neighbors; every minister of the church has his proper calling, by which he earns the bread of his family; he who cannot or will not do the church's work for nothing is not wanted in her service. Even our lawyers (pointing to General Ferguson and another present, who are the regular lawyers of the church) are paid nothing for their services. I am the only person in the church who has not a regular calling apart from the church's service, and I never received one farthing from her treasury; if I obtain anything from the tithing house, I am charged with and pay for it just as anyone else would. The clerks in the tithing store are paid like other clerks; but no one is ever paid for any service pertaining to the ministry. We think a man who cannot make his living aside from the ministry of Christ unsuited to that office.

I am called rich, and consider myself worth $250,000; but no dollar of it was ever paid me by the church, nor for any service as a minister of the everlasting Gospel. I lost nearly all I had when we were broken up in Missouri and driven from that state. I was nearly stripped again when Joseph Smith was murdered and we were driven from Illinois; but nothing was ever made up to me by the church, nor by anyone. I believe I know how to acquire property and how to take care of it.

H.G. — Can you give me any rational explanation of the aversion and hatred with which your people are generally regarded by those among whom they have lived and with whom they have been brought directly in contact?

B.Y. — No other explanation than is afforded by the crucifixion of Christ and the kindred treatment of God's ministers, prophets, and saints in all ages.

H.G. — I know that a new sect is always decried and traduced; that it is hardly ever deemed respectable to belong to one; that the Baptists, Quakers, Methodists, Universalists, etc., have each in their turn been regarded in the infancy of their sect as the offscouring of the earth; yet I cannot remember that either of them were ever generally represented and regarded by the older sects of their early days as thieves, robbers, murderers.

B.Y. — If you will consult the contemporary Jewish account of the life and acts of Jesus Christ, you will find that He and His disciples were accused of every abominable deed and purpose, robbery and murder included. Such a work is still extant and may be found by those who seek it.

H.G. — What do you say of the so-called Danites, or Destroying Angels, belonging to your church?

B.Y. — What do *you* say? I know of no such band, no such persons or organization. I hear of them only in the slanders of our enemies.

H.G. — With regard, then, to the grave question on which your doctrines and practices are avowedly at war with those of the Christian world — that of a plurality of wives — is the system of your church acceptable to the majority of its women?

B.Y. — They could not be more adverse to it than I was when it was first revealed to us as the divine will. I think they generally accept it, as I do, as the will of God.

H.G. — How general is polygamy among you?

B.Y. — I could not say. Some of those present (heads of the church) have each but one wife; others have more; each determines what is his individual duty.

H.G. — What is the largest number of wives belonging to any one man?

B.Y. — I have fifteen; I know no one who has more; but some of those sealed to me are old ladies whom I regard rather as mothers than wives, but whom I have taken home to cherish and support.

H.G. — Does not the apostle Paul say that a bishop should be "the husband of one wife"?

B.Y. — So we hold. We do not regard any but a married man as fitted for the office of bishop. But the apostle does not forbid a bishop having more wives than one.

H.G. — Does not Christ say that he who puts away his wife, or marries one whom another has put away, commits adultery!

B.Y. — Yes; and I hold that no man should ever put away his wife except for adultery — not always even for that. Such is *my* individual view of the matter. I do not say that wives have never been put away in our church, but that I do not approve of the practice.

H.G. — How do you regard what is commonly termed the Christian Sabbath?

B.Y. — As a divinely appointed day of rest. We enjoin all to rest from secular labor on that day. We would have no man enslaved to the Sabbath, but we enjoin all to respect and enjoy it.

Such is, as nearly as I can recollect, the substance of nearly two hours' conversation, wherein much was said incidentally that would not be worth reporting, even if I could remember and reproduce it, and wherein others bore a part; but as President Young is the first minister of the Mormon Church and bore the principal part in the conversation, I have reported his answers alone to my questions and observations. The others appeared uniformly to defer to his views and to acquiesce fully in his responses and explanations. He spoke readily, not always with grammatical accuracy but with no appearance of hesitation or reserve and with no apparent desire to conceal anything, nor did he repel any of my questions as impertinent. He was very plainly dressed in thin summer clothing, and with no air of sanctimony or fanaticism. In appearance, he is a portly, frank, good-natured, rather thickset man of fifty-five, seeming to enjoy life and to be in no particular hurry to get to heaven.

His associates are plain men, evidently born and reared to life of labor, and looking as little like crafty hypocrites or swindlers as any body of men I ever met. The absence of cant or snuffle from their manner was marked and general; yet, I think I may fairly say that their Mormonism has not impoverished them — that they were generally poor men when they embraced it and are now in very comfortable circumstances, as men averaging three or four wives apiece certainly need to be. . . .

The degradation (or, if you please, the restriction) of woman to the single office of childbearing and its accessories is an inevitable consequence of the system here paramount. I have not observed a sign in the streets, an advertisement in the journals of this Mormon metropolis, whereby a woman proposes to do anything whatever. No Mormon has ever cited to me his wife's or any woman's opinion on any subject; no Mormon woman has been introduced or has spoken to me; and, though I have been asked to visit Mormons in their houses, no one has spoken of his wife (or wives) desiring to see me, or his desiring me to make her (or their) acquaintance, or voluntarily indicated the existence of such a being or beings.

I will not attempt to report our talk on this subject; because, unlike what I have given above, it assumed somewhat the character of a disputation, and I could hardly give it impartially; but one remark made by President Young I think I can give accurately, and it may serve as a sample of all that was offered on that side. It was in these words, I think exactly: "If I did not consider myself competent to transact a certain business without taking my wife's or any woman's counsel with regard to it, I think I ought to let that business alone."

The spirit with regard to woman of the entire Mormon, as of all other polygamic systems, is fairly displayed in this avowal.

23.

Henry David Thoreau: A Plea for Captain John Brown

John Brown, whose career in Kansas had led some to think him a madman, conceived a quixotic plan in 1859 whereby he hoped to bring about a general slave uprising in the South. On October 16 he led a group of about twenty men in a raid on the federal arsenal at Harpers Ferry, Virginia (now West Virginia), in the hope of obtaining weapons with which to arm the slaves. The few Negroes that Brown was able to attract to his venture showed little interest and probably did not know what to make of it. Sporadic fighting occurred for two days around the arsenal. On October 18, a detachment of one hundred marines commanded by Colonel Robert E. Lee and including Lieutenant J. E. B. Stuart subdued Brown and his men. Brown was indicted for treason on October 25. Five days later Thoreau became the first man to champion Brown publicly, delivering the following speech to his protesting fellow townsmen. A month later, when he heard that Brown had been executed, Thoreau said: "I heard, to be sure, that he had been hanged, but I did not know what that meant — and not after any number of days shall I believe it. Of all the men who are said to be my contemporaries, it seems to me that John Brown is the only one who has not died."

Source: *Echoes of Harper's Ferry*, James Redpath, ed., Boston, 1860.

I trust that you will pardon me for being here. I do not wish to force my thoughts upon you, but I feel forced myself. Little as I know of Captain Brown, I would fain do my part to correct the tone and the statements of the newspapers, and of my countrymen generally, respecting his character and actions. It costs us nothing to be just. We can at least express our sympathy with and admiration of him and his companions, and that is what I now propose to do. . . .

When the troubles in Kansas began, he sent several of his sons thither to strengthen the party of the free state men, fitting them out with such weapons as he had; telling them that if the troubles should increase and there should be need of him, he would follow to assist them with his hand and counsel. This, as you all know, he soon after did; and it was through his agency, far more than any other's, that Kansas was made free. . . .

I should say that he was an old-fashioned man in his respect for the Constitution and his faith in the permanence of this Union. Slavery he deemed to be wholly opposed to these, and he was its determined foe.

He was by descent and birth a New England farmer, a man of great common sense, deliberate and practical as that class is, and tenfold more so. He was like the best of those who stood at Concord Bridge once, on Lexington Common, and on Bunker Hill, only he was firmer and higher principled than any that I have chanced to hear of as there. It was no Abolition lecturer that converted him. Ethan Allen and Stark, with whom he may in some respects be compared, were rangers in a lower and less important field. They could bravely face their country's foes, but he had the courage to face his country herself when she was in the wrong. A Western writer says, to account for his escape from so many perils, that he was concealed under a "rural exterior"; as if, in that prairie land, a hero should, by good rights, wear a citizen's dress only.

He did not go to the college called Harvard, good old Alma Mater as she is. He was not fed on the pap that is there furnished. As he phrased it, "I know no more of grammar than one of your calves." But he went to the great university of the West, where he sedulously pursued the study of liberty, for which he had early betrayed a fondness, and, having taken many degrees, he finally commenced the public practice of humanity in Kansas, as you all know. Such were *his humanities,* and not any study of grammar. He would have left a Greek accent slanting the wrong way and righted up a falling man.

He was one of that class of whom we hear a great deal, but, for the most part, see nothing at all — the Puritans. It would be in vain to kill him. He died lately in the time of Cromwell, but he reappeared here. Why should he not? Some of the Puritan stock are said to have come over and settled in New England. They were a class that did something else than celebrate their forefathers' day and eat parched corn in remembrance of that time. They were neither Democrats nor Republicans but men of simple habits, straightforward, prayerful; not thinking much of rulers who did not fear God, not making many compromises, nor seeking after available candidates. . . .

He was never able to find more than a score or so of recruits whom he would accept, and only about a dozen, among them his sons, in whom he had perfect faith. When he was here, some years ago, he showed to a few a little manuscript book — his "orderly book," I think he called it — containing the names of his company in Kansas and the rules by which they bound themselves; and he stated that several of them had already sealed the contract with their blood. When someone remarked that, with the addition of a chaplain, it would

have been a perfect Cromwellian troop, he observed that he would have been glad to add a chaplain to the list if he could have found one who could fill that office worthily. It is easy enough to find one for the United States Army. I believe that he had prayers in his camp morning and evening, nevertheless.

He was a man of Spartan habits, and at sixty was scrupulous about his diet at your table, excusing himself by saying that he must eat sparingly and fare hard as became a soldier or one who was fitting himself for difficult enterprises, a life of exposure.

A man of rare common sense and directness of speech, as of action; a Transcendentalist above all, a man of ideas and principles — that was what distinguished him — not yielding to a whim or transient impulse but carrying out the purpose of a life. I noticed that he did not overstate anything but spoke within bounds. I remember, particularly, how, in his speech here, he referred to what his family had suffered in Kansas, without ever giving the least vent to his pent-up fire. It was a volcano with an ordinary chimney flue. Also referring to the deeds of certain border ruffians, he said, rapidly paring away his speech, like an experienced soldier, keeping a reserve of force and meaning, "They had a perfect right to be hung."

He was not in the least a rhetorician, was not talking to Buncombe or his constituents anywhere, had no need to invent anything but to tell the simple truth and communicate his own resolution; therefore, he appeared incomparably strong, and eloquence in Congress and elsewhere seemed to me at a discount. It was like the speeches of Cromwell compared with those of an ordinary king. . . .

As for his recent failure, we do not know the facts about it. It was evidently far from being a wild and desperate attempt. His enemy Mr. Vallandigham is compelled to say that "it was among the best planned and executed conspiracies that ever failed."

Not to mention his other successes, was it a failure, or did it show a want of good management, to deliver from bondage a dozen human beings and walk off with them by broad daylight, for weeks if not months, at a leisurely pace, through one state after another for half the length of the North, conspicuous to all parties, with a price set upon his head, going into a court-room on his way and telling what he had done, thus convincing Missouri that it was not profitable to try to hold slaves in his neighborhood? And this, not because the government menials were lenient but because they were afraid of him.

Yet he did not attribute his success, fool-ishly, to "his star" or to any magic. He said, truly, that the reason why such greatly superior numbers quailed before him was, as one of his prisoners confessed, because they *lacked a cause* — a kind of armor which he and his party never lacked. When the time came, few men were found willing to lay down their lives in defense of what they knew to be wrong ; they did not like that this should be their last act in this world.

But to make haste to *his* last act and its effects.

The newspapers seem to ignore, or per-haps are really ignorant of the fact, that there are at least as many as two or three individuals to a town throughout the North who think much as the present speaker does about him and his enterprise. I do not hesi-tate to say that they are an important and growing party. We aspire to be something more than stupid and timid chattels, pre-tending to read history and our Bibles, but desecrating every house and every day we breathe in. Perhaps anxious politicians may prove that only seventeen white men and five Negroes were concerned in the late en-terprise; but their very anxiety to prove this might suggest to themselves that all is not told.

Why do they still dodge the truth? They are so anxious because of a dim conscious-ness of the fact, which they do not distinct-ly face, that at least a million of the free inhabitants of the United States would have rejoiced if it had succeeded. They at most only criticize the tactics. Though we wear no crepe, the thought of that man's position and probable fate is spoiling many a man's day here at the North for other thinking. If anyone who has seen him here can pursue successfully any other train of thought, I do not know what he is made of. If there is any such who gets his usual allowance of sleep, I will warrant him to fatten easily un-der any circumstances which do not touch his body or purse. I put a piece of paper and a pencil under my pillow, and when I could not sleep, I wrote in the dark.

On the whole, my respect for my fellow-men, except as one may outweigh a million, is not being increased these days. I have no-ticed the cold-blooded way in which news-paper writers and men generally speak of this event, as if an ordinary malefactor, though one of unusual "pluck" — as the governor of Virginia is reported to have said, using the language of the cockpit, "the gamest man he ever saw" — had been caught and were about to be hung. He was not dreaming of his foes when the governor thought he looked so brave. It turns what sweetness I have to gall to hear, or hear of, the remarks of some of my neighbors.

When we heard at first that he was dead, one of my townsmen observed that "he died as the fool dieth"; which, pardon me, for an instant suggested a likeness in him dying to my neighbor living. Others, cra-ven-hearted, said disparagingly, that "he threw his life away," because he resisted the government. Which way have they thrown *their* lives, pray? such as would praise a man for attacking singly an ordinary band of thieves or murderers. I hear another ask, Yankee-like, "What will he gain by it?" as if he expected to fill his pockets by this en-terprise. Such a one has no idea of gain but in this worldly sense. If it does not lead to a "surprise" party, if he does not get a new pair of boots, or a vote of thanks, it must be a failure. "But he won't gain anything by it."

Well, no, I don't suppose he could get four-and-sixpence a day for being hung, take the year round; but then he stands a chance to save a considerable part of his soul — and *such* a soul! — when *you* do not. No doubt you can get more in your market for a quart of milk than for a quart of blood, but that is not the market that heroes carry their blood to. Such do not know that like the seed is the fruit and that, in the moral world, when good seed is planted good fruit is inevitable and does not depend on our watering and cultivating; that when you plant, or bury, a hero in his field, a crop of heroes is sure to spring up. This is a seed of such force and vitality, that it does not ask our leave to germinate. . . .

The modern Christian is a man who has consented to say all the prayers in the liturgy, provided you will let him go straight to bed and sleep quietly afterward. All his prayers begin with "Now I lay me down to sleep," and he is forever looking forward to the time when he shall go to his *"long rest."* He has consented to perform certain old, established charities, too, after a fashion, but he does not wish to hear of any new-fangled ones; he doesn't wish to have any supplementary articles added to the contract to fit it to the present time. He shows the whites of his eyes on the Sabbath, and the blacks all the rest of the week.

The evil is not merely a stagnation of blood but a stagnation of spirit. Many, no doubt, are well-disposed but sluggish by constitution and by habit, and they cannot conceive of a man who is actuated by higher motives than they are. Accordingly, they pronounce this man insane, for they know that *they* could never act as he does as long as they were themselves. . . .

I read all the newspapers I could get within a week after this event, and I do not remember in them a single expression of sympathy for these men. I have since seen one noble statement, in a Boston paper, not editorial. Some voluminous sheets decided not to print the full report of Brown's words to the exclusion of other matter. It was as if a publisher should reject the manuscript of the New Testament and print Wilson's last speech. The same journal which contained this pregnant news was chiefly filled, in parallel columns, with the reports of the political conventions that were being held. But the descent to them was too steep. They should have been spared this contrast, been printed in an extra at least.

To turn from the voices and deeds of earnest men to the *cackling* of political conventions! Office seekers and speechmakers who do not so much as lay an honest egg but wear their breasts bare upon an egg of chalk! Their great game is the game of straws, or rather that universal aboriginal game of the platter, at which the Indians cried *hub, hub!* Exclude the reports of religious and political conventions and publish the words of a living man.

But I object not so much to what they have omitted as to what they have inserted. Even the *Liberator* called it "a misguided, wild, and apparently insane — effort." As for the herd of newspapers and magazines, I do not chance to know an editor in the country who will deliberately print anything which he knows will ultimately and permanently reduce the number of his subscribers. They do not believe that it would be expedient. How then can they print truth? If we do not say pleasant things, they argue, nobody will attend to us. And so they do like some traveling auctioneers, who sing an obscene song in order to draw a crowd around them.

Republican editors, obliged to get their sentences ready for the morning edition and accustomed to look at everything by the twilight of politics, express no admiration, nor true sorrow even, but call these men "deluded fanatics," "mistaken men" — "insane" or "crazed." It suggests what a *sane* set of editors we are blessed with, *not* "mistaken men"; who know very well on which side their bread is buttered, at least.

A man does a brave and humane deed, and at once, on all sides, we hear people and parties declaring, "I didn't do it, nor countenance *him* to do it, in any conceivable way. It can't be fairly inferred from my past career." I, for one, am not interested to hear you define your position. I don't know that I ever was or ever shall be. I think it is mere egotism or impertinent at this time. Ye needn't take so much pains to wash your skirts of him. No intelligent man will ever be convinced that he was any creature of yours. He went and came, as he himself informs us, "under the auspices of John Brown and nobody else." The Republican Party does not perceive how many his *failure* will make to vote more correctly than they would have them. They have counted the votes of Pennsylvania & Co., but they have not correctly counted Captain Brown's vote. He has taken the wind out of their sails, the little wind they had, and they may as well lie to and repair. . . .

The slave ship is on her way, crowded with its dying victims; new cargoes are being added in midocean; a small crew of slaveholders, countenanced by a large body of passengers, is smothering 4 million under the hatches; and yet the politician asserts that the only proper way by which deliverance is to be obtained is by "the quiet diffusion of the sentiments of humanity," without any "outbreak." As if the sentiments of humanity were ever found unaccompanied by its deeds, and you could disperse them, all finished to order, the pure article, as easily as water with a watering pot, and so lay the dust. What is that that I hear cast overboard? The bodies of the dead that have found deliverance. That is the way we are "diffusing" humanity and its sentiments with it.

Prominent and influential editors, accustomed to deal with politicians, men of an infinitely lower grade, say, in their ignorance, that he acted "on the principle of revenge." They do not know the man. They must enlarge themselves to conceive of him. I have no doubt that the time will come when they will begin to see him as he was. They have got to conceive of a man of faith and of religious principle, and not a politician nor an Indian; of a man who did not wait till he was personally interfered with or thwarted in some harmless business before he gave his life to the cause of the oppressed.

If Walker may be considered the representative of the South, I wish I could say that Brown was the representative of the North. He was a superior man. He did not value his bodily life in comparison with ideal things. He did not recognize unjust human laws but resisted them as he was bid. For once we are lifted out of the trivialness and dust of politics into the region of truth and manhood. No man in America has ever stood up so persistently and effectively for the dignity of human nature, knowing himself for a man and the equal of any and all governments. In that sense he was the most American of us all.

He needed no babbling lawyer, making false issues, to defend him. He was more than a match for all the judges that American voters, or office holders of whatever grade, can create. He could not have been tried by a jury of his peers, because his peers did not exist. When a man stands up serenely against the condemnation and vengeance of mankind, rising above them literally *by a whole body* — even though he were of late the vilest murderer who has settled that matter with himself — the spectacle is a sublime one — didn't ye know it, ye Liberators, ye Tribunes, ye Republicans? and we become criminal in comparison. Do yourselves the honor to recognize him. He needs none of your respect.

As for the Democratic journals, they are

not human enough to affect me at all. I do not feel indignation at anything they may say.

I am aware that I anticipate a little, that he was still, at the last accounts, alive in the hands of his foes; but that being the case, I have all along found myself thinking and speaking of him as physically dead.

I do not believe in erecting statues to those who still live in our hearts, whose bones have not yet crumbled in the earth around us, but I would rather see the statue of Captain Brown in the Massachusetts Statehouse yard than that of any other man whom I know. I rejoice that I live in this age — that I am his contemporary.

What a contrast, when we turn to that political party which is so anxiously shuffling him and his plot out of its way and looking around for some available slaveholder, perhaps, to be its candidate, at least for one who will execute the Fugitive Slave Law, and all those other unjust laws which he took up arms to annul!

Insane! A father and six sons, and one son-in-law, and several more men besides — as many, at least, as twelve disciples — all struck with insanity at once; while the same tyrant holds with a firmer grip than ever his 4 million slaves, and a thousand sane editors, his abettors, are saving their country and their bacon! Just as insane were his efforts in Kansas. Ask the tyrant who is his most dangerous foe, the sane man or the insane. Do the thousands who know him best, who have rejoiced at his deeds in Kansas, and have afforded him material aid there, think him insane? Such a use of this word is a mere trope with most who persist in using it, and I have no doubt that many of the rest have already in silence retracted their words.

Read his admirable answers to Mason and others. How they are dwarfed and defeated by the contrast! On the one side, half-brutish, half-timid questioning; on the other, truth, clear as lightning, crashing into

their obscene temples. They are made to stand with Pilate, and Gesler, and the Inquisition. How ineffectual their speech and action! And what a void their silence! They are but helpless tools in this great work. It was no human power that gathered them about this preacher.

What have Massachusetts and the North sent a few *sane* representatives to Congress for, of late years? to declare with effect what kind of sentiments? All their speeches put together and boiled down — and probably they themselves will confess it — do not match for manly directness and force, and for simple truth, the few casual remarks of crazy John Brown, on the floor of the Harpers Ferry engine house — that man whom you are about to hang, to send to the other world, though not to represent *you* there.

No, he was not our representative in any sense. He was too fair a specimen of a man to represent the like of us. Who, then, *were* his constituents? If you read his words understandingly, you will find out. In his case there is no idle eloquence, no made nor maiden speech, no compliments to the oppressor. Truth is his inspirer and earnestness the polisher of his sentences. He could afford to lose his Sharps rifles, while he retained his faculty of speech, a Sharps rifle of infinitely surer and longer range. . . .

We talk about a *representative* government; but what a monster of a government is that where the noblest faculties of the mind, and the *whole* heart, are not *represented*. A semi-human tiger or ox, stalking over the earth, with its heart taken out and the top of its brain shot away. Heroes have fought well on their stumps when their legs were shot off, but I never heard of any good done by such a government as that.

The only government that I recognize — and it matters not how few are at the head of it or how small its army — is that power that establishes justice in the land, never that which establishes injustice. What shall we think of a government to which all the truly brave and just men in the land are enemies, standing between it and those whom it oppresses? A government that pretends to be Christian and crucifies a million Christs every day!

Treason! Where does such treason take its rise? I cannot help thinking of you as you deserve, ye governments. Can you dry up the fountains of thought? High treason, when it is resistance to tyranny here below, has its origin in, and is first committed by, the power that makes and forever recreates man. When you have caught and hung all these human rebels, you have accomplished nothing but your own guilt, for you have not struck at the fountainhead. You presume to contend with a foe against whom West Point cadets and rifled cannon *point* not. Can all the art of the cannon founder tempt matter to turn against its maker? Is the form in which the founder thinks he casts it more essential than the constitution of it and of himself?

The United States have a coffle of 4 million slaves. They are determined to keep them in this condition; and Massachusetts is one of the confederated overseers to prevent their escape. Such are not all the inhabitants of Massachusetts, but such are they who rule and are obeyed here. It was Massachusetts, as well as Virginia, that put down this insurrection at Harpers Ferry. She sent the Marines there, and she will have to pay the penalty of her sin. . . .

It was [Brown's] peculiar doctrine that a man has a perfect right to interfere by force with the slaveholder in order to rescue the slave. I agree with him. They who are continually shocked by slavery have some right to be shocked by the violent death of the slaveholder, but no others. Such will be more shocked by his life than by his death. I shall not be forward to think him mistaken in his method who quickest succeeds to liberate the slave. I speak for the slave when I say that I prefer the philanthropy of Cap-

tain Brown to that philanthropy which neither shoots me nor liberates me. At any rate, I do not think it is quite sane for one to spend his whole life in talking or writing about this matter, unless he is continuously inspired, and I have not done so. A man may have other affairs to attend to. I do not wish to kill nor to be killed, but I can foresee circumstances in which both these things would be by me unavoidable.

We preserve the so-called peace of our community by deeds of petty violence every day. Look at the policemen's billy and handcuffs! Look at the jail! Look at the gallows! Look at the chaplain of the regiment! We are hoping only to live safely on the outskirts of *this* provisional army. So we defend ourselves and our hen roosts and maintain slavery. I know that the mass of my countrymen think that the only righteous use that can be made of Sharps rifles and revolvers is to fight duels with them when we are insulted by other nations, or to hunt Indians, or shoot fugitive slaves with them, or the like. I think that for once the Sharps rifles and the revolvers were employed in a righteous cause. The tools were in the hands of one who could use them.

The same indignation that is said to have cleared the temple once, will clear it again. The question is not about the weapon but the spirit in which you use it. No man has appeared in America, as yet, who loved his fellowman so well and treated him so tenderly. He lived for him. He took up his life and he laid it down for him. What sort of violence is that which is encouraged, not by soldiers but by peaceable citizens, not so much by laymen as by ministers of the gospel, not so much by the fighting sects as by the Quakers, and not so much by Quaker men as by Quaker women? . . .

Who is it whose safety requires that Captain Brown be hung? Is it indispensable to any Northern man? Is there no resource but to cast these men also to the Minotaur? If you do not wish it, say so distinctly.

While these things are being done, beauty stands veiled and music is a screeching lie. Think of him — of his rare qualities! Such a man as it takes ages to make and ages to understand; no mock hero, nor the representative of any party. A man such as the sun may not rise upon again in this benighted land. To whose making went the costliest material, the finest adamant; sent to be the redeemer of those in captivity; and the only use to which you can put him is to hang him at the end of a rope! You who pretend to care for Christ crucified, consider what you are about to do to him who offered himself to be the savior of 4 million men. . . .

I am here to plead his cause with you. I plead not for his life but for his character — his immortal life; and so it becomes your cause wholly and is not his in the least. Some 1,800 years ago, Christ was crucified; this morning, perchance, Captain Brown was hung. These are the two ends of a chain which is not without its links. He is not Old Brown any longer; he is an angel of light.

I see now that it was necessary that the bravest and humanest man in all the country should be hung. Perhaps he saw it himself. I *almost fear* that I may yet hear of his deliverance, doubting if a prolonged life, if *any* life, can do as much good as his death.

24.

JOHN BROWN: Last Speech to the Court

After his futile attempt to bring about a slave uprising in October 1859, John Brown was charged with treason and condemned to death. He made the following speech to the court on November 2, a month before he was hanged. Brown's raid on the federal arsenal at Harpers Ferry heightened Southern fears and provoked official disapproval throughout the North. "That affair, in its philosophy, corresponds with the many attempts . . . at the assassination of kings and emperors," said Abraham Lincoln, who at the time was hopeful of obtaining the presidential nomination a year later, and who knew that he could not be elected without Southern support. "An enthusiast broods over the oppression of a people till he fancies himself commissioned by Heaven to liberate them. He ventures the attempt, which ends in little else than his own execution." A few Northerners, however, were sympathetic to Brown — including Thoreau and Emerson, who declared that Brown's martyrdom would "make the gallows glorious like the cross."

Source: *The Life, Trial and Execution of Captain John Brown . . . Compiled from Official and Authentic Sources,* New York, 1859, pp. 94-95.

I HAVE, MAY IT PLEASE THE COURT, a few words to say.

In the first place, I deny everything but what I have all along admitted, of a design on my part to free the slaves. I intended, certainly, to have made a clean thing of that matter, as I did last winter when I went into Missouri and there took slaves without the snapping of a gun on either side, moved them through the country, and finally leaving them in Canada. I designed to have done the same thing again, on a larger scale. That was all I intended to do. I never did intend murder, or treason, or the destruction of property, or to excite or incite the slaves to rebellion, or to make insurrection.

I have another objection, and that is that it is unjust that I should suffer such a penalty. Had I interfered in the manner which I admit, and which I admit has been fairly proved — for I admire the truthfulness and candor of the greatest portion of the witnesses who have testified in this case — had I so interfered in behalf of the rich, the powerful, the intelligent, the so-called great, or in behalf of any of their friends, either father, mother, brother, sister, wife, or children, or any of that class, and suffered and sacrificed what I have in this interference, it would have been all right; and every man in this court would have deemed it an act worthy of reward rather than punishment.

This court acknowledges, too, as I suppose, the validity of the law of God. I see a book kissed here which I suppose to be the Bible, or at least the New Testament, which teaches me that all things whatsoever I would that men should do to me, I should do even so to them. It teaches me, further, to remember them that are in bonds as bound with them. I endeavored to act up to that instruction. I say I am yet too young to understand that God is any respecter of persons. I believe that to have interfered as I have done — as I have always freely admitted I have done — in behalf of His despised poor is no wrong but right.

Now, if it is deemed necessary that I should forfeit my life for the furtherance of the ends of justice and mingle my blood further with the blood of my children and with the blood of millions in this slave country whose rights are disregarded by wicked, cruel, and unjust enactments — I say, let it be done!

Let me say one word further.

I feel entirely satisfied with the treatment I have received on my trial. Considering all the circumstances, it has been more generous than I expected. But I feel no consciousness of guilt. I have stated from the first what was my intention and what was not. I never had any design against the liberty of any person, nor any disposition to commit treason, or excite slaves to rebel, or make any general insurrection. I never encouraged any man to do so but always discouraged any idea of that kind.

Let me say, also, in regard to the statements made by some of those who were connected with me. I fear it has been stated by some of them that I have induced them to join me. But the contrary is true. I do not say this to injure them but as regretting their weakness. Not one but joined me of his own accord, and the greater part at their own expense. A number of them I never saw and never had a word of conversation with till the day they came to me; and that was for the purpose I have stated.

Now, I am done.

All men born free and equal ?

25.

"John Brown's Body"

John Brown's execution brought together three of the most extraordinary figures in America's history. The colonel of marines who was in charge of the affair was Robert E. Lee, later to lead the Confederate armies against the Union. One of the militiamen was John Wilkes Booth, who would commit the last tragic act in the tragedy that was the Civil War. And, of course, there was John Brown himself, who "never again," in Lloyd Lewis' words, "after that day's work, was . . . to be clearly a man any more in anybody's memory; thereafter he was to the South a gathering thunderhead on the Northern sky, promise of the hurricane to come. Thereafter he was to the North a song." And what a song! The Union soldiers sang this "greatest of the world's war songs," as it has been called, throughout the war. They sang it quickly, lightly, as they marched into battle, and slowly, mournfully, after the many defeats. The words are simplicity itself, and yet we sing them still.

JOHN BROWN'S BODY

John Brown's body lies a-moldering in the grave,
John Brown's body lies a-moldering in the grave,
John Brown's body lies a-moldering in the grave,
    But his soul goes marching on.

Chorus:
Glory, glory, hallelujah!
Glory, glory, hallelujah!
Glory, glory, hallelujah!
    His soul goes marching on!

John Brown died that the slaves might be free,
John Brown died that the slaves might be free,
John Brown died that the slaves might be free,
    But his soul goes marching on.

He's gone to be a soldier in the army of the Lord,
He's gone to be a soldier in the army of the Lord,
He's gone to be a soldier in the army of the Lord,
    And his soul is marching on.

The stars of heaven are looking kindly down,
The stars of heaven are looking kindly down,
The stars of heaven are looking kindly down,
    On the grave of old John Brown.

26.

Daniel Decatur Emmett and Albert Pike: "Dixie"

Dan Emmett wrote "Dixie" for Bryant's Minstrels, who first performed it in New York, probably in the late fall of 1859. The song soon reverberated through the land: people clapped their hands to it; soldiers in both North and South sang it merrily; Abe Lincoln loved it. And many wrote lyrics for it. Albert Pike, a Southern poet, produced an "improved" version, eliminating the dialect and the "vulgarisms"; but it is Emmett's version that is remembered. (We reprint both here.) During the war, "Dixie" became the favorite Confederate marching song. After Appomattox, Lincoln was heard to remark that "the song is federal property now."

Source: *Heart Songs*, Cleveland, 1909.
   War Songs and Poems of the Southern Confederacy 1861-1865,
   H. M. Wharton, ed., n.p., 1904.

DIXIE

I wish I was in de land ob cotton,
Old times dar am not forgotten;
   Look away, look away, look away,
      Dixie land!
In Dixie land whar I was born in,
Early on one frosty mornin',
   Look away, look away, look away,
      Dixie land!

Chorus:
Den I wish I was in Dixie!
   Hooray! hooray!
In Dixie's land I'll take my stand
   To lib an' die in Dixie,
Away, away, away down south in
      Dixie!
Away, away, away down south in
      Dixie!

Old missus marry Will de weaber,
Willium was a gay deceaber;
   Look away, look away, look away,
      Dixie land!
When he put his arm around 'er,
He look as fierce as a forty-pounder,
   Look away, look away, look away,
      Dixie land!

His face was sharp as a butcher cleaber,
But dat did not seem to greab 'er;
   Look away, look away, look away,
      Dixie land!
Will run away, missus took a decline, O,
Her face was the color of bacon rhine, O,
   Look away, look away, look away,
      Dixie land!

While missus lib, she lib in clover,
When she die, she die all over;
  Look away, look away, look away,
    Dixie land!
How could she act de foolish part
An' marry a man to break her heart?
  Look away, look away, look away,
    Dixie land!

Now here's a health to de nex' old
    missus,
An' all de gals dat want to kiss us;
  Look away, look away, look away,
    Dixie land!
An' if you want to dribe away sorrow,
Come an' hear dis song tomorrow,
  Look away, look away, look away,
    Dixie land!

              DANIEL DECATUR EMMETT

DIXIE

Southrons, hear your country call you!
Up, lest worse than death befall you!
  To arms! To arms! To arms, in Dixie!
Lo! all the beacon-fires are lighted —
Let all hearts be now united!
  To arms! To arms! To arms, in Dixie!
    Advance the flag of Dixie!
      Hurrah! Hurrah!
For Dixie's land we take our stand,
    And live or die for Dixie!
      To arms! To arms!
    And conquer peace for Dixie!
      To arms! To arms!
    And conquer peace for Dixie!

Hear the Northern thunders mutter!
Northern flags in South winds flutter!

Send them back your fierce defiance!
Stamp upon the accursed alliance!

Fear no danger! Shun no labor!
Lift up rifle, pike, and saber!
Shoulder pressing close to shoulder,
Let the odds make each heart bolder!

How the South's great heart rejoices
At your cannons' ringing voices!
For faith betrayed and pledges broken,
Wrongs inflicted, insults spoken.

Strong as lions, swift as eagles,
Back to their kennels hunt these beagles!
Cut the unequal bonds asunder!
Let them hence each other plunder!

Swear upon your country's altar
Never to submit or falter,
Till the spoilers are defeated,
Till the Lord's work is completed.

Halt not till our Federation
Secures among earth's powers its station!
Then at peace, and crowned with glory,
Hear your children tell the story!

If the loved ones weep in sadness,
Victory soon shall bring them
    gladness —
  To arms! To arms! To arms, in Dixie!
Exultant pride soon banish sorrow,
Smiles chase tears away tomorrow.
  To arms! To arms! To arms, in Dixie!
    Advance the flag of Dixie!
      Hurrah! Hurrah!
For Dixie's land we take our stand,
    And live or die for Dixie!
      To arms! To arms!
    And conquer peace for Dixie!
      To arms! To arms!
    And conquer peace for Dixie!
              ALBERT PIKE

1860

27.

OLIVER WENDELL HOLMES: The Brahmin Caste of New England

Oliver Wendell Holmes coined the term "Brahmin" to refer to the class of New England society to which he himself belonged, along with other prominent writers like Longfellow and James Russell Lowell. This class was marked by the traditional aristocratic virtues of birth, rearing, and education, as well as foreign travel and a scholarly profession. The term, which became a favorite of literary critics, was also used to denote disciplined artistry in poetry, as opposed to the reliance upon inspiration. Holmes first made use of the term in the introductory chapter to his novel Elsie Venner, *which was serialized as* The Professor's Story *in the* Atlantic Monthly *before its publication in 1861. The chapter is reprinted here.*

Source: *Atlantic Monthly*, January 1860.

THERE IS NOTHING in New England corresponding to the feudal aristocracies of the Old World. Whether it be owing to the stock from which we were derived, or to the practical working of our institutions, or to the abrogation of the technical "law of honor," which draws a sharp line between the personally responsible class of "gentlemen" and the unnamed multitude of those who are not expected to risk their lives for an abstraction — whatever be the cause — we have no such aristocracy here as that which grew up out of the military systems of the Middle Ages.

What our people mean by "aristocracy" is merely the richer part of the community that live in the tallest houses, drive real carriages (not "kerridges"), kid-glove their hands and French-bonnet their ladies' heads, give parties where the persons who call them by the above title are not invited, and have a provokingly easy way of dressing, walking, talking, and nodding to people, as if they felt entirely at home and would not be embarrassed in the least if they met the governor, or even the President of the United States, face to face. Some of these great folks are really well-bred, some of them are only purse-proud and assuming, but they form a class and are named as above in the common speech.

It is in the nature of large fortunes to diminish rapidly when subdivided and distributed. A million is the unit of wealth now and here in America. It splits into four handsome properties; each of these into four good inheritances; these, again, into scanty competences for four ancient maidens, with whom it is best the family should die out, unless it can begin again as its great grandfather did. Now a million is a kind of golden cheese, which represents in a compendious form the summer's growth of a fat meadow of craft or commerce; and as this kind of meadow rarely bears more than one crop, it is pretty certain that sons and grandsons will not get another golden cheese out of it, whether they milk the same cows or turn in new ones.

In other words, the millionocracy, considered in a large way, is not at all an affair of persons and families, but a perpetual fact of money with a variable human element, which a philosopher might leave out of consideration without falling into serious error. Of course, this trivial and fugitive fact of personal wealth does not create a permanent class, unless some special means are taken to arrest the process of disintegration in the third generation. This is so rarely done, at least successfully, that one need not live a very long life to see most of the rich families he knew in childhood more or less reduced, and the millions shifted into the hands of the country boys who were sweeping stores and carrying parcels when the now-decayed gentry were driving their chariots, eating their venison over silver chafing dishes, drinking Madeira chilled in embossed coolers, wearing their hair in powder, and casing their legs in white topped boots with silken tassels.

There is, however, in New England, an aristocracy, if you choose to call it so, which has a far greater character of permanence. It has grown to be a *caste*, not in any odious sense, but, by the repetition of the same influences, generation after generation, it has acquired a distinct organization and physiognomy, which not to recognize is mere stupidity, and not to be willing to describe would show a distrust of the good nature and intelligence of our readers, who like to have us see all we can and tell all we see.

If you will look carefully at any class of students in one of our colleges, you will have no difficulty in selecting specimens of two different aspects of youthful manhood. Of course I shall choose extreme cases to illustrate the contrast between them. In the first, the figure is perhaps robust, but often otherwise — inelegant, partly from careless attitudes, partly from ill-dressing — the face is uncouth in feature, or at least common; the mouth, coarse and unformed; the eye, unsympathetic, even if bright; the movements of the face are clumsy, like those of the limbs; the voice, unmusical; and the enunciation, as if the words were coarse castings instead of fine carvings. The youth of the other aspect is commonly slender; his face is smooth and apt to be pallid; his features are regular and of a certain delicacy; his eye is bright and quick; his lips play over the thought he utters as a pianist's fingers dance over their music; and his whole air, though it may be timid and even awkward, has nothing clownish. If you are a teacher, you know what to expect from each of these young men. With equal willingness, the first will be slow at learning; the second will take to his books as a pointer or a setter to his fieldwork.

The first youth is the common country boy, whose race has been bred to bodily labor. Nature has adapted the family organization to the kind of life it has lived. The hands and feet, by constant use, have got more than their share of development; the organs of thought and expression, less than their share. The finer instincts are latent and must be developed. A youth of this kind is raw material in its first stage of elaboration. You must not expect too much of any such. Many of them have force of will and character and become distinguished in practical life; but very few of them ever become great scholars. A scholar is almost always the son of scholars or scholarly persons.

That is exactly what the other young man is. He comes of the *Brahmin caste of New England*. This is the harmless, inoffensive, untitled aristocracy to which I have re-

Oliver Wendell Holmes, 1863

ferred, and which I am sure you will at once acknowledge. There are races of scholars among us in which aptitude for learning, and all these marks of it I have spoken of, are congenital and hereditary. Their names are always on some college catalogue or other. They break out every generation or two in some learned labor which calls them up after they seem to have died out. At last some newer name takes their place, it may be; but you inquire a little and you find it is the blood of the Edwardses or the Chaunceys or the Ellerys or some of the old historic scholars disguised under the altered name of a female descendant.

I suppose there is not an experienced instructor anywhere in our Northern states who will not recognize at once the truth of this general distinction. But the reader who has never been a teacher will very probably object that some of our most illustrious public men have come direct from the homespun-clad class of the people, and he may, perhaps, even find a noted scholar or two whose parents were masters of the English alphabet, but of no other.

It is not fair to pit a few chosen families

against the great multitude of those who are continually working their way up into the intellectual classes. The results which are habitually reached by hereditary training are occasionally brought about without it. There are natural filters as well as artificial ones; and though the great rivers are commonly more or less turbid, if you will look long enough, you may find a spring that sparkles as no water does which drips through your apparatus of sands and sponges. So there are families which refine themselves into intellectual aptitude without having had much opportunity for intellectual acquirements.

A series of felicitous crosses develops an improved strain of blood and reaches its maximum perfection at last in the large uncombed youth who goes to college and startles the hereditary class leaders by striding past them all. That is nature's republicanism; thank God for it, but do not let it make you illogical. The race of the hereditary scholar has exchanged a certain portion of its animal vigor for its new instincts, and it is hard to lead men without a good deal of animal vigor. The scholar who comes by nature's special grace from an unworn stock of broad-chested sires and deep-bosomed mothers must always overmatch an equal intelligence with a compromised and lowered vitality. A man's breathing and digestive apparatus (one is tempted to add *muscular*) are just as important to him on the floor of the Senate as his thinking organs. You broke down in your great speech, did you? Yes, your grandfather had an attack of dyspepsia in '82, after working too hard on his famous Election Sermon. All this does not touch the main fact — our scholars come chiefly from a privileged order, just as our best fruits come from well-known grafts, though now and then a seedling apple, like the Northern Spy, or a seedling pear, like the Seckel, springs from a nameless ancestry and grows to be the pride of all the gardens in the land.

28.

Elizabeth Cady Stanton: The Natural Rights of Civilized Women

Until the end of the nineteenth century, American women were generally denied political and legal rights. In 1869 Wyoming, while still a territory, was the first to grant women's suffrage. The Nineteenth, or Women's Suffrage, Amendment was ratified in 1920. The crusade for women's rights and suffrage that led to these events was launched in 1848 at Seneca Falls, New York, with the first women's rights convention, organized chiefly by Elizabeth Cady Stanton, one of the leaders of the women's rights movement. The convention adopted her resolution declaring "that it is the duty of the women of this country to secure to themselves their sacred right to the elective franchise." On February 18, 1860, Mrs. Stanton gave the following address to the New York legislature on the bill for woman suffrage that was pending before the state senate. It was not until 1917 that New York granted women the right to vote.

Source: *History of Woman Suffrage,* Elizabeth Cady Stanton *et al.,* eds., New York, 1881, Vol. I, pp. 679-685.

Gentlemen of the Judiciary:

There are certain natural rights as inalienable to civilization as are the rights of air and motion to the savage in the wilderness. The natural rights of the civilized man and woman are government, property, and harmonious development of all their powers, and the gratification of their desires. There are a few people we now and then meet who, like Jeremy Bentham, scout the idea of natural rights in civilizations and pronounce them mere metaphors, declaring that there are no rights aside from those the law confers. If the law made man too, that might do, for then he could be made to order to fit the particular niche he was designed to fill. But inasmuch as God made man in His own image with capacities and powers as boundless as the universe, whose exigencies no mere human law can meet, it is evident that the man must ever stand first; the law but the creature of his wants; the lawgiver but the mouthpiece of humanity. If, then, the nature of a being decides its rights, every individual comes into this world with rights that are not transferable. He does not bring them like a pack on his back that may be stolen from him, but they are a component part of himself, the laws which insure his growth and development. The individual may be put in the stocks, body and soul, he may be dwarfed, crippled, killed, but his rights no man can get; they live and die with him.

Though the atmosphere is forty miles deep all round the globe, no man can do more than fill his own lungs. No man can see, hear, or smell but just so far; and though hundreds are deprived of these senses, his are not the more acute. Though rights have been abundantly supplied by the good Father, no man can appropriate to himself those that belong to another. A citizen can have but one vote, fill but one office, though thousands are not permitted to do either. These axioms prove that woman's poverty does not add to man's wealth, and if, in the plenitude of his power, he should secure to her the exercise of all her God-given rights, her wealth could not bring poverty to him.

There is a kind of nervous unrest always manifested by those in power whenever new claims are started by those out of their own immediate class. The philosophy of this is very plain. They imagine that if the rights of this new class be granted, they must, of necessity, sacrifice something of what they already possess. They cannot divest themselves of the idea that rights are very much like lands, stocks, bonds, and mortgages, and that if every new claimant be satisfied, the supply of human rights must in time run low. You might as well carp at the birth of every child lest there should not be enough air left to inflate your lungs; at the success of every scholar for fear that your drafts at the fountain of knowledge could not be so long and deep; at the glory of every hero lest there be no glory left for you. . . .

If the object of government is to protect the weak against the strong, how unwise to place the power wholly in the hands of the strong. Yet that is the history of all governments, even the model republic of these United States. You who have read the history of nations from Moses down to our last election, where have you ever seen one class looking after the interests of another? Any of you can readily see the defects in other governments and pronounce sentence against those who have sacrificed the masses to themselves; but when we come to our own case, we are blinded by custom and self-interest. Some of you who have no capital can see the injustice which the laborer suffers; some of you who have no slaves can see the cruelty of his oppression; but who of you appreciate the galling humiliation, the refinements of degradation to which women (the mothers, wives, sisters,

and daughters of freemen) are subject in this last half of the 19th century? How many of you have ever read even the laws concerning them that now disgrace your statute books? In cruelty and tyranny they are not surpassed by any slaveholding code in the South . . . in fact they are worse by just so far as woman from her social position, refinement, and education is on a more equal ground with the oppressor. . . .

Blackstone declares that the husband and wife are one, and learned commentators have decided that one is the husband. In all civil codes you will find them classified as one. Certain rights and immunities, such and such privileges are to be secured to white male citizens. What have women and Negroes to do with rights? What know they of government, war, or glory?

The prejudice against color, of which we hear so much, is no stronger than that against sex. It is produced by the same cause and manifested very much in the same way. The Negro's skin and the woman's sex are both *prima facie* evidence that they were intended to be in subjection to the white Saxon man. The few social privileges which the man gives the woman he makes up to the Negro in civil rights. The woman may sit at the same table and eat with the white man; the free Negro may hold property and vote. The woman may sit in the same pew with the white man in church; the free Negro may enter the pulpit and preach. Now, with the black man's right to suffrage, the right unquestioned, even by Paul, to minister at the altar, it is evident that the prejudice against sex is more deeply rooted and more unreasonably maintained than that against color. As citizens of a republic, which should we most highly prize, social privileges or civil rights? The latter, most certainly.

To those who do not feel the injustice and degradation of the condition, there is something inexpressibly comical in man's "citizen woman." It reminds me of those monsters I used to see in the Old World, head and shoulders woman, and the rest of the body sometimes fish and sometimes beast. I used to think — What a strange conceit! But now I see how perfectly it represents a man's idea! Look over all his laws concerning us and you will see just enough of woman to tell of her existence; all the rest is submerged or made to crawl upon the earth. . . .

Man is in such a labyrinth of contradictions with his marital and property rights; he is so befogged on the whole question of maidens, wives, and mothers that, from pure benevolence, we should relieve him from this troublesome branch of legislation. We should vote and make laws for ourselves. Do not be alarmed, dear ladies! You need spend no time reading Grotius, Coke, Pufendorf, Blackstone, Bentham, Kent, and Story to find out what you need. We may safely trust the shrewd selfishness of the white man, and consent to live under the same broad code where he has so comfortably ensconced himself. Any legislation that will do for man, we may abide by most cheerfully. . . .

But, say you, we would not have woman exposed to the grossness and vulgarity of public life, or encounter what she must at the polls. When you talk, gentlemen, of sheltering woman from the rough winds and revolting scenes of real life, you must be either talking for effect or wholly ignorant of what the facts of life are. The man, whatever he is, is known to the woman. She is the companion, not only of the accomplished statesman, the orator, and the scholar; but the vile, vulgar, brutal man has his mother, his wife, his sister, his daughter. Yes, delicate, refined, educated women are in daily life with the drunkard, the gambler, the licentious man, the rogue, and the villain; and if man shows out what he is anywhere, it is at his own hearthstone. There are over 40,000 drunkards in this state. All these are bound by the ties of family to some woman. Allow but a mother and a wife to each, and you have over 80,000

women. All these have seen their fathers, brothers, husbands, sons in the lowest and most debased stages of obscenity and degradation. In your own circle of friends, do you not know refined women whose whole lives are darkened and saddened by gross and brutal associations?

Now, gentlemen, do you talk to woman of a rude jest or jostle at the polls where noble, virtuous men stand ready to protect her person and her rights, when alone in the darkness and solitude and gloom of night she has trembled on her own threshold awaiting the return of a husband from his midnight revels? — when stepping from her chamber she has beheld her royal monarch, her lord and master — her legal representative — the protector of her property, her home, her children, and her person, down on his hands and knees slowly crawling up the stairs? Behold him in her chamber — in her bed! The fairy tale of *Beauty and the Beast* is far too often realized in life. Gentlemen, such scenes as woman has witnessed at her own fireside where no eye save Omnipotence could pity, no strong arm could help, can never be realized at the polls, never equaled elsewhere this side the bottomless pit. No, woman has not hitherto lived in the clouds surrounded by an atmosphere of purity and peace; but she has been the companion of man in health, in sickness, and in death, in his highest and in his lowest moments. She has worshiped him as a saint and an orator, and pitied him as madman or a fool.

In paradise man and woman were placed together, and so they must ever be. They must sink or rise together. If man is low and wretched and vile, woman cannot escape the contagion, and any atmosphere that is unfit for woman to breathe is not fit for man. Verily, the sins of the fathers shall be visited upon the children to the third and fourth generation. You, by your unwise legislation, have crippled and dwarfed womanhood by closing to her all honorable and lucrative means of employment, have driven

"Ye May Session of Ye Woman's Rights Convention — Ye Orator of Ye
Day Denouncing Ye Lords of Creation"; cartoon in "Harper's," 1859

her into the garrets and dens of our cities
where she now revenges herself on your innocent sons, sapping the very foundations
of national virtue and strength. Alas! for the
young men just coming on the stage of action who soon shall fill your vacant places,
our future senators, our presidents, the expounders of our constitutional law! Terrible
are the penalties we are now suffering for
the ages of injustice done to woman.

Again it is said that the majority of wom-
en do not ask for any change in the laws;
that it is time enough to give them the
elective franchise when they as a class demand it.

Wise statesmen legislate for the best interests of the nation; the state, for the highest good of its citizens; the Christian, for
the conversion of the world. Where would
have been our railroads, our telegraphs, our
ocean steamers, our canals and harbors, our
arts and sciences if government had withheld the means from the far-seeing minority? This state established our present system of common schools, fully believing that
educated men and women would make better citizens than ignorant ones. In making
this provision for the education of its children, had they waited for a majority of the
urchins of this state to petition for schools,
how many, think you, would have asked to
be transplanted from the street to the

schoolhouse? Does the state wait for the
criminal to ask for his prison house; the insane, the idiot, the deaf and dumb for his
asylum? Does the Christian in his love to
all mankind wait for the majority of the benighted heathen to ask him for the Gospel?
No; unasked and unwelcomed, he crosses
the trackless ocean, rolls off the mountain
of superstition that oppresses the human
mind, proclaims the immortality of the soul,
the dignity of manhood, the right of all to
be free and happy.

No, gentlemen, if there is but one woman in this state who feels the injustice of her
position, she should not be denied her inalienable rights because the common household drudge and silly butterfly of fashion
are ignorant of all laws, both human and
divine. Because they know nothing of governments or rights and therefore ask nothing, shall my petitions be unheard? I stand
before you, the rightful representative of
woman, claiming a share in the halo of glory that has gathered round her in the ages;
and by the wisdom of her past words and
works, her peerless heroism and self-sacri-
fice, I challenge your admiration; and moreover claiming, as I do, a share in all her
outrages and sufferings, in the cruel injustice, contempt, and ridicule now heaped
upon her, in her deep degradation, hopeless
wretchedness, by all that is helpless in her

present condition, that is false in law and public sentiment, I urge your generous consideration; for as my heart swells with pride to behold woman in the highest walks of literature and art, it grows big enough to take in those who are bleeding in the dust.

Now do not think, gentlemen, we wish you to do a great many troublesome things for us. We do not ask our legislators to spend a whole session in fixing up a code of laws to satisfy a class of most unreasonable women. We ask no more than the poor devils in the Scripture asked, "Let us alone." In mercy, let us take care of ourselves, our property, our children, and our homes. True, we are not so strong, so wise, so crafty as you are, but if any kind friend leaves us a little money, or we can by great industry earn fifty cents a day, we would rather buy bread and clothes for our children than cigars and champagne for our legal protectors.

There has been a great deal written and said about protection. We as a class are tired of one kind of protection, that which leaves us everything to do, to dare, and to suffer, and strips us of all means for its accomplishment. We would not tax man to take care of us. No, the Great Father has endowed all His creatures with necessary powers for self-support, self-defense, and protection. We do not ask man to represent us; it is hard enough in times like these for man to carry backbone enough to represent himself. So long as the mass of men spend most of their time on the fence, not knowing which way to jump, they are surely in no condition to tell us where we had better stand. In pity for man, we would no longer hang like a millstone round his neck. Undo what man did for us in the Dark Ages and strike out all special legislation for us; strike the words "white male" from all your constitutions and then, with fair sailing, let us sink or swim, live or die, survive or perish together.

At Athens, an ancient apologue tells us, on the completion of the temple of Minerva, a statue of the goddess was wanted to occupy the crowning point of the edifice. Two of the greatest artists produced what each deemed his masterpiece. One of these figures was the size of life, admirably designed, exquisitely finished, softly rounded, and beautifully refined. The other was of Amazonian stature and so boldly chiseled that it looked more like masonry than sculpture. The eyes of all were attracted by the first and turned away in contempt from the second. That, therefore, was adopted and the other rejected almost with resentment, as though an insult had been offered to a discerning public. The favored statue was accordingly borne in triumph to the place for which it was designed in the presence of applauding thousands, but as it receded from their upturned eyes, all at once agaze upon it, the thunders of applause unaccountably died away — a general misgiving ran through every bosom — the mob themselves stood like statues, as silent and as petrified, for, as it slowly went up and up, the soft expression of those chiseled features, the delicate curves and outlines of the limbs and figure became gradually fainter and fainter; and when, at last, it reached the place for which it was intended, it was a shapeless ball enveloped in mist.

Of course, the idol of the hour was not clamored down as rationally as it had been cried up, and its dishonored rival, with no goodwill and no good looks on the part of the chagrined populace, was reared in its stead. As it ascended, the sharp angles faded away, the rough points became smooth, the features full of expression, the whole figure radiant with majesty and beauty. The rude hewn mass that before had scarcely appeared to bear even the human form assumed at once the divinity which it represented, being so perfectly proportioned to the dimensions of the building and to the elevation on which it stood, that it seemed as though Pallas herself had alighted upon the pinnacle of the temple in person to receive the homage of her worshipers.

The woman of the 19th century is the shapeless ball in the lofty position which she was designed fully and nobly to fill. The place is not too high, too large, too sacred for woman, but the type that you have chosen is far too small for it. The woman we declare unto you is the rude, misshapen, unpolished object of the successful artist. From your standpoint, you are absorbed with the defects alone. The true artist sees the harmony between the object and its destination. Man, the sculptor, has carved out his ideal, and applauding thousands welcome his success. He has made a woman that, from his low standpoint, looks fair and beautiful, a being without rights, or hopes, or fears but in him, neither noble, virtuous, nor independent.

Where do we see, in church or state, in schoolhouse or at the fireside, the much-talked-of moral power of woman? Like those Athenians, we have bowed down and worshiped in woman beauty, grace, and exquisite proportions, the soft and beautifully rounded outline, her delicacy, refinement, and silent helplessness; all well when she is viewed simply as an object of sight, never to rise one foot above the dust from which she sprung. But if she is to be raised up to adorn a temple or represent a divinity; if she is to fill the niche of wife and counselor to true and noble men; if she is to be the mother, the educator of a race of heroes or martyrs, of a Napoleon, or a Jesus; then must the type of womanhood be on a larger scale than that yet carved by man.

In vain would the rejected artist have reasoned with the Athenians as to the superiority of his production; nothing short of the experiment they made could have satisfied them. And what of your experiment, what of your wives, your homes? Alas! for the folly and vacancy that meet you there! But for your clubhouses and newspapers, what would social life be to you? Where are your beautiful women — your frail ones, taught to lean lovingly and confidingly on man? Where are the crowds of educated dependents, where the long line of pensioners on man's bounty? Where all the young girls taught to believe that marriage is the only legitimate object of a woman's pursuit — they who stand listlessly on life's shores, waiting, year after year, like the sick man at the pool of Bethesda for someone to come and put them in? These are they who by their ignorance and folly curse almost every fireside with some human specimen of deformity or imbecility. These are they who fill the gloomy abodes of poverty and vice in our vast metropolis. These are they who patrol the streets of our cities to give our sons their first lessons in infamy. These are they who fill our asylums and make night hideous with their cries and groans.

The women who are called masculine, who are brave, courageous, self-reliant, and independent, are they who in the face of adverse winds have kept one steady course upward and onward in the paths of virtue and peace; they who have taken their gauge of womanhood from their own native strength and dignity; they who have learned for themselves the will of God concerning them. This is our type of womanhood. Will you help us raise it up, that you too may see its beautiful proportions, that you may behold the outline of the goddess who is yet to adorn your temple of freedom?

We are building a model republic; our edifice will one day need a crowning glory. Let the artists be wisely chosen. Let them begin their work. Here is a temple to liberty, to human rights, on whose portals behold the glorious declaration, "All men are created equal." The sun has never yet shone upon any of man's creations that can compare with this. The artist who can mold a statue worthy to crown magnificence like this must be godlike in his conceptions, grand in his comprehensions, sublimely beautiful in his power of execution. The woman — the crowning glory of the model republic among the nations of the earth — what must she not be? *(Loud applause.)*

29.

Henry Wadsworth Longfellow: "The Children's Hour"

"The Children's Hour" is one of the many "domestic" poems that endeared Longfellow to his wide audience during the nineteenth century but have had the effect of alienating him from moderns, who tend to find these small-scale masterpieces sentimental and even vapid. (A still more famous example is "There was a little girl,/ And she had a little curl/ Right in the middle of her forehead./ When she was good/ She was very very good,/ But when she was bad she was horrid.") "The Children's Hour" was probably written about 1860, and published in the volume containing the first series of Tales of a Wayside Inn *(1863). It could not have been written after 1861, when the death of his wife plunged Longfellow into despair. The "geography" of the poem becomes clear when one visits Longfellow's home in Cambridge, Massachusetts — the stairway is still there, as is the study where the poet worked, and the visitor can hear in his imagination "The sound of a door that is opened,/ And voices soft and sweet."*

Source: *Complete Poetical Works*, Cambridge Edition, Boston, 1893.

❦ THE CHILDREN'S HOUR

Between the dark and the daylight,
  When the night is beginning to lower,
Comes a pause in the day's occupations
  That is known as the Children's Hour.

I hear in the chamber above me
  The patter of little feet,
The sound of a door that is opened,
  And voices soft and sweet.

From my study I see in the lamplight,
  Descending the broad hall stair,
Grave Alice, and laughing Allegra,
  And Edith with golden hair.

A whisper, and then a silence:
  Yet I know by their merry eyes
They are plotting and planning together
  To take me by surprise.

A sudden rush from the stairway,
  A sudden raid from the hall!
By three doors left unguarded
  They enter my castle wall!

They climb up into my turret
  O'er the arms and back of my chair;
If I try to escape, they surround me;
  They seem to be everywhere.

They almost devour me with kisses,
  Their arms about me entwine,
Till I think of the Bishop of Bingen
  In his Mouse-Tower on the Rhine!

Do you think, O blue-eyed banditti,
  Because you have scaled the wall,
Such an old mustache as I am
  Is not a match for you all!

I have you fast in my fortress,
  And will not let you depart,
But put you down into the dungeon
  In the round-tower of my heart.

And there will I keep you forever,
  Yes, forever and a day,
Till the walls shall crumble to ruin,
  And molder in dust away.

30.

Abraham Lincoln: Address at Cooper Union

Following his debates with Stephen Douglas in 1858, Lincoln, who had become a national figure, began to carry the message of the Republican Party outside of Illinois. When he arrived in New York, after a lengthy tour of the Midwest, he was regarded as a presidential prospect. Thus his audience at the Cooper Union, on February 27, 1860, was a distinguished one, and he prepared his address with more than usual care. The result has always been regarded as one of his greatest efforts — among the most brilliant speeches in American political history. It received an enthusiastic reception and Lincoln now became the most likely to lead the Party ticket in November.

Source: Nicolay-Hay, V, pp. 293-328.

Mr. President and Fellow Citizens of New York:

The facts with which I shall deal this evening are mainly old and familiar; nor is there anything new in the general use I shall make of them. If there shall be any novelty, it will be in the mode of presenting the facts, and the inferences and observations following that presentation.

In his speech last autumn at Columbus, Ohio, as reported in the *New York Times,* Senator Douglas said:

> Our fathers, when they framed the government under which we live, understood this question just as well, and even better, than we do now.

I fully endorse this, and I adopt it as a text for this discourse. I so adopt it because it furnishes a precise and an agreed starting point for a discussion between Republicans and that wing of the Democracy headed by Senator Douglas. It simply leaves the inquiry: What was the understanding those fathers had of the question mentioned?

What is the frame of government under which we live? The answer must be: the Constitution of the United States. That Constitution consists of the original, framed in 1787, and under which the present government first went into operation; and twelve subsequently framed amendments, the first ten of which were framed in 1789.

Who were our fathers that framed the Constitution? I suppose the "thirty-nine" who signed the original instrument may be fairly called our fathers who framed that part of the present government. It is almost exactly true to say they framed it, and it is altogether true to say they fairly represented the opinion and sentiment of the whole nation at that time. Their names, being familiar to nearly all and accessible to quite all, need not now be repeated.

I take these "thirty-nine," for the present, as being "our fathers who framed the government under which we live." What is the question which, according to the text, those fathers understood "just as well, and even better, than we do now"?

It is this: Does the proper division of local from federal authority, or anything in the Constitution, forbid our federal government to control as to slavery in our federal territories?

Upon this, Senator Douglas holds the affirmative and Republicans the negative. This affirmation and denial form an issue; and this issue, this question, is precisely what the text declares our fathers understood "better than we."

Let us now inquire whether the "thirty-nine," or any of them, ever acted upon this question; and if they did, how they acted upon it, how they expressed that better understanding.

In 1784, three years before the Constitution, the United States then owning the Northwestern Territory and no other, the Congress of the Confederation had before them the question of prohibiting slavery in that territory; and four of the "thirty-nine," who afterward framed the Constitution, were in that Congress and voted on that question. Of these, Roger Sherman, Thomas Mifflin, and Hugh Williamson voted for the prohibition, thus showing that, in their understanding, no line dividing local from federal authority, nor anything else, properly forbade the federal government to control as to slavery in federal territory. The other of the four, James McHenry, voted against the prohibition, showing that for some cause he thought it improper to vote for it.

In 1787, still before the Constitution, but while the Convention was in session framing it, and while the Northwestern Territory still was the only territory owned by the United States, the same question of prohibiting slavery in the territory again came before the Congress of the Confederation; and two more of the "thirty-nine," who afterward signed the Constitution, were in that Congress and voted on the question. They were William Blount and William Few; and they both voted for the prohibition, thus showing that in their understanding no line dividing local from federal authority, nor anything else, properly forbade the federal government to control as to slavery in federal territory. This time the prohibition became a law, being part of what is now well known as the Ordinance of '87.

The question of federal control of slavery in the territories seems not to have been directly before the Convention which framed the original Constitution; and hence it is not recorded that the "thirty-nine," or any of them, while engaged on that instrument, expressed any opinion on that precise question.

In 1789, by the first Congress which sat under the Constitution, an act was passed to enforce the Ordinance of '87, including the prohibition of slavery in the Northwestern Territory. The bill for this act was reported by one of the "thirty-nine," Thomas Fitzsimmons, then a member of the House of Representatives from Pennsylvania. It went through all its stages without a word of opposition, and finally passed both branches without ayes and nays, which is equivalent to a unanimous passage. In this Congress there were sixteen of the thirty-nine fathers who framed the original Constitution. They were John Langdon, Nicholas Gilman, William S. Johnson, Roger Sherman, Robert Morris, Thomas Fitzsimmons, William Few, Abraham Baldwin, Rufus King, William Paterson, George Clymer, Richard Bassett, George Read, Pierce Butler, Daniel Carroll, and James Madison.

This shows that, in their understanding, no line dividing local from federal authority, nor anything in the Constitution, properly forbade Congress to prohibit slavery in the federal territory; else both their fidelity to correct principle and their oath to support the Constitution would have constrained them to oppose the prohibition.

Again, George Washington, another of the "thirty-nine," was then President of the United States and, as such, approved and signed the bill, thus completing its validity as a law and thus showing that, in his understanding, no line dividing local from federal authority, nor anything in the Constitution, forbade the federal government to control as to slavery in federal territory.

No great while after the adoption of the original Constitution, North Carolina ceded to the federal government the country now constituting the state of Tennessee; and a few years later Georgia ceded that which now constitutes the states of Mississippi and Alabama. In both deeds of cession it was made a condition by the ceding states that the federal government should not prohibit slavery in the ceded country. Besides this, slavery was then actually in the ceded country. Under these circumstances, Congress, on taking charge of these countries, did not absolutely prohibit slavery within them. But they did interfere with it — take control of it — even there, to a certain extent.

In 1798 Congress organized the territory of Mississippi. In the act of organization they prohibited the bringing of slaves into the territory from any place without the United States, by fine, and giving freedom to slaves so brought. This act passed both branches of Congress without yeas and nays. In that Congress were three of the "thirty-nine" who framed the original Constitution. They were John Langdon, George Read, and Abraham Baldwin. They all, probably, voted for it. Certainly they would have placed their opposition to it upon record if, in their understanding, any line dividing local from federal authority, or anything in the Constitution, properly forbade the federal government to control as to slavery in federal territory.

In 1803 the federal government purchased the Louisiana country. Our former territorial acquisitions came from certain of our own states; but this Louisiana country was acquired from a foreign nation. In 1804 Congress gave a territorial organization to that part of it which now constitutes the state of Louisiana. New Orleans, lying within that part, was an old and comparatively large city. There were other considerable towns and settlements, and slavery was extensively and thoroughly intermingled with the people. Congress did not, in the Territorial Act, prohibit slavery; but they did interfere with it — take control of it — in a more marked and extensive way than

they did in the case of Mississippi. The substance of the provision therein made in relation to slaves was:

1. That no slave should be imported into the territory from foreign parts.

2. That no slave should be carried into it who had been imported into the United States since the 1st day of May, 1798.

3. That no slave should be carried into it, except by the owner, and for his own use as a settler; the penalty in all the cases being a fine upon the violator of the law and freedom to the slave.

This act also was passed without ayes or nays. In the Congress which passed it, there were two of the "thirty-nine." They were Abraham Baldwin and Jonathan Dayton. As stated in the case of Mississippi, it is probable they both voted for it. They would not have allowed it to pass without recording their opposition to it if, in their understanding, it violated either the line properly dividing local from federal authority or any provision of the Constitution.

In 1819-20 came and passed the Missouri question. Many votes were taken, by yeas and nays, in both branches of Congress, upon the various phases of the general question. Two of the "thirty-nine," Rufus King and Charles Pinckney, were members of that Congress. Mr. King steadily voted for slavery prohibition and against all compromises, while Mr. Pinckney as steadily voted against slavery prohibition and against all compromises. By this, Mr. King showed that, in his understanding, no line dividing local from federal authority, nor anything in the Constitution, was violated by Congress prohibiting slavery in federal territory; while Mr. Pinckney, by his votes, showed that, in his understanding, there was some sufficient reason for opposing such prohibition in that case.

The cases I have mentioned are the only acts of the "thirty-nine," or of any of them, upon the direct issue which I have been able to discover.

To enumerate the persons who thus acted as being four in 1784, two in 1787, seventeen in 1789, three in 1798, two in 1804, and two in 1819-20, there would be thirty of them. But this would be counting John Langdon, Roger Sherman, William Few, Rufus King, and George Read each twice, and Abraham Baldwin three times. The true number of those of the "thirty-nine" whom I have shown to have acted upon the question, which, by the text, they understood better than we, is twenty-three, leaving sixteen not shown to have acted upon it in any way.

Here, then, we have twenty-three out of our thirty-nine fathers, "who framed the government under which we live," who have, upon their official responsibility and their corporal oaths, acted upon the very question which the text affirms they "understood just as well, and even better, than we do now"; and twenty-one of them — a clear majority of the whole "thirty-nine" — so acting upon it as to make them guilty of gross political impropriety and willful perjury if, in their understanding, any proper division between local and federal authority, or anything in the Constitution they had made themselves and sworn to support, forbade the federal government to control as to slavery in the federal territories. Thus the twenty-one acted; and, as actions speak louder than words, so actions under such responsibility speak still louder.

Two of the twenty-three voted against congressional prohibition of slavery in the federal territories in the instances in which they acted upon the question. But for what reasons they so voted is not known. They may have done so because they thought a proper division of local from federal authority, or some provision or principle of the Constitution, stood in the way; or they may, without any such question, have voted against the prohibition on what appeared to them to be sufficient grounds of expediency. No one who has sworn to support the Constitution can conscientiously vote for what he understands to be an unconstitutional measure, however expedient he may think it; but one may and ought to vote against a measure which he deems constitutional if, at the same time, he deems it inexpedient. It, therefore, would be unsafe to set down even the two who voted against the prohibition as having done so because, in their understanding, any proper division of local from federal authority, or anything in the Constitution, forbade the federal government to control as to slavery in federal territory.

The remaining sixteen of the "thirty-nine," so far as I have discovered, have left no record of their understanding upon the direct question of federal control of slavery in the federal territories. But there is much reason to believe that their understanding upon that question would not have appeared different from that of their twenty-three compeers had it been manifested at all.

For the purpose of adhering rigidly to the text, I have purposely omitted whatever understanding may have been manifested by any person, however distinguished, other than the thirty-nine fathers who framed the original Constitution; and, for the same reason, I have also omitted whatever understanding may have been manifested by any of the "thirty-nine" even on any other phase of the general question of slavery. If we should look into their acts and declarations on those other phases, as the foreign slave trade, and the morality and policy of slavery generally, it would appear to us that on the direct question of federal control of slavery in federal territories, the sixteen, if they had acted at all, would probably have acted just as the twenty-three did. Among that sixteen were several of the most noted antislavery men of those times — as Dr. Franklin, Alexander Hamilton, and Gouverneur Morris — while there was not one now known to have been otherwise, unless it may be John Rutledge of South Carolina.

The sum of the whole is that, of our thirty-nine fathers who framed the original Constitution, twenty-one — a clear majority of the whole — certainly understood that no proper division of local from federal authority, nor any part of the Constitution, forbade the federal government to control slavery in the federal territories; while all the rest had probably the same understanding. Such, unquestionably, was the understanding of our fathers who framed the original Constitution; and the text affirms that they understood the question "better than we."

But, so far, I have been considering the understanding of the question manifested by the framers of the original Constitution. In and by the original instrument, a mode was provided for amending it; and, as I have already stated, the present frame of "the government under which we live" consists of that original and twelve amendatory articles framed and adopted since. Those who now insist that federal control of slavery in federal territories violates the Constitution point us to the provisions which they suppose it thus violates; and, as I understand, they all fix upon provisions in these amendatory articles, and not in the original instrument. The Supreme Court, in the Dred Scott case, plant themselves upon the Fifth Amendment, which provides that no person shall be deprived of "life, liberty, or property without due process of law"; while Senator Douglas and his peculiar adherents plant themselves upon the Tenth Amendment, providing that "the powers not delegated to the United States by the Constitution . . . are reserved to the states respectively, or to the people."

Now, it so happens that these amendments were framed by the first Congress which sat under the Constitution, the identical Congress which passed the act, already mentioned, enforcing the prohibition of slavery in the Northwestern Territory. Not only was it the same Congress but they were the identical, same individual men who, at the same session and at the same time within the session, had under consideration and in progress toward maturity these constitutional amendments and this act prohibiting slavery in all the territory the nation then owned. The constitutional amendments were introduced before and passed after the act enforcing the Ordinance of '87; so that, during the whole pendency of the act to enforce the ordinance, the constitutional amendments were also pending.

The seventy-six members of that Congress, including sixteen of the framers of the original Constitution, as before stated, were preeminently our fathers who framed that part of "the government under which we live," which is now claimed as forbidding the federal government to control slavery in the federal territories.

Is it not a little presumptuous in anyone at this day to affirm that the two things which that Congress deliberately framed and carried to maturity at the same time are absolutely inconsistent with each other? And does not such affirmation become impudently absurd when coupled with the other affirmation, from the same mouth, that those who did the two things alleged to be inconsistent understood whether they really were inconsistent better than we — better than he who affirms that they are inconsistent?

It is surely safe to assume that the thirty-nine framers of the original Constitution and the seventy-six members of the Congress which framed the amendments thereto, taken together, do certainly include those who may be fairly called "our fathers who framed the government under which we live." And so assuming, I defy any man to show that any one of them ever, in his whole life, declared that in his understanding any proper division of local from federal authority, or any part of the Constitution, forbade the federal government to control as to slavery in the federal territories.

I go a step further. I defy anyone to

show that any living man in the whole world ever did, prior to the beginning of the present century (and I might almost say prior to the beginning of the last half of the present century), declare that, in his understanding, any proper division of local from federal authority, or any part of the Constitution, forbade the federal government to control as to slavery in the federal territories. To those who now so declare I give not only "our fathers who framed the government under which we live" but, with them, all other living men within the century in which it was framed among whom to search, and they shall not be able to find the evidence of a single man agreeing with them.

Now and here, let me guard a little against being misunderstood. I do not mean to say we are bound to follow implicitly in whatever our fathers did. To do so would be to discard all the lights of current experience, to reject all progress, all improvement. What I do say is that if we would supplant the opinions and policy of our fathers in any case, we should do so upon evidence so conclusive, and argument so clear, that even their great authority, fairly considered and weighed, cannot stand; and most surely not in a case whereof we ourselves declare they understood the question better than we.

If any man at this day sincerely believes that a proper division of local from federal authority, or any part of the Constitution, forbids the federal government to control as to slavery in the federal territories, he is right to say so and to enforce his position by all truthful evidence and fair argument which he can. But he has no right to mislead others, who have less access to history and less leisure to study it, into the false belief that "our fathers who framed the government under which we live" were of the same opinion, thus substituting falsehood and deception for truthful evidence and fair argument. If any man at this day sincerely believes "our fathers who framed the government under which we live" used

and applied principles in other cases which ought to have led them to understand that a proper division of local from federal authority, or some part of the Constitution, forbids the federal government to control as to slavery in the federal territories, he is right to say so. But he should, at the same time, brave the responsibility of declaring that, in his opinion, he understands their principles better than they did themselves; and especially should he not shirk that responsibility by asserting that they "understood the question just as well, and even better than we do now."

But enough! Let all who believe that "our fathers who framed the government under which we live understood this question just as well, and even better than we do now" speak as they spoke and act as they acted upon it. This is all Republicans ask — all Republicans desire — in relation to slavery. As those fathers marked it, so let it be again marked, as an evil not to be extended but to be tolerated and protected only because of and so far as its actual presence among us makes that toleration and protection a necessity. Let all the guarantees those fathers gave it be, not grudgingly but fully and fairly, maintained. For this Republicans contend, and with this, so far as I know or believe, they will be content.

And now, if they would listen — as I suppose they will not — I would address a few words to the Southern people.

I would say to them: You consider yourselves a reasonable and a just people; and I consider that in the general qualities of reason and justice you are not inferior to any other people. Still, when you speak of us Republicans, you do so only to denounce us as reptiles, or, at the best, as no better than outlaws. You will grant a hearing to pirates or murderers, but nothing like it to "Black Republicans." In all your contentions with one another, each of you deems an unconditional condemnation of "Black Republicanism" as the first thing to be attended to. Indeed, such condemnation of us seems to be an indispensable prerequisite — license, so to speak — among you to be admitted or permitted to speak at all. Now, can you or not be prevailed upon to pause and to consider whether this is quite just to us, or even to yourselves? Bring forward your charges and specifications, and then be patient long enough to hear us deny or justify.

You say we are sectional. We deny it. That makes an issue; and the burden of proof is upon you. You produce your proof; and what is it? Why, that our party has no existence in your section, gets no votes in your section. The fact is substantially true; but does it prove the issue? If it does, then in case we should, without change of principle, begin to get votes in your section, we should thereby cease to be sectional. You cannot escape this conclusion; and, yet, are you willing to abide by it? If you are, you will probably soon find that we have ceased to be sectional, for we shall get votes in your section this very year. You will then begin to discover, as the truth plainly is, that your proof does not touch the issue. The fact that we get no votes in your section is a fact of your making and not of ours.

And if there be fault in that fact, that fault is primarily yours, and remains so until you show that we repel you by some wrong principle or practice. If we do repel you by any wrong principle or practice, the fault is ours; but this brings you to where you ought to have started, to a discussion of the right or wrong of our principle. If our principle, put in practice, would wrong your section for the benefit of ours, or for any other object, then our principle, and we with it, are sectional and are justly opposed and denounced as such. Meet us, then, on the question of whether our principle, put in practice, would wrong your section; and so meet us as if it were possible that something may be said on our side. Do you accept the challenge? No! Then you really

believe that the principle which "our fathers who framed the government under which we live" thought so clearly right as to adopt it, and endorse it again and again, upon their official oaths, is in fact so clearly wrong as to demand your condemnation without a moment's consideration.

Some of you delight to flaunt in our faces the warning against sectional parties given by Washington in his Farewell Address. Less than eight years before Washington gave that warning, he had, as President of the United States, approved and signed an act of Congress enforcing the prohibition of slavery in the Northwestern Territory, which act embodied the policy of the government upon that subject up to and at the very moment he penned that warning; and about one year after he penned it, he wrote Lafayette that he considered that prohibition a wise measure, expressing in the same connection his hope that we should at some time have a confederacy of free states.

Bearing this in mind, and seeing that sectionalism has since arisen upon this same subject, is that warning a weapon in your hands against us, or in our hands against you? Could Washington himself speak, would he cast the blame of that sectionalism upon us, who sustain his policy, or upon you, who repudiate it? We respect that warning of Washington, and we commend it to you, together with his example pointing to the right application of it.

But you say you are conservative — eminently conservative — while we are revolutionary, destructive, or something of the sort. What is conservatism? Is it not adherence to the old and tried against the new and untried? We stick to, contend for the identical old policy on the point in controversy which was adopted by "our fathers who framed the government under which we live"; while you, with one accord, reject, and scout, and spit upon that old policy, and insist upon substituting something new. True, you disagree among yourselves as to what that substitute shall be. You are divided on new propositions and plans, but you are unanimous in rejecting and denouncing the old policy of the fathers.

Some of you are for reviving the foreign slave trade; some for a congressional slave code for the territories; some for Congress forbidding the territories to prohibit slavery within their limits; some for maintaining slavery in the territories through the judiciary; some for the "gur-reat pur-rinciple" that "if one man would enslave another, no third man should object," fantastically called "popular sovereignty"; but never a man among you is in favor of federal prohibition of slavery in federal territories, according to the practice of "our fathers who framed the government under which we live." Not one of all your various plans can show a precedent or an advocate in the century within which our government originated. Consider, then, whether your claim of conservatism for yourselves and your charge of destructiveness against us are based on the most clear and stable foundations.

Again, you say we have made the slavery question more prominent than it formerly was. We deny it. We admit that it is more prominent, but we deny that we made it so. It was not we, but you, who discarded the old policy of the fathers. We resisted, and still resist, your innovation; and thence comes the greater prominence of the question. Would you have that question reduced to its former proportions? Go back to that old policy. What has been will be again, under the same conditions. If you would have the peace of the old times, readopt the precepts and policy of the old times.

You charge that we stir up insurrections among your slaves. We deny it; and what is your proof? Harpers Ferry! John Brown!! John Brown was no Republican; and you have failed to implicate a single Republican in his Harpers Ferry enterprise. If any member of our party is guilty in that matter, you know it, or you do not know it. If you do know it, you are inexcusable for not designating the man and proving the fact. If you do not know it, you are inexcusable for asserting it, and especially for persisting in the assertion after you have tried and failed to make the proof. You need not be told that persisting in a charge which one does not know to be true is simply malicious slander.

Some of you admit that no Republican designedly aided or encouraged the Harpers Ferry affair, but still insist that our doctrines and declarations necessarily lead to such results. We do not believe it. We know we hold no doctrine and make no declaration which were not held to and made by "our fathers who framed the government under which we live." You never dealt fairly by us in relation to this affair. When it occurred, some important state elections were near at hand, and you were in evident glee with the belief that, by charging the blame upon us, you could get an advantage of us in those elections. The elections came, and your expectations were not quite fulfilled. Every Republican man knew that, as to himself at least, your charge was a slander, and he was not much inclined by it to cast his vote in your favor.

Republican doctrines and declarations are accompanied with a continual protest against any interference whatever with your slaves or with you about your slaves. Surely this does not encourage them to revolt. True, we do, in common with "our fathers who framed the government under which we live," declare our belief that slavery is wrong; but the slaves do not hear us declare even this. For anything we say or do, the slaves would scarcely know there is a Republican Party. I believe they would not, in fact, generally know it but for your misrepresentations of us in their hearing. In your political contests among yourselves, each faction charges the other with sympathy with Black Republicanism; and then, to give point to the charge, defines Black Republicanism to simply be insurrection, blood, and thunder among the slaves.

Slave insurrections are no more common now than they were before the Republican Party was organized. What induced the Southampton insurrection twenty-eight years ago, in which at least three times as many lives were lost as at Harpers Ferry? You can scarcely stretch your very elastic fancy to the conclusion that Southampton was "got up by Black Republicanism." In the present state of things in the United States, I do not think a general, or even a very extensive, slave insurrection is possible. The indispensable concert of action cannot be attained. The slaves have no means of rapid communication; nor can incendiary freemen, black or white, supply it. The explosive materials are everywhere in parcels, but there neither are, nor can be supplied, the indispensable connecting trains.

Much is said by Southern people about the affection of slaves for their masters and mistresses; and a part of it, at least, is true. A plot for an uprising could scarcely be devised and communicated to twenty individuals before some one of them, to save the life of a favorite master or mistress, would divulge it. This is the rule; and the slave revolution in Haiti was not an exception to it but a case occurring under peculiar circumstances. The Gunpowder Plot of British history, though not connected with slaves, was more in point. In that case only about twenty were admitted to the secret; and yet one of them, in his anxiety to save a friend, betrayed the plot to that friend, and, by consequence, averted the calamity. Occasional poisonings from the kitchen, and open or stealthy assassinations in the field, and local revolts extending to a score or so will continue to occur as the natural results of slavery; but no general insurrection of slaves, as I think, can happen in this country for a long time. Whoever much fears, or

much hopes, for such an event will be alike disappointed.

In the language of Mr. Jefferson, uttered many years ago,

> It is still in our power to direct the process of emancipation and deportation peaceably, and in such slow degrees, as that the evil will wear off insensibly; and their places be, *pari passu* [with equal step], filled up by free white laborers. If, on the contrary, it is left to force itself on, human nature must shudder at the prospect held up.

Mr. Jefferson did not mean to say, nor do I, that the power of emancipation is in the federal government. He spoke of Virginia; and, as to the power of emancipation, I speak of the slaveholding states only. The federal government, however, as we insist, has the power of restraining the extension of the institution, the power to insure that a slave insurrection shall never occur on any American soil which is now free from slavery.

John Brown's effort was peculiar. It was not a slave insurrection. It was an attempt by white men to get up a revolt among slaves, in which the slaves refused to participate. In fact, it was so absurd that the slaves, with all their ignorance, saw plainly enough it could not succeed. That affair, in its philosophy, corresponds with the many attempts, related in history, at the assassination of kings and emperors. An enthusiast broods over the oppression of a people till he fancies himself commissioned by heaven to liberate them. He ventures the attempt, which ends in little else than his own execution. Orsini's attempt on Louis Napoleon and John Brown's attempt at Harpers Ferry were, in their philosophy, precisely the same. The eagerness to cast blame on old England in the one case and on New England in the other does not disprove the sameness of the two things.

And how much would it avail you if you could, by the use of John Brown, Helper's book, and the like, break up the Republican organization? Human action can be modified to some extent, but human nature cannot be changed. There is a judgment and a feeling against slavery in this nation which cast at least a million and a half of votes. You cannot destroy that judgment and feeling — that sentiment — by breaking up the political organization which rallies around it. You can scarcely scatter and disperse an army which has been formed into order in the face of your heaviest fire; but if you could, how much would you gain by forcing the sentiment which created it out of the peaceful channel of the ballot box into some other channel? What would that other channel probably be? Would the number of John Browns be lessened or enlarged by the operation?

But you will break up the Union rather than submit to a denial of your constitutional rights.

That has a somewhat reckless sound; but it would be palliated, if not fully justified, were we proposing, by the mere force of numbers, to deprive you of some right plainly written down in the Constitution. But we are proposing no such thing.

When you make these declarations, you have a specific and well-understood allusion to an assumed constitutional right of yours to take slaves into the federal territories and to hold them there as property. But no such right is specifically written in the Constitution. That instrument is literally silent about any such right. We, on the contrary, deny that such a right has any existence in the Constitution, even by implication.

Your purpose, then, plainly stated, is that you will destroy the government unless you be allowed to construe and force the Constitution as you please on all points in dispute between you and us. You will rule or ruin in all events.

This, plainly stated, is your language. Perhaps you will say the Supreme Court has decided the disputed constitutional question in your favor. Not quite so. But waiving the lawyer's distinction between dictum and decision, the Court has decided the question for you in a sort of way. The Court has substantially said it is your constitutional right to take slaves into the federal territories and to hold them there as property. When I say the decision was made in a sort of way, I mean it was made in a divided court, by a bare majority of the judges, and they not quite agreeing with one another in the reasons for making it; that it is so made as that its avowed supporters disagree with one another about its meaning; and that it was mainly based upon a mistaken statement of fact — the statement in the opinion that "the right of property in a slave is distinctly and expressly affirmed in the Constitution."

An inspection of the Constitution will show that the right of property in a slave is not "distinctly and expressly affirmed" in it. Bear in mind, the judges do not pledge their judicial opinion that such right is impliedly affirmed in the Constitution; but they pledge their veracity that it is "distinctly and expressly" affirmed there — "distinctly," that is, not mingled with anything else — "expressly," that is, in words meaning just that, without the aid of any inference and susceptible of no other meaning.

If they had only pledged their judicial opinion that such right is affirmed in the instrument by implication, it would be open to others to show that neither the word "slave" nor "slavery" is to be found in the Constitution, nor the word "property" even, in any connection with language alluding to the things slave, or slavery; and that wherever in that instrument the slave is alluded to, he is called a "person"; and wherever his master's legal right in relation to him is alluded to, it is spoken of as "service or labor which may be due" — as a debt payable in service or labor. Also it would be open to show, by contemporaneous history, that this mode of alluding to slaves and slavery, instead of speaking of them, was employed on purpose to exclude from the Constitution the idea that there could be property in man.

To show all this is easy and certain.

When this obvious mistake of the judges shall be brought to their notice, is it not reasonable to expect that they will withdraw the mistaken statement and reconsider the conclusion based upon it?

And then it is to be remembered that "our fathers who framed the government under which we live," the men who made the Constitution, decided this same constitutional question in our favor long ago: decided it without division among themselves when making the decision; without division among themselves about the meaning of it after it was made; and, so far as any evidence is left, without basing it upon any mistaken statement of facts.

Under all these circumstances, do you really feel yourselves justified to break up this government unless such a court decision as yours is shall be at once submitted to as a conclusive and final rule of political action? But you will not abide the election of a Republican President! In that supposed event, you say, you will destroy the Union; and then, you say, the great crime of having destroyed it will be upon us! That is cool. A highwayman holds a pistol to my ear and mutters through his teeth, "Stand and deliver or I shall kill you, and then you will be a murderer!"

To be sure, what the robber demanded of me — my money — was my own; and I had a clear right to keep it; but it was no more my own than my vote is my own; and the threat of death to me to extort my money, and the threat of destruction to the Union to extort my vote, can scarcely be distinguished in principle.

A few words now to Republicans. It is exceedingly desirable that all parts of this great Confederacy shall be at peace and in harmony one with another. Let us Republicans do our part to have it so. Even though much provoked, let us do nothing through passion and ill temper. Even though the Southern people will not so much as listen to us, let us calmly consider their demands and yield to them if, in our deliberate view of our duty, we possibly can. Judging by all they say and do, and by the subject and nature of their controversy with us, let us determine, if we can, what will satisfy them.

Will they be satisfied if the territories be unconditionally surrendered to them? We know they will not. In all their present complaints against us, the territories are scarcely mentioned. Invasions and insurrections are the rage now. Will it satisfy them if, in the future, we have nothing to do with invasions and insurrections? We know it will not. We so know because we know we never had anything to do with invasions and insurrections; and yet this total abstaining does not exempt us from the charge and the denunciation.

The question recurs: What will satisfy them? Simply this: We must not only let them alone but we must somehow convince them that we do let them alone. This, we know by experience, is no easy task. We have been so trying to convince them from the very beginning of our organization, but with no success. In all our platforms and speeches we have constantly protested our purpose to let them alone; but this has had no tendency to convince them. Alike unavailing to convince them is the fact that they have never detected a man of us in any attempt to disturb them.

These natural and apparently adequate means all failing, what will convince them? This, and this only: cease to call slavery wrong, and join them in calling it right. And this must be done thoroughly, done in acts as well as in words. Silence will not be tolerated; we must place ourselves avowedly with them. Senator Douglas' new sedition law must be enacted and enforced, suppressing all declarations that slavery is wrong, whether made in politics, in presses, in pulpits, or in private. We must arrest and return their fugitive slaves with greedy pleasure. We must pull down our free-state constitutions. The whole atmosphere must be disinfected from all taint of opposition to slavery before they will cease to believe that all their troubles proceed from us.

I am quite aware they do not state their case precisely in this way. Most of them would probably say to us, "Let us alone; do nothing to us, and say what you please about slavery." But we do let them alone — have never disturbed them — so that, after all, it is what we say which dissatisfies them. They will continue to accuse us of doing until we cease saying.

I am also aware they have not as yet, in terms, demanded the overthrow of our free-state constitutions. Yet those constitutions declare the wrong of slavery with more solemn emphasis than do all other sayings against it; and when all these other sayings shall have been silenced, the overthrow of these constitutions will be demanded and nothing be left to resist the demand. It is nothing to the contrary that they do not demand the whole of this just now. Demanding what they do, and for the reason they do, they can voluntarily stop nowhere short of this consummation. Holding, as they do, that slavery is morally right and socially elevating, they cannot cease to demand a full national recognition of it as a legal right and a social blessing.

Nor can we justifiably withhold this on any ground save our conviction that slavery is wrong. If slavery is right, all words, acts, laws, and constitutions against it are themselves wrong, and should be silenced and swept away. If it is right, we cannot justly object to its nationality, its universality; if it is wrong, they cannot justly insist upon its extension, its enlargement. All they ask we could readily grant, if we thought slavery right; all we ask they could as readily grant,

if they thought it wrong. Their thinking it right and our thinking it wrong is the precise fact upon which depends the whole controversy. Thinking it right, as they do, they are not to blame for desiring its full recognition as being right; but thinking it wrong, as we do, can we yield to them? Can we cast our votes with their view and against our own? In view of our moral, social, and political responsibilities, can we do this?

Wrong as we think slavery is, we can yet afford to let it alone where it is, because that much is due to the necessity arising from its actual presence in the nation; but can we, while our votes will prevent it, allow it to spread into the national territories and to overrun us here in these free states? If our sense of duty forbids this, then let us stand by our duty fearlessly and effectively. Let us be diverted by none of those sophistical contrivances wherewith we are so industriously plied and belabored — contrivances such as groping for some middle ground between the right and the wrong, vain as the search for a man who should be neither a living man nor a dead man; such as a policy of "don't care" on a question about which all true men do care; such as Union appeals beseeching true Union men to yield to disunionists, reversing the divine rule, and calling, not the sinners but the righteous, to repentance; such as invocations to Washington, imploring men to unsay what Washington said and undo what Washington did.

Neither let us be slandered from our duty by false accusations against us, nor frightened from it by menaces of destruction to the government, nor of dungeons to ourselves. Let us have faith that right makes might, and in that faith let us, to the end, dare to do our duty as we understand it.

Billy, I fear that I shall meet with some terrible end.
ABRAHAM LINCOLN, prediction to William Herndon, often repeated

31.

Walt Whitman: "I Hear America Singing"

"I Hear America Singing" is one of the numerous "Inscriptions," as they were called by their author — in a modern prose work such small introductory pieces would be called epigraphs — that Whitman composed, at various times, for Leaves of Grass. This one was written in 1860; it appeared for the first time in its final form in the 1867 edition of the work. Whitman has been charged with the mere making of lists — of things, of persons, of ideas — and passing them off as poetry. "I Hear America Singing" is such a list, but its effectiveness is undeniable, and the notion that America is a great choral symphony made up of the individual voices of her citizens, going about their various tasks and "Singing with open mouths their strong melodious songs," is a haunting one.

Source: *Leaves of Grass*, New York, 1867.

❦ I HEAR AMERICA SINGING

I hear America singing, the varied carols I hear,
Those of mechanics, each one singing his as it should be blithe and strong,
The carpenter singing his as he measures his plank or beam,
The mason singing his as he makes ready for work, or leaves off work,
The boatman singing what belongs to him in his boat, the deck-hand singing on the
     steamboat deck,
The shoemaker singing as he sits on his bench, the hatter singing as he stands,
The wood-cutter's song, the ploughboy's on his way in the morning, or at noon
     intermission or at sundown,
The delicious singing of the mother, or of the young wife at work, or of the girl
     sewing or washing,
Each singing what belongs to him or her and to none else,
The day what belongs to the day — at night the party of young fellows,
     robust, friendly,
Singing with open mouths their strong melodious songs.

32.

HENRY WHEELER SHAW ("JOSH BILLINGS"): An Essa on the Muel

Henry Wheeler Shaw, essayist, epigrammatist, humorist, and one-time auctioneer in Poughkeepsie, New York, believed he could write, but few people read him. He believed he had things to say, but few people listened. In his early forties, Shaw decided to change his literary style and pose as a philosopher named Josh Billings. His essays, with their grotesque misspellings, immediately delighted many people and were reprinted in newspapers across America. When someone once criticized his spelling, he replied: "I hold that a man haz az much rite tew spell a word as it iz pronounsed az he haz tew pronounse it the way it ain't spelt." The following essay, which appeared in a New York newspaper in 1860, was the first to bring Shaw national attention.

Source: *Everybody's Friend, or; Josh Billing's Encyclopedia and Proverbial Philosophy of Wit and Humor,* Hartford, 1874, pp. 163-164.

THE MUEL IS HAF HOSS and haf Jackass, and then kums tu a full stop, natur diskovering her mistake.

Tha weigh more, akordin tu their heft, than enny other kreetur, except a crowbar.

Tha kant hear enny quicker, nor further than the hoss, yet their ears are big enuff for snow shoes.

You kan trust them with enny one whose life aint worth enny more than the mules. The only wa tu keep the mules into a paster, is tu turn them into a medder jineing, and let them jump out.

Tha are reddy for use, just as soon as they will du tu abuse.

Tha haint got enny friends, and will live on huckle berry brush, with an ocasional chanse at Kanada thistels.

Tha are a modern invenshun, i dont think the Bible deludes tu them at tall.

Tha sel for more money than enny other domestik animile. Yu kant tell their age by looking into their mouth, enny more than you kould a Mexican cannons. Tha never hav no dissease that a good club wont heal.

If tha ever die tha must kum rite tu life agin, for i never herd noboddy sa "ded mule."

Tha are like sum men, verry korrupt at harte; ive known them tu be good mules for 6 months, just tu git a good chanse to kick sumbody.

I never owned one, nor never mean to, unless thare is a United Staits law passed, requiring it.

The only reason why tha are pashunt, is bekause tha are ashamed ov themselfs.

I have seen eddikated mules in a sirkus.

Tha kould kick, and bite, tremenjis. I would not sa what I am forced tu sa again the mule, if his birth want an outrage, and man want tu blame for it.

Enny man who is willing tu drive a mule, ought to be exempt by law from running for the legislatur.

Tha are the strongest creeturs on earth, and heaviest ackording tu their sise; I herd tell ov one who fell oph from the tow path, on the Eri kanawl, and sunk as soon as he touched bottom, but he kept rite on towing the boat tu the nex stashun, breathing thru his ears, which stuck out ov the water about 2 feet 6 inches; i didn't see this did, but an auctioneer told me ov it, and i never knew an auctioneer tu lie unless it was absolutely convenient.

33.

The Pony Express

One ephemeral moment in the history of the American West that has been glamorized in legend far out of proportion to its actual usefulness is the Pony Express. This short-lived, limited, and ruinously expensive venture began in April 1860 and ended eighteen months later with the opening of the transcontinental telegraph. It operated as a mail-carrying relay system from St. Joseph, Missouri, to Sacramento, California, along what was called the Oregon-California Trail. The following glowing account of the Pony Express was published shortly after the operation began.

Source: *Hutchings' California Magazine,* July 1860.

WE ARE NOT ABOUT TO INSIST that the Pony Express is the greatest of all the great enterprises of modern times, nor are we contemplating the running down of others by way of proving that this individual one is particularly and preeminently *the* enterprise of the present day; but we shall show that in speed of transmitting news and letters, nothing has ever equaled it on this continent.

We remember with what enthusiastic welcoming the first Overland Mail was received here, on the 10th of October, 1858, which had made the trip from St. Louis to San Francisco, via Los Angeles, in the unprecedented short time of twenty-three days and twenty-one hours. This was a great achievement and should not be overlooked, especially as a better average of speed has been made from that time to this, almost in every instance anticipating the mail steamer's news.

Nor should we overlook the demonstration of joy everywhere manifest when the pioneer mail steamship, the *California,* plowed the waters of the bay, on the 28th day of February, 1850; and the actual benefits that have arisen from passenger and mail transportation by the steamships of this and other companies from that time to this, with all their high prices and abuses — and heaven knows they have been high enough and bad enough. Yet, to suppose them out of the way before the Pacific Railroad is built would be to suppose one of the most deplorable extremities to which California could be reduced, especially as it would be utterly impossible to convey, overland, the thirty or more drayloads of mail matter sent by every steamer; to say nothing of the 400 or more passengers that depart semi-monthly for the Atlantic ports.

We wish to offer no plea in justification of the exorbitant rates of passage charged, nor the overcrowding and other abuses to which travelers have to submit, simply because they cannot help themselves; but to ask a question arising from the circumstances of the case. "After all, what could we do without them — at least, until the railroad is built?" and which at present appears very doubtful. Therefore, while we remember the one with just exultation and pride, let us not forget the other in ingratitude — however great the humiliation we may feel — that through the selfish conniving of interested politicians, who cannot be accredited with being statesmen, a greater good, the Pacific Railroad, is indefinitely postponed. With this brief allusion to these valuable public enterprises, we can, with a better conscience, proceed to speak of a private one of equal importance, in a new and commercial point of view — THE PONY.

This express was established by Majors, Russell & Co., whose principal office is at Leavenworth, Mo., and who have had the mail contract from St. Joseph, Mo., to Salt Lake City for several years. When gold had been discovered and mining settlements began to flourish at Pike's Peak, this enterprising company organized a branch express to that point also.

Early in the present year, the plans for the establishing of the Pony Express from St. Joseph to San Francisco were perfected, and Major Solomon, U.S. marshal for California, was authorized to select and procure as fine a collection of fleet-footed and muscular horses as could be found in the state. This accomplished, Mr. W. W. Finney was dispatched as general road agent, and who arrived here in March last, with the intention of starting the Pony on the 1st day of April, ensuing. But owing to the difficulty of arranging the stations beyond Placerville, on account of several severe snow-storms having rendered the trails almost impassable, it was found next to impossible to get feed for the animals and provisions for the men packed out at any price; and but for the kindness of Mr. Halliday, who promptly cashed the drafts of the company, a still further delay would have been inevitable. Yet owing to this well-timed assistance, Mr. Finney was enabled to purchase trains of pack mules and thus prosecute the work of stocking the stations, which he did with untiring energy.

All things being in readiness, early on the morning of the 3rd of April, the "Pony" was placed at the door of the Alta Telegraph Company, on Montgomery Street, San Francisco, decked with a small U.S. flag on each side of his head, and a neat pair of leather bags *in* the *mochila* [leather covering] of the saddle, on which was painted "Pony Express." At a few minutes before 4 o'clock P.M. of the same day, in order to be in time for the Sacramento boat, the first messenger left the office on his arduous undertaking.

At 5 P.M. of the same day, the first Pony Express was dispatched from St. Joseph, with St. Louis dates up to the time of starting.

As many of our readers have probably never crossed this portion of the continent, perhaps they would like to accompany the Pony — at least in imagination — for the purpose of seeing the country; which, if it be not as instructive or as lifelike as an actual trip, can be taken in less time, at a smaller expense, and with considerable less fatigue, danger, inconvenience, and exposure than is traveled by every expressman on the route.

The moment the St. Joseph's ferryboat touches the western side of the Missouri River, the "rider" mounts his steed and dashes up the steep bank and across the heavily timbered alluvium on the margin of the stream. The beautiful, undulating country, carpeted with green or covered with flowers; the songs of the birds; the wild bees prospecting for honey; even the delicious flavor of the strawberries that grow in bounteous profusion on every hand are alike unheeded — for onward he hastens.

The loud peals of thunder and the fierce flashes of lightning, or even the falling of the drenching rain, detains him not. What though the storm-swollen banks of the streams are full to overflowing, so that even the landmarks for crossing are altogether invisible, it deters him not; for in it he plunges and speeds along on his rapid course, undismayed.

Whether sun-dried or soaked, snow-covered or frozen, by day or by night, in starlight or darkness, be he lonely or merry, forward he hastens, until the thrice-welcome station is just there, in sight, when he leaps from his saddle, and with full heart rejoices that his task for the present is fully accomplished.

Here, another, whose horse, like himself, has been waiting, perhaps without shelter, quickly takes the *mochila*, which contains all the letters. On his saddle he throws it, then jumps to his seat, shouts a hearty "Goodnight, boys," and is lost in the distance. He rides on alone, over prairies and mountains, whether uphill or down, on rough ground or smooth, among true friends or foes, he hies swiftly on, until, in the shadowy distance, the relay is seen and his duty's performed.

Again and again, from station to station, this is often repeated, until, from the Carson across the Sierras, a message announces the "Pony's arrival," with news from St. Louis in eight days or less.

34.

Defense of a Negro Pioneer Land Claim

The following selection is concerned with the right of Negroes to own property. If, in consequence of the Dred Scott decision, Negroes were not citizens, did it also follow that they could not own property? Sylvester Gray had staked his land claim prior to the court decision of 1857. In 1860 the federal government confiscated his land and to recover it he sent a petition to Congress. His petition of March 23 and the action taken on it by the Senate Committee on Public Lands on May 19 are reprinted below.

Source: National Archives, Record Group 46, Records of the U.S. Senate,
        Committee on Public Lands.
        36 Congress, 1 Session, Senate Committee Report No. 230.

I.

Petition of SYLVESTER GRAY

To the Senate and House of Representatives:

The petition of Sylvester Gray, a freeman of color, respectfully shows: That on the 7th day of August, 1856, he settled upon the northwest quarter of Section 14, Township 48, Range 13, of lands of the United States subject to sale at the Land Office at Superior, Wis.; that, under the Preemption Act of 1841, he filed his declaratory state-

36 Cong. 3
1 Sess. 3 ✓

Petition

of Sylvester Gray, a
free man of color,
praying that a
patent may be
issued to him for
land settled and
improved by him
under the preemption
act of 1841.

National Archives

Gray's petition to Congress, 1860

ment on the 14th of August, 1856, at the said Land Office; and, upon the 20th of June, 1857, located the said tract, containing 160 acres, with Military Bounty Land Warrant No. 39,006, issued under the act of 1855, and received from the register at Superior a certificate of such location.

Your petitioner further alleges that, in erecting a dwelling place, clearing land, and other labor and improvements upon said tract, he expended the sum of $223 (see memorandum herewith); which expenses and improvements were made with a view to making said tract a home for himself and family; it having been the practice of the General Land Office to allow entries or locations by persons of his description under the Preemption Act aforesaid.

But your petitioner has been recently informed, by a letter from the commissioner of the General Land Office, that on the 27th of January, 1860, his said location was canceled for the reason that he is a "man of color"; and his warrant has been returned to him.

Your petitioner begs leave to state that he

has understood that the action of the General Land Office in his case was had in pursuance of the decision of the Supreme Court of the United States, in Dred Scott's case, that persons of African descent could not be considered as citizens of the United States.

But your petitioner further begs leave to call the attention of your honorable body to the fact that his settlement and improvements, as aforesaid, were made prior to the date of that decision; for which reason, and that he may not be compelled to sustain the loss which would otherwise result to him, he respectfully asks that a law may be passed directing that a patent be issued to him for the land before described upon his surrendering to the commissioner of the General Land Office the warrant aforesaid.

Cost of Claim	
Original expense of building	$ 65.00
″ ″ clearing land	48.00
Subsequent expense of various improvements & labor	110.00
	$223.00

II.

Report of the Senate Committee on Public Lands

THE COMMITTEE ON PUBLIC LANDS, to whom was referred the case of Sylvester Gray, a freeman of color, praying that a patent may issue to him for land settled and improved by him, under the Preemption Act of 1841, having had the same under consideration, respectfully report:

That it appears that the said Gray claims, by preemption, the northwest quarter of Section Fourteen, in Township Forty-eight, of Range Thirteen, in the Fond du Lac Land District, Wisconsin, under Warrant No. 39,006, issued under act of 1855.

On the 27th January, 1860, the claim of

Gray was examined and canceled by the Interior Department upon the grounds that he was not a citizen of the United States, being a freeman of color, in accordance with the decision of the Supreme Court in the Dred Scott case. (*Vide* report of the commissioner of the General Land Office on the subject.)

Previous, however, to that decision, a different rule of action prevailed and was recognized by the government as correct, as will be seen by reference to the following opinion of a former attorney general:

Office of the Attorney General,
March 15, 1843.

Sir:

I have the honor to submit herewith a letter from the commissioner of the General Land Office, and request your opinion on the question therein stated, viz.: Whether a freeman of color, in the case presented, can be admitted to the privileges of a preemptioner under the act of 4th September, 1841? I enclose, also, a communication from the register of the Land Office at Edwardsville, Illinois, containing a statement of facts in the case, together with the usual declaratory statement of the applicants.

I have delayed giving an opinion on the subject because I was desirous of bestowing upon it a very deliberate consideration. The result is that I am of opinion that a freeman of color, a native of this country, may be admitted to the privileges of a preemptioner under the 10th Section of the act of 4th September, 1841.

It is not necessary, in my view of the matter, to discuss the question how far a freeman of color may be a citizen, in the highest sense of that word; that is, one who enjoys in the fullest manner all the *jura civilatis* under the Constitution of the United States. It is the plain meaning of the act to give the right of preemption to all denizens; and any foreigner who had filed his declaration of intention to become a citizen is rendered at once capable of holding land.

I conceive the purpose of the lawgiver to be only to exclude *aliens*, in the proper acceptation of the word — men born and living under the *ligeance* of a foreign power — from the enjoyment of the contemplated privileges. This acceptation of the word "citizen" is familiar in questions of a national character, arising during war in the prize courts, and might easily be illustrated by reference to the analogies of the law and the provisions of other statutes.

Now, free people of color are not *aliens;* they enjoy universally (while there has been no express statutable provision to the contrary) the rights of denizens. Even in the slaveholding states, they are capable of all the rights of contract and property. In all nations, without exception, ancient and modern, in which domestic slavery has existed, even the *slave* is distinguished from the *alien.* He is a part of the family, and as soon as he passes into the class of freemen, is considered as at once capable of all the *rights* which mere birth under the *ligeance* of a country bestows. How far a political *status* may be acquired is a different question, but his civil *status* is that of a complete denizenship. Therefore, free people of color, having always hitherto been admitted to share in the benefit of the preemption laws, I see nothing in the law of 1841 requiring a man to be a denizen that necessarily excludes them.

I have the honor to be, sir, your obedient servant,

H. S. LEGARE

Your Committee have, therefore, reported a bill for the relief of the said Sylvester Gray and recommend its passage.

Fourth of July parade in New York City, 1860

IRREPRESSIBLE CONFLICT

Events in the late 1850s made further compromise over the slavery issue impossible. Tensions were building throughout the country. Northerners who had bitterly resented the passing of the Fugitive Slave Law protested the Dred Scott Decision, which seemed to sanction the expansion of slavery. There were frequent minor skirmishes for possession of escaped slaves. Senator Charles Sumner, leader of the anti-slavery bloc in Congress, was brutally beaten by Preston Brooks, an outraged Southerner. The border fighting in Kansas and John Brown's futile raid on the federal arsenal at Harper's Ferry convinced the country that there was no hope of avoiding what Sen. William Seward had called the "irrepressible conflict." Seward had made his prediction on Oct. 25, 1858, just ten days after the last Lincoln-Douglas debate. With Lincoln's election the South was confirmed in its course of secession.

"Lincoln House," home of William J. Vaughn and a station on the underground railway, Christian County, Illinois; (right) 5 generations of a slave family, all born on the plantation of J. J. Smith, Beaufort, South Carolina; (below) slave quarters on a plantation in South Carolina, 1860

Preparing cotton for the gin on the J. J. Smith plantation, 1862; photographed by Timothy O'Sullivan; (left) slave nurse and her white charge, about 1860; (below) expulsion of Negroes and Abolitionists from a meeting at the Tremont Temple in Boston, 1860, after they attempted to break up the proceedings

(Above) Stephen A. Douglas, photographed at the time of the debates with Lincoln (right)

Springfield hall where Lincoln was chosen to oppose Douglas and made his "house-divided" speech

View of Harpers Ferry, Virginia (now West Virginia) scene of John Brown's raid

Handbill warning people to stay away from the vicinity of John Brown's execution, 1859

Daguerreotype of John Brown made in the year prior to the Harpers Ferry raid

PROCLAMATION!

IN pursuance of instructions from the Governor of Virginia, notice is hereby given to all whom it may concern,

That, as heretofore, particularly from now until after Friday next the 2nd of December, STRANGERS found within the County of Jefferson, and Counties adjacent, having no known and proper business here, and who cannot give a satisfactory account of themselves, will be at once arrested.

That on, and for a proper period before that day, strangers and especially parties, approaching under the pretext of being present at the execution of John Brown, whether by Railroad or otherwise, will be met by the Military and turned back or arrested without regard to the amount of force, that may be required to affect this, and during the said period and especially on the 2nd of December, the citizens of Jefferson and the surrounding country are EMPHATICALLY warned to remain at their homes armed and guard their own property.

Information received from reliable sources, clearly indicates that by so doing they will best consult their own interests.

No WOMEN or CHILDREN will be allowed to come near the place of execution.

WM. B. TALLIAFERRO, Maj. Gen Com. troops,
S. BASSETT FRENCH, Military Sec'y.
THOMAS C. GREEN, Mayor,
ANDREW HUNTER, Asst. Pros. Att'y.
JAMES W. CAMPBELL, Sheriff.

November 26th, '59.   Spirit Print

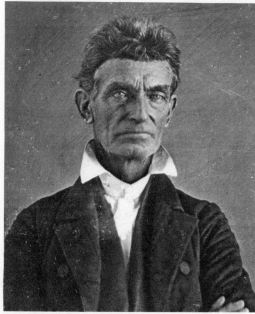

Lincoln and Hannibal Hamlin, as representatives of the more moderate wing of the Republican Party, were able to undermine many of the sources of Democratic strength in the North. Since the bulk of the population lay in the North, victory there was decisive. Lincoln carried all the free states (Douglas won three electoral votes in New Jersey), the Southern Democrat John C. Breckinridge carried eleven slave states, Douglas won Missouri, and three border slave states went to John Bell, the Constitional Union candidate.

(Top) Cartoon from the 1860 election shows three of the candidates, Lincoln, Douglas, and Breckinridge, tearing the nation to shreds, while the Union candidate, Bell, applies glue from a tiny, useless pot; (left) Lincoln, photographed in 1860 by Alexander Hesler; (below) Lincoln is shown riding uncomfortably on the Republican platform carried by Greeley and a Negro

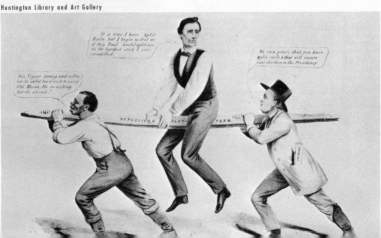

PROGRESSIVE DEMOCRACY—PROSPECT OF A SMASH UP.

1860 Republican cartoon describes the split within the Democratic Party in striking terms

John Bell, Constitutional Union candidate

John Breckinridge, candidate of Southern Democrats after break with the regular party

South Carolina seceded from the Union on Dec. 20, 1860, followed by Mississippi, Alabama, Florida, Georgia, Louisiana, and Texas. Arkansas formally seceded on May 6, 1861, though state troops had seized the federal arsenal in February. Virginia, Tennessee, and North Carolina joined the secession only after the hostilities had begun. Several states were sharply divided; western Virginia became the Union state of West Virginia in 1863. The Confederate States of America was formed on Feb. 8, 1861.

(Top) South Carolina Institute Hall, Charleston, where the Ordinance of Secession was ratified, December 20, 1860; (left) Edmund Ruffin, an early leader of secession movement in Virginia, author of a book defending the slave economy. He fired the first shot against Sumter and committed suicide at end of the war. (Below) Mass meeting endorsing the call for secession convention

THE "SECESSION MOVEMENT".

As other states charge wildly after the "Secession Humbug," Georgia detours temporarily

(Below) Jefferson Davis, Confederate president;
(right) W. L. Yancy, minister to Great Britain

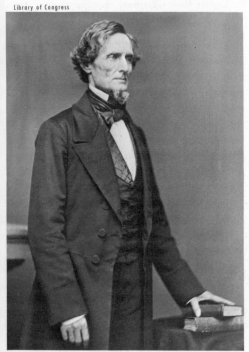

Citizens of Charleston watch the bombardment of Ft. Sumter from waterfront rooftops; (below) the Confederate flag flies over Sumter after its surrender, April 14, 1861

35.

Herman Melville: "Misgivings"

In 1866 Herman Melville published a collection of poems about the Civil War. At the time of its publication, Melville ha ceased to be an active writer and had taken a job as a customs inspector in New York City. In a prose supplement to the collection Melville pleaded for benevolent treatment of the South, though he detested slavery. "It is enough," he wrote, "for all practical purposes, if the South have been taught by the terrors of civil war to feel that Secession, like Slavery, is against Destiny; that both now lie buried in one grave; that her fate is linked with ours; and that together we comprise the Nation." "Misgivings," written in 1860, is from the collection.

Source: *Battle-Pieces and Aspects of the War*, New York, 1866.

MISGIVINGS

When ocean-clouds over inland hills
  Sweep storming in late autumn brown,
And horror the sodden valley fills,
  And the spire falls crashing in the town,

I muse upon my country's ills —
  The tempest bursting from the waste of Time
On the world's fairest hope linked with man's foulest crime.

Nature's dark side is heeded now —
  (Ah! optimist-cheer disheartened flown) —
A child may read the moody brow
  Of yon black mountain lone.
With shouts the torrents down the gorges go,
  And storms are formed behind the storm we feel:
The hemlock shakes in the rafter, the oak in the driving keel.

36.

Party Platforms of 1860

*Four major political parties took part in the election of 1860. Each party was
basically sectional in orientation, yet each hoped to provide overall solutions for the
critical problems that divided the nation. The Constitutional Union Party, founded
in 1859, called for devotion to the Union and the Constitution but took no stand on
the vital issues of the day. The Republican Party united the interests of the Northeast
and the Northwest and pledged itself to exclude slavery from the territories. The
Democrats were divided over the issue of slavery. The "Douglas" Democrats held
to the principle of "popular sovereignty," arguing that Congress had no right to
intervene on the slavery issue. When the Douglas platform was adopted, the Democratic
Party split into two factions, and a Southern wing, led by John C. Breckinridge,
reconvened in Baltimore and issued a pro-slavery platform. The four party platforms
are printed below.*

Source: *The National Conventions and Platforms of the Political Parties 1789-1905,*
Thomas H. McKee, ed., Baltimore, 1906, pp. 108-117.

I.

Constitutional Union Platform

Whereas, experience has demonstrated
that platforms adopted by the partisan conventions of the country have had the effect
to mislead and deceive the people, and at
the same time to widen the political divisions of the country, by the creation and
encouragement of geographical and sectional parties; therefore,

Resolved, that it is both the part of patriotism and of duty to *recognize* no political
principles other than THE CONSTITUTION OF
THE COUNTRY, THE UNION OF THE STATES,
AND THE ENFORCEMENT OF THE LAWS; and
that, as representatives of the Constitutional
Union men of the country in national convention assembled, we hereby pledge ourselves to maintain, protect, and defend, separately and unitedly, these great principles
of public liberty and national safety against
all enemies, at home and abroad, believing

that thereby peace may once more be restored to the country, the rights of the
people and of the states reestablished, and
the government again placed in that condition of justice, fraternity, and equality
which, under the example and Constitution
of our fathers, has solemnly bound every
citizen of the United States to maintain a
more perfect Union, establish justice, insure
domestic tranquillity, provide for the common defense, promote the general welfare,
and secure the blessings of liberty to ourselves and our posterity.

II.

Republican Platform

Resolved, that we, the delegated representatives of the Republican electors of the
United States, in convention assembled, in
discharge of the duty we owe to our constituents and our country, unite in the following declarations:

1. That the history of the nation, during the last four years, has fully established the propriety and necessity of the organization and perpetuation of the Republican Party, and that the causes which called it into existence are permanent in their nature, and now, more than ever before, demand its peaceful and constitutional triumph.

2. That the maintenance of the principles promulgated in the Declaration of Independence and embodied in the federal Constitution, "That all men are created equal; that they are endowed by their Creator with certain inalienable rights; that among these are life, liberty, and the pursuit of happiness; that, to secure these rights, governments are instituted among men, deriving their just powers from the consent of the governed," is essential to the preservation of our republican institutions; and that the federal Constitution, the rights of the states, and the Union of the states must and shall be preserved.

3. That to the Union of the states this nation owes its unprecedented increase in population, its surprising development of material resources, its rapid augmentation of wealth, its happiness at home and its honor abroad; and we hold in abhorrence all schemes for disunion, come from whatever source they may. And we congratulate the country that no Republican member of Congress has uttered or countenanced the threats of disunion so often made by Democratic members, without rebuke and with applause from their political associates; and we denounce those threats of disunion, in case of a popular overthrow of their ascendancy, as denying the vital principles of a free government, and as an avowal of contemplated treason, which it is the imperative duty of an indignant people sternly to rebuke and forever silence.

4. That the maintenance inviolate of the rights of the states, and especially the right of each state to order and control its own domestic institutions according to its own judgment exclusively, is essential to that balance of power on which the perfection and endurance of our political fabric depend; and we denounce the lawless invasion by armed force of the soil of any state or territory, no matter under what pretext, as among the gravest of crimes.

5. That the present Democratic administration has far exceeded our worst apprehensions, in its measureless subserviency to the exactions of a sectional interest, as especially evinced in its desperate exertions to force the infamous Lecompton Constitution upon the protesting people of Kansas; in construing the personal relations between master and servant to involve an unqualified property in persons; in its attempted enforcement everywhere, on land and sea, through the intervention of Congress and of the federal courts, of the extreme pretensions of a purely local interest; and in its general and unvarying abuse of the power entrusted to it by a confiding people.

6. That the people justly view with alarm the reckless extravagance which pervades every department of the federal government; that a return to rigid economy and accountability is indispensable to arrest the systematic plunder of the public treasury by favored partisans; while the recent startling developments of frauds and corruptions at the federal metropolis show that an entire change of administration is imperatively demanded.

7. That the new dogma that the Constitution, of its own force, carries slavery into any or all of the territories of the United States is a dangerous political heresy, at variance with the explicit provisions of that instrument itself, with contemporaneous exposition, and with legislative and judicial precedent; is revolutionary in its tendency and subversive of the peace and harmony of the country.

8. That the normal condition of all the territory of the United States is that of freedom; that as our republican fathers, when they had abolished slavery in all our national territory, ordained that "no person

should be deprived of life, liberty, or property without due process of law," it becomes our duty, by legislation, whenever such legislation is necessary, to maintain this provision of the Constitution against all attempts to violate it; and we deny the authority of Congress, of a territorial legislature, or of any individuals to give legal existence to slavery in any territory of the United States.

9. That we brand the recent reopening of the African slave trade, under the cover of our national flag, aided by perversions of judicial power, as a crime against humanity and a burning shame to our country and age; and we call upon Congress to take prompt and efficient measures for the total and final suppression of that execrable traffic.

10. That in the recent vetoes by their federal governors of the acts of the legislatures of Kansas and Nebraska prohibiting slavery in those territories, we find a practical illustration of the boasted Democratic principles of nonintervention and popular sovereignty embodied in the Kansas-Nebraska Bill, and a demonstration of the deception and fraud involved therein.

11. That Kansas should, of right, be immediately admitted as a state under the constitution recently formed and adopted by her people and accepted by the House of Representatives.

12. That, while providing revenue for the support of the general government by duties upon imports, sound policy requires such an adjustment of these imposts as to encourage the development of the industrial interests of the whole country; and we commend that policy of national exchanges which secures to the workingmen liberal wages; to agriculture, remunerative prices; to mechanics and manufacturers, an adequate reward for their skill, labor, and enterprise; and to the nation, commercial prosperity and independence.

13. That we protest against any sale or alienation to others of the public lands held by actual settlers, and against any view of the free-homestead policy which regards the settlers as paupers or suppliants for public bounty; and we demand the passage by Congress of the complete and satisfactory homestead measure which has already passed the House.

14. That the Republican Party is opposed to any change in our naturalization laws or any state legislation by which the rights of citizens hitherto accorded to immigrants from foreign lands shall be abridged or impaired; and in favor of giving a full and efficient protection to the rights of all classes of citizens, whether native or naturalized, both at home and abroad.

15. That appropriations by Congress for river and harbor improvements of a national character, required for the accommodation and security of an existing commerce, are authorized by the Constitution and justified by the obligation of government to protect the lives and property of its citizens.

16. That a railroad to the Pacific Ocean is imperatively demanded by the interests of the whole country; that the federal government ought to render immediate and efficient aid in its construction; and that, as preliminary thereto, a daily overland mail should be promptly established.

17. Finally, having thus set forth our distinctive principles and views, we invite the cooperation of all citizens, however differing on other questions, who substantially agree with us in their affirmance and support.

III.

Democratic Platform (Douglas)

1. *Resolved,* that we, the Democracy of the Union, in convention assembled, hereby declare our affirmance of the resolutions unanimously adopted and declared as a platform of principles by the Democratic Convention at Cincinnati in the year 1856, believing that Democratic principles are un-

changeable in their nature when applied to the same subject matters; and we recommend as the only further resolutions the following:

Inasmuch as difference of opinion exists in the Democratic Party as to the nature and extent of the powers of a territorial legislature, and as to the powers and duties of Congress, under the Constitution of the United States, over the institution of slavery within the territories,

2. *Resolved,* that the Democratic Party will abide by the decision of the Supreme Court of the United States upon the questions of constitutional law.

3. *Resolved,* that it is the duty of the United States to afford ample and complete protection to all its citizens, whether at home or abroad, and whether native or foreign.

4. *Resolved,* that one of the necessities of the age, in a military, commercial, and postal point of view, is speedy communication between the Atlantic and Pacific states; and the Democratic Party pledge such constitutional government aid as will insure the construction of a railroad to the Pacific Coast at the earliest practicable period.

5. *Resolved,* that the Democratic Party are in favor of the acquisition of the island of Cuba on such terms as shall be honorable to ourselves and just to Spain.

6. *Resolved,* that the enactments of state legislatures to defeat the faithful execution of the Fugitive Slave Law are hostile in character, subversive of the Constitution, and revolutionary in their effect.

7. *Resolved,* that it is in accordance with the true interpretation of the Cincinnati platform that, during the existence of the territorial governments, the measure of restriction, whatever it may be, imposed by the federal Constitution on the power of the territorial legislature over the subject of the domestic relations, as the same has been or shall hereafter be finally determined by the Supreme Court of the United States, should be respected by all good citizens and

enforced with promptness and fidelity by every branch of the general government.

IV.

Democratic Platform (Breckinridge)

Resolved, that the platform adopted by the Democratic Party at Cincinnati be affirmed, with the following explanatory resolutions:

1. That the government of a territory organized by an act of Congress is provisional and temporary, and during its existence all citizens of the United States have an equal right to settle with their property in a territory, without their rights either of person or property being destroyed or impaired by congressional or territorial legislation.

2. That it is the duty of the federal government, in all its departments, to protect, when necessary, the rights of persons and property in the territories and wherever else its constitutional authority extends.

3. That when settlers in a territory, having an adequate population, form a state constitution, the right of sovereignty commences, and, being consummated by admission into the Union, they stand on an equal footing with the people of other states; and the state thus organized ought to be admitted into the federal Union, whether its constitution prohibits or recognizes the institution of slavery.

4. That the Democratic Party are in favor of the acquisition of the island of Cuba on such terms as shall be honorable to ourselves and just to Spain at the earliest practicable moment.

5. That the enactments of state legislatures to defeat the faithful execution of the Fugitive Slave Law are hostile in character, subversive of the Constitution, and revolutionary in their effect.

6. That the democracy of the United States recognize it as the imperative duty of this government to protect the naturalized citizen in all his rights, whether at home or

in foreign lands, to the same extent as its native-born citizens.

Whereas, one of the greatest necessities of the age, in a political, commercial, postal, and military point of view, is a speedy communication between the Pacific and Atlantic coasts; therefore,

Be it resolved, that the National Demo-

cratic Party do hereby pledge themselves to use every means in their power to secure the passage of some bill, to the extent of the constitutional authority of Congress, for the construction of a Pacific railroad from the Mississippi River to the Pacific Ocean at the earliest practicable moment.

37.

Georgia Debate on Secession

When news of Lincoln's election reached Georgia, a proposal was placed before the legislature to call a special convention to consider whether the state should secede. Realizing its critical situation, the Georgia legislature sought counsel from leading political figures of the state. All Southerners were fearful of the new President, but they were divided over what action the South should take. The die-hard secessionists demanded that the South secede before Lincoln took office. The moderates believed the South should wait until the federal government took some overt action against it. Two leading statesmen of Georgia, Robert Toombs, a secessionist, and Alexander Stephens, a moderate, debated the issue of secession before the legislature on November 13-14, 1860. The two men were devoted friends. When Stephens finished his speech, Toombs moved that cheers be given for his opponent. Stephens' speech reached even Lincoln, a friend from congressional days, who gave him assurances that he would not interfere with slavery in the South. By February 1, 1861, a month before the inauguration, all of the deep South, including Georgia, had left the Union. Following are excerpts of the speeches by Toombs and Stephens.

Source: Moore, I, Supplement, Document 67.
        Moore, I, Document 147 1/2.

I.

ROBERT TOOMBS: For Secession

I VERY MUCH REGRET, in appearing before you at your request, to address you on the present state of the country and the prospect before us, that I can bring you no good tidings. The stern, steady march of

events has brought us in conflict with our nonslaveholding confederates upon the fundamental principles of our compact of Union. We have not sought this conflict; we have sought too long to avoid it; our forbearance has been construed into weakness, our magnanimity into fear, until the vindication of our manhood, as well as the defense of our rights, is required at our hands. The door of conciliation and compromise is finally closed by our adversaries, and it remains only to us to meet the conflict with the dignity and firmness of men worthy of freedom.

We need no declaration of independence. Above eighty-four years ago, our fathers won that by the sword from Great Britain, and above seventy years ago, Georgia, with the twelve other confederates, as free, sovereign, and independent states, having perfect governments already in existence, for purposes and objects clearly expressed and with powers clearly defined, erected a common agent for the attainment of these purposes by the exercise of those powers, and called this agent the United States of America.

The basis, the cornerstone of this government, was the perfect equality of the free, sovereign, and independent states which made it. They were unequal in population, wealth, and territorial extent; they had great diversities of interests, pursuits, institutions, and laws; but they had common interests, mainly exterior, which they proposed to protect by this common agent — a constitutional united government — without in any degree subjecting their inequalities and diversities to federal control or action. . . .

We had a large common domain, already added by the several states for the common benefit of all; purchase and war might make large additions to this common domain; hence, the power over existing and future territories, with the stipulation to admit new states, was conferred. Being independent states, in such close proximity, acts seriously affecting the tranquillity of some might be done by others; fugitives from labor and justice in one might seek sanctuary in others, producing strife, and bloodshed, and insecurity; therefore the power was conferred in the common agent and the duty imposed by the compact upon each confederate to remedy these evils. These were the main objects for forming the federal government; the powers it possesses were conferred chiefly with the view of securing them. . . .

The instant the government was organized, at the very first Congress, the Northern states evinced a general desire and purpose to use it for their own benefit and to pervert its powers for sectional advantage; and they have steadily pursued that policy to this day. They demanded a monopoly of the business of shipbuilding, and got a prohibition against the sale of foreign ships to citizens of the United States, which exists to this day. They demanded a monopoly of the coasting trade, in order to get higher freights than they could get in open competition with the carriers of the world. Congress gave it to them, and they yet hold this monopoly. And now, today, if a foreign vessel in Savannah offer to take your rice, cotton, grain, or lumber to New York, or any other American port, for nothing, your laws prohibit it, in order that Northern shipowners may get enhanced prices for doing your carrying. . . .

Even the fishermen of Massachusetts and New England demand and receive from the public treasury about $500,000 per annum as a pure bounty on their business of catching codfish. The North, at the very first Congress, demanded and received bounties, under the name of protection, for every trade, craft, and calling which they pursue; and there is not an artisan in brass, or iron, or wood, or weaver, or spinner in wool or cotton, or a calicomaker, or ironmaster, or a coal owner in all of the Northern or Middle states who has not received what he calls the protection of his government on his industry to the extent of from 15 to 200 percent from the year 1791 to this day. They will not strike a blow, or stretch a muscle, without bounties from the government.

No wonder they cry aloud for the glorious Union; they have the same reason for praising it that craftsmen of Ephesus had for shouting, "Great is Diana of the Ephesians," whom all Asia and the world worshiped. By it they got their wealth; by it they levy tribute on honest labor. It is true that this policy has been largely sustained by the South; it is true that the present tariff was sustained by an almost unanimous vote of the South; but it was a reduction — a reduction necessary from the plethora of the revenue; but the policy of the North soon made it inadequate to meet the public expenditure by an enormous and profligate increase of the public expenditure; and at the last session of Congress they brought in and passed through the House the most atrocious tariff bill that ever was enacted, raising the present duties from 20 to 250 percent above the existing rates of duty. . . .

Thus stands the account between the North and the South. Under its ordinary and most favorable action, bounties and protection to every interest and every pursuit in the North, to the extent of at least $50 million per annum, besides the expenditure of at least $60 million out of every $70 million of the public expenditure among them, thus making the Treasury a perpetual fertilizing stream to them and their industry, and a suction pump to drain away our substance and parch up our lands.

With these vast advantages, ordinary and extraordinary, one would have supposed the North would have been content, and would have at least respected the security and tranquillity of such obedient and profitable brethren; but such is not human nature. They despised the patient victims of their avarice, and they very soon began a war upon our political rights and social institutions, marked by every act of perfidy and treachery which could add a darker hue to such a warfare. In 1820, the Northern party (and I mean by that term now and whenever else it is used, or its equivalent, in these remarks, the Antislavery or Abolition Party

of the North) endeavored to exclude the state of Missouri from admission into the Union, because she chose to protect African slavery in the new state. In the House, where they had a majority, they rejected her application, and a struggle ensued, when some half a dozen of Northern men gave way and admitted the state, but upon condition of the exclusion of slavery from all that country acquired from France by the treaty of 1802 lying north of 36°30′ N latitude, and outside of the state of Missouri.

This act of exclusion violated the express provisions of the treaty of 1802, to which the national faith was pledged; violated the well-settled policy of the government, at least from Adams' administration to that day, and has, since slavery was adjudicated by the Supreme Court of the United States, violated the Constitution itself. When we acquired California and New Mexico, this party, scorning all compromises and all concessions, demanded that slavery should be forever excluded from them and all other acquisitions of the republic, either by purchase or conquest, forever. This position of this Northern party brought about the troubles of 1850 and the political excitement of 1854.

The South at all times demanded nothing but equality in the common territories, equal enjoyment of them with their property to that extended to Northern citizens and their property — nothing more. They said, we pay our part in all the blood and treasure expended in their acquisition. Give us equality of enjoyment, equal right to expansion — it is as necessary to our prosperity as yours. In 1790 we had less than 800,000 slaves. Under our mild and humane administration of the system, they have increased above 4 million. The country has expanded to meet this growing want; and Florida, Alabama, Mississippi, Louisiana, Texas, Arkansas, Kentucky, Tennessee, and Missouri have received this increasing tide of African labor; before the end of this century, at precisely the same rate of increase, the Africans among us in a subordinate condition will amount to 11 million persons. What shall be done with them?

We must expand or perish. We are constrained by an inexorable necessity to accept expansion or extermination. Those who tell you that the territorial question is an abstraction, that you can never colonize another territory without the African slave trade are both deaf and blind to the history of the last sixty years. All just reasoning, all past history condemn the fallacy. The North understand it better — they have told us for twenty years that their object was to pen up slavery within its present limits — surround it with a border of free states, and, like the scorpion surrounded with fire, they will make it sting itself to death. One thing at least is certain, that whatever may be the effect of your exclusion from the territories, there is no dispute but that the North mean it, and adopt it as a measure hostile to slavery upon this point.

They all agree, they are unanimous in Congress, in the states, on the rostrum, in the sanctuary — everywhere they declare that slavery shall not go into the territories. They took up arms to drive it out of Kansas; and Sharp's rifles were put into the hands of assassins by Abolition preachers to do their work. Are they mistaken? No; they are not. The party put it into their platform at Philadelphia — they have it in the cornerstone of their Chicago platform; Lincoln is on it — pledged to it. Hamlin is on it, and pledged to it; every Abolitionist in the Union, in or out of place, is openly pledged in some manner to drive us from the common territories.

This conflict, at least, is irrepressible — it is easily understood — we demand the equal right with the North to go into the common territories with all of our property, slaves included, and to be there protected in its peaceable enjoyment by the federal government, until such territories may come into the Union as equal states — then we admit them with or without slavery, as the people themselves may decide for themselves. Will you surrender this principle? The day you do this base, unmanly deed you embrace political degradation and death.

But this is only one of the points of the case; the North agreed to deliver up fugitives from labor. In pursuance of this clause of the Constitution, Congress, in 1797, during Washington's administration, passed a Fugitive Slave Law. That act never was faithfully respected all over the North, but it was not obstructed by state legislation until within the last thirty years; but the spirit of hostility to our rights became more active and determined, and in 1850 that act was found totally insufficient to recover and return fugitives from labor; therefore the act of 1850 was passed. The passage of that act was sufficient to rouse the demon of Abolition all over the North. The pulpit, the press, Abolition societies, popular assemblages belched forth nothing but imprecations and curses upon the South and the honest men of the North who voted to maintain the Constitution. And thirteen states of the Union, by the most solemn acts of legislation, willfully, knowingly, and corruptly perjured themselves, and annulled this law within their respective limits.

I say willfully, knowingly, and corruptly. The Constitution is plain — it was construed in 1793 by Washington and the Second Congress. In the Senate, the bill for the rendition of fugitives was unanimously passed, and nearly unanimously passed by the House of Representatives, and signed by Washington. All the courts of the United States, federal and state, from the Supreme Court of the United States to the justice courts of all the states whose actions have ever come under my notice, construed

Valentine Museum, Cook Collection
Robert Toombs

this Constitution to mean and intend the rendition of fugitive slaves by law of Congress, which might be aided, not thwarted, by state legislation, until the decision of the Supreme Court of Wisconsin held otherwise, and that decision was unanimously overruled by Northern and Southern judges in the Supreme Court, and which Court, in the same case, unanimously affirmed the constitutionality of the act of 1850. But these acts were not only annulled by the Abolition legislatures but annulled under circumstances of atrocity and aggravation unknown to the legislation of any civilized people in the world. Some of them punish us with penitentiary punishment as felons for even claiming our own slaves within their limits, even by his own consent; others by ingenious contrivances prevent the possibility of your sustaining your rights in their limits, where they seek to compel you to go, and then punish you by fine and infamous punishments for asserting your rights and failing to get them. This is the

fidelity of our brethren (!) to their plighted faith — their oft-repeated oaths! . . .

I have shown you what this party has done and declared in the national councils, in the state legislatures, by and through their Executive departments. Let us examine what they are at as private citizens. By the laws of nations, founded on natural justice, no nation, nor the subjects or citizens of any nation, have the right to disturb the peace or security of any other nation or people, much less to conspire, excite insurrection, discontent, or the commission of crimes among them, and all these are held to be good causes of war. For twenty years this party has, by Abolition societies, by publications made by them, by the public press, through the pulpit and their own legislative halls, and every effort — by reproaches, by abuse, by vilification, by slander — to disturb our security, our tranquillity — to excite discontent between the different classes of our people, and to excite our slaves to insurrection. No nation in the world would submit to such conduct from any other nation. I will not willingly do so from this Abolition Party.

I demand the protection of my state government, to whom I owe my allegiance. I wish it distinctly understood that it is the price of my allegiance. You are here, constitutional legislators — I make the demand today of you. Gentlemen, I have thus shown you the violations of our constitutional rights by our confederates; I have shown you that they are plain, palpable, deliberate, and dangerous; that they are committed by the Executive, Legislative, and Judicial departments of the state governments of our confederates — that all their wrongs are approved by the people of these states. I say the time has come to redress these acknowledged wrongs and to avert even greater evils, of which these are but the signs and symbols.

But I am asked, why do you demand action now? The question is both appropriate and important; it ought to be frankly met. The Abolitionists say you are raising a clamor because you were beaten in the election. The falsity of this statement needs no confirmation. Look to our past history for its refutation. Some excellent citizens and able men in Georgia say the election of any man constitutionally is no cause for a dissolution of the Union. That position is calculated only to mislead and not to enlighten. It is not the issue. I say the election of Lincoln, with all of its surroundings, is sufficient. What is the significance of his election? It is the endorsement, by the non-slaveholding states, of all those acts of aggression upon our rights by all these states, legislatures, governors, judges, and people. He is elected by the perpetrators of these wrongs with the purpose and intent to aid and support them in wrongdoing.

Hitherto, the Constitution has had on its side the federal executive, whose duty it is to execute the laws and Constitution against these malefactors. It has earnestly endeavored to discharge that duty. Relying upon its power and good faith to remedy these wrongs, we have listened to conservative counsels, trusting to time, to the federal executive, and to a returning sense of justice in the North. The executive has been faithful — the federal judiciary have been faithful — the President has appointed sound judges, sound marshals, and other subordinate officers to interpret and to execute the laws. With the best intentions, they have all failed — our property has been stolen, our people murdered; felons and assassins have found sanctuary in the arms of the party which elected Mr. Lincoln. The executive power, the last bulwark of the Constitution to defend us against these enemies of the Constitution, has been swept away, and we now stand without a shield, with bare bosoms presented to our enemies, and we demand at your hands the sword for our de-

fense, and if you will not give it to us, we will take it — take it by the divine right of self-defense, which governments neither give nor can take away.

Therefore, redress for past and present wrongs demands resistance to the rule of Lincoln and his Abolition horde over us; he comes at their head to shield and protect them in the perpetration of these outrages upon us, and, what is more, he comes at their head to aid them in consummating their avowed purposes by the power of the federal government. Their main purpose, as indicated by all their acts of hostility to slavery, is its final and total abolition. His party declare it; their acts prove it. He has declared it; I accept his declaration. The battle of the irrepressible conflict has hitherto been fought on his side alone. We demand service in this war. Surely no one will deny that the election of Lincoln is the endorsement of the policy of those who elected him, and an endorsement of his own opinions.

The opinions of those who elected him are to be found in their solemn acts under oath — in their state governments, endorsed by their constituents. To them I have already referred. They are also to be found in the votes of his supporters in Congress — also endorsed by the party, by their return. Their opinions are to be found in the speeches of Seward, and Sumner, and Lovejoy, and their associates and confederates in the two houses of Congress. Since the promotion of Mr. Lincoln's party, all of them speak with one voice, and speak trumpet-tongued their fixed purpose to outlaw $4 billion of our property in the territories, and to put it under the ban of the empire in the states where it exists. They declare their purpose to war against slavery until there shall not be a slave in America, and until the African is elevated to a social and political equality with the white man. Lincoln endorses them and their principles, and in his own speeches declares the conflict irrepressible and enduring, until slavery is everywhere abolished.

Hitherto, they have carried on this warfare by state action, by individual action, by appropriation, by the incendiary's torch and the poisoned bowl. They were compelled to adopt this method because the federal executive and the federal judiciary were against them. They will have possession of the federal executive with its vast power, patronage, prestige of legality, its Army, its Navy, and its revenue on the 4th of March next. Hitherto, it has been on the side of the Constitution and the right; after the 4th of March it will be in the hands of your enemy. Will you let him have it? [*Cries of "No, no. Never."*]

Then strike while it is yet today. Withdraw your sons from the Army, from the Navy, and every department of the federal public service. Keep your own taxes in your own coffers — buy arms with them and throw the bloody spear into this den of incendiaries and assassins, and let God defend the right.

But you are advised to wait, send soft messages to their brethren, to beg them to relent, to give you some assurances of their better fidelity for the future. What more can you get from them under this government? You have the Constitution — you have its exposition by themselves for seventy years — you have their oaths — they have broken all these, and will break them again. They tell you everywhere, loudly and defiantly, you shall have no power, no security until you give up the right of governing yourselves according to your own will — until you submit to theirs. For this is the meaning of Mr. Lincoln's irrepressible conflict — this is his emphatic declaration to all the world. Will you heed it? For myself, like the Athenian ambassador, I will take no security but this, that it shall not be in the power of our enemies to injure my country if they desire it. Nothing but ruin will follow delay. The enemy on the 4th of March will entrench himself behind a quintuple wall of defense. Executive power, judiciary (Mr. Seward has already proclaimed its reformation), Army, Navy, and Treasury. Twenty years of labor and toil and taxes all expended upon preparation would not make up for the advantage your enemies would gain if the rising sun on the 5th of March should find you in the Union. Then strike while it is yet time.

But we are told that secession would destroy the fairest fabric of liberty the world ever saw, and that we are the most prosperous people in the world under it. The arguments of tyranny as well as its acts always reenact themselves. The arguments I now hear in favor of this Northern connection are identical in substance and almost in the same words as those which were used in 1775 and 1776 to sustain the British connection. We won liberty, sovereignty, and independence by the American Revolution — we endeavored to secure and perpetuate these blessings by means of our Constitution. The very men who use these arguments admit that this Constitution, this compact is violated, broken, and trampled under foot by the Abolition Party. Shall we surrender the jewels because their robbers and incendiaries have broken the casket? Is this the way to preserve liberty? I would as lief surrender it back to the British Crown as to the Abolitionists. I will defend it from both. Our purpose is to defend those liberties. What baser fate could befall us or this great experiment of free government than to have written upon its tomb: "Fell by the hands of Abolitionists and the cowardice of its natural defenders." If we quail now, this will be its epitaph.

We are said to be a happy and prosperous people. We have been, because we have hitherto maintained our ancient rights and liberties — we will be until we surrender them. They are in danger; come, freemen, to the rescue. If we are prosperous, it is due to God, ourselves, and the wisdom of our state government. We have an Executive, Legislative, and Judicial department at home, professing and entitled to the confidence of the people. I have already vainly asked for the law of the federal government that promotes our prosperity. I have shown you many that retard that prosperity — many that drain our coffers for the benefit of our bitterest foes. I say bitterest foes — show me the nation in the world that hates, despises, vilifies, or plunders us like our Abolition "brethren" in the North. There is none.

I can go to England or France, or any other country in Europe with my slave without molestation or violating any law. I can go anywhere except in my own country, whilom [formerly] called "the glorious Union"; here alone am I stigmatized as a felon; here alone am I an outlaw; here alone am I under the ban of the empire; here alone I have neither security nor tranquillity; here alone are organized governments ready to protect the incendiary, the assassin who burns my dwelling or takes my life or those of my wife and children; here alone are hired emissaries paid by brethren to glide through the domestic circle and intrigue insurrection with all of its nameless horrors.

My countrymen, "if you have nature in you, bear it not." Withdraw yourselves from such a confederacy; it is your right to do so — your duty to do so. I know not why the Abolitionists should object to it, unless they want to torture and plunder you. If they resist this great sovereign right, make another war of independence, for that then will be the question; fight its battles over again — reconquer liberty and independence. As for me, I will take any place in the great conflict for rights which you may assign. I will take none in the federal government during Mr. Lincoln's administration.

If you desire a senator after the 4th of March, you must elect one in my place. I have served you in the state and national councils for nearly a quarter of a century without once losing your confidence. I am yet ready for the public service when honor and duty call. I will serve you anywhere where it will not degrade and dishonor my country. Make my name infamous forever, if you will, but save Georgia. I have pointed out your wrongs, your danger, your duty. You have claimed nothing but that rights be respected and that justice be done. Emblazon it on your banner — fight for it, win it, or perish in the effort.

II.

Alexander H. Stephens: Against Secession

I appear before you tonight at the request of members of the legislature and others to speak of matters of the deepest interest that can possibly concern us all of an earthly character. There is nothing — no question or subject connected with this life — that concerns a free people so intimately as that of the government under which they live. We are now, indeed, surrounded by evils. Never since I entered upon the public stage has the country been so environed with difficulties and dangers that threatened the public peace and the very existence of society as now. I do not now appear before you at my own instance. It is not to gratify desire of my own that I am here. Had I consulted my own ease and pleasure I should not be before you; but, believing that it is the duty of every good citizen to give his counsels and views whenever the country is in danger, as to the best policy to be pursued, I am here. For these reasons, and these only, do I bespeak a calm, patient, and attentive hearing.

My object is not to stir up strife but to allay it; not to appeal to your passions but to your reason. Good governments can never be built up or sustained by the impulse of passion. I wish to address myself to your good sense, to your good judgment, and, if after hearing you disagree, let us agree to disagree, and part as we met, friends. We all have the same object, the same interest. That people should disagree in republican governments, upon questions of public policy, is natural. That men should disagree upon all matters connected with human investigation, whether relating to science or human conduct, is natural. Hence, in free governments, parties will arise. But a free people should express their different opinions with liberality and charity, with no acrimony toward those of their fellows, when honestly and sincerely given. These are my feelings tonight.

Let us, therefore, reason together. It is not my purpose to say aught to wound the feelings of any individual who may be present; and if in the ardency with which I shall express my opinions I shall say anything which may be deemed too strong, let it be set down to the zeal with which I advocate my own convictions. There is with me no intention to irritate or offend.

The first question that presents itself is — Shall the people of the South secede from the Union in consequence of the election of Mr. Lincoln to the presidency of the United States? My countrymen, *I tell you frankly, candidly, and earnestly that I do not think that they ought.* In my judgment, the election of no man, constitutionally chosen to that high office, is sufficient cause for any state to separate from the Union. It ought to stand by and aid still in maintaining the Constitution of the country. To make a point of resistance to the government, to withdraw from it because a man has been constitutionally elected, puts us in the wrong. We are pledged to maintain the Constitution. Many of us have sworn to support it. Can we, therefore, for the mere election of a man to the presidency, and that, too, in accordance with the prescribed forms of the Constitution, make a point of resistance to the government without becoming the breakers of that sacred instrument ourselves, withdraw ourselves from it? Would we not be in the wrong?

Whatever fate is to befall this country, let it never be laid to the charge of the people of the South, and especially to the people of Georgia, that we were untrue to our national engagements. Let the fault and the wrong rest upon others. If all our hopes are to be blasted, if the republic is to go down, let us be found to the last moment standing on the deck, with the Constitution of the United States waving over our heads. Let the fanatics of the North break the Constitution, if such is their fell purpose. Let the responsibility be upon them. I shall speak presently more of their acts; but let not the South, let us not be the ones to commit the aggression. We went into the election with this people. The result was different from what we wished; but the election has been constitutionally held. Were we to make a point of resistance to the government and go out of the Union on that account, the record would be made up hereafter against us.

But it is said Mr. Lincoln's policy and principles are against the Constitution, and that if he carries them out it will be destructive of our rights. Let us not anticipate a threatened evil. If he violates the Constitution then will come our time to act. Do not let us break it because, forsooth, he may. If he does, that is the time for us to strike. I think it would be injudicious and unwise to do this sooner. I do not anticipate that Mr. Lincoln will do anything to jeopard our safety or security, whatever may be his spirit to do it; for he is bound by the constitutional checks which are thrown around him, which at this time render him powerless to do any great mischief.

This shows the wisdom of our system. The President of the United States is no emperor, no dictator — he is clothed with no absolute power. He can do nothing unless he is backed by power in Congress. The House of Representatives is largely in the majority against him.

In the Senate he will also be powerless. There will be a majority of four against him. This, after the loss of Bigler, Fitch, and others, by the unfortunate dissensions of the National Democratic Party in their states. Mr. Lincoln cannot appoint an officer without the consent of the Senate — he cannot form a cabinet without the same consent. He will be in the condition of George III (the embodiment of Toryism), who had to ask the Whigs to appoint his ministers, and was compelled to receive a cabinet utterly opposed to his views; and so Mr. Lincoln will be compelled to ask of the Senate to choose for him a cabinet; if the Democracy of that body choose to put him on such terms. He will be compelled to do this or let the government stop, if the National Democratic men — for that is their name at the North — the conservative men in the Senate, should so determine. Then, how can Mr. Lincoln obtain a cabinet which would aid him or allow him to violate the Constitution?

Why, then, I say, should we disrupt the ties of this Union when his hands are tied, when he can do nothing against us? I have heard it mooted that no man in the state of Georgia, who is true to her interests, could hold office under Mr. Lincoln. But, I ask, who appoints to office? Not the President alone; the Senate has to concur. No man can be appointed without the consent of the Senate. Should any man then refuse to hold office that was given to him by a Democratic Senate? . . . In my judgment, I say under such circumstances, there would be no possible disgrace for a Southern man to hold office. No man will be suffered to be appointed, I have no doubt, who is not true to the Constitution, if Southern senators are true to their trusts, as I cannot permit myself to doubt that they will be. . . .

My countrymen, I am not of those who believe this Union has been a curse up to this time. True men, men of integrity, entertain different views from me on this subject. I do not question their right to do so; I would not impugn their motives in so doing. Nor will I undertake to say that this government of our fathers is perfect. There is nothing perfect in this world of a human origin. Nothing connected with human nature, from man himself to any of his works. You may select the wisest and best men for your judges, and yet how many defects are there in the administration of justice? You may select the wisest and best men for your legislators, and yet how many defects are apparent in your laws? And it is so in our government. . . .

I come now to the main question put to me, and on which my counsel has been asked. That is, what the present legislature should do in view of the dangers that threaten us, and the wrongs that have been done us by several of our confederate states in the Union, by the acts of their legislatures nullifying the Fugitive Slave Law, and in direct disregard of their constitutional obligations. What I shall say will not be in the spirit of dictation. It will be simply my own judgment for what it is worth. It proceeds from a strong conviction that according to it our rights, interests, and honor — our present safety and future security — can be maintained without yet looking to the last resort, the *ultima ratio regum*. That should not be looked to until all else fails. That may come. On this point I am hopeful but not sanguine. But let us use every patriotic effort to prevent it while there is ground for hope.

If any view that I may present, in your

judgment, be inconsistent with the best interests of Georgia, I ask you as patriots not to regard it. After hearing me and others whom you have advised with, act in the premises according to your own conviction of duty as patriots. I speak now particularly to the members of the legislature present. There are, as I have said, great dangers ahead. Great dangers may come from the election I have spoken of. If the policy of Mr. Lincoln and his Republican associates shall be carried out, or attempted to be carried out, no man in Georgia will be more willing or ready than myself to defend our rights, interest, and honor at every hazard, and to the last extremity.

What is this policy? It is, in the first place, to exclude us by an act of Congress from the territories with our slave property. He is for using the power of the general government against the extension of our institutions. Our position on this point is and ought to be, at all hazards, for perfect equality between all the states, and the citizens of all the states, in the territories, under the Constitution of the United States. If Congress should exercise its power against this, then I am for standing where Georgia planted herself in 1850. These were plain propositions which were then laid down in her celebrated platform as sufficient for the disruption of the Union if the occasion should ever come; on these Georgia has declared that she will go out of the Union; and for these she would be justified by the nations of the earth in so doing.

I say the same; I said it then; I say it now — if Mr. Lincoln's policy should be carried out. I have told you that I do not think his bare election sufficient cause; but if his policy should be carried out in violation of any of the principles set forth in the Georgia Platform, that would be such an act of aggression which ought to be met as therein provided for. If his policy shall be carried out in repealing or modifying the Fugitive Slave Law so as to weaken its efficacy, Georgia has declared that she will in the last resort disrupt the ties of the Union, and I say so too. . . .

Now, upon another point, and that the most difficult and deserving your most serious consideration, I will speak. That is the course which this state should pursue toward these Northern states which, by their legislative acts, have attempted to nullify the Fugitive Slave Law. I know that in some of these states their acts pretend to be based upon the principles set forth in the case of *Prigg* against *Pennsylvania.* That decision did proclaim the doctrine that the state officers are not bound to carry out the provisions of a law of Congress; that the federal government cannot impose duties upon state officials; that they must execute their own laws by their own officers. And this may be true. But still it is the duty of the states to deliver fugitive slaves, as well as the duty of the general government to see that it is done.

Northern states, on entering into the federal compact, pledged themselves to surrender such fugitives; and it is in disregard of their obligations that they have passed laws which even tend to hinder or obstruct the fulfillment of that obligation. They have violated their plighted faith; what ought we to do in view of this? That is the question. What is to be done? By the law of nations you would have a right to demand the carrying out of this article of agreement, and I do not see that it should be otherwise with respect to the states of this Union. And in case it be not done, we would, by these principles, have the right to commit acts of reprisal on these faithless governments, and seize upon their property, or that of their citizens wherever found. The states of this Union stand upon the same footing with foreign nations in this respect. But by the law of nations we are equally bound, before proceeding to violent measures, to set forth our grievances before the offending government, to give them an opportunity to redress the wrong. Has our state yet done this? I think not. . . .

Let us, therefore, not act hastily in this matter. Let your committee on the state of the republic make out a bill of grievances; let it be sent by the governor to those faithless states, and if reason and argument shall be tried in vain — all shall fail to induce them to return to their constitutional obligations — I would be for retaliatory measures, such as the governor has suggested to you. This mode of resistance in the Union is in our power. It might be effectual, and, if in the last resort, we would be justified in the eyes of nations, not only in separating from them but by using force. . . .

In view of all these questions of difficulty, let a convention of the people of Georgia be called, to which they may be all referred. Let the sovereignty of the people speak. . . .

Should Georgia determine to go out of the Union, I speak for one, though my views might not agree with them, whatever the result may be, I shall bow to the will of her people. Their cause is my cause, and their destiny is my destiny; and I trust this will be the ultimate course of all. The greatest curse that can befall a free people is civil war.

But, as I said, let us call a convention of the people; let all these matters be submitted to it, and when the will of a majority of the people has thus been expressed, the whole state will present one unanimous voice in favor of whatever may be demanded; for I believe in the power of the people to govern themselves when wisdom prevails and passion is silent. . . .

Another thing I would have that convention to do. Reaffirm the Georgia Platform

with an additional plank in it. Let that plank be the fulfillment of the obligation on the part of those states to repeal these obnoxious laws as a condition of our remaining in the Union. Give them time to consider it, and I would ask all states south to do the same thing.

I am for exhausting all that patriotism can demand before taking the last step. I would invite, therefore, South Carolina to a conference. I would ask the same of all the other Southern states, so that if the evil has got beyond our control, which God, in His mercy, grant may not be the case, let us not be divided among ourselves — but, if possible, secure the united cooperation of all the Southern states; and then, in the face of the civilized world, we may justify our action; and, with the wrong all on the other side, we can appeal to the God of battles to aid us in our cause.

But let us not do anything in which any portion of our people may charge us with rash or hasty action. It is certainly a matter of great importance to tear this government asunder. You were not sent here for that purpose. I would wish the whole South to be united if this is to be done; and I believe if we pursue the policy which I have indicated this can be effected.

In this way our sister Southern states can be induced to act with us, and I have but little doubt that the states of New York and Pennsylvania and Ohio, and the other Western states, will compel their legislatures to recede from their hostile attitudes if the others do not. Then, with these, we would go on without New England if she chose to stay out. . . .

If all this fails, we shall at least have the satisfaction of knowing that we have done our duty and all that patriotism could require.

38.

Southern Secession

*With the election in 1860 of Abraham Lincoln, who won the electoral votes of no
states south of the Mason-Dixon line, the political balance was upset and the South
lost whatever influence it had over the policies of the national government. Most
Southerners were convinced that the election of a Republican President meant
the Southern way of life was doomed. Resisting the counsel of moderates like
Alexander Stephens of Georgia, who warned on the eve of secession that the Southern
people "are wild with passion and frenzy, doing they know not what," South Carolina
became the first state to secede from the Union on December 20. It was soon
followed by six other Southern states. The Mississippi resolutions of November 30,
1860, which preceded the adoption of a secession ordinance, provide one of the most
concise statements on the causes of secession. South Carolina presented its
"Declaration" of the causes which induced its secession on December 24. Mississippi
formally seceded on January 9, 1861, becoming the second state to do so.*

Source: *Laws of the State of Mississippi, Passed at a Called Session of the Mississippi Legislature
held in . . . Jackson, November, 1860*, Jackson, 1860, pp. 43-45.
Moore, I, Document 3.

I.

Mississippi Resolutions

Whereas, the constitutional Union was
formed by the several states in their separate sovereign capacity for the purpose of
mutual advantage and protection;

That the several states are distinct sovereignties, whose supremacy is limited so far
only as the same has been delegated by voluntary compact to a federal government,
and, when it fails to accomplish the ends
for which it was established, the parties to
the compact have the right to resume, each
state for itself, such delegated powers;

That the institution of slavery existed pri-
or to the formation of the federal Constitution, and is recognized by its letter, and all
efforts to impair its value or lessen its dura-

tion by Congress, or any of the free states,
is a violation of the compact of Union and
is destructive of the ends for which it was
ordained, but in defiance of the principles of
the Union thus established, the people of
the Northern states have assumed a revolutionary position toward the Southern states;

That they have set at defiance that provision of the Constitution which was intended to secure domestic tranquillity among
the states and promote their general welfare, namely: "No person held to service or
labor in one state, under the laws thereof,
escaping into another shall, in consequence
of any law or regulation therein, be discharged from such service or labor, but shall
be delivered up, on claim of the party to
whom such service or labor may be due";

That they have by voluntary associations,
individual agencies, and state legislation in-

terfered with slavery as it prevails in the slaveholding states;

That they have enticed our slaves from us and, by state intervention, obstructed and prevented their rendition under the Fugitive Slave Law;

That they continue their system of agitation obviously for the purpose of encouraging other slaves to escape from service, to weaken the institution in the slaveholding states by rendering the holding of such property insecure, and as a consequence its ultimate abolition certain;

That they claim the right and demand its execution by Congress, to exclude slavery from the territories, but claim the right of protection for every species of property owned by themselves;

That they declare in every manner in which public opinion is expressed their unalterable determination to exclude from admittance into the Union any new state that tolerates slavery in its constitution and thereby force Congress to a condemnation of that species of property;

That they thus seek by an increase of Abolition states "to acquire two-thirds of both houses," for the purpose of preparing an amendment to the Constitution of the United States abolishing slavery in the states, and so continue the agitation that the proposed amendment shall be ratified by the legislatures of three-fourths of the states;

That they have, in violation of the comity of all civilized nations and in violation of the comity established by the Constitution of the United States, insulted and outraged our citizens when traveling among them for pleasure, health, or business, by taking their servants and liberating the same, under the forms of state laws, and subjecting their owners to degrading and ignominious punishment;

That to encourage the stealing of our property they have put at defiance that provision of the Constitution which declares that fugitives from justice into another state, on demand of the executive authority of that state from which he fled, shall be delivered up;

That they have sought to create domestic discord in the Southern states by incendiary publications;

That they encouraged a hostile invasion of a Southern state to excite insurrection, murder, and rapine;

That they have deprived Southern citizens of their property and continue an unfriendly agitation of their domestic institutions, claiming for themselves perfect immunity from external interference with their domestic policy;

We of the Southern states alone made an exception to that universal quiet;

That they have elected a majority of electors for President and Vice-President on the ground that there exists an irreconcilable conflict between the two sections of the Confederacy in reference to their respective systems of labor and in pursuance of their hostility to us and our institutions, thus declaring to the civilized world that the powers of this government are to be used for the dishonor and overthrow of the Southern section of this great Confederacy. Therefore:

Be it resolved by the legislature of the state of Mississippi that, in the opinion of those who now constitute the said legislature, the secession of each aggrieved state is the proper remedy for these injuries.

II.

South Carolina Declarations

THE PEOPLE of the state of South Carolina, in convention assembled, on the 2nd day of April, A.D. 1852, declared that the frequent violations of the Constitution of the United States by the federal government, and its encroachments upon the reserved rights of the states, fully justified this state in their withdrawal from the federal Union; but in deference to the opinions and wishes of the other slaveholding states, she forbore at that time to exercise this right. Since that time, these encroachments have continued to increase, and further forbearance ceases to be a virtue.

And, now, the state of South Carolina, having resumed her separate and equal place among nations, deems it due to herself, to the remaining United States of America, and to the nations of the world, that she should declare the immediate causes which have led to this act.

In the year 1765, that portion of the British empire embracing Great Britain undertook to make laws for the government of that portion composed of the thirteen American colonies. A struggle for the right of self-government ensued, which resulted, on the 4th of July, 1776, in a Declaration, by the colonies, "that they are, and of right ought to be, *free and independent states;* and that, as free and independent states, they have full power to levy war, conclude peace, contract alliances, establish commerce, and to do all other acts and things which independent states may of right do."

They further solemnly declared that whenever any "form of government becomes destructive of the ends for which it was established, it is the right of the people to alter or abolish it, and to institute a new government." Deeming the government of Great Britain to have become destructive of these ends, they declared that the colonies "are absolved from all allegiance to the British Crown, and that all political connection between them and the state of Great Britain is, and ought to be, totally dissolved."

In pursuance of this Declaration of Independence, each of the thirteen states proceeded to exercise its separate sovereignty; adopted for itself a constitution, and appointed officers for the administration of government in all its departments — Legis-

lative, Executive, and Judicial. For purposes of defense, they united their arms and their counsels, and, in 1778, they entered into a league known as the Articles of Confederation, whereby they agreed to entrust the administration of their external relations to a common agent, known as the Congress of the United States, expressly declaring, in the 1st Article, "that each state retains its sovereignty, freedom, and independence, and every power, jurisdiction, and right which is not, by this Confederation, expressly delegated to the United States in Congress assembled."

Under this Confederation, the War of the Revolution was carried on; and on the 3rd of September, 1783, the contest ended, and a definite treaty was signed by Great Britain, in which she acknowledged the independence of the colonies in the following terms:

> Article I. His Britannic Majesty acknowledges the said United States, viz.: New Hampshire, Massachusetts Bay, Rhode Island and Providence Plantations, Connecticut, New York, New Jersey, Pennsylvania, Delaware, Maryland, Virginia, North Carolina, South Carolina, and Georgia, to be *free, sovereign, and independent states;* that he treats with them as such; and, for himself, his heirs, and successors, relinquishes all claims to the government, propriety, and territorial rights of the same and every part thereof.

Thus were established the two great principles asserted by the colonies, namely, the right of a state to govern itself; and the right of a people to abolish a government when it becomes destructive of the ends for which it was instituted. And concurrent with the establishment of these principles was the fact that each colony became and was recognized by the mother country as a *free, sovereign, and independent state.*

In 1787, deputies were appointed by the states to revise the Articles of Confederation; and on Sept. 17, 1787, these deputies recommended, for the adoption of the states, the Articles of Union, known as the Constitution of the United States.

The parties to whom this Constitution was submitted were the several sovereign states; they were to agree or disagree, and when nine of them agreed, the compact was to take effect among those concurring; and the general government, as the common agent, was then to be invested with their authority.

If only nine of the thirteen states had concurred, the other four would have remained as they then were — separate, sovereign states, independent of any of the provisions of the Constitution. In fact, two of the states did not accede to the Constitution until long after it had gone into operation among the other eleven; and during that interval, they each exercised the functions of an independent nation.

By this Constitution, certain duties were imposed upon the several states, and the exercise of certain of their powers was restrained, which necessarily impelled their continued existence as sovereign states. But, to remove all doubt, an amendment was added which declared that the powers not delegated to the United States by the Constitution, nor prohibited by it to the states, are reserved to the states respectively, or to the people. On the 23rd of May, 1788, South Carolina, by a convention of her people, passed an ordinance assenting to this Constitution, and afterward altered her own constitution to conform herself to the obligations she had undertaken.

Thus was established, by compact between the states, a government with defined objects and powers, limited to the express words of the grant. This limitation left the whole remaining mass of power subject to the clause reserving it to the states or the people, and rendered unnecessary any specification of reserved rights. We hold that the government thus established is subject to the two great principles asserted in the Declaration of Independence; and we hold further that the mode of its formation subjects it to a third fundamental principle, namely, the law of compact. We maintain that in every compact between two or more parties, the obligation is mutual; that the failure of one of the contracting parties to perform a material part of the agreement entirely releases the obligation of the other; and that, where no arbiter is provided, each party is remitted to his own judgment to determine the fact of failure, with all its consequences.

In the present case, the fact is established with certainty. We assert that fourteen of the states have deliberately refused for years past to fulfill their constitutional obligations, and we refer to their own statutes for the proof.

The Constitution of the United States, in its 4th Article, provides as follows: "No person held to service or labor in one state, under the laws thereof, escaping into another shall, in consequence of any law or regulation therein, be discharged from such service or labor, but shall be delivered up, on claim of the party to whom such service or labor may be due."

This stipulation was so material to the compact that without it that compact would not have been made. The greater number of the contracting parties held slaves, and they had previously evinced their estimate of the value of such a stipulation by making it a condition in the ordinance for the government of the territory ceded by Virginia, which obligations, and the laws of the general government, have ceased to effect the objects of the Constitution. The states of Maine, New Hampshire, Vermont, Massachusetts, Connecticut, Rhode Island, New York, Pennsylvania, Illinois, Indiana, Michigan, Wisconsin, and Iowa have enacted laws which either nullify the acts of Congress or render useless any attempt to execute them. In many of these states the fugitive is discharged from the service of labor claimed, and in none of them has the state government complied with the stipulation made in the Constitution.

The state of New Jersey, at an early day, passed a law in conformity with her constitutional obligation; but the current of antislavery feeling has led her more recently to enact laws which render inoperative the remedies provided by her own laws and by the laws of Congress. In the state of New York even the right of transit for a slave has been denied by her tribunals; and the states of Ohio and Iowa have refused to surrender to justice fugitives charged with murder and with inciting servile insurrection in the state of Virginia. Thus the constitutional compact has been deliberately broken and disregarded by the nonslaveholding states; and the consequence follows that South Carolina is released from her obligation.

The ends for which this Constitution was framed are declared by itself to be "to form a more perfect union, to establish justice, insure domestic tranquillity, provide for the common defense, promote the general welfare, and secure the blessings of liberty to ourselves and our posterity." These ends it endeavored to accomplish by a federal government in which each state was recognized as an equal and had separate control over its own institutions. The right of property in slaves was recognized by giving to free persons distinct political rights; by giving them the right to represent, and burdening them with direct taxes for, three-fifths of their slaves; by authorizing the importation of slaves for twenty years; and by stipulating for the rendition of fugitives from labor.

We affirm that these ends for which this government was instituted have been defeated, and the government itself has been destructive of them by the action of the nonslaveholding states. Those states have assumed the right of deciding upon the propriety of our domestic institutions; and have denied the rights of property established in fifteen of the states and recognized by the Constitution. They have denounced as sinful the institution of slavery; they have permitted the open establishment among them of societies, whose avowed object is to disturb the peace of and eloign the property of the citizens of other states. They have encouraged and assisted thousands of our slaves to leave their homes; and, those who remain, have been incited by emissaries, books, and pictures to servile insurrection.

For twenty-five years this agitation has been steadily increasing, until it has now secured to its aid the power of the common government. Observing the *forms* of the Constitution, a sectional party has found, within that article establishing the Executive Department, the means of subverting the Constitution itself. A geographical line has been drawn across the Union, and all the states north of that line have united in the election of a man to the high office of President of the United States whose opinions and purposes are hostile to slavery. He is to be entrusted with the administration of the common government, because he has declared that that "Government cannot endure permanently half slave, half free," and that the public mind must rest in the belief that slavery is in the course of ultimate extinction.

This sectional combination for the subversion of the Constitution has been aided, in some of the states, by elevating to citizenship persons who, by the supreme law of the land, are incapable of becoming citizens; and their votes have been used to inaugurate a new policy, hostile to the South and destructive of its peace and safety.

On the 4th of March next this party will take possession of the government. It has announced that the South shall be excluded from the common territory, that the judicial tribunal shall be made sectional, and that a war must be waged against slavery until it shall cease throughout the United States.

The guarantees of the Constitution will then no longer exist; the equal rights of the states will be lost. The slaveholding states will no longer have the power of self-government or self-protection, and the federal government will have become their enemy.

Sectional interest and animosity will deepen the irritation; and all hope of remedy is rendered vain by the fact that the public opinion at the North has invested a great political error with the sanctions of a more erroneous religious belief.

We, therefore, the people of South Carolina, by our delegates in convention assembled, appealing to the Supreme Judge of the world for the rectitude of our intentions, have solemnly declared that the Union heretofore existing between this state and the other states of North America is dissolved; and that the state of South Carolina has resumed her position among the nations of the world, as [a] separate and independent state, with full power to levy war, conclude peace, contract alliances, establish commerce, and to do all other acts and things which independent states may of right do.

39.

James Buchanan: The Impending Disruption of the Union

During the critical four months that intervened between Lincoln's election in November 1860 and his inauguration in March 1861, President James Buchanan was faced with the problem of secession. The Southerners in his Cabinet were creating confusion and dissension. The secretary of war, a Virginia slaveholder, ordered arms and ammunition transferred from Northern arsenals to the South. In his last annual message to Congress on December 3, 1860, the President did not take a strong stand in asserting federal authority because Jeremiah S. Black, the attorney general, advised him that a state could not be legally coerced by the federal government. Two weeks after the message was delivered, South Carolina seceded from the Union.

Source: Richardson, V, pp. 626-653.

Fellow Citizens of the Senate and House of Representatives:

Throughout the year since our last meeting the country has been eminently prosperous in all its material interests. The general health has been excellent, our harvests have been abundant, and plenty smiles throughout the land. Our commerce and manufactures have been prosecuted with energy and industry, and have yielded fair and ample returns. In short, no nation in the tide of time has ever presented a spectacle of great-er material prosperity than we have done until within a very recent period.

Why is it, then, that discontent now so extensively prevails, and the union of the states, which is the source of all these blessings, is threatened with destruction?

The long continued and intemperate interference of the Northern people with the question of slavery in the Southern states has at length produced its natural effects. The different sections of the Union are now arrayed against each other, and the time has arrived, so much dreaded by the father of his country, when hostile geographical parties have been formed.

I have long foreseen and often forewarned my countrymen of the now impending danger. This does not proceed solely from the claim on the part of Congress or the territorial legislatures to exclude slavery from the territories, nor from the efforts of different states to defeat the execution of the Fugitive Slave Law. All or any of these evils might have been endured by the South without danger to the Union (as others have been) in the hope that time and reflection might apply the remedy. The immediate peril arises not so much from these causes as from the fact that the incessant and violent agitation of the slavery question throughout the North for the last quarter of a century has at length produced its malign influence on the slaves and inspired them with vague notions of freedom.

Hence a sense of security no longer exists around the family altar. This feeling of peace at home has given place to apprehensions of servile insurrections. Many a matron throughout the South retires at night in dread of what may befall herself and children before the morning. Should this apprehension of domestic danger, whether real or imaginary, extend and intensify itself until it shall pervade the masses of the Southern people, then disunion will become inevitable.

Self-preservation is the first law of nature and has been implanted in the heart of man by his Creator for the wisest purpose; and no political union, however fraught with blessings and benefits in all other respects, can long continue if the necessary consequence be to render the homes and firesides of nearly half the parties to it habitually and hopelessly insecure. Sooner or later the bonds of such a union must be severed. It is my conviction that this fatal period has not yet arrived, and my prayer to God is that He would preserve the Constitution and the Union throughout all generations.

But let us take warning in time and remove the cause of danger. It cannot be denied that for five-and-twenty years the agitation at the North against slavery has been incessant. In 1835 pictorial handbills and inflammatory appeals were circulated extensively throughout the South of a character to excite the passions of the slaves, and, in the language of General Jackson, "to stimulate them to insurrection and produce all the horrors of a servile war." This agitation has ever since been continued by the public press, by the proceedings of state and county conventions, and by Abolition sermons and lectures. The time of Congress has been occupied in violent speeches on this neverending subject, and appeals, in pamphlet and other forms, endorsed by distinguished names, have been sent forth from this central point and spread broadcast over the Union.

How easy would it be for the American people to settle the slavery question forever and to restore peace and harmony to this distracted country! They, and they alone, can do it. All that is necessary to accomplish the object, and all for which the slave states have ever contended, is to be let alone and permitted to manage their domestic institutions in their own way. As sovereign states they, and they alone, are responsible before God and the world for the slavery existing among them. For this the people of the North are not more responsible and have no more right to interfere than with similar institutions in Russia or in Brazil.

Upon their good sense and patriotic forbearance I confess I still greatly rely. Without their aid it is beyond the power of any President, no matter what may be his own political proclivities, to restore peace and harmony among the states. Wisely limited and restrained as is his power under our Constitution and laws, he alone can accomplish but little for good or for evil on such a momentous question.

And this brings me to observe that the

election of any one of our fellow citizens to the office of President does not of itself afford just cause for dissolving the Union. This is more especially true if his election has been effected by a mere plurality and not a majority of the people, and has resulted from transient and temporary causes, which may probably never again occur. In order to justify a resort to revolutionary resistance, the federal government must be guilty of "a deliberate, palpable, and dangerous exercise" of powers not granted by the Constitution. The late presidential election, however, has been held in strict conformity with its express provisions.

How, then, can the result justify a revolution to destroy this very Constitution? Reason, justice, a regard for the Constitution, all require that we shall wait for some overt and dangerous act on the part of the President-elect before resorting to such a remedy. It is said, however, that the antecedents of the President-elect have been sufficient to justify the fears of the South that he will attempt to invade their constitutional rights. But are such apprehensions of contingent danger in the future sufficient to justify the immediate destruction of the noblest system of government ever devised by mortals? From the very nature of his office and its high responsibilities, he must necessarily be conservative. The stern duty of administering the vast and complicated concerns of this government affords in itself a guarantee that he will not attempt any violation of a clear constitutional right.

After all, he is no more than the chief executive officer of the government. His province is not to make but to execute the laws. And it is a remarkable fact in our history that, notwithstanding the repeated efforts of the antislavery party, no single act has ever passed Congress, unless we may possibly except the Missouri Compromise, impairing in the slightest degree the rights of the South to their property in slaves; and it may also be observed, judging from present indications, that no probability exists of the passage of such an act by a majority of both houses, either in the present or the next Congress. Surely under these circumstances we ought to be restrained from present action by the precept of Him who spoke as man never spoke, that "sufficient unto the day is the evil thereof." The day of evil may never come unless we shall rashly bring it upon ourselves.

It is alleged as one cause for immediate secession that the Southern states are denied equal rights with the other states in the common territories. But by what authority are these denied? Not by Congress, which has never passed, and I believe never will pass, any act to exclude slavery from these territories; and certainly not by the Supreme Court, which has solemnly decided that slaves are property, and, like all other property, their owners have a right to take them into the common territories and hold them under the protection of the Constitution.

So far, then, as Congress is concerned, the objection is not to anything they have already done but to what they may do hereafter. It will surely be admitted that this apprehension of future danger is no good reason for an immediate dissolution of the Union. It is true that the territorial legislature of Kansas, on the 23rd of February, 1860, passed in great haste an act over the veto of the governor declaring that slavery "is and shall be forever prohibited in this territory." Such an act, however, plainly violating the rights of property secured by the Constitution, will surely be declared void by the judiciary whenever it shall be presented in a legal form.

Only three days after my inauguration, the Supreme Court of the United States solemnly adjudged that this power did not exist in a territorial legislature. Yet such has been the factious temper of the times that the correctness of this decision has been extensively impugned before the people, and the question has given rise to angry political conflicts throughout the country. Those

James Buchanan; photo by Brady

who have appealed from this judgment of our highest constitutional tribunal to popular assemblies would, if they could, invest a territorial legislature with power to annul the sacred rights of property. This power Congress is expressly forbidden by the federal Constitution to exercise. Every state legislature in the Union is forbidden by its own constitution to exercise it. It cannot be exercised in any state except by the people in their highest sovereign capacity, when framing or amending their state constitution.

In like manner, it can only be exercised by the people of a territory represented in a convention of delegates for the purpose of framing a constitution preparatory to admission as a state into the Union. Then, and not until then, are they invested with power to decide the question whether slavery shall or shall not exist within their limits. This is an act of sovereign authority and not of subordinate territorial legislation. Were it otherwise, then, indeed, would the equality of the states in the territories be destroyed, and the rights of property in slaves would depend, not upon the guarantees of the Constitution but upon the shifting majorities of an irresponsible territorial legislature. Such a doctrine, from its intrinsic unsoundness, cannot long influence any considerable portion of our people, much less can it afford a good reason for a dissolution of the Union.

The most palpable violations of constitutional duty which have yet been committed consist in the acts of different state legislatures to defeat the execution of the Fugitive Slave Law. It ought to be remembered, however, that for these acts neither Congress nor any President can justly be held responsible. Having been passed in violation of the federal Constitution, they are therefore null and void. All the courts, both state and national, before whom the question has arisen, have from the beginning declared the Fugitive Slave Law to be constitutional. The single exception is that of a state court in Wisconsin; and this has not only been reversed by the proper appellate tribunal but has met with such universal reprobation that there can be no danger from it as a precedent.

The validity of this law has been established over and over again by the Supreme Court of the United States with perfect unanimity. It is founded upon an express provision of the Constitution requiring that fugitive slaves who escape from service in one state to another shall be "delivered up" to their masters. Without this provision it is a well-known historical fact that the Constitution itself could never have been adopted by the Convention. In one form or other, under the acts of 1793 and 1850, both being substantially the same, the Fugitive Slave Law has been the law of the land from the days of Washington until the present moment. Here, then, a clear case is presented in which it will be the duty of the next President, as it has been my own, to act with vigor in executing this supreme law against the conflicting enactments of state legislatures. Should he fail in the performance of this high duty, he will then have manifested a disregard of the Constitution and laws, to the great injury of the people of nearly one-half of the states of the Union.

But are we to presume in advance that he will thus violate his duty? This would be at war with every principle of justice and of Christian charity. Let us wait for the overt act. The Fugitive Slave Law has been carried into execution in every contested case since the commencement of the present administration, though often, it is to be regretted, with great loss and inconvenience to the master and with considerable expense to the government. Let us trust that the state legislatures will repeal their unconstitutional and obnoxious enactments. Unless this shall be done without unnecessary delay, it is impossible for any human power to save the Union.

The Southern states, standing on the basis of the Constitution, have a right to demand this act of justice from the states of the North. Should it be refused, then the Constitution, to which all the states are parties, will have been willfully violated by one portion of them in a provision essential to the domestic security and happiness of the remainder. In that event the injured states, after having first used all peaceful and constitutional means to obtain redress, would be justified in revolutionary resistance to the government of the Union.

I have purposely confined my remarks to revolutionary resistance, because it has been claimed within the last few years that any state, whenever this shall be its sovereign will and pleasure, may secede from the Union in accordance with the Constitution and without any violation of the constitutional rights of the other members of the confederacy; that as each became parties to the Union by the vote of its own people assembled in convention, so any one of them may retire from the Union in a similar manner by the vote of such a convention.

In order to justify secession as a constitutional remedy, it must be on the principle that the federal government is a mere voluntary association of states, to be dissolved at pleasure by any one of the contracting parties. If this be so, the confederacy is a rope of sand, to be penetrated and dissolved by the first adverse wave of public opinion in any of the states. In this manner our thirty-three states may resolve themselves into as many petty, jarring, and hostile republics, each one retiring from the Union without responsibility whenever any sudden excitement might impel them to such a course. By this process a Union might be entirely broken into fragments in a few weeks which cost our forefathers many years of toil, privation, and blood to establish.

Such a principle is wholly inconsistent with the history as well as the character of the federal Constitution. After it was framed with the greatest deliberation and care, it was submitted to conventions of the people of the several states for ratification. Its provisions were discussed at length in these bodies, composed of the first men of the country. Its opponents contended that it conferred powers upon the federal government dangerous to the rights of the states, while its advocates maintained that under a fair construction of the instrument there was no foundation for such apprehensions.

In that mighty struggle between the first intellects of this or any other country, it never occurred to any individual, either among its opponents or advocates, to assert or even to intimate that their efforts were all vain labor, because the moment that any state felt herself aggrieved she might secede from the Union. What a crushing argument would this have proved against those who dreaded that the rights of the states would be endangered by the Constitution! The truth is that it was not until many years after the origin of the federal government that such a proposition was first advanced. It was then met and refuted by the conclusive arguments of General Jackson, who in his message of the 16th of January, 1833, transmitting the nullifying ordinance of South Carolina to Congress, employs the following language:

The right of the people of a single state to absolve themselves at will and without the consent of the other states from their most solemn obligations, and hazard the liberties and happiness of the millions composing this Union, cannot be acknowledged. Such authority is believed to be utterly repugnant both to the principles upon which the general government is constituted and to the objects which it is expressly formed to attain.

It is not pretended that any clause in the Constitution gives countenance to such a theory. It is altogether founded upon inference, not from any language contained in the instrument itself but from the sovereign character of the several states by which it was ratified. But is it beyond the power of a state, like an individual, to yield a portion of its sovereign rights to secure the remainder? In the language of Mr. Madison, who has been called the Father of the Constitution:

It was formed by the states; that is, by the people in each of the states acting in their highest sovereign capacity, and formed, consequently, by the same authority which formed the state constitutions. . . . Nor is the government of the United States, created by the Constitution, less a government, in the strict sense of the term, within the sphere of its powers, than the governments created by the constitutions of the states are within their several spheres. It is, like them, organized into Legislative, Executive, and Judiciary departments. It operates, like them, directly on persons and things, and, like them, it has at command a physical force for executing the powers committed to it.

It was intended to be perpetual and not to be annulled at the pleasure of any one of the contracting parties. The old Articles of Confederation were entitled "Articles of Confederation and Perpetual Union between the States," and by the 13th Article it is expressly declared that "the articles of this Confederation shall be inviolably observed by every state, and the Union shall be perpetual." The Preamble to the Constitution of the United States, having express reference to the Articles of Confederation, recites that it was established "in order to form a more perfect union." And yet it is contended that this "more perfect union" does not include the essential attribute of perpetuity.

But that the Union was designed to be perpetual appears conclusively from the nature and extent of the powers conferred by the Constitution on the federal government. These powers embrace the very highest attributes of national sovereignty. They place both the sword and the purse under its control. Congress has power to make war and to make peace, to raise and support armies and navies, and to conclude treaties with foreign governments. It is invested with the power to coin money and to regulate the value thereof, and to regulate commerce with foreign nations and among the several states. It is not necessary to enumerate the other high powers which have been conferred upon the federal government. In order to carry the enumerated powers into effect, Congress possesses the exclusive right to lay and collect duties on imports, and, in common with the states, to lay and collect all other taxes.

But the Constitution has not only conferred these high powers upon Congress but it has adopted effectual means to restrain the states from interfering with their exercise. For that purpose it has in strong prohibitory language expressly declared that:

No state shall enter into any treaty, alliance, or confederation; grant letters of marque and reprisal; coin money; emit bills of credit; make anything but gold and silver coin a tender in payment of debts; pass any bill of attainder, *ex post facto* law, or law impairing the obligation of contracts.

OLD MOTHER BUCHANAN AT WHEATLAND.

Cartoon from "Harper's Weekly" depicting Buchanan's justification
of his actions leading up to the outbreak of the Civil War

Moreover,

> No state shall, without the consent of
> the Congress lay any imposts or duties
> on imports or exports, except what may
> be absolutely necessary for executing its
> inspection laws.

And if they exceed this amount, the excess shall belong to the United States. And,

> No state shall without the consent of
> Congress lay any duty of tonnage, keep
> troops or ships of war in time of peace,
> enter into any agreement or compact
> with another state or with a foreign
> power, or engage in war, unless actually
> invaded or in such imminent danger as
> will not admit of delay.

In order still further to secure the uninterrupted exercise of these high powers
against state interposition, it is provided
that:

> This Constitution and the laws of the
> United States which shall be made in
> pursuance thereof, and all treaties made
> or which shall be made under the au-
> thority of the United States, shall be the
> supreme law of the land, and the judges
> in every state shall be bound thereby,
> anything in the constitution or laws of
> any state to the contrary notwithstand-
> ing.

The solemn sanction of religion has been
superadded to the obligations of official
duty, and all senators and representatives of
the United States, all members of state legislatures, and all executive and judicial officers "both of the United States and of the
several states, shall be bound by oath or affirmation to support this Constitution."

In order to carry into effect these powers,
the Constitution has established a perfect
government in all its forms — legislative,
executive, and judicial; and this government
to the extent of its powers acts directly
upon the individual citizens of every state,
and executes its own decrees by the agency
of its own officers. In this respect it differs
entirely from the government under the old
Confederation, which was confined to making requisitions on the states in their sovereign character. This left it in the discretion of each whether to obey or to refuse,
and they often declined to comply with
such requisitions. It thus became necessary
for the purpose of removing this barrier and
"in order to form a more perfect union" to
establish a government which could act directly upon the people and execute its own
laws without the intermediate agency of the

states. This has been accomplished by the Constitution of the United States. In short, the government created by the Constitution, and deriving its authority from the sovereign people of each of the several states, has precisely the same right to exercise its power over the people of all these states in the enumerated cases that each one of them possesses over subjects not delegated to the United States, but "reserved to the states respectively or to the people."

To the extent of the delegated powers the Constitution of the United States is as much a part of the constitution of each state and is as binding upon its people as though it had been textually inserted therein.

This government, therefore, is a great and powerful government, invested with all the attributes of sovereignty over the special subjects to which its authority extends. Its framers never intended to implant in its bosom the seeds of its own destruction, nor were they, at its creation, guilty of the absurdity of providing for its own dissolution. It was not intended by its framers to be the baseless fabric of a vision, which at the touch of the enchanter would vanish into thin air, but a substantial and mighty fabric, capable of resisting the slow decay of time and of defying the storms of ages. Indeed, well may the jealous patriots of that day have indulged fears that a government of such high powers might violate the reserved rights of the states, and wisely did they adopt the rule of a strict construction of these powers to prevent the danger. But they did not fear, nor had they any reason to imagine, that the Constitution would ever be so interpreted as to enable any state by her own act, and without the consent of her sister states, to discharge her people from all or any of their federal obligations.

It may be asked, then — Are the people of the states without redress against the tyranny and oppression of the federal government? By no means. The right of resistance on the part of the governed against the oppression of their governments cannot be denied. It exists independently of all constitutions, and has been exercised at all periods of the world's history. Under it, old governments have been destroyed and new ones have taken their place. It is embodied in strong and express language in our own Declaration of Independence. But the distinction must ever be observed that this is revolution against an established government and not a voluntary secession from it by virtue of an inherent constitutional right. In short, let us look the danger fairly in the face. Secession is neither more nor less than revolution. It may or it may not be a justifiable revolution, but still it is revolution.

What, in the meantime, is the responsibility and true position of the executive? He is bound by solemn oath, before God and the country, "to take care that the laws be faithfully executed," and from this obligation he cannot be absolved by any human power. But what if the performance of this duty, in whole or in part, has been rendered impracticable by events over which he could have exercised no control? Such at the present moment is the case throughout the state of South Carolina so far as the laws of the United States to secure the administration of justice by means of the federal judiciary are concerned. All the federal officers within its limits through whose agency alone these laws can be carried into execution have already resigned. We no longer have a district judge, a district attorney, or a marshal in South Carolina. In fact, the whole machinery of the federal government necessary for the distribution of remedial justice among the people has been demolished, and it would be difficult, if not impossible, to replace it.

The only acts of Congress on the statute book bearing upon this subject are those of Feb. 28, 1795, and March 3, 1807. These authorize the President, after he shall have ascertained that the marshal, with his *posse comitatus*, is unable to execute civil or criminal process in any particular case, to call forth the militia and employ the army and navy to aid him in performing this service, having first by proclamation commanded the insurgents "to disperse and retire peaceably to their respective abodes within a limited time." This duty cannot by possibility be performed in a state where no judicial authority exists to issue process, and where there is no marshal to execute it, and where, even if there were such an officer, the entire population would constitute one solid combination to resist him.

The bare enumeration of these provisions proves how inadequate they are without further legislation to overcome a united opposition in a single state, not to speak of other states who may place themselves in a similar attitude. Congress alone has power to decide whether the present laws can or cannot be amended so as to carry out more effectually the objects of the Constitution.

The same insuperable obstacles do not lie in the way of executing the laws for the collection of the customs. The revenue still continues to be collected as heretofore at the customhouse in Charleston, and should the collector unfortunately resign a successor may be appointed to perform this duty.

Then, in regard to the property of the United States in South Carolina. This has been purchased for a fair equivalent, "by the consent of the legislature of the state," "for the erection of forts, magazines, arsenals," etc., and over these the authority "to exercise exclusive legislation" has been expressly granted by the Constitution to Congress. It is not believed that any attempt will be made to expel the United States from this property by force; but if in this I should prove to be mistaken, the officer in command of the forts has received orders to act strictly on the defensive. In such a contingency the responsibility for consequences would rightfully rest upon the heads of the assailants.

Apart from the execution of the laws, so far as this may be practicable, the executive has no authority to decide what shall be the relations between the federal government and South Carolina. He has been invested with no such discretion. He possesses no power to change the relations heretofore existing between them, much less to acknowledge the independence of that state. This would be to invest a mere executive officer with the power of recognizing the dissolution of the confederacy among our thirty-three sovereign states. It bears no resemblance to the recognition of a foreign de facto government, involving no such responsibility. Any attempt to do this would, on his part, be a naked act of usurpation. It is therefore my duty to submit to Congress the whole question in all its bearings. The course of events is so rapidly hastening forward that the emergency may soon arise when you may be called upon to decide the momentous question whether you possess the power by force of arms to compel a state to remain in the Union. I should feel myself recreant to my duty were I not to express an opinion on this important subject.

The question fairly stated is: Has the Constitution delegated to Congress the power to coerce a state into submission which is attempting to withdraw or has actually withdrawn from the confederacy? If answered in the affirmative, it must be on the principle that the power has been conferred upon Congress to declare and to make war against a state. After much serious reflection, I have arrived at the conclusion that no such power has been delegated to Congress or to any other department of the federal government. It is manifest upon an inspection of the Constitution that this is not among the specific and enumerated powers granted to Congress, and it is equally apparent that its exercise is not "necessary and proper for carrying into execution" any one of these powers. So far from this power having been delegated to Congress, it was expressly refused by the Convention which framed the Constitution.

It appears from the proceedings of that

body that on the 31st of May, 1787, the clause "authorizing an exertion of the force of the whole against a delinquent state" came up for consideration. Mr. Madison opposed it in a brief but powerful speech, from which I shall extract but a single sentence. He observed:

The use of force against a state would look more like a declaration of war than an infliction of punishment, and would probably be considered by the party attacked as a dissolution of all previous compacts by which it might be bound.

Upon his motion the clause was unanimously postponed and was never, I believe, again presented. Soon afterward, on the 8th of June, 1787, when incidentally adverting to the subject, he said: "Any government for the United States formed on the supposed practicability of using force against the unconstitutional proceedings of the states would prove as visionary and fallacious as the government of Congress," evidently meaning the then existing Congress of the old Confederation.

Without descending to particulars, it may be safely asserted that the power to make war against a state is at variance with the whole spirit and intent of the Constitution. Suppose such a war should result in the conquest of a state; how are we to govern it afterward? Shall we hold it as a province and govern it by despotic power? In the nature of things, we could not by physical force control the will of the people and compel them to elect senators and representatives to Congress and to perform all the other duties depending upon their own volition and required from the free citizens of a free state as a constituent member of the confederacy.

But if we possessed this power, would it be wise to exercise it under existing circumstances? The object would doubtless be to preserve the Union. War would not only present the most effectual means of destroying it but would vanish all hope of its peaceable reconstruction. Besides, in the fraternal conflict, a vast amount of blood and treasure would be expended, rendering future reconciliation between the states impossible. In the meantime, who can foretell what would be the sufferings and privations of the people during its existence?

The fact is that our Union rests upon public opinion and can never be cemented by the blood of its citizens shed in civil war. If it cannot live in the affections of the people, it must one day perish. Congress possesses many means of preserving it by conciliation, but the sword was not placed in their hand to preserve it by force.

But may I be permitted solemnly to invoke my countrymen to pause and deliberate before they determine to destroy this, the grandest temple which has ever been dedicated to human freedom since the world began? It has been consecrated by the blood of our fathers, by the glories of the past, and by the hopes of the future. The Union has already made us the most prosperous, and ere long will, if preserved, render us the most powerful nation on the face of the earth. In every foreign region of the globe the title of American citizen is held in the highest respect, and when pronounced in a foreign land it causes the hearts of our countrymen to swell with honest pride. Surely, when we reach the brink of the yawning abyss, we shall recoil with horror from the last fatal plunge.

By such a dread catastrophe the hopes of the friends of freedom throughout the world would be destroyed, and a long night of leaden despotism would enshroud the nations. Our example for more than eighty years would not only be lost but it would be quoted as a conclusive proof that man is unfit for self-government.

It is not every wrong — nay, it is not every grievous wrong — which can justify a resort to such a fearful alternative. This ought to be the last desperate remedy of a despairing people, after every other constitutional means of conciliation had been exhausted. We should reflect that under this free government there is an incessant ebb and flow in public opinion. The slavery question, like everything human, will have its day. I firmly believe that it has reached and passed the culminating point. But if in the midst of the existing excitement the Union shall perish, the evil may then become irreparable.

Congress can contribute much to avert it by proposing and recommending to the legislatures of the several states the remedy for existing evils which the Constitution has itself provided for its own preservation. This has been tried at different critical periods of our history, and always with eminent success. It is to be found in the 5th Article, providing for its own amendment. Under this article, amendments have been proposed by two-thirds of both houses of Congress, and have been "ratified by the legislatures of three-fourths of the several states," and have consequently become parts of the Constitution. To this process the country is indebted for the clause prohibiting Congress from passing any law respecting an establishment of religion or abridging the freedom of speech or of the press or of the right of petition. To this we are also indebted for the Bill of Rights, which secures the people against any abuse of power by the federal government. Such were the apprehensions justly entertained by the friends of state rights at that period as to have rendered it extremely doubtful whether the Constitution could have long survived without those amendments.

Again the Constitution was amended by the same process, after the election of President Jefferson by the House of Representatives, in February 1803. This amendment was rendered necessary to prevent a recurrence of the dangers which had seriously threatened the existence of the government during the pendency of that election. The article for its own amendment was intended to secure the amicable adjustment of conflicting constitutional questions, like the present, which might arise between the governments of the states and that of the United States. This appears from contemporaneous history.

In this connection I shall merely call attention to a few sentences in Mr. Madison's justly celebrated report, in 1799, to the legislature of Virginia. In this he ably and conclusively defended the resolutions of the preceding legislature against the strictures of several other state legislatures. These were mainly founded upon the protest of the Virginia legislature against the "Alien and Sedition Acts," as "palpable and alarming infractions of the Constitution." In pointing out the peaceful and constitutional remedies — and he referred to none other — to which the states were authorized to resort on such occasions, he concludes by saying:

> The legislatures of the states might have made a direct representation to Congress with a view to obtain a rescinding of the two offensive acts, or they might have represented to their respective senators in Congress their wish that two-thirds thereof would propose an explanatory amendment to the Constitution; or two-thirds of themselves, if such had been their option, might by an application to Congress have obtained a convention for the same object.

This is the very course which I earnestly recommend in order to obtain an "explanatory amendment" of the Constitution on the subject of slavery. This might originate with Congress or the state legislatures, as may be deemed most advisable to attain the object. The explanatory amendment might be confined to the final settlement of the true construction of the Constitution on three special points:

1. An express recognition of the right of property in slaves in the states where it now exists or may hereafter exist.

2. The duty of protecting this right in all the common territories throughout their territorial existence, and until they shall be admitted as states into the Union, with or without slavery, as their constitutions may prescribe.

3. A like recognition of the right of the master to have his slave who has escaped from one state to another restored and "delivered up" to him, and of the validity of the Fugitive Slave Law enacted for this purpose, together with a declaration that all state laws impairing or defeating this right are violations of the Constitution, and are consequently null and void. It may be objected that this construction of the Constitution has already been settled by the Supreme Court of the United States, and what more ought to be required? The answer is that a very large proportion of the people of the United States still contest the correctness of this decision, and never will cease from agitation and admit its binding force until clearly established by the people of the several states in their sovereign character. Such an explanatory amendment would, it is believed, forever terminate the existing dissensions and restore peace and harmony among the states.

It ought not to be doubted that such an appeal to the arbitrament established by the Constitution itself would be received with favor by all the states of the confederacy. In any event, it ought to be tried in a spirit of conciliation before any of these states shall separate themselves from the Union.

40.

War or Compromise

In his last annual message to Congress on December 3, 1860, President Buchanan tried to avert the drift toward secession and war by urging Congress to satisfy some of the South's grievances. As a conciliatory gesture to the South, he proposed an "explanatory" constitutional amendment dealing with the rights of slave owners. The President's speech spurred a compromise movement. Senator Benjamin F. Wade of Ohio, a leader of the antislavery faction, was a firm opponent of compromise, a position he passionately defended in a speech to the Senate on December 17. Southerners regarded his speech as an example of Republican intolerance. One of the numerous compromise plans was the "Crittenden Compromise," proposed by Senator John J. Crittenden of Kentucky on December 18. The plan was defeated four days later because the Republicans refused to consider extending slavery into the territories. Wade's speech and the Crittenden resolutions are reprinted here.

Source: Horace Greeley, *The American Conflict: A History of the Great Rebellion, etc., etc.*, Vol. I, Hartford, 1865, pp. 375-377.

I.

BENJAMIN F. WADE:
Opposition to Compromise

THE REPUBLICAN PARTY holds the same opinion, so far as I know, with regard to your "peculiar institution" that is held by every civilized nation on the globe. We do not differ in public sentiment from England, France, Germany, and Italy on the subject of slavery.

I tell you frankly that we *did* lay down the principle in our platform, that we would prohibit, if we had the power, slavery from invading another inch of the free soil of this government. I stand to that principle today. I have argued it to 500,000 people, and *they* stand by it; they have commissioned *me* to stand by it; and, so help me God, I will! I say to you, while we hold this doctrine to the end, there is no Republican, or convention of Republicans, or Republican paper that pretends to have any right in your states to interfere with your peculiar and local institutions. On the other hand, our platform repudiates the idea that we have any right, or harbor any ultimate intention, to invade or interfere with your institution in your own states. . . .

I have disowned any intention, on the part of the Republican Party, to harm a hair of your heads. We hold to no doctrine that can possibly work you any inconvenience, any wrong, any disaster. We have been, and shall remain, faithful to all the laws — studiously so. It is not, by your own confessions, that Mr. Lincoln is expected to commit any overt act by which you may be injured. You will not even wait for any, you say; but, by anticipating that the government *may* do you an injury, you will put an end to it; which means, simply and squarely, that you intend to rule or ruin this government. . . .

As to compromises, I supposed that we had agreed that the day of compromises was at an end. The most solemn we have made have been violated and are no more. Since I have had a seat in the Senate, one of considerable antiquity was swept from our statute book; and when in the minority, I stood up here and asked you to withhold your hands — that it was a solemn, sacred compact between nations — what was the reply? That it was nothing but an act of Congress, and could be swept away by the same majority which enacted it. That *was* true in fact and true in law; and it showed the weakness of compromises. . . .

We beat you on the plainest and most palpable issue ever presented to the Ameri-

can people, and one which every man understood; and now, when we come to the capital, we tell you that our candidates must and shall be inaugurated, must and shall administer this government precisely as the Constitution prescribes. It would not only be humiliating but highly dishonorable to us if we listened to any compromise by which we should set aside the honest verdict of the people. When it comes to that, you have no government, but anarchy intervenes, and civil war may follow; and all the evils that human imagination can raise may be consequent on such a course as that. The American people would lose the sheet anchor of their liberties whenever it is denied on this floor that a majority, fairly given, shall rule.

I know not what others may do; but I tell you that, with that verdict of the people in my pocket, and standing on the platform on which these candidates were elected, I would suffer anything before I would compromise in any way. I deem it no case where we have a right to extend courtesy and generosity. The absolute right, the most sacred that a free people can bestow upon any man, is their verdict that gives him a full title to the office he holds. If we cannot stand there, we cannot stand anywhere; and, my friends, any other verdict would be as fatal to you as to us.

II.

JOHN J. CRITTENDEN: Compromise Resolutions

Whereas, serious and alarming dissensions have arisen between the Northern and the Southern states concerning the rights and security of the rights of the slaveholding states, and especially their rights in the common territory of the United States; *And whereas,* it is eminently desirable and proper that these dissensions which now threaten the very existence of this Union should be permanently quieted and settled

Sen. John Crittenden from Kentucky who tried unsuccessfully to work out a compromise between the North and South in 1860; photo by Brady

by constitutional provisions, which shall do equal justice to all sections and thereby restore to the people that peace and goodwill which ought to prevail between all the citizens of the United States; therefore:

Resolved, by the Senate and House of Representatives of the United States of America, in Congress assembled (two-thirds of both houses concurring), that the following articles be, and are hereby, proposed and submitted as amendments to the Constitution of the United States, which shall be valid, to all intents and purposes, as part of said Constitution, when ratified by conventions of three-fourths of the several states:

Article I. In all the territory of the United States now held, or hereafter acquired, situated north of latitude 36°30′, slavery or involuntary servitude, except as a punishment for crime, is prohibited while such territory shall remain under territorial government. In all the territory south of said line of latitude, slavery of the African race is hereby recognized as existing and shall not be interfered with by Congress, but shall be protected as property by all the departments of the territorial government during its continuance. And when any territory, north or south of said line, within such boundaries as Congress may prescribe, shall contain the population requisite for a member of Congress, according to the then federal ratio of representation of the people of the United States, it shall, if its form of government be republican, be admitted into the Union on an equal footing with the original states, with or without slavery, as the constitution of such new state may provide.

Article II. Congress shall have no power to abolish slavery in places under its exclusive jurisdiction, and situate within the limits of states that permit the holding of slaves.

Article III. Congress shall have no power to abolish slavery within the District of Columbia so long as it exists in the adjoining states of Virginia and Maryland, or either, nor without the consent of the inhabitants, nor without just compensation first made to such owners of slaves as do not consent to such abolishment. Nor shall Congress, at any time, prohibit officers of the federal government, or members of Congress whose duties require them to be in said district, from bringing with them their slaves, and holding them as such during the time their duties may require them to remain there, and afterward taking them from the district.

Article IV. Congress shall have no power to prohibit or hinder the transportation of slaves from one state to another, or to a territory in which slaves are, by law, permitted to be held, whether that transportation be by land, navigable rivers, or by the sea.

Article V. That, in addition to the provisions of the third paragraph of the 2nd Section of the 4th Article of the Constitution of the United States, Congress shall have power to provide by law, and it shall be its duty to provide, that the United States shall pay to the owner who shall apply for it the full value of his fugitive slaves in all cases where the marshal, or other officer whose duty it was to arrest said fugitive, was prevented from so doing by violence or intimidation, or where, after arrest, said fugitive was rescued by force, and the owner thereby prevented and obstructed in the pursuit of his remedy for the recovery of his fugitive slave under the said clause of the Constitution and the laws made in pursuance thereof. And in all such cases, when the United States shall pay for such fugitive, they shall have the right, in their own name, to sue the county in which said violence, intimidation, or rescue was committed, and recover from it, with interest and damages, the amount paid by them for said fugitive slave. And the said county, after it has paid said amount to the United States, may, for its indemnity, sue and recover from the wrongdoers or rescuers by whom the owner was prevented from the recovery of his fugitive slave, in like manner as the owner himself might have sued and recovered.

Article VI. No future amendment of the Constitution shall affect the five preceding articles; nor the third paragraph of the 2nd Section of the 1st Article of the Constitution; nor the third paragraph of the 2nd Section of the 4th Article of said Constitution; and no amendment shall be made to the Constitution which shall authorize or give to Congress any power to abolish or interfere with slavery in any of the states by whose laws it is, or may be, allowed or permitted.

And whereas, also, besides those causes of dissension embraced in the foregoing amendments proposed to the Constitution of the United States, there are others which come within the jurisdiction of Congress, and may be remedied by its legislative power; *And whereas,* it is the desire of Congress, as far as its power will extend, to remove all just cause for the popular discontent and agitation which now disturb the peace of the country and threaten the stability of its institutions; therefore:

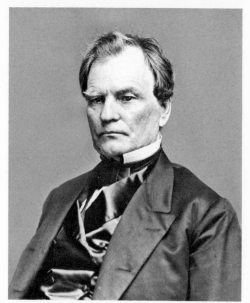

Benjamin Wade, senator from Ohio who urged strong military action on the part of the North when the Civil War broke out

Resolved, by the Senate and House of Representatives, in Congress assembled, that the laws now in force for the recovery of fugitive slaves are in strict pursuance of the plain and mandatory provisions of the Constitution, and have been sanctioned as valid and constitutional by the judgment of the Supreme Court of the United States; that the slaveholding states are entitled to the faithful observance and execution of those laws; and that they ought not to be repealed, or so modified or changed as to impair their efficiency, and that laws ought to be made for the punishment of those who attempt, by rescue of the slave or other illegal means, to hinder or defeat the due execution of said laws.

2. That all state laws which conflict with the fugitive slave acts of Congress, or any other constitutional acts of Congress, or which, in their operation, impede, hinder, or delay the free course and due execution of any of said acts, are null and void by the plain provisions of the Constitution of the United States; yet those state laws, void as they are, have given color to practices and led to consequences which have obstructed

the due administration and execution of acts of Congress, and especially the acts for the delivery of fugitive slaves; and have thereby contributed much to the discord and commotion now prevailing. Congress, therefore, in the present perilous juncture, does not deem it improper, respectfully and earnestly, to recommend the repeal of those laws to the several states which have enacted them, or such legislative corrections or explanations of them as may prevent their being used or perverted to such mischievous purposes.

3. That the act of the 18th of September, 1850, commonly called the Fugitive Slave Law, ought to be so amended as to make the fee of the commissioner, mentioned in the 8th Section of the act, equal in amount in the cases decided by him,

whether his decision be in favor of or against the claimant. And, to avoid misconstruction, the last clause of the 5th Section of said act, which authorizes the person holding a warrant for the arrest or detention of a fugitive slave to summon to his aid the *posse comitatus,* and which declares it to be the duty of all good citizens to assist him in its execution, ought to be so amended as to expressly limit the authority and duty to cases in which there shall be resistance, or danger of resistance or rescue.

4. That the laws for the suppression of the African slave trade, and especially those prohibiting the importation of slaves into the United States, ought to be more effectual, and ought to be thoroughly executed; and all further enactments necessary to those ends ought to be promptly made.

41.

John Sherman: Secession Means War

"I see some signs of hope, but it is probably a deceptive light," wrote Congressman John Sherman to his brother, William Tecumseh Sherman, early in January 1861. For American statesmen the period between Lincoln's election on November 6, 1860, and his inauguration on March 4, 1861, was an agonizing one. South Carolina seceded on December 20. The congressional attempt to reconcile North and South failed on December 22 when the "Crittenden Compromise" was defeated. President Buchanan seemed unable to take any decisive action to avert the secession threat. In the following letter of December 22 to a group of Philadelphians, John Sherman summed up his views on the crisis that faced the nation. He enclosed a copy in a letter to his brother, written January 6, 1861.

Source: *The Sherman Letters,* Rachel Sherman Thorndike, ed., New York, 1894, pp. 92-104.

FIDELITY TO PRINCIPLE is demanded by the highest patriotism. The question is not whether this or that policy should prevail but whether we shall allow the government to be broken into fragments by disappointed partisans condemned by four-fifths of the people. It is the same question answered by

General Jackson in his proclamation of 1833. It is the same question answered by Henry Clay in the Senate in 1850. It is the same question answered by Madison and Jefferson and recently by Wade and Johnson. It is a question which, I feel assured, every one of you will answer, in the patriotic language of General Jackson — "The Union, it must be preserved."

Such would be the voice of the whole country, if the government was not now administered by those who not only permit treason but actually commit it, by turning the powers of the government against itself. They kill the government they have sworn to maintain and defend, because the people, whose agents they are, have condemned them. In this spirit we have seen a secretary of the treasury, charged with the financial credit of the government, offering for sale the bonds of the government and, at the same moment, declaring that it will be overthrown and that he would aid in overthrowing it. We see other high officers receiving pay for services to the government and yet, at the same moment, plotting its destruction. We see the treasury robbed by subordinate officers amid the general ruin. Stranger still, we see the President of the United States acknowledging his duty to execute the laws but refusing to execute them. He admits that the Constitution is the supreme law; that neither a state nor the citizens of a state can disregard it; and yet, armed as he is with all the executive power, he refuses even to protect the property of the United States against armed violence. He will not hear General Cass, the head of his Cabinet. He will not heed General Scott, the head of the Army. He has transferred to Southern states more than 100,000 arms, of the newest pattern and most effective caliber, to be turned against the government.

The American people are now trembling with apprehension lest the President allows our officers and soldiers to be slaughtered at their posts for want of the aid which he has refused, or, what is far more disgraceful, shall order the flag of the Union to be lowered without resistance to lawless force.

Treason sits in the councils, and timidity controls the executive power. The President listens to and is controlled by threats. He theorizes about coercing a state when he should be enforcing the laws against rebellious citizens. He admits that the states have surrendered the power to make treaties, coin money, and regulate commerce, and yet we will probably have the novel and ridiculous farce of a negotiation between the President and a state for the surrender of forts and arsenals and sovereignty. Congress can do nothing, for the laws now are sufficient, if executed. Impeachment is too slow a remedy. The Constitution provided against every probable vacancy in the office of President, but did not provide for utter imbecility.

The people, alarmed, excited, yet true to the Union and the Constitution, are watching with eager fear lest the noble government, baptized in the blood of the Revolution, shall be broken into fragments before the President-elect shall assume the functions of his office.

What pretext is given for this alarming condition of affairs, for every treasonable act has its pretext? We are told that the people of the Southern states *apprehend* that Mr. Lincoln will deprive them of their constitutional rights. It is not claimed that, as yet, their rights have been invaded, but upon an *apprehension* of evil, they will break up the most prosperous government the providence of God ever allowed to man.

We know very well how groundless are their apprehensions, but we are not even allowed to say so to our fellow citizens of the South. So wild is their apprehension that even such statesmen as Stephens, Johnson, Hill, Botts, and Pettigrew, when they say, "wait, wait, till we see what this Republican Party will attempt," are denounced as Abolitionists — submissionists. You know very well that we do not propose to interfere in the slightest degree with slavery in the states. We know that our leader, for whose election you rejoice, has, over and over again, affirmed his opposition to the abolition of slavery in the District of Columbia, except upon conditions that are not likely to occur; to any interference with the

John Sherman, senator from Ohio

interstate slave trade; and that he will enforce the constitutional right of the citizens of the slave states to recapture their fugitive slaves when they escape from service into the free states.

We know very well that the great objects which those who elected Mr. Lincoln expect him to accomplish will be to secure to free labor its just right to the territories of the United States; to protect, as far as practicable, by wise revenue laws, the labor of our people; to secure the public lands to actual settlers, instead of to nonresident speculators; to develop the internal resources of the country by opening new means of communication between the Atlantic and the Pacific; and to purify the administration of the government from the pernicious influences of jobs, contracts, and unreasonable party warfare.

But, some of you may say, all this is very well, but what will you do to save the Union? Why don't you compromise?

Gentlemen, remember that we are just recovering from the dishonor of breaking a legislative compromise. We have been struggling against all the powers of the government for six years to secure practically what was expressly granted by a compromise. We have succeeded. Kansas is now free. The Missouri restriction is now practically restored by the incipient constitution of Kansas, and safer yet by the will of her people. The baptism of strife through which she has passed has only strengthened the prohibition. There let it stand.

But our political opponents, who have dishonored the word "compromise," who trampled, without a moment's hesitation, upon a compromise when they expected to gain by it, now ask us to again compromise by securing slavery south of a geographical line. To this we might fairly say: There is no occasion for compromise. We have done no wrong; we have no apologies to make and no concessions to offer. You chose your ground, and we accepted your issue. We have beaten you, and you must submit, as we have done in the past, and as we should have done if the voice of the people had been against us. As good citizens you must obey the laws and respect the constituted authorities. But we will meet new questions of administration with a liberal spirit. Without surrendering our convictions in the least, we may now dispose of the whole territorial controversy by the exercise of unquestioned congressional power.

The only territory south of the line (except that which, by treaty with Indian tribes, cannot be included within the jurisdiction of a state) is New Mexico. She has now population enough for admission as a state. Let Congress admit her as a state, and then she has the acknowledged right to form, regulate, change, or modify her domestic institutions. She has now a nominal slave code framed and urged upon her by territorial officers. Practically, slavery does not exist there. It never can be established there. In a region where the earth yields her increase only by the practice of irrigation, slave labor will not be employed. At any rate, it is better to settle all questions about slavery there by admitting the territory as a state. While a territory, it is insisted that slavery shall be protected in it. We insist that Congress may prohibit it and that the people have an undisputed right to exclude slaves. Why not, by terminating their territorial condition, determine this controversy? The same course might now properly be adopted with all the territories of the United States.

In each of the territories there are now small settlements scattered along the lines of transit. Within five years, the least populous will contain sufficient population for a representative in Congress. Dakota, Washington, Nevada, and Jefferson [Colorado] are destined soon to be as familiar to us as Kansas and Nebraska. It is well worthy the consideration of the old states, whether it is not better to dispense with all territorial organizations — always expensive and turbulent — and, at once, to carve the whole into states of convenient size for admission. This was the Jeffersonian plan, which did not contemplate territories but states. It was also sanctioned by General Taylor and, but for his death, would have been adopted.

This is an easy, effectual remedy, within the power of Congress, and in its nature an irrevocable act. There is no necessity of an amendment to the Constitution. It is not at all probable that two-thirds of both houses of Congress and three-fourths of the states can agree to any amendments. Why attempt it, unless to invite new conquests, new acquisitions, to again arouse sectional animosities? We know that if Mexico is acquired, the South will demand it for slavery and the North for free institutions. We must forgo, for the present, new conquests, unless the love of acquisition is stronger than the love of domestic peace.

Suppose it to be conceded that the Constitution should be amended, what amendment will satisfy the South? Nothing less than the protection of slavery in the territories. But our people have pronounced against it. All who voted for Mr. Lincoln or Mr. Douglas — over 3,300,000 citizens — voted against this claim. Less than 1 million voted for it. Should the great majority yield to a meager minority, especially under threats of disunion? This minority demand that slavery be protected by the Constitution. Our fathers would not allow the word "slave" or "slavery" in the Constitution, when all the states but one were slaveholding. Shall we introduce these words when a majority of the states are free and when the progress of civilization has arrayed the world against slavery? If the love of peace, and ease, and office should tempt politicians and merchants to do it, the people will rebel. I assure you, whatever may be the consequence, they will not yield their moral convictions by strengthening the influence of slavery in this country.

Recent events have only deepened this feeling. The struggle to establish slavery in Kansas; the frequent murders and mobbings, in the South, of Northern citizens; the present turbulence and violence of Southern society; the manifest fear of the freedom of speech and of the press; the danger of insurrection; and now the attempt to subvert the government rather than submit to a constitutional election — these events, disguise it as you may, have aroused a counterirritation in the North that will not allow its representatives to yield, merely for peace, more than is prescribed by the letter and spirit of the Constitution. Every guarantee of this instrument ought to be faithfully and religiously observed. But when it is proposed to change it, to secure new guarantees to slavery, to extend and protect it, you awake and arouse the antislavery feeling of the North to war against slavery everywhere.

I am, therefore, opposed to any change in the Constitution and to any compromise that will surrender any of the principles sanctioned by the people in the recent contest. If the personal-liberty bills of any state infringe upon the Constitution, they should at once be repealed. Most of them have slumbered upon the statute book for years. They are now seized upon by those who are plotting disunion as a pretext. We should give them no pretext. It is always right and proper for each state to apply to state laws the test of the Constitution.

It is a remarkable fact that none of the border free states — New Jersey, Pennsylvania, Ohio, Indiana, Illinois, nor Iowa — have any such upon their statute books. The laws of these states against kidnaping are similar to those of Virginia and Kentucky. The laws of other states, so called, have never operated to release a single fugitive slave and may be regarded simply as a protest of those states against the harsh features of the Fugitive Slave Law. So far as they infringe upon the Constitution, or impair, in the least, a constitutional right, they are void and ought to be repealed.

I venture the assertion that there have been more cases of kidnaping of free Negroes in Ohio than of peaceable or unlawful rescue of fugitive slaves in the whole United States. It has been shown that the law of recapture and the penalties of rescue have been almost invariably executed. Count up all the cases of rescue of Negroes in the North, and you can find in your newspapers more cases of unlawful lynching and murder of white men in the South. These cases have now become so frequent and atrocious as to demand the attention of the general government. The same article of the Constitution that secures the recapture of fugitives from service and justice also secures the rights of citizens of Pennsylvania and Ohio to all the immunities and privileges of citizens of the several states. No law has been passed by Congress to secure this constitutional right. No executive authority interposes to protect our citizens, and yet we hear no threats of retaliation or rebellion from Northern citizens or Northern states. So, I trust, it may ever be.

The great danger that now overshadows us does not arise from real grievances. Plotters for disunion avail themselves of the weakness of the executive to precipitate revolution. South Carolina has taken the lead. The movement would be utterly insignificant if confined to that state. She is still in the Union, and neither the President nor Congress has the power to consent to her withdrawal. This can only be by a change in the Constitution, or by the acquiescence of the people of the other states. The defense of the property of the United States and the collection of the revenues need not cause the shedding of blood, unless she commences a contest of physical force. The increase, in one year, of our population is greater than her entire population, white and black. Either one of several congressional districts in the West has more white inhabitants than she has. Her military power is crippled by the preponderance of her slaves. However brave and gallant and spirited her people may be, and no one disputes these traits, yet it is manifest she is weak in physical force. This great government might well treat with indulgence paper secession, or the resolves of her convention and legislature, without invoking physical force to enforce the laws among her citizens.

Without disrespect to South Carolina, it would be easy to show that Shays's Rebellion and the Whiskey Insurrection involved the government in greater danger than the solitary secession of South Carolina. But the movement becomes imposing when we are assured that several powerful states will very soon follow in the lead of South Carolina; and when we know that other states, still more powerful, sympathize with the seceding states, to the extent of opposing, and perhaps resisting, the execution of the laws in the seceding states.

In this view of the present condition of public affairs, it becomes the people of the United States seriously to consider whether the government shall be arrested in the execution of its undisputed powers by the citizens of one or more states, or whether we shall test the power of the government to defend itself against dissolution. Can a separation take place without war? If so, where will be the line? Who shall possess this magnificent capital, with all its evidences of progress and civilization? Shall the mouth of the Mississippi be separated from its sources? Who shall possess the territories? Suppose these difficulties to be overcome; suppose that in peace we should huckster and divide up our nationality, our flag, our history, all the recollections of the past; suppose all these difficulties overcome, how can two rival republics, of the same race of men, divided only by a line or a river for thousands of miles, with all the present difficulties aggravated by separation, avoid forays, disputes, and war? How can we travel our future march of progress in Mexico, or on the high seas, or on the Pacific slope, without collision? It is impossible. To peaceably accomplish such results, we must change the nature of man.

Disunion is war! God knows, I do not threaten it, for I will seek to prevent it in every way possible. I speak but the logic of facts, which we should not conceal from each other. It is either hostilities between the government and the seceding states; or, if separation is yielded peaceably, it is a war of factions — a rivalry of insignificant communities, hating each other, and contemned by the civilized world. If war results, what a war it will be! Contemplate the North and South in hostile array against each other. If these sections do not know each other *now*, they will *then*.

We are a nation of military men, naturally turbulent because we are free, accustomed to arms, ingenious, energetic, brave, and strong. The same qualities that have enabled a single generation of men to develop the resources of a continent would enable us to destroy more rapidly than we have constructed. It is idle for individuals of either section to suppose themselves superi-

or in military power. The French and English tried that question for a thousand years. We ought to know it now. The result of the contest will not depend upon the first blow or the first year, but blood shed in civil war will yield its baleful fruits for generations.

How can we avert a calamity at which humanity and civilization shudder? I know no way but to cling to the government framed by our fathers, to administer it in a spirit of kindness but, in all cases, without partiality to enforce the laws. No state can release us from the duty of obeying the laws. The ordinance or act of a state is no defense for treason, nor does it lessen the moral guilt of that crime. Let us cling to each other in the hope that our differences will pass away, as they often have in times past. For the sake of peace, for the love of civil liberty, for the honor of our name, our race, our religion, let us preserve the Union, loving it better as the clouds grow darker. I am willing to unite with any man, whatever may have been his party relations, whatever may be his views of the existing differences, who is willing to rely on the Constitution as it is for his rights, and who is willing to maintain and defend the Union under all circumstances, against all enemies, at home or abroad.

Pardon me, gentlemen for writing you so fully. I feel restrained, by the custom of the House of Representatives, from engaging there in political debate; and yet I feel it is the duty of every citizen to prepare his countrymen for grave events that will test the strength and integrity of the government.

Believing that our only safety is in a firm enforcement of the laws, and that Mr. Lincoln will execute that duty without partiality, I join my hearty congratulations with yours that he is so soon to be the President of the United States.

1861

42.

James Russell Lowell: The Government's Right to Self-Defense

As editor of the Atlantic Monthly *from 1857 to 1861, James Russell Lowell wrote many political essays on the critical issues facing the nation. In the following piece, Lowell argued that the South by seceding had negated the basic principle of democracy — majority rule — and that the North had no choice but to defend that principle.*

Source: *Atlantic Monthly,* February 1861: "E Pluribus Unum."

THE THEORY that the best government is that which governs least seems to have been accepted literally by Mr. Buchanan, without considering the qualifications to which all general propositions are subject. His course of conduct has shown up its absurdity, in cases where prompt action is required, as effectually as Buckingham turned into ridicule the famous verse

My wound is great, because it is so small,

by instantly adding

Then it were greater, were it none at all.

Mr. Buchanan seems to have thought that if to govern little was to govern well, then to do nothing was the perfection of policy. But there is a vast difference between letting well alone and allowing bad to become worse by a want of firmness at the outset. If Mr. Buchanan, instead of admitting the right of secession, had declared it to be, as it plainly is, rebellion, he would not only have received the unanimous support of the free states but would have given confidence to the loyal, reclaimed the wavering, and disconcerted the plotters of treason in the South.

Either we have no government at all or else the very word implies the right, and therefore the duty, in the governing power of protecting itself from destruction and its property from pillage. But for Mr. Buchanan's acquiescence, the doctrine of the right of secession would never for a moment have bewildered the popular mind. It is simply mob law under a plausible name. Such a claim might have been fairly enough urged under the old Confederation; though even then it would have been summarily dealt with, in the case of a Tory colony, if the necessity had arisen. But the very fact that we have a national Constitution and legal methods for testing, preventing, or punishing any infringement of its provisions demonstrates the absurdity of any such assumption of right now. When the states surrendered their power to make war, did they make the single exception of the United States, and reserve the privilege of declaring war against them at any moment? . . .

The United States are . . . a unitary and indivisible nation, with a national life to protect, a national power to maintain, and national rights to defend against any and every assailant, at all hazards. Our national existence is all that gives value to American citizenship. Without the respect which nothing but our consolidated character could inspire, we might as well be citizens of the toy republic of San Marino for all the protection it would afford us. If our claim to a national existence was worth a seven-years' war to establish, it is worth maintaining at any cost; and it is daily becoming more apparent that the people, so soon as they find that secession means anything serious, will not allow themselves to be juggled out of their rights, as members of one of the great powers of the earth, by a mere quibble of constitutional interpretation.

We have been so much accustomed to the Buncombe style of oratory, to hearing men offer the pledge of their lives, fortunes, and sacred honor on the most trivial occasions, that we are apt to allow a great latitude in such matters, and only smile to think how small an advance any intelligent pawnbroker would be likely to make on securities of this description. . . . Our Southern brethren have been especially given to these orgies of loquacity, and have so often solemnly assured us of their own courage and of the warlike propensities, power, wealth, and general superiority of that part of the universe which is so happy as to be represented by them, that, whatever other useful impression they have made, they insure our never forgetting the proverb about the woman who talks of her virtue.

South Carolina, in particular, if she has hitherto failed in the application of her enterprise to manufacturing purposes of a more practical kind, has always been able to match every yard of printed cotton from the North with a yard of printed fustian, the product of her own domestic industry. We have thought no harm of this so long as no act of Congress required the reading of the *Congressional Globe*. We submitted to the general dispensation of long-windedness and short-meaningness as to any other providential visitation, endeavoring only to hold fast our faith in the divine government of the world in the midst of so much that was past understanding. . . .

The country is weary of being cheated with plays upon words. The United States are a nation and not a mass meeting; theirs is a government and not a caucus — a government that was meant to be capable, and is capable, of something more than the helpless *please don't* of a village constable; they have executive and administrative officers that are not mere puppet figures to go through the motions of an objectless activity, but arms and hands that become supple to do the will of the people so soon as that will becomes conscious and defines its purpose. It is time that we turned up our definitions in some more trustworthy dictionary than that of avowed disunionists and their more dangerous because more timid and cunning accomplices.

Rebellion smells no sweeter because it is called "secession," nor does "order" lose its divine precedence in human affairs because a knave may nickname it "coercion." Secession means chaos, and coercion, the exercise of legitimate authority. You cannot dignify the one nor degrade the other by any verbal charlatanism. The best testimony to the virtue of coercion is the fact that no wrongdoer ever thought well of it. The thief in jail, the mob leader in the hands of the police, and the murderer on the drop will be unanimous in favor of this new heresy of the unconstitutionality of constitutions, with its Newgate Calendar of confessors, martyrs, and saints. Falstaff's famous regiment would have volunteered to a man for its propagation or its defense. . . .

If secession be a right, then the moment of its exercise is wholly optional with those possessing it. . . . Within the limits of the Constitution, two sovereignties cannot coexist; and yet what practical odds does it make if a state becomes sovereign by simply declaring herself so? The legitimate consequence of secession is not that a state becomes sovereign but that, so far as the general government is concerned, she has outlawed herself, nullified her own existence as a state, and become an aggregate of riotous men who resist the execution of the laws.

We are told that coercion will be civil war; and so is a mob civil war till it is put down. In the present case, the only coercion called for is the protection of the public property and the collection of the federal revenues. If it be necessary to send troops to do this, they will not be sectional, as it is the fashion nowadays to call people who insist on their own rights and the maintenance of the laws, but federal troops, representing the will and power of the whole confederacy. A danger is always great so long as we are afraid of it; and mischief like that now gathering head in South Carolina may soon become a danger if not swiftly dealt with. . . .

It cannot be too distinctly stated or too often repeated that the discontent of South Carolina is not one to be allayed by any concessions which the free states can make with dignity or even safety. It is something more radical and of longer standing than distrust of the motives or probable policy of the Republican Party. It is neither more nor less than a disbelief in the very principles on which our government is founded. So long as they practically retained the government of the country, and could use its power and patronage to their own advantage, the plotters were willing to wait; but the moment they lost that control, by the breaking up of the Democratic Party, and saw that their

chance of ever regaining it was hopeless, they declared openly the principles on which they have all along been secretly acting.

Denying the constitutionality of special protection to any other species of property or branch of industry, and in 1832 threatening to break up the Union unless their theory of the Constitution in this respect were admitted, they went into the late presidential contest with a claim for extraordinary protection to a certain kind of property already the only one endowed with special privileges and immunities. Defeated overwhelmingly before the people, they now question the right of the majority to govern, except on their terms, and threaten violence in the hope of extorting from the fears of the free states what they failed to obtain from their conscience and settled convictions of duty. Their quarrel is not with the Republican Party but with the theory of democracy. . . .

But the present question is one altogether transcending all limits of party and all theories of party policy. It is a question of national existence; it is a question whether Americans shall govern America, or whether a disappointed clique shall nullify all government now and render a stable government difficult hereafter; it is a question not whether we shall have civil war under certain contingencies but whether we shall prevent it under any. It is idle, and worse than idle, to talk about Central Republics that can never be formed. We want neither Central Republics nor Northern Republics, but our own Republic and that of our fathers, destined one day to gather the whole continent under a flag that shall be the most august in the world. Having once known what it was to be members of a grand and peaceful constellation, we shall not believe, without further proof, that the laws of our gravitation are to be abolished and we flung forth into chaos, a hurly-burly of jostling and splintering stars, whenever Robert Toombs or Robert Thett, or any other Bob of the secession kite, may give a flirt of self-importance.

The first and greatest benefit of government is that it keeps the peace, that it ensures every man his right, and not only that, but the permanence of it. In order to do this, its first requisite is stability; and this once firmly settled, the greater the extent of conterminous territory that can be subjected to one system and one language and inspired by one patriotism, the better. That there should be some diversity of interests is perhaps an advantage, since the necessity of legislating equitably for all gives legislation its needful safeguards of caution and largeness of view. A single empire embracing the whole world, and controlling, without extinguishing, local organizations and nationalities, has been not only the dream of conquerors but the ideal of speculative philanthropists. Our own dominion is of such extent and power that it may, so far as this continent is concerned, be looked upon as something like an approach to the realization of such an ideal. But for slavery, it might have succeeded in realizing it; and in spite of slavery, it may. One language, one law, one citizenship over thousands of miles, and a government on the whole so good that we seem to have forgotten what government means. These are things not to be spoken of with levity, privileges not to be surrendered without a struggle.

43.

FERNANDO WOOD: Proposal for the Secession of New York City

Foreseeing the outbreak of civil war, the business interests of New York City, which had heavy investments in the South, felt threatened by the policy of the Republican Party. Fernando Wood, mayor of New York, had built a powerful political machine with the aid of the financial and commercial interests of the city. The Republican legislature of New York State feared Wood's machine and tried on several occasions to undermine his power. On January 6, 1861, the mayor delivered the following message to the city government, in which he recommended that New York City become a "free city" and that it stay out of the impending conflict and maintain its prosperity by dealing with both sides. Ironically, the mayor's fears for the economic welfare of his city were unfounded. With the coming of war, the city's economy was caught up in the rapid industrial and commercial expansion of the North.

Source: McPherson, pp. 42-44.

To the Honorable the Common Council:

Gentlemen:

We are entering upon the public duties of the year under circumstances as unprecedented as they are gloomy and painful to contemplate. The great trading and producing interests of not only the city of New York but of the entire country are prostrated by a monetary crisis; and, although similar calamities have before befallen us, it is the first time that they have emanated from causes having no other origin than that which may be traced to political disturbances. Truly, may it now be said, "We are in the midst of a revolution *bloodless* AS YET." Whether the dreadful alternative implied as probable in the conclusion of this prophetic quotation may be averted, "no human ken can divine."

It is quite certain that the severity of the storm is unexampled in our history, and if the disintegration of the federal government, with the consequent destruction of all the material interests of the people, shall not follow, it will be owing more to the interposition of Divine Providence than to the inherent preventive power of our institutions or the intervention of any other human agency.

It would seem that a dissolution of the federal Union is inevitable. Having been formed originally on a basis of general and mutual protection but separate local independence, each state reserving the entire and absolute control of its own domestic affairs, it is evidently impossible to keep them together longer than they deem themselves fairly treated by each other or longer than the interests, honor, and fraternity of the people of the several states are satisfied. Being a government created by *opinion,* its continuance is dependent upon the continuance of the sentiment which formed it. It cannot be preserved by coercion or held together by force. A resort to this last dreadful alternative would of itself destroy not only the government but the lives and property of the people.

If these forebodings shall be realized and a separation of the states shall occur, momentous considerations will be presented to the corporate authorities of this city. We must provide for the new relations which will necessarily grow out of the new condition of public affairs.

It will not only be necessary for us to settle the relations which we shall hold to other cities and states but to establish, if we can, new ones with a portion of our own state. Being the child of the Union, having drawn our sustenance from its bosom and

Library of Congress

Fernando Wood, mayor of New York, opposed the Lincoln administration's conduct of the Civil War

arisen to our present power and strength through the vigor of our mother, when deprived of her maternal advantages, we must rely upon our own resources and assume a position predicated upon the new phase which public affairs will present, and upon the inherent strength which our geographical, commercial, political, and financial preeminence imparts to us.

With our aggrieved brethren of the slave states we have friendly relations and a common sympathy. We have not participated in the warfare upon their constitutional rights or their domestic institutions. . . . Our ships have penetrated to every clime, and so have New York capital, energy, and enterprise found their way to every state, and, indeed, to almost every county and town of the American Union. If we have derived sustenance from the Union, so have we in return disseminated blessings for the common benefit of all. Therefore, New York has a right to expect, and should endeavor to preserve, a continuance of uninterrupted intercourse with every section.

It is however, folly to disguise the fact

that, judging from the past, New York may have more cause of apprehension from aggressive legislation of our own state than from external dangers. We have already largely suffered from this cause. For the past five years our interests and corporate rights have been repeatedly trampled upon. Being an integral portion of the state, it has been assumed, and in effect tacitly admitted on our part by nonresistance, that all political and governmental power over us rested in the state legislature. Even the common right of taxing ourselves for our own gov-. ernment has been yielded, and we are not permitted to do so without this authority. . . .

Thus it will be seen that the political connection between the people of the city and the state has been used by the latter to our injury. The legislature, in which the present partisan majority has the power, has become an instrument by which we are plundered to enrich their speculators, lobby agents, and Abolition politicians. . . .

How we shall rid ourselves of this odious and oppressive connection, it is not for me to determine. It is certain that a dissolution cannot be peacefully accomplished except by the consent of the legislature itself. Whether this can be obtained or not is, in my judgment, doubtful. Deriving so much advantage from its power over the city, it is not probable that a partisan majority will consent to a separation — and the resort to force by violence and revolution must not be thought of for an instant. We have been distinguished as an orderly and law-abiding people. Let us do nothing to forfeit this character or to add to the present distracted condition of public affairs.

Much, no doubt, can be said in favor of the justice and policy of a separation. . . . Why should not New York City, instead of supporting by her contributions in revenue two-thirds of the expenses of the United States, become also equally independent? As a free city, with but nominal duty on imports, her local government could be sup-ported without taxation upon her people. Thus we could live free from taxes and have cheap goods nearly duty free. In this she would have the whole and united support of the Southern states, as well as all the other states to whose interests and rights under the Constitution she has always been true.

It is well for individuals or communities to look every danger square in the face and to meet it calmly and bravely. As dreadful as the severing of the bonds that have hitherto united the states has been in contemplation, it is now apparently a stern and inevitable fact. We have now to meet it with all the consequences, whatever they may be. If the confederacy is broken up, the government is dissolved; and it behooves every distinct community, as well as every individual, to take care of themselves.

When disunion has become a fixed and certain fact, why may not New York disrupt the bands which bind her to a venal and corrupt master — to a people and a party that have plundered her revenues, attempted to ruin her commerce, taken away the power of self-government, and destroyed the confederacy of which she was the proud Empire City? Amid the gloom which the present and prospective condition of things must cast over the country, New York, as a *free city*, may shed the only light and hope of a future reconstruction of our once blessed confederacy.

But I am not prepared to recommend the violence implied in these views. In stating this argument in favor of freedom, "peaceably if we can, forcibly if we must," let me not be misunderstood. The redress can be found only in appeals to the magnanimity of the people of the whole state. The events of the past two months have no doubt effected a change in the popular sentiment of the state and national politics. This change may bring us the desired relief, and we may be able to obtain a repeal of the law to which I have referred and a consequent restoration of our corporate rights.

44.

Economic Reasons for Secession

Chief among the rationales for secession was the economic argument that an independent South would prosper more outside the Union. It could conduct trade directly with Europe and find a profitable market for its agriculture. British interest in Southern textiles would support the cotton industry. A revival of the slave trade would lower the cost of labor and aid in the development of Southern manufacturing. The following editorial supporting these economic reasons for secession appeared in the New Orleans Daily Crescent *on January 21, 1861.*

Source: *New Orleans Daily Crescent,* January 21, 1861.

THERE IS THIS DIFFERENCE between the Northern and Southern states which illustrates the exact nature of the quarrel between the two sections: that, while the Southern states in the Union would have interposed no objection to the secession of any Northern state, the Northern states, on the other hand, are thrown into a perfect paroxysm of rage at the mere whisper of an intention to secede on the part of any state of the South.

Thus, if at any time within the last ten years Massachusetts had threatened to leave the Union, the idea, so far from being unpalatable to the South, would have been hailed with the liveliest demonstrations of joy and satisfaction. The South would have bid her go and go quickly, and have esteemed it a happy riddance. But, on the other hand, when any Southern state proposes to leave the Union, Massachusetts becomes intensely disgusted thereat, and considers herself very much insulted and scandalized.

Why is this? Why is it that the South is perfectly willing for the North to secede, while the reverse is true of the North as respects the South? In social life, when two persons are together and the presence of one is known to be distasteful to the other, the remedy of withdrawal is universally admitted. But for the offending and offensive party to follow up the withdrawing party and insist upon forcing his company upon him when he knows it to be irksome and hateful is a breach of every canon of good manners and polite society.

When the North tells us that we have no right to withdraw from the Union, we answer that we are perfectly willing to stay in the Union if *they themselves* will withdraw! We will not question *their* right to secede, but, on the contrary, will concede it cheerfully. We would perhaps prefer this arrangement to the other. The South, which claims the right of secession for itself, is equally ready and willing to grant the same right to the North; and we will undertake to pledge the Southern states that if those of the North wish to secede from the Union, not only will no objection be raised but, as to a large majority of them, the secession will be accounted a most fortunate and happy circumstance for us.

But as the Northern states will *not* leave the Union, as in common decency they ought to do seeing that they are so unhappy about the countenance the Union is supposed to give to the institution of slavery, there is no alternative to the South except to withdraw for herself. As it is manifestly impossible for the two sections to get along together in peace and harmony, and as the North, which might withdraw without objection, refuses to do so, we are driven to the necessity of withdrawing ourselves, painful as it appears to be to our loving and considerate friends and brethren of the states of the North.

But why is there such objection made to the withdrawal of the South? We are told by Abolition orators and organs that the South is a poor, miserable region; that most of the wealth, the enterprise, and the intelligence of the nation is in the North; that the Southern people, as was said by Sumner in the Senate, are identified with, and apologists for, an institution essentially "barbaric"; that our section is unable to support a mail system, and that we are pensioners, to that extent, of the federal government; that we are, in short, a semi-civilized, God-forsaken people, a long ways behind the "great North" in the arts, in refinement, in education, in enterprise, and in everything else that constitutes what they call "civilization." One would suppose they would be eager to be relieved of association with a people of whom they have so poor an opinion. So far the contrary, however, they are, as we have before said, mortally offended at the bare idea of our dissolving with them our political connection.

There must be a reason for this, as there is for everything else, and the reason is plain enough. All that they say about the South is false, and, what is more, they know it to be false. They know that the South is the main prop and support of the federal system. They know that it is Southern productions that constitute the surplus wealth of the nation and enables us to import so largely from foreign countries. They know that it is their import trade that draws from the people's pockets $60 million or $70 million per annum, in the shape of duties, to be expended mainly in the North and in the protection and encouragement of Northern interests. They know that it is the export of Southern productions, and the corresponding import of foreign goods, that gives profitable employment to their shipping. They know that the bulk of the duties is paid by the Southern people, though first collected at the North, and that, by the iniquitous operation of the federal government, these duties are mainly expended among the Northern people.

They know that they can plunder and pillage the South, as long as they are in the same Union with us, by other means such as fishing bounties, navigation laws, robberies of the public lands, and every other possible mode of injustice and peculation. They know that in the Union they can steal Southern property in slaves without risking civil war, which would be certain to occur if such a thing were done from the independent South. And, above and beyond all this, is the Puritanic love of mean tyranny and cold-blooded, inexorable oppression, which the Union enables them to cherish and reduce to practice — coupled with the Pharisaical boast of "holier than thou," which they are constantly uttering as a reproach to the South — both of which feelings are innate in the descendants of the Pilgrims, and have become a part of their nature, which they could not get rid of if they wished.

These are the reasons why these people do not wish the South to secede from the Union. They are enraged at the prospect of being despoiled of the rich feast upon which they have so long fed and fattened, and which they were just getting ready to enjoy with still greater *goût* [relish] and gusto. They are mad as hornets because the prize slips them just as they are ready to grasp it. Their fruitless wailing and frantic rage only serve to confirm the South in her inflexible determination to break up an alliance which is as unnatural as it is to us oppressive and degrading.

45.

JEFFERSON DAVIS: Inaugural Address

*As a senator from Mississippi in the pre-Civil War period, Jefferson Davis was one of
the influential politicians of his times. Between 1858 and 1860 he delivered speeches
in both North and South urging the preservation of the Union. During the presidential
campaign of 1860 he attempted to discourage secessionist sentiment. On January 21,
1861, after his own state seceded from the Union, he delivered an eloquent plea for peace
in his farewell speech to the Senate. Three weeks later, representatives of the seceded
states met at Montgomery and elected Davis president of the Confederate States of
America. He was surprised at the news of his election. His wife recorded his reaction
in her memoirs, published in 1890: ". . . when reading the telegram he looked so grieved
that I feared some evil had befallen our family." Unlike most of the Southern leaders,
Davis had expected war and hoped to become the commander in chief of the Southern
armies. Yet his first act as president of the Confederacy was to send a commission to
Washington to negotiate a peaceful settlement with the government. Lincoln refused to
receive his commission. In a state of poor health and with grave doubts about his ability
to serve as president and about the South's ability to fight a war, Davis delivered his
Inaugural Address on February 18, 1861.*

Source: Moore, I, Document 37.

Gentlemen of the Congress of the Confederate States of America, Friends, and Fellow Citizens:

Called to the difficult and responsible station of chief magistrate of the provisional government which you have instituted, I approach the discharge of the duties assigned me with a humble distrust of my abilities, but with a sustaining confidence in the wisdom of those who are to guide and aid me in the administration of public affairs, and an abiding faith in the virtue and patriotism of the people. Looking forward to the speedy establishment of a permanent government to take the place of this, and which by its greater moral and physical power will be better able to combat with the many difficulties which arise from the conflicting interests of separate nations, I enter upon the duties of the office to which I have been chosen with the hope that the beginning of our career as a Confederacy may not be obstructed by hostile opposition to our enjoyment of the separate existence and independence we have asserted, and which, with the blessing of Providence, we intend to maintain.

Our present condition, achieved in a manner unprecedented in the history of nations, illustrates the American idea that governments rest upon the consent of the governed, and that it is the right of the people to alter or abolish governments whenever they become destructive to the ends for which they were established. The declared compact of the Union from which we have withdrawn was to establish justice, insure domestic tranquillity, provide for the common defense, promote the general welfare, and secure the blessings of liberty to ourselves and our posterity; and when, in the judgment of the sovereign states now composing this Confederacy, it has been perverted from the purposes for which it was ordained, and ceased to answer the ends for which it was established, a peaceful appeal to the ballot box declared that, so far as they are concerned, the government created by that compact should cease to exist.

In this they merely asserted the right which the Declaration of Independence of 1776 defined to be "inalienable." Of the time and occasion of its exercise, they, as sovereigns, were the final judges, each for itself. The impartial, enlightened verdict of mankind will vindicate the rectitude of our conduct; and He who knows the hearts of men will judge of the sincerity with which we labored to preserve the government of our fathers in its spirit.

The right solemnly proclaimed at the birth of the States, and which has been affirmed and reaffirmed in the bills of rights of the states subsequently admitted into the Union of 1789, undeniably recognizes in the people the power to resume the authority delegated for the purposes of government. Thus the sovereign states here represented proceeded to form this Confederacy; and it is by the abuse of language that their act has been denominated revolution. They formed a new alliance, but within each state its government has remained. The rights of person and property have not been disturbed. The agent through whom they communicated with foreign nations is changed, but this does not necessarily interrupt their international relations. Sustained by the consciousness that the transition from the former Union to the present Confederacy has not proceeded from a disregard on our part of our just obligations or any failure to perform every constitutional duty,

Chicago Historical Society

Jefferson Davis; photographed by Brady about 1860

moved by no interest or passion to invade the rights of others, anxious to cultivate peace and commerce with all nations, if we may not hope to avoid war, we may at least expect that posterity will acquit us of having needlessly engaged in it. Doubly justified by the absence of wrong on our part, and by wanton aggression on the part of others, there can be no cause to doubt the courage and patriotism of the people of the Confederate States will be found equal to any measure of defense which soon their security may require.

An agricultural people, whose chief interest is the export of a commodity required in every manufacturing country, our true policy is peace and the freest trade which our necessities will permit. It is alike our interest and that of all those to whom we would sell, and from whom we would buy, that there should be the fewest practicable restrictions upon the interchange of commodities. There can be but little rivalry between ours and any manufacturing or navigating community, such as the Northeastern states of the American Union. It must follow, therefore, that mutual interest would invite to goodwill and kind offices. If, however, passion or lust of dominion should cloud the judgment or inflame the ambition of those states, we must prepare to meet the emergency and maintain by the final arbitrament of the sword the position which we have assumed among the nations of the earth.

We have entered upon a career of independence, and it must be inflexibly pursued through many years of controversy with our late associates of the Northern states. We have vainly endeavored to secure tranquillity and obtain respect for the rights to which we were entitled. As a necessity, not a choice, we have resorted to the remedy of separation, and henceforth our energies must be directed to the conduct of our own affairs and the perpetuity of the Confederacy which we have formed. If a just perception of mutual interest shall permit us peaceably to pursue our separate political career, my most earnest desire will have been fulfilled. But if this be denied us, and the integrity of our territory and jurisdiction be assailed, it will but remain for us with firm resolve to appeal to arms and invoke the blessing of Providence on a just cause.

As a consequence of our new condition, and with a view to meet anticipated wants, it will be necessary to provide a speedy and efficient organization of the branches of the Executive Department having special charge of foreign intercourse, finance, military affairs, and the postal service. For purposes of defense, the Confederate States may, under ordinary circumstances, rely mainly upon their militia; but it is deemed advisable, in the present condition of affairs, that there should be a well-instructed, disciplined army, more numerous than would usually be required on a peace establishment. I also suggest that, for the protection of our harbors and commerce on the high seas, a navy adapted to those objects will be required.

These necessities have, doubtless, engaged the attention of Congress.

With a constitution differing only from that of our fathers insofar as it is explanatory of their well-known intent, freed from sectional conflicts, which have interfered with the pursuit of the general welfare; it is not unreasonable to expect that states from which we have recently parted may seek to unite their fortunes to ours under the government which we have instituted. For this your constitution makes adequate provision; but beyond this, if I mistake not, the judgment and will of the people are that reunion with the states from which they have separated is neither practicable nor desirable. To increase the power, develop the resources, and promote the happiness of the Confederacy, it is requisite that there should be so much homogeneity that the welfare of every portion would be the aim of the whole. Where this does not exist, antagonisms are engendered which must and should result in separation.

Actuated solely by a desire to preserve our own rights and promote our own welfare, the separation of the Confederate States has been marked by no aggression upon others and followed by no domestic convulsion. Our industrial pursuits have received no check, the cultivation of our fields progresses as heretofore, and even should we be involved in war, there would be no considerable dimunition in the production of the staples which have constituted our exports, in which the commercial world has an interest scarcely less than our own. This common interest of producer and consumer can only be intercepted by an exterior force which should obstruct its transmission to foreign markets — a course of conduct which would be detrimental to manufacturing and commercial interests abroad.

Should reason guide the action of the government from which we have separated, a policy so detrimental to the civilized world, the Northern states included, could not be dictated by even a stronger desire to inflict injury upon us; but if it be otherwise, a terrible responsibility will rest upon it, and the suffering of millions will bear testimony to the folly and wickedness of our aggressors. In the meantime there will remain to us, besides the ordinary remedies before suggested, the well-known resources for retaliation upon the commerce of an enemy.

Experience in public stations of a subordinate grade to this which your kindness has conferred, has taught me that care and toil and disappointments are the price of official elevation. You will see many errors to forgive, many deficiencies to tolerate; but you shall not find in me either want of zeal or fidelity to the cause that is to me the highest in hope and of most enduring affection. Your generosity has bestowed upon me an undeserved distinction, one which I neither sought nor desired. Upon the continuance of that sentiment, and upon your wisdom and patriotism, I rely to direct and support me in the performance of the duties required at my hands.

We have changed the constituent parts but not the system of government. The Constitution formed by our fathers is that of these Confederate States. In their exposition of it, and in the judicial construction it has received, we have a light which reveals its true meaning. Thus instructed as to the just interpretation of that instrument, and ever remembering that all offices are but trusts held for the people, and that delegated powers are to be strictly construed, I will hope by due diligence in the performance of my duties, though I may disappoint your expectation, yet to retain, when retiring, something of the goodwill and confidence which will welcome my entrance into office.

It is joyous in the midst of perilous times to look around upon a people united in heart, when one purpose of high resolve animates and actuates the whole; where the sacrifices to be made are not weighed in the balance against honor, right, liberty, and equality. Obstacles may retard, but they cannot long prevent the progress of a movement sanctioned by its justice and sustained by a virtuous people. Reverently let us invoke the God of our fathers to guide and protect us in our efforts to perpetuate the principles which by His blessing they were able to vindicate, establish, and transmit to their posterity. And with a continuance of His favor ever gratefully acknowledged, we may hopefully look forward to success, to peace, to prosperity.

———◆———

My friends, no one, not in my situation, can appreciate my feeling of sadness at this parting. To this place and the kindness of these people I owe everything. Here I have lived a quarter of a century and have passed from a young to an old man. Here my children have been born, and one is buried. I now leave, not knowing when, or whether ever, I may return, with a task before me greater than that which rested upon Washington. Without the assistance of that Divine Being who ever attended him, I cannot succeed. With that assistance I cannot fail. Trusting in Him who can go along with me, and remain with you, and be everywhere for good, let us confidently hope that all will yet be well. To His care commending you, as I hope in your prayers you will commend me, I bid you an affectionate farewell.

ABRAHAM LINCOLN, address on leaving Springfield, Feb. 11, 1861

46.

Henry Timrod: "Ethnogenesis"

Henry Timrod was unrecognized as a poet until the Southern secession and the Civil War. The emotions that stirred the South in 1860-1861 led to a flowering of his poetic talents, and by the time the Confederacy was formed he was regarded as the South's poet laureate. The following poem was written while Timrod was attending the First Southern Congress, at Montgomery, in February 1861. Originally titled "Ode, on the Meeting of the Southern Congress," it was first printed in the Charleston Mercury *on September 26. In the poem Timrod eloquently sings of the birth of the new nation, expresses the patriotic spirit of his countrymen, and presents his ideas of the South's mission and of the Southern character.*

Source: *Poems,* Memorial Edition, Richmond, Va., 1901.

ETHNOGENESIS

I

Hath not the morning dawned with added
    light?
And shall not evening call another star
Out of the infinite regions of the night,
To mark this day in Heaven? At last, we
    are
A nation among nations; and the world
Shall soon behold in many a distant port
    Another flag unfurled!
Now, come what may, whose favor need
    we court?
And, under God, whose thunder need we
    fear?
Thank Him who placed us here
Beneath so kind a sky — the very sun
Takes part with us; and on our errands run
All breezes of the ocean; dew and rain
Do noiseless battle for us; and the year,
And all the gentle daughters in her train,
March in our ranks, and in our service
    wield
    Long spears of golden grain!
A yellow blossom as her fairy shield,
June flings her azure banner to the wind,

While in the order of their birth
Her sisters pass, and many an ample field
Grows white beneath their steps, till now,
    behold,
    Its endless sheets unfold
The snow of Southern summers! Let the
    earth
Rejoice! beneath those fleeces soft and warm
    Our happy land shall sleep
    In a repose as deep
As if we lay entrenched behind
Whole leagues of Russian ice and
    Arctic storm!

II

And what if, mad with wrongs themselves
    have wrought,
    In their own treachery caught,
    By their own fears made bold,
    And leagued with him of old,
Who long since in the limits of the North,
Set up his evil throne, and warred with
    God —
What if, both mad and blinded in their rage
Our foes should fling us down their
    mortal gage,
And with a hostile step profane our sod!

We shall not shrink, my brothers, but go
  forth
To meet them, marshaled by the Lord
  of Hosts,
And overshadowed by the mighty ghosts
Of Moultrie and Eutaw — who shall foil
Auxiliars such as these? Nor these alone,
  But every stock and stone
  Shall help us; but the very soil,
And all the generous wealth it gives to toil,
And all for which we love our noble land,
Shall fight beside, and through us; sea and
  strand,
The heart of woman, and her hand,
Tree, fruit, and flower, and every influence,
  Gentle, or grave, or grand;
  The winds in our defense
Shall seem to blow; to us the hills shall
  lend
  Their firmness and their calm;
And in our stiffened sinews we shall blend
  The strength of pine and palm!

III

Nor would we shun the battleground,
  Though weak as we are strong;
Call up the clashing elements around,
  And test the right and wrong!
On one side, creeds that dare to teach
What Christ and Paul refrained to preach;
Codes built upon a broken pledge,
And charity that whets a poniard's edge;
Fair schemes that leave the neighboring
  poor
To starve and shiver at the schemer's door,
While in the world's most liberal ranks
  enrolled,
He turns some vast philanthropy to gold;
Religion, taking every mortal form
But that a pure and Christian faith makes
  warm,
Where not to vile fanatic passion urged,
Or not in vague philosophies submerged,
Repulsive with all Pharisaic leaven,
And making laws to stay the laws of
  Heaven!
And on the other, scorn of sordid gain,
Unblemished honor, truth without a stain,

Faith, justice, reverence, charitable wealth,
And, for the poor and humble, laws which
  give,
Not the mean right to buy the right to live,
  But life, and home, and health!
To doubt the end were want of trust in
  God,
  Who, if He has decreed
That we must pass a redder sea
  Than that which rang to Miriam's holy
  glee,
  Will surely raise at need
  A Moses with his rod!

IV

But let our fears — if fears we have — be
  still,
And turn us to the future! Could we climb
Some mighty Alp, and view the coming
  time,
The rapturous sight would fill
  Our eyes with happy tears!
Not only for the glories which the years
Shall bring us; not for lands from sea to
  sea,
And wealth, and power, and peace, though
  these shall be;
But for the distant peoples we shall bless,
And the hushed murmurs of a world's
  distress:
For, to give labor to the poor,
  The whole sad planet o'er,
And save from want and crime the
  humblest door,
Is one among the many ends for which
  God makes us great and rich!
The hour perchance is not yet wholly ripe
When all shall own it, but the type
Whereby we shall be known in every land
Is that vast gulf which lips our Southern
  strand,
And through the cold, untempered ocean
  pours
Its genial streams, that far off Arctic shores,
May sometimes catch upon the softened
  breeze
Strange tropic warmth and hints of summer
  seas.

47.

Compromise Resolutions of the House of Representatives

In the hope of maintaining the Union, moderates in Congress sought to adopt compromise resolutions on the question of slavery. On December 6, 1860, the House of Representatives established the Committee of Thirty-Three, having one member from each state, with the aim of proposing legislation that would assure the South that its "peculiar institution" would remain intact where it existed, while assuring the North that slavery would not be extended into the territories. The Committee made the following two proposals to the House on February 27, 1861, both of which were adopted. However, the Committee could reach no agreement on the issue of slavery in the territories.

Source: McPherson, pp. 58-59.

Resolved by the Senate and House of Representatives of the United States of America, in Congress assembled, that all attempts on the part of the legislatures of any of the states to obstruct or hinder the recovery and surrender of fugitives from service or labor are in derogation of the Constitution of the United States, inconsistent with the comity and good neighborhood that should prevail among the several states, and dangerous to the peace of the Union.

Resolved, that the several states be respectfully requested to cause their statutes to be revised, with a view to ascertain if any of them are in conflict with or tend to embarrass or hinder the execution of the laws of the United States made in pursuance of the 2nd Section of the 4th Article of the Constitution of the United States for the delivery up of persons held to labor by the laws of any state and escaping therefrom; and the Senate and House of Representatives earnestly request that all enactments having such tendency be forthwith repealed, as required by a just sense of constitutional obligations and by a due regard for the peace of the republic; and the President of the United States is requested to communicate these resolutions to the governors of the several states, with a request that they will lay the same before the legislatures thereof respectively.

Resolved, that we recognize slavery as now existing in fifteen of the United States by the usages and laws of those states; and we recognize no authority, legally or otherwise, outside of a state where it so exists, to interfere with slaves or slavery in such states, in disregard of the rights of their owners or the peace of society.

Resolved, that we recognize the justice and propriety of a faithful execution of the Constitution and laws made in pursuance thereof on the subject of fugitive slaves, or fugitives from service or labor, and discountenance all mobs or hindrances to the execution of such laws, and that citizens of each state shall be entitled to all the privileges and immunities of citizens in the several states.

Resolved, that we recognize no such conflicting elements in its composition, or sufficient cause from any source, for a dissolution of this government; that we were not sent here to destroy but to sustain and harmonize the institutions of the country, and to see that equal justice is done to all parts of the same; and finally, to perpetuate its existence on terms of equality and justice to all the states.

Resolved, that a faithful observance, on the part of all the states, of all their constitutional obligations to each other and to the federal government is essential to the peace of the country.

Resolved, that it is the duty of the federal government to enforce the federal laws, protect the federal property, and preserve the Union of these states.

Resolved, that each state be requested to revise its statutes, and if necessary, so to amend the same as to secure, without legislation by Congress, to citizens of other states traveling therein, the same protection as citizens of such state enjoy; and also to protect the citizens of other states traveling or sojourning therein against popular violence or illegal summary punishment, without trial in due form of law, for imputed crimes.

Resolved, that each state be also respectfully requested to enact such laws as will prevent and punish any attempt whatever in such state to recognize or set on foot the lawless invasion of any other state or territory.

Resolved, that the President be requested to transmit copies of the foregoing resolutions to the governors of the several states, with a request that they be communicated to their respective legislatures.

So the joint resolution was passed.

Be it resolved by the Senate and House of Representatives of the United States of America, in Congress assembled, two-thirds of both houses concurring, that the following article be proposed to the legislatures of the several states as an amendment to the Constitution of the United States, which, when ratified by three-fourths of said legislatures, shall be valid, to all intents and purposes, as a part of the said Constitution, namely:

> Article XII. No amendment of this Constitution having for its object any interference within the states with the relation between their citizens and those described in Section 2 of Article I of the Constitution as "all other persons" shall originate with any state that does not recognize that relation within its own limits, or shall be valid without the assent of every one of the states composing the Union.

Before the vote was taken Mr. Corwin [Committee member from Ohio] offered the following substitute for the above article:

> Article XII. No amendment shall be made to the Constitution which will authorize or give to Congress the power to abolish or interfere, within any state, with the domestic institutions thereof, including that of persons held to labor or service by the laws of said state.

Which was agreed to.

Say to the seceded states, "Wayward sisters, depart in peace."
GENERAL WINFIELD SCOTT, letter to William H. Seward, March 3, 1861

All we ask is to be left alone.
JEFFERSON DAVIS, "Inaugural Address," Feb. 18, 1861

48.

John J. Crittenden: The Union at Any Price

The Crittenden Compromise, presented to Congress on December 18, 1860, had been defeated. On January 3, 1861, Senator Crittenden of Kentucky put a resolution before the Senate that his Compromise be submitted to a popular vote. Supporting the resolution, Senator Douglas said: "I prefer compromise to war. I prefer concession to a dissolution of the Union." The House endorsed it; the Senate voted it down. On March 2, 1861, the day before Congress adjourned, Crittenden made yet another unsuccessful plea to the Senate to save the Union. He did, however, help persuade Kentucky to remain in it. The plea of March 2 is reprinted here in part.

Source: *Globe*, 36 Cong., 2 Sess., pp. 1375-1379.

Mr. President:

It is an admitted fact that our Union, to some extent, has already been dismembered; and that further dismemberment is impending and threatened. It is a fact that the country is in danger. This is admitted on all hands. . . . Remedies have been proposed, resolutions have been offered proposing for adoption measures which it was thought would satisfy the country and preserve as much of the Union as remained to us at least, if they were not enough at once to recall the seceding states to the Union. We have passed none of these measures. . . .

Mr. President, the cause of this great discontent in the country, the cause of the evils which we now suffer and which we now fear originates chiefly from questions growing out of the respective territorial rights of the different states and the unfortunate subject of slavery. I have said before to my brother senators that I do not appear on this occasion as the advocate of slavery; I appear here as the advocate of Union. I want to preserve that from overthrow; and I am suggesting that policy, which, according to my poor judgment, is adequate to the object. . . .

We are likely soon to part, and what a spectacle do we present? We have done nothing. The country is inflamed, and nothing has been done to quench the destroying fire; yet, that is our business here, to preserve the Union, to make the people contented and happy. That is our great and high mission. The country is in flames, and nothing has been done to extinguish the fire. What, senators and Mr. President, is to be the consequence of it? No one can exactly answer; but the question must awaken the forebodings of every man within the reach of my voice. What consequence will follow from our failure to do anything? God only knows. They are fearful to think of, in my judgment. I do not know what they will be.

I fear for further revolution — for revolution to such an extent as to destroy, in effect, this Union. I hope not. I would advise against it. I would say to the people, the distraction which exists in the opinions of those that constitute Congress are such that they cannot agree upon any measures now; you may think and feel that justice is denied you; it may be so; but is denied you by whom? In a time of high party excitement, by one Congress. Your Constitution is so framed as to give you, in a short period, many congresses. The power returns to the people of electing their representatives; and this government is worth being patient for and worth bearing a great deal for. Be patient and bear it, even though you think you are wronged. Rather bear the wrongs you have than fly to others which you know not of.

Hold fast to the Union. The Union is the instrument by which you may obtain redress, by which you will in the end obtain redress. Congress may err. It may err from error of judgment, from passion, from excitement, from party heats; they will not last always. The principles upon which your government was founded recognize all these frailties, recognize all these sources of occasional and temporary wrong and injustice, but they furnish a remedy for it. They furnish a remedy in the often-recurring elections which the people make. It is not for the first offense that dismemberment and disunion are justified. Hold fast to the Union. There is safety, tried safety, known safety; and that same Union is the best assurance you can have of eventually obtaining from your fellow citizens a generous recompense for all the wrongs you have received and a generous remedy against any wrongs hereafter.

These are my feelings, and this would be my advice. My advice is that of a Union man earnest for its preservation; and without the fullness of my heart, the words which I utter are worth nothing. This would be my advice at all times upon this question and upon every question which threatened the Union: stay in the Union and strive in the Union. We may have had evidences enough here of the impossibility of obtaining any agreement from our Northern brethren to these measures of policy which I have offered. I will not call them a compromise, for that seems to offend gentlemen; though I was willing that each of our brethren, North and South, might think, by the word compromise, that, in a generous and affectionate spirit and

sentiment, nominally, at least, he had given up something. But gentlemen object to the term, if the stern, warlike cry of "no compromise" is heard, like the ancient cry of the Roman conqueror. When oppression was complained of, they answered it by a *vae victis* — woe to the conquered — now translated, "no compromise." . . .

Take our dogmas; take our platforms; it is not sufficient that you obey the Constitution; it is not sufficient that you adhere to the Union; go out of the Constitution; go out of the Union; look at our platform; study that; that is the idol to which you must bow down; otherwise, "no compromise" — woe to you. Sir, this is not the language of the heart or of the judgment. It is the language of excitement. It may be uttered by good men; but it is the language of passion. It is the language of excitement. It regards nothing here to be a compromise that is within the Constitution.

These amendments only ask you to make some additions to your Constitution because of the altered state of things. When we met here at the commencement of the session, you had fifteen states which adopted the same system of labor — involuntary servitude. The Constitution was framed to a state of things when almost every state in the Union, with but one exception, adopted that system of labor. You have now in the Union, of those who acknowledge this system of labor within it, only eight of those states — supposing Texas out.

In the old Constitution, when almost all were slave states, you gave guarantees that fugitives from one state to another should be returned. Now there has got up what is unknown to the Constitution, an agitation against slaveholding which the Constitution recognizes, for which the Constitution did not disqualify or place any inequality upon the states holding it. There has been got up in our country questions arising out of that, beyond the limits of the Constitution, which rest above the Constitution, and which are worked up into platforms, and to which the obedience of all other sections is demanded. Now, my brother senators, is there anything like that in the Constitution, in fact or in truth? Did not the Constitution intend to leave us free on that question as regards ourselves? Did it not intend to leave the states choosing to adopt that system of labor just as free as it intended to leave them in regard to other questions? It seems so to me.

Sir, another reason for my confidence is that this cry of *vae victis,* or "no compromise," is not the sentiment of the American people. Although we have been unable to agree upon anything here, is it known to any senator, the oldest and the most experienced, either in his own experience or what happened in the country before his time, that there ever was such an expression of public opinion given within so short a time as has been given here in reference to these very propositions? What is the number of petitions forwarded? I suppose, if I should say we have received petitions from not less than a quarter of a million, I should be within bounds. In addition to that, societies everywhere have been petitioning in the name of their whole body. State legislatures have memorialized, and, in fact, petitioned Congress in the name of the people of their states. I do not know how many. The chief agents of the great railroad companies, owning railroads in value to the amount of more than $300 million, traversing the country from north to south in every direction, have petitioned in favor of the adoption of these propositions of peace, and they, gentlemen of the highest standing and the highest respectability, have declared that as far as all their travels extended along all these mighty railroads, they have found the people, with great unanimity, of the same opinion, and in favor of the adoption of these propositions.

Now, sir, I do not want confidence in legislators. I have been one of them too often and too long to endeavor to cast any discredit upon them, or the differences of opinion which exist among them. I do not intend to do any such thing; but I intend to say this: that my confidence in the intelligence and public virtue of the people is greater than it is in any body of their representatives. The people have given me assurances upon this subject by these petitions, that right will eventually be done; that they, the true sovereigns of the country, will take this subject into consideration; and that they will not allow them and their children, and their children's children, scattered about through all this land, to go to war with one another upon such a comparative trifle. . . .

Through this great nation common blood flows. What man is there here that is not of a blood, flowing — meandering — perhaps through every state in the Union? And we talk about not compromising a family quarrel; and that is to be held up as patriotism, or party fidelity. In the name of God, who is it that will adopt that policy? We are one people in blood; in language one; in thoughts one; we read the same books; we feed on the same meats; we go to the same schools; we belong to the same communion. If, as we go through this quarrelsome world, we meet with our little difficulties, if we wish to carry with us grateful hearts of the blessings we have enjoyed, we shall be bound to compromise with the difficulties that must occur on all the ways of the world that are trodden by governments on earth. It is our infirmity to have such difficulties. Let it be our magnanimity and our wisdom to compromise and settle them.

Do not believe, my fellow citizens of the North, my brother senators of the North, that I am urging this upon you as a bargain. I am only proposing the measure which I believe, and which my judgment suggests to me, as most for your benefit, and most for my benefit; most for the benefit of your states, of my state, and of the states of all of us. That is the spirit in which I propose it. I would not take the most paltry right from you to give it to the South. I would not detract a particle from your honor in order to give anything like a triumph to any section of the country. You are as much my countrymen as anybody. I claim the whole country as my country; and as yet the alienation is not such between us and even these seceding brethren that I could not travel through it and feel as if I was still in my own country. I feel an assurance that, by a right system of policy here, even they would return.

Now, I would have the South, I would have the border states, as they are commonly called — those that yet remain out of secession — to stand by you, trust to you, and trust to the people. A great many, if not a majority, of their Northern brethren have given them assurances of their sympathy for them, and that justice shall be done them. I believe it. They are assurances given by kindness, by patriotism, and will be redeemed; and that kindness, that sympathy which exists in the North will attract others. It is the standard of humanity and the standard of patriotism; and one after another they will crowd around it, until the states shall come and make peace offering to their brethren, instead of crying out "no compromise." I believe in this. I would have the border states believe in this. Our Northern fellow citizens have entitled themselves to this confidence by their action upon these very resolutions. Thousands, and tens and hundreds of thousands, have come here and petitioned for them; the states have petitioned for them. All this is an evidence of kindness that ought to bind the heart of the Southern states. At any rate, it ought to affect their judgment as to the future.

You will see by this that, even if nothing be done, I am not for secession. No, sir; I was born and bred in the state of Kentucky; and as to my native state, old Kentucky, I shall say to her more freely than to others: I desire to see you stand by the Union of the country; do not go off until an imperious necessity forces you; give to the world a long, continued evidence of your constancy, your patriotism, and your fidelity to the Constitution. Stand by it; you have stood there heretofore manfully; you have literally founded this faith upon a rock; this faith is founded upon a rock and you have engraven the sentiment there. The stone which you contributed to the unfinished monument of Washington in this city bore upon its Kentucky marble front these words: "Kentucky was the first to enter the Union after the adoption of the Constitution; she will be the last to leave it." That sentiment she has engraven in marble; and it now stands sanctified still more by forming a portion of the monument of George Washington. I want to see her true to that great sentiment. It swells the heart to hear it. There is nothing, as it seems to me, in all the hopes and all the triumphs that secession can promise itself equal to the proud swelling of the heart at these noble and patriotic sentiments. . . .

When rebellion and revolution shall have passed over this whole land, I want to see old Kentucky, even in that day of desolation, standing up, if left alone on the wasted field, brave and collected, with the flag of the Union in her hands, standing upon the great field like the last hero of a battle; and then, when the Union is no more, and she stands there, the image of patriotism, of honor, and of heroism and of fidelity to the Union to the last day of the Union, it will be time enough for her to consider what next shall be done.

My principle, and the doctrine I teach, is — take care of the Union; compromise it; do anything for it; it is the palladium — so General Washington called it — of your rights; take care of it, and it will take care of you. Yes, sir; let us take care of the Union, and it will certainly take care of us. That is the proposition which I teach.

49.

Abraham Lincoln: First Inaugural Address

Abraham Lincoln wrote the first draft of his First Inaugural Address in Springfield, in January 1861. According to William Herndon, his law partner and biographer, he used only a handful of sources, among them Henry Clay's famous speech of 1850, the U.S. Constitution, and Andrew Jackson's Proclamation against Nullification. Lincoln reworked the speech countless times, always with an eye toward expressing a more conciliatory position. In referring to Southern secession, he changed "treasonable" to "revolutionary." His first draft ended on a warlike note: "You can forbear the assault upon it [the government]; I cannot shrink from the defense of it. With you, and not with me, is the solemn question of 'Shall it be peace, or a sword?'" On Seward's advice, he substituted a sentimental appeal to his countrymen's pride in their common heritage. During the days preceding the inauguration the capital was rife with rumors of violence and assassination. Tension mounted as thousands of soldiers took their places in and around the Capitol. On March 4, ten thousand people heard the President, an unusually small gathering owing to the widespread fear of violence. The address evoked some applause but little enthusiasm. But in the week that followed, wrote Carl Sandburg in his biography of Lincoln, "[the address] was the most widely read and closely scrutinized utterance that had ever come from an American President." The political positions had indeed hardened. Many Southern editorials asserted that the address was an act of war, while Northern papers saw it as a peace offering.

Source: Richardson, VI, pp. 5-12.

In compliance with a custom as old as the government itself, I appear before you to address you briefly and to take, in your presence, the oath prescribed by the Constitution of the United States to be taken by the President "before he enters on the execution of his office."

I do not consider it necessary, at present, for me to discuss those matters of administration about which there is no special anxiety or excitement. Apprehension seems to exist among the people of the Southern states that, by the accession of a Republican administration, their property and their peace and personal security are to be endangered. There has never been any reasonable cause for such apprehension. Indeed, the most ample evidence to the contrary has all the while existed and been open to their inspection. It is found in nearly all the published speeches of him who now addresses you.

I do but quote from one of those speeches when I declare that "I have no purpose, directly or indirectly, to interfere with the institution of slavery in the states where it exists. I believe I have no lawful right to do so, and I have no inclination to do so." Those who nominated and elected me did so with full knowledge that I had made this and many similar declarations, and had never recanted them. And, more than this, they placed in the platform, for my acceptance, and as a law to themselves and to me, the clear and emphatic resolution which I now read:

Resolved, that the maintenance inviolate of the rights of the states, and especially the right of each state, to order and control its own domestic institutions according to its own judgment exclusively is essential to that balance of power on which the perfection and endurance of our political fabric depend; and we denounce the lawless invasion by armed force of the soil of any state or territory, no matter under what pretext, as among the gravest of crimes.

I now reiterate these sentiments; and, in doing so, I only press upon the public attention the most conclusive evidence, of which the case is susceptible, that the property, peace, and security of no section are to be in any way endangered by the now incoming administration. I add, too, that all the protection which, consistently with the Constitution and the laws, can be given will be cheerfully given to all the states when lawfully demanded, for whatever cause — as cheerfully to one section as to another.

There is much controversy about the delivering up of fugitives from service or labor. The clause I now read is as plainly written in the Constitution as any other of its provisions:

> No person held to service or labor in one state, under the laws thereof, escaping into another, shall, in consequence of any law or regulation therein, be discharged from such service or labor, but shall be delivered up on claim of the party to whom such service or labor may be due.

It is scarcely questioned that this provision was intended by those who made it for the reclaiming of what we call fugitive slaves; and the intention of the lawgiver is the law.

All members of Congress swear their support to the whole Constitution — to this provision as much as to any other. To the proposition, then, that slaves whose cases come within the terms of this clause "shall be delivered up," their oaths are unanimous. Now, if they would make the effort in good temper, could they not, with nearly equal unanimity, frame and pass a law by means of which to keep good that unanimous oath?

There is some difference of opinion whether this clause should be enforced by national or by the state authority; but surely that difference is not a very material one. If the slave is to be surrendered, it can be of but little consequence to him or to others by which authority it is done. And should anyone, in any case, be content that his oath shall go unkept on a merely unsubstantial controversy as to *how* it shall be kept?

Again, in any law upon this subject, ought not all the safeguards of liberty known in civilized and humane jurisprudence to be introduced, so that a freeman be not, in any case, surrendered as a slave? And might it not be well, at the same time, to provide by law for the enforcement of that clause in the Constitution which guarantees that "the citizen of each state shall be entitled to all privileges and immunities of citizens in the several states"?

I take the official oath today with no mental reservations and with no purpose to construe the Constitution or laws by any hypercritical rules. And while I do not choose now to specify particular acts of Congress as proper to be enforced, I do suggest that it will be much safer for all, both in official and private stations, to conform to and abide by all those acts which stand unrepealed than to violate any of them, trusting to find impunity in having them held to be unconstitutional.

It is seventy-two years since the first inauguration of a President under our national Constitution. During that period fifteen different and greatly distinguished citizens have, in succession, administered the executive branch of the government. They have conducted it through many perils, and generally with great success. Yet, with all this scope of precedent, I now enter upon the same task for the brief constitutional term of four years under great and peculiar difficulties.

A disruption of the federal Union, heretofore only menaced, is now formidably attempted.

I hold that, in contemplation of universal law and of the Constitution, the Union of these states is perpetual. Perpetuity is implied, if not expressed, in the fundamental law of all national governments. It is safe to assert that no government proper ever had a provision in its organic law for its own termination. Continue to execute all the express provisions of our national Constitution, and the Union will endure forever — it being impossible to destroy it except by some action not provided for in the instrument itself.

Again, if the United States be not a government proper, but an association of states in the nature of contract merely, can it, as a contract, be peaceably unmade by less than all the parties who made it? One party to a contract may violate it — break it, so to speak — but does it not require all to lawfully rescind it? Descending from these general principles, we find the proposition that in legal contemplation, the Union is perpetual, confirmed by the history of the Union itself.

The Union is much older than the Constitution. It was formed, in fact, by the Articles of Association in 1774. It was matured and continued by the Declaration of Independence in 1776. It was further matured, and the faith of all the then thirteen states expressedly plighted and engaged, that it should be perpetual by the Articles of Confederation of 1778. And finally, in 1787, one of the declared objects for ordaining and establishing the Constitution, was "to form a more perfect Union."

But if destruction of the Union by one or by a part only of the states be lawfully possible, the Union is less perfect than before the Constitution, having lost the vital element of perpetuity.

It follows from these views that no state, upon its own mere motion, can lawfully get out of the Union — that resolves and ordinances to that effect are legally void; and that acts of violence within any state or states against the authority of the United States are insurrectionary or revolutionary, according to circumstances.

I therefore consider that, in view of the Constitution and the laws, the Union is unbroken; and to the extent of my ability, I shall take care, as the Constitution itself expressly enjoins upon me, that the laws of the Union be faithfully executed in all the states. Doing this I deem to be only a simple duty on my part; and I shall perform it, so far as practicable, unless my rightful masters, the American people, shall withhold the requisite means or in some authoritative manner direct the contrary.

I trust this will not be regarded as a menace but only as the declared purpose of the Union that it will constitutionally defend and maintain itself. In doing this, there needs to be no bloodshed or violence; and there shall be none unless it be forced upon the national authority.

The power confided to me will be used to hold, occupy, and possess the property and places belonging to the government, and to collect the duties and imposts; but beyond what may be necessary for these objects, there will be no invasion — no using of force against or among the people anywhere.

Where hostility to the United States, in any interior locality, shall be so great and universal as to prevent competent resident citizens from holding the federal offices, there will be no attempt to force obnoxious strangers among the people for that object. While the strict legal right may exist in the government to enforce the exercise of these offices, the attempt to do so would be so irritating, and so nearly impracticable withal, that I deem it best to forego, for the time, the uses of such offices.

The mails, unless repelled, will continue to be furnished in all parts of the Union.

So far as possible, the people everywhere shall have that sense of perfect security which is most favorable to calm thought and reflection.

The course here indicated will be followed unless current events and experience shall show a modification or change to be proper; and in every case and exigency, my best discretion will be exercised, according to circumstances actually existing, and with a view and a hope of a peaceful solution of the national troubles, and the restoration of fraternal sympathies and affections.

That there are persons in one section or another who seek to destroy the Union at all events and are glad of any pretext to do it, I will neither affirm or deny; but if there be such, I need address no word to them. To those, however, who really love the Union, may I not speak?

Before entering upon so grave a matter as the destruction of our national fabric, with all its benefits, its memories, and its hopes, would it not be wise to ascertain precisely why we do it? Will you hazard so desperate a step while there is any possibility that any portion of the ills you fly from have no real existence? Will you, while the certain ills you fly to are greater than all the real ones you fly from — will you risk the commission of so fearful a mistake?

All profess to be content in the Union if all constitutional rights can be maintained. Is it true, then, that any right plainly written in the Constitution has been denied? I think not. Happily, the human mind is so constituted that no party can reach to the audacity of doing this. Think, if you can, of a single instance in which a plainly written provision of the Constitution has ever been denied. If, by the mere force of numbers, a majority should deprive a minority of any clearly written constitutional right, it might, in a moral point of view, justify revolution — certainly would, if such right were a vital one. But such is not our case.

All the vital rights of minorities and of individuals are so plainly assured to them by affirmations and negations, guarantees and prohibitions, in the Constitution that controversies never arise concerning them. But no organic law can ever be framed with a provision specifically applicable to every question which may occur in practical administration. No foresight can anticipate nor any document of reasonable length contain express provisions for all possible questions. Shall fugitives from labor be surrendered by national or by state authority? The Constitution does not expressly say. *May* Congress prohibit slavery in the territories? The Constitution does not expressly say. *Must* Congress protect slavery in the territories? The Constitution does not expressly say.

From questions of this class spring all our constitutional controversies, and we divide upon them into majorities and minorities. If the minority will not acquiesce, the majority must, or the government must cease. There is no other alternative; for continuing the government is acquiescence on one side or the other. If a minority, in such case, will secede rather than acquiesce, they make a precedent which in turn will divide and ruin them; for a minority of their own will secede from them whenever a majority refuses to be controlled by such minority.

For instance, why may not any portion of a new confederacy, a year or two hence, arbitrarily secede again, precisely as portions of the present Union now claim to secede from it? All who cherish disunion sentiments are now being educated to the exact temper of doing this. Is there such perfect identity of interests among the states to compose a new Union as to produce harmony only and prevent renewed secession?

Plainly, the central idea of secession is the essence of anarchy. A majority, held in restraint by constitutional checks and limitations, and always changing easily with deliberate changes of popular opinions and sentiments, is the only true sovereign of a free people. Whoever rejects it does of necessity fly to anarchy or to despotism. Unanimity is impossible. The rule of a minority, as a permanent arrangement, is wholly inadmissible; so that, rejecting the majority principle, anarchy or despotism in some form is all that is left.

I do not forget the position assumed by some, that constitutional questions are to be decided by the Supreme Court; nor do I deny that such decisions must be binding in any case upon the parties to a suit as to the object of that suit, while they are also entitled to very high respect and consideration, in all parallel cases, by all other departments of the government. And while it is obviously possible that such decision may be erroneous in any given case, still the evil effect following it, being limited to that particular case, with the chance that it may be overruled and never become a precedent for other cases, can better be borne than could the evils of a different practice.

At the same time, the candid citizen must confess that if the policy of the government, upon vital questions affecting the whole people, is to be irrevocably fixed by decisions of the Supreme Court, the instant they are made, in ordinary litigation between parties in personal actions, the people will have ceased to be their own rulers, having, to that extent, practically resigned their government into the hands of that eminent tribunal.

Nor is there, in this view, any assault upon the Court or the judges. It is a duty from which they may not shrink to decide cases properly brought before them; and it is no fault of theirs if others seek to turn their decisions to political purposes.

One section of our country believes slavery is *right* and ought to be extended, while the other believes it is *wrong* and ought not to be extended. This is the only substantial dispute. The fugitive slave clause of the Constitution and the law for the suppression of the foreign slave trade are each as well enforced, perhaps, as any law can ever be in a community where the moral sense of the people imperfectly supports the law itself. The great body of the people abide by the dry legal obligation in both cases,

and a few break over in each. This, I think, cannot be perfectly cured; and it would be worse in both cases *after* the separation of the sections than before. The foreign slave trade, now imperfectly suppressed, would be ultimately revived without restriction in one section; while fugitive slaves, now only partially surrendered, would not be surrendered at all by the other.

Physically speaking, we cannot separate. We cannot remove our respective sections from each other, nor build an impassable wall between them. A husband and wife may be divorced, and go out of the presence and beyond the reach of each other; but the different parts of our country cannot do this. They cannot but remain face to face; and intercourse, either amicable or hostile, must continue between them. Is it possible, then, to make that intercourse more advantageous or more satisfactory *after* separation than *before*? Can aliens make treaties easier than friends can make laws? Can treaties be more faithfully enforced between aliens than laws can among friends? Suppose you go to war, you cannot fight always; and when, after much loss on both sides and no gain on either, you cease fighting, the identical old questions as to terms of intercourse are again upon you.

This country, with its institutions, belongs to the people who inhabit it. Whenever they shall grow weary of the existing government, they can exercise their *constitutional* right of amending it or their *revolutionary* right to dismember or overthrow it. I cannot be ignorant of the fact that many worthy and patriotic citizens are desirous of having the national Constitution amended. While I make no recommendation of amendments, I fully recognize the rightful authority of the people over the whole subject, to be exercised in either of the modes prescribed in the instrument itself; and I should, under existing circumstances, favor rather than oppose a fair opportunity being afforded the people to act upon it.

I will venture to add that, to me, the

convention mode seems preferable, in that it allows amendments to originate with the people themselves, instead of only permitting them to take or reject propositions originated by others, not especially chosen for the purpose, and which might not be precisely such as they would wish to either accept or refuse. I understand a proposed amendment to the Constitution — which amendment, however, I have not seen — has passed Congress, to the effect that the federal government shall never interfere with the domestic institutions of the states, including that of persons held to service. To avoid misconstruction of what I have said, I depart from my purpose not to speak of particular amendments so far as to say that, holding such a provision to now be implied constitutional law, I have no objection to its being made express and irrevocable.

The chief magistrate derives all his authority from the people, and they have conferred none upon him to fix terms for the separation of the states. The people themselves can do this also if they choose; but the executive, as such, has nothing to do with it. His duty is to administer the present government, as it came to his hands, and to transmit it, unimpaired by him, to his successor. Why should there not be a patient confidence in the ultimate justice of the people? Is there any better or equal hope in the world? In our present differences, is either party without faith of being in the right?

If the Almighty Ruler of nations, with His eternal truth and justice, be on your side of the North, or on yours of the South, that truth and that justice will surely prevail, by the judgment of this great tribunal, the American people. By the frame of the government under which we live, this same people have wisely given their public servants but little power for mischief; and have, with equal wisdom, provided for the return of that little to their own hands at very short intervals. While the people retain

their virtue and vigilance, no administration, by any extreme of wickedness or folly, can very seriously injure the government in the short space of four years.

My countrymen, one and all, think calmly and *well* upon this whole subject. Nothing valuable can be lost by taking time. If there be an object to *hurry* any of you, in hot haste, to a step which you would never take *deliberately*, that object will be frustrated by taking time; but no good object can be frustrated by it.

Such of you as are now dissatisfied still have the old Constitution unimpaired, and, on the sensitive point, the laws of your own framing under it; while the new administration will have no immediate power, if it would, to change either.

If it were admitted that you who are dissatisfied hold the right side in the dispute, there still is no single good reason for precipitate action. Intelligence, patriotism, Christianity, and a firm reliance on Him, who has never yet forsaken this favored land, are still competent to adjust, in the best way, all our present difficulty.

In *your* hands, my dissatisfied fellow countrymen, and not in *mine* is the momentous issue of civil war. The government will not assail *you*. You can have no conflict without being yourselves the aggressors. *You* have no oath registered in heaven to destroy the government, while *I* shall have the most solemn one to "preserve, protect, and defend" it.

I am loathe to close. We are not enemies but friends. We must not be enemies. Though passion may have strained, it must not break our bonds of affection.

The mystic chords of memory, stretching from every battlefield and patriot grave to every living heart and hearthstone all over this broad land, will yet swell the chorus of the Union, when again touched, as surely they will be, by the better angels of our nature.

50.

A Plan to Avoid Civil War

William H. Seward joined the Republican Party in 1855 and had high hopes for the 1860 presidential nomination. Although the nomination of Lincoln was a blow to his ambitions, he campaigned ardently for the party and for its candidate. When Lincoln made him secretary of state, he probably envisaged himself as becoming the dominant figure in the administration, believing himself to be the man best able to avert war. Gideon Welles, Lincoln's secretary of the navy, once commented that "Seward liked to be called premier." On April 1, 1861, Seward saw an opportunity to exert his influence over Lincoln and sent a memorandum to the President offering his views on how to formulate policy. On the same day, Lincoln replied to Seward, emphasizing that the President alone was ultimately responsible for policy, though making sure not to alienate his secretary of state.

Source: Nicolay-Hay, VI, pp. 234-237.

I.

WILLIAM H. SEWARD: Suggestions to the President on Domestic and Foreign Policy

SOME THOUGHTS for the President's consideration, April 1, 1861:

First. We are at the end of a month's administration and yet without a policy, either domestic or foreign.

Second. This, however, is not culpable, and it has even been unavoidable. The presence of the Senate, with the need to meet applications for patronage, has prevented attention to other and more grave matters.

Third. But further delay to adopt and prosecute our policies for both domestic and foreign affairs would not only bring scandal on the administration but danger upon the country.

Fourth. To do this we must dismiss the applicants for office. But how? I suggest that we make the local appointments forthwith, leaving foreign or general ones for ulterior and occasional action.

Fifth. The policy at home. I am aware that my views are singular and perhaps not sufficiently explained. My system is built upon this idea as a ruling one, namely, that we must CHANGE THE QUESTION BEFORE THE PUBLIC FROM ONE UPON SLAVERY, OR ABOUT SLAVERY, for a question upon UNION OR DISUNION. In other words, from what would be regarded as a party question to one of patriotism or union.

The occupation or evacuation of Fort Sumter, although not in fact a slavery or a party question, is so regarded. Witness the temper manifested by the Republicans in the free states, and even by the Union men in the South.

I would therefore terminate it as a safe means for changing the issue. I deem it fortunate that the last administration created the necessity.

For the rest, I would simultaneously defend and reinforce all the ports in the Gulf and have the Navy recalled from foreign stations to be prepared for a blockade. Put the island of Key West under martial law.

This will raise distinctly the question of union or disunion. I would maintain every fort and possession in the South.

For foreign nations, I would demand explanations from Spain and France, categorically, at once. I would seek explanations from Great Britain and Russia, and send agents into Canada, Mexico, and Central America to rouse a vigorous continental spirit of independence on this continent against European intervention. And, if satisfactory explanations are not received from Spain and France, would convene Congress and declare war against them.

But whatever policy we adopt, there must be an energetic prosecution of it.

For this purpose it must be somebody's business to pursue and direct it incessantly. Either the President must do it himself, and be all the while active in it, or devolve it on some member of his Cabinet. Once adopted, debates on it must end, and all agree and abide.

It is not in my especial province; but I neither seek to evade nor assume responsibility.

II.

Abraham Lincoln: Reply to Seward

Since parting with you, I have been considering your paper dated this day, and entitled "Some Thoughts for the President's Consideration." The first proposition in it is: "*First.* We are at the end of a month's administration and yet without a policy, either domestic or foreign."

At the beginning of that month, in the inaugural, I said: "The power confided to me will be used to hold, occupy, and possess the property and places belonging to the government, and to collect the duties and imposts." This had your distinct approval at the time; and, taken in connection with the order I immediately gave General Scott directing him to employ every means in his power to strengthen and hold the forts, comprises the exact domestic policy you now urge, with the single exception that it does not propose to abandon Fort Sumter.

Again, I do not perceive how the reinforcement of Fort Sumter would be done on a slavery or a party issue, while that of Fort Pickens would be on a more national and patriotic one.

The news received yesterday in regard to Santo Domingo certainly brings a new item within the range of our foreign policy; but up to that time we have been preparing circulars and instructions to ministers and the like, all in perfect harmony, without even a suggestion that we had no foreign policy.

Upon your closing propositions — that "whatever policy we adopt, there must be an energetic prosecution of it. For this purpose it must be somebody's business to pursue and direct it incessantly. Either the President must do it himself, and be all the while active in it, or devolve it on some member of his Cabinet. Once adopted, debates on it must end, and all agree and abide" — I remark that if this must be done, I must do it. When a general line of policy is adopted, I apprehend there is no danger of its being changed without good reason, or continuing to be a subject of unnecessary debate; still, upon points arising in its progress, I wish, and suppose I am entitled to have, the advice of all the Cabinet.

51.

ROBERT E. LEE: Resignation from the United States Army

Robert E. Lee was a colonel in the U.S. Army when Confederate soldiers fired on Fort Sumter. Lee was devoted to the Union and could not rationally justify secession. But stronger than his commitments to the Union were the emotional ties to his home state, born out of his family's deep roots in Virginia. On April 18, 1861, he was offered the field command of the U.S. Army but declined the offer. General Winfield Scott, a close friend, advised him either to resign his commission or to accept the assignment. The following day the Virginia convention voted to secede. Lee was torn between his conscience, which would not allow him to bear arms against his homeland, and his devotion to the Union. Even on April 20, when he resigned from the U.S. Army, Lee had hoped he would not have to participate in a war he detested. That day he wrote the following letters to General Scott and to his sister, Mrs. Anne Marshall. Three days later Virginia named him commander of its army.

Source: *Personal Reminiscences, Anecdotes, and Letters of Gen. Robert E. Lee,* J. William Jones, ed., New York, 1875, pp. 138-140.

Letter to General Winfield Scott

General:

Since my interview with you on the 18th instant, I have felt that I ought no longer to retain my commission in the Army. I, therefore, tender my resignation, which I request you will recommend for acceptance. It would have been presented at once but for the struggle it has cost me to separate myself from a service to which I have devoted the best years of my life and all the ability I possessed.

During the whole of that time — more than a quarter of a century — I have experienced nothing but kindness from my superiors and the most cordial friendship from my comrades. To no one, General, have I been as much indebted as to yourself for uniform kindness and consideration; and it has always been my ardent desire to meet your approbation. I shall carry to the grave the most grateful recollections of your kind consideration, and your name and fame will always be dear to me.

Save in defense of my native state, I never desire again to draw my sword.

Be pleased to accept my most earnest wishes for the continuance of your happiness and prosperity.

Letter to Anne Marshall

My Dear Sister:

I am grieved at my inability to see you. . . . I have been waiting for a "more convenient season," which has brought to many before me deep and lasting regret.

Now we are in a state of war, which will yield to nothing. The whole South is in a state of revolution, into which Virginia, after a long struggle, has been drawn; and though I recognize no necessity for this state of things, and would have forborne and pleaded to the end for redress of grievances, real or supposed, yet in my own person I had to meet the question whether I should take part against my native state.

With all my devotion to the Union and the feeling of loyalty and duty of an American citizen, I have not been able to make up my mind to raise my hand against my relatives, my children, my home. I have, therefore, resigned my commission in the Army, and, save in defense of my native state, with the sincere hope that my poor services may never be needed, I hope I may never be called on to draw my sword. I know you will blame me; but you must think as kindly of me as you can, and believe that I have endeavored to do what I thought right.

To show you the feeling and struggle it has cost me, I send you a copy of my letter of resignation. I have no time for more. . . .

May God guard and protect you and yours, and shower upon you everlasting blessings.

52.

Jefferson Davis: War Message

Jefferson Davis was elected president of the Confederate States of America on February 9, 1861. When Fort Sumter fell to Confederate batteries in the harbor of Charleston, South Carolina, on April 14, 1861, President Lincoln responded with a call for 75,000 volunteers to put down the "insurrection." Davis, regarding this as an act of war, summoned the Confederate Congress into special session, and presented his plans for common defense. The Congress responded by granting Davis sweeping powers. His message, delivered on April 29, is regarded by most historians as his ablest state paper.

Source: Moore, I, Document 117.

IT IS MY PLEASING DUTY to announce to you that the constitution framed for the establishment of a permanent government of the Confederate States of America has been ratified by the several conventions of each of those states which were referred to to inaugurate the said government in its full proportions and upon its own substantial basis of the popular will. It only remains that elections should be held for the designation of the officers to administer it.

There is every reason to believe that at no distant day other states, identical in political principles and community of interests with those which you represent, will join this Confederacy, giving to its typical constellation increased splendor; to its government of free, equal, and sovereign states a wider sphere of usefulness; and to the friends of constitutional liberty a greater security for its harmonious and perpetual existence.

It was not, however, for the purpose of making this announcement that I have deemed it my duty to convoke you at an earler day than that fixed by yourselves for your meeting.

The declaration of war made against this Confederacy by Abraham Lincoln, President of the United States, in his proclamation issued on the 15th day of the present month, renders it necessary, in my judgment, that you should convene at the earliest practicable moment to devise the measures necessary for the defense of the country.

The occasion is, indeed, an extraordinary one. It justifies me in giving a brief review of the relations heretofore existing between us and the states which now unite in warfare against us, and a succinct statement of the events which have resulted, to the end that mankind may pass intelligent and impartial judgment on our motives and objects.

During the war waged against Great Britain by her colonies on this continent, a common danger impelled them to a close alliance and to the formation of a Confederation by the terms of which the colonies, styling themselves states, entered severally into a firm league of friendship with each other for their common defense, the security of their liberties, and their mutual and general welfare, binding themselves to assist each other against all force offered to, or attacks made upon them, or any of them, on account of religion, sovereignty, trade, or any other pretense whatever.

In order to guard against any misconstruction of their compact, the several states made an explicit declaration in a distinct article — that each state retain its sovereignty, freedom, and independence, and every power of jurisdiction and right which is not by this said Confederation expressly delegated to the United States in Congress assembled under this contract of alliance.

The war of the Revolution was successfully waged, and resulted in the treaty of peace with Great Britain in 1783, by the terms of which the several states were each by name recognized to be independent.

The Articles of Confederation contained a clause whereby all alterations were prohibited, unless confirmed by the legislatures of every state after being agreed to by the Congress; and, in obedience to this provision, under the resolution of Congress of the 21st of February, 1787, the several states appointed delegates for the purpose of revising the Articles of Confederation, and reporting to Congress and the several legislatures such alterations and provisions therein as shall, when agreed to in Congress and confirmed by the states, render the Federal Constitution adequate to the exigencies of the government and the preservation of the Union.

It was by the delegates chosen by the several states under the resolution just quoted that the Constitution of the United States was formed in 1787 and submitted to the several states for ratification, as shown by the 7th Article, which is in these words: "The ratification of the conventions of nine states shall be sufficient for the establishment of this Constitution between the states so ratifying the same."

I have [emphasized] certain words in the resolutions just made for the purpose of attracting attention to the singular and marked caution with which the states endeavored in every possible form to exclude the idea that the separate and independent sovereignty of each state was merged into one common government or nation; and the earnest desire they evinced to impress on the Constitution its true character — that of a compact between independent states — the Constitution of 1787, however, omitting the clause already recited from the Articles of Confederation which provided in explicit terms that each state retained its sovereignty and independence.

Some alarm was felt in the states when invited to ratify the Constitution lest this omission should be construed into an abandonment of their cherished principles, and they refused to be satisfied until amendments were added to the Constitution, placing beyond any pretense of doubt the reservation by the states of their sovereign rights and powers not expressly delegated to the United States by the Constitution.

Strange, indeed, must it appear to the impartial observer that it is nonetheless true that all these carefully worded clauses proved unavailing to prevent the rise and growth in the Northern states of a political school which has persistently claimed that the government set above and over the states an organization created by the states to secure the blessings of liberty and independence against foreign aggression has been gradually perverted into a machine for their control in their domestic affairs.

The creature has been exalted above its creator — the principles have been made subordinate to the agent appointed by themselves.

The people of the Southern states, whose almost exclusive occupation was agriculture, early perceived a tendency in the Northern states to render a common government subservient to their own purposes by imposing burdens on commerce as protection to their manufacturing and shipping interests.

Long and angry controversies grew out of these attempts, often successful, to benefit one section of the country at the expense of the other, and the danger of disruption arising from this cause was enhanced by the fact that the Northern population was increasing by emigration and other causes more than the population of the South.

By degrees, as the Northern states gained preponderance in the national Congress, self-interest taught their people to yield ready assent to any plausible advocacy of their right as majority to govern the minority. Without control, they learn to listen with impatience to the suggestion of any constitutional impediment to the exercise of their will, and so utterly have the principles of the Constitution been corrupted in the Northern mind that, in the Inaugural Address delivered by President Lincoln in March last, he asserts a maxim which he plainly deems to be undeniable — that the theory of the Constitution requires, in all cases, that the majority shall govern. And, in another memorable instance, the same chief magistrate did not hesitate to liken the relations between states and the United States to those which exist between the county and the state in which it is situated and by which it was created.

This is the lamentable and fundamental error in which rests the policy that has culminated in his declaration of war against these Confederate States.

In addition to the long-continued and deep-seated resentment felt by the Southern states at the persistent abuse of the powers they had delegated to the Congress for the purpose of enriching the manufacturing and shipping classes of the North at the expense of the South, there has existed for nearly half a century another subject of discord, involving interests of such transcendent magnitude as at all times to create the apprehension in the minds of many devoted lovers of the Union that its permanence was impossible.

When the several states delegated certain powers to the United States Congress, a large portion of the laboring population were imported into the colonies by the mother country. In twelve out of the thirteen states, Negro slavery existed, and the right of property existing in slaves was protected by law; this property was recognized in the Constitution, and provision was made against its loss by the escape of the slave.

The increase in the number of slaves by foreign importation from Africa was also secured by a clause forbidding Congress to prohibit the slave trade anterior to a certain date, and in no clause can there be found any delegation of power to the Congress to authorize it in any manner to legislate to the prejudice, detriment, or discouragement of the owners of that species of property, or excluding it from the protection of the government.

The climate and soil of the Northern states soon proved unpropitious to the continuance of slave labor, while the reverse being the case in the South, made unrestricted free intercourse between the two sections unfriendly.

The Northern states consulted their own interests by selling their slaves to the South and prohibiting slavery between their limits. The South were willing purchasers of property suitable to their wants, and paid the price of the acquisition without harboring a suspicion that their quiet possession was to be disturbed by those who were not only in want of constitutional authority but, by good faith as vendors, from disquieting a title emanating from themselves.

As soon, however, as the Northern states that prohibited African slavery within their limits had reached a number sufficient to give their representation a controlling vote in the Congress, a persistent and organized system of hostile measures against the rights of the owners of slaves in the Southern states was inaugurated and gradually extended. A series of measures was devised and prosecuted for the purpose of rendering insecure the tenure of property in slaves.

Fanatical organizations, supplied with money by voluntary subscriptions, were assiduously engaged in exciting among the slaves a spirit of discontent and revolt. Means were furnished for their escape from their owners and agents secretly employed to entice them to abscond.

The constitutional provision for their rendition to their owners was first evaded, then openly denounced as a violation of conscientious obligation and religious duty. Men were taught that it was a merit to elude, disobey, and violently oppose the execution of the laws enacted to secure the performance of the promise contained in the constitutional compact. Often, owners of slaves were mobbed and even murdered in open day solely for applying to a magistrate for the arrest of a fugitive slave.

The dogmas of the voluntary organization soon obtained control of the legislatures of many of the Northern states, and laws were passed for the punishment, by ruinous fines and long-continued imprisonment in [jails] and penitentiaries, of citizens of the Southern states who should dare ask of the officers of the law for the recovery of their property. Emboldened by success, on the theater of agitation and aggression, against the clearly expressed constitutional rights of the Congress, senators and representatives were sent to the common councils of the nation, whose chief title to this distinction consisted in the display of a spirit of ultra-fanaticism, and whose business was not to promote the general welfare or ensure domestic tranquillity but to awaken the bitterest hatred against the citizens of sister states by violent denunciations of their institutions.

The transactions of public affairs was impeded by the repeated efforts to usurp powers not delegated by the Constitution, for the purpose of impairing the security of property in slaves, and reducing those states which held slaves to a condition of inferiority.

Finally, a great party was organized for the purpose of obtaining the administration of the government, with the avowed object of using its power for the total exclusion of the slave states from all participation in the benefits of the public domain acquired by all the states in common, whether by conquest or purchase, surrounded them entirely by states in which slavery should be prohibited, thus rendering the property in slaves so insecure as to be comparatively worthless, and thereby annihilating in effect property worth thousands of millions of dollars. This party, thus organized, succeeded in the month of November last in the election of its candidate for the presidency of the United States.

In the meantime, under the mild and genial climate of the Southern states, and the increasing care for the well-being and comfort of the laboring classes, dictated alike by interest and humanity, the African slaves had augmented in number from about 600,000, at the date of the adoption of the constitutional compact, to upward of 4 million.

In a moral and social condition, they had been elevated from brutal savages into docile, intelligent, and civilized agricultural laborers, and supplied not only with bodily comforts but with careful religious instruction, under the supervision of a superior race. Their labor had been so directed as not only to allow a gradual and marked amelioration of their own condition but to convert hundreds of thousands of square miles of the wilderness into cultivated lands covered with a prosperous people. Towns and cities had sprung into existence, and it rapidly increased in wealth and population under the social system of the South.

The white population of the Southern slaveholding states had augmented from about 1,250,000, at the date of the adoption of the Constitution, to more than 8,500,000 in 1860, and the productions of the South in cotton, rice, sugar, and tobacco, for the full development and continuance of which the labor of African slaves was and is indispensable, had swollen to an amount which formed nearly three-fourths of the export of the whole United States, and had become absolutely necessary to the wants of civilized man.

With interests of such overwhelming magnitude imperiled, the people of the Southern states were driven by the conduct of the North to the adoption of some course of action to avoid the dangers with which they were openly menaced. With this view, the legislatures of the several states invited the people to select delegates to conventions to be held for the purpose of determining for themselves what measures were best to be adopted to meet so alarming a crisis in their history.

Here it may be proper to observe that, from a period as early as 1798, there had existed in all of the states of the Union a party almost uninterruptedly in the majority based upon the creed that each state was, in the last resort, the sole judge as well of its wrongs as of the mode and measures of redress. Indeed, it is obvious that under the law of nations this principle is an axiom as applied to the relations of independent sovereign states, such as those which had united themselves under the constitutional compact.

The Democratic Party of the United States repeated, in its successful canvass in 1836, the deduction made in numerous previous political contests that it would faithfully abide by and uphold the principles laid down in the Kentucky and Virginia legislatures of 1799, and that it adopts those principles as constituting one of the main foundations of its political creed.

The principles thus emphatically announced embrace that to which I have already adverted — the right of each state to judge of and redress the wrongs of which it complains. Their principles were maintained by overwhelming majorities of the people of all the states of the Union at different elections, especially in the election of Mr. Jefferson in 1805, Mr. Madison in 1809, and Mr. Pierce in 1852. In the exercise of a right so ancient, so well established and so necessary for self-preservation, the people of the Confederate States, in their conventions, determined that the wrongs which they had suffered and the evils with which they were menaced required that they should revoke the delegation of powers to the Federal government which they had ratified in their several conventions.

They consequently passed ordinances resuming all their rights as sovereign and independent states, and dissolved their connection with the other states of the Union. Having done this, they proceeded to form a new compact among themselves by new Articles of Confederation, which have been also ratified by conventions of the several states, with an approach to unanimity far exceeding that of the conventions which adopted the constitution of 1787. They have organized their new government in all its departments. The functions of the executive, legislative, and judicial magistrates are performed in accordance with the will of the people as displayed not merely in a cheerful acquiescence but in the enthusiastic support of the government thus established by themselves; and but for the interference of the government of the United States, this legitimate exercise of a people to self-government has been manifested in every possible form.

Scarce had you assembled in February last, when, prior even to the inauguration of the chief magistrate you had elected, you expressed your desire for the appointment of commissioners, and for the settlement of all questions of disagreement between the two governments upon principles of right, justice, equity, and good faith.

It was my pleasure as well as my duty to cooperate with you in this work of peace. Indeed, in my address to you on taking the oath of office, and before receiving from you the communication of this resolution, I had said that "as a necessity, not as a choice, we have resorted to the remedy of separating, and henceforth our energies must be directed to the conduct of our own affairs and the perpetuity of the Confederacy which we have formed. If a just perception of mutual interest shall permit us to peaceably pursue our separate political career, my most earnest desire will then have been fulfilled."

It was in furtherance of these accordant views of the Congress and the executive that I made choice of three discreet, able, and distinguished citizens who repaired to Washington. Aided by their cordial cooperation and that of the secretary of state, every effort compatible with self-respect and the dignity of the Confederacy was exhausted before I allowed myself to yield to the conviction that the government of the United States was determined to attempt the conquest of this people, and that our cherished hopes of peace were unobtainable.

On the arrival of our commissioners in Washington on the 5th of March, they postponed, at the suggestion of a friendly intermediator, doing more than giving informal notice of their arrival. This was done with a view to afford time to the President of the United States, who had just been inaugurated, for the discharge of other pressing official duties in the organization of his administration before engaging his attention in the object of their mission.

It was not until the 12th of the month that they officially addressed the secretary of state, informing him of the purpose of their arrival, and stating in the language of their instructions their wish to make to the government of the United States overtures for the opening of negotiations, assuring the government of the United States that the president, congress, and people of the Confederate States desired a peaceful solution of these great questions; that it was neither their interest nor their wish to make any demand which is not founded on the strictest principles of justice, nor to do any act to injure their late confederates.

To this communication no formal reply was received until the 8th of April. During the interval, the commissioners had consented to waive all questions of form, with the firm resolve to avoid war if possible. They went so far even as to hold, during that long period, unofficial intercourse through an intermediary, whose high position and character inspired the hope of success, and through whom constant assurances were received from the government of the United States of its peaceful intentions — of its determination to evacuate Fort Sumter; and, further, that no measures would be introduced changing the existing status prejudicial to the Confederate States; that in the event of any change in regard to Fort Pickens, notice would be given to the commissioners.

The crooked path of diplomacy can scarcely furnish an example so wanting in courtesy, in candor and directness as was the course of the United States government toward our commissioners in Washington. . . .

Early in April the attention of the whole country was attracted to extraordinary preparations for an extensive military and naval expedition in New York and other Northern ports. These preparations commenced in secrecy, for an expedition whose destination was concealed, and only became known when nearly completed, and on the 5th, 6th, and 7th of April, transports and vessels of war with troops, munitions, and military supplies, sailed from Northern ports, bound southward.

Alarmed by so extraordinary a demonstration, the commissioners requested the delivery of an answer to their official communication of the 12th of March, and the reply dated on the 15th of the previous month, from which it appears that during the whole interval, while the commissioners were receiving assurances calculated to inspire hope of the success of their mission, the secretary of state and the President of the United States had already determined to hold no intercourse with them whatever — to refuse even to listen to any proposals

they had to make — and had profited by the delay created by their own assurances in order to prepare secretly the means for effective hostile operations.

That these assurances were given has been virtually confessed by the government of the United States by its act of sending a messenger to Charleston to give notice of its purpose to use force if opposed in its intention of supplying Fort Sumter. No more striking proof of the absence of good faith in the confidence of the government of the United States toward the Confederacy can be required than is contained in the circumstances which accompanied this notice.

According to the usual course of navigation, the vessels composing the expedition, and designed for the relief of Fort Sumter, might be looked for in Charleston Harbor on the 9th of April. Yet our commissioners in Washington were detained under assurances that notice should be given of any military movement. The notice was not addressed to them, but a messenger was sent to Charleston to give notice to the governor of South Carolina, and the notice was so given at a late hour on the 8th of April, the eve of the very day on which the fleet might be expected to arrive.

That this maneuver failed in its purpose was not the fault of those who controlled it. A heavy tempest delayed the arrival of the expedition and gave time to the commander of our forces at Charleston to ask and receive instructions of the government. Even then, under all the provocation incident to the contemptuous refusal to listen to our commissioners, and the treacherous course of the government of the United States, I was sincerely anxious to avoid the effusion of blood, and directed a proposal to be made to the commander of Fort Sumter, who had avowed himself to be nearly out of provisions, that we would abstain from directing our fire on Fort Sumter if he would promise to not open fire on our forces unless first attacked. This proposal was refused. The conclusion was that the design of the United States was to place the besieging force at Charleston between the simultaneous fire of the fleet. The fort should, of course, be at once reduced. This order was executed by General Beauregard with skill and success, which were naturally to be expected from the well-known character of that gallant officer; and, although the bombardment lasted some thirty-three hours, our flag did not wave over the battered walls until after the appearance of the hostile fleet off Charleston.

Fortunately, not a life was lost on our side, and we were gratified in being prepared. The necessity of a useless effusion of blood by the prudent caution of the officers who commanded the fleet, in abstaining from the evidently futile effort to enter the harbor for the relief of Major Anderson, was spared.

I refer to the report of the secretary of war, and the papers accompanying it, for further particulars of this brilliant affair.

In this connection I cannot refrain from a well-deserved tribute to the noble state, the eminently soldierly qualities of whose people were conspicuously displayed. The people of Charleston for months had been irritated by the spectacle of a fortress held within their principal harbor as a standing menace against their peace and independence — built in part with their own money — its custody confided with their long consent to an agent who held no power over them other than such as they had themselves delegated for their own benefit, intended to be used by that agent for their own protection against foreign attack. How it was held out with persistent tenacity as a means of offense against them by the very government which they had established for their own protection is well known. They had beleaguered it for months, and felt entire confidence in their power to capture it, yet yielded to the requirements of discipline, curbed their impatience, submitted without complaint to the unaccustomed hardships, labors, and privations of a protracted siege; and when at length their patience was relieved by the signal for attack, and success had crowned their steady and gallant conduct, even in the very moment of triumph they evinced a chivalrous regard for the feelings of the brave but unfortunate officer who had been compelled to lower his flag.

All manifestations or exultations were checked in his presence. Their commanding general, with their cordial approval and consent of his government, refrained from imposing any terms that would wound the sensibility of the commander of the fort. He was permitted to retire with the honors of war, to salute his flag, to depart freely with all his command, and was escorted to the vessel on which he embarked with the highest marks of respect from those against whom his guns had so recently been directed.

Not only does every event connected with the siege reflect the highest honor on South Carolina, but the forbearance of her people and of this government from making any harangue of a victory obtained under circumstances of such peculiar provocation attest, to the fullest extent, the absence of any purpose beyond securing their own tranquillity and the sincere desire to avoid the calamities of war.

Scarcely had the President of the United States received intelligence of the failure of the scheme which he had devised for the reinforcement of Fort Sumter when he issued the declaration of war against this Confederacy, which has prompted me to convoke you. In this extraordinary production that high functionary affects total ignorance of the existence of an independent government, which, possessing the entire and enthusiastic devotion of its people, is exercising its functions without question over seven sovereign states, over more than

5 million people, and over a territory whose area exceeds 500,000 square miles.

He terms sovereign states "combinations too powerful to be suppressed in the ordinary course of judicial proceedings, or by the powers vested in the marshals by law."

He calls for an army of 75,000 men to act as the *posse comitatus* [body of men summoned to assist in preserving the public peace] in aid of the process of the courts of justice in states where no courts exist, whose mandates and decrees are not cheerfully obeyed and respected by a willing people.

He avows that the first service to be assigned to the forces which have been called out will not be to execute the processes of courts but to capture forts and strongholds situated within the admitted limits of this Confederacy and garrisoned by its troops, and declares that this effort is intended to maintain the perpetuity of popular government.

He concludes by commanding the persons composing the "combinations" aforesaid, to wit, the 5 million inhabitants of these states, to retire peaceably to their respective abodes within twenty days.

Apparently contradictory as are the terms of this singular document, one point was unmistakably evident. The President of the United States calls for an army of 75,000 men, whose first service was to be to capture our forts. It was a plain declaration of war which I was not at liberty to disregard because of my knowledge that under the Constitution of the United States the President was usurping a power granted exclusively to the Congress.

He is the sole organ of communication between that country and foreign powers. The law of nations did not permit me to question the authority of the executive of a foreign nation to declare war against this Confederacy. Although I might have refrained from taking active measures for our defense, if the states of the Union had all

imitated the action of Virginia, North Carolina, Arkansas, Kentucky, Tennessee, and Missouri by denouncing it as an unconstitutional usurpation of power to which they refuse to respond, I was not at liberty to disregard the fact that many of the states seemed quite content to submit to the exercise of the powers assumed by the President of the United States, and were actively engaged in levying troops for the purpose indicated in the proclamation. Deprived of the aid of Congress, at the moment I was under the necessity of confining my action to a call on the states for volunteers for the common defense, in accordance with the authority you had confided to me before your adjournment.

I deemed it proper, further, to issue a proclamation inviting applications from persons disposed to aid in our defense in private armed vessels on the high seas, to the end that preparations might be made for the immediate issue of letters of marque and reprisal, which you alone, under the Constitution, have the power to grant.

I entertain no doubt that you will concur with me in the opinion that in the absence of an organized navy, it will be eminently expedient to supply their place with private armed vessels, so happily styled by the publicists of the United States the militia of the sea, and so often and justly relied on by them as an efficient and admirable instrument of defensive warfare.

I earnestly recommend the immediate passage of a law authorizing me to accept the numerous proposals already received.

I cannot close this review of the acts of the government of the United States without referring to a proclamation issued by their President under date of the 19th inst., in which, after declaring that an insurrection has broken out in this Confederacy against the government of the United States, he announces a blockade of all the ports of these states, and threatens to punish as pirates all persons who shall molest any vessel of the United States under letters of marque issued by this government. Notwithstanding the authenticity of this proclamation, you will concur with me that it is hard to believe that it could have emanated from a President of the United States.

Its announcement of a mere paper blockade is so manifestly a violation of the law of nations that it would seem incredible that it could have been issued by authority; but conceding this to be the case, so far as the executive is concerned, it will be difficult to satisfy the people of these states that their late confederates will sanction its declarations; will determine to ignore the usages of civilized nations; and will inaugurate a war of extermination on both sides by treating as pirates open enemies acting under the authority of commissions issued by an organized government.

If such proclamation was issued, it could only have been published under the sudden influence of passion, and we may rest assured that mankind will be spared the horrors of the conflict it seems to invite.

53.

ABRAHAM LINCOLN: A War to Preserve the Union

After the surrender of Fort Sumter on April 14, 1861, Lincoln immediately issued a proclamation calling for 75,000 soldiers to suppress the insurrection. At the same time he called for a special session of Congress to convene on the Fourth of July. When the session convened, Lincoln explained the case against the South, outlined the measures he had taken against the rebellion, and defined the purpose of the war. At this early stage, even Lincoln did not foresee the bloody and protracted struggle that lay ahead. Lincoln's message is reprinted below.

Source: Richardson, VI, pp. 20-31.

Fellow Citizens of the Senate and House of Representatives:

Having been convened on an extraordinary occasion, as authorized by the Constitution, your attention is not called to any ordinary subject of legislation.

At the beginning of the present presidential term, four months ago, the functions of the Federal government were found to be generally suspended within the several states of South Carolina, Georgia, Alabama, Mississippi, Louisiana, and Florida, excepting only those of the Post Office Department.

Within these states all the forts, arsenals, dockyards, customhouses, and the like, including the movable and stationary property in and about them, had been seized and were held in open hostility to this government, excepting only Forts Pickens, Taylor, and Jefferson, on and near the Florida coast, and Fort Sumter, in Charleston Harbor, South Carolina. The forts thus seized had been put in improved condition, new ones had been built, and armed forces had been organized and were organizing, all avowedly with the same hostile purpose.

The forts remaining in the possession of the Federal government in and near those states were either besieged or menaced by warlike preparations, and especially Fort Sumter was nearly surrounded by well-protected hostile batteries, with guns equal in quality to the best of its own and out-numbering the latter as perhaps ten to one. A disproportionate share of the Federal muskets and rifles had somehow found their way into these states, and had been seized to be used against the government. Accumulations of the public revenue lying within them had been seized for the same object. The Navy was scattered in distant seas, leaving but a very small part of it within the immediate reach of the government. Officers of the Federal Army and Navy had resigned in great numbers, and, of those resigning, a large proportion had taken up arms against the government. Simultaneously and in connection with all this the purpose to sever the Federal Union was openly avowed. In accordance with this purpose, an ordinance had been adopted in each of these states declaring the states respectively to be separated from the national Union. A formula for instituting a combined government of these states had been promulgated, and this illegal organization, in the character of Confederate States, was already invoking recognition, aid, and intervention from foreign powers.

Finding this condition of things and believing it to be an imperative duty upon the incoming executive to prevent, if possible, the consummation of such attempt to destroy the Federal Union, a choice of means to that end became indispensable. This choice was made and was declared in the inaugural address. The policy chosen looked to the exhaustion of all peaceful measures before a resort to any stronger ones. It sought only to hold the public places and property not already wrested from the government and to collect the revenue, relying for the rest on time, discussion, and the ballot box. It promised a continuance of the mails at government expense to the very people who were resisting the government, and it gave repeated pledges against any disturbance to any of the people or any of their rights. Of all that which a President might constitutionally and justifiably do in

such a case, everything was forborne without which it was believed possible to keep the government on foot.

On the 5th of March, the present incumbent's first full day in office, a letter of Major Anderson, commanding at Fort Sumter, written on the 28th of February and received at the War Department on the 4th of March, was by that department placed in his hands. This letter expressed the professional opinion of the writer that reenforcements could not be thrown into that fort within the time for his relief rendered necessary by the limited supply of provisions, and with a view of holding possession of the same, with a force of less than 20,000 good and well-disciplined men. This opinion was concurred in by all the officers of his command, and their memoranda on the subject were made enclosures of Major Anderson's letter.

The whole was immediately laid before Lieutenant General Scott, who at once concurred with Major Anderson in opinion. On reflection, however, he took full time, consulting with other officers, both of the Army and the Navy, and at the end of four days came reluctantly, but decidedly, to the same conclusion as before. He also stated at the same time that no such sufficient force was then at the control of the government or could be raised and brought to the ground within the time when the provisions in the fort would be exhausted. In a purely military point of view this reduced the duty of the administration in the case to the mere matter of getting the garrison safely out of the fort.

It was believed, however, that to so abandon that position under the circumstances would be utterly ruinous; that the necessity under which it was to be done would not be fully understood; that by many it would be construed as a part of a *voluntary* policy; that at home it would discourage the friends of the Union, embolden its adversaries, and go far to insure to the latter a recognition abroad; that, in fact, it would be our national destruction consummated. This could not be allowed. Starvation was not yet upon the garrison, and ere it would be reached, Fort Pickens might be reenforced. This last would be a clear indication of *policy*, and would better enable the country to accept the evacuation of Fort Sumter as a military *necessity*.

An order was at once directed to be sent for the landing of the troops from the steamship *Brooklyn* into Fort Pickens. This order could not go by land but must take the longer and slower route by sea. The first return news from the order was received just one week before the fall of Fort Sumter. The news itself was that the officer commanding the *Sabine*, to which vessel the troops had been transferred from the *Brooklyn*, acting upon some quasi-armistice of the late administration (and of the existence of which the present administration, up to the time the order was dispatched, had only too vague and uncertain rumors to fix attention), had refused to land the troops. To now reenforce Fort Pickens before a crisis would be reached at Fort Sumter was impossible, rendered so by the near exhaustion of provisions in the latter named fort. In precaution against such a conjuncture, the government had a few days before commenced preparing an expedition, as well-adapted as might be, to relieve Fort Sumter, which expedition was intended to be ultimately used or not, according to circumstances. The strongest anticipated case for using it was now presented, and it was resolved to send it forward.

As had been intended in this contingency, it was also resolved to notify the governor of South Carolina that he might expect an attempt would be made to provision the fort, and that if the attempt should not be resisted there would be no effort to throw in men, arms, or ammunition without further notice, or in case of an attack upon the fort. This notice was accordingly given, whereupon the fort was attacked and bombarded to its fall, without even awaiting the arrival of the provisioning expedition.

It is thus seen that the assault upon and reduction of Fort Sumter was in no sense a matter of self-defense on the part of the assailants. They well knew that the garrison in the fort could by no possibility commit aggression upon them. They knew — they were expressly notified — that the giving of bread to the few brave and hungry men of the garrison was all which would on that occasion be attempted, unless themselves, by resisting so much, should provoke more They knew that this government desired to keep the garrison in the fort, not to assail them but merely to maintain visible possession, and thus to preserve the Union from actual and immediate dissolution, trusting, as hereinbefore stated, to time, discussion, and the ballot box for final adjustment; and they assailed and reduced the fort for precisely the reverse object — to drive out the visible authority of the Federal Union, and thus force it to immediate dissolution.

That this was their object the executive well understood; and having said to them in the inaugural address, "You can have no conflict without being yourselves the aggressors," he took pains not only to keep this declaration good but also to keep the case so free from the power of ingenious sophistry as that the world should not be able to misunderstand it. By the affair at Fort Sumter, with its surrounding circumstances, that point was reached. Then and thereby the assailants of the government began the conflict of arms, without a gun in sight or in expectancy to return their fire, save only the few in the fort, sent to that harbor years before for their own protection, and still ready to give that protection in whatever was lawful. In this act, discarding all else, they have forced upon the country the distinct issue: "Immediate dissolution or blood."

And this issue embraces more than the fate of the United States. It presents to the whole family of man the question whether a constitutional republic, or democracy — a government of the people by the same people — can or cannot maintain its territorial integrity against its own domestic foes. It presents the question whether discontented individuals, too few in numbers to control administration according to organic law in any case, can always, upon the pretenses made in this case, or on any other pretenses, or arbitrarily without any pretense, break up their government and thus practically put an end to free government upon the earth. It forces us to ask — Is there in all republics this inherent and fatal weakness? Must a government of necessity be too *strong* for the liberties of its own people, or too *weak* to maintain its own existence?

So viewing the issue, no choice was left but to call out the war power of the government and so to resist force employed for its destruction by force for its preservation. . . .

It might seem at first thought to be of little difference whether the present movement at the South be called "secession" or "rebellion." The movers, however, well understand the difference. At the beginning they knew they could never raise their treason to any respectable magnitude by any name which implies *violation* of law. They knew their people possessed as much of moral sense, as much of devotion to law and order, and as much pride in and reverence for the history and government of their common country as any other civilized and patriotic people. They knew they could make no advancement directly in the teeth of these strong and noble sentiments. Accordingly, they commenced by an insidious debauching of the public mind. They invented an ingenious sophism, which, if conceded, was followed by perfectly logical steps through all the incidents to the complete destruction of the Union. The sophism itself is that any state of the Union may

consistently with the national Constitution, and therefore *lawfully* and *peacefully*, withdraw from the Union without the consent of the Union or of any other state. The little disguise that the supposed right is to be exercised only for just cause, themselves to be the sole judge of its justice, is too thin to merit any notice.

With rebellion thus sugarcoated, they have been drugging the public mind of their section for more than thirty years, and until at length they have brought many good men to a willingness to take up arms against the government the day *after* some assemblage of men have enacted the farcical pretense of taking their state out of the Union who could have been brought to no such thing the day *before*.

This sophism derives much, perhaps the whole, of its currency from the assumption that there is some omnipotent and sacred supremacy pertaining to a state — to each state of our Federal Union. Our states have neither more nor less power than that reserved to them in the Union by the Constitution, no one of them ever having been a state out of the Union. The original ones passed into the Union even before they cast off their British colonial dependence, and the new ones each came into the Union directly from a condition of dependence, excepting Texas; and even Texas, in its temporary independence, was never designated a state. The new ones only took the designation of states on coming into the Union, while that name was first adopted for the old ones in and by the Declaration of Independence. Therein the "United Colonies" were declared to be "free and independent states"; but even then the object plainly was not to declare their independence of *one another* or of the *Union*, but directly the contrary, as their mutual pledge and their mutual action before, at the time, and afterward abundantly show.

The express plighting of faith by each and all of the original thirteen in the Articles of

Confederation, two years later, that the Union shall be perpetual is most conclusive. Having never been states, either in substance or in name, outside of the Union, whence this magical omnipotence of "state rights," asserting a claim of power to lawfully destroy the Union itself? Much is said about the "sovereignty" of the states, but the word even is not in the national Constitution, nor, as is believed, in any of the state constitutions. What is a "sovereignty" in the political sense of the term? Would it be far wrong to define it "a political community without a political superior"? Tested by this, no one of our states, except Texas, ever was a sovereignty; and even Texas gave up the character on coming into the Union, by which act she acknowledged the Constitution of the United States and the laws and treaties of the United States made in pursuance of the Constitution to be for her the supreme law of the land.

The states have their status in the Union, and they have no other legal status. If they break from this, they can only do so against law and by revolution. The Union, and not themselves separately, procured their independence and their liberty. By conquest or purchase the Union gave each of them whatever of independence and liberty it has. The Union is older than any of the states, and, in fact, it created them as states. Originally some dependent colonies made the Union, and in turn the Union threw off their old dependence for them and made them states, such as they are. Not one of them ever had a state constitution independent of the Union. Of course it is not forgotten that all the new states framed their constitutions before they entered the Union, nevertheless dependent upon and preparatory to coming into the Union.

Unquestionably the states have the powers and rights reserved to them in and by the national Constitution; but among these surely are not included all conceivable powers, however mischievous or destructive, but at most such only as were known in the world at the time as governmental powers; and certainly a power to destroy the government itself had never been known as a governmental — as a merely administrative — power. This relative matter of national power and state rights, as a principle, is no other than the principle of *generality* and *locality*. Whatever concerns the whole should be confided to the whole — to the general government — while whatever concerns only the state should be left exclusively to the state. This is all there is of original principle about it. Whether the national Constitution in defining boundaries between the two has applied the principle with exact accuracy is not to be questioned. We are all bound by that defining without question.

What is now combated is the position that secession is *consistent* with the Constitution — is *lawful* and *peaceful*. It is not contended that there is any express law for it, and nothing should ever be implied as law which leads to unjust or absurd consequences. . . .

The seceders insist that our Constitution admits of secession. They have assumed to make a national constitution of their own, in which of necessity they have either *discarded* or *retained* the right of secession, as they insist it exists in ours. If they have discarded it, they thereby admit that on principle it ought not to be in ours. If they have retained it, by their own construction of ours they show that to be consistent they must secede from one another whenever they shall find it the easiest way of settling their debts or effecting any other selfish or unjust object. The principle itself is one of disintegration and upon which no government can possibly endure.

If all the states save one should assert the power to drive that one out of the Union, it is presumed the whole class of seceder politicians would at once deny the power and denounce the act as the greatest outrage upon state rights. But suppose that precisely the same act, instead of being called "driving the one out," should be called "the seceding of the others from that one," it would be exactly what the seceders claim to do, unless, indeed, they make the point that the one, because it is a minority, may rightfully do what the others, because they are a majority, may not rightfully do. These politicians are subtle and profound on the rights of minorities. They are not partial to that power which made the Constitution and speaks from the Preamble, calling itself "We, the people."

It may well be questioned whether there is today a majority of the legally qualified voters of any state, except, perhaps, South Carolina, in favor of disunion. There is much reason to believe that the Union men are the majority in many, if not in every other one, of the so-called seceded states. The contrary has not been demonstrated in any one of them. It is ventured to affirm this even of Virginia and Tennessee; for the result of an election held in military camps, where the bayonets are all on one side of the question voted upon, can scarcely be considered as demonstrating popular sentiment. At such an election all that large class who are at once *for* the Union and *against* coercion would be coerced to vote against the Union. . . .

This is essentially a people's contest. On the side of the Union it is a struggle for maintaining in the world that form and substance of government whose leading object is to elevate the condition of men; to lift artificial weights from all shoulders; to clear the paths of laudable pursuit for all; to afford all an unfettered start and a fair chance in the race of life. Yielding to partial and temporary departures, from necessity, this is the leading object of the government for whose existence we contend. . . .

Our popular government has often been called an experiment. Two points in it our people have already settled — the successful *establishing* and the successful *administering* of it. One still remains: its successful *maintenance* against a formidable internal attempt to overthrow it. It is now for them to dem-

onstrate to the world that those who can fairly carry an election can also suppress a rebellion; that ballots are the rightful and peaceful successors of bullets, and that when ballots have fairly and constitutionally decided, there can be no successful appeal back to bullets; that there can be no successful appeal except to ballots themselves at succeeding elections. Such will be a great lesson of peace, teaching men that what they cannot take by an election neither can they take it by a war; teaching all the folly of being the beginners of a war.

Lest there be some uneasiness in the minds of candid men as to what is to be the course of the government toward the Southern states after the rebellion shall have been suppressed, the executive deems it proper to say it will be his purpose then, as ever, to be guided by the Constitution and the laws, and that he probably will have no different understanding of the powers and duties of the Federal government relatively to the rights of the states and the people under the Constitution than that expressed in the inaugural address.

He desires to preserve the government, that it may be administered for all as it was administered by the men who made it. Loyal citizens everywhere have the right to claim this of their government, and the government has no right to withhold or neglect it. It is not perceived that in giving it there is any coercion, any conquest, or any subjugation in any just sense of those terms.

The Constitution provides, and all the states have accepted the provision, that "the United States shall guarantee to every state in this Union a republican form of government." But if a state may lawfully go out of the Union, having done so it may also discard the republican form of government; so that to prevent its going out is an indispensable *means* to the *end* of maintaining the guaranty mentioned; and when an end is lawful and obligatory, the indispensable means to it are also lawful and obligatory.

It was with the deepest regret that the

executive found the duty of employing the war power in defense of the government forced upon him. He could but perform this duty or surrender the existence of the government. No compromise by public servants could in this case be a cure; not that compromises are not often proper, but that no popular government can long survive a marked precedent that those who carry an election can only save the government from immediate destruction by giving up the main point upon which the people gave the election. The people themselves, and not their servants, can safely reverse their own deliberate decisions.

As a private citizen the executive could not have consented that these institutions shall perish; much less could he in betrayal of so vast and so sacred a trust as these free people had confided to him. He felt that he had no moral right to shrink, not even to count the chances of his own life, in what might follow. In full view of his great responsibility he has so far done what he has deemed his duty. You will now, according to your own judgment, perform yours. He sincerely hopes that your views and your action may so accord with his as to assure all faithful citizens who have been disturbed in their rights of a certain and speedy restoration to them under the Constitution and the laws.

And having thus chosen our course, without guile and with pure purpose, let us renew our trust in God and go forward without fear and with manly hearts.

54.

ETHEL LYNN BEERS: "All Quiet Along the Potomac To-Night"

"All Quiet Along the Potomac To-Night," written by Ethel Lynn Beers, a New York poet, first appeared in Harper's Weekly *on November 30, 1861. According to H. M. Wharton, a compiler of war songs, "there was no poem written during the war that had a wider popularity than this." A year after its appearance in the North, a Southern newspaper reprinted the poem, claiming that it had been found on the dead body of a soldier. Later the poem was transformed into a Confederate song by John Hill Hewitt. Southerners believed the poem was written either by Lamar Fontaine or Thaddeus Oliver, both Southerners, though there is little evidence to support this claim.*

Source: *Famous Songs and Those Who Made Them,* Helen K. Johnson and
         Frederic Dean, eds., New York, 1895, pp. 94-95.

⚱ ALL QUIET ALONG THE POTOMAC TO-NIGHT

"All quiet along the Potomac," they say,
    "Except here and there a stray picket
Is shot, as he walks on his beat, to and fro,
    By a rifleman hid in the thicket.

'Tis nothing — a private or two now and then
    Will not count in the news of the battle;
Not an officer lost, only one of the men
    Moaning out all alone the death rattle."

All quiet along the Potomac to-night,
    Where the soldiers lie peacefully dreaming,
Their tents in the rays of the clear autumn moon,
    And the light of their watch-fires are gleaming.
A tremulous sigh, as the gentle night wind
    Through the forest leaves softly is creeping,
While the stars up above, with their glittering eyes,
    Keep guard, for the army is sleeping.

There's only the sound of the lone sentry's tread,
    As he tramps from the rock to the fountain,
And thinks of the two on the low trundle bed,
    Far away in the cot on the mountain.
His musket falls slack — his face, dark and grim,
    Grows gentle with memories tender,
As he mutters a prayer for the children asleep,
    And their mother — "may Heaven defend her."

Then drawing his sleeve roughly over his eyes,
    He dashes off tears that are welling;
And gathers his gun closer up to his breast,
    As if to keep down the heart's swelling.
He passes the fountain, the blasted pine tree,
    And his footstep is lagging and weary:
Yet onward he goes, through the broad belt of light,
    Toward the shades of the forest so dreary.

Hark! was it the night wind that rustles the leaves?
    Was it the moonlight so wondrously flashing?
It looked like a rifle! "Ha! Mary, good-bye!"
    And his lifeblood is ebbing and splashing.
"All quiet along the Potomac to-night,"
    No sound save the rush of the river;
While soft falls the dew on the face of the dead,
    The picket's off duty forever.

55.

Benjamin F. Butler: Negro Refugees in the Northern Army

During the Civil War, thousands of slaves fled the Confederacy and sought refuge behind the Union lines. These fugitive slaves presented the government with a difficult legal problem. Benjamin F. Butler was a major general of the Union Army in command of Fortress Monroe in Virginia. When the problem of refugee slaves arose, he took the initiative and refused to return them, declaring the slaves "contraband of war." This judgment was upheld by the administration. On July 30, 1861, he sent a report, part of which is reprinted here, to the secretary of war, Simon Cameron, justifying his action.

Source: Moore, II, Document 132.

IN THE VILLAGE OF HAMPTON there were a large number of Negroes, composed in a great measure of women and children of the men who had fled thither within my lines for protection, who had escaped from marauding parties of Rebels who had been gathering up able-bodied blacks to aid them in constructing their batteries on the James and York rivers. I have employed the men in Hampton in throwing up entrenchments, and they were working zealously and efficiently at that duty, saving our soldiers from that labor under the gleam of the midday sun. The women were earning substantially their own subsistence in washing, marketing, and taking care of the clothes of the soldiers, and rations were being served out to the men who worked for the support of the children.

But by the evacuation of Hampton, rendered necessary by the withdrawal of troops, leaving me scarcely 5,000 men outside the fort, including the force at Newport News, all these black people were obliged to break up their homes at Hampton, fleeing across the creek within my lines for protection and support. Indeed, it was a most distressing sight to see these poor creatures, who had trusted to the protection of the arms of the United States, and who aided the troops of the United States in their enterprise, to be thus obliged to flee from their homes, and the homes of their masters who had deserted them, and become fugitives from fear of the return of the Rebel soldiery, who had threatened to shoot the men who had wrought for us and to carry off the women who had served us to a worse than Egyptian bondage. I have, therefore, now, within the Peninsula, this side of Hampton Creek, 900 Negroes, 300 of whom are able-bodied men, 30 of whom are men substantially past hard labor, 175 women, 225 children under the age of 10 years, and 170 between 10 and 18 years, and many more coming in. The questions which this state of facts presents are very embarrassing.

First, what shall be done with them? Second, what is their state and condition?

Upon these questions I desire the instruction of the department.

The first question, however, may perhaps be answered by considering the last. Are these men, women, and children slaves? Are they free? Is their condition that of men, women, and children, or of property, or is it a mixed relation? What their *status* was under the Constitution and laws, we all know. What has been the effect of rebellion and a state of war upon that *status*? When I adopted the theory of treating the able-bodied Negro fit to work in the trenches as property liable to be used in aid of rebellion, and so contraband of war, that condition of things was insofar met, as I then and still believe, on a legal and constitutional basis. But now a new series of questions arises.

Passing by women, the children, certainly, cannot be treated on that basis; if property, they must be considered the encumbrance rather than the auxiliary of an army, and, of course, in no possible legal relation could be treated as contraband. Are they property? If they were so, they have been left by their masters and owners, deserted, thrown away, abandoned, like the wrecked vessel upon the ocean. Their former possessors and owners have causelessly, traitorously, rebelliously, and, to carry out the figure, practically abandoned them to be swallowed up by the winter storm of starvation. If property, do they not become the property of the salvors? But we, their salvors, do not need and will not hold such property, and will assume no such ownership. Has not, therefore, all proprietary relation ceased? Have they not become, thereupon, men, women, and children?

No longer under ownership of any kind, the fearful relics of fugitive masters, have they not, by their masters' acts and the state of war, assumed the condition, which we hold to be the normal one, of those made in God's image? Is not every constitutional, legal, and moral requirement, as well to the runaway master as their relinquished slaves, thus answered? I confess that my own mind is compelled by this reasoning to look upon them as men and women. If not freeborn, yet free, manumitted, sent forth from the hand that held them never to be reclaimed.

Of course, if this reasoning, thus imperfectly set forth, is correct, my duty, as a humane man, is very plain. I should take the same care of these men, women, and children, houseless, homeless, and unprovided for, as I would of the same number of men, women, and children who, for their attachment to the Union, had been driven or allowed to flee from the Confederate States. I should have no doubt on this question had I not seen it stated that an order had been issued by General McDowell, in his department, substantially forbidding all fugitive slaves from coming within his lines or being harbored there.

Is that order to be enforced in all military departments? If so, who are to be considered fugitive slaves? Is a slave to be considered fugitive whose master runs away and leaves him? Is it forbidden to the troops to aid or harbor within their lines the Negro children who are found therein, or is the soldier, when his march has destroyed their means of subsistence, to allow them to starve because he has driven off the Rebel masters? Now, shall the commander of a regiment or battalion sit in judgment upon the question, whether any given black man has fled from his master, or his master fled from him?

Indeed, how are the freeborn to be distinguished? Is one any more or less a fugitive slave because he has labored upon the Rebel entrenchments? If he has so labored, if I understand it, he is to be harbored. By the reception of which, are the Rebels most to be distressed by taking those who have wrought all their Rebel masters desired, masked their battery or those who have refused to labor and left the battery unmasked?

I have very decided opinions upon the subject of this order. It does not become me to criticize it, and I write in no spirit of criticism, but simply to explain the full difficulties that surround the enforcing it. If the enforcement of that order becomes the policy of the government, I, as a soldier, shall be bound to enforce it steadfastly, if not cheerfully. But if left to my own discretion, as you may have gathered from my reasoning, I should take a widely different course from that which it indicates.

In a loyal state, I would put down a servile insurrection. In a state of rebellion, I would confiscate that which was used to oppose my arms, and take all that property which constituted the wealth of that state and furnished the means by which the war is prosecuted, besides being the cause of the war; and if, in so doing, it should be objected that human beings were brought to the free enjoyment of life, liberty, and the pursuit of happiness, such objection might not require much consideration.

Pardon me for addressing the secretary of war directly upon this question, as it involves some political considerations as well as propriety of military action.

56.

An Alliance Between the Confederacy and the Indians

Upon the outbreak of war, Union soldiers were withdrawn from the frontier posts, leaving the western Indians exposed to Confederate influence. Five great Indian tribes — the Cherokees, Creeks, Choctaws, Chickasaws, and Seminoles — wished to remain neutral, but on November 22, 1861, the Confederacy established authority over them by organizing the Indian territory north of Texas and west of Arkansas. Albert Pike, a Confederate brigadier general in charge of the Indian territory, was commissioned in the summer of 1861 to negotiate treaties with the Indians in order to protect the western flank of the Confederacy. Pike soon won the friendship of most of the tribes, though many Indians resisted Confederate pressure and some remained loyal to the Union. On August 12, 1861, Pike successfully negotiated the following treaty creating an Indian alliance. It was one of several such treaties he negotiated with Indian tribes.

Source: Ainsworth, 4th series, I, pp. 542-546.

ARTICLES OF A CONVENTION entered into and concluded at the Wichita agency, near the False Washita River, in the country leased from the Choctaws and Chickasaws, on August 12, 1861, between the Confederate States of America, by Albert Pike, their commissioner with full powers, appointed by the president by virtue of an act of the congress in that behalf, of the one part, and the Pen-e-tegh-ca band of the Ne-um or Comanches, and the tribes and bands of Wichitas, Cado-Ha-da-chos, Hue-cos, Ta-hua-ca-ros, A-na-dagh-cos, Ton-ca-wes, Ai-o-nais, Ki-chais, Shawnees, and Delawares residing in the said leased country, by their respective chiefs and headmen, who have signed these articles, of the other part.

Article I. The Pen-e-tegh-ca band of the Ne-um or Comanches, and the tribes and bands of the Wichitas, Cado-Ha-da-chos, Hue-cos, Ta-hua-ca-ros, A-na-dagh-cos, Ton-ca-wes, Ai-o-nais, Ki-chais, Shawnees, and Delawares now residing within the country north of Red River and south of the Canadian, and between the 98th and 100th parallels of west longitude, leased for them and other tribes from the Choctaw and Chickasaw nations, do hereby place themselves under the laws and protection of the Confederate States of America in peace and war forever.

Article II. The Confederate States of America do hereby promise and engage themselves to be during all time the friends and protectors of the Pen-e-tegh-ca band of the Ne-um, and of the Wichitas, Cado-Ha-da-chos, Hue-cos, Ta-hua-ca-ros, A-na-dagh-cos, Ton-ca-wes, Ai-o-nais, Ki-chais, Shawnees, and Delawares residing, or that may hereafter come to reside, in the said leased country; and that they will not allow them henceforward to be in anywise troubled or molested by any power or people, state or person, whatever.

Article III. The reserves at present occupied by the said several tribes and bands may continue to be occupied by them if they are satisfied therewith; and if any of them are not, the tribe or tribes, band or bands dissatisfied may select other reserves instead of those now occupied by them, in the same leased country, with the concurrence and assent of the agent of the Confederate States for the reserve Indians, at any time within two years from the day of the signing of these articles.

Article IV. Each reserve shall be of sufficient extent of good arable and grazing land amply to supply the needs of the tribe or band that is to occupy it; and each shall have a separate reserve, unless two or more

elect to settle and reside together and hold their reserves in common. The reserves shall, as far as practicable, be defined by natural boundaries that may be described, and so far as this is not practicable, by permanent monuments and definite courses and distances; and full and authentic descriptions of the reserves shall be made out and preserved by the Confederate States.

Article V. Each tribe or band shall have the right to possess, occupy, and use the reserve allotted to it as long as grass shall grow and water run, and the reserves shall be their own property, like their horses and cattle.

Article VI. The members of all the said several bands and tribes of Indians shall have the right, henceforward forever, to hunt and kill game in all the unoccupied part of the said leased country without let or molestation from any quarter.

Article VII. There shall be perpetual peace and brotherhood between the Pen-e-tegh-ca band of the Ne-um or Comanches, and the tribes and bands of the Wichitas, Cado-Ha-da-chos, Hue-cos, Ta-hua-ca-ros, A-na-dagh-cos, Ton-ca-wes, Ai-o-nais, Ki-chais, Shawnees, and Delawares, between each of them and each and all of the others; and every injury or act of hostility which either has heretofore sustained at the hands of the other shall be forgiven and forgotten.

Article VIII. The said several tribes and bands shall henceforth be good neighbors to each other, and there shall be a free and friendly intercourse among them. And it is hereby agreed by all that the horses, cattle, and other stock and property of each tribe or band and of every person of each is his or its own, and that no tribe or band nor any person belonging to any tribe or band shall or will hereafter kill, take away, or injure any such property of another tribe or band or of any member of any tribe or band, or in any other way do them any harm.

Article IX. There shall be perpetual peace

and brotherhood between each and all of said tribes and bands and the Cherokee, Mus-ko-ki, Seminole, Choctaw, and Chickasaw nations; and the chiefs and headmen of each of the said tribes and bands shall do all in their power to take and return any Negroes, horses, or other property stolen from white men or from persons who belong to the Cherokee, Mus-ko-ki, Seminole, Choctaw, or Chickasaw nation, and to catch and give up any person among them who may kill or steal or do any other very wrong thing.

Article X. None of the laws of the Choctaws and Chickasaws shall ever be in force in the said leased country so as to affect any of the members of the said several tribes and bands, but only as to their own people who may settle therein; and they shall never interfere in any way with the reserves, improvements, or property of the reserve Indians.

Article XI. It is distinctly understood by the said several tribes and bands that the state of Texas is one of the Confederate States, and joins this convention, and signs it when the commissioner signs it, and is bound by it; and that all hostilities and enmities between it and them are now ended and are to be forgotten and forgiven on both sides.

Article XII. None of the braves of the said tribes and bands shall go upon the warpath against any enemy whatever, except with the consent of the agent, nor hold any councils or talks with any white men or other Indians without his knowledge and consent. And the Confederate States will not permit improper persons to live among them, but only such persons as are employed by the Confederate States and traders licensed by them, who shall sell to the Indians and buy from them at fair prices, under such regulations as the president shall make.

Article XIII. To steal a horse or any other article of property from an Indian or a white man shall hereafter be considered disgraceful, and the chiefs will discountenance it by every means in their power; for if they should not, there never could be any permanent peace.

Article XIV. The Confederate States ask nothing of the Pen-e-tegh-cas, Wichitas, Cado-Ha-da-chos, Hue-cos, Ta-hua-caros, A-na-dagh-cos, Ton-ca-wes, Ai-o-nais, Ki-chais, Shawnees, and Delawares, except that they will settle upon their reserves, become industrious, and prepare to support themselves, and live in peace and quietness; and in order to encourage and assist them in their endeavors to become able to support themselves, the Confederate States agree to continue to furnish them rations of provisions in the same manner as they are now doing, to include also sugar and coffee, salt, soap, and vinegar, for such time as may be necessary to enable them to feed themselves. They agree to furnish each tribe or band with 20 cows and calves for every 50 persons contained in the same, and 1 bull for every 40 cows and calves; and also to furnish to all of said tribes and bands together 250 stock hogs, all of which animals shall be distributed by the agent to such persons and families as shall, in his judgment, be most proper to receive them and most likely to take care of them.

And they also agree to furnish, for the use of the said tribes and bands, such number of draft oxen, wagons, carts, plows, shovels, hoes, pickaxes, spades, scythes, rakes, axes, and seeds as may be necessary, in addition to their present supply, to enable them to farm successfully. They also agree to furnish each tribe or band annually with such quantities as the agent shall estimate for, and the superintendent require, of all such articles as are mentioned and contained in the schedule hereunto annexed, marked A; to be issued and delivered to them by the agent.

Article XV. The Confederate States will maintain one agency for the said tribes and bands at the present agency house or some other suitable and convenient location, at which the agent shall continually reside; and they do promise the said tribes and bands that they shall never be abandoned by the agent, and that he shall not be often nor for any long time away from his agency.

Article XVI. The Confederate States will also employ and pay an interpreter for each language spoken among the said tribes and bands, and also one blacksmith, who shall also be a gunsmith, one striker, and one wagonmaker, for all; all of whom shall reside at the agency; and they will furnish from time to time such tools and such supplies of iron, steel, and wood as may be needed for the work of the said tribes and bands; and will also furnish all the people of said tribes and bands who may be sick with medicines and medical service at the agency, where a physician shall be employed to reside for their benefit exclusively. They will also employ for five years, and as much longer as the president shall please, a farmer for each reserve to instruct the Indians in cultivating the soil, so that they may soon be able to feed themselves; and will erect such a number of horse mills to grind their corn as the superintendent shall consider to be necessary in order to accommodate all. And the stock and animals to be given to the tribes and bands shall be in charge of the farmers, that they may not be foolishly killed or left to perish by neglect.

Article XVII. The Confederate States also agree to erect such buildings for the mills and the blacksmith shops, and houses for the farmers and interpreters as have been erected among the other Indian tribes, and also to assist the said Indians in building houses for themselves, and in digging wells for water, and opening their lands.

Article XVIII. The said bands and tribes agree to remain upon their reserves, and not at any time to leave them in order to make crops elsewhere. And if they should leave

Brigadier Gen. Albert Pike, CSA, authorized to recruit the Indians' support for the Confederacy

them, the Confederate States shall not be bound any longer to feed them or make them presents or give them any assistance.

Article XIX. The Confederate States also agree to furnish each warrior of the said tribes and bands who has not a gun with a flintlock rifle and ammunition, which he agrees never to sell or give away; and the Confederate States will punish any trader or other white man who may purchase one from them.

Article XX. The Confederate States invite all the other bands of the Ne-um or Comanches to abandon their wandering life and settle within the leased country aforesaid, and do promise them in that case the same protection and care as is hereby promised to said tribes and bands now residing therein; and that there shall be allotted to them reserves of good land, of sufficient extent to be held and owned by them forever; and that all the other promises made by these articles shall be considered as made to them also, as well as to the tribes and bands now residing on reserves; and that the same presents shall be made them and assistance given them in all respects; and the same things in all respects are hereby also offered the Cai-a-was and agreed to be given them if they will settle in said country, atone for the murders and robberies they have lately committed, and show a resolution to lead an honest life; to which end the Confederate States send the Cai-a-was with this talk the wampum of peace and the bullet of war, for them to take their choice now and for all time to come.

Article XXI. The Confederate States hereby guarantee to the members of the aforesaid tribes and bands full indemnity for any horses or any other property that may be killed or stolen from them by any citizen of the Confederate States, or by Indians of any other tribe or band: *Provided,* that the property, if stolen, cannot be recovered and restored, and that sufficient proof is produced to satisfy the agent that it was killed or stolen within the limits of the Confederate States.

Article XXII. If any difficulty should hereafter arise between any of the bands or tribes in consequence of the killing of anyone, of the stealing or killing of horses, cattle, or other stock, or of injury in any other way to person or property, the same shall be submitted to the agent of the Confederate States, who shall settle and decide the same equitably and justly, to which settlement all parties agree to submit, and such atonement and satisfaction shall be made as he shall direct.

Article XXIII. In order that the friendship which now exists between the said several tribes and bands of Indians and the people of the Confederate States and of the Choctaw and Chickasaw nations may not be interrupted by the conduct of individuals, it is hereby agreed that if any white man or any Choctaw or Chickasaw injures an Indian of any one of said tribes and bands, or if any one of them injures a white man or a Choctaw or Chickasaw, no private revenge or retaliation shall take place, nor shall the Choctaws or Chickasaws try the person who does the wrong and punish him in their courts, but he shall be tried and punished by the Confederate States; and the life of every person belonging to said tribes and bands shall be of the same value as the life of a white man; and any Indian or white man who kills one of them without cause shall be hung by the neck until he is dead.

Article XXIV. It is further hereby agreed by the Confederate States that all the Texan troops now within the limits of the said leased country shall be withdrawn across Red River, and that no Texan troops shall hereafter be stationed in forts or garrisons in the said country or be sent into the same, except in the service of the Confederate States and when on the warpath against the Cai-a-was or other hostile Indians.

Article XXV. This convention shall be obligatory on the tribes and bands whose chiefs and headmen signed the same from the day of its date, and on the Confederate States from and after its ratification by the proper authority.

In perpetual testimony whereof, the said Albert Pike, as commissioner with plenary powers of the Confederate States of America to the Indian nations and tribes west of Arkansas, for and on behalf of the said Confederate States, does now hereunto set his hand and affix the seal of his arms; and the undersigned chiefs and headmen, for and on behalf of their respective tribes and bands, do now hereunto respectively set their hands and affix their seals.

Indians is pizen wherever found.
CHARLES FARRAR BROWNE ("ARTEMUS WARD"), *Artemus Ward: His Book*

"The Great Union Meeting in Union Square"; photographed in New York City by Anthony, April 1861

THE WAR, 1861 - 1863

Whether the firing on Sumter was a local incident or the inevitable first shot is beyond determination. Once the war officially began, enthusiasm ran high on both sides. And on both sides the general expectation was for a short war, relatively simple in execution and sure in outcome. It took three months for the North to learn otherwise at Bull Run; the South was buoyantly optimistic a bit longer, and failed to press its advantage or to organize a total effort. As the prospect of a long and arduous war became clear, support began to wane, particularly in the North, and the need for a

well-developed overall strategy became obvious in both capitals. As the North recovered from its early miscalculations, and as the South failed to take the offensive, the tide began to turn. When the North gained control of the Mississippi in 1863, the South was effectively cut in half; for the South, caught between the great river and the blockade, there remained little hope. Innovations in weaponry and tactics made this the first "modern war"; combined with the miscalculations, misjudgements, and outright blunders on either side, they also made it an incredibly vicious and costly one.

(Above) The Inauguration of Abraham Lincoln as President, March 4, 1861; (right) portrait of Lincoln by Mathew Brady, 1861

Elected by a mere plurality, Lincoln was regarded by the South as a purely sectional President; thus his election became the signal for secession. Like outgoing President Buchanan, Lincoln held secession to be unconstitutional, yet he was not eager to employ coercion to preserve the Union. The first weeks of his administration became a waiting period, as each side maneuvered for position and tried to force the other into the first blow and thus responsibility for whatever might follow. The South lost, as Lincoln fulfilled his inaugural pledge to maintain federal property in the departed states.

Confederate volunteers at the start of the war

Union volunteer photographed by Brady, 1861

Tintype of a Civil War soldier on horseback, about 1862; by an unknown photographer

Battle of Bull Run, July 1861: (Above) Col. Burnside's Rhode Island brigade in action; drawing by Alfred R. Waud; (below) Confederate dead

(Above) Battle of Winchester, Va., May 1862; pencil drawing by Alfred Waud

Bull Run, the first major engagement of the war, took place at Manassas Junction, only 30 mi. from Washington and a vital link in Richmond's railroad connection with the West. The battle turned into a rout of the North. The South failed, however, to pursue the retreating Union Army back to Washington and thus gained no advantage. The disaster hardened the North's view of the war, and brought the able Gen. McClellan to command and organize the Army of the Potomac.

(Left) Gen. Robert E. Lee, commander of the Confederate Army, photographed in 1865; (below) Capt. Tichball and his staff at Fair Oaks, Va., in 1862

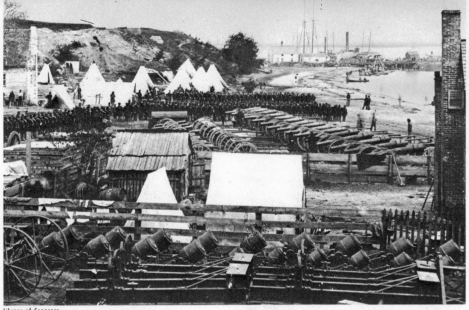

Withstanding constant criticism of his inaction, McClellan devoted the winter of 1861-62 to training his army. After several delays, he formally began his Richmond campaign in March. Contrary to his expectations, it was a long campaign, and ultimately failed, though he did inflict serious losses on Lee's Army of Northern Virginia. He was in a strong position when a bickering Washington called for his withdrawal and demotion.

(Above) Federal ordnance awaiting transport from Yorktown, 1862; (left) Lincoln conferring with McClellan at Antietam, 1862; (below) troop inspection at Cumberland Landing

Antietam Bridge just after the battle in October 1862

Antietam battlefield: dead along the west side of Hagerstown Pike, September 1862

Scene outside Dunkard Church where the Confederates held off a Union threat, Antietam

Embarkation of the 9th Army Corps at Acquia Creek Landing, Feb. 1863; photo by Gardner

(Above left) Stonewall Jackson, photo by Brady; (above right) Pvt. Thomas Jefferson Rushin, from a Georgia regiment; both men were killed at Chancellorsville; (below) Civil War artillery

The war in the West was decisive compared to the long stalemate in the East. Despite occasional reverses, the Union's western commanders, notably Grant, succeeded in cutting the Southern forces in two and securing all of western Tennessee. A drive down the Mississippi brought Grant to Vicksburg by the summer of 1862, while Farragut, with the iron-clad vessels which played a large role in Union success, came upriver and took New Orleans. The western campaign successfully set up Winfield Scott's original "anaconda" strategy of encirclement.

(Above) Confederate battery at Vicksburg, 1863; (left) U. S. Grant in 1863; photo by Brady; (below) gun and mortar boats on the Mississippi engaging Confederate forts and batteries on the island and mainland

(Above) Chambersburg Pike and the surrounding fields, scene of the first day's battle at Gettysburg, July 1863; (below left) General Pickett, leader of the Confederates' desperate charge on the third day of battle; (below right) George Meade, Union general in command at Gettysburg

Regiment in anti-cavalry square; method used by Gen. John Buford's troops at Gettysburg

The Battle of Gettysburg, July 1-3, 1863, was of critical importance to the course of the war. The decisive defeat of Lee's army turned back a daring offensive aimed at capturing desperately needed supplies and undermining Northern resolves to continue the fighting. To win the war, Lee had only to keep from being destroyed until the North tired of it all. The Confederacy also hoped to gain long-expected foreign support with a dramatic sweep north.

(Right) Body of Confederate soldier of Ewell's Corps; (below) dead Rebel soldier at the foot of Little Round Top; photo by Gardner

The struggle for eastern Tennessee was far more bitter than the earlier Union success in the western part of the state. Rosecrans and his Union forces occupied Chattanooga but found themselves trapped, besieged by Bragg and Longstreet. Grant, new western commander, put Thomas in command of the Cumberland Army and undertook an attack on Bragg. The storming of Lookout Mountain and Missionary Ridge forced Bragg's retreat and put nearly all of eastern Tennessee in Union hands.

(Top) Grant (on the left) with other officers on Lookout Mountain; (right) Gen. Thomas, nicknamed "Rock of Chickamauga" for his stand against the Confederates; (bottom) Fort Sherman in Chattanooga, Tenn.

57.

"Song of the Mississippi Volunteers"

Many men and women on both sides in the Civil War described their experiences in songs and poems. The soldiers themselves wrote many songs, among them this one, which became popular throughout the South, especially (it is said) among children.

🎵 SONG OF THE MISSISSIPPI VOLUNTEERS

O, I would not marry a conscript a-hidin' in the wood,
I'd rather marry a volunteer and do my country good —
Soldier boy, o soldier boy, a soldier boy for me,
If ever I get married, a soldier's wife I'll be.

> *Chorus:*
> We go walking on the green grass thus, thus, thus.
> Come all ye fair and pretty maids and walk along with us.
> So pretty and so fair as you take yourselves to be,
> I'll choose you for a partner, come walk along with me.

O, I would not marry a lawyer who's pleading at the bar,
I'd rather marry a soldier boy who wears a Southern star.
O, I would not be a lady that Southrons call a belle,
I'd rather be a soldier boy and hear the Yankees yell.

O, I would not be a nursemaid and hear the children squall,
I'd rather be a volunteer and face a cannon ball.
O, I would not be a farmer who's toiling in the sun,
I'd rather be a soldier boy and see the Yankees run.

O, I would not be a miller who grinds the people's grain,
I'd rather be a soldier boy who walks through wind and rain —
Soldier boy, o soldier boy, a soldier boy for me,
If ever I get married, a soldier's wife I'll be.

58.

Abraham Lincoln: Military Proclamations and Civil Law

In July 1861 Lincoln appointed John Charles Frémont major general in charge of the department of the West, with headquarters in St. Louis. Frémont's task was enormous, for he had to organize an army in a slave state that was generally disloyal to the Union. He was equipped with few arms and faced active insurrection in the state. In order to deter further rebellion, Frémont on his own authority issued a proclamation on August 30, confiscating the property of disloyal Missourians and freeing their slaves. Lincoln regarded Frémont's proclamation as legally unjustifiable and countermanded it. Antislavery men disapproved of the President's action. Lincoln was especially surprised when one of his closest political friends, Senator Orville Browning of Illinois, objected to his action. On September 22, 1861, Lincoln sent the following explanatory letter to the senator.

Source: Nicolay-Hay, VI, pp. 357-361.

Yours of the 17th is just received; and coming from you, I confess it astonishes me. That you should object to my adhering to a law which you had assisted in making and presenting to me less than a month before is odd enough. But this is a very small part.

General Frémont's proclamation as to confiscation of property and the liberation of slaves is purely political and not within the range of military law or necessity. If a commanding general finds a necessity to seize the farm of a private owner for a pasture, an encampment, or a fortification, he has the right to do so, and to so hold it as long as the necessity lasts; and this is within military law because within military necessity. But to say the farm shall no longer belong to the owner, or his heirs, forever, and this as well when the farm is not needed for military purposes as when it is, is purely

political, without the savor of military law about it.

And the same is true of slaves. If the general needs them, he can seize them and use them; but when the need is past, it is not for him to fix their permanent future condition. That must be settled according to laws made by lawmakers and not by military proclamations. The proclamation in the point in question is simply "dictatorship." It assumes that the general may do anything he pleases — confiscate the lands and free the slaves of loyal people, as well as of disloyal ones. And going the whole figure, I have no doubt, would be more popular with some thoughtless people than that which has been done! But I cannot assume this reckless position nor allow others to assume it on my responsibility.

You speak of it as being the only means of saving the government. On the contrary it is itself the surrender of the government. Can it be pretended that it is any longer the government of the United States — any government of Constitution and laws — wherein a general or a President may make permanent rules of property by proclamation?

I do not say Congress might not with propriety pass a law on the point, just such as General Frémont proclaimed. I do not say I might not, as a member of Congress, vote for it. What I object to is that I, as President, shall expressly or impliedly seize and exercise the permanent legislative functions of the government.

So much as to principle. Now as to policy. No doubt the thing was popular in some quarters, and would have been more so if it had been a general declaration of emancipation. The Kentucky legislature would not budge till that proclamation was modified; and General Anderson telegraphed me that on the news of General Frémont having actually issued deeds of manumission, a whole company of our volunteers threw down their arms and disbanded. I was so assured as to think it probable that the very arms we had furnished Kentucky would be turned against us. I think to lose Kentucky is nearly the same as to lose the whole game. Kentucky gone, we cannot hold Missouri, nor, as I think, Maryland. These all against us, and

the job on our hands is too large for us. We would as well consent to separation at once, including the surrender of this capitol.

On the contrary, if you will give up your restlessness for new positions and back me manfully on the grounds upon which you and other kind friends gave me the election and have approved in my public documents, we shall go through triumphantly. You must not understand I took my course on the proclamation because of Kentucky. I took the same ground in a private letter to General Frémont before I heard from Kentucky.

You think I am inconsistent because I did not also forbid General Frémont to shoot men under the proclamation. I understand that part to be within military law; but I also think, and so privately wrote General Frémont, that it is impolitic in this, that our adversaries have the power, and will certainly exercise it, to shoot as many of our men as we shoot of theirs. I did not say this in the public letter, because it is a subject I prefer not to discuss in the hearing of our enemies.

There has been no thought of removing General Frémont on any ground connected with his proclamation; and if there has been any wish for his removal on any ground, our mutual friend Sam Glover can probably tell you what it was. I hope no real necessity for it exists on any ground.

Let us determine to die here, and we will conquer. There is Jackson standing like a stone wall. Rally behind the Virginians!
GENERAL BERNARD ELLIOTT BEE, at first Battle of Bull Run.
General Jackson was ever afterward "Stonewall" Jackson.

59.

A Southern Christian View of Slavery

One of the many bonds between the North and the South that was broken by the Civil War was religious unity. On May 16, 1861, the Presbyterian Assembly met in Philadelphia. Only a minority of Southern presbyteries was represented. When a Northern clergyman called for an oath of allegiance to the Federal government, the Southern clergymen defected. On December 4, Presbyterian clergymen of the South met at Augusta, Georgia, to establish the General Assembly of the Presbyterian Church in the Confederate States of America. The Assembly adopted a statement drafted by James Henley Thornwell, a prominent South Carolina Presbyterian clergyman, the purpose of which was to justify the church's secession from the parent church. A political moderate and opponent of the church's participation in secular affairs such as the slavery issue prior to 1860, Thornwell became a champion of the Confederacy and one of the strongest advocates of slavery in the South. The part of the Address dealing with the slavery question is reprinted here.

Source: *Minutes of the General Assembly of the Presbyterian Church in the Confederate States of America,* Vol. I, Augusta, Ga., 1861, Appendix, pp. 55-59.

THE ANTAGONISM of Northern and Southern sentiment on the subject of slavery lies at the root of all the difficulties which have resulted in the dismemberment of the federal Union, and involved us in the horrors of an unnatural war.

The Presbyterian Church in the United States has been enabled by the Divine Grace to pursue, for the most part, an eminently conservative, because a thoroughly scriptural, policy in relation to this delicate question. It has planted itself upon the word of God and utterly refused to make slaveholding a sin or nonslaveholding a term of communion. But though both sections are agreed as to this general principle, it is not to be disguised that the North exercises a deep and settled antipathy to slavery itself, while the South is equally zealous in its defense. Recent events can have no

other effect than to confirm the antipathy on the one hand and strengthen the attachment on the other.

The Northern section of the church stands in the awkward predicament of maintaining, in one breath, that slavery is an evil which ought to be abolished and of asserting, in the next, that it is not a sin to be visited by exclusion from communion of the saints. The consequence is that it plays partly into the hands of Abolitionists and partly into the hands of slaveholders and weakens its influence with both. It occupies the position of a prevaricating witness whom neither party will trust. It would be better, therefore, for the moral power of the Northern section of the church to get entirely quit of the subject.

At the same time, it is intuitively obvious that the Southern section of the church, while even partially under the control of those who are hostile to slavery, can never have free and unimpeded access to the slave population. Its ministers and elders will always be liable to some degree of suspicion. In the present circumstances, Northern alliance would be absolutely fatal. It would utterly preclude the church from a wide and commanding field of usefulness.

This is too dear a price to be paid for a nominal union. We cannot afford to give up these millions of souls and consign them, so far as our efforts are concerned, to hopeless perdition for the sake of preserving an outward unity which, after all, is an empty shadow. If we would gird ourselves heartily and in earnest for the work which God has set before us, we must have the control of our ecclesiastical affairs and declare ourselves separate and independent.

And here we may venture to lay before the Christian world our views as a church upon the subject of slavery. We beg a candid hearing.

In the first place, we would have it distinctly understood that, in our ecclesiastical capacity, we are neither the friends nor the foes of slavery, that is to say, we have no commission either to propagate or abolish it. The policy of its existence or nonexistence is a question which exclusively belongs to the state. We have no right, as a church, to enjoin it as a duty or to condemn it as a sin. Our business is with the duties which spring from the relation; the duties of the masters, on the one hand, and of their slaves, on the other. These duties we are to proclaim and to enforce with spiritual sanctions. The social, civil, political problems connected with this great subject transcend our sphere, as God has not entrusted to His church the organization of society, the construction of governments, nor the allotment of individuals to their various stations. The church has as much right to preach to the monarchies of Europe and the despotism of Asia the doctrines of republican equality as to preach to the governments of the South the extirpation of slavery. This position is impregnable unless it can be shown that slavery is a sin. Upon every other hypothesis, it is so clearly a question for the state that the proposition would never for a moment have been doubted had there not been a foregone conclusion in relation to its moral character. Is slavery, then, a sin?

In answering this question, as a church, let it be distinctly borne in mind that the only rule of judgment is the written word of God. The church knows nothing of the intuitions of reason or the deductions of philosophy, except those reproduced in the Sacred Canon. She has a positive constitution in the Holy Scriptures and has no right to utter a single syllable upon any subject except as the Lord puts words in her mouth. She is founded, in other words, upon express *revelation*. Her creed is an authoritative testimony of God and not a speculation, and what she proclaims, she must proclaim with the infallible certitude of faith and not with the hesitating assent of an opinion. The question, then, is brought within a narrow compass: Do the Scriptures directly or indirectly condemn slavery as a sin? If they do not, the dispute is ended, for the church, without forfeiting her character, dares not go beyond them.

Now, we venture to assert that if men had drawn their conclusions upon this subject only from the Bible, it would no more have entered into any human head to denounce slavery as a sin than to denounce monarchy, aristocracy, or poverty. The truth is, men have listened to what they falsely considered as primitive intuitions, or as necessary deductions from primitive cognitions, and then have gone to the Bible to confirm the crotchets of their vain philosophy. They have gone there determined to find a particular result, and the consequence is that they leave with having made, instead of having interpreted, Scripture. Slavery is no new thing. It has not only existed for ages in the world but it has existed, under every dispensation of the covenant of grace, in the Church of God.

Indeed, the first organization of the church as a visible society, separate and distinct from the unbelieving world, was inaugurated in the family of a slaveholder. Among the very first persons to whom the seal of circumcision was affixed were the slaves of the father of the faithful, some born in his house and others bought with his money. Slavery again reappears under the Law. God sanctions it in the first table of the Decalogue, and Moses treats it as an institution to be regulated, not abolished; legitimated and not condemned. We come down to the age of the New Testament, and we find it again in the churches founded by the apostles under the plenary inspiration of the Holy Ghost. These facts are utterly amazing, if slavery is the enormous sin which its enemies represent it to be. It will not do to say that the Scriptures have treated it only in a general, incidental way, without any clear implication as to its moral character. Moses surely made it the subject of express and positive legislation, and the apostles are equally explicit in inculcating the duties which spring from both sides of the relation. They treat slaves as bound to obey and inculcate obedience as an office of religion — a thing wholly self-contradictory if the authority exercised over them were unlawful and iniquitous.

But what puts this subject in a still clearer light is the manner in which it is sought to extort from the Scriptures a contrary testimony. The notion of direct and explicit condemnation is given up. The attempt is to show that the genius and spirit of Christianity are opposed to it — that its great cardinal principles of virtue are utterly against it. Much stress is laid upon the Golden Rule and upon the general denunciations of tyranny and oppression. To all this we reply that no principle is clearer than that a case positively excepted cannot be included under a general rule.

Let us concede, for a moment, that the law of love, and the condemnation of tyranny and oppression seem logically to involve, as a result, the condemnation of slavery; yet, if slavery is afterwards expressly mentioned and treated as a lawful relation, it obviously follows, unless Scripture is to be interpreted as inconsistent with itself, that slavery is, by necessary implication, excepted. The Jewish law forbade, as a general rule, the marriage of a man with his brother's wife. The same law expressly enjoined the same marriage in a given case. The given case was, therefore, an exception, and not to be treated as a violation of the general rule. The law of love has always been the law of God. It was enunciated by Moses almost as clearly as it was enunciated by Jesus Christ. Yet, notwithstanding this law, Moses and the apostles alike sanctioned the relation of slavery.

The conclusion is inevitable, either that the law is not opposed to it or that slavery is an excepted case. To say that the prohibition of tyranny and oppression include slavery is to beg the whole question. Tyranny and oppression involve either the unjust usurpation or the unlawful exercise of power. It is the unlawfulness, either in its principle or measure, which constitutes the core of the sin. Slavery must, therefore, be proved to be unlawful before it can be referred to any such category. The master may, indeed, abuse his power, but he oppresses, not simply as a master but as a wicked master.

But, apart from all this, the law of love is simply the inculcation of universal equity. It implies nothing as to the existence of various ranks and gradations in society. The interpretation which makes it repudiate slavery would make it equally repudiate all social, civil, and political inequalities. Its meaning is not that we should conform ourselves to the arbitrary expectations of others but that we should render unto them precisely the same measure which, if we were in their circumstance, it would be reasonable and just in us to demand at their hands. It condemns slavery, therefore, only upon the supposition that slavery is a sinful relation — that is, he who extracts the prohibition of slavery from the Golden Rule begs the very point in dispute.

We cannot prosecute the argument in detail, but we have said enough, we think, to vindicate the position of the Southern church. We have assumed no new attitude. We stand exactly where the Church of God has always stood — from Abraham to Moses, from Moses to Christ, from Christ to the reformers, and from the reformers to ourselves. We stand upon the foundation of the prophets and apostles, Jesus Christ himself being the chief cornerstone. Shall we be excluded from the fellowship of our brethren in other lands because we dare not depart from the charter of our faith? Shall we be branded with the stigma of reproach because we cannot consent to corrupt the word of God to suit the intuitions of an infidel philosophy? Shall our names be cast out as evil and the finger of scorn pointed at us because we utterly refuse to break our communion with Abraham, Isaac and Jacob, with Moses, David and Isaiah, with apostles, prophets, and martyrs, with all the noble army of confessors who have gone to glory from slaveholding countries and from a slaveholding church, without ever having dreamed that they were living in mortal sin by conniving at slavery in the midst of them? If so, we shall take consolation in the cheering consciousness that the Master has accepted us.

We may be denounced, despised, and cast out of the synagogues of our brethren. But while they are wrangling about the distinctions of men according to the flesh, we shall go forward in our divine work and confidently anticipate that, in the great day, as the consequence of our humble labors, we shall meet millions of glorified spirits who have come up from the bondage of earth to a nobler freedom than human philosophy ever dreamed of. Others, if they please, may spend their time in declaiming on the tyranny of earthly masters; it will be our aim to resist the real tyrants which oppress the soul — sin and Satan. These are the foes against whom we shall find it employment enough to wage a successful war. And to this holy war it is the purpose of our church to devote itself with redoubled energy. We feel that the souls of our slaves are a solemn trust, and we shall strive to present them faultless and complete before the presence of God.

Indeed, as we contemplate their condition in the Southern states, and contrast it with that of their fathers before them and that of their brethren in the present day in their native land, we cannot but accept it as a gracious providence that they have been brought in such numbers to our shores and redeemed from the bondage of barbarism and sin. Slavery to them has certainly been overruled for the greatest good. It has been a link in the wondrous chain of providence, through which many sons and daughters have been made heirs of the heavenly inheritance. The providential result is, of course, no justification if the thing is intrinsically wrong; but it is certainly a matter of devout thanksgiving, and no obscure intimation of the will and purpose of God and of the consequent duty of the church. We cannot forbear to say, however, that the general operation of the system is kindly and benevolent; it is a real and effective discipline, and, without it, we are profoundly persuaded that the African race in the midst of us can never be elevated in the scale of being. As long as that race, in its comparative degradation, coexists, side by side with the white, bondage is its normal condition.

As to the endless declamation about human rights, we have only to say that human rights are not a fixed but a fluctuating quantity. Their sum is not the same in any two nations on the globe. The rights of Englishmen are one thing, the rights of Frenchmen, another. There is a minimum without which a man cannot be responsible; there is a maximum which expresses the highest degree of civilization and of Christian culture. The education of the species consists in its ascent along this line. As you go up, the number of rights increases, but the number of individuals who possess them diminishes. As you come down the line, rights are diminished, but the individuals are multiplied. It is just the opposite of the predicamental scale of the logicians. There, comprehension diminishes as you ascend and extension increases, and comprehension increases as you descend and extension diminishes.

Now, when it is said that slavery is inconsistent with human rights, we crave to understand what point in this line is the slave conceived to occupy. There are, no doubt, many rights which belong to other men — to Englishmen, to Frenchmen, to his master, for example — which are denied to him. But is he fit to possess them? Has God qualified him to meet the responsibilities which their possession necessarily implies? His place in the scale is determined by his competency to fulfill its duties. There are other rights which he certainly possesses, without which he could neither be human nor accountable. Before slavery can be charged with doing him injustice, it must be shown that the minimum which falls to his lot at the bottom of the line is out of proportion to his capacity and culture — a thing which can never be done by abstract speculation.

The truth is, the education of the human race for liberty and virtue is a vast providential scheme, and God assigns to every man, by a wise and holy degree, the precise place he is to occupy in the great moral school of humanity. The scholars are distributed into classes according to their competency and progress. For God is in history.

To avoid the suspicion of a conscious weakness of our cause, when contemplated from the side of pure speculation, we may advert for a moment to those pretended intuitions which stamp the reprobation of humanity upon this ancient and hoary institution. We admit that there are primitive principles in morals which lie at the root of human consciousness. But the question is, how are we to distinguish them? The subjective feeling of certainty is no adequate criterion, as that is equally felt in reference to crotchets and hereditary prejudices. The very point is to know when this certainty indicates a primitive cognition and when it does not. There must, therefore, be some eternal test, and whatever cannot abide that test has no authority as a primary truth. That test is an inward necessity of thought, which in all minds at the proper stage of maturity is absolutely universal.

Whatever is universal is natural. We are willing that slavery should be tried by this standard. We are willing to abide by the testimony of the race, and if man, as man, has everywhere condemned it — if all human laws have prohibited it as crime — if it stands in the same category with malice, murder, and theft, then we are willing, in the name of humanity, to renounce it, and to renounce it forever. But what if the overwhelming majority of mankind have approved it? What if philosophers and statesmen have justified it, and the laws of all nations acknowledged it; what then becomes of these luminous intuitions? They are an *ignis fatuus*, mistaken for a star.

We have now, brethren, in a brief compass, for the nature of this address admits only of an outline, opened to you our whole hearts upon this delicate and vexed subject. We have concealed nothing. We have sought to conciliate no sympathy by appeals to your charity. We have tried our cause by the word of God; and though protesting against its authority to judge in a question concerning the duty of the church, we have not refused to appear at the tribunal of reason.

Are we not right, in view of all the preceding considerations, in remitting the social, civil, and political problems connected with slavery to the state? Is it not a subject, save in the moral duties which spring from it, which lies beyond the province of the church? Have we any right to make it an element in judging of Christian character? Are we not treading in the footsteps of the flock? Are we not acting as Christ and His apostles have acted before us? Is it not enough for us to pray and labor, in our lot, that all men may be saved without meddling as a church with the technical distinction of their civil life?

We leave the matter with you. We offer you the right hand of fellowship. It is for you to accept it or reject it. We have done our duty. We can do no more. Truth is more precious than union, and if you cast us out as sinners, the breach of charity is not with us as long as we walk according to the light of the written word.

60.

Patriotic Songs of North and South

Every war manifests its spirit in songs. One of the most popular songs of the North was "The Battle-Cry of Freedom," composed by George Frederick Root, a professional songwriter. The song was written a few hours after President Lincoln called for troops to put down the insurrection in Virginia. "The Bonnie Blue Flag" was one of the most popular Confederate songs, commemorating an early Confederate flag of solid blue with a white star. It was written by "the little Irishman," Harry McCarty, who grew famous singing it all over the South. According to one compiler of Confederate war songs, the people "went wild with excitement" when they heard the first familiar strains.

Source: *Heart Songs*, Cleveland, 1909.
   War Songs and Poems of the Southern Confederacy 1861-1865,
   H. M. Wharton, ed., n.p., 1904.

ℬ THE BATTLE-CRY OF FREEDOM

Yes, we'll rally round the flag, boys, we'll rally once again,
   Shouting the battle-cry of freedom,
We will rally from the hillside, we'll gather from the plain,
   Shouting the battle-cry of freedom.

Chorus:
The Union forever, hurrah! boys, hurrah!
Down with the traitor, up with the star,
While we rally round the flag, boys, rally once again,
Shouting the battle-cry of freedom.

We are springing to the call of our brothers gone before,
   Shouting the battle-cry of freedom,
And we'll fill the vacant ranks with a million freemen more,
   Shouting the battle-cry of freedom.

We will welcome to our numbers the loyal, true, and brave,
   Shouting the battle-cry of freedom,
And although they may be poor, not a man shall be a slave,
   Shouting the battle-cry of freedom.

So we're springing to the call from the East and from the West,
   Shouting the battle-cry of freedom,
And we'll hurl the rebel crew from the land we love the best,
   Shouting the battle-cry of freedom.

GEORGE FREDERICK ROOT

◈ THE BONNIE BLUE FLAG

We are a band of brothers
   And native to the soil,
Fighting for the property
   We gained by honest toil;
And when our rights were threatened,
   The cry rose near and far —
"Hurrah for the Bonnie Blue Flag
   That bears the single star!"

Chorus:
Hurrah! hurrah!
For Southern rights, hurrah!
Hurrah for the Bonnie Blue Flag
That bears the single star.

As long as the Union
   Was faithful to her trust,
Like friends and like brothers
   Both kind were we and just;
But now, when Northern treachery
   Attempts our rights to mar,

We hoist on high the Bonnie Blue Flag
   That bears the single star.

First gallant South Carolina
   Nobly made the stand,
Then came Alabama,
   Who took her by the hand;
Next quickly Mississippi,
   Georgia and Florida,
All raised on high the Bonnie Blue Flag
   That bears the single star.

And here's to old Virginia —
   The Old Dominion State —
With the young Confed'racy
   At length has linked her fate.
Impelled by her example,
   Now other states prepare
To hoist on high the Bonnie Blue Flag
   That bears the single star.

Then here's to our Confed'racy,
  Strong are we and brave,
Like patriots of old we'll fight
  Our heritage to save.
And rather than submit to shame,
  To die we would prefer;
So cheer for the Bonnie Blue Flag
  That bears the single star.

Then cheer, boys, cheer;
  Raise the joyous shout,
For Arkansas and North Carolina
  Now have both gone out;
And let another rousing cheer
  For Tennessee be given,
The single star of the Bonnie Blue Flag
  Has grown to be eleven.

HARRY McCARTY

61.

War, Industry, and Invention

During the Civil War, Scientific American, *a New York periodical founded in 1845, published a series of editorials pointing out that, although the war was having grave effects on society in general and impoverishing the South, it was stimulating industry and invention in the North. Week after week, the magazine catalogued Northern achievements, and in the following editorial of December 28, 1861, it summed up the year's progress.*

Source: *Scientific American*, December 28, 1861: "The Old Year's Progress."

AT THE CLOSE OF THE YEAR 1860, we congratulated our readers upon a year of unexampled national prosperity. Never before had the fields and orchards of our husbandmen yielded so profusely, or our manufacturers and merchants enjoyed a period of more profitable success. It would have afforded us intense pleasure had we been able to close our present volume in the same tones of peaceful gladness; but in thousands of workshops, factories, and farms, the hammer, the saw, and the plow have been laid aside for the sword, the rifle, and the cannon, and our country has become one vast camp of armed men. Fierce battles have been fought, and many brave men have fall-

en and now "sleep the sleep which knows no waking." Still there is much to cheer and awaken faith and hope for the future. Many philosophers believe that wars are tribulations which exert similar influences among the nations that thunderstorms do upon the atmosphere. They are evils while they exist, but when the clouds are dispersed, men breathe a purer and more serene atmosphere. May this be the happy consummation of our national troubles!

Although the vast insurrection has exerted a disorganizing influence upon many manufactures and other branches of business, it is really wonderful to witness the elasticity of our people and the facility with which they have adapted themselves to altered circumstances. Many old branches of industry have been destroyed, but new ones have sprung up, and there is now a great amount of industrial prosperity enjoyed in most of the manufacturing sections of our country.

The war has stimulated the genius of our people and directed it to the service of our country. Sixty-six new inventions relating to engines, implements, and articles of warfare have been illustrated in our columns, with no less than 147 figures. These embrace a great variety of cannon, rifles, shells, shot, tents, kits, and almost all articles found in the military vocabulary. Rodman's monster cannon, Dahlgren's howitzers, De Brame's revolving cannon, Winslow's steel cannon, and several others have been thus brought before the public. No man can really be intelligent in matters relating to modern warfare unless he has made himself acquainted with these inventions.

Other departments of industry have also been well represented. Our inventors have not devoted themselves exclusively to the invention of destructive implements; they have also cultivated the arts of peace. In the present volume of the *Scientific American* — extending only over six months — 160 different subjects have been illustrated, averaging from three to four figures each. It would take up too much space to enumer-ate all these; but in thus summing up our yearly progress in a general way, we can safely assert that for original and well-studied efforts of genius, they equal if they do not surpass the inventions of any former year. And as the number of patents issued is a very good exponent of the progress of our country, we can point to no less than 2,919, which is equal to the number (2,910) issued in 1857 — four years ago. When the defection of eleven states and the distractions of our country are taken into consideration, it is not too much to assert that our inventors have done better last year than ever before, and that inventions are perhaps the most safe and profitable sources of investment in times of war as well as peace.

Considering the nature and extent of the tremendous struggle in which our country is engaged, we have really great reason as a people to feel grateful and call this a prosperous year after all. Never before have our fields yielded so bountifully. The great West is surcharged with wheat and corn, and we are in the happy condition of enjoying a surplus of the necessaries of life. In thus viewing the past, we can still say with cheerfulness, "Thy face, old year, has been deeply furrowed by scars and tears, but it has also been illuminated with many sunny smiles."

1861 - 1864

62.

Mary Boykin Chesnut: Diary of a Southern Belle

Mary Boykin Chesnut was the daughter of a governor of South Carolina and the wife of a U.S. senator from the same state who later became a military aide to Jefferson Davis. Prior to the war, the Chesnuts lived comfortably on an estate in South Carolina, where Mrs. Chesnut kept a journal and occasionally wrote poetry and prose. With secession and the imminence of war, Mrs. Chesnut found herself torn between her dislike of slavery and her love for her land and people. In a state of emotional turmoil, she began to transform her lighthearted journal into an explosive diary that grew to 400,000 words in four years. "Few private papers and fewer public documents," remarks Louis Untermeyer, "give a greater sense of the havoc brought about by the Civil War than the diary of Mary Boykin Chesnut." Portions of her diary, beginning in February 1861 and continuing through September 1864, are reprinted here.

Source: *A Diary From Dixie*, Isabella D. Martin and Myrta L. Avary, eds., New York, 1905.

Montgomery, Alabama

February 19, 1861. The brand-new Confederacy is making or remodeling its constitution. Everybody wants Mr. Davis to be general in chief or president. Keitt and Boyce and a party preferred Howell Cobb for president. And the fire-eaters *per se* wanted Barnwell Rhett.

My brother Stephen brought the officers of the "Montgomery Blues" to dinner. "Very soiled Blues," they said, apologizing for their rough condition. Poor fellows! They had been a month before Fort Pickens and not allowed to attack it. They said

Colonel Chase built it, and so were sure it was impregnable. Colonel Lomax telegraphed to Governor Moore if he might try to take it, "Chase or no Chase," and got for his answer, "No." "And now," say the Blues, "we have worked like niggers, and when the fun and fighting begin, they send us home and put regulars there." They have an immense amount of powder. The wheel of the car in which it was carried took fire. There was an escape for you! We are packing a hamper of eatables for them.

I am despondent once more. If I thought them in earnest because at first they put their best in front, what now? We have to meet tremendous odds by pluck, activity, zeal, dash, endurance of the toughest, military instinct. We have had to choose born leaders of men who could attract love and secure trust. Everywhere political intrigue is as rife as in Washington. . . .

February 25. Find everyone working very hard here. As I dozed on the sofa last night, could hear the scratch, scratch of my husband's pen as he wrote at the table until midnight.

After church today, Captain Ingraham called. He left me so uncomfortable. He dared to express regrets that he had to leave the United States Navy. He had been stationed in the Mediterranean, where he liked to be and expected to be these two years and to take those lovely daughters of his to Florence. Then came Abraham Lincoln and rampant black Republicanism, and he must lay down his life for South Carolina. He, however, does not make any moan. He says we lack everything necessary in naval gear to retake Fort Sumter. Of course, he only expects the navy to take it. He is a fish out of water here. He is one of the finest sea captains; so I suppose they will soon give him a ship and send him back to his own element.

At dinner, Judge —— was loudly abusive of congress. He said: "They have trampled the constitution underfoot. They have provided President Davis with a house." He was disgusted with the folly of parading the president at the inauguration in a coach drawn by four white horses. Then someone said Mrs. Fitzpatrick was the only lady who sat with the congress. After the inaugural she poked Jeff Davis in the back with her parasol that he might turn and speak to her. "I am sure that was democratic enough," said someone.

Governor Moore came in with the latest news — a telegram from Governor Pickens to the president — "that a war steamer is lying off the Charleston bar laden with re-enforcements for Fort Sumter, and what must we do?" Answer: "Use your own discretion!" There is faith for you, after all is said and done. It is believed there is still some discretion left in South Carolina fit for use.

Everybody who comes here wants an office, and the many who, of course, are disappointed raise a cry of corruption against the few who are successful. I thought we had left all that in Washington. Nobody is willing to be out of sight, and all will take office.

"Constitution" Browne says he is going to Washington for twenty-four hours. I mean to send by him to Mary Garnett for a bonnet ribbon. If they take him up as a traitor, he may cause a civil war. War is now our dread. Mr. Chesnut told him not to make himself a bone of contention.

Everybody means to go into the army. If Sumter is attacked, then Jeff Davis' troubles will begin. The Judge says a military despotism would be best for us — anything to prevent a triumph of the Yankees. All right, but every man objects to any despot but himself.

Mr. Chesnut, in high spirits, dines today with the Louisiana delegation. Breakfasted with "Constitution" Browne, who is appointed assistant secretary of state, and so does not go to Washington. There was at table the man who advertised for a wife, with the wife so obtained. She was not pretty. We dine at Mr. Pollard's and go to a ball afterward at Judge Bibb's. The *New York Herald* says Lincoln stood before Washington's picture at his inauguration, which was taken by the country as a good sign. We are always frantic for a good sign. Let us pray that a Caesar or a Napoleon may be sent us. That would be our best sign of success. But they still say, "No war." Peace let it be, kind Heaven! . . .

March 5. We stood on the balcony to see our Confederate flag go up. Roars of cannon, etc., etc. Miss Sanders complained (so said Captain Ingraham) of the deadness of the mob. "It was utterly spiritless," she said; "no cheering, or so little, and no enthusiasm." Captain Ingraham suggested that gentlemen "are apt to be quiet," and this was "a thoughtful crowd, the true mob element with us just now is hoeing corn." And yet! It is uncomfortable that the idea has gone abroad that we have no joy, no pride in this thing. The band was playing "Massa in the Cold, Cold Ground." Miss Tyler, daughter of the former President of the United States, ran up the flag.

Captain Ingraham pulled out of his pocket some verses sent to him by a Boston girl. They were well rhymed and amounted to this: she held a rope ready to hang him, though she shed tears when she remembered his heroic rescue of Koszta. Koszta, the rebel! She calls us rebels, too. So it depends upon whom one rebels against — whether to save or not shall be heroic.

I must read Lincoln's inaugural. Oh, "comes he in peace, or comes he in war, or to tread but one measure as Young Lochinvar?" Lincoln's aim is to seduce the border states.

The people, the natives, I mean, are astounded that I calmly affirm, in all truth and candor, that if there were awful things in society in Washington, I did not see or hear of them. One must have been hard to please who did not like the people I knew in Washington. . . .

March 11. In full conclave tonight, the drawing room crowded with judges, governors, senators, generals, congressmen. They were exalting John C. Calhoun's hospitality. He allowed everybody to stay all night who chose to stop at his house. An ill-mannered person, on one occasion, refused to attend family prayers. Mr. Calhoun said to the servant, "Saddle that man's horse and let him go." From the traveler, Calhoun would take no excuse for the "Deity offended." I believe in Mr. Calhoun's hospitality but not in his family prayers. Mr. Calhoun's piety

was of the most philosophical type, from all accounts.

The latest news is counted good news; that is, the last man who left Washington tells us that Seward is in the ascendency. He is thought to be the friend of peace. The man did say, however, that "that serpent Seward is in the ascendency just now." . . .

Tuesday. Now this, they say, is positive: "Fort Sumter is to be released, and we are to have no war." After all, far too good to be true. Mr. Browne told us that, at one of the peace intervals (I mean intervals in the interest of peace), Lincoln flew through Baltimore, locked up in an express car. He wore a Scotch cap.

We went to the congress. Governor Cobb, who presides over that august body, put James Chesnut in the chair and came down to talk to us. He told us why the pay of congressmen was fixed in secret session and why the amount of it was never divulged — to prevent the lodging-house and hotel people from making their bills of a size to cover it all. "The bill would be sure to correspond with the pay," he said.

In the hotel parlor we had a scene. Mrs. Scott was describing Lincoln, who is of the cleverest Yankee type. She said: "Awfully ugly, even grotesque in appearance, the kind who are always at the corner stores, sitting on boxes, whittling sticks, and telling stories as funny as they are vulgar." Here I interposed: "But Stephen A. Douglas said one day to Mr. Chesnut, 'Lincoln is the hardest fellow to handle I have ever encountered yet.' " Mr. Scott is from California and said Lincoln is "an utter American specimen, coarse, rough, and strong; a good-natured, kind creature; as pleasant tempered as he is clever, and if this country can be joked and laughed out of its rights he is the kindhearted fellow to do it. Now if there is a war and it pinches the Yankee pocket instead of filling it ——"

Here a shrill voice came from the next

room (which opened upon the one we were in by folding doors thrown wide open) and said: "Yankees are no more mean and stingy than you are. People at the North are just as good as people at the South." The speaker advanced upon us in great wrath.

Mrs. Scott apologized and made some smooth, polite remark, though evidently much embarrassed. But the vinegar face and curly pate refused to receive any concessions and replied: "That comes with a very bad grace after what you were saying," and she harangued us loudly for several minutes. Someone in the other room giggled outright, but we were quiet as mice. Nobody wanted to hurt her feelings. She was one against so many. If I were at the North, I should expect them to belabor us and should hold my tongue. We separated North from South because of incompatibility of temper. We are divorced because we have hated each other so. If we could only separate, a *"separation à l'agréable,"* as the French say it, and not have a horrid fight for divorce.

The poor exile had already been insulted, she said. She was playing "Yankee Doodle" on the piano before breakfast to soothe her wounded spirit, and the Judge came in and calmly requested her to "leave out the Yankee while she played the Doodle." The Yankee end of it did not suit our climate, he said; was totally out of place and had got out of its latitude.

A man said aloud: "This war talk is nothing. It will soon blow over. Only a fuss gotten up by that Charleston clique." Mr. Toombs asked him to show his passports, for a man who uses such language is a suspicious character.

Charleston, South Carolina

April 13. Fort Sumter has been on fire. Anderson has not yet silenced any of our guns. So the aides, still with swords and red sashes by way of uniform, tell us. But the sound of those guns makes regular meals impossible. None of us go to table. Tea trays pervade the corridors going everywhere. Some of the anxious hearts lie on their beds and moan in solitary misery. Mrs. Wigfall and I solace ourselves with tea in my room. These women have all a satisfying faith. "God is on our side," they say. When we are shut in, Mrs. Wigfall and I ask "Why?" "Of course, He hates the Yankees," we are told. "You'll think that well of Him."

Not by one word or look can we detect any change in the demeanor of these Negro servants. Lawrence sits at our door, sleepy and respectful and profoundly indifferent. So are they all, but they carry it too far. You could not tell that they even heard the awful roar going on in the bay, though it has been dinning in their ears night and day. People talk before them as if they were chairs and tables. They make no sign. Are they stolidly stupid, or wiser than we are; silent and strong, biding their time?

So tea and toast came; also came Colonel Manning, red sash and sword, to announce that he had been under fire, and didn't mind it. He said gaily: "It is one of those things a fellow never knows how he will come out until he has been tried. Now I know I am a worthy descendant of my old Irish hero of an ancestor, who held the British officer before him as a shield in the Revolution and backed out of danger gracefully." We talked of St. Valentine's eve, or the maid of Perth, and the drop of the white doe's blood that sometimes spoiled all.

The war steamers are still there, outside the bar. And there are people who thought the Charleston bar "no good" to Charleston. The bar is the silent partner, or sleeping partner, and in this fray it is doing us yeoman service.

April 15. I did not know that one could live such days of excitement. Someone called: "Come out! There is a crowd coming." A mob it was, indeed, but it was headed by Colonels Chesnut and Manning. The crowd was shouting and showing these two as messengers of good news. They were escorted to Beauregard's headquarters. Fort Sumter had surrendered! Those upon the housetops shouted to us, "The fort is on fire." That had been the story once or twice before.

When we had calmed down, Colonel Chesnut, who had taken it all quietly enough, if anything more unruffled than usual in his serenity, told us how the surrender came about. Wigfall was with them on Morris Island when they saw the fire in the fort; he jumped in a little boat, and with his handkerchief as a white flag, rowed over. Wigfall went in through a porthole. When Colonel Chesnut arrived shortly after and was received at the regular entrance, Colonel Anderson told him he had need to pick his way warily for the place was all mined. As far as I can make out, the fort surrendered to Wigfall. But it is all confusion. Our flag is flying there. Fire engines have been sent for to put out the fire. Everybody tells you half of something and then rushes off to tell something else or to hear the last news. . . .

Richmond, Virginia

June 27. At the depot in Richmond, Mr. Mallory, with Wigfall and Garnett, met us. We had no cause to complain of the warmth of our reception. They had a carriage for us, and our rooms were taken at the Spotswood. But then the people who were in the rooms engaged for us had not departed at the time they said they were going. They lingered among the delights of Richmond, and we knew of no law to make them keep their words and go. Mrs. Preston had gone for a few days to Manassas. So we took her room. Mrs. Davis is as kind as ever. She met us in one of the corridors accidentally and asked us to join her party

and to take our meals at her table. Mr. Preston came, and we moved into a room so small there was only space for a bed, washstand, and glass over it. My things were hung up out of the way on nails behind the door.

As soon as my husband heard we had arrived, he came, too. After dinner he sat smoking, the solitary chair of the apartment tilted against the door as he smoked, and my poor dresses were fumigated. I remonstrated feebly. "War times," said he; "nobody is fussy now. When I go back to Manassas tomorrow, you will be awfully sorry you snubbed me about those trumpery things up there." So he smoked the pipe of peace, for I knew that his remarks were painfully true. As soon as he was once more under the enemy's guns, I would repent in sackcloth and ashes.

Captain Ingraham came with Colonel Lamar. The latter said he could only stay five minutes; he was obliged to go back at once to his camp. That was a little before eight. However, at twelve he was still talking to us on that sofa. We taunted him with his fine words to the F.F.V. crowd before the Spotswood: "Virginia has no grievance. She raises her strong arm to catch the blow aimed at her weaker sisters." He liked it well, however, that we knew his speech by heart.

This Spotswood is a miniature world. The war topic is not so much avoided as that everybody has some personal dignity to take care of and everybody else is indifferent to it. I mean the "personal dignity of" *autrui.* In this wild confusion everything likely and unlikely is told you, and then everything is as flatly contradicted. At any rate, it is safest not to talk of the war.

Trescott was telling us how they laughed at little South Carolina in Washington. People said it was almost as large as Long Island, which is hardly more than a tail feather of New York. Always there is a child who sulks and won't play; that was our role. And we were posing as San Marino and all model-spirited, though small, republics, pose.

He tells us that Lincoln is a humorist. Lincoln sees the fun of things; he thinks if they had left us in a corner or out in the cold awhile pouting, with our fingers in our mouth, by hook or by crook he could have got us back, but Anderson spoiled all.

In Mrs. Davis' drawing room last night, the president took a seat by me on the sofa where I sat. He talked for nearly an hour. He laughed at our faith in our own powers. We are like the British. We think every Southerner equal to three Yankees at least. We will have to be equivalent to a dozen now. After his experience of the fighting qualities of Southerners in Mexico, he believes that we will do all that can be done by pluck and muscle, endurance, and dogged courage, dash, and red-hot patriotism. And yet his tone was not sanguine. There was a sad refrain running through it all. For one thing, either way, he thinks it will be a long war. That floored me at once. It has been too long for me already. Then he said, before the end came, we would have many a bitter experience. He said only fools doubted the courage of the Yankees or their willingness to fight when they saw fit. And now that we have stung their pride, we have roused them till they will fight like devils. . . .

July 27. Mrs. Davis' drawing room last night was brilliant, and she was in great force. Outside, a mob called for the president. He did speak — an old war-horse who scents the battlefields from afar. His enthusiasm was contagious. They called for Colonel Chesnut, and he gave them a capital speech, too. As public speakers say sometimes, "It was the proudest moment of my life." I did not hear a great deal of it, for always, when anything happens of any moment, my heart beats up in my ears; but the distinguished Carolinians who crowded round told me how good a speech he made.

I was dazed. There goes the "Dead March" for some poor soul.

Today, the president told us at dinner that Mr. Chesnut's eulogy of Bartow in the congress was highly praised. Men liked it. Two eminently satisfactory speeches in twenty-four hours is doing pretty well. And now I could be happy, but this cabinet of ours are in such bitter quarrels among themselves — everybody abusing everybody.

Last night, while those splendid descriptions of the battle were being given to the crowd below from our windows, I said: "Then, why do we not go on to Washington?" "You mean why did they not; the opportunity is lost." Mr. Barnwell said to me: "Silence, we want to listen to the speaker"; and Mr. Hunter smiled compassionately, "Don't ask awkward questions."

Kirby Smith came down on the turnpike in the very nick of time. Still, the heroes who fought all day and held the Yankees in check deserve credit beyond words, or it would all have been over before the Joe Johnston contingent came. It is another case of the eleventh-hour scrape; the eleventh-hour men claim all the credit, and they who bore the heat and brunt and burden of the day do not like that.

Everybody said at first, "Pshaw! There will be no war." Those who foresaw evil were called ravens, ill-foreboders. Now the same sanguine people all cry, "The war is over" — the very same who were packing to leave Richmond a few days ago. Many were ready to move on at a moment's warning, when the good news came. There are such owls everywhere.

But, to revert to the other kind, the sage and circumspect, those who say very little, but that little shows they think the war barely begun. Mr. Rives and Mr. Seddon have just called. Arnoldus Van der Horst came to see me at the same time. He said there was no great show of victory on our side until 2 o'clock, but when we began to win, we did it in double-quick time. I mean, of course, the battle last Sunday.

Arnold Harris told Mr. Wigfall the news from Washington last Sunday. For hours the telegrams reported at rapid intervals, "Great victory," "Defeating them at all points." The couriers began to come in on horseback, and at last, after 2 or 3 o'clock, there was a sudden cessation of all news. About nine messengers with bulletins came on foot or on horseback — wounded, weary, draggled, footsore, panic-stricken — spreading in their path, on every hand, terror and dismay. That was our opportunity. Wigfall can see nothing that could have stopped us, and when they explain why we did not go to Washington, I understand it all less than ever. Yet here we will dilly-dally, and congress orate, and generals parade, until they in the North get up an army three times as large as McDowell's, which we have just defeated.

Trescott says this victory will be our ruin. It lulls us into a fool's paradise of conceit at our superior valor, and the shameful farce of their flight will wake every inch of their manhood. It was the very fillip they needed. There are a quieter sort here who know their Yankees well. They say if the thing begins to pay — government contracts and all that — we will never hear the end of it, at least, until they get their pay in some way out of us. They will not lose money by us. Of that we may be sure. Trust Yankee shrewdness and vim for that.

There seems to be a battle raging at Bethel, but no mortal here can be got to think of anything but Manassas. Mrs. McLean says she does not see that it was such a great victory, and if it be so great, how can one defeat hurt a nation like the North.

John Waties fought the whole battle over for me. Now I understand it. Before this, nobody would take the time to tell the thing consecutively, rationally, and in order. Mr. Venable said he did not see a braver thing done than the cool performance of a

Columbia Negro. He carried his master a bucket of ham and rice, which he had cooked for him, and he cried: "You must be so tired and hungry, marster; make haste and eat." This was in the thickest of the fight, under the heaviest of the enemy's guns.

The Federal congressmen had been making a picnic of it; their luggage was all ticketed to Richmond. Cameron has issued a proclamation. They are making ready to come after us on a magnificent scale. They acknowledge us at last foemen worthy of their steel. The Lord help us, since England and France won't, or don't. If we could only get a friend outside and open a port.

One of these men told me he had seen a Yankee prisoner who asked him "what sort of a diggins Richmond was for trade." He was tired of the old concern and would like to take the oath and settle here. They brought us handcuffs found in the debacle of the Yankee army. For whom were they? Jeff Davis, no doubt, and the ringleaders. "Tell that to the marines." We have outgrown the handcuff business on this side of the water. . . .

August 27. The North is consolidated; they move as one man, with no states but an army organized by the central power. Russell in the Northern camp is cursed of Yankees for that Bull Run letter. Russell, in his capacity of Englishman, despises both sides. He divides us equally into North and South. He prefers to attribute our victory at Bull Run to Yankee cowardice rather than to Southern courage. He gives no credit to either side; for good qualities, we are after all mere Americans! Everything not "national" is arrested. It looks like the business of Seward.

I do not know when I have seen a woman without knitting in her hand. Socks for the soldiers is the cry. One poor man said he had dozens of socks and but one shirt. He preferred more shirts and fewer stockings. We make a quaint appearance with this twinkling of needles and the everlasting sock dangling below. . . .

Columbia, South Carolina

April 29, 1862. A grand smash, the news from New Orleans fatal to us. Met Mr. Weston. He wanted to know where he could find a place of safety for 200 Negroes. I looked into his face to see if he were in earnest; then to see if he were sane. There was a certain set of 200 Negroes that had grown to be a nuisance. Apparently all the white men of the family had felt bound to stay at home to take care of them. There are people who still believe Negroes property — like Noah's neighbors, who insisted that the deluge would only be a little shower after all.

These Negroes, however, were Plowden Weston's, a totally different part of speech. He gave field rifles to one company and $40,000 to another. He is away with our army at Corinth. So I said: "You may rely upon Mr. Chesnut, who will assist you to his uttermost in finding a home for these people. Nothing belonging to that patriotic gentleman shall come to grief if we have to take charge of them on our own place." Mr. Chesnut did get a place for them, as I said he would.

Had to go to the governor's or they would think we had hoisted the black flag. Heard there we are going to be beaten as Cortez beat the Mexicans — by superior arms. Mexican bows and arrows made a poor showing in the face of Spanish accouterments. Our enemies have such superior weapons of war; we, hardly any but what we capture from them in the fray. The Saxons and the Normans were in the same plight.

War seems a game of chess, but we have an unequal number of pawns to begin with. We have knights, kings, queens, bishops, and castles enough. But our skillful generals, whenever they cannot arrange the board

to suit them exactly, burn up everything and march away. We want them to save the country. They seem to think their whole duty is to destroy ships and save the army.

Mr. Robert Barnwell wrote that he had to hang his head for South Carolina. We had not furnished our quota of the new levy, 5,000 men. Today, Colonel Chesnut published his statement to show that we have sent 13,000, instead of the mere number required of us; so Mr. Barnwell can hold up his head again.

May 24. The enemy are landing at Georgetown. With a little more audacity, where could they not land? But we have given them such a scare, they are cautious. If it be true, I hope some cool-headed white men will make the Negroes save the rice for us. It is so much needed. They say it might have been done at Port Royal with a little more energy. South Carolinians have pluck enough, but they only work by fits and starts; there is no continuous effort; they can't be counted on for steady work. They will stop to play or enjoy life in some shape.

Without let or hindrance, Halleck is being reenforced. Beauregard, unmolested, was making some fine speeches and issuing proclamations while we were fatuously looking for him to make a tiger's spring on Huntsville. Why not? Hope springs eternal in the Southern breast. . . .

Columbia is the place for good living, pleasant people, pleasant dinners, pleasant drives. I feel that I have put the dinners in the wrong place. They are the climax of the good things here. This is the most hospitable place in the world, and the dinners are worthy of it.

In Washington, there was an endless succession of state dinners. I was kindly used. I do not remember ever being condemned to two dull neighbors; on one side or the other was a clever man, so I liked Washington dinners.

In Montgomery, there were a few dinners — Mrs. Pollard's, for instance — but the society was not smoothed down or in shape. Such as it was it was given over to balls and suppers. In Charleston, Mr. Chesnut went to gentlemen's dinners all the time; no ladies present. Flowers were sent to me, and I was taken to drive and asked to tea. There could not have been nicer suppers, more perfect of their kind than were to be found at the winding up of those festivities.

In Richmond, there were balls, which I did not attend — very few to which I was asked: the MacFarlands' and Lyons', all I can remember. James Chesnut dined out nearly every day. But then the breakfasts — the Virginia breakfasts — where were always pleasant people. Indeed, I have had a good time everywhere — always clever people, and people I liked, and everybody so good to me.

Here in Columbia, family dinners are the specialty. You call, or they pick you up and drive home with you. "Oh, stay to dinner!" and you stay gladly. They send for your husband, and he comes willingly. Then comes a perfect dinner. You do not see how it could be improved; and yet they have not had time to alter things or add because of the unexpected guests. They have everything of the best — silver, glass, china, table linen and damask, etc. And then the planters live "within themselves," as they call it. From the plantations come mutton, beef, poultry, cream, butter, eggs, fruits, and vegetables. . . .

June 6. Paul Hayne, the poet, has taken rooms here. My husband came and offered to buy me a pair of horses. He says I need more exercise in the open air. "Come, now, are you providing me with the means of a rapid retreat?" said I. "I am pretty badly equipped for marching."

Mrs. Rose Greenhow is in Richmond. One-half of the ungrateful Confederates say Seward sent her. My husband says the Confederacy owes her a debt it can never pay. She warned them at Manassas, and so they got Joe Johnston and his Paladins to appear upon the stage in the very nick of time. In Washington they said Lord Napier left her a legacy to the British Legation, which accepted the gift, unlike the British nation, who would not accept Emma Hamilton and her daughter Horatia, though they were willed to the nation by Lord Nelson. . . .

June 10. General Scott, on Southern soldiers, says, we have *élan*, courage, woodcraft, consummate horsemanship, endurance of pain equal to the Indians, but that we will not submit to discipline. We will not take care of things or husband our resources. Where we are, there is waste and destruction. If it could all be done by one wild, desperate dash, we would do it. But he does not think we can stand the long, blank months between the acts — the waiting! We can bear pain without a murmur, but we will not submit to be bored, etc.

Now, for the other side. Men of the North can wait; they can bear discipline; they can endure forever. Losses in battle are nothing to them. Their resources in men and materials of war are inexhaustible, and if they see fit they will fight to the bitter end. Here is a nice prospect for us — as comfortable as the old man's croak at Mulberry, "Bad times, worse coming."

Mrs. McCord says, "In the hospital the better born, that is, those born in the purple, the gentry, those who are accustomed to a life of luxury, are the better patients. They endure in silence. They are hardier, stronger, tougher, less liable to break down than the sons of the soil." "Why is that?" I asked; and she answered, "Something in man that is more than the body."

I know how it feels to die. I have felt it again and again. For instance, someone calls out, "Albert Sidney Johnston is killed." My heart stands still. I feel no more. I am, for so many seconds, so many minutes, I know not how long, utterly without sensation of any kind — dead; and then there is that great throb, that keen agony of physical pain, and the works are wound up again. The ticking of the clock begins, and I take up the burden of life once more. Some day it will stop too long, or my feeble heart will be too worn out to make that awakening jar, and all will be over. I do not think when the end comes that there will be any difference, except the miracle of the new windup throb. And now good news is just as exciting as bad. "Hurrah, Stonewall has saved us!" The pleasure is almost pain because of my way of feeling it.

Miriam's Luryea and the coincidences of his life. He was born Moses and is the hero of the bombshell. His mother was at a hotel in Charleston when kindhearted Anna De Leon Moses went for her sister-in-law and gave up her own chamber that the child might be born in the comfort and privacy of a home. Only our people are given to such excessive hospitality. So little Luryea was born in Anna De Leon's chamber. After Chickahominy, when he, now a man, lay mortally wounded, Anna Moses, who was living in Richmond, found him, and she brought him home, though her house was crowded to the doorsteps. She gave up her chamber to him, and so, as he had been born in her room, in her room he died.

June 12. New England's Butler, best known to us as "Beast" Butler, is famous or infamous now. His amazing order to his soldiers at New Orleans and comments on it are in everybody's mouth. We hardly expected from Massachusetts behavior to shame a Comanche. . . .

Richmond, Virginia

January 1, 1864. General Hood's an awful flatterer — I mean an awkward flatterer. I told him to praise my husband to someone else, not to me. He ought to praise me to somebody who would tell my husband, and then praise my husband to another person who would tell me. Man and wife are too much one person; to wave a compliment straight in the face of one about the other is not graceful.

One more year of "Stonewall" would have saved us. Chickamauga is the only battle we have gained since "Stonewall" died, and no results follow as usual. "Stonewall" was not so much as killed by a Yankee; he was shot by his own men; that is hard. General Lee can do no more than keep back Meade. "One of Meade's armies, you mean," said I, "for they have only to double on him when Lee whips one of them."

Gen. Edward Johnston says he got Grant a place — *esprit de corps,* you know. He could not bear to see an old army man driving a wagon; that was when he found him out West, put out of the army for habitual drunkenness. He is their right man, a bullheaded Suwarrow. He don't care a snap if men fall like the leaves fall; he fights to win, that chap does. He is not distracted by a thousand side issues; he does not see them. He is narrow and sure — sees only in a straight line. Like Louis Napoleon, from a battle in the gutter, he goes straight up. Yes, as with Lincoln, they have ceased to carp at him as a rough clown, no gentleman, etc. You never hear now of Lincoln's nasty fun; only of his wisdom. Doesn't take much soap and water to wash the hands that the rod of empire sway. They talked of Lincoln's drunkenness, too. Now, since Vicksburg, they have not a word to say against Grant's habits. He has the disagreeable habit of not retreating before irresistible veterans.

General Lee and Albert Sidney Johnston show blood and breeding. They are of the Bayard and Philip Sidney order of soldiers. Listen: If General Lee had had Grant's resources, he would have bagged the last Yankee or have had them all safe back in Massachusetts. "You mean if he had not the weight of the Negro question upon him?" "No, I mean if he had Grant's unlimited allowance of the powers of war — men, money, ammunition, arms."

Mrs. Ould says Mrs. Lincoln found the gardener of the White House so nice, she would make him a major general. Lincoln remarked to the secretary: "Well, the little woman must have her way sometimes." . . .

Columbia, South Carolina

March 24. Yesterday, we went to the capitol grounds to see our returned prisoners. We walked slowly up and down until Jeff Davis was called upon to speak. There I stood, almost touching the bayonets when he left me. I looked straight into the prisoners' faces, poor fellows. They cheered with all their might, and I wept for sympathy and enthusiasm. I was very deeply moved. These men were so forlorn, so dried up and shrunken, with such a strange look in some of their eyes; others so restless and wild looking; others, again, placidly vacant, as if they had been dead to the world for years. A poor woman was too much for me. She was searching for her son. He had been expected back. She said he was taken prisoner at Gettysburg. She kept going in and out among them with a basket of provisions she had brought for him to eat. It was too pitiful. She was utterly unconscious of the crowd. The anxious dread, expectation, hurry, and hope which led her on showed in her face.

A sister of Mrs. Lincoln is here. She brings the freshest scandals from Yankeeland. She says she rode with Lovejoy. A friend of hers commands a black regiment. Two Southern horrors — a black regiment and Lovejoy.

September 21. Went with Mrs. Rhett to hear Dr. Palmer. I did not know before how utterly hopeless was our situation. This man is so eloquent, it was hard to listen and not give way. Despair was his word, and martyrdom. He offered us nothing more in this world than the martyr's crown. He is not for slavery, he says; he is for freedom, and the freedom to govern our own country as we see fit. He is against foreign interference in our state matters. That is what Mr. Palmer went to war for, it appears. Every day shows that slavery is doomed the world over; for that he thanked God. He spoke of our agony, and then came the cry, "Help us, O God! Vain is the help of man." And so we came away shaken to the depths.

The end has come. No doubt of the fact. Our army has so moved as to uncover Macon and Augusta. We are going to be wiped off the face of the earth. What is there to prevent Sherman taking General Lee in the rear? We have but two armies, and Sherman is between them now.

September 24. These stories of our defeats in the valley fall like blows upon a dead body. Since Atlanta fell, I have felt as if all were dead within me forever. Captain Ogden, of General Chesnut's staff, dined here today. Had ever brigadier, with little or no brigade, so magnificent a staff? The reserves, as somebody said, have been secured only by robbing the cradle and the grave — the men too old, the boys too young. Isaac Hayne, Edward Barnwell, Bacon, Ogden, Richardson, Miles are the picked men of the agreeable world.

———◆———

If the people [of Georgia] raise a howl against my barbarity and cruelty, I will answer that war is war, and not popularity-seeking.

GENERAL WILLIAM TECUMSEH SHERMAN, during his march to the sea

1862

63.

John S. Rock: Negro Hopes for Emancipation

Many Negroes saw in the Civil War the promise of emancipation. One of the most prominent Negro leaders was Dr. John S. Rock, a Boston physician and attorney and the first Negro lawyer admitted to the bar of the U.S. Supreme Court. His speeches have a contemporary ring, for he was one of the few leaders who looked beyond the immediate issues of the war to ask what would become of the free Negro in a white society. In a speech delivered in 1858 he sought to answer his own question. "When the avenues to wealth are opened to us," he declared, "we will then become educated and wealthy, and then the roughest looking colored man that you ever saw . . . will be pleasanter than the harmonies of Orpheus, and black will be a very pretty color." The speech reprinted below was given on January 23, 1862, before the Massachusetts Anti-Slavery Society.

Source: *Liberator*, February 14, 1862.

Ladies and Gentlemen:

I am here not so much to make a speech as to add a little more *color* to this occasion.

I do not know that it is right that I should speak at this time, for it is said that we have talked too much already; and it is being continually thundered in our ears that the time for speechmaking has ended, and the time for action has arrived. Perhaps this is so. This may be the theory of the people, but we all know that the *active* idea has found but little sympathy with either of our great military commanders or the national executive; for they have told us, again and again, that "patience is a cure for all sores," and that we must wait for the "good time," which, to us, has been long a-coming.

It is not my desire, neither is it the time for me, to criticize the government, even if I had the disposition so to do. The situation of the black man in this country is far from being an enviable one. Today, our heads are in the lion's mouth, and we must get them out the best way we can. To contend against the government is as difficult as it is to sit in Rome and fight with the pope. It is probable that, if we had the malice of the Anglo-Saxon, we would watch our chances and seize the first opportunity to take our revenge. If we attempted this, the odds would be against us, and the first thing we should know would be — *nothing!* The most of us are capable of perceiving that the man who spits against the wind spits in his own face!

While Mr. Lincoln has been more conservative than I had hoped to find him, I recognize in him an honest man, striving to redeem the country from the degradation and shame into which Mr. Buchanan and his predecessors have plunged it.

This nation is mad. In its devoted attachment to the Negro, it has run crazy after him; and now, having caught him, hangs on with a deadly grasp, and says to him, with more earnestness and pathos than Ruth expressed to Naomi, "Where thou goest, I will go; where thou lodgest, I will lodge; thy people shall be my people, and thy God my God." . . .

I do not deny that there is a deep and cruel prejudice lurking in the bosoms of the white people of this country. It is much more abundant in the North than in the South. Here, it is to be found chiefly among the higher and lower classes; and there is no scarcity of it among the poor whites at the South.

The cause of this prejudice may be seen at a glance. The educated and wealthy class despise the Negro because they have robbed him of his hard earnings or, at least, have got rich off the fruits of his labor; and they believe if he gets his freedom, their fountain will be dried up, and they will be obliged to seek business in a new channel. Their "occupation will be gone." The lowest class hate him because he is poor, as they are, and is a competitor with them for the same labor. The poor, ignorant white man, who does not understand that the interest of the laboring classes is mutual, argues in this wise: "Here is so much labor to be performed, that darkey does it. If he was gone, I should have his place." The rich and the poor are both prejudiced from interest, and not because they entertain vague notions of justice and humanity.

While uttering my solemn protest against this American vice, which has done more than any other thing to degrade the American people in the eyes of the civilized world, I am happy to state that there are many who have never known this sin, and many others who have been converted to the truth by the "foolishness of antislavery preaching," and are deeply interested in the welfare of the race, and never hesitate to use their means and their influence to help break off the yoke that has been so long crushing us. I thank them all and hope the number may be multiplied, until we shall have a people who will know no man save by his virtues and his merits.

Now, it seems to me that a blind man can see that the present war is an effort to nationalize, perpetuate, and extend slavery in this country. In short, slavery is the cause of the war: I might say, is *the* war itself. Had it not been for slavery, we should have had no war! Through 240 years of indescribable tortures, slavery has wrung out of the blood, bones, and muscles of the Negro hundreds of millions of dollars and helped much to make this nation rich. At the same time, it has developed a volcano which has burst forth, and, in a less number of days than years, has dissipated this wealth and rendered the government bankrupt! And, strange as it may appear, you still cling to this monstrous iniquity, notwithstanding it is daily sinking the country lower and lower! Some of our ablest and best men have been sacrificed to appease the wrath of this American god. . . .

The government wishes to bring back the country to what it was before. This is possible; but what is to be gained by it? If we are fools enough to retain the cancer that is eating out our vitals, when we can safely extirpate it, who will pity us if we see our mistake when we are past recovery? The Abolitionists saw this day of tribulation and reign of terror long ago, and warned you of it; *but you would not hear!* You now say that it is their agitation which has brought about this terrible civil war! That is to say, your friend sees a slow match set near a keg of gunpowder in your house and timely warns you of the danger which he sees is inevitable; you despise his warning, and, after the explosion, say, if he had not told you of it, it would not have happened!

Now, when some leading men who hold with the policy of the President, and yet pretend to be liberal, argue that while they are willing to admit that the slave has an undoubted right to his liberty, the master has an equal right to his property; that to liberate the slave would .be to injure the master, and a greater good would be accomplished to the country in these times by the loyal master's retaining his property than by giving to the slave his liberty — I do not understand it so. Slavery is treason against God, man, and the nation. The master has no right to be a partner in a conspiracy which has shaken the very foundation of the government. Even to apologize for it, while in open rebellion, is to aid and abet in treason. The master's right to his property in human flesh cannot be equal to the slave's right to his liberty.

The former right is acquired, either by kidnaping or unlawful purchase from kidnapers, or inheritance from kidnapers. The very claim invalidates itself. On the other hand, liberty is the inalienable right of every human being; and liberty can make no compromise with slavery. . . .

Today, when it is a military necessity, and when the safety of the country is dependent upon emancipation, our humane political philosophers are puzzled to know what would become of the slaves if they were emancipated! The idea seems to prevail that the poor things would suffer if robbed of the glorious privileges that they now enjoy! If they could not be flogged, half starved, and work to support in ease and luxury those who have never waived an opportunity to outrage and wrong them, they would pine away and die! Do you imagine that the Negro can live outside of slavery? Of course, now, they can take care of themselves and their masters too; but if you give them their liberty, must they not suffer?

Have you never been able to see through all this? Have you not observed that the location of this organ of sympathy is in the pocket of the slaveholder and the man who shares in the profits of slave labor? Of course you have; and pity those men who have lived upon their ill-gotten wealth. You know, if they do not have somebody to work for them, they must leave their gilded *salons,* and take off their coats and roll up their sleeves, and take their chances among the *live* men of the world. This, you are aware, these respectable gentlemen will not do, for they have been so long accustomed to live by robbing and cheating the Negro that they are sworn never to work while they can live by plunder.

Can the slaves take care of themselves? What do you suppose becomes of the thousands who fly, ragged and penniless, from the South every year, and scatter themselves throughout the free states of the North? Do they take care of themselves? I am neither ashamed nor afraid to meet this question. Assertions like this, long uncontradicted, seem to be admitted as established facts. I ask your attention for one moment to the fact that colored men at the North are shut out of almost every avenue to wealth, and, yet, strange to say, the proportion of paupers is much less among us than among you!

Are the beggars in the streets of Boston colored men? In Philadelphia, where there is a larger free colored population than is to be found in any other city in the free states, and where we are denied every social privilege, and are not even permitted to send our children to the schools that we are taxed to support, or to ride in the city horsecars, yet even there we pay taxes enough to support our own poor, and have a balance of a few thousand in our favor, which goes to support those "poor whites" who "can't take care of themselves."

Many of those who advocate emancipation as a military necessity seem puzzled to know what is best to be done with the slave if he is set at liberty. Colonization in Africa, Haiti, Florida, and South America are favorite theories with many well-informed persons. This is really interesting! No wonder Europe does not sympathize with you. You are the only people, claiming to be civilized, who take away the rights of those whose color differs from your own. If you find that you cannot rob the Negro of his labor and of himself, you will banish him! What a sublime idea! You are certainly a great people! What is your plea? Why, that the slaveholders will not permit us to live among them as freemen, and that the air of northern latitudes is not good for us! Let me tell you, my friends, *the slaveholders are not the men we dread!* They do not desire to have us removed. The Northern proslavery men have done the free people of color tenfold more injury than the Southern slaveholders. In the South, it is simply a question of dollars and cents. The slaveholder cares no more for you than he does for me. They enslave their own children and sell them, and they would as soon enslave white men as black men.

The secret of the slaveholder's attachment to slavery is to be found in the dollar, and *that* he is determined to get without working for it. There is no prejudice against color among the slaveholders. Their social system and 1 million mulattoes are facts which no arguments can demolish. If the slaves were emancipated, they would remain where they are. Black labor in the South is at a premium. The freeman of color there has always had the preference over the white laborer. Many of you are aware that Southerners will do a favor for a free colored man when they will not do it for a white man in the same condition in life. They believe in their institution because it supports them. . . .

Other countries are held out as homes for us. Why is this? Why is it that the people from all other countries are invited to come here, and we are asked to go away? Is it to make room for the refuse population of Europe? . . . Does anyone pretend to deny that this is our country, or that much of the wealth and prosperity found here is the result of the labor of our hands? . . . The free people of color have succeeded, in spite of every effort to crush them, and we are today a living refutation of that shameless assertion that we "can't take care of ourselves" in a state of freedom. . . .

When the orange is squeezed, we throw it aside. The black man is a good fellow while he is a slave and toils for nothing; but the moment he claims his own flesh and blood and bones, he is a most obnoxious creature, and there is a proposition to get rid of him! He is happy while he remains a poor, degraded, ignorant slave, without even the right to his own offspring. While in this condition, the master can ride in the same carriage, sleep in the same bed, and nurse from the same bosom. But give this same slave the right to use his own legs, his hands, his body, and his mind, and this happy and desirable creature is instantly transformed into a miserable and loathsome wretch, fit only to be colonized somewhere near the mountains of the moon or eternally banished from the presence of all civilized beings. You must not lose sight of the fact that it is the emancipated slave and the free colored man whom it is proposed to remove — not the slave. This country and climate are perfectly adapted to Negro slavery; it is the free black that the air is not good for! What an idea! A country good for slavery and not good for freedom! . . . *All the emigration and colonization societies that have been formed have been auxiliaries of the Slave Power and established for this purpose and the grand desire to make money out of our necessities.* . . .

I do not regard this trying hour as a dark one. The war that has been waged on us for more than two centuries has opened our eyes and caused us to form alliances, so that instead of acting on the defensive, we are now prepared to attack the enemy. This is simply a change of tactics. I think I see the finger of God in all this. Yes, *there* is the handwriting on the wall: *I come not to bring peace, but the sword. Break every yoke, and let the oppressed go free. I have heard the groans of my people and am come down to deliver them! . . .*

This rebellion for slavery means something! Out of it emancipation must spring. I do not agree with those men who see no hope in this war. There is nothing in it but hope. Our cause is onward. As it is with the sun, the clouds often obstruct his vision, but in the end we find there has been no standing still. It is true the government is but little more antislavery now than it was at the commencement of the war; but while fighting for its own existence, it has been obliged to take slavery by the throat and, sooner or later, *must* choke her to death.

64.

JULIA WARD HOWE: "The Battle Hymn of the Republic"

In her Reminiscences *(1899), Julia Ward Howe told the story of how she came to write "The Battle Hymn of the Republic." Returning from a visit to an army camp near Washington, in the company of her minister and a band of soldiers, she joined in singing the refrain of "John Brown's Body," which greatly pleased the soldiers. Her minister, Mr. Clarke, then asked her: "Mrs. Howe, why do you not write some good words for that stirring tune?" She replied that she had often wished to but was as yet uninspired. "I went to bed that night," she said, ". . . and as I lay waiting for the dawn, the long lines of the desired poem began to twine themselves in my mind. . . . I said to myself, I must get up and write these verses down, lest I fall asleep again and forget them. . . . I scrawled the verses almost without looking at the paper." The poem was published in the* Atlantic Monthly *in February 1862; she received a fee of $4. The poem, sung to the tune of "John Brown's Body," became the most famous hymn of the Union. It was Lincoln's favorite war song. After being showered with praise for her poem, Mrs. Howe was moved to say: "I wish very much that it may do some service in time of peace, which, I pray God, may never more be broken."*

Source: *Atlantic Monthly*, February 1862.

❧ THE BATTLE HYMN OF THE REPUBLIC

Mine eyes have seen the glory of the coming of the Lord;
He is trampling out the vintage where the grapes of wrath are stored;
He hath loosed the fateful lightning of His terrible swift sword;
    His truth is marching on.
     Chorus:
    Glory, glory, hallelujah,
    Glory, glory, hallelujah,
    Glory, glory, hallelujah,
       His truth is marching on.

I have seen Him in the watch-fires of a hundred circling camps;
They have builded Him an altar in the evening dews and damps;
I can read His righteous sentence by the dim and flaring lamps;
     His day is marching on.

I have read a fiery gospel writ in burnished rows of steel:
"As ye deal with My contemners, so with you My grace shall deal;
Let the Hero, born of woman, crush the serpent with His heel,
     Since God is marching on."

He has sounded forth the trumpet that shall never call retreat;
He is sifting out the hearts of men before His judgment seat:
Oh! be swift, my soul, to answer Him! be jubilant, my feet!
     Our God is marching on.

In the beauty of the lilies Christ was born across the sea,
With a glory in His bosom that transfigures you and me:
As He died to make men holy, let us die to make men free,
     While God is marching on.

65.

CHARLES SUMNER: Resolutions on Secession and Reconstruction

In October of 1861, Senator Charles Sumner of Massachusetts became one of the first prominent statesmen to urge emancipation and worked harder than any other man to see the goal realized. On February 11, 1862, Sumner presented to the Senate the following resolutions on secession and reconstruction. The resolutions reflected his famous doctrine that, by seceding, the Southern states had lost all their rights under the Constitution and, in effect, had committed political suicide.

Source: McPherson, pp. 322-323.

Resolutions declaratory of the relations between the United States and the territory once occupied by certain states, and now usurped by pretended governments, without constitutional or legal right.

Whereas certain states, rightfully belonging to the Union of the United States, have, through their respective governments, wickedly undertaken to abjure all those duties by which their connection with the Union was maintained; to renounce all allegiance to the Constitution; to levy war upon the national government; and, for the consummation of this treason, have unconstitutionally and unlawfully confederated together, with the declared purpose of putting an end by force to the supremacy of the Constitution within their respective limits;

And whereas this condition of insurrection, organized by pretended governments, openly exists in South Carolina, Georgia, Florida, Alabama, Mississippi, Louisiana, Texas, Arkansas, Tennessee, and Virginia, except in eastern Tennessee and western Virginia, and has been declared by the President of the United States, in a proclamation duly made in conformity with an act of Congress, to exist throughout this territory, with the exceptions already named;

And whereas the extensive territory thus usurped by these pretended governments and organized into a hostile confederation belongs to the United States, as an inseparable part thereof, under the sanctions of the Constitution, to be held in trust for the inhabitants in the present and future generations, and is so completely interlinked with the Union that it is forever dependent thereupon;

And whereas the Constitution, which is the supreme law of the land, cannot be displaced in its rightful operation within this territory, but must ever continue the supreme law thereof, notwithstanding of the doings of any pretended governments, acting singly or in confederation, in order to put an end to its supremacy; therefore,

1. *Resolved,* that any vote of secession or other act by which any state may undertake to put an end to the supremacy of the Constitution within its territory is inoperative and void against the Constitution, and when sustained by force it becomes a practical *abdication* by the state of all rights under the Constitution, while the treason which it involves still further works an instant *forfeiture* of all those functions and powers essential to the continued existence of the state as a body politic, so that from that time forward the territory falls under the exclusive jurisdiction of Congress as other territory, and the state being, according

to the language of the law, *felo-de-se,* ceases to exist.

2. That any combination of men assuming to act in place of such state, attempting to ensnare or coerce the inhabitants thereof into a confederation hostile to the Union, is rebellious, treasonable, and destitute of all moral authority; and that such combination is a usurpation incapable of any constitutional existence and utterly lawless, so that everything dependent upon it is without constitutional or legal support.

3. That the termination of a state under the Constitution necessarily causes the termination of those peculiar local institutions which, having no origin in the Constitution or in those natural rights which exist independent of the Constitution, are upheld by the sole and exclusive authority of the state.

4. That slavery, being a peculiar local institution, derived from local laws, without any origin in the Constitution or in natural rights, is upheld by the sole and exclusive authority of the state, and must therefore cease to exist legally or constitutionally when the state on which it depends no longer exists; for the incident cannot survive the principal.

5. That in the exercise of its exclusive jurisdiction over the territory once occupied by the states, it is the duty of Congress to see that the supremacy of the Constitution is maintained in its essential principles, so that everywhere in this extensive territory slavery shall cease to exist practically, as it has already ceased to exist constitutionally or legally.

6. That any recognition of slavery in such territory, or any surrender of slaves under the pretended laws of the extinct states by any officer of the United States, civil or military, is a recognition of the pretended governments, to the exclusion of the jurisdiction of Congress under the Constitution, and is in the nature of aid and comfort to the rebellion that has been organized.

7. That any such recognition of slavery or surrender of pretended slaves, besides being a recognition of the pretended governments, giving them aid and comfort, is a denial of the rights of persons who, by the extinction of the states, have become free, so that under the Constitution they cannot again be enslaved.

8. That allegiance from the inhabitant and protection from the government are corresponding obligations, dependent upon each other, so that while the allegiance of every inhabitant of this territory, without distinction of color or class, is due to the United States, and cannot in any way be defeated by the action of any pretended government, or by any pretense of property or claim to service, the corresponding obligation of protection is at the same time due by the United States to every such inhabitant, without distinction of color or class; and it follows that inhabitants held as slaves, whose paramount allegiance is due to the United States, may justly look to the national government for protection.

9. That the duty directly cast upon Congress by the extinction of the states is reinforced by the positive prohibition of the Constitution that "no state shall enter into any confederation," or "without the consent of Congress keep troops or ships of war in time of peace, or enter into any agreement or compact with another state," or "grant letters of marque and reprisal," or "coin money," or "emit bills of credit," or "without the consent of Congress lay any duties on imports or exports," all of which have been done by these pretended governments, and also by the positive injunction of the Constitution, addressed to the nation, that "the United States shall guarantee to every state in this Union a republican form of government"; and that in pursuance of this duty cast upon Congress, and further enjoined by the Constitution, Congress will assume complete jurisdiction of such vacated territory where such unconstitutional and illegal things have been attempted, and will proceed to establish therein republican forms of government under the Constitution; and in the execution of this trust will provide carefully for the protection of all the inhabitants thereof, for the security of families, the organization of labor, the encouragement of industry, and the welfare of society, and will in every way discharge the duties of a just, merciful, and paternal government.

We, on our side, are praying to Him to give us victory, because we believe we are right; but those on the other side pray to Him, look for victory, believing they are right. What must He think of us?

ABRAHAM LINCOLN

66.

WILLIAM H. SEWARD: American and European Interests in Mexico

In the decade preceding the Civil War, the American government was apprehensive about possible European intervention in the Americas. Mexico, beset by civil war, was forced to suspend payments on its foreign debts. On the pretext that European lives and property in Mexico were threatened, France, Spain, and England agreed to a joint military expedition to Mexico in October 1861 and invited the American government to participate. Secretary of State Seward declined. European soldiers landed in Mexico in 1862. When French Emperor Napoleon III's plan to establish a monarchy in Mexico became known, Spain and England withdrew. Napoleon installed Austrian Archduke Maximilian as emperor of Mexico, and, in effect, Mexico became a French protectorate. The Civil War made it impossible for the United States to intervene. On March 3, 1862, Seward sent the following dispatch to the American minister to England, Charles Francis Adams, explaining the U.S. attitude toward this violation of the Monroe Doctrine.

Source: 37 Congress, 2 Session, House Document No. 100, pp. 207-208.

WE OBSERVE INDICATIONS of a growing opinion in Europe that the demonstrations which are being made by Spanish, French, and British forces against Mexico are likely to be attended with a revolution in that country, which will bring in a monarchical government there, in which the crown will be assumed by some foreign prince.

This country is deeply concerned in the peace of nations, and aims to be loyal, at the same time, in all its relations, as well to the allies as to Mexico. The President has therefore instructed me to submit his views on the new aspect of affairs to the parties concerned. He has relied upon the assurances given to this government by the allies that they were seeking no political objects and only a redress of grievances. He does not doubt the sincerity of the allies, and his confidence in their good faith, if it could be shaken, would be reinspired by explanations apparently made in their behalf that the governments of Spain, France, and Great Britain are not intending to intervene and will not intervene to effect a change of the constitutional form of government now existing in Mexico, or to produce any political change there in opposition to the will of the Mexican people. Indeed, he understands the allies to be unanimous in declaring that the proposed revolution in Mexico is moved only by Mexican citizens now in Europe.

The President, however, deems it his duty to express to the allies, in all candor and frankness, the opinion that no monarchical government which could be founded in Mexico, in the presence of foreign navies and armies in the waters and upon the soil of Mexico, would have any prospect of security or permanency. Second, that the instability of such a monarchy there would be enhanced if the throne should be assigned to any person not of Mexican nativity. That under such circumstances the new government must speedily fall unless it could draw into its support European alliances, which, relating back to the present invasion, would, in fact, make it the beginning of a permanent policy of armed European monarchical intervention, injurious and practically hostile to the most general system of government on the continent of America, and this would be the beginning rather than the ending of revolution in Mexico.

These views are grounded upon some knowledge of the political sentiments and habits of society in America.

In such a case it is not to be doubted that the permanent interests and sympathies of this country would be with the other American republics. It is not intended on this occasion to predict the course of events which might happen as a consequence of the proceeding contemplated, either on this continent or in Europe. It is sufficient to say that, in the President's opinion, the emancipation of this continent from European control has been the principal feature in its history during the last century. It is not probable that a revolution in the contrary direction would be successful in an immediately succeeding century, while population in America is so rapidly increasing, resources so rapidly developing, and society so steadily forming itself upon principles of democratic American government. Nor is it necessary to suggest to the allies the improbability that European nations could steadily agree upon a policy favorable to such a counterrevolution as one conducive to their own interests, or to suggest that, however studiously the allies may act to avoid lend-

Library of Congress

William H. Seward; photo by Brady

ing the aid of their land and naval forces to domestic revolutions in Mexico, the result would nevertheless be traceable to the presence of those forces there, although for a different purpose, since it may be deemed certain that but for their presence there no such revolution could probably have been attempted or even conceived.

The Senate of the United States has not, indeed, given its official sanction to the precise measures which the President has proposed for lending our aid to the existing government in Mexico, with the approval of the allies, to relieve it from its present embarrassments. This, however, is only a question of domestic administration. It would be very erroneous to regard such a disagreement as indicating any serious difference of opinion in this government or among the American people in their cordial good wishes for the safety, welfare, and stability of the republican system of government in that country.

67.

Abraham Lincoln: A Plea for Compensated Emancipation

Compensated emancipation was a scheme to allow the government to free the slaves and reimburse slave-owners. The Republican platform of 1860 recognized it as a desirable solution to the slavery issue. President Lincoln initially viewed it as the best solution because it was gradual and would distribute the financial burden of emancipation. In addition, he hoped the plan would appeal to the border states. In response to growing antislavery sentiment, Lincoln sent the following special message to Congress urging a joint resolution on compensated emancipation on March 6, 1862. Congress approved the resolution, but the border states failed to support it. The plan was realized only in the District of Columbia by an act of Congress on April 16, 1862.

Source: Richardson, VI, pp. 68-69.

I RECOMMEND THE ADOPTION of a joint resolution by your honorable bodies, which shall be substantially as follows:

> *Resolved,* that the United States ought to cooperate with any state which may adopt gradual abolishment of slavery, giving to such state pecuniary aid, to be used by such state, in its discretion, to compensate for the inconveniences, public and private, produced by such change of system.

If the proposition contained in the resolution does not meet the approval of Congress and the country, there is the end; but if it does command such approval, I deem it of importance that the states and people immediately interested should be at once distinctly notified of the fact, so that they may begin to consider whether to accept or reject it. The Federal government would find its highest interest in such a measure as one of the most efficient means of self-preservation. The leaders of the existing insurrection entertain the hope that this government will ultimately be forced to acknowledge the independence of some part of the disaffected region, and that all the slave states north of such part will then say, "The Union for which we have struggled being already gone, we now choose to go with the Southern section." To deprive them of this hope substantially ends the rebellion, and the initiation of emancipation completely deprives them of it as to all the states initiating it.

The point is not that *all* the states tolerating slavery would very soon, if at all, initiate emancipation but that, while the offer is equally made to all, the more northern shall by such initiation make it certain to the more southern that in no event will the former ever join the latter in their proposed confederacy. I say "initiation" because, in my judgment, gradual and not sudden emancipation is better for all. In the mere financial or pecuniary view, any member of Congress with the census tables and Treasury reports before him can readily see for himself how very soon the current expenditures of this war would purchase, at fair valuation, all the slaves in any named state. Such a proposition on the part of the general government sets up no claim of a right by Federal authority to interfere with slavery within state limits, referring, as it does, the absolute control of the subject in each case to the state and its people immediately interested. It is proposed as a matter of perfectly free choice with them.

In the annual message last December, I thought fit to say "the Union must be preserved, and hence all indispensable means must be employed." I said this not hastily but deliberately. War has been made and continues to be an indispensable means to this end. A practical reacknowledgment of the national authority would render the war unnecessary, and it would at once cease. If, however, resistance continues, the war must also continue; and it is impossible to foresee all the incidents which may attend and all the ruin which may follow it. Such as may seem indispensable or may obviously prom-

ise great efficiency toward ending the struggle must and will come.

The proposition now made (though an offer only), I hope it may be esteemed no offense to ask whether the pecuniary consideration tendered would not be of more value to the states and private persons concerned than are the institution and property in it in the present aspect of affairs.

While it is true that the adoption of the proposed resolution would be merely initiatory, and not within itself a practical measure, it is recommended in the hope that it would soon lead to important practical results. In full view of my great responsibility to my God and to my country, I earnestly beg the attention of Congress and the people to the subject.

68.

Rose O'Neal Greenhow: Diary of a Confederate Spy

Rose O'Neal Greenhow was an untiring Confederate spy who operated out of Washington in the first year of the Civil War. She claimed to have contributed to the Confederate victory at Bull Run by learning in advance of the Northern strategy and informing General Beauregard. The government was aware that she was spying but could never find out how. She was jailed but carried on from her cell. The government at last threw up its hands and sentenced the lady spy to exile in the South. Instead, Mrs. Greenhow sailed to England to raise funds for the Confederacy. She was returning to the United States, with a substantial amount of gold, in 1864; but, before reaching the Carolina coast, was shipwrecked and drowned. Mrs. Greenhow kept a diary, an excerpt from which, dated March 25, 1862, is reprinted here.

Source: *My Imprisonment*, London, 1863.

THIS DAY I RECEIVED A SUMMONS to appear before United States commissioners for the trial of state prisoners. I decided to obey the summons as I felt some curiosity to know in what manner the trial would be conducted, what was the nature of the

charges against me, and to what results it would be likely to lead.

It was one of those raw, uncomfortable days in which the cold penetrated to the marrow. The sun was obscured by clouds as dark as Yankee deeds, and heavy flakes of

Mrs. Rose Greenhow and her daughter in Old Capitol Prison in Washington

snow were falling thick and fast. As I drove through the avenue from the prison to the provost marshal's office, which was at the other end of the city, the filth and desolation were appalling, for even in those first days of the occupation the effects had not been so visible. However, I had no time for reflection upon the contrast which the present and the past presented, as by this time the carriage drew near the provost marshal's. But here truly was there room for comparison.

This had been the house of Mrs. Gwin, one of the most elegant and agreeable in the city; and, as I passed up through the filthy halls and stairs, and the filthy crowd of soldiers and civilians who lined the way, my mind instinctively reverted to the gay and brilliant scenes in which I had mingled in that house, and the goodly company who had enjoyed its hospitality.

I was conducted to the third story, and put in a room without fire, and kept there until my hands and feet were completely benumbed with cold. A guard was stationed at the door, who rattled his musket in order that I should have a comfortable sense of his proximity. Numbers of officers in gay uniforms came in, upon one pretext or another, in order to stare at me. I was detained in this manner for nearly an hour, when the superintendent of the Old Capitol Prison, Mr. Wood, in whose custody I was still regarded as being, came to conduct me before the commissioners, whose presence I reached with difficulty — a passage being forced for me to pass through the soldiers who filled the antechamber.

Arriving before the door of the room in which the commissioners held their séance, it was thrown open, my name announced, and the commissioners advanced to receive me, with ill-concealed embarrassment. I bowed to them saying, "Gentlemen, resume your seats" (for they were still standing). "I recognize the embarrassment of your positions; it was a mistake in your government to have selected gentlemen for this mission. You have, however, shown me but scant courtesy in having kept me waiting your pleasure for nearly an hour in the cold."

They apologized, protesting their ignorance of my arrival, etc. Some few complimentary remarks followed, and I now took a survey of the scene.

A large table was placed in the middle of the room, at the upper end of which sat General Dix, and at the other extremity, Governor Fairfield. Mr. Webster, private secretary of Mr. Seward — as secretary of the commission — sat at a small table a little to the left of General Dix; and two other persons at a similar table to the rear of Governor Fairfield. My own seat was midway between the commissioners, in full view of the whole party.

Large piles of papers lay before General Dix, which he fingered uneasily, and seemed uncertain what to do. Governor Fairfield made some unimportant remark, to which I replied, "I suppose this is a mimic court, and I can answer or not, according to my own discretion."

One of the reporters now said, "If you

please to speak louder, madam." I rose from my seat and said to General Dix, "If it is your object to make a *spectacle* of me and furnish reports for the newspapers, I shall have the honor to withdraw from this presence."

Hereupon both of the commissioners arose and protested that they had no such intention; but that it was necessary to take notes in order to lay before the President and Congress. I then resumed my seat; and Governor Fairfield continued in a strain in no respects different from that of an ordinary conversation held in a drawing room; and to which I replied sarcastically or caustically, as suited my purpose; and a careless listener would have imagined that the commissioner was endeavoring with plausible argument to defend the government, rather than criminate me.

Finally, and after it had continued some time, I said, "But when is this dreadful ordeal — this trial for treason which has been heralded to the world with so much circumstance — to commence? For I can scarcely believe that I have been brought from my prison on this inclement day for the purpose of this very facetious and irrelevant conversation, or be induced to regard it in the light of a formal trial for life, liberty, and estate, attainder of blood, and all the other ills of feudal times."

At this the subordinates laughed outright. Governor Fairfield colored, attempted to speak several times, and changed his mind; and finally said, "General Dix, you are so much better acquainted with Mrs. Greenhow, suppose you continue the examination?"

I laughingly said, "Commence it, for I hold that it has not begun."

General Dix turned over and over again the papers before him, which were my letters seized by the detective police, and which, though relevant to the subject matter, had no legal importance or bearing at this time. He selected one, laying his hand

upon it, but still hesitated. I watched him keenly.

At last he said, "You are charged with treason."

"I deny it, sir. During the eight months of my imprisonment I have had ample time to study the Constitution of the United States, and there is no act or provision in it which will justify a charge of that nature against me."

"And so you deny the charge of treason?"

"I do, sir, most emphatically; and, moreover, retort the charge against yourself as being the minister of a President who has violated the Constitution, destroyed the personal rights of the citizen, and inaugurated revolution. At this moment, sir, you are presiding at, and conducting, a trial unlawful in every sense, and without even a pretense of the legal form prescribed; for the Constitution of the United States is very precise and specific as to the mode in which a trial for treason shall be conducted. It requires that the charge for treason shall be sustained by two respectable witnesses, which you could not find in all Yankeedom."

He then held up the letter which he had selected. I immediately recognized it as the one I had caused to be mailed in Baltimore. . . . I held out my hand, saying, "Let me see it." After a moment of indecision he gave it to me. I glanced my eye over its contents and returned it to him, saying, "It is rather a clever letter, is it not?"

General Dix replied, "Mrs. Greenhow requires no new testimony in favor of her ability in the use of her pen."

I bowed my head, "Well, General, what next have you to say?"

"You are charged, madam, with having caused a letter which you wrote to the secretary of state to be published in Richmond."

"That can scarcely be brought forward as

one of the causes for my arrest, as I was some three months a prisoner when that letter was written; and I, myself, regarded its undue publicity (prior to its publication at Richmond) as a grave cause of complaint against the secretary of state."

"You are charged, madam, with holding communication with the enemy in the South."

"If this were an established fact, you could not be surprised at it. I am a Southern woman, and I thank God that no drop of Yankee blood ever polluted my veins; and as all that I have ever honored or respected have been driven by ruthless despotism to seek shelter there, it would seem the most natural thing in life that I should have done so."

"How is it, madam, that you have managed to communicate in spite of the vigilance exercised over you?"

"That is my secret, sir; and, if it be any satisfaction to you to know it, I shall, in the next forty-eight hours, make a report to my government at Richmond of this rather farcical trial for treason."

"General McClellan, madam, charges you with having obtained a thorough knowledge of his plans, and of forcing him consequently four times to change them."

At this I smilingly shrugged my shoulders, without reply, saying, "Well, what else?"

After a few moments General Dix said, "Governor, I think we have nothing else to say to Mrs. Greenhow?" To which Governor Fairfield replied, "No, sir, I think not."

Of course I do not pretend to relate the entire conversation — for it could not be called an examination — but have gleaned the most important points. I now said, "It seems to me a little extraordinary that, after such grave charges as that of penetrating Cabinet secrets and fathoming and thwarting the plans of commanding generals, no curiosity should have been felt to arrive at the source of my so-called treason, if only

as a measure of prevention for the future, as it is but reasonable to suppose I must have had able coadjutors high in the national councils; and that this information must have sought me at my own house, as it can be clearly established that I have never crossed the threshold of a Lincolnite."

"Oh, that reminds me," resumed General Dix. "Did Lieutenant Sheldon ever take out communications for you?"

"Oh, certainly, by authority of the provost marshal. But if you wish to criminate Lieutenant Sheldon, you had better send for him and question him on that subject, as I certainly should not betray him or anyone else who might have rendered me a service."

General Dix asked, "Where is Lieutenant Sheldon?"

Mr. Webster replied, "With his regiment in Virginia."

General Dix then said, "I shall be very glad to serve you, madam, and shall certainly advise the government to allow you to go south, or consult your wishes in any other respects"; that he regretted deeply my extreme bitterness, for which he could see no reason, etc.

I replied, "That is the difference between *meum* and *tuum*. I have been now eight months a prisoner, subject during that period to every insult and outrage which capricious tyranny could invent; my property stolen and destroyed; shut up in close imprisonment; and actually suffering the torments of hunger.

"To this treatment has my child of eight years been also exposed, thereby seriously impairing her health. Not content with this, I have been daily assailed in the journals of the administration and sought to be dragged down to the level of the inmates of your White House. Knowing me then as you do, it will not seem strange that, instead of crushing, this system should have excited my contemptuous defiance and undying hatred.

"On examining this evidence, you can but smile at the absurdity of the charges, and the extreme care not to extract any information from me. I have, however, sir, to return my most sincere thanks to you and your colleague for the delicacy and kind feeling which has characterized your bearing toward me, and to congratulate you upon the conclusion of a task which can be but little in unison with the feelings of gentlemen."

Thereupon, both commissioners advanced and shook hands, and expressed an earnest hope that I would very soon be sent south.

69.

David Ross Locke ("Petroleum V. Nasby"): Ameriky for White Men

David Ross Locke was one of the most influential political satirists during the Civil War. He was opposed to slavery and the political hypocrisy of his day. Seeking a way to impress his ideas forcefully upon people, he assumed a satiric pose under the pseudonym Petroleum V. Nasby. He began writing letters that appeared in country newspapers and later in the Toledo Blade, *which he edited. He created Nasby in the image of an illiterate, hypocritical, cowardly, and dissolute country preacher whose manner of speech was styled after Artemus Ward. Every opinion Nasby held — pro-slavery, pro-Southern, anti-war — condemned itself because of the vicious character of the man. Lincoln was one of Locke's greatest admirers and relished the occasion to read Nasby letters to visitors. Lincoln once quipped: "For the genius to write like Nasby, I would gladly give up my office." Locke wrote his letters from 1861 to 1887. The following letter is dated April 2, 1862.*

Source: *The Struggles, Social, Financial and Political of Petroleum V. Nasby,*
etc., etc., Boston, 1888: "Negro Emigration."

THERE IS NOW fifteen niggers, men, wimin, and childern, or ruther, mail, femail, and yung, in Wingert's Corners, and yisterday another arrove. I am bekomin alarmed, for, ef they inkreese at this rate, in suthin over sixty years they'll hev a majority in the town, and may, ef they git mean enuff, tyrannize over us, even ez we air tyrannizin over them. The danger is imminent! Alreddy our poor white inhabitants is out uv employment to make room for that nigger; even now our shops and factories is full uv that nigger, to the great detriment uv a white inhabitant who hez a family to support, and our poor-house and jail is full uv him.

I implore the peeple to wake up. Let us hold a mass meetin to take this subgik into considerashen, and, that biznis may be expeditid, I perpose the adopshen uv a series uv preamble and resolooshens, suthin like the follerin, to-wit:

Wareas, we vew with alarm the acksun uv the President uv the U.S., in recommendin the immejit emansipashun uv the slaves uv our misgidid Suthern brethrin, and his evident intenshun uv kolonizin on em in the North, and the heft on em in Wingert's Corners; and

Wareas, in the event uv this imigrashun, our fellow-townsman, Abslum Kitt, and others, whose families depend upon their labor for support, wood be throde out of employment; and

Wareas, when yoo giv a man a hoss, yoo air obleeged to also make him a present uv a silver-platid harnis and a $650 buggy, so ef we let the nigger live here, we are in dooty bound to marry him off-hand; and

Wareas, when this stait uv affares arrives our kentry will be no fit place for men uv educashen and refinement; and

Wareas, any man heving the intellek uv a brass-mounted jackass kin easily see that the two races want never intendid to live together; and

Wareas, bein in the magority, we kin do as we please, and ez the nigger aint no vote he kant help hisself; therefore be it

Resolved, that the crude, undeodorizd Afrikin is a disgustin obgik.

Resolved, that the Convenshun, when it hez its feet washed, smells sweeter than the Afrikin in his normal condishun, and is therefore his sooperior.

Resolved, that the niggers be druv out uv Wingert's Corners, and that sich property ez they may hev accumulatid be confiscatid, and the proceeds applide to the follerin purposes, to-wit:

Payment uv the bills of the last Dimekratik Centrel Committee; payment uv the disintrestid patriots ez got up this meetin; the balance to remane in my hands.

Resolved, that the Ablishnists who oppose these resolushens all want to marry a nigger.

Resolved, that Dr. Petts, in rentin a part uv his bildin to niggers, hez struck a blow at the very foundashens uv sosiety.

Fellow-whites, arouse! The enemy is onto us! Our harths is in danger! When we hev a nigger for judge — niggers for teachers — niggers in pulpits — when niggers rool and controle society, then will yoo remember this warnin!

Arouse to wunst! Rally agin Conway! Rally agin Sweet! Rally agin Hegler! Rally agin Hegler's family! Rally agin the porter at the Reed House! Rally agin the cook at the Crook House! Rally agin the nigger widder in Vance's Addishun! Rally agin Missis Umstid! Rally agin Missis Umstid's childern by her first husband! Rally agin Missis Umstid's childern by her sekkund husband! Rally agin all the rest uv Missis Umstid's childern! Rally agin the nigger that cum yisterday! Rally agin the saddleculurd girl that yoost to be hear! Ameriky for white men!

70.

Thaddeus Stevens: Concerning Wartime Taxes in the North

As chairman of the House Ways and Means Committee, Thaddeus Stevens wielded great power over all revenue bills and other congressional measures affecting the war. While his views on war policy differed sharply from the administration's, in the area of finance he gave Lincoln loyal support. He carried through the House legislation authorizing the government to float loans. He created new forms of taxation against great opposition and made them effective. On April 8, 1862, the House was engaged in its final debate on an important internal revenue bill. At the end of the debate, Stevens defined the bill in the remarks reprinted below. The bill was passed the same day.

Source: *Globe*, 37 Cong., 2 Sess., pp. 1576-1577.

I will assume that every loyal man admits the necessity of everything required to extinguish this wicked rebellion. To do that requires armies and navies. To sustain them money is absolutely necessary; for the soldiers of the republic must not go unpaid, whatever it may cost the civilian. Money can be had only through loans; but loans cannot be had unless, at the same time, means be provided for paying punctually the interest. This nation must never repudiate her debts. This brings us to the direct question, how much must be annually raised to pay such interest? If the war were to end now or within sixty days, we could tell very nearly.

I suppose our debt on the 1st day of July next will not be less than $800 million. When, some time since, I had occasion to address the House on the Treasury Note Bill, I stated our daily expenses at $2 million. They are now, and have been for some time past, over $3 million a day. It is plain, therefore, that the sum I have stated will be rather below than above our indebt-edness at the end of this fiscal year. The interest, at 7.30, will require about $60 million annually. How much this will be increased by the necessary sacrifice of our bonds, owing to the unfortunate specie clause in our Treasury Note Bill, it is hard to conjecture. The ordinary peace expenses of government will not be less than $70 million + $60 million; these together will be $130 million, independent of the increase in our pension list. My learned colleague from Vermont estimates the revenue from this bill and from customs at $163 million. We have been so little accustomed to national taxation that our statistics and means of ascertaining the actual product of this bill are very scanty. Any estimates must necessarily be very imperfect. Much will depend on the amount of trade and the prosperity of domestic industry.

I am fearful that my colleague has overestimated the amount for the first year. But for the second year, when the stock on hand which will escape this tax shall have been consumed, I believe the amount will go considerably above his estimate. But as the amount of interest for the first year will be considerably less than the second year, I have a confident hope that this bill, with our other revenue, will raise at least $15 million beyond the interest and ordinary expenses of government. If our debt should not be increased beyond $1,200,000,000, and commerce should revive. I believe, in after years, we shall have a surplus of $50 million to apply to the reduction of the debt.

This calculation is merely hypothetical, as I cannot foresee the course of the government in dealing with this rebellion. If they should use the legitimate means in their power, I have no doubt that in ninety days the rebels might be so crippled that our army could safely be reduced to 100,000 men, and five-sixths of the present expenses saved. In that case, I feel no hesitancy in predicting that not another dollar of taxes need ever be imposed on the people to defray our whole debt. If the government should further determine, in accordance with the practice of nations, the dictates of wisdom and of justice to make the property of the rebels pay the expenses of the war which they have so wantonly caused, this tax need never be collected beyond the second year. But if the administration should deem it wise to prolong the war, and suffer the loyal citizens to be oppressed, to show mercy to traitors, the people must expect further and heavier burdens.

In selecting the objects of taxation, the committee have found it necessary to visit many articles which they would have gladly spared. They have, however, laid no burdens on those who have but small means. They have exempted property and business below the value of $600 so that the poor man's tenement shall not be disturbed by the tax gatherer. For the same reason, they have laid no poll tax. They have, no doubt, notwithstanding their best efforts, failed to equalize the burden to the extent which

they desired. They have attempted to raise the largest sums from articles of luxury and from the large profits of wealthy men.

But even on these articles the tax is light compared with that of other countries. Take spirits as a sample. You may call it a luxury or a nuisance, as best suits your taste. The excise in England is $2.50 per gallon; here, 15 cents. Tobacco stands in the same list. Even now, when England has reduced her tariff, her duty on the raw material is 72 cents per pound; on manufactured, or cigars, $2.16; on snuff, $1.44; on stems and scraps, 72 cents. In this bill, the raw material is free; manufactured, 10 cents per pound; cigars, 10 cents; smoking, 5 cents; snuff, 8 cents; scraps, nothing. Where we have laid a tax on the domestic article, the committee have adopted the principle of laying compensatory duties on the foreign article when imported. This we deem necessary to retain the home market and not to discriminate against our own industry.

The income tax has been found very difficult to adjust so as to escape double taxation. But the committee thought it would be manifestly unjust to allow the large money operators and wealthy merchants, whose incomes might reach hundreds of thousands of dollars, to escape from their due proportion of the burden. They hope they have succeeded in excluding from this tax the articles and subjects of gain and profit which are taxed in another form.

The committee have been greatly embarrassed by the Canadian reciprocity treaty. They have been obliged to omit many articles which, with a light tax, would have produced a large revenue. This is but one of many illustrations of the evil of commercial treaties, which are in direct violation of the letter and spirit of the Constitution. The treaty-making power has no more right to regulate commerce than it has to declare war and raise armies and navies.

I have no fear that the loyal people of the free states will complain of any burdens which may be necessary to vindicate the authority of the Union, and establish on a firm basis the principle of self-government and the inalienable rights of man. So long as this money is honestly and economically expended, they will not repine. While the rich and the thrifty will be obliged to contribute largely from the abundance of their means, we have the consolation to know that no burdens have been imposed on the industrious laborer and mechanic; that the food of the poor is untaxed; and that no one will be affected by the provisions of this bill whose living depends solely on his manual labor.

71.

The Homestead Act

The desire for free land had motivated wave after wave of westward migrations from early colonial days. By the 1850s, important figures like Horace Greeley and organizations like the labor unions and the Free Soil Party were urging the passage of homestead legislation. The first homestead bill was presented to Congress in 1846. Senator Wade of Ohio called the legislation a "great question of land to the landless," and Congress finally passed a Homestead Act in 1860, but President Buchanan vetoed it. Southerners opposed it on the grounds that it would result in the settling of the territories by antislavery people; employers opposed it because they feared that it would deplete the labor market, and thus bring about an increase in wages. The Republican platform in 1860 promised a new homestead bill, and Lincoln's victory, along with the secession of the Southern states, insured its passage. On May 20, 1862, President Lincoln signed the Homestead Act into law. The Act, reprinted below, has been the basis of all subsequent public land policy.

Source: *Statutes*, XII, pp. 392-393.

An act to secure homesteads to actual settlers on the public domain.

Be it enacted by the Senate and House of Representatives of the United States of America, in Congress assembled, that any person who is the head of a family, or who has arrived at the age of twenty-one years, and is a citizen of the United States, or who shall have filed his declaration of intention to become such, as required by the naturalization laws of the United States, and who has never borne arms against the United States government or given aid and comfort to its enemies, shall, from and after January 1, 1863, be entitled to enter one quarter section or a less quantity of unappropriated public lands, upon which said person may have filed a preemption claim, or which may, at the time the application is made, be subject to preemption at $1.25, or less, per acre; or 80 acres or less of such unappropriated lands, at $2.50 per acre, to be located in a body, in conformity to the legal subdivisions of the public lands, and after the same shall have been surveyed: *Provided,* that any person owning or residing on land may, under the provisions of this act, enter other land lying contiguous to his or her said land, which shall not, with the land so already owned and occupied, exceed in the aggregate 160 acres.

Section 2. *And be it further enacted,* that the person applying for the benefit of this act shall, upon application to the register of the Land Office in which he or she is about to make such entry, make affidavit before the said register or receiver that he or she is the head of a family, or is twenty-one or more years of age, or shall have performed service in the Army or Navy of the United States, and that he has never borne arms against the government of the United States or given aid and comfort to its enemies, and that such application is made for his or her exclusive use and benefit, and that said entry is made for the purpose of actual settlement and cultivation and not, either directly or indirectly, for the use or benefit of any other person or persons whomsoever; and upon filing the said affidavit with the register or receiver, and on payment of $10, he or she shall thereupon be permitted to enter the quantity of land specified.

Provided, however, that no certificate shall be given or patent issued therefor until the expiration of five years from the date of such entry; and if, at the expiration of such time, or at any time within two years thereafter, the person making such entry — or if he be dead, his widow; or in case of her death, his heirs or devisee; or in case of a widow making such entry, her heirs or devisee, in case of her death — shall prove by two credible witnesses that he, she, or they have resided upon or cultivated the same for the term of five years immediately succeeding the time of filing the affidavit aforesaid, and shall make affidavit that no part of said land has been alienated, and that he

has borne true allegiance to the government of the United States; then, in such case, he, she, or they, if at that time a citizen of the United States, shall be entitled to a patent, as in other cases provided for by law.

And provided, further, that in case of the death of both father and mother, leaving an infant child or children under twenty-one years of age, the right and fee shall inure to the benefit of said infant child or children; and the executor, administrator, or guardian may, at any time within two years after the death of the surviving parent, and in accordance with the laws of the state in which such children for the time being have their domicile, sell said land for the benefit of said infants, but for no other purpose; and the purchaser shall acquire the absolute title by the purchase, and be entitled to a patent from the United States, on payment of the office fees and sum of money herein specified. . . .

Section 5. *And be it further enacted,* that if, at any time after the filing of the affidavit, as required in the 2nd Section of this act, and before the expiration of the five years aforesaid, it shall be proven, after due notice to the settler, to the satisfaction of the register of the Land Office, that the person having filed such affidavit shall have actually changed his or her residence, or abandoned the said land for more than six months at any time, then, and in that event, the land so entered shall revert to the government.

Section 6. . . . *Provided, further,* that no person who has served, or may hereafter serve, for a period of not less than fourteen days in the Army or Navy of the United States, either regular or volunteer, under the laws thereof, during the existence of an actual war, domestic or foreign, shall be deprived of the benefits of this act on account of not having attained the age of twenty-one years.

72.

Public Lands for the Benefit of Agriculture and the Mechanic Arts

Agricultural organizations and advocates of vocational training urged Congress for many years to enact laws setting aside public lands for the establishment of agricultural and vocational schools. Illinois, in 1853, was one of the first states to make public lands available for such purposes. In 1857, Representative Justin Morrill of Vermont introduced a bill before the House to provide grants of public lands for agricultural and vocational colleges. Congress passed the bill, but mainly because of Southern opposition President Buchanan vetoed it. A similar bill, known as the Morrill Act, was passed in 1862 and signed by President Lincoln on July 2. Over the years, the law granted 13 million acres of public land to the states for educational purposes, and was, according to Henry Steele Commager, "with the exception of the Act of 1785, the most important piece of legislation on behalf of education ever passed." The text of the Morrill Act follows.

Source: *Statutes*, XII, pp. 503-505.

An Act donating Public Lands to the several States and Territories which may provide Colleges for the Benefit of Agriculture and the Mechanic Arts.

Be it enacted by the Senate and House of Representatives of the United States of America, in Congress assembled, that there be granted to the several states, for the purposes hereinafter mentioned, an amount of public land, to be apportioned to each state a quantity equal to 30,000 acres for each senator and representative in Congress to which the states are respectively entitled by the apportionment under the census of 1860: *Provided*, that no mineral lands shall be selected or purchased under the provisions of this act.

Section 2. *And be it further enacted*, that the land aforesaid, after being surveyed, shall be apportioned to the several states in

sections or subdivisions of sections, not less than one-quarter of a section; and whenever there are public lands in a state subject to sale at private entry at $1.25 per acre, the quantity to which said state shall be entitled shall be selected from such lands within the limits of such state; and the secretary of the interior is hereby directed to issue to each of the states in which there is not the quantity of public lands subject to sale at private entry at $1.25 per acre, to which said state may be entitled under the provisions of this act, land scrip to the amount in acres for the deficiency of its distributive share; said scrip to be sold by said states and the proceeds thereof applied to the uses and purposes prescribed in this act, and for no other use or purpose whatsoever: *Provided*, that in no case shall any state to which land scrip may thus be issued be allowed to locate the same within the limits of any other state, or of any territory of the United States, but their assignees may thus locate said land scrip upon any of the unappropriated lands of the United States subject to sale at private entry at $1.25, or less, per acre: *And provided further,* that not more than 1 million acres shall be located by such assignees in any one of the states: *And provided further,* that no such location shall be made before one year from the passage of this act.

Section 3. *And be it further enacted,* that all the expenses of management, superintendence and taxes from date of selection of said lands, previous to their sales, and all expenses incurred in the management and disbursement of the moneys which may be received therefrom, shall be paid by the states to which they may belong, out of the treasury of said states, so that the entire proceeds of the sale of said lands shall be applied without any diminution whatever to the purposes hereinafter mentioned.

Section 4. *And be it further enacted,* that all moneys derived from the sale of the lands aforesaid by the state to which the lands are apportioned, and from the sales of land scrip hereinbefore provided for, shall be invested in stocks of the United States, or of the states, or some other safe stocks, yielding not less than 5 percent upon the par value of said stocks; and that the moneys so invested shall constitute a perpetual fund, the capital of which shall remain forever undiminished (except so far as may be provided in Section 5 of this act) and the interest of which shall be inviolably appropriated, by each state which may take and claim the benefit of this act, to the endowment, support, and maintenance of at least one college where the leading object shall be, without excluding other scientific and classical studies, and including military tactics, to teach such branches of learning as are related to agriculture and the mechanic arts, in such manner as the legislatures of the states may respectively prescribe, in or-

der to promote the liberal and practical education of the industrial classes in the several pursuits and professions in life.

Section 5. *And be it further enacted,* that the grant of land and land scrip hereby authorized shall be made on the following conditions, to which, as well as to the provisions hereinbefore contained, the previous assent of the several states shall be signified by legislative acts:

First, if any portion of the fund invested, as provided by the foregoing section, or any portion of the interest thereon, shall, by any action or contingency be diminished or lost, it shall be replaced by the state to which it belongs, so that the capital of the fund shall remain forever undiminished; and the annual interest shall be regularly applied without diminution to the purposes mentioned in the 4th Section of this act, except that a sum, not exceeding 10 percent upon the amount received by any state under the provisions of this act, may be expended for the purchase of lands for sites or experimental farms, whenever authorized by the respective legislatures of said states.

Second, no portion of said fund, nor the interest thereon, shall be applied, directly or indirectly, under any pretense whatever, to the purchase, erection, preservation, or repair of any building or buildings.

Third, any state which may take and claim the benefit of the provisions of this act shall provide, within five years, at least not less than one college, as described in the 4th Section of this act, or the grant to such state shall cease; and said state shall be bound to pay the United States the amount received of any lands previously sold, and that the title to purchasers under the state shall be valid.

Fourth, an annual report shall be made regarding the progress of each college, recording any improvements and experiments made, with their cost and results, and such other matters, including state industrial and economical statistics, as may be supposed useful; one copy of which shall be transmitted by mail free, by each, to all the other colleges which may be endowed under the provisions of this act, and also one copy to the secretary of the interior.

Fifth, when lands shall be selected from those which have been raised to double the minimum price, in consequence of railroad grants, they shall be computed to the states at the maximum price, and the number of acres proportionally diminished.

Sixth, no state while in a condition of rebellion or insurrection against the government of the United States shall be entitled to the benefit of this act.

Seventh, no state shall be entitled to the benefits of this act unless it shall express its acceptance thereof by its legislature within two years from the date of its approval by the President.

Section 6. *And be it further enacted*, that land scrip issued under the provisions of this act shall not be subject to location until after January 1, 1863.

Section 7. *And be it further enacted*, that the land officers shall receive the same fees for locating land scrip issued under the provisions of this act as is now allowed for the location of military bounty land warrants under existing laws: *Provided*, their maximum compensation shall not be thereby increased.

Section 8. *And be it further enacted*, that the governors of the several states to which scrip shall be issued under this act shall be required to report annually to Congress all sales made of such scrip until the whole shall be disposed of, the amount received for the same, and what appropriation has been made of the proceeds.

73.

"The Brass-Mounted Army"

Most famous songs of the Civil War were partisan songs like "The Bonnie Blue Flag" and "John Brown's Body," which expressed the patriotic spirit of the North or the South. "The Brass-Mounted Army," though a Confederate song, is rare in that it does not express partisanship at all, but treats an eternal theme of all armies — the conflict between the simple soldier and the officer.

THE BRASS-MOUNTED ARMY

Oh, soldiers I've concluded to make a little song,
And if I tell no falsehood there can be nothing wrong;
If any be offended at what I have to sing,
Then surely his own conscience applies the bitter sting.

> *Chorus:*
> Oh, how do you like the army,
> The brass-mounted army,
> The high-falutin' army,
> Where eagle buttons rule?

Whiskey is a monster, and ruins great and small,
But in our noble army, headquarters gets it all.
They drink it when there's danger, although it seems too hard,
But if a private touches it they put him "under guard."

And when we meet the ladies we're bound to go it sly,
Headquarters are the pudding, and the privates are the pie!
They issue standing orders to keep us all in line,
For if we had a showing, the brass would fail to shine.

At every big plantation or Negro-holders yard,
Just to save the property, the general puts a guard;
The sentry's then instructed to let no private pass —
The rich man's house and table are fixed to suit the "brass."

I have to change this story, so beautiful and true,
But the poor man and widow must have a line or two;
For them no guard is stationed, their fences oft are burned,
And property molested, as long ago you've learned.

The army's now much richer than when the war begun.
It furnishes three tables where once it had but one;
The first is richly loaded with chickens, goose, and duck,
The next with pork and mutton, the third with good old buck.

Our generals eat the poultry, and buy it very cheap,
Our colonels and our majors devour the hog and sheep;
The privates are contented (except when they can steal)
With beef and corn bread plenty to make a hearty meal.

Sometimes we get so hungry we're bound to press a pig,
Then the largest stump in Dixie we're sure to have to dig;
And when we fret, an officer who wears long-legged boots,
With neither judge nor jury, puts us on "double roots."

These things, and many others, are truly hard to me,
But still I'll be contented, and fight for liberty
And when the war is over, oh what a jolly time!
We'll be our own commanders and sing much sweeter rhymes.

We'll see our loving sweethearts, and sometimes kiss them too,
We'll eat the finest rations, and bid old buck adieu;
There'll be no generals with orders to compel,
Long boots and eagle buttons, forever fare ye well!

> *Last chorus:*
> And thus we'll leave the army,
> The brass-mounted army
> The high-falutin' army,
> Where the eagle buttons rule.

74.

GEORGE B. MCCLELLAN: Advice to the President on Conducting the War

In war and peace, one of the firmest principles of American constitutionalism has been the supremacy of civil over military authority. During the Civil War, Lincoln was confronted on numerous occasions with attempts of generals to usurp civil authority. General George McClellan, who disapproved of Lincoln's conduct of the war, made an attempt to impose his military views on the President that, according to Henry Steele Commager, was "the most spectacular attempt of this kind in our history." General McClellan, commanding the Army of the Potomac, wrote the following letter to Lincoln on July 7, 1862.

Source: McPherson, pp. 385-386.

YOU HAVE BEEN FULLY INFORMED that the Rebel Army is in the front, with the purpose of overwhelming us by attacking our positions or reducing us by blocking our river communications. I cannot but regard our condition as critical, and I earnestly desire, in view of possible contingencies, to lay before your excellency, for your private consideration, my general views concerning the existing state of the rebellion, although they do not strictly relate to the situation of this Army, or strictly come within the scope of my official duties.

These views amount to convictions and are deeply impressed upon my mind and heart. Our cause must never be abandoned; it is the cause of free institutions and self-government. The Constitution and the Union must be preserved, whatever may be the cost in time, treasure, and blood. If secession is successful, other dissolutions are clearly to be seen in the future. Let neither military disaster, political faction, nor foreign war shake your settled purpose to enforce the equal operation of the laws of the United States upon the people of every state.

The time has come when the government must determine upon a civil and military policy, covering the whole ground of our national trouble.

The responsibility of determining, declaring, and supporting such civil and military policy, and of directing the whole course of national affairs in regard to the rebellion, must now be assumed and exercised by you, or our cause will be lost. The Constitution gives you power, even for the present terrible exigency.

This rebellion has assumed the character of a war; as such it should be regarded, and it should be conducted upon the highest principles known to Christian civilization. It should not be a war looking to the subjugation of the people of any state, in any event. It should not be at all a war upon population but against armed forces and political organizations. Neither confiscation of property, political executions of persons, territorial organization of states, or forcible abolition of slavery should be contemplated for a moment.

In prosecuting the war, all private property and unarmed persons should be strictly protected, subject only to the necessity of military operations; all private property taken for military use should be paid or receipted for; pillage and waste should be treated as high crimes; all unnecessary trespass sternly prohibited; and offensive demeanor by the military toward citizens promptly rebuked. Military arrests should not be tolerated, except in places where active hostilities exist; and oaths, not required by enactments constitutionally made, should be neither demanded nor received.

Military government should be confined to the preservation of public order and the protection of political right. Military power should not be allowed to interfere with the relations of servitude, either by supporting or impairing the authority of the master, except for repressing disorder, as in other cases. Slaves, contraband under the act of Congress, seeking military protection should receive it. The right of the government to appropriate permanently to its own service claims to slave labor should be asserted and the right of the owner to compensation therefor should be recognized. This principle might be extended, upon grounds of military necessity and security, to all the slaves of a particular state, thus working manumission in such state; and in Missouri, perhaps in western Virginia also, and possibly even in Maryland, the expediency of such a measure is only a question of time. A system of policy thus constitutional, and pervaded by the influences of Christianity and freedom, would receive the support of almost all truly loyal men, would deeply impress the Rebel masses and all foreign nations, and it might be humbly hoped that it would commend itself to the favor of the Almighty.

Unless the principles governing the future conduct of our struggle shall be made known and approved, the effort to obtain requisite forces will be almost hopeless. A declaration of radical views, especially upon slavery, will rapidly disintegrate our present armies.

The policy of the government must be supported by concentrations of military power. The national forces should not be dispersed in expeditions, posts of occupation, and numerous armies, but should be mainly collected into masses and brought to bear upon the armies of the Confederate States. Those armies thoroughly defeated, the political structure which they support would soon cease to exist.

In carrying out any system of policy which you may form, you will require a commander in chief of the Army, one who possesses your confidence, understands your views, and who is competent to execute your orders by directing the military forces of the nation to the accomplishment of the objects by you proposed. I do not ask that place for myself. I am willing to serve you in such position as you may assign me, and I will do so as faithfully as ever subordinate served superior.

I may be on the brink of eternity; and as I hope forgiveness from my Maker, I have written this letter with sincerity toward you and from love for my country.

———◆———

My dear McClellan: If you don't want to use the Army I should like to borrow it for a while. Yours respectfully, A. Lincoln.

ABRAHAM LINCOLN, unsent letter protesting against McClellan's "waiting campaign" of 1862

75.

Discussion of War Aims

Horace Greeley, editor of the New York Tribune, *was one of the most vigorous and influential opponents of slavery in the North. He insisted that the principal object of the Civil War was the abolition of slavery. In the first year of the war he advocated immediate emancipation. On August 19, 1862, in a signed editorial in the* Tribune *entitled "The Prayer of Twenty Millions," Greeley criticized Lincoln for failing to make slavery the dominant issue of the war and compromising moral principles for political motives. Greeley's attack stunned Lincoln, who had been for months seeking a reasonable way to end slavery. Lincoln's reply to Greeley on August 22 was one of his clearest formulations of the aims of his war policy.*

Source: Moore, I, Supplement, Document 85.

I.

HORACE GREELEY:
Freeing the Slaves

Dear Sir:

I do not intrude to tell you — for you must know already — that a great proportion of those who triumphed in your election, and of all who desire the unqualified suppression of the rebellion now desolating our country, are sorely disappointed and deeply pained by the policy you seem to be pursuing with regard to the slaves of Rebels. I write only to set succinctly and unmistakably before you what we require, what we think we have a right to expect, and of what we complain.

I. We require of you, as the first servant of the republic, charged especially and preeminently with this duty, that you EXECUTE THE LAWS. Most emphatically do we demand that such laws as have been recently enacted, which therefore may fairly be presumed to embody the public will and to be dictated by the *present* needs of the republic, and which, after due consideration, have received your personal sanction, shall by you be carried into full effect and that you publicly and decisively instruct your subordinates that such laws exist, that they are binding on all functionaries and citizens, and that they are to be obeyed to the letter.

II. We think you are strangely and disastrously remiss in the discharge of your official and imperative duty with regard to the emancipating provisions of the new Confiscation Act. Those provisions were designed to fight slavery with liberty. They prescribe that men loyal to the Union, and willing to shed their blood in her behalf, shall no longer be held, with the nation's consent, in bondage to persistent, malignant traitors, who for twenty years have been plotting and for sixteen months have been fighting to divide and destroy our country. Why these traitors should be treated with tenderness by you, to the prejudice of the dearest rights of loyal men, we cannot conceive.

III. We think you are unduly influenced

by the councils, the representations, the menaces, of certain fossil politicians hailing from the border Slave states. Knowing well that the heartily, unconditionally loyal portion of the white citizens of those states do not expect nor desire that slavery shall be upheld to the prejudice of the Union — for the truth of which we appeal not only to every Republican residing in those states but to such eminent loyalists as H. Winter Davis, Parson Brownlow, the Union Central Committee of Baltimore, and to the *Nashville Union* — we ask you to consider that slavery is everywhere the inciting cause and sustaining base of treason: the most slaveholding sections of Maryland and Delaware being this day, though under the Union flag, in full sympathy with the rebellion, while the free labor portions of Tennessee and of Texas, though writhing under the bloody heel of treason, are unconquerably loyal to the Union.

So emphatically is this the case that a most intelligent Union banker of Baltimore recently avowed his confident belief that a majority of the present legislature of Maryland, though elected as and all professing to be Unionists, are at heart desirous of the triumph of the Jeff Davis conspiracy, and when asked how they could be won back to loyalty, replied — "Only by the complete abolition of slavery."

It seems to us the most obvious truth that whatever strengthens or fortifies slavery in the border states strengthens also treason and drives home the wedge intended to divide the Union. Had you, from the first, refused to recognize in those states, as here, any other than unconditional loyalty — that which stands for the Union, whatever may become of slavery — those states, would have been, and would be, far more helpful and less troublesome to the defenders of the Union than they have been, or now are.

IV. We think timid counsels in such a crisis calculated to prove perilous, and probably disastrous. It is the duty of a government so wantonly, wickedly assailed by rebellion as ours has been to oppose force to force in a defiant, dauntless spirit. It cannot afford to temporize with traitors, nor with semi-traitors. It must not bribe them to behave themselves, nor make them fair promises in the hope of disarming their causeless hostility. Representing a brave and high-spirited people, it can afford to forfeit anything else better than its own self-respect, or their admiring confidence. For our government even to seek, after war has been made on it, to dispel the affected apprehensions of armed traitors that their cherished privileges may be assailed by it is to invite insult and encourage hopes of its own downfall. The rush to arms of Ohio, Indiana, Illinois, is the true answer at once to the rebel raids of John Morgan and the traitorous sophistries of Beriah Magoffin.

V. We complain that the Union cause has suffered and is now suffering immensely from mistaken deference to Rebel slavery. Had you, sir, in your inaugural address, unmistakably given notice that in case the rebellion already commenced were persisted in and your efforts to preserve the Union and enforce the laws should be resisted by armed force, *you would recognize no loyal person as rightfully held in slavery by a traitor,* we believe the rebellion would therein have received a staggering if not fatal blow. At that moment, according to the returns of the most recent elections, the Unionists were a large majority of the voters of the Slave states. But they were composed in good part of the aged, the feeble, the wealthy, the timid — the young, the reckless, the aspiring, the adventurous had already been largely lured by the gamblers and Negro traders, the politicians by trade and the conspirators by instinct, into the toils of treason. Had you then proclaimed that rebellion would strike the shackles from the slaves of every traitor, the wealthy and the cautious would have been supplied with a powerful inducement to remain loyal.

As it was, every coward in the South soon became a traitor from fear; for loyalty was perilous, while treason seemed comparatively safe. Hence the boasted unanimity of the South — a unanimity based on Rebel terrorism and the fact that immunity and safety were found on that side, danger and probable death on ours. The Rebels, from the first, have been eager to confiscate, imprison, scourge, and kill; we have fought wolves with the devices of sheep. The result is just what might have been expected. Tens of thousands are fighting in the Rebel ranks today whose original bias and natural leanings would have led them into ours.

VI. We complain that the Confiscation Act which you approved is habitually disregarded by your generals, and that no word of rebuke for them from you has yet reached the public ear. Frémont's Proclamation and Hunter's Order favoring emancipation were promptly annulled by you; while Halleck's Number Three, forbidding fugitives from slavery to Rebels to come within his lines — an order as unmilitary as inhuman, and which received the hearty approbation of every traitor in America — with scores of like tendency, have never provoked even your remonstrance.

We complain that the officers of your armies have habitually repelled rather than invited the approach of slaves who would have gladly taken the risks of escaping from their Rebel masters to our camps, bringing intelligence often of inestimable value to the Union cause. We complain that those who *have* thus escaped to us, avowing a willingness to do for us whatever might be required, have been brutally and madly repulsed, and often surrendered to be scourged, maimed, and tortured by the ruffian traitors who pretend to own them. We complain that a large proportion of our regular Army officers, with many of the volunteers, evince far more solicitude to uphold slavery than to put down the rebellion.

And, finally, we complain that you, Mr. President, elected as a Republican, knowing well what an abomination slavery is and how emphatically it is the core and essence of this atrocious rebellion, seem never to interfere with these atrocities and never give a direction to your military subordinates, which does not appear to have been conceived in the interest of slavery rather than of freedom. . . .

VIII. On the face of this wide earth, Mr. President, there is not one disinterested, determined, intelligent champion of the Union cause who does not feel that all attempts to put down the rebellion and at the same time uphold its inciting cause are preposterous and futile; that the rebellion, if crushed out tomorrow, would be renewed within a year if slavery were left in full vigor; that Army officers who remain to this day devoted to slavery can at best be but halfway loyal to the Union; and that every hour of deference to slavery is an hour of added and deepened peril to the Union. I appeal to the testimony of your ambassadors in Europe. It is freely at your service, not at mine. Ask them to tell you candidly whether the seeming subserviency of your policy to the slaveholding, slavery-upholding interest is not the perplexity, the despair of statesmen of all parties, and be admonished by the general answer!

IX. I close as I began with the statement that what an immense majority of the loyal millions of your countrymen require of you is a frank, declared, unqualified, ungrudging execution of the laws of the land, more especially of the Confiscation Act. That act gives freedom to the slaves of Rebels coming within our lines, or whom those lines may at any time enclose — we ask you to render it due obedience by publicly requiring all your subordinates to recognize and obey it. The Rebels are everywhere using the late anti-Negro riots in the North, as they have long used your officers' treatment of Negroes in the South, to convince the slaves that they have nothing to hope from a Union success, that we mean in that case to sell them into a bitter bondage to defray the cost of the war.

Let them impress this as a truth on the great mass of their ignorant and credulous bondmen, and the Union will never be restored — never. We cannot conquer 10 million people united in solid phalanx against us, powerfully aided by Northern sympathizers and European allies. We must have scouts, guides, spies, cooks, teamsters, diggers, and choppers from the blacks of the South, whether we allow them to fight for us or not, or we shall be baffled and repelled.

As one of the millions who would gladly have avoided this struggle at any sacrifice but that of principle and honor, but who now feel that the triumph of the Union is indispensable, not only to the existence of our country but to the well-being of mankind, I entreat you to render a hearty and unequivocal obedience to the law of the land.

II.

ABRAHAM LINCOLN:
Saving the Union

Dear Sir:

I have just read yours of the 19th, addressed to myself through the *New York Tribune*. If there be in it any statements or assumptions of fact which I may know to be erroneous, I do not now and here controvert them. If there be in it any inferences which I may believe to be falsely drawn, I do not now and here argue against them. If there be perceptible in it an impatient and dictatorial tone, I waive it in deference to an old friend, whose heart I have always supposed to be right.

As to the policy I "seem to be pursuing," as you say, I have not meant to leave anyone in doubt.

I would save the Union. I would save it the shortest way under the Constitution. The sooner the national authority can be restored, the nearer the Union will be "the Union as it was." If there be those who would not save the Union unless they could at the same time *save* slavery, I do not agree with them. If there be those who would not save the Union unless they could at the same time *destroy* slavery, I do not agree with them. My paramount object in this struggle *is* to save the Union, and is *not* either to save or destroy slavery. If I could save the Union without freeing *any* slave, I would do it; and if I could save it by freeing *all* the slaves, I would do it; and if I could do it by freeing some and leaving others alone, I would also do that.

What I do about slavery and the colored race I do because I believe it helps to save this Union; and what I forbear I forbear because I do *not* believe it would help to save the Union. I shall do *less* whenever I shall believe what I am doing hurts the cause, and I shall do *more* whenever I shall believe doing more will help the cause. I shall try to correct errors when shown to be errors; and I shall adopt new views so fast as they shall appear to be true views.

I have here stated my purpose according to my view of *official* duty, and I intend no modification of my oft-expressed *personal* wish that all men, everywhere, could be free.

As I would not be a slave, so I would not be a master. Whatever differs from this, to the extent of the difference, is no democracy.
ABRAHAM LINCOLN, "Fragment on Slavery," Aug. 1, 1858

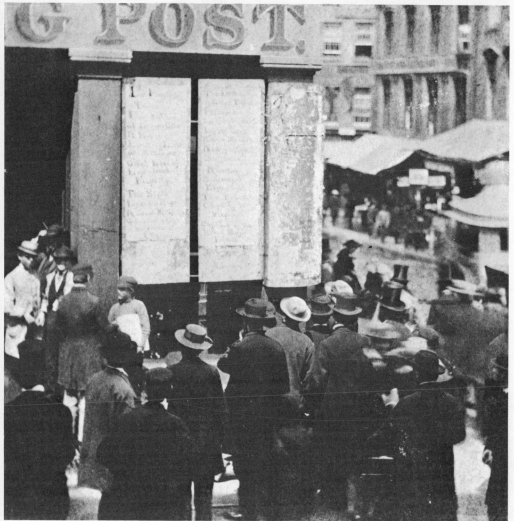

Civil War bulletin board in New York; from a stereograph

THE HOME FRONT

The effectiveness of war mobilization and, ultimately, of the war effort itself depended upon the economic and social resources at the disposal of the two governments. The North had heavy material superiority — manpower, capital, manufacturing, natural resources, transportation — which the South could not hope to match. The South was further hampered by the difficulty of coordinated mobilization for war under a political system based on the absolute sovereignty of the states. The overall strategy of the war, however, favored the South. Victory could be had simply by not being defeated, inflicting damage and casualties until the North tired of the effort. The North, on the other hand, could win only by conquering and occupying the entire Confederacy. The relative unpopularity of the war in the North and the highly emotional nature of the Southern cause further offset the material disparity of the two nations. In the final analysis, however, the economic power of the North was decisive.

View of Richmond, Va., in 1863

New Orleans: this engraving and the one above from "The War with the South," by Tomes

(Below) The waterfront of Galveston, Texas, in the late 1850s

Meeting Street, Charleston, S.C., in 1865; St. Michael's Church is in right center. Photo by Brady

The grounds of Buen Ventura in Savannah, Georgia, photographed in 1864 by George Barnard, who marched with Sherman's army

View of the Savannah waterfront taken at the same time by Barnard

(Top) Tredegor Iron Works in Richmond, Va., 1865; (center) Vulcan Iron Works in Charleston, S.C., the key manufacturer of arms for the Confederacy; photographed in 1865; (bottom) Confederate Powder Works in Augusta, Ga.

The industrial capacity of the North was its great advantage. Much of the South's initial supply of war material came from the capture of federal arsenals throughout the South, and as the war continued the Confederacy was seriously handicapped by its lack of productive capacity. Without a well-developed system of roads and railways, distribution was also a major problem. When the North gained control of the Mississippi and, by blockading Southern ports, cut off the South's cotton trade with England — its sole source of income — the ultimate defeat of the Confederacy became inevitable.

(Above) Cambria Iron Works in Pennsylvania during the late 1860s

(Right) Arsenal and Musket Factory in Harpers Ferry, West Virginia

(Below) Lithograph of the Armory of Colt's Patent Fire Arms Manufacturing Co., Hartford, in 1866

(Above) Broadway, New York City, in 1860; from a stereograph by Anthony; (below left) Grand Central Depot, New York; photographed by Ropes & Co.; (below right) skating pond in Central Park, New York

Boston scenes: (Above left) view from an anchored balloon by J. W. Black, 1860; America's earliest extant aerial photo; (above right) harbor and East Boston; Soule photo; (below left) Brattle Street from Southworth and Hawes studio; (below right) State Street; Bierstadt stereograph

Poeston Mill, New York

(Left) Countryside view by an unknown photographer

Horse-drawn sleigh on a street in Newark, N.J., 1863

Mauch Chunk and Mount Pisgah in the coal mining regions of Pennsylvania

View of Chicago looking north from the new courthouse dome; photo by Hessler in 1858

Jefferson, Wis., in 1857; lithograph from a sketch by L. Kurz

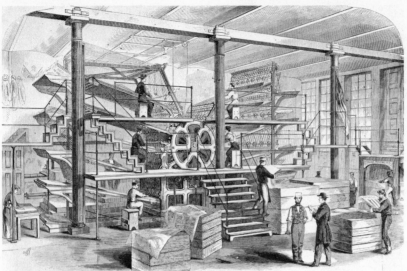

(Above) Press room of the New York "Tribune," 1861, when Greeley was editor; (left) Gleason's publishing offices in Boston, opened in 1852

As both journalism and warfare entered their modern phases, Northern newspapers and magazines sent more than 150 correspondents to the field to cover the war. Extensive news coverage was made possible by the telegraph, the recently established news agency in New York, and the new art of photography. Mathew Brady, the pioneer in the field, organized photographic teams that recorded the men and the scenes of the war in more than 7,000 photographs. Such complete and detailed documentation was unprecedented and marked a new direction in popular journalism.

Duff Green, newspaper entrepreneur; James G. Bennett, New York "Herald"

Horace Greeley

(Above) Photo wagon used by Mathew Brady when on location during the Civil War to enable him to process the wet collodion plates; (left) Mathew Brady, 1863; (right) Alfred R. Waud, artist for "Harper's" sketching at Gettysburg; photo by T. H. O'Sullivan, 1863

Pencil drawing by Arthur Lumley showing Gen. Wilcox and his troops relaxing on Caroline Street, Fredericksburg, Va., prior to battle, 1862. The drawing shows the artist's instructions to the engraver who will render it into a finished state for publication

I RECEIVE A LETTER WHICH TELLS THE AGONIZING FACT... I'M DRAFTED.

AM SENT WITH DESPATCHES, A PERILOUS DUTY, DEATH OR GLORY!

I DELIVER DESPATCHES, SAVE THE ARMY, AND AM MADE A BRIGADIER GENERAL!

(Above) Series of drawings by W. A. Stephens comically tracing the making of a hero

(Right) Boy in uniform of the Union Army; photo by Addis

(Below) John Burns, 80-year-old citizen of Gettysburg who fought with the Union Army during the battle

(Above) Union troops encamped at Westover, the mansion originally inhabited by William Byrd; (right) making clothes for the boys in the Confederate Army; etching by Adalbert Volck; (below) departure from the old homestead in rural Virginia

Attack on the Tribune offices during the riots that broke out after the first published draft call, 1863

The war was initially fought by volunteers on both sides, but as enthusiasm waned, conscription was instituted. Though probably more effective as a stimulus to volunteering than as a direct source of manpower, the draft evoked widespread resistance. The inequity of the exemption system, based on cash, together with a general dissatisfaction with the war and hostility toward the Negro among laboring and immigrant groups, led to riots. In New York, hundreds were killed or wounded in four days (July 13-16, 1863).

HOW TO ESCAPE THE DRAFT.

(Above) Rioters attacking Negroes as the cause of the war; (left) New York provost guard firing on the rioters in an attempt to disperse them

76.

Negro Opposition to Lincoln's Offer of Colonization

*On August 14, 1862, President Lincoln received a committee of Northern Negro
leaders at the White House to hear his views on Negro emigration, an idea he favored
throughout the early years of the war. Earlier, in April, Congress had provided
$100,000 for the colonization abroad of freed Negroes of the District of Columbia.
One of the Negroes at the meeting kept a record of Lincoln's remarks that was
published in Carl Sandburg's* Abraham Lincoln: The War Years. *The
President said to them: "You and we are different races. . . . This physical difference
is a great disadvantage to us both. . . . Your race are suffering, in my judgment, the
greatest wrong inflicted on any people. But even when you cease to be slaves, you
are yet far removed from being placed on an equality with the white race. . . . But
for your race among us there could not be war. . . . It is better for us both, therefore,
to be separated." Lincoln concluded by advancing a plan for voluntary colonization
of freed Negroes in Central America and asked the committee to consider his offer.
On August 20, a mass meeting of Negroes in Newtown, Long Island, adopted the
following resolutions as a reply to the President.*

Source: *Liberator*, September 12, 1862.

WE, THE COLORED CITIZENS of Queens
County, N.Y., having met in mass meeting,
according to public notice, to consider the
speech of Abraham Lincoln, President of
the United States, addressed to a committee
of Free Colored Men, called at his request
at the White House in Washington, on
Thursday, August 14, 1862, and to express
our views and opinions of the same; and
whereas, the President desires to know in
particular our views on the subject of being
colonized in Central America or some other
foreign country, we will take the present
opportunity to express our opinions most
respectfully and freely, since as loyal Union
colored Americans and Christians we feel
bound to do so.

First, we rejoice that we are colored

Americans, but deny that we are a "different race of people," as God has made of
one blood all nations that dwell on the face
of the earth, and has hence no respect of
men in regard to color, neither ought men
to have respect to color, as they have not
made themselves or their color.

Second, the President calls our attention
particularly to this question: "Why should
we leave this country?" This, he says, is
perhaps the first question for proper consideration. We will answer this question by
showing why we should remain in it. This
is our country by birth, consequently we
are acclimated and in other respects better
adapted to it than to any other country.
This is our native country; we have as
strong attachment naturally to our native

hills, valleys, plains, luxuriant forests, flowing streams, mighty rivers, and lofty mountains as any other people. Nor can we fail to feel a strong attachment to the whites with whom our blood has been commingling from the earliest days of this our country. Neither can we forget and disown our white kindred. This is the country of our choice, being our fathers' country.

Third, again, we are interested in its welfare above every other country; we love this land and have contributed our share to its prosperity and wealth. This we have done by cutting down forests, subduing the soil, cultivating fields, constructing roads, digging canals. We have, too, given our aid in building cities and villages, in building and supporting churches and schools. We have aided in procuring its mineral resources, as coal, iron, and the precious metals; helped in the construction of railroads, bridges, telegraph lines, steamboats and ships; assisted in cattle breeding, raising various kinds of produce, as corn, wheat, oats, potatoes, cotton, rice, tobacco, and leading staples of the country, etc. In these ways, and many others too numerous to be named here, we have aided the nation in her growth and progress and contributed to her general prosperity.

Fourth, again, we believe, too, we have the right to have applied to ourselves those rights named in the Declaration of Independence, "that all men are born free and equal, and have certain inalienable rights, among which are life, liberty, and the pursuit of happiness" — rights which we have derived from the Creator — since we helped to gain our country's independence, under Washington, on her battlefields as well as in the cornfields; and we helped to maintain the same in 1814 under General Jackson at New Orleans; and are willing and ready even now to fight our country's battles against slaveholding traitors and rebels, who are slaying thousands of freemen and seeking the very lifeblood of

the nation; and we hope and believe that the time is not far distant when, instead of being called upon to leave our country, the loyal and just people of the country will pass judgment on the men who stopped the million of our brave hearts, strong arms, and willing hands, desiring to fight our country's battles in her most trying hour and sorest need.

While bleeding and struggling for her life against slaveholding traitors, and, at this very time, when our country is struggling for life and 1 million freemen are believed to be scarcely sufficient to meet the foe, we are called upon by the President of the United States to leave this land and go to another country, to carry out his favorite scheme of colonization. But at this crisis, we feel disposed to refuse the offers of the President, since the call of our suffering country is too loud and imperative to be unheeded.

Again, the President says that Congress has placed a sum of money at his disposition for the purpose of aiding the colonization of the people of African descent, or some portion of them, in some country; therefore making it his duty, as it had been a long time his inclination, to favor that course. Our answer is this: There is no country like our own. Why not declare slavery abolished and favor our peaceful colonization in the Rebel states, or some portion of them? We are all in favor of this, and we believe the majority of those who elected you to the office of the chief magistrate of the nation are in favor, also, of this measure. We believe that this would be a wise and just policy, and would receive the approbation of God and all good men. We would cheerfully return there and give our most willing aid to deliver our loyal colored brethren and other Unionists from the tyranny of rebels to our government.

We colored people are all loyal men, which is more than any other class of people in the country can say. There are

Yankee, English, Scotch, German, and French rebels, but no colored rebels; and let us add, Mr. President, that no one suffers by our presence but rebels and traitors: and if we were permitted to fight our country's battles and an army of colored men were permitted to march into those Rebel states, well-armed and equipped, we believe, with your excellency, that the Rebels would suffer from our presence, but the Union would be saved without spades and shovels.

Congress has also passed the Confiscation and Emancipation Bill. Now, if the President is disposed to give the colored people the benefits guaranteed by that bill and de-clare the Rebel states Free states, we would colonize ourselves in our native states, without the aid of the government, and the President might use the money to defray the expenses of the war.

In conclusion, we would say that, in our belief, the speech of the President has only served the cause of our enemies who wish to insult and mob us, as we have, since its publication, been repeatedly insulted and told that we must leave the country. Hence we conclude that the policy of the President toward the colored people of this country *is a mistaken policy.*

77.

ALEXANDER WALKER: Butler's Brutality in the South

Alexander Walker, a journalist and a leading Louisiana secessionist, was working in New Orleans when the Union Army led by Major General Benjamin F. Butler occupied the city on May 1, 1862. As military governor of New Orleans, Butler proved to be harsh and often unjustifiably punitive. When Walker dared to criticize Butler's policy, he was arrested and imprisoned at Ship Island, Mississippi. While in prison Walker sent the following letter to Jefferson Davis. The letter, which depicted Butler's brutality, was written on September 13, 1862. Butler's Order No. 28, referred to by Walker, that Southern women showing contempt to Northern officers "be regarded and held liable to be treated as a woman of the town plying her avocation" aroused indignation in the North and elicited protests from foreign countries. The increasing irregularity of Butler's administration and the embarrassment which this caused led to his removal on December 16.

Source: Ainsworth, Additions and Corrections to 2nd Series, IV, pp. 880-885.

A CLOSE PRISONER on this desolate island with some fifty others of my fellow citizens, I have thought it my duty at every risk to communicate to you some, at least, of the incidents of the administration of the brutal tyrant who has been sent by the United States government to oppress, rob, assault, and trample upon our people in every manner which the most fiendish ingenuity and most wanton cruelty could devise and in gross violation of all the laws and usages of the most remorseless wars between civilized and even savage nations and tribes.

Previous to my committal to Ship Island as a close prisoner, where I was consigned with seven other respectable citizens to a small hut, fifteen feet by twenty, exposed to rain and sun, without permission to leave except for a bath in the sea once or twice a week, I had prepared an elaborate statement of the outrages perpetrated by Butler upon our people, or rather of the more flagrant ones, which I committed to Reverdy Johnson, a commissioner of the United States who had been sent out to investigate and report upon certain transactions of Butler. Mr. Johnson received this document, but stated that his mission related exclusively to certain issues which had arisen between Butler and the foreign consuls. He manifested, however, some sympathy for our wronged people and some disgust for the excesses and villainies of Butler. Shortly after Mr. Johnson's departure, I was sent to Ship Island.

A description of the causes and circumstances of the imprisonment of our citizens who are now held on this island will afford some of the mildest illustrations of Butler's brutality. There are about sixty prisoners here, all of whom are closely confined in portable houses and furnished with the most wretched and unwholesome condemned soldiers' rations. Some are kept at hard labor on the fort; several, in addition to labor, are compelled to wear a ball and chain, which is never removed. Among these is Mr. Shepherd, a respectable, elderly, and weakly citizen, who is charged with secreting certain papers belonging to the naval officer of the Confederate States, which the latter left in his charge when he departed from New Orleans. Mr. Shepherd had the proof that the officer who had deposited these documents afterward returned and took them and that they had been carried into the Confederate States. This testi-

mony Butler would not receive and declared that, if it existed, it would make no difference in his case.

Doctor Moore, a dealer in drugs, is also at hard labor with ball and chain, on the charge of having sent a few ounces of quinine into the Confederate States. There are five prisoners condemned and employed at hard labor on the charge of intending to break their parole as prisoners of war, captured at Fort Jackson. There is also a delicate youth from the country who is subjected to the same treatment on the charge of being a guerrilla, the term which Butler applies to the partisan rangers organized under the act of congress of the Confederate States. Alderman Beggs, on the charge of denouncing those who, having taken the oath to the Confederate States, afterward swore allegiance to the United States, and Mr. Keller, a vendor of books, stationery, and scientific apparatus, on the charge of permitting a clerk to placard the word "Chickahominy" on a skeleton which was suspended in his show window for sale for the use of students of anatomy, are condemned also to close imprisonment and hard labor for two years. The others mentioned above are condemned for a longer period.

A like condemnation and punishment were imposed upon Judge John W. Andrews, a most respectable citizen, recently a member of the judiciary of the state, of the legislature, and of the City Council, and a prominent merchant. This gentleman is advanced in years and in very delicate health. There is little hope that his health can long sustain his present burdens and hardships. The circumstances of Mrs. Phillips' imprisonment are probably known to you. As, however, I desire this to be an authentic and studiously accurate statement of the facts, I will here relate them.

In the raid of the U.S. troops near Warrenton, Miss., a young officer named De Kay was mortally wounded. He died in

New Orleans, and an attempt was made by the Federal authorities to get up a pompous funeral ceremony and procession in honor of so "gallant and heroic a young officer" who had fallen in an expedition which had no other purpose or object but the pillage of defenseless farms and villages. The efforts to excite the sympathies of our people on this occasion proved a ridiculous failure and the funeral ceremony had no aspect of solemnity or even propriety, a long line of carriages composing the cortege designed for the Union citizens being all empty.

As this procession passed the residence of P. Phillips, Esq., Mrs. Phillips, standing on the balcony with several lady friends, was observed by some Federal officer to smile, so it was charged. She was immediately arrested and taken before Butler, who, in the most brutal and insolent manner, sought to terrify the heroic lady. In this he did not succeed. While denying that her gaiety had any reference whatever to the funeral ceremony, Mrs. Phillips refused to make any apologies or concessions to the vulgar tyrant. Thereupon, she was condemned to close imprisonment in a filthy guardroom, thence to be transported to Ship Island, where she was to be held in close confinement for two years, with no other fare but soldiers' rations; no intercourse or correspondence with any person except through General Butler. This sentence was published in the newspapers, accompanied by words of the grossest insult and most vulgar ribaldry, in which Mrs. Phillips was denounced as "not a common but an uncommon bad woman," referring to his proclamation, denounced by Lord Palmerston and the whole civilized world as "so infamous," in which his soldiers are authorized to treat "as common women plying their profession" all who may manifest any contempt or discourtesy toward them.

To add further insult, in the order condemning Mr. Keller, it was made part of his sentence to permit him to hold converse and intercourse with Mrs. Phillips, to which condition this honest man was induced to protest from the belief that his fellow prisoner was a notorious courtesan of the city who bore the name of Phillips. This protest was published in the paper with Butler's order granting the request of Keller, so as to convey to the world the idea that a poor vendor of periodicals declined association with a lady of the highest respectability, the wife of a distinguished lawyer and ex-member of Congress. I can bear personal testimony to the rigorous execution of the sentence against Mrs. Phillips, having been imprisoned for weeks in a building adjoining to that which she was never allowed to leave. Such was the treatment of a delicate lady of the highest refinement, the mother of nine children.

The case of Judge Andrews presents another striking example of the brutality and dishonesty of Butler. The charge against him imputed the horrid crime of having received and exhibited, nine months before the arrival of Butler in the city, a cross which had been sent to him by a young friend in our army at Manassas and which, it was represented, was made of the bones of a Yankee soldier. No proof whatever was adduced that such exhibition had ever been made by Judge Andrews in exultation, and the cross, after being received, was destroyed before Butler arrived in the city. In his first interview with the authorities of the city, Butler had declared that he would take no cognizance of any acts committed before he occupied the city and established martial law therein. This solemn and oft-repeated pledge he has violated in a thousand instances. . . .

So much for the prisoners at Ship Island, with the facts of whose cases I am personally acquainted. I refrain from any reference to my own case, hard as my doom is, closely confined on this island with all my property appropriated by the enemy and my family placed under strict espionage and subject to many annoyances, insults, and discomforts. With all its trials and hardships the condition of the prisoners here is quite easy and endurable compared with that of those who are confined in the damp and unwholesome casemates of Forts Jackson and Saint Philip, on the Mississippi, and in Fort Pickens, on Santa Rosa Island.

Among the latter is the mayor of the city, who has been imprisoned for four months for the offense of writing a letter to Butler protesting against his order relative to the treatment of the ladies of the city and declaring his inability to maintain the peace of the city if the Federal soldiers were thus authorized to insult and outrage our women at their own pleasure and will. The secretary of the mayor, who wrote the letter signed by the mayor, was included in the same committal and imprisonment. Several members of the Council, for like or smaller offenses, suffer the same punishment.

Doctor Porter, a wealthy dentist and citizen, is imprisoned for requiring the Citizens' Bank, the pet bank and place of deposit of Butler and his agent in his vast schemes of corruption and extortion, to pay checks in the currency which Butler alone allowed the banks to pay. George C. Laurason, formerly collector of the port of New Orleans, suffers a like penalty for applying for a passport to go to Europe, where his family now is. Thomas Murray, as president of that benevolent institution known as the Free Market, which supplied the families of the soldiers with the means of subsistence; Charles Heidsieck, a French citizen, the owner of the celebrated wine manufactory in France; Mr. Dacres and other British citizens; Mr. Mire, a wealthy and highly respectable Spanish citizen, the owner of extensive sawmills in Florida and the contractor to supply the French Navy with timber, are all imprisoned at Fort Pickens for endeavoring to pass the lines without taking the oath prescribed by Butler for foreigners, which oath requires them to reveal to the United States all information they may have respecting the acts and designs of the Confederate States on pain of being regarded and treated as enemies and spies. There are, too, many prisoners who are confined on the information of political and personal enemies as dangerous characters for offenses alleged to have been committed by them months and years before Butler's arrival in the city.

Doctor McPhevroa, an elderly and most respectable citizen, was condemned to the casemates of Fort Jackson for speaking in a circle of his friends of Butler's proclamation, No. 28, that relative to the ladies of New Orleans, as "infamous," the very epithet which Lord Palmerston in the House of Commons declared as the only appropriate one. Dr. Warren Stone, the distinguished surgeon and philanthropist, was consigned to a like punishment for refusing to recognize an individual who had been announced as president of a Union association and, yet, who a few months before had made in public a most violent speech against the Yankees and had advised our people to cut the throats of all invaders.

Several ladies of the highest social position have been imprisoned for the expression of sympathy with the Confederates and the wearing of ribbons of certain colors. Mrs. Dubois, an elderly lady long engaged in the business of teaching our children, was imprisoned on the charge of not being able to account for certain keys and books belonging to the schools, which were never in her possession. All the members of the Finance Committee of the City Council are imprisoned for authorizing the subscription of the city to the fund for its defense; and several hundred of our citizens who subscribed to this fund have been compelled to pay 25 percent of their subscription to Butler, under threat of imprisonment at hard labor. To swell this exaction to the sum of $300,000, all the cotton factors of the city who had united in a circular address to the planters advising them not to send their cotton to New Orleans were assessed in sums of $500 and $250, which they had to pay or go to prison.

The treatment of a venerable citizen named Roberts, a farmer living a short distance from Baton Rouge, is one of peculiar atrocity. A son of Mr. Roberts, a soldier of the Confederate Army, having come on sick leave to see his parents, a detachment of the Twenty-first Indiana Regiment was sent to arrest him. The young man, hearing the approach of armed men, went out to meet them, when several shots were fired by the Indianians, one of which killed young Roberts. The father, seeing the danger of his son, seized a gun and fired through the door, slightly wounding Colonel McMillan, the commander of the detachment. He was then arrested and charged with having killed his own son, and was taken with the rest of his family from his house, the body of his son being brought out and laid on the ground. The building, all the outhouses, barns, and stables were burned to the ground, and his mules, horses, and cattle were driven off to the Federal camp. Old Mr. Roberts was condemned to close imprisonment for twenty years, and this imprisonment he is now undergoing at Fort Pickens. . . .

A Mr. Levy, a respectable merchant, was imprisoned for one month for stating to a Federal that he heard that Baton Rouge had been evacuated, when it really had been evacuated. Another citizen was arrested in the cars and imprisoned for saying that the distress for cotton in England would soon increase; and another for repeating what had been published in the *Delta* that "Richmond had fallen," such a remark being regarded as ironical after the Confederate victories in the first days of July. A great many have been imprisoned on the information of their slaves that they had concealed or destroyed arms, and the informers emancipated. Mr. Lathrop, a respectable lawyer, is

now undergoing, in the parish prison, a sentence of two years' imprisonment for "kidnaping" his own slave, who had been appropriated by a Federal officer. This sentence, Butler declared, was intended as a warning to the people not to interfere with the servants of his officers, meaning the slaves of our citizens appropriated by them.

A number of our citizens, enrolled as partisan rangers or in the state militia, have been closely imprisoned and threatened with death as guerrillas or pirates. W. E. Seymour, late a captain in one of the regiments in the defense of the state and honorably paroled, is a close prisoner at Fort Saint Philip and his property all confiscated on account of an obituary notice which appeared in his own paper, the *Bulletin*, of his father, the late gallant Col. I. G. Seymour, of the Sixth Louisiana, who fell in the battle at Gaines' Mill. The writer of the article, Mr. Devis, an old and infirm citizen, was subjected to a like punishment and is now a prisoner at Fort Pickens. Besides these instances, there are a great many citizens who have only escaped imprisonment by the payment of large fines, and in many cases by corrupting Federal officers of influence.

To enumerate the cases of confiscation by order of Butler, and in many cases even by the order of his subordinates, would exceed the bounds I have affixed to this report. I have, however, kept a record of these cases and will communicate them at some other time. Suffice it to say that nearly all the large and commodious houses of our citizens, especially those of absentees and officers in our army and government, have been thus appropriated. Officers of no higher grade than lieutenants occupy houses which have cost our citizens $30,000, and where furniture has been removed, and, when deficient, any articles which the appropriators may deem necessary to their comfort are purchased at the expense of the owners of the property. The wives and families of our citizens are frequently ejected from their houses to make way for coarse Federal officers and the Negro women whom they appropriate as their wives and concubines. Ships have been loaded with costly articles of furniture stolen — they say confiscated — from our citizens and transmitted North to the families of Federal officers. Many a house in New England is even now resounding with the tones of pianos thus stolen from the parlors of our citizens. A vast amount of silver has been appropriated in like manner. The example set by Butler in appropriating the house of General Twiggs's minor heir and furnishing it in a most lavish and luxurious style at the expense of the estate, and in transmitting the plate and swords of the deceased veteran to Lowell; the seizure and removal to the North of the statue of Washington by Powers and of the state library from the capital at Baton Rouge, have been extensively followed by Butler's subordinates.

Nor have I here space to expose the extortions of Butler through the agency of his brother, an abandoned gambler and speculator, who has compelled our citizens by all kinds of threats to sell their property to him at rates fixed by him, who has monopolized all the shipping employed by the United States to transport the produce thus forced from our people, who has acted as broker to obtain remissions of penalties and the restoration of fugitive slaves, in many cases on condition of the payment of half their value and on pledges of half of the growing crops. In this manner have the plantations within fifty miles of New Orleans been taxed. Many of them, unable to secure even these terms, have been depopulated.

You have doubtless been made acquainted with the proceedings of Butler to compel our citizens to take the oath of allegiance to the United States — the prohibition of all trade to those who have not taken the oath and the seizure of their funds in bank. The last device will be to compel all those who do not take that oath to register themselves as enemies of the United States, when they will be either imprisoned or driven from the city and their property confiscated. These orders, especially the oath requirement, are applicable as well to women as to men. Indeed, the malice of Butler against females is more bitter and insatiable than that against males. A placard in his office in large letters bears this inscription: "The venom of the she adder is as dangerous as that of the he adder."

And this is but a feeble and deficient presentment of the enormities and brutalities of this cowardly and brutal monster. It is in vain that some of his subordinates remonstrate and protest against many of his acts. He will permit no one to thwart his two great objects — to bid highest for the favor of the Northern mob and to accumulate a vast fortune by extortion and plunder. The extent to which this latter purpose is carried will surpass all similar efforts of great robbers from Verres down.

I content myself with this mere epitome of Butler's crimes. At some other more favorable occasion I will present them in greater detail and with the authentic proofs which I cannot now command. It would not be becoming in me to solicit or suggest that some steps be taken by the president and government of the Confederate States to correct and to avenge these wrongs done our people. I have full confidence that all will be done in that behalf which can be done. I cannot but say, however, that a feeling prevails among our people that they have been forgotten or abandoned by the government for which they suffer, or an apprehension that the true state of affairs is not known or appreciated by our government. That this may not any longer be the case I have incurred the peril of writing this memoir in a close prison on a desolate island, with a Federal sentinel at the door and the broadside of a Federal frigate frowning upon all in the bay.

78.

John Greenleaf Whittier: "Barbara Frietchie"

"This poem was written in strict conformity to the account of the incident as I had it from respectable and trustworthy sources," wrote Whittier of this very famous, very sentimental, and yet very successful ballad. "It has since been the subject of a good deal of conflicting testimony, and the story was probably incorrect in some of its details. It is admitted by all that Barbara Frietchie was no myth, but a worthy and highly esteemed gentlewoman, intensely loyal and a hater of the Slavery Rebellion, holding her Union flag sacred and keeping it with her Bible; that when the Confederates halted before her house, and entered her dooryard, she denounced them in vigorous language, shook her cane in their faces, and drove them out; and when General Burnside's troops followed close upon Jackson's, she waved her flag and cheered them." But does it really matter whether the story is true? It is a wonderful story nevertheless.

Source: *Complete Poetical Works*, Cambridge Edition, Boston, 1894.

❦ BARBARA FRIETCHIE

Up from the meadows rich with corn,
Clear in the cool September morn,

The clustered spires of Frederick stand
Green-walled by the hills of Maryland.

Round about them orchards sweep,
Apple and peach tree fruited deep,

Fair as the garden of the Lord
To the eyes of the famished rebel horde,

On that pleasant morn of the early fall
When Lee marched over the mountain
   wall;

Over the mountains winding down,
Horse and foot, into Frederick town.

Forty flags with their silver stars,
Forty flags with their crimson bars,

Flapped in the morning wind: the sun
Of noon looked down, and saw not one.

Up rose old Barbara Frietchie then,
Bowed with her fourscore years and ten;

Bravest of all in Frederick town,
She took up the flag the men hauled
   down;

In her attic window the staff she set,
To show that one heart was loyal yet.

Up the street came the rebel tread,
Stonewall Jackson riding ahead.

Under his slouched hat left and right
He glanced; the old flag met his sight.

"Halt!" — the dust-brown ranks stood
   fast.
"Fire!" — out blazed the rifle blast.

It shivered the window, pane and sash;
It rent the banner with seam and gash.

Quick, as it fell, from the broken staff
Dame Barbara snatched the silken scarf.

She leaned far out on the window sill,
And shook it forth with a royal will.

"Shoot, if you must, this old gray head,
But spare your country's flag," she said.

A shade of sadness, a blush of shame,
Over the face of the leader came;

The nobler nature within him stirred
To life at that woman's deed and word;

"Who touches a hair of yon gray head
Dies like a dog! March on!" he said.

All day long through Frederick street
Sounded the tread of marching feet:

All day long that free flag tossed
Over the heads of the rebel host.

Ever its torn folds rose and fell
On the loyal winds that loved it well;

And through the hill-gaps sunset light
Shone over it with a warm good-night.

Barbara Frietchie's work is o'er,
And the Rebel rides on his raids no more.

Honor to her! and let a tear
Fall, for her sake, on Stonewall's bier.

Over Barbara Frietchie's grave,
Flag of Freedom and Union, wave!

Peace and order and beauty draw
Round thy symbol of light and law;

And ever the stars above look down
On thy stars below in Frederick town!

79.

Anonymous: Dilemma of a Norwegian Immigrant

Between 1836 and 1900, over half a million Norwegians emigrated, causing Norway a greater loss of population owing to emigration to America than any other European country except Ireland. In the 1840s Norwegian immigrants sent home letters glowing with praise for America. In one such letter a Norwegian wrote: "What an impression it would make on a poor highlander's imagination to be told that some day he might eat wheat bread every day and pork at least three times a week!" The Norwegian government, worried about the loss of population, made efforts to offset these optimistic accounts by publishing some woeful tales about America. A Norwegian immigrant from Dodge County, Minnesota, was prompted by wartime conditions on the frontier to write the following letter, which a Norwegian newspaper, Morgenbladet, *gladly printed on November 22, 1862, hoping to discourage further emigration. Nevertheless, after the war, the tide of Norwegian emigration to America continued to increase.*

Source: Blegen, pp. 425-427.

AT THIS TIME life is not very pleasant in this so-called wonderful America. The country is full of danger, and at no time do we feel any security for our lives or property. A week ago in our county (Dodge County in southeastern Minnesota), the name of every citizen between eighteen and forty-five years of age was taken down, regardless of whether he, like myself, was married or not. Next month (October) there is to be a levy

People escaping from the Indian massacre of 1862 in Minnesota; photo by Adrian J. Ebell

of soldiers for military service, and our county alone is to supply 118 men, in addition to those who have already enlisted as volunteers.

Last week we, therefore, all had to leave our harvesting work and our weeping wives and children and appear at the place of enlistment, downcast and worried. We waited until 6 o'clock in the afternoon. Then, finally, the commissioner arrived, accompanied by a band, which continued playing for a long time to encourage us and give us a foretaste of the joys of war. But we thought only of its sorrows, and, despite our reluctance, had to give our name and age. To tempt people to enlist as volunteers, everybody who would volunteer was offered $225, out of which $125 is paid by the county and $100 by the state. Several men then enlisted, Yankees and Norwegians; and we others, who preferred to stay at home and work for our wives and children, were ordered to be ready at the next levy. Then who is to go will be decided by drawing lots. In the meantime, we were forbidden to leave the county without special permission, and we were also told that no one would get a passport to leave the country. Dejected, we went home, and now we are in a mood of uncertainty and tension, almost like prisoners of war in this formerly so free country. Our names have been taken down — perhaps I shall be a soldier next

month and have to leave my home, my wife, child, and everything I have been working for over so many years.

But this is not the worst of it. We have another and far more cruel enemy nearby, namely, the Indians. They are raging, especially in northwestern Minnesota, and perpetrate cruelties which no pen can describe. As yet they have not appeared in our fairly densely populated districts, but still they are not more than ten or fifteen Norwegian miles away. Every day, settlers come through here who have had to abandon everything they owned to escape a most painful death. Several Norwegians have been killed and many women have been captured. They chase the women together in groups and make them herd the cattle they have seized.

When the Indians are on horseback, they rush with the speed of a whirlwind across the vast prairies. You are not safe from them anywhere, for they are as cunning as they are bold. The other evening we received the frightening message that they have been seen in our neighborhood; so we hitched our horses and made ready to leave our house and all our property and escape from the savages under the cover of darkness. But it was a false alarm, God be praised, and for this time we could rest undisturbed. How terrible it is thus, every moment, to expect that you will be attacked, robbed, and perhaps murdered! We do not go to bed any night without fear, and my rifle is always loaded.

But may the will of the Lord be done. We must not grumble, for He may still save us. It is true that some cavalry have been dispatched against these hordes, but they will not avail much, for the Indians are said to be more than 10,000 strong. Besides, they are so cunning that it is not easy to get the better of them. Sometimes they disguise themselves in ordinary farmers' clothes and stalk their victims noiselessly. Thus, they recently attacked some Norwegians who were working at their threshing machine suspecting no danger. The men were all killed, the horses stolen, and the machine and the whole crop burned.

From this you may see how we live: on the one hand, the prospect of being carried off as cannon fodder to the South; on the other, the imminent danger of falling prey to the Indians; add to this the heavy war tax that everybody has to pay whether he is enlisted as a soldier or not. You are better off who can live at home in peaceful Norway. God grant us patience and fortitude to bear these heavy burdens.

80.

James Sloan Gibbons: "Three Hundred Thousand More"

James Sloan Gibbons, like his contemporary John Greenleaf Whittier, was a Quaker Abolitionist whose pacifist principles were compromised by the Civil War. In 1862 Lincoln called for 300,000 more volunteers; and Gibbons, remembering that a group of Quakers was the first to vote against slavery in 1688, was inspired to write the poem "We Are Coming, Father Abraham, Three Hundred Thousand More" as a stirring call to fight "for freedom's sake." The New York Evening Post *published the poem on July 16, 1862, unsigned, and for a long time its authorship was attributed to the* Post's *editor, William Cullen Bryant. Later set to music by Stephen Foster and Luther Emerson, it became a favorite song of the Union.*

THREE HUNDRED THOUSAND MORE

We are coming, Father Abraham, three hundred thousand more,
From Mississippi's winding stream and from New England's shore;
We leave our ploughs and workshops, our wives and children dear,
With hearts too full for utterance, with but a silent tear;
We dare not look behind us, but steadfastly before.
We are coming, Father Abraham, three hundred thousand more!

If you look across the hilltops that meet the northern sky,
Long moving lines of rising dust your vision may descry;
And now the wind an instant tears the cloudy veil aside,
And floats aloft our spangled flag, in glory and in pride;
And bayonets in the sunlight gleam, and bands brave music pour.
We are coming, Father Abraham, three hundred thousand more!

If you look all up our valleys where the growing harvests shine,
You may see our sturdy farmer boys fast forming into line;
And children from their mothers' knees are pulling at the weeds,
And learning how to reap and sow, against their country's needs;
And a farewell group stands weeping at every cottage door —
We are coming, Father Abraham, three hundred thousand more!

You have called us and we're coming, by Richmond's bloody tide,
To lay us down for freedom's sake, our brothers' bones beside;
Or from foul treason's savage grasp to wrench the murderous blade,
And in the face of foreign foes its fragments to parade.
Six hundred thousand loyal men and true have gone before —
We are coming, Father Abraham, three hundred thousand more!

81.

JOSEPH EMERSON BROWN: Opposition to Conscription in the Confederacy

As governor of Georgia, Joseph Brown was an early advocate of secession and a loyal supporter of the Confederacy. When the war led, however, to a centralization of power by the Confederate government, Brown fell into conflict with the Confederacy. He was a fanatical defender of the doctrine of state sovereignty and on numerous occasions charged the Confederacy with exceeding its constitutional authority. Early in the war Brown disputed President Davis' authority to appoint officers to command Georgia troops. In April 1862 the Confederate Congress passed the first national conscription act in America, and Governor Brown wrote the following letter of protest to Davis on April 22.

Source: Ainsworth, 4th series, I, pp. 1082-1085.

Dear Sir:

So soon as I received from the secretary of war official notice of the passage by Congress of the Conscription Act, placing in the military service of the Confederate States all white men between the ages of eighteen and thirty-five years, I saw that it was impossible for me longer to retain in the field the Georgia state troops without probable collision and conflict with the Confederate authorities in the face of the enemy. I therefore acquiesced in the necessity which compelled me to transfer the state forces to the command of the Confed-erate general at Savannah, and tendered to General Lawton, who commands the Military District of Georgia, not only the conscripts in the state army but also those not conscripts for the unexpired term of their enlistment. General Lawton accepted the command with the assurance that he would interfere as little as possible with the company and regimental organizations of the troops. This assurance I trust the government will permit him to carry out in the same spirit of liberality in which it was given. If the state regiments are broken up and the conscripts belonging to them forced into other organizations against their consent, it will have a very discouraging effect. If the regiments and companies were preserved and permission given to the officers to fill up their ranks by recruits, there would be no doubt of their ability to do so, and I think they have a just right to expect this privilege.

Georgia has promptly responded to every call made upon her by you for troops, and has always given more than you asked. She has now about 60,000 in the field. Had you called upon her executive for 20,000 more (if her just quota), they would have been furnished without delay. The plea of necessity, so far at least as this state is concerned, cannot be set up in defense of the Conscription Act. When the government of the United States disregarded and attempted to trample upon the rights of the states, Georgia set its power at defiance and seceded from the Union rather than submit to the consolidation of all power in the hands of the central or federal government. The Conscription Act not only put it in the power of the executive of the Confederacy to disorganize her troops, which she was compelled to call into the field for her own defense in addition to her just quota because of the neglect of the Confederacy to place sufficient troops upon her coast for her defense, which would have required less than half the number she has sent to the field, but also places it in his power to destroy her state government by disbanding her lawmaking power.

The constitution of this state makes every male citizen who has attained the age of twenty-one years eligible to a seat in the House of Representatives of the General Assembly, and everyone who has attained the age of twenty-five, eligible to a seat in the Senate. There are a large number of the members of the General Assembly between the ages of eighteen and thirty-five. They are white citizens of the Confederate States, and there is no statute in the state, and I am aware of none in the Confederate States' code, which exempts them from military duty. They, therefore, fall within the provisions of the Conscription Act.

It may become necessary for me to convene the General Assembly in extra session; or, if not, the regular session will commence the first Wednesday in November. When the members meet at the capitol, if not sooner, they might be claimed as conscripts by a Confederate officer and arrested with a view to carry them to some remote part of the Confederacy as recruits to fill up some company now in service. They have no military power, and could only look to the executive of the state for military protection; and I cannot hesitate to say that in such case I should use all the remaining military force of the state in defense of a coordinate constitutional branch of the government.

I can, therefore, permit no enrollment of the members of the General Assembly under the Conscription Act. The same is true of the judges of the Supreme and Superior courts should any of them fall within the ages above mentioned, and of the secretaries of the executive department, the heads and necessary clerks of the other departments of the state government, and the tax collectors and receivers of the different counties, who are now in the midst of their duties and are not permitted by law to supply substitutes, and whose duties must be performed or the revenues of the state cannot be collected. The same remark applies to the staff of the commander in chief. There is no statute exempting them from military duty for the reason that they are at all times subject to the command of the governor and are not expected to go into the ranks. The state's quartermaster, commissary, ordnance, and engineer departments fall within the same rule. The major generals, brigadier generals, and other field officers of the militia would seem to be entitled to like consideration.

Again, the Western and Atlantic Railroad is the property of the state and is under the control and management of the governor. It is a source of revenue to the state, and its successful management is a matter of great military importance both to the state and the Confederacy. I now have an efficient force of officers and workmen upon the road, and must suspend operations if all between eighteen and thirty-five are taken away from the road. I would also invite your attention to the further fact that the state owns and controls the Georgia Military Institute, at Marietta, and now has in the institute over 125 cadets, a large proportion of whom are within the age of conscripts. If they are not exempt, this most important institution is broken up. I must not omit in this connection the students of the state university and of the other colleges of the state. These valuable institutions of learning must also be suspended if the law is enforced against the students.

I would also respectfully call your attention to the further fact that in portions of our state where the slave population is heavy almost the entire white male population capable of bearing arms (except the overseers on the plantations) are now in the military service of the Confederacy. Most of these overseers are over eighteen and under thirty-five. If they are carried to the field, thousands of slaves must be left without overseers, and their labor not only lost at a time when there is great need of it in the production of provisions and supplies for our armies, but the peace and safety of helpless women and children must be imperiled for want of protection against bands of idle slaves who must be left to roam over the country without restraint.

It is also worthy of remark that a large proportion of our best mechanics and of the persons engaged in the various branches of manufacturing now of vital importance to the success of our cause are within the ages which subject them to the provisions of the Conscription Act. My remark that I cannot permit the enrollment of such state officers as are necessary to the existence of the state government and the working of the state road does not of course apply to persons

engaged in the other useful branches of industry considered of paramount importance; but I must ask, in justice to the people of this state, that such exemptions among these classes be made as the public necessities may require.

As you are all well aware, the military operations of the government cannot be carried on without the use of all our railroads, and the same necessity exists for the exemption of all other railroad officers and workmen which exists in the case of the state road. There are doubtless other important interests not herein enumerated which will readily occur to you which must be kept alive or the most serious consequences must ensue. The constitution gives to congress the power to provide for organizing, arming, and disciplining the militia, and for governing such part of them as may be employed in the service of the Confederate States, reserving to the states, respectively, the appointment of the officers and the authority of training the militia according to the discipline prescribed by congress. The Conscription Act gives the president the power to enroll the entire militia of the states between eighteen and thirty-five, and takes from states their constitutional right to appoint the officers and to train the militia. While the act does not leave to the states the appointment of a single officer to command the militia employed in the service of the Confederate States under its provisions, it places it in the power of the president to take a major general of the militia of a state, if he is not thirty-five years of age, and place him in the ranks of the C. S. Army, under the command of a third lieutenant appointed by the president, and to treat him as a deserter if he refuses to obey the call and submit to the command of the subaltern placed over him.

I do not wish to be understood in any portion of this letter to refer to the intentions of the president, but only to the extraordinary powers given him by the act. This act not only disorganizes the military systems of all the states but consolidates almost the entire military power of the states in the Confederate executive with the appointment of the officers of the militia, and enables him at his pleasure to cripple or destroy the civil government of each state by arresting and carrying into the Confederate service the officers charged by the state constitution with the administration of the state government.

I notice, by a perusal of the Conscription Act, that the president may, with the consent of the governors of the respective states, employ state officers in the enrollment of the conscripts. While I shall throw no obstructions in the way of the general enrollment of persons embraced within the act, except as above stated, I do not feel that it is the duty of the executive of a state to employ actually the officers of the state in the execution of a law which virtually strips the state of her constitutional military powers, and, if fully executed, destroys the legislative department of her government, making even the sessions of her General Assembly dependent upon the will of the Confederate executive.

I therefore respectfully decline all connection with the proposed enrollment and propose to reserve the question of the constitutionality of the act and its binding force upon the people of this state for their consideration at a time when it may less seriously embarrass the Confederacy in the prosecution of the war. You will much oblige by informing me of the extent to which you propose making exemptions, if any, in favor of the interests above mentioned, and such others as you may consider of vital importance. The question is one of the greatest interest to our people, and they are anxious to know your pleasure in the premises.

82.

ANONYMOUS: Financial Resources of the North

Though the first months of the Civil War were marked by business uncertainty in the North, the war soon stimulated an unrivaled economic boom. In October 1862 the Knickerbocker *magazine, a popular New York monthly, though lukewarm toward Lincoln's policies, published an article praising the economic changes that the war had produced in the North and reflecting the Northerners' buoyant optimism about their growing prosperity.*

Source: *Knickerbocker*, October 1862: "The Financial Resources of the United States."

NOTHING HAS SO ASTONISHED EUROPE in modern times as the magnitude of the scale on which the American republic carries on the war for the maintenance of its own integrity. For the enormous expenditure of men and money, and the vastness of the theater on which the military operations are conducted, there is no parallel in the history of any European nation, not excepting even France, under the regime of the elder Napoleon. There is no civil war to be compared with it in extent, either in ancient or modern times. It is a war commensurate with the gigantic features of the country, its vast area, bounded by two oceans; its mighty rivers, watering valleys of wonderful fertility; and its inexhaustible agricultural, mineral, manufacturing, and commercial resources. The war is commensurate, too, with the tremendous issues involved in the result; the continued existence, or the dissolution of the great American Union; the preservation of law and order, or the prevalence of anarchy and political chaos; the solution of the problem of self-government, by the final triumph of democratic institutions, or by the failure of that which the founders of the government regarded as "an experiment," a triumph or a failure affecting the interest, the liberties, and the destinies of millions of the living human race, and of millions still unborn in both worlds.

Already 1 million of volunteers have been called into the field, with 300,000 drafted men in reserve; and an immense naval force has been improvised to operate on the seacoast and navigable rivers of the enemy. By land and water the conflict has been carried on for eighteen months, with the most lavish expenditure for arms, of the best construction known to modern art and science; for the most improved equipments and for all the munitions and appliances of war of the most costly description. It is hardly necessary to say that to maintain such an army and navy, and to wage such a war, involves a corresponding outlay and financial resources so immense that no European power could attempt it without certain bankruptcy.

Hence, when hostilities were fairly inaugurated, and our government commenced its preparations upon such a gigantic scale, the great financial organs of England laughed to scorn the idea of the United States without a dollar in its treasury, and with doubtful credit in Europe, being able to carry on the struggle for any length of time. The leading journals of London labored so sedulously to depreciate the American war loan in advance that the calcula-

tion was that the government would be checkmated at the very outset by a refusal on the part of foreigners to take the new bonds. But how little these expounders of British public opinion could appreciate the patriotism or the resources of the loyal states of the Union may be judged by the fact that the immediate wants of the government were supplied by banks and individuals; and that the secretary of the treasury decided not to offer the loan in any foreign market but to negotiate it exclusively in the United States, though he estimated the expenditure till July 1863, which was the most remote period he had calculated for the termination of the war, at $830 million. Indeed it was expected by some of the ablest financiers, not only in England but here, that the expenses would amount for the two years and a quarter to $1,000 million.

But we are happy to say that the estimate even of Mr. Chase is above the mark. The first year of a war costs more in proportion to the number of men enrolled than subsequent years. The national debt on the 1st of July, 1862, was $504,500,000; the debt on the 1st of July, 1863, calculating from the data of the last year, will be only $626 million after applying the revenue from duties on imports and the estimated proceeds of the direct or internal tax.

English writers congratulate their country on the favorable comparison which its expenditures during its greatest wars present when placed side by side with the expenditures of this war for the Union. They say that the average yearly amount of the British loan, from 1793 to 1815, was under $150 million; and that in the very first year, the 20 million of loyal population at the North borrow twice as much as England borrowed in her direst extremity in one year, when her population was 18 million, and when she had been groaning for generations under the pressure of taxation. . . .

Admitting the data to be correct, we ask

to what conclusion does the reasoning tend? It does not prove that our expenditures are more extravagant than those of England, or more likely to result in bankruptcy. It only shows that we can better afford a larger expenditure. What is extravagance in one man would not be in another. It depends on the means of each. If our means to meet the expenditure of our war were only equal to the means of England then there might be some force in the argument. The resources of England are limited and for the most part artificial and worn out, and her people are impoverished by accumulated taxation. Our resources are fresh and boundless and continually growing; our people have been hitherto almost untaxed, and wealth is so diffused among them that they can bear, without feeling it very severely, an amount of taxation that would grind the British people to powder.

Besides, it is not intended that the war should be a long one. The idea is that it be an expensive and short one, and such wars are the cheapest in the end. It might suit the policy of the British Empire to extend a war over many years. That would never suit the policy of the American government or harmonize with the interests of the American people. To enable them to cultivate the arts of peace, and to prevent future war, is one of the chief designs of the present conflict. Hence the great sacrifices which have been so cheerfully made. We admit that to carry on the contest very long upon its present scale would be to use up the resources even of the United States, and that it must be speedily brought to an end from sheer exhaustion, and this is still more true of the enemy. A long war under the circumstances is, therefore, impossible.

The American mode is rapidity in everything. The jog-trot, slow-coach style of European wars does not suit the genius of our people. They are quick in perceiving the situation of affairs. Their intelligence and general education give them that advantage. Hence, in the most warmly contested elections, the moment the result is known the beaten party acquiesce with perfect good humor. In this struggle now pending, which appears to be at its crisis, if the Southern Confederacy is defeated in a decisive battle, the rebellious states will probably submit with the best grace they can. If the Rebels should succeed in winning two or three more great battles, it is extremely probable that the feeling of the majority of the people of the North would soon develop itself by unmistakable symptoms, that their Southern brethren should be allowed to depart from the Union and permanently establish a separate confederacy. We are a practical people and will not adhere long to a theory if it does not produce the promised fruit.

Now let us examine the capabilities of the nation to meet the war debt, consisting of loan by act of February 1861, of $25 million; Treasury notes, 6 percent, $10 million; Treasury notes, 730 and 365, together with demand notes, $250 million; legal tender demand notes, February 25, 1862, $150 million, of which $50 million were to take up the demand notes of July 17, 1861. Additional legal tender notes, July 11, 1862, $150 million, of which $35 million may be of lower denomination than $5; coupons, or registered bonds, not exceeding $500 million, bearing interest at 6 percent, into which the Treasury notes are convertible; lastly, stamps as currency, $40 million.

Though the secretary of the treasury is authorized to issue the foregoing securities, he does not necessarily issue them to the full amount. Accordingly, on the 29th of May last, the whole funded debt of the United States, including the loans of 1842, 1847, 1858, and 1860, was $491,446,184, at an average interest of 4³⁵/₁₀₀ percent, as reported by Mr. Chase himself; and the actual debt on July 1, 1862, we know to be $504,500,000; the estimated debt, July 1, 1863, after applying the direct tax to its reduction, $626 million.

Now what is this compared with the debt

of Great Britain, which in round numbers is $4 billion, and requiring each year to be paid for interest and management, $127,695,701, against $26 million, the probable interest of our debt, July 1, 1863? The English debt would, therefore, be nearly seven times as great, and the interest nearly five times that of the interest of the debt of the United States, while the ability to pay would be greatly inferior. It is the mass of the people and not the rich who pay the taxes. Now what is the condition of a large number of the people of England? Mr. Pashley, in his work on "Pauperism," states that of that population, 3 million belong to "an ignorant, degraded, and pauper class," and actually receive parish relief in the course of every year, while a still larger class are but little less ignorant, degraded, and miserable. The interest of the English debt is equal to $4.36 per head; the interest of the French debt is $110 million, and is $3.04 per head; the interest of the American debt is $1.14 per head. The national debt of England will never be paid. The debt of the United States will be paid off, principal and interest, in a very few years. Our national debt in 1816 was $127,500,000; the population, 8,500,000. The burden of the interest was 90 cents per head; the principal, $14.81. The valuation of the property averaged per head, from 1816 to 1835, about $250. The entire debt was extinguished in 1835, leaving a large surplus in the Treasury. The value of the property in the loyal states, in 1860, was $11 billion, or $477 per head. We are, therefore, better able to extinghish the present debt in fifteen years than we were the former debt in twenty years. In sixteen years, an average payment of about $43 million per annum would completely wipe it out. . . .

War and direct taxation were new to us; and it was with extreme difficulty that Congress, from fear of the unpopularity of the measure, could be induced to pass the national tax bill, which is expected to produce

$200 million. Had it not been adopted, the depreciation of the paper issued by the government would have entailed financial ruin. As it is, the depreciation is about 20 percent; so that a $5 demand note is only worth $4 in gold. What would it have been had not Mr. Chase's recommendation been embodied in a law, at the last moment? The new paper currency would soon share the fate of the French assignats and the Continental money issued during the Revolutionary War.

In 1775, Congress issued $3 million; in 1776, an issue was made to the amount of $20 million; in 1777, another issue, reaching the sum of $26,426,000. There were nearly $50 million issued in all; and the price then fell so low that 4 paper dollars were only worth 1 in silver. In 1778, Congress issued $66,963,269 in convertible paper currency; and at the end of that year, 45 paper dollars could be purchased for 1 silver dollar. In 1780, the government issued $83 million of this money; and the price was 100 paper dollars for 1 in silver. In 1781, the issue was $12,587,000; and the price in June of that year was 1,000 paper dollars in exchange for 1 silver dollar. Such was the result of an excessive issue of inconvertible paper money. . . .

The total issue of the Continental money was $362,546,822, which was a circulation far in excess of the wants of 4 million population, having at that time but little trade or commerce. The number of notes issued by Mr. Chase for circulation among 20 million of a trading and commercial population does not exceed the wants of the community, and, therefore, it cannot be depreciated like the Continental money and French assignats; but let Mr. Chase continue to issue more of these notes, year after year, by the authority of Congress, and make no provision for their redemption, and they would soon become of the same value as the Continental money. But the fact of the notes being convertible into bonds, bearing 6 percent interest, and the interest being payable in specie, and the other fact that a tax has been laid to pay the interest, and gradually extinguish the principal of all the war loans and liabilities of the government, will save the present issues from much further depreciation. The direct tax will be ample to cover the ground.

As for the tariff, it is not likely — owing to the great falling off in the imports — to do more than pay the ordinary expenses of the government — say $60 million per annum. And here we may observe that the curtailment of imports is to be regarded rather as an evidence of prudent economy than of the inability to purchase. Persons engaged in the dry goods business have, no doubt, suffered by the change, but not the general community. Our exports have been immense during the past year — particularly in breadstuffs, our control of which has compelled Europe to keep the peace to us. Corn, and not cotton, is now king. The ships bearing our commerce whiten every sea. Our agricultural and mining interests are in a most flourishing condition; and our manufactures were never more active than at present. The tariff is prohibitory of many foreign articles which formerly competed successfully with our domestic manufactures; and the enormous expenditures for the war have stimulated those branches of native industry which embrace articles as are used by the army and navy.

The effect of so large a circulation of money cannot but have a beneficial effect upon the internal trade of the country, while the burden of repayment of the debt will be distributed over a great many years; and posterity, which has an equal interest in the objects of the war with the present generation, will have to pay a share of the expense. Hitherto, the Northern territory of the Union has been saved from the destructive ravages of war, involving great loss of property and the interruption of the operations of agricultural trade and every description of business. Nor is it possible that the Southern armies can ever penetrate the North, except for a brief space, beyond the border. We may, therefore, safely calculate upon immunity from future invasion.

The loss of population would be the greatest loss of all, were it not that Europe stands ready to fill up the chasm; so that at the end of the next decade — provided the war ceases before the expiration of another year — there would be no evidence of the effects of the conflict as far as the diminution of population is concerned. In 1816, the population of the United States was 8,500,000; by the last census it was 31,500,000. During the decade between 1850 and 1860, the population increased 4,500,000, or nearly 20 percent. Population is the wealth of nations, because it supplies the labor; and the demand for labor here is unbounded. Every settler from Europe not only contributes his labor but many of the emigrants bring money with them, thus swelling the national wealth. The loss of population by the war will soon, therefore, be repaired by the continual living stream from Europe. With the South the case is different, and time would not repair the ravages of the war so rapidly, as the current of emigration from Europe is chiefly directed to the Northern states.

The injurious effects of the war are scarcely perceptible as yet. Only let the struggle terminate before the 1st of next July, and in three or four years the country would be as prosperous and happy as ever — such is the buoyancy of the American people. In 1837 a commercial revulsion seemed to threaten universal ruin. In two or three years the tide of prosperity set in again, and disaster was forgotten. It was the same in the disastrous panic of 1857. In two years the recuperation of business was complete; the dry goods trade was in full vigor, and all went merry as a marriage bell. When the Civil War broke out, the country was in the very acme of prosperity; and soon after the war shall have closed, the prosperity of the republic will rise to a higher point than it ever did before.

Notwithstanding the enormous wars in which Napoleon had been engaged, he expended in the course of nine years, in public improvements, upward of $200 million. And what were the resources of the French Empire compared with those of the United States! The area of the country is more than 2 billion acres — including immense tracts of the richest virgin soil in the world — inviting the plowshare to make it productive of wealth untold.

For the future of the country we have no fears. When the element of disunion, North as well as South, is crushed, the republic will spread over this vast continent like a banyan tree; each branch will put forth its root, and each root will become a stem of the great parent tree — *e pluribus unum.* — a spectacle of growth and prosperity such as the world has never seen.

83.

ANTHONY TROLLOPE: American and European Cities

Anthony Trollope was an English novelist whose business ability led to his being sent on professional missions to the West Indies and to Egypt and, in 1861, to the United States. His journeys resulted in several travel books and essays, and his impressions of America were published in a volume entitled North America, *in 1862. In the following excerpt he discusses the differences between American and English cities, using Milwaukee as an example. It is interesting to note that his generally admiring account of America contrasts sharply with the bitter reflections of his mother, Frances, whose* Domestic Manners of the Americans *had been published in 1832.*

Source: *North America*, Philadelphia, 1862, Vol. I, Ch. 9.

MILWAUKEE IS A PLEASANT TOWN, a very pleasant town, containing 45,000 inhabitants. How many of my readers can boast that they know anything of Milwaukee, or even have heard of it? To me its name was unknown until I saw it on huge railway placards stuck up in the smoking rooms and lounging halls of all American hotels.

It is the big town of Wisconsin, whereas Madison is the capital. It stands immediately on the western shore of Lake Michigan and is very pleasant. Why it should be so and why Detroit should be the contrary, I can hardly tell; only I think that the same verdict would be given by any English tourist.

It must be always borne in mind that 10,000 or 40,000 inhabitants in an American town, and especially in any new Western town, is a number which means much more than would be implied by any similar number as to an old town in Europe. Such a population in America consumes double the amount of beef which it would in England, wears double the amount of clothes, and demands double as much of the comforts of life.

If a census could be taken of the watches, it would be found, I take it, that the American population possessed among them nearly double as many as would the English; and I fear also that it would be found

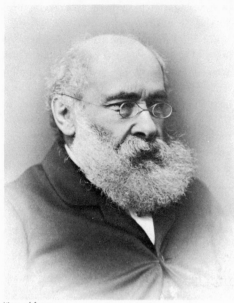

Anthony Trollope

that many more of the Americans were readers and writers by habit. In any large town in England it is probable that a higher excellence of education would be found than in Milwaukee, and also a style of life into which more of refinement and more of luxury had found its way. But the general level of these things, of material and intellectual well-being — of beef, that is, and book learning — is no doubt infinitely higher in a new American than in an old European town.

Such an animal as a beggar is as much unknown as a mastodon. Men out of work and in want are almost unknown. I do not say that there are none of the hardships of life . . . but want is not known as a hardship in these towns, nor is that dense ignorance in which so large a proportion of our town populations is still steeped. And then the town of 40,000 inhabitants is spread over a surface which would suffice in England for a city of four times the size.

Our towns in England — and the towns, indeed, of Europe generally — have been built as they have been wanted. No aspiring ambition as to hundreds of thousands of people warmed the bosoms of their first founders. Two or three dozen men required habitations in the same locality, and clustered them together closely. Many such have failed and died out of the world's notice. Others have thrived, and houses have been packed on to houses, till London and Manchester, Dublin and Glasgow have been produced. Poor men have built, or have had built for them, wretched lanes, and rich men have erected grand palaces. From the nature of their beginnings such has, of necessity, been the manner of their creation.

But in America, and especially in Western America, there has been no such necessity and there is no such result. The founders of cities have had the experience of the world before them. They have known of sanitary laws as they began. That sewerage, and water, and gas, and good air would be needed for a thriving community has been to them as much a matter of fact as are the well-understood combinations between timber and nails, and bricks and mortar. They have known that water carriage is almost a necessity for commercial success, and have chosen their sites accordingly. Broad streets cost as little, while land by the foot is not yet of value to be regarded as those which are narrow; and therefore the sites of towns have been prepared with noble avenues and imposing streets.

A city at its commencement is laid out with an intention that it shall be populous. The houses are not all built at once, but there are the places allocated for them. The streets are not made, but there are the spaces. Many an abortive attempt at municipal greatness has so been made and then all but abandoned. There are wretched villages, with huge, straggling, parallel ways, which will never grow into towns. They are the failures — failures in which the pioneers of civilization, frontier men as they call themselves, have lost their tens of thousands of dollars. But when the success comes, when the happy hit has been made, and the ways of commerce have been truly foreseen with a cunning eye, then a great and prosperous city springs up, ready-made as it were, from the earth. Such a town is Milwaukee, now containing 45,000 inhabitants, but with room apparently for double that number; with room for four times that number, were men packed as closely there as they are with us.

In the principal business streets of all these towns one sees vast buildings. They are usually called blocks, and often so denominated in large letters on their front, as Portland Block, Devereux Block, Buel's Block. Such a block may face to two, three, or even four streets and, as I presume, has generally been a matter of one special speculation. It may be divided into separate houses, or kept for a single purpose, such as that of a hotel, or grouped into shops below and into various sets of chambers above. I have had occasion in various towns to mount the stairs within these blocks and have generally found some portion of them vacant — have sometimes found the greater portion of them vacant. Men build on an enormous scale, three times, ten times as much as is wanted. The only measure of size is an increase on what men have built before.

Monroe P. Jones, the speculator, is very probably ruined, and then begins the world again, nothing daunted. But Jones's Block remains, and gives to the city in its aggregate a certain amount of wealth. Or the block becomes at once of service and finds tenants. In which case Jones probably sells it and immediately builds two others twice as big. That Monroe P. Jones will encounter ruin is almost a matter of course; but then he is none the worse for being ruined. It hardly makes him unhappy. He is greedy

of dollars with a terrible covetousness; but he is greedy in order that he may speculate more widely. He would sooner have built Jones's tenth block with a prospect of completing a twentieth than settle himself down at rest for life as the owner of a Chatsworth or a Woburn. As for his children, he has no desire of leaving them money. Let the girls marry. And for the boys — for them it will be good to begin as he began. If they cannot build blocks for themselves, let them earn their bread in the blocks of other men. So Monroe P. Jones, with his $1 million accomplished, advances on to a new frontier, goes to work again on a new city, and loses it all. . . .

Jones is undoubtedly the man for the West. It is that love of money to come, joined to a strong disregard for money made, which constitutes the vigorous frontier mind, the true pioneering organization. Monroe P. Jones would be a great man to all posterity if only he had a poet to sing of his valor.

It may be imagined how large in proportion to its inhabitants will be a town which spreads itself in this way. There are great houses left untenanted, and great gaps left unfilled. But if the place be successful, if it promises success, it will be seen at once that there is life all through it. Omnibuses, or streetcars working on rails, run hither and thither. The shops that have been opened are well filled. The great hotels are thronged. The quays are crowded with vessels, and a general feeling of progress pervades the place. It is easy to perceive whether or not an American town is going ahead. The days of my visit to Milwaukee were days of civil war and national trouble, but in spite of civil war and national trouble Milwaukee looked healthy.

———◆———

Almost any man knows how to earn money, but not one in a million knows how to spend it. If he had known so much as this, he would never have earned it.
HENRY DAVID THOREAU, *Journal*

84.

Israel Benjamin: The Spirit of America

Israel Benjamin was born in Rumania in 1818. Retiring as a merchant in 1845, he was inspired by the memory of the twelfth-century Spanish rabbi and traveler, Benjamin of Tudela, who became famous for his writings on medieval Jews, to travel the world and visit its Jewish communities. Calling himself Benjamin the Second, he reached America in 1859. Intensely fascinated by what he saw, and initially aiming to enlighten the world about the Jews, he began to envisage himself as the redeemer of America's sins, which he judged "an illness that must arouse the liveliest apprehensions. . . . The United States stands at the brink of the precipice and runs the risk of a fall." Benjamin's journey through America inspired him to write a two-volume work, Drei Jahre in Amerika 1859-1862, *from which a chapter is reprinted here.*

Source: *Three Years in America 1859-1862*, translated by Charles Reznikoff, Philadelphia, 1956, Vol. I, pp. 93-99.

WE HAVE BEFORE US a little brochure, a lecture on "America and its Destiny," delivered by a lady in New York, because — so she says — "the spirits" determined that she deliver the lecture there. The statement was believed, and people came streaming from all sides to listen to the revelations of the spirit that ruled the lady.

That single fact characterizes the spirit of America. It is to be regretted that such a crude delusion could find admirers and partisans among a people whom Morse and Mitchell in their geography call "the most enlightened." How can one still be angry at magic, witchcraft, or the other superstitious notions which mankind has cherished all along if "the most enlightened people" find pleasure in such frauds, and have Mormons, Millerites, and similar strange sects among them! Why still speak of the delusions of the Middle Ages if with our own eyes we see that "the most enlightened" people run to the representative of such superstition

and if one can be sure that the more absurd and sillier a thing is, the more numerous its admirers, helpers, and defenders!

The peaceful and serene spectator at such exhibitions might almost completely doubt the existence of sound common sense and is almost ready to believe that the world is most easily ruled by the swindlers and the sly. It is harsh to say this, but it must be said: He is no true friend who only flatters his neighbor and gilds the spots in his character or excuses them. He is also no friend of the American people who increases and supports the self-delusion and self-complacency from which the Americans suffer. A true friend says a truthful word at the right time even if it has a bitter sound (Prov. 12:17).

The writer of these lines loves this land and this people as his own and has chosen both out of a free choice without compulsion. He should consequently be permitted to speak freely, provided he does not speak out of a mania for blaming and faultfinding.

Above all we must — as a naturalized American permit me to say "we" — make mention of the fact that it is a great self-delusion to maintain that we are "the most enlightened people." In our fatherland we have not a single seat of learning that can be compared to the little universities of Padua, Jena, Goettingen, or Halle, to say nothing of the famous universities of England or France, those in Berlin, St. Petersburg, and Vienna. This is one of the surest measures of culture. Enlightenment is not a plant that grows wild, that springs out of the ground without any trouble and labor; it is rather a blossom that will never flower without the helping hand of man. From what sources, then, have we drawn the unusually illuminating principles, opinions, or doctrines? Enlightenment must have its conductor as well as electricity if it is to become part of a vast community; and the best conductor is the schools and the press.

Our public schools are no more than twenty years old and are still handicapped by the lack of that which new institutions lack generally. The superficiality of our colleges, academies, and seminaries has become proverbial. Young ladies study astronomy before they can spell properly; young men receive their doctorate after they have gone through a thoroughly confused mass of Greek, Latin, mathematics, French, German, physics, chemistry, history, geography, logic, metaphysics, ethics, and still other studies, in two or three years, and that without a firm grasp of any one of them. Tailors, cobblers, farmers, or clerks in stores are turned into physicians in thirty-two weeks; policemen, watchmen, and constables suddenly become lawyers; every man feels that he has the ability to be a preacher, teacher, politician, statesman, and diplomat and soon finds his public and his sphere of influence.

This utterly ridiculous superficiality is nevertheless by far not so stupid and dis-

gusting as the pedantry of our self-educated schoolmasters and pedagogues who kill the spirit with words and formulas. Can we regard this as a fountain of enlightenment which has educated us to be "the most enlightened people"? What then are the merits of the model schools, gymnasia, and universities? One must not deceive oneself: the schools are still too young and the colleges too superficial to make an enlightened people of us.

The press likewise is not strong enough to make up for what the schools lack. Only too often it is governed by inadequate principles, so that it only aims at making money; or by superficiality, so that by means of pictures and other ways it tries to supply what it otherwise lacks. In this, too, other nations are far ahead and there is still no paper that can be considered the equal of the press of London, or the French and German periodicals.

We are also far behind in this respect: every kind of depravity finds its defenders and patrons in the press if they only pay well enough. Thus it is that our press is not always a lighthouse for the community, not always the great lever for noble and illustrious purposes, not the honest and faithful expounder of the events of the day, not the torch that carries progress and knowledge; but rather at times merely a commercial enterprise in the hands of a group which publicizes only such things which, according to all expectation, will yield the most profit.

One often looks in vain for the serious or the love of truth; so much the oftener one runs into articles that are merely sensational, into bombastic words and immoral announcements. The press here is not the mistress but too often only the wretched handmaiden of the people, picking up the crumbs of news that fall from the richly laden table of mankind. Such a press could never, and can never, lift a people to the highest degree of enlightenment.

A glance at the current literature likewise

does not make us happy. If we except a few names with a good old reputation, we have no better authors, no scholars more brilliant, no men of talent in the arts more illustrious to point to. We shall be answered by those who point to the greatest, loftiest blessing of our land, saying: "It is the freedom for which our fathers bled and died, it is the Constitution and the laws which the wise men, our ancestors, have left us, that have made us the most enlightened of people." It would be more correct to say: "That should have made us such."

In such a school quite another kind of student should be found; with such examples to shine before us, quite another spirit should animate us. Our Constitution and institutions merely show that the fathers of the republic were very enlightened. What is the condition now of that Constitution, in theory and in practice? We must be silent. Where is the Constitution? Where is our freedom? We ask this often and receive no answer.

Future generations will be astounded to learn from history that from 400,000 to 500,000 volunteers took up arms to defend the Constitution of their land and that nowhere could this most enlightened people find a man to lead these mighty columns, this mountain rolling onward to victory, so that it might in a short time shatter its weaker opponent, and that immigrant Germans and Irish had to be summoned to act as spearhead. The generations to come will read to their amazement how 22 million freemen, who arose in the majestic strength of a lion and were aided by the wealth of a Croesus, who stood up with the firm conviction that they were defending only their sacred possessions and that the iron dice of death were rolling only for the sake of right, could suddenly remain motionless, utterly inactive, that the lion would no longer shake his mane in anger and terrify the foe by the paralyzing thunder of his voice.

Is there, in the history of the world, an-

other page on which the like is to be read? The great army of the Persians which invaded Greece was not inactive; the great army of Napoleon, which poured over Russia, fought; the Austrians in Italy defended themselves. Where in history did a nation ever rise to such great fame and mighty strength without begetting great and mighty spirits who took over the leadership? One has only to think of the generals of the French Revolution. We stand with all our might, with our love for the Constitution, with our longing for peace and unity and with our myriads of soldiers, our mighty arms — have we no one who can lead us, guide us happily to victory, and must we now live to see defeats like that of Manassas? Who knows how much time must still pass before the old spirit reawakens, when more illustrious deeds will cause the first defeats of this struggle to be forgotten.[1]

Our present distress arose out of no organic defects of the government but has its origin in a kind of demagogism to be found in many lands. . . . The present situation in the Northern states — the misfortunes that they have suffered, blow upon blow, at the beginning of the war just broken out — has encouraged the enemies of the American Constitution to condemn it utterly and to represent it as a vain effort. Without wishing to appear as its defender, I cannot refrain from mentioning the present state of affairs and to shed some light on its various aspects. The current state of mind, brought about and continued by the war, emphatically calls for such an explanation.

From the outset the baser passions of the volatile multitude were aroused and bloody feuds were the natural and necessary result. Our struggle then began because of the abuse of freedom and of wealth, just as a man, through excessive pleasure and immoderation, can kill himself.

1. To our joy the fortunes of war have turned for the better (beginning of 1862).

This abuse of the boundless wealth of our land and of freedom occurred in two ways: first, through materialism and then through the neglect of learning. Fast as our steamers speed at sea and our locomotives fly over the Western plains, faster still we raced into materialism and corruption. To make money! This has, at present, a magnetic charm and enchantment! Public officials accept positions and others long for them simply to enrich themselves. They care nothing about working for the common good, and have set no noble goal for themselves; no pure motive animates them.

True enough, there are exceptions. For a few, honor and the public good are the stars that guide them; but, for the great majority, the important thing is the money that this service provides. Did anyone ever hear of so many officials turned traitor as we have had in the few months of our political disturbances? The reason is elementary; treason is more profitable than loyalty, and he who is only loyal for money quickly turns traitor if the seducer pays more.

Money makes a man respected here, honored and prized — people ask: What is he worth? And, according to the amount of his possessions, he is a statesman, a scholar. An honorable man without money is not respected at all; he is considered a nobody; he is treated as though superfluous. On the other hand, we heap all honors on a rich scoundrel, on a well-to-do blockhead, on a wealthy ignoramus, and almost crawl before him. Only at election time, when everyone has his right to vote, does respect for the poorest come into its own.

Almost every man is therefore driven to try to become a merchant, a banker, a speculator, a manufacturer, or tries to capture a position that will yield money. The child hears from its father, the pupil from his teacher, the student from his professor, that gold creates an almighty power in every circle of society. The greed for it is thus nourished with our life's blood at the expense of

all nobler, better, and higher feelings, and at the sacrifice of our spiritual capacities and our happiness. Thousands sacrifice their health and their lives to the service of Mammon and as a result of this general and prevailing passion the human spirit is completely neglected. Tied to the making of money ever since childhood, the beauty of nature is stunted and so is the charm of education in the humanities, the truth of science, the sublimity of art, the holiness of religion, morality, truth, honor, and virtue.

Everything is pushed into the background and takes a subordinate place. This is the focal point of our corruption, around which it revolves. How can one still wonder at the multitude of dishonest officials and traitors? They walk along the same path as the others; they, too, are making money like the rest; and in no way are they different from the multitude. How can one still be surprised that the most impudent demagogues try to stir up the basest passions so that, once the election is over, they might find compensation in a well-paid post. When these things happen, why should one complain that neither talent nor true greatness exist? Everyone only wishes to make money and that as fast and as safely as they can.

Herein, as I said, lies the root of the sickness and this is the dangerous cancer. The spirit of the American people is sick in a fashion that must arouse the greatest anxiety and that should never have occurred in a constitutional state. Thus it has happened that now, after we have done business for fifty years, and, to be sure, most successfully, we stand on the brink of an abyss and run the danger of plunging down if someone or other does not soon appear to help us with rede and deed.

We come now to the second point mentioned above — knowledge. This, too, like everything else, is only the slave and the handmaiden of the passions that can only be goaded on by the pursuit of money. We have no love for knowledge for its own sake; we do not turn to it as to the sun that illuminates our path, but look on it as merchandise. We find shops for politics, working places of professional politicians who manufacture politics, and working rooms of priests in which religion is dispensed. The occupation of a professor, a scholar, a clergyman, a rabbi and preacher is regarded as his business. "That is his business." We have no time to do anything for ourselves and want our fellow creatures to earn money like ourselves.

We are pleased to find ready, for our comfort, the shoes, boots, clothes, caps, even medicines, magnetic pills, galvanized chains, health, morals, religion, truth, or any other article which they have manufactured. Therefore, any absurdity or madness, if only mad enough, creates a stir in this country and men have faith in it. Deception, quackery, misrepresentation, ridiculous or childish superstition — they all pay and whatever its name it is profitable for a while until it must give way before something newer, from Barnum down to a fortune-teller, from Dr. Townsend's sarsaparilla down to the different bitter cordials made by Jon Smith and Mueller, to Mr. Lederer of New York. We are so often deceived because we want to be deceived.

Knowledge cannot flourish under such conditions, and since this is the situation that prevails generally, we came to the conclusion that is reached everywhere: everyone knows everything and can do anything. The facts here teach that we know everything and understand how to set to work at anything without having studied it or engaged in it before.

We met a professor in this country who stepped down to become a bookbinder and bookseller, that is to say, to become a good man. Having failed in the mission of his life, instead of devoting himself to knowledge, to perfecting himself and developing his knowledge further, he had to drive himself, like the rest about him, to make the most money in his own fashion. We met an astronomer, who was excellent in his field but who, in addition, engaged in the ordinary work of an engineer. Many doctors who never studied a thing do best of all; they rely on boasting and bragging and in this they do not miscalculate. Quacks, swindlers, and the great native intellects brag and are, in almost all places, the representatives of the intelligentsia.

Everyone must admit that our learning is still on a very low level. To be sure, we are still too young a nation to enter the ranks of other nations and to be able to match their men of distinction with names of equal importance, but if we continue on the same way that we have gone, if our young people continue their studies as until now, knowledge will never blossom here.

The students have no time to busy themselves for long with earnest studies, but must hurry on. And yet, nothing can be studied thoroughly in a hurry.

It is no trick to be a captain when the sea is quiet. But, when the storm rages, the experienced seaman proves himself. As long as peace and unity reigned upon our ship of state, every man was good enough and capable for a public office. But now, at the first storm, the result of our foolish system can be seen: everyone understands and can do everything. Nevertheless, the judgment of God, through which we now must pass, will show us how small we are in our inflated pride; it will teach us that there are loftier and more important interests than gold and luxury. For as little as it is the highest calling of an individual to amass goods and chattels, no more can it be the highest calling of an entire nation which, after all, consists only of individuals. It will teach us that man has been chosen by Providence to progress in the good, the true, and the beautiful and also that upon this blood-soaked place of God's election welfare and blessing will blossom forth for America and all mankind.

85.

EMILY DICKINSON: Two Poems

Emily Dickinson is widely acclaimed as America's greatest woman poet. Though she wrote nearly 2,000 poems, only 7 were printed during her lifetime, and those without her consent. Her poetic genius flowered during the Civil War; in 1862 alone, she wrote some 360 poems. But she refused any publicity, after a critic and friend, Thomas Higginson, advised her against publishing her works. "Publication," she wrote, "is the auction of the mind." As one of her poems puts it: "How dreary to be somebody!/ How public, like a frog,/ To tell your name the livelong day/ To an admiring bog!" The following two poems were written in 1862.

Source: *Poems*, Mabel L. Todd and T. W. Higginson, eds., Boston, 1890.
 Poems, T. W. Higginson and Mabel L. Todd, eds., 2nd series, Boston, 1891.

I CANNOT LIVE WITH YOU

I cannot live with you,
It would be life,
And life is over there
Behind the shelf

The sexton keeps the key to,
Putting up
Our life, his porcelain,
Like a cup

Discarded of the housewife,
Quaint or broken;
A newer Sèvres pleases,
Old ones crack.

I could not die with you,
For one must wait
To shut the other's gaze down —
You could not.

And I, could I stand by
And see you freeze,
Without my right of frost,
Death's privilege?

Nor could I rise with you,
Because your face
Would put out Jesus',
That new grace

Glow plain and foreign
On my homesick eye,
Except that you, than he
Shone closer by.

They'd judge us — how?
For you served heaven, you know,
Or sought to;
I could not,

Because you saturated sight,
And I had no more eyes
For sordid excellence
As Paradise.

And were you lost, I would be,
Though my name
Rang loudest
On the heavenly fame.

And were you saved,
And I condemned to be
Where you were not,
That self were hell to me.

So we must keep apart,

You there, I here,
With just the door ajar
That oceans are,
And prayer,
And that pale sustenance,
Despair!

❧ I LIKE TO SEE IT LAP THE MILES

I like to see it lap the miles,
And lick the valleys up,
And stop to feed itself at tanks;
And then, prodigious, step

Around a pile of mountains,
And, supercilious, peer
In shanties by the sides of roads;
And then a quarry pare

To fit its sides, and crawl between,
Complaining all the while
In horrid, hooting stanza;
Then chase itself down hill

And neigh like Boanerges;
Then, punctual as a star,
Stop — docile and omnipotent —
At its own stable door.

86.

Orestes A. Brownson: The Preservation of Catholic Orthodoxy in America

American intellectuals in the nineteenth century were not noted for their consistency ("Consistency," as Emerson said, "is the hobgoblin of little minds"), but Orestes A. Brownson probably outdid all of his contemporaries in flitting from one position and faith to another. A man of vast contradictions who espoused numerous causes, he at one time championed the workingman but later became a vehement critic of democracy. He at one time avowed revolution as the worker's only true recourse against big business, but later adopted an autocratic view of politics. He at one time attacked the priesthood as despotic and corrupt, but later became an ardent Catholic. His conversion occurred in 1844, and his polemical writings of the next two decades reflected his new religious outlook. The following selection comprises part of an article, "Catholic Schools and Education," that he published in 1862.

Source: *Brownson's Quarterly Review*, January 1862.

The great body of our Catholics, no doubt, wish to Americanize and conform to the civilization of the country, but they have hitherto Americanized, so far as they have Americanized at all, in a Southern rather than in a Northern sense. The type of the Americanism they aim to adopt is in Maryland, not in Massachusetts; Baltimore, not Boston; and nothing can exceed the hostility of the Maryland type, which, properly speaking, is the Virginia type, to the Boston or New England type. Indeed, it is these two orders of civilization that meet in mortal combat in the civil war which now threatens the integrity of the American nation. The war is a struggle for life and death, a struggle between a civilization based on slavery, represented by the South, and a civilization based on constitutional liberty and the rights of men, represented by the Free states.

And, in this struggle, if, as is the fact, the interest and loyalty of Catholics lead them in large numbers to take sides with the North, their sympathies are very generally with the South; and we cannot doubt that, if the South were the loyal party, they would much more readily fight with the South than they now fight with the North. Even, then, where our Catholics aim to be American, it is not American in the sense of the highest, truest, and most advanced Americanism; but in the sense of the lowest, the least advanced, that which is least remote from barbarism, and the furthest removed from that which the church as well as humanity demands and never ceases to struggle to obtain.

We are also borne out in our views by the political history of the country. Politically, the Southern leaders have for a long time formed their association with the least intelligent, the least advanced classes in the Free states, and these Southern leaders are those our Catholic population have followed with the most alacrity. This fact proves, on the one hand, that the South represents the lowest order of civilization in the country, and that Catholics are more easily engaged in supporting it than in supporting the superior civilization represented by the Northern states. It is not too much to say that the great influx of the Catholic peasantry of different European states into the country and the conferring on them, almost on their arrival, of political franchises have done not a little to corrupt our politics

and to lower the standard of our civilization. Their orthodoxy, as yet, has done less to advance than their inferior civilization has done to corrupt and lower our civilization and morals. . . .

Now, the objection to Catholic schools, especially those for the people at large, is that they tend, and for a time at least must tend, to perpetuate the association of orthodoxy with this inferior civilization and thus injure alike the country and the church. These schools must be taught chiefly by foreigners, or, if not by foreigners, at least by those whose sympathies and connections, tastes and habits are un-American; because what is wanted by their founders and supporters is not simply the preservation of orthodoxy but the perpetuation of the foreignism hitherto associated with it. Schools which should associate real Americanism with orthodoxy would be hardly less offensive or more acceptable to them than the public schools themselves. They must, therefore, be conducted and taught by men who will keep up the old association and prevent the association of real Americanism with orthodoxy. Yet it is precisely this latter association which is desirable both for civilization and for religion, and it is only by breaking the old association and forming the new in good faith, as we are in fact required to do by orthodoxy itself, that Catholics can cease to be in this country an isolated foreign colony, or a band of emigrants encamped for the night and ready to strike their tents and take up their line of march on the morrow for some other place.

These are some of the reasons which have led many of our most intelligent, most earnest and devout Catholics to form their unfavorable judgment of Catholic schools and Catholic education as they now are, and for some time are likely to be, in the United States. They are solid reasons as far as they go and fully justify the dissatisfaction with them we began by recognizing.

They prove that here and elsewhere, but especially here, Catholic education, or the education given by Catholics, is below the wants of the age and country, and prove that, from the seminary down to the primary school, it stands in need, whether we consult the interest of orthodoxy or that of civilization, of a wide, deep, and thorough reform. Yet, after long reflection and much hesitation, some would say opposition, we must say that we do not regard them as sufficient reasons for abandoning the movement for Catholic schools and education supported by our bishops and clergy. . . .

That we are to have schools and colleges of our own, under the control of Catholics, we take it is a "fixed fact". Whether the movement for them is premature or not, it is idle, if nothing worse, to war against it. Let us say, then, to those who regard the education actually given by Catholics as we do, and who have not seen their way clear to the support of primary schools under the control of Catholics as a substitute, in the case of Catholic children, for the common schools of the country, that we regard it as our duty now to accept the movement, and labor not to arrest it or to embarrass it but to reform and render truly Catholic the whole system of Catholic education from the highest grade to the lowest. Let it be our work not to destroy Catholic education but to reform and advance it. The first care of all Catholics should be the preservation of orthodoxy, and, in the actual state of our Catholic population, it may be that orthodoxy will be better preserved by schools under Catholic direction than it can be by sending our children to the public schools.

The objections we have set forth are, after all, only temporary and accidental. They grow out of the present and past state of our Catholic population, and must disappear under the slow but effectual operation of time and causes already in operation among us. We might gain something under the point of view of civilization by adopting the schools of the country; but, as our prel-

ates and clergy are strongly opposed to them and have done much to bring them into disrepute with Catholics, we should probably lose, under the point of view of orthodoxy, more than would thus be gained. Schools under the control of Catholics will, at least, teach the catechism, and though they may in fact teach it as a dead letter rather than as a quickening spirit, it is better that it should be taught as a dead letter than not be taught at all. It is only by preserving the dogma intact that we do or can preserve the Christian ideal or have the slightest chance of securing our final destiny. The hopes of the world for time and eternity are dependent on the preservation of the orthodox faith.

The reform in our schools and in education will go on just in proportion as it goes on in our Catholic community itself, and perhaps even much faster. The dissatisfaction we hear expressed with our collegiate education for boys and with that of our conventual schools for girls is an encouraging symptom; it proves that there is, after all, a growing Americanization of our Catholic population, and that the need of an education less European and more truly American is daily becoming more widely and more deeply felt. It will be more widely and more deeply felt still as time goes on and as Catholics become more generally naturalized in habit, feeling, and association, as well as in law. . . .

Then our schools will assume their true character and position, and exert a truly Catholic influence. They will preserve orthodoxy not as a dead letter, not as isolated and inoperative dogmas, but as a quickening spirit, as living and operative truth. Then, under the point of view of civilization, instead of tending to recall a dead past, they will accept the living present and associate the living civilization of the day with the orthodox faith — reunite in a living and productive whole the scattered members of the torn and bleeding body of truth, and aid both the church and the nation in carrying forward our civilization to the last term of its progress. Then our schools will send out living men, live with the love of God and of man — men of large minds, of liberal studies, and generous aims — men inspired by faith and genius, who will take the command of their age, breathe their whole souls into it, inform it with their own love of truth, and raise it to the level of their own high and noble aspirations.

87.

NATHANIEL HAWTHORNE: Lincoln and the American Character

In March of 1862 Nathaniel Hawthorne was a member of a Massachusetts delegation that presented a gift to President Lincoln. Hawthorne's impressions of the President were drawn together in a sketch that appeared in an article, "Chiefly About War Matters," in the Atlantic Monthly *for July 1862. The sketch was expanded and later published in* Tales, Sketches and Other Papers. *Though Hawthorne failed to see many facets of Lincoln's greatness, especially his literary gift, his portrait was glowing. The qualities he admired most in the President were his basic humility and his humanity.*

Source: *Tales, Sketches and Other Papers,* Boston, 1883.

THERE WAS ONE . . . PERSONAGE, in the class of statesmen, whom I should have been truly mortified to leave Washington without seeing; since (temporarily, at least, and by force of circumstances) he was the man of men. But a private grief had built up a barrier about him, impeding the customary free intercourse of Americans with their chief magistrate; so that I might have come away without a glimpse of this very remarkable physiognomy, save for a semiofficial opportunity of which I was glad to take advantage. The fact is, we were invited to annex ourselves, as supernumeraries, to a deputation that was about to wait upon the President, from a Massachusetts whip factory, with a present of a splendid whip.

Our immediate party consisted only of four or five (including Major Ben Perley Poore, with his notebook and pencil), but we were joined by several other persons who seemed to have been lounging about the precincts of the White House, under the spacious porch, or within the hall, and who swarmed in with us to take the chances of a presentation. Nine o'clock had been appointed as the time for receiving the deputation, and we were punctual to the moment; but not so the President, who sent us word that he was eating his breakfast and would come as soon as he could. His appetite, we were glad to think, must have been a pretty fair one; for we waited about half an hour in one of the antechambers, and then were ushered into a reception room, in one corner of which sat the secretaries of war and of the treasury, expecting, like ourselves, the termination of the presidential breakfast. During this interval there were several new additions to our group, one or two of whom were in a working garb, so that we formed a very miscellaneous collection of people, mostly unknown to each other, and without any common sponsor, but all with an equal right to look our head servant in the face.

By and by there was a little stir on the staircase and in the passageway, and in lounged a tall, loose-jointed figure, as of an exaggerated Yankee port and demeanor, whom (as being about the homeliest man I ever saw, yet by no means repulsive or disagreeable) it was impossible not to recognize as Uncle Abe.

Unquestionably, Western man though he be, and Kentuckian by birth, President Lincoln is the essential representative of all Yankees, and the veritable specimen, physically, of what the world seems determined to regard as our characteristic qualities. It is the strangest and yet the fittest thing in the jumble of human vicissitudes that he, out of so many millions, unlooked for, unselected by any intelligible process that could be based upon his genuine qualities, unknown to those who chose him, and unsuspected of what endowments may adapt him for his tremendous responsibility, should have found the way open for him to fling his lank personality into the chair of state — where, I presume, it was his first impulse to throw his legs on the council table and tell the cabinet ministers a story.

There is no describing his lengthy awkwardness, nor the uncouthness of his movement; and yet it seemed as if I had been in the habit of seeing him daily and had shaken hands with him a thousand times in some village street; so true was he to the aspect of the pattern American, though with a certain extravagance which, possibly, I exaggerated still further by the delighted eagerness with which I took it in. If put to guess his calling and livelihood, I should have taken him for a country schoolmaster as soon as anything else. He was dressed in a rusty black frock coat and pantaloons, unbrushed, and worn so faithfully that the suit had adapted itself to the curves and angularities of his figure and had grown to be an outer skin of the man. He had shabby slippers on his feet. His hair was black, still unmixed with gray, stiff, somewhat bushy, and had apparently been acquainted with neither brush nor comb that morning, after the disarrangement of the pillow; and as to a nightcap, Uncle Abe probably knows nothing of such effeminacies. His complexion is dark and sallow, betokening, I fear, an insalubrious atmosphere around the White House; he has thick black eyebrows and an impending brow; his nose is large, and the lines about his mouth are very strongly defined.

The whole physiognomy is as coarse a one as you would meet anywhere in the length and breadth of the states; but, withal, it is redeemed, illuminated, softened, and brightened by a kindly though serious look out of his eyes and an expression of homely sagacity that seems weighted with rich results of village experience. A great deal of native sense; no bookish cultivation, no refinement; honest at heart, and thoroughly so, and yet, in some sort, sly — at least, endowed with a sort of tact and wisdom that are akin to craft, and would impel him, I think, to take an antagonist in flank, rather than to make a bull-run at him right in front. But, on the whole, I like this sallow, queer, sagacious visage, with the homely human sympathies that warmed it; and, for my small share in the matter, would as lief have Uncle Abe for a ruler as any man whom it would have been practicable to put in his place.

Immediately on his entrance the President accosted our member of Congress, who had us in charge, and, with a comical twist of his face, made some jocular remark about the length of his breakfast. He then greeted us all round, not waiting for an introduction, but shaking and squeezing everybody's hand with the utmost cordiality, whether the individual's name was announced to him or not. His manner toward us was wholly without pretense, but yet had a kind of natural dignity, quite sufficient to keep the forwardest of us from clapping him on the shoulder and asking him for a story. A mutual acquaintance being established, our leader took the whip out of its case and began to read the address of presentation. The whip was an exceedingly long one, its handle wrought in ivory (by some artist in the Massachusetts State Prison, I believe) and ornamented with a medallion of the President, and other equally beautiful devices; and along its whole length there was a succession of golden bands and ferrules. The address was shorter than the whip, but equally well made, consisting chiefly of an explanatory description of these artistic designs, and closing with a hint that the gift was a suggestive and emblematic one, and that the President would recognize the use to which such an instrument should be put.

This suggestion gave Uncle Abe rather a delicate task in his reply, because, slight as the matter seemed, it apparently called for some declaration, or intimation, or faint foreshadowing of policy in reference to the conduct of the war, and the final treatment of the Rebels. But the President's Yankee aptness and not-to-be-caughtness stood him in good stead, and he jerked or wiggled himself out of the dilemma with an uncouth dexterity that was entirely in character; although, without his gesticulation of eye and mouth — and especially the flourish of the whip, with which he imagined himself touching up a pair of fat horses — I doubt whether his words would be worth recording, even if I could remember them.

The gist of the reply was that he accepted the whip as an emblem of peace, not punishment; and, this great affair over, we retired out of the presence in high good humor, only regretting that we could not have seen the President sit down and fold up his legs (which is said to be a most extraordinary spectacle), or have heard him tell one of those delectable stories for which he is so celebrated. A good many of them are afloat upon the common talk of Washington, and are certainly the aptest, pithiest, and funniest little things imaginable; though, to be

sure, they smack of the frontier freedom, and would not always bear repetition in a drawing room or on the immaculate page of the *Atlantic*.

Good heavens! What liberties have I been taking with one of the potentates of the earth, and the man on whose conduct more important consequences depend than on that of any other historical personage of the century! But with whom is an American citizen entitled to take a liberty if not with his own chief magistrate? However, lest the above allusions to President Lincoln's little peculiarities (already well known to the country and to the world) should be misinterpreted, I deem it proper to say a word or two in regard to him of unfeigned respect and measurable confidence. He is evidently a man of keen faculties, and, what is still more to the purpose, of powerful character. As to his integrity, the people have that intuition of it which is never deceived.

Before he actually entered upon his great office, and for a considerable time afterward there is no reason to suppose that he adequately estimated the gigantic task about to be imposed on him or, at least, had any distinct idea how it was to be managed; and I presume there may have been more than one veteran politician who proposed to himself to take the power out of President Lincoln's hands into his own, leaving our honest friend only the public responsibility for the good or ill success of the career. The extremely imperfect development of his statesmanly qualities, at that period, may have justified such designs. But the President is teachable by events, and has now spent a year in a very arduous course of education; he has a flexible mind, capable of much expansion and convertible toward far loftier studies and activities than those of his early life; and if he came to Washington a backwoods humorist, he has already transformed himself into as good a statesman (to speak moderately) as his prime minister.

1863

88.

Abraham Lincoln: Emancipation Proclamation

In the popular mind the Emancipation Proclamation transformed the Civil War from a struggle to preserve the Union into a crusade for human freedom. But at the time of its issuance, its actual provisions had already largely been enacted into law by Congress, which had provided for the freeing of slaves of owners hostile to the Union, the prohibition of slavery in the District of Columbia and the territories, and the freeing of slave-soldiers. The Emancipation Proclamation actually did not free a single slave, since the regions in which it authorized emancipation were under Confederate control, and in the border states where emancipation might have been effected, it was not authorized. It did, however, tremendously boost Union morale, breed disaffection in the South, and bolster support for the Union cause in Europe. The real significance of the document lay in the political factors that brought it to fruition and in the delicate political balance it preserved. By the summer of 1862, Lincoln had exhausted all other schemes short of full emancipation. Freed Negroes in the North had objected to his offer of colonization; the border states disapproved of his proposal of compensated emancipation; and Abolitionists were demanding a more radical course. The military position of the North had deteriorated when on July 22, 1862, Lincoln called together his Cabinet to discuss emancipation. The President later described this fateful day in a conversation with the painter Frank Carpenter. "Things had gone on from bad to worse," said Lincoln, "until I felt that we had reached the end of our rope. . . . We had about played our last card, and must change our tactics, or lose the game!" Lincoln had prepared a draft of the proclamation prior to the Cabinet meeting, "without consultation with or the knowledge of the Cabinet." The majority of the Cabinet were enthusiastic, including William Seward, who raised, however, an objection to its timing. Seward argued that Lincoln should postpone the proclamation until the Union had achieved some military success, otherwise "it may be viewed as the last measure of an exhausted government, a cry for help." Lincoln heeded this advice. After the decisive Battle of Antietam (September 17) stopped Lee's advance upon Washington, Lincoln issued a preliminary proclamation and the Emancipation Proclamation as reprinted here was issued on January 1, 1863.

Source: *Statutes*, XII, pp. 1268-1269.

Whereas, on the 22nd day of September, in the year of our Lord 1862, a proclamation was issued by the President of the United States, containing, among other things, the following, to wit:

That on the 1st day of January, in the year of our Lord 1863, all persons held as slaves within any state or designated part of a state, the people whereof shall then be in rebellion against the United States, shall be then, thenceforward, and forever free; and the executive government of the United States, including the military and naval authority thereof, will recognize and maintain the freedom of such persons and will do no act or acts to repress such persons, or any of them, in any efforts they may make for their actual freedom.

That the executive will, on the 1st day of January aforesaid, by proclamation, designate the states and parts of states, if any, in which the people thereof, respectively, shall then be in rebellion against the United States; and the fact that any state or the people thereof shall on that day be in good faith represented in the Congress of the United States by members chosen thereto at elections wherein a majority of the qualified voters of such states shall have participated shall, in the absence of strong countervailing testimony, be deemed conclusive evidence that such state and the people thereof are not then in rebellion against the United States.

Now, therefore, I, Abraham Lincoln, President of the United States, by virtue of the power in me vested as commander in chief of the Army and Navy of the United States, in time of actual armed rebellion against the authority and government of the United States, and as a fit and necessary war measure for suppressing said rebellion, do, on this 1st day of January, in the year of our Lord 1863, and in accordance with my purpose so to do, publicly proclaimed for the full period of 100 days from the day first above mentioned, order and designate as the states and parts of states wherein the people thereof, respectively, are this day in rebellion against the United States the following, to wit:

Arkansas, Texas, Louisiana (except the parishes of St. Bernard, Plaquemines, Jefferson, St. John, St. Charles, St. James, Ascension, Assumption, Terrebonne, Lafourche, St. Mary, St. Martin, and Orleans, including the city of New Orleans), Mississippi, Alabama, Florida, Georgia, South Carolina, North Carolina, and Virginia (except the forty-eight counties designated as West Virginia, and also the counties of Berkeley, Accomac, Northampton, Elizabeth City, York, Princess Anne, and Norfolk, including the cities of Norfolk and Portsmouth), and which excepted parts are for the present left precisely as if this proclamation were not issued.

And, by virtue of the power and for the purpose aforesaid, I do order and declare that all persons held as slaves within said designated states and parts of states are, and henceforward shall be, free; and that the executive government of the United States, including the military and naval authorities thereof, will recognize and maintain the freedom of said persons.

And I hereby enjoin upon the people so declared to be free to abstain from all violence, unless in necessary self-defense; and I recommend to them that, in all cases when allowed, they labor faithfully for reasonable wages.

And I further declare and make known that such persons of suitable condition will be received into the armed service of the United States to garrison forts, positions, stations, and other places, and to man vessels of all sorts in said service.

And upon this act, sincerely believed to be an act of justice, warranted by the Constitution upon military necessity, I invoke the considerate judgment of mankind and the gracious favor of Almighty God.

89.

Songs About Freedom

The Civil War produced both war songs and freedom songs. Two examples of the latter are reprinted here. "Many Thousand Gone" was modeled after the old Negro spirituals, but was infused with a secular political content, and gained popularity shortly after the Emancipation Proclamation in 1863. This anthem of liberation became a marching song among Negro soldiers fighting in the Union Army. "Kingdom Coming," composed by Henry Clay Work in 1861, also came to represent, in 1863, the Negro's joy in his freedom. The Union Army later sang it while marching into Richmond after Lee's surrender.

Source: *Immortal Songs of Camp and Field*, Louis A. Banks, ed., Cleveland, 1899, pp. 140-144.

❧ MANY THOUSAND GONE

No more auction block for me,
No more, no more,
No more auction block for me,
Many thousand gone.

No more driver's lash for me,
No more, no more,
No more driver's lash for me,
Many thousand gone.

No more peck of salt for me,
No more, no more,
No more peck of salt for me,
Many thousand gone.

No more iron chain for me,
No more, no more,
No more iron chain for me,
Many thousand gone.

❧ KINGDOM COMING

Say, darkeys, hab you seen de massa,
Wid de muff-stash on his face,
Go long de road some time dis mornin',
Like he gwine to leab de place?
He seen a smoke, way up de ribber,
Whar de Linkum gumboats lay;
He took his hat, an' lef berry sudden,
An' I spec he's run away!

Chorus:

De massa run? ha, ha!
De darkey stay? ho, ho!
It mus' be now de kingdom comin',
An' de year ob Jubilo!

He six foot one way, two foot tudder,
An' he weigh tree hundred pound.
His coat so big, he couldn't pay de tailor,
An' it won't go half way round.
He drill so much dey call him Cap'an,
And he get so drefful tanned,
I spec he try an' fool dem Yankees
For to tink he's contraband.

De darkeys feel so lonesome libing
In de log-house on de lawn,
Dey move dar tings to massa's parlor
For to keep it while he's gone.
Dar's wine an' cider in de kitchen,
An' de darkeys dey'll hab some;
I spose dey'll all be confiscated
When de Linkum sojers come.

De oberseer he made us trubbel,
An' he dribe us round a spell;
We lock him up in de smoke-house cellar,
Wid de key trown in de well.
De whip is lost, de hand-cuff's broken,
But de massa'll hab his pay.
He's ole enough, big enough, ought to known better
Dan to went an' run away.

HENRY CLAY WORK

90.

ABRAHAM LINCOLN: Appointment of General Hooker

On December 13, 1862, the Union Army suffered a crushing defeat at Fredericksburg. The defeat was complicated by friction between the commanding general, Ambrose Burnside, and some of his subordinate officers, particularly General "Fighting Joe" Hooker, who openly criticized Burnside's conduct of the campaign. Lincoln reluctantly removed Burnside and with great misgivings appointed Hooker as commander of the Army of the Potomac. Lincoln was aware of Hooker's vanity and intemperance, and in the following letter of January 26, 1863, the President attempted both to admonish and to reassure his new commander.

Source: Nicolay-Hay, VIII, pp. 206-207.

General:

I have placed you at the head of the Army of the Potomac. Of course I have done this upon what appear to me to be sufficient reasons, and yet I think it best for you to know that there are some things in regard to which I am not quite satisfied with you. I believe you to be a brave and skillful soldier, which of course I like. I also believe you do not mix politics with your profession, in which you are right. You have confidence in yourself, which is a valuable if not an indispensable quality. You are ambitious, which, within reasonable bounds, does good rather than harm; but I think that during General Burnside's command of the army you have taken counsel of your ambition and thwarted him as much as you could, in which you did a great wrong to the country and to a most meritorious and honorable brother officer.

I have heard, in such a way as to believe it, of your recently saying that both the army and the government needed a dictator. Of course it was not for this, but in spite of it, that I have given you the command. Only those generals who gain successes can set up dictators. What I now ask of you is military success, and I will risk the dictatorship. The government will support you to the utmost of its ability, which is neither more nor less than it has done and will do for all commanders. I much fear that the spirit which you have aided to infuse into the army, of criticizing their commander and withholding confidence from him, will now turn upon you. I shall assist you as far as I can to put it down. Neither you nor Napoleon, if he were alive again, could get any good out of an army while such a spirit prevails in it. And now beware of rashness. Beware of rashness, but with energy and sleepless vigilance go forward and give us victories.

91.

John Lansing Burrows: Opposition to the Theater in Time of War

Prior to the Civil War, Southern critics openly admitted that the South had generally been unproductive in the fine arts. The war nourished an artistic flowering, and the Southern theater soon became a prominent institution. Though productions were uneven in quality, theaters were usually packed. Many actors toured throughout the South, but the theatrical center was Richmond, Virginia. The most illustrious house was the Richmond New Theatre, completed in February 1863. Some Southerners, however, were repelled by the theater, regarding it as a frivolous, even immoral, institution that distracted people from the seriousness of the war. The Reverend John Burrows echoed this opinion in a sermon on February 8, 1863, at the First Baptist Church in Richmond, reprinted here in part.

Source: *The New Richmond Theatre. A Discourse, Delivered on Sunday, February 8, 1863, in the First Baptist Church, Richmond, Va.*, Richmond, 1863.

TOMORROW NIGHT the New Richmond Theatre is to be opened. I deem it fitting, in addition to the notices so liberally given through the daily press, to give this public notice from the pulpit. With surprising energy and regardless of cost in these pinching times of war, a splendid building with most costly decorations has been reared from the ashes of the old. Builders, artists, workmen have devoted themselves with an enterprise and industry that would be praiseworthy if, in any sense, their work were useful in these pressing times of war. Enough able-bodied men have escaped from the conscription, have, perhaps, purchased the right to keep away from the camp and the battle in order to accomplish this magnificent work, for a consideration. The work is completed; the decorations are finished; and tomorrow night the New Richmond Theatre is to be opened.

A strong corps of actors, male and female, have been secured, and, in addition to them, "twenty *gentlemen* for the chorus and the ballet." No cripples from the battlefields are these — they can sing and dance; they can mimic fighting on the stage. For the serious work of repelling a real enemy, they have neither taste nor heart. But they can sing while the country groans and dance while the cars are bringing, in sad funeral procession, the dead to their very doors, and the dismal ambulance bears the sick and the wounded under the very glare of their lights and within the sound of their music. They keep themselves out of the war for the noble duty of amusing the populace.

Should they not, in these times, be especially encouraged, particularly by those whose own brave sons are in the camp or in the hospital, or whose mangled bodies are moldering in uncoffined graves? Does it not seem a peculiarly happy time for theatrical amusements? Shall we all go and laugh and clap to the music and the dance while the grasp of relentless foes is tightening upon the throats of our sons, and the armed heels of trampling hosts are bruising the bosom of our beloved motherland?

What fitter time for opening a theater in the capital of our bleeding country, unless it could have been on the evening of the battle of Malvern Hill or of Fredericksburg? But enterprise and industry could not secure the completion of the building in time for those bloody days, or we should, doubtless, have had the theater open every night while the battle raged by day around the very suburbs of Richmond. "A strong stock company," and "twenty gentlemen for the chorus and the ballet," besides artists, musicians, etc., etc. Men enough, perhaps, to form an effective artillery company deny themselves the patriotic desire to aid in defending the country against assailing foes in order that they may devote themselves, fellow citizens, to your amusement.

I find, in my heart, no sympathy with that austere and morose idea of religion which forbids a laugh and prohibits recreation and amusement. I find no pleasure in tracing the wrinkles of seventy upon the brow of seventeen. It is contrary to nature and piety to curb and cramp, perpetually, the cheerful impulses of the young heart and force it into the unnatural faith that gloom is godliness and that innocent mirth is but the outburst of depravity. If God had not meant we should laugh, He would not

have created the risible nerves and muscles. From the severer duties and struggles of life there may be and there ought to be relaxations and mere pleasures in every family and in every community. Sincere and intelligent piety is always cheerful, and Christians are enjoined in the word to rejoice and to "rejoice evermore." I am not disposed, therefore, to insist upon any captious or churlish denunciation of the theater merely because it is a place of amusement. . . .

Yet there is much to be learned at the theater which can hardly be learned anywhere else. Sentiments of impiety and blasphemy may be so deeply stamped upon the memory as never to be eradicated, either by the motive to piety on earth or by the fires of hell. Among the lessons of the stage are very often such as these: simple honesty and truth are folly and vulgarity; religion is bigotry or hypocrisy, and the humbly pious are fools and fanatics; fraud and falsehood are justifiable as means to an end; murderers and duelists are model men; suicides are worthy of high eulogium; libertines and seducers are noble and generous; chastity is prudishness or affectation. All that is popularly vicious is adorned and rendered attractive, and all that is unpopularly virtuous is degraded as meanness or folly. That such is the general character of the plays that draw, I think, cannot be denied.

I cannot now dwell more particularly upon the general character of the plays that draw the largest crowds. It is hardly a secret that blasphemy and obscenity, vulgarity and scurrility are the seasoning, at least, of the drama, by a liberal use of which the sparse morality which it contains is made palatable. One can scarcely be wise in swallowing an ounce of poison for the sake of the grain of nutriment that may be in it.

And these theories of the stage are often practically illustrated in the auditory. The apprentice to vice can gain in the theater new insight into the principles of his chosen trade. They are developed in the curses and blasphemy of "the pit"; in the shameless impudence of the "third tier"; in the drunkenness and riot of the gallery; and often in the fashionable ribaldry of the boxes. There is red-hot iron for searing the conscience of the shrinking and sensitive, and prepared fuel for the burning depravity of the heart.

Does the moral character more than the scholastic attainments of the actors entitle them to the position they assume as professors in this school of morality and virtue? . . .

I shall not be deterred from a conscientious discharge of duty by the wincings of a false modesty or the frowns of a morbid sensitiveness. I suppose this announcement to mean what is meant by "the third tier" elsewhere and everywhere. In plain words, it is a flaunting advertisement in your daily papers, that the New Richmond Theatre is a public assignation house, where any vile man may be introduced to an infamous woman by paying the price of a ticket. It is a part of the building especially appropriated to harlots, where your sons may meet them and by their enticements be drawn into the very depths of debasement and vice. It is expressly designed by the architect, fitted up and decorated that it may be used for these infamous purposes.

If any other building in our city were so appropriated, and an advertisement were offered setting forth the facts to any of our newspaper proprietors, they would reject the advertisement with disgust; but, because it is a theater, and this is an essential part of such an establishment as conducted in these days, the infamous advertisement finds a place in our public prints. And this assignation arrangement is declared to be essential to the support of the theater. Attempts were made in Boston and New York to dispense with this revolting feature, and they proved failures.

Oh! did we dare to speak the whole truth on this subject, were it proper to speak of what many in this community know before such an audience as this, the theater would be so intimately associated with the brothel that the naming of the one would, as quickly as the naming of the other, bring the blush to the cheek of a virtuous woman and teach her as sensitively to shrink from mingling with the prostitutes of the one as of the other.

Is it a shame to speak of these things? How much blacker is the shame to the community that they are permitted and encouraged. We are to have inaugurated, tomorrow night, in this capital of our new Confederacy, one of these nefarious establishments, which have been the disgrace of European and Northern cities, to be conducted on precisely the same principles and for the same ends.

Away, then, with the impudent and preposterous plea that the theater, as it is, is a school of morals. It is what it always has been, a school of immorality and vice. I could as readily conceive of a church in hell as a theater in heaven, and in proportion as the virtue of a community is assimilated to the purity of heaven, or based upon the principles of God's Word, will the good regard with shame and scorn the licentiousness and blasphemy of the theater. . . .

And now, I ask, in all seriousness, is a theater, so conducted as this New Richmond Theatre is evidently to be, worthy the patronage and presence of reputable people? That there will be crowds nightly gathered within its walls is very probable. There are, alas! in our community enough of the vile, the unprincipled, and the mere pleasure-loving to support such an institution liberally. There are also many very respectable people who will seek for amusement without regard to the influence of their example upon others. It may be that some very decent fathers and mothers will take their sons and even their daughters to a place, a portion of which they know is set apart for vilest assignations, where libertines parade their shameless profligacy, where the infamous wait for the vicious.

None of this congregation shall do this without honest and faithful warning; without an exposure of the influences to which they choose to subject themselves and their children.

I am not morose or puritanic. My religion is not of the gloomy type. God has made men to be cheerful and happy. The ringing laugh of innocent enjoyment I love to hear. I am no enemy to pleasure. I take delight in witnessing the sports of childhood and youth. I strive to cultivate and exhibit a cheerful, joyous spirit. But life has

its stern, grave duties, and whatever unfits the mind and heart for these; whatever creates a distaste for their earnest fulfillment; whatever sullies the innocency of the heart, or perverts and distorts the nobler faculties of the soul; whatever ministers to the development of a prurient imagination at the expense of the more practicable and serviceable powers of the mind, is injury to the individual and a mischief to society.

All this, and more than this, I believe to be the influence of the stage in its best aspects, and even without the infamous associations to which I have alluded. You cannot visit the theater and love it and remain innocent and pure.

92.

WILLIAM TECUMSEH SHERMAN: The Press and Wartime Security

The North was the underdog in the early part of the Civil War, and it seemed to some Northern statesmen that this was owing in part to the Confederate Army's ability to gather intelligence. Union officers, particularly General William T. Sherman, placed the blame for the lack of wartime security on Northern newspapers. General Sherman wrote the following letter to his brother, Senator John Sherman of Ohio, on February 18, 1863, reflecting the prevailing military viewpoint. While there is some truth in his view, it was a fact that Confederate spies operating in the capital were also an invaluable source of information.

Source: *The Sherman Letters*, Rachel Sherman Thorndike, ed., New York, 1894, pp. 191-193.

My Dear Brother:

We have reproached the South for arbitrary conduct in coercing their people; at last we find we must imitate their example. We have denounced their tyranny in filling their armies with conscripts, and now we

must follow her example. We have denounced their tyranny in suppressing freedom of speech and the press, and here, too, in time, we must follow their example. The longer it is deferred the worse it becomes. Who gave notice of McDowell's movement on Manassas and enabled Johnston so to reinforce Beauregard that our army was defeated? The press. Who gave notice of the movement on Vicksburg? The press. Who has prevented all secret combinations and movements against our enemy? The press. . . .

In the South this powerful machine was at once scotched and used by the Rebel government, but in the North was allowed to go free. What are the results? After arousing the passions of the people till the two great sections hate each other with a hate hardly paralleled in history, it now begins to stir up sedition at home, and even to encourage mutiny in our armies. What has paralyzed the Army of the Potomac? Mutual jealousies kept alive by the press. What has enabled the enemy to combine so as to hold Tennessee after we have twice crossed it with victorious armies? What defeats and will continue to defeat our best plans here and elsewhere? The press.

I cannot pick up a paper but tells of our situation here, in the mud, sickness, and digging a canal in which we have little faith. But our officers attempt secretly to cut two other channels, one into Yazoo by an old pass and one through Lake Providence into Tensas, Black, Red, etc., whereby we could turn not only Vicksburg, Port Hudson, but also Grand (Gulf), Natchez,

Ellis Cliff, Fort Adams, and all the strategic points on the main river; and the busy agents of the press follow up and proclaim to the world the whole thing, and instead of surprising our enemy we find him felling trees and blocking passages that would without this have been in our possession, and all the real effects of surprise are lost. I say with the press unfettered as now we are defeated to the end of time. 'Tis folly to say the people must have news.

Every soldier can and does write to his family and friends, and all have ample opportunities for so doing; and this pretext forms no good reason why agents of the press should reveal prematurely all our plans and designs. We cannot prevent it. Clerks of steamboats, correspondents in disguise or openly, attend each army and detachment, and presto! appear in Memphis and St. Louis minute accounts of our plans and designs. These reach Vicksburg by telegraph from Hernando and Holly Springs before we know of it. The only two really successful military strokes out here have succeeded because of the absence of newspapers, or by throwing them off the trail. Halleck had to make a simulated attack on Columbus to prevent the press giving notice of his intended move against Forts Henry and Donelson. We succeeded in reaching the Post of Arkansas before the correspondents could reach the papers.

It is a newspaper's duty to print the news, and raise hell.
Wilbur F. Storey, Statement of Aims of the *Chicago Times*, which Storey edited, 1861

93.

Resolutions Against Foreign Mediation

At the outset of the Civil War, Confederate leaders expected French and English intervention on their behalf because of the latter's seeming dependence on "King Cotton" to supply the textile industries. But England was as much dependent on Northern wheat, and profited by trading with both sides. On November 1, 1862, Emperor Napoleon III of France urged cooperation by France, England, and Russia to end the war. He offered mediation on the basis of a six months' armistice and the lifting of the North's blockade of the South. This meant virtual recognition of Southern independence. England and Russia rejected the proposal, but Napoleon, the following February, again proposed mediation. Apprehensive of European policy, Senator Charles Sumner, chairman of the Committee on Foreign Affairs, presented the following resolutions against foreign mediation that Congress passed on March 3, 1863.

Source: McPherson, pp. 346-347.

Whereas it appears from the diplomatic correspondence submitted to Congress that a proposition, friendly in form, looking to pacification through foreign mediation, has been made to the United States by the emperor of the French and promptly declined by the President. *And whereas* the idea of mediation or intervention in some shape may be regarded by foreign governments as practicable, and such governments, through this misunderstanding, may be led to proceedings tending to embarrass the friendly relations which now exist between them and the United States. *And whereas,* in order to remove for the future all chance of misunderstanding on this subject, and to secure for the United States the full enjoyment of that freedom from foreign interference which is one of the highest rights of independent states, it seems fit that Congress should declare its convictions thereon: Therefore, —

Resolved (the House of Representatives concurring), that while, in times past, the United States have sought and accepted the friendly mediation or arbitration of foreign powers for the pacific adjustment of international questions where the United States were the party of the one part and some other sovereign power the party of the other part; and while they are not disposed to misconstrue the natural and humane desire of foreign powers to aid in arresting domestic troubles, which, widening in their influence, have afflicted other countries, especially in view of the circumstance, deeply regretted by the American people, that the blow aimed by the rebellion at the national life has fallen heavily upon the laboring population of Europe; yet, notwithstanding these things, Congress cannot hesitate to regard every proposition of foreign interference in the present contest as so far unreasonable and inadmissable that its only explanation will be found in a misunderstanding of the true state of the question and of the real character of the war in which the republic is engaged.

2. That the United States are now grappling with an unprovoked and wicked rebellion, which is seeking the destruction of the republic that it may build a new power, whose cornerstone, according to the confession of its chiefs, shall be slavery; that for the suppression of this rebellion, and thus to save the republic and to prevent the establishment of such a power, the national government is now employing armies and fleets in full faith that through these efforts all the purpose of conspirators and rebels will be crushed; that while engaged in this struggle, on which so much depends, any proposition from a foreign power, whatever form it may take, having for its object the arrest of these efforts, is, just in proportion to its influence, an encouragement to the rebellion and to its declared principles, and, on this account, is calculated to prolong and embitter the conflict, to cause increased expenditure of blood and treasure, and to postpone the much-desired day of peace; that, with these convictions, and not doubting that every such proposition, although made with good intent, is injurious to the national interests, Congress will be obliged to look upon any further attempt in the same direction as an unfriendly act which it earnestly deprecates, to the end that nothing may occur abroad to strengthen the rebellion or to weaken those relations of goodwill with foreign powers which the United States are happy to cultivate.

3. That the rebellion from its beginning, and far back even in the conspiracy which preceded its outbreak, was encouraged by the hope of support from foreign powers; that its chiefs frequently boasted that the people of Europe were so far dependent upon regular supplies of the great Southern staple that, sooner or later, their governments would be constrained to take side with the rebellion in some effective form, even to the extent of forcible intervention, if the milder form did not prevail; that the rebellion is now sustained by this hope, which every proposition of foreign interference quickens anew, and that, without this life-giving support, it must soon yield to the just and paternal authority of the national government; that considering these things, which are aggravated by the motive of the resistance thus encouraged, the United States regret that foreign powers have not frankly told the chiefs of the rebellion that the work in which they are engaged is hateful, and that a new government such as they seek to found with slavery as its acknowledged cornerstone, and with no other declared object of separate existence, is so far shocking to civilization and the moral sense of mankind that it must not expect welcome or recognition in the commonwealth of nations.

4. That the United States, confident in the justice of their cause, which is the cause, also, of good government and of human rights everywhere among men; anxious for the speedy restoration of peace which shall secure tranquillity at home and remove all occasion of complaint abroad; and awaiting with well-assured trust the final suppression of the rebellion through which all these things, rescued from present danger, will be secured forever, and the republic, one and indivisible, triumphant over its enemies, will continue to stand an example to mankind, *hereby announce,* as their unalterable purpose, that the war will be vigorously prosecuted according to the humane principles of Christian states until the rebellion shall be suppressed. And they reverently invoke upon their cause the blessings of Almighty God.

5. That the President be requested to transmit a copy of these resolutions, through the secretary of state, to the ministers of the United States in foreign countries, that the declaration and protest herein set forth may be communicated by them to the government to which they are accredited.

94.

Clement L. Vallandigham: A Plea to Stop the War

Clement Vallandigham, an Ohio lawyer and congressman, became the most famous of the Peace Democrats, or "Copperheads," who wished to end the war at any cost. His roots in Virginia inspired him with a devotion to the South, but far stronger was his devotion to the cause of peace. In a speech at Cooper Union on November 2, 1860, Vallandigham asserted he would never "as a Representative in the Congress of the United States, vote one dollar of money whereby one drop of American blood should be shed in a civil war." Throughout the war years he made speeches in the North against the war and the administration. Republicans branded him a traitor, while many war-weary Northerners extolled him as an apostle of freedom. The following speech, given before the Democratic Union Association in New York City on March 7, 1863, was one of several that led to his arrest for treason on May 5, 1863. Lincoln subsequently banished him to the Confederacy.

Source: *Speeches, Arguments, Addresses, and Letters of Clement L. Vallandigham,* New York, 1864, pp. 479-502.

THE MEN WHO ARE IN POWER at Washington, extending their agencies out through the cities and states of the Union and threatening to reinaugurate a reign of terror, may as well know that we comprehend precisely their purpose. I beg leave to assure you that it cannot and will not be permitted to succeed. The people of this country endorsed it once because they were told that it was essential to "the speedy suppression or crushing out of the rebellion" and the restoration of the Union; and they so loved the Union of these states that they would consent, even for a little while, under the false and now broken promises of the men in power, to surrender those liberties in order that the great object might, as was promised, be accomplished speedily.

They have been deceived; instead of crushing out the rebellion, the effort has been to crush out the spirit of liberty. The conspiracy of those in power is not so much for a vigorous prosecution of the war against rebels in the South as against the democracy in peace at home. . . .

I am ready to submit to many things that I think had better not be attempted, just so long as assemblages of the people and the ballot, which are the great correctives of evil and which were intended by our fathers to be the machinery by which peaceable revolution should be accomplished in our government, remain untouched; but I say to the administration: "Lay not your hands at the foundation of the fabric of our liberties: you may lop off a branch here and there, and it will survive; we may tolerate that for the sake of a greater good hereafter; but whenever you reach forth your hand to strike at the very vitals of public liberty, then the people must and will determine in their sovereign capacity what remedy the occasion demands. . . ."

Coming immediately from Washington,

having witnessed, with the common satisfaction of the people of this country, the expiration of the Thirty-seventh Congress, I am here to speak, in the first place, briefly of some things which have been done in that body during the recent session and the session which preceded it. I will not go back so far as the extra session when general insanity prevailed throughout the country, and when the representatives of the people were, perhaps, to a larger degree excusable; because while they had doubtless contributed to that insanity, it was reflected back upon them again; but after a period given for meditation, after the logic of events had begun to work out, after the experiment of war had been tried for one year, it seems to me that wise men, men in whose hands you can with safety deposit the power that belongs to you, should have meditated a little while, and with some degree of wisdom have proceeded to legislate for the true interests of the country. Did they do it?

What has been the legislation financially, to begin with that? Where were we then? What was your currency? Gold. How much have you seen lately of it? You read of it in the stock market, impalpable, invisible — a thing that belongs to the past; it will go into the collections of those who have a curiosity for coins. What is your currency now? Greenbacks; nor is that all. Postage currency, and to what extent? Nearly a thousand millions already. That is what is offered to you. It is the entertainment to which you were invited, or rather which you were compelled to accept though not invited to, in 1860.

Your public debt — what was it then? The enormous sum of $71 million. Would you not be willing to compromise on that today? No doubt even they to whom that word "compromise" is most odious, who feel toward it as Romeo toward the word "banishment," would be very willing to settle the debt of this country at $71 million.

It is now, actually or prospectively, because the appropriations reach that extent — $2,277,000,000.

That is the sum which this Congress has appropriated. They have given to this tremendous debt the power that belongs to it by the issuing of what is called a government currency, binding everybody by some sort of paper tie to the government — by the establishment of a grand national paper mill, a national bank, and through the other schemes of finance which were formed in the brain, or found a lodgment there somehow or other, of the secretary of the treasury. They have, by this instrumentality, obtained absolute control of the entire country. Through a tax law, the like of which never was imposed upon any but a conquered people, they have possession, actually or prospectively, of the entire property of the people of the country. Thus the purse, through the swift and anxious servility of a Congress which was intended by our fathers to be the watchful guardian of the people's money and the people's property, is now absolutely and unqualifiedly for two years at the disposal of the Executive of the United States.

In ordinary times, the control of that purse was regarded by the jealous lovers of liberty, by the men who preceded those in power, by the men who sat in your places twenty, thirty, or forty years ago, as one of the instruments of despotism — then even when our revenue was down as low as $20 million. It was then that, with jealousy, with the most scrutinizing care, every appropriation of money was allowed to pass through the House of Representatives or the Senate of the United States. And yet this Congress, since the 4th of July, 1861, some twenty months or less, has appropriated, as I have said, the enormous sum, and put it at the disposal of the President of the United States, of $2,277,000,000. And for what? To control that which in part is the lifeblood of the nation, its business, its currency, all that enter into the business transactions of life.

Part of it was intended in the beginning as a fund wherewith to set up the Negro trade. It entered the mind of Mr. Lincoln that the idea of compensated emancipation, as he calls it, must be carried out practically, and it found a place in his message and was repeated in the annual message, and that most delicate term to conceal a most odious thing — compensated emancipation — was given to it with the vain idea of deceiving the people — compensated emancipation meaning, being interpreted into good old-fashioned English — *Greenback Abolition.*

The minority in the Senate and in the House, through their pertinacity of purpose, surrounded though they were by bayonets and by despotic power on every side, succeeded at last in defeating this scheme for the purchase of Negroes; but nearly all the other plans were consummated. Thus, as I have said, the purse was placed under the control of the executive for two years. . . .

And now, as to that other great weapon of government — the sword. . . . Not only have . . . 937,000 enlisted men and . . . 300,000 drafted men — indeed, I might say . . . 1,237,000 enlisted men, for the draft was used only to compel and procure enlistments — not only have all these men been sent into the field, or at least made to appear on the payrolls, but in the very expiring hours of the Congress, which died and went to its own place at 12 o'clock on the 4th of March, your misrepresentatives — for such they had become — not speaking the voice of the people, did attempt to clothe the President with the power of conscripting every man in the United States between the ages of twenty and forty-five — to compel him to enter the Army and enable the President to keep up a war which, by that bill itself, he and they confess to be against the will of the people. . . .

Thus, so far as it is possible, by an enactment having the form of law, the Congress of the United States have surrendered, absolutely, the entire military power of the country to the President. Now, if in possession of the purse and the sword absolutely and unqualifiedly, for two years, there be anything else wanting which describes a dictatorship, I beg to know what it is. Why did they not imitate the manhood of the old Roman senators when the exigency of the Republic, in their judgment, demanded it, and declare Mr. Lincoln a dictator in terms? That was alone absolutely what they meant — instead of, cowardlike, undertaking, in the form of law and by the abuse of constitutional power, to give the same authority and the same agencies to establish a despotism as would have been implied by the direct creation of a dictatorship. . . .

As originally proposed, the bill not only would have but the 3 or 4 million males between twenty and forty-five under the military control of the President, as commander in chief, but would also have placed every man, woman, and child, by virtue of the two provisions that were stricken out, also in his power. Our civil rights would have been gone, and our judiciary undermined, and he would have been an absolute and uncontrolled dictator, with the power of Cincinnatus, but without one particle of his virtues.

Yet, unfortunately, while this much was accomplished on that bill, the same tyrannical power was conferred by another bill which passed both houses, and is now, so far as forms are concerned, a law of the land — at least an act of the Thirty-seventh Congress. It authorizes the President, whom the people made, whom the people had chosen by the ballot box under the Constitution and laws, to suspend the writ of habeas corpus all over the United States; to say that because there is a rebellion in South Carolina, a man shall not have freedom of speech, freedom of the press, or any of his rights untrammeled in the state of New York, or 1,000 miles distant. That was the very question upon which the people passed judgment in the recent elections, more, perhaps, than any other question. . . .

The Constitution gives the power to Congress, and to Congress alone, to suspend the writ of habeas corpus, but it can only be done in case of invasion or rebellion, and then only when the public safety requires it; and in the opinion of the best jurists of the land, and indeed of everyone previous to these times, Congress could only suspend this writ in places actually in rebellion or actually invaded. That is the Constitution. And whenever this question shall be tried before a court in the state of New York, or Ohio, or Wisconsin, or anywhere else, before honest and fearless judges worthy of the place they occupy, the decision will be that it is unconstitutional, . . .

The foreigner who seeks citizenship takes an express oath to support the Constitution of the United States. The man born under the tyranny of Austria or Russia — these used to be tyrannies before we had one of our own — that man born thus, with all his ideas formed upon the model of such governments, comes here; and yet it never entered into the heads of our fathers, from the beginning down to the present day, to require of him, through the naturalization laws, the taking of any other oath than to withdraw his allegiance to any foreign potentate and support the Constitution. But our own native-born citizens, and foreigners who have become citizens, who have taken that oath, are required, notwithstanding their innocence, to take this other oath. And though the informers, despicable as the vermin are, have failed to invent or devise any accusation whereby he can be held, he is required to take it; and if he refuse, he is then to remain imprisoned during the pleasure of the President of the United States. These are our liberties, forsooth!

Was it this which you were promised, in 1860, in that grand "Wide Awake" campaign, when banners were borne through your streets inscribed "Free speech, free press, and free men"? And all this has been accomplished, so far as the forms of the law go, by the Congress which has just expired. Now, I repeat again, that if there is anything wanting to make up a complete and absolute despotism, as iron and inexorable in its character as the worst despotisms of the Old World, or the most detestable of modern times, even to Bomba's of Naples, I am unable to comprehend what it is.

All this, gentlemen, infamous and execrable as it is, is enough to make the blood of the coldest man who has one single appreciation in his heart of freedom to boil with indignation. Still, so long as they leave to us free assemblages, free discussion, and a free ballot, I do not want to see, and will not encourage or countenance, any other mode of ridding ourselves of it.

We are ready to try these questions in that way; but I have only to repeat what I said a little while ago, that when the attempt is made to take away those other rights, and the only instrumentalities peaceably of reforming and correcting abuses — free assemblages, free speech, free ballot, and free elections — THEN THE HOUR WILL HAVE ARRIVED WHEN IT WILL BE THE DUTY OF FREEMEN TO FIND SOME OTHER AND EFFICIENT MODE OF DEFENDING THEIR LIBERTIES.

Our fathers did not inaugurate the Revolution of 1776, they did not endure the sufferings and privations of a seven years' war to escape from the mild and moderate control of a constitutional monarchy like that of England, to be at last, in the third generation, subjected to a tyranny equal to that of any upon the face of the globe.

But, sir, I repeat, that it will not, in my judgment, come to this. I do not believe that this administration will undertake to deprive us of that right. I do not think it will venture, for one moment, to attempt to prevent, under any pretext whatever, the assembling together of the people for the fair discussion of their measures and policy. I do not believe it, because it seems to me with all the folly and madness which have been manifested in those high places, they must foresee what will inevitably follow. . . .

In the beginning you were told that the purpose of all the power, previous to the recent legislation of Congress, given to or usurped by the executive, was for the maintenance of the Constitution and the restoration of the Union; and with that love for both, which is the highest honor to this people and its only apology (and it will be so recorded) for submitting to what we have done, the people made sacrifices, gave money, sent forth their firstborn at the call of the executive as no other people ever did since the world began. There never was such a struggle in any age or any country. Why? Because the President and all under him did repeatedly and distinctly declare that the sole purpose was to uphold the Constitution which our fathers had made and the Union which that Constitution established, and to which we owed all our greatness and prosperity.

The people of America were willing to sacrifice all these for that great good. It was so said in the President's annual message of the 4th of July, as it had been in his proclamation of the 15th of April, calling forth the militia, in the beginning. It was in the orders and proclamations of every Federal general for the first eight or ten months after he entered the Southern states. The day after the Battle of Bull Run, by a vote unanimous save two, Congress declared that the sole purpose of the war should be the maintenance of the Constitution, the restoration of the Union, and the enforcement of the laws; and when these objects were accomplished, the war should cease, without touching the domestic institutions, slavery included, in the Southern states. That pledge was given, and under it an army of

600,000 men was at once raised; and it was repeated in every form till toward the close of the second session of Congress. Then the Abolition senators and representatives began first to demand a change in the policy of the administration, they began to proclaim that the war must be no longer for the Union and the Constitution but for the abolition of slavery in the Southern states.

Now, sir, I repeat it and defy contradiction, that not a soldier enlisted, out of the first 900,000, for any other purpose than the restoration of the Union and the maintenance of the Constitution. There was not one single officer, so far as his public declarations were concerned, whatever may have been the secret purposes of his heart, that did not openly declare that the moment this object was changed to the abolition of slavery, he would throw up his commission and resign. Yes, the very men who, for the last four or five weeks in the army — the officers — I do not mean your private soldiers, they who do picket duty, who stand in the front ranks, who brave the iron hail and leaden rain of the stormy battlefield, the men who sacrifice their lives for the paltry sum of $13 a month, the noble, brave men, who, if they were at home, would give us their votes, as their sympathies are still with us; I speak of your officers only — your majors, your lieutenant colonels, colonels, brigadiers, and major generals, each one of them seeking promotion, and drawing his salary of $2,000, $3,000, $4,000, $5,000, $6,000, and $7,000 a year, and whose interest it is that the war be made eternal.

They are the men who have been holding these meetings of regiments so-called, concocting resolutions, or rather adopting resolutions concocted in Indianapolis, Columbus, Springfield, or Washington, and sent down to be clothed in form as an expression of the opinion of the regiments, but, in fact, the expression of the officers alone. They are the men who have solemnly declared, at home and in the Army, that the moment this became an Abolition war, they would resign and come back to us, and yet they are now sending out these missiles to us their peers — threatening messages that they mean to come back and "whip" the Democratic traitors and secessionists of the North.

Now, I tell these shoulder-strapped gentlemen who are looking to the White House instead of at the enemy that when they have succeeded in the mission for which they were sent out; when upon the battlefield they have put down those who are now in arms against them, it will be time enough to talk about coming back. But if they imagine for one moment that any man here is to be frightened by their insolent messages, they know not the spirit of the freemen who remain at home. . . .

If there be any man in the Democratic or Republican Party who still thinks that war can restore the Union as it was and maintain the Constitution as it is, I have no quarrel with him tonight. I assume his position for the sake of argument — it is not mine, and never was; but let it be so for a moment. You say that a war prosecuted for this purpose must thus result. Have you the power to change the purpose? Can you compel Abraham Lincoln to withdraw his proclamation? Can you repeal the legislation of the Congress that is now defunct? If you cannot, the war must go on upon the basis on which it is now prosecuted — and you believe that it will end in death to the Union, the Constitution, and to liberty.

What position, then, do you occupy before your countrymen in still advocating the so-called vigorous prosecution of the war? Vigorous prosecution! For what? By your own declaration — disunion, separation, destruction, despotism. Dare any man stand before an assembly of freemen and advocate the objects or the results, at least, of such a war? And yet what inconsistency for anyone claiming intelligence to declare that al-

though it must so result, and although he has not the power to change the policy of the administration, it is the duty of every man to support that administration in its policy. I deny it; and for one, at least, I will not do it. If I had believed originally, as I did not believe, that it was possible to restore this Union by force, if I had occupied the position of hundreds and thousands of Democrats, as well as the great mass of the Republican Party, I would proclaim tonight that, inasmuch as this is the policy and we have not the power to change it, that then our duty would be, and is, to advocate henceforth to the end A VIGOROUS PROSECUTION OF PEACE FOR THE UNION.

I will not consent to put the entire purse of the country and the sword of the country into the hands of the executive, giving him despotic and dictatorial power to carry out an object which I avow before my countrymen is the destruction of their liberties and the overthrow of the Union of these states. I do not comprehend the honesty of such declarations or of the men who make them. I know that the charge is brought against myself, personally, and against many of us. I have not spent a moment in replying to it — the people will take care of all that.

The charge has been made against us — all who are opposed to the policy of this administration and opposed to this war — that we are for "peace on any terms." It is false. I am not, but I am for an immediate stopping of the war and for honorable peace. I am for peace for the sake of the Union of these states. More than that — I am for peace, and would be, even if the Union could not be restored, as I believe it can be; because without peace, permitting this administration for two years to exercise its tremendous powers, the war still existing, you will not have one remnant of civil liberty left among yourselves. The exercise of these tremendous powers, the apology for which is the existence of this war, is utterly incompatible with the stability of the

Constitution and of constitutional liberty.

I am not for "peace on any terms"; I would not be with any country on the globe. Honor is also the life of the nation, and it is never to be sacrificed. I have as high and proud a sense of honor, and have a right to have it, as any man in the South, and I love my country too well, and cherish its honor too profoundly, for one single moment to consent to a dishonorable peace. Yes, the whole country; every state; and I, unlike some of my own party, and unlike thousands of the Abolition Party, believe still, before God, that the Union can be reconstructed and will be. That is my faith, and I mean to cling to it as the wrecked mariner clings to the last plank amid the shipwreck. But when I see that the experiment of blood has failed from the beginning, as I believed it would fail, I am not one of those who proclaim now that we shall have separation and disunion. I am for going back to the instrumentality through which this Union was first made, and by which alone it can be restored.

I am for peace, because it is the first step toward conciliation and compromise. You cannot move until you have first taken that indispensable preliminary — a cessation of hostilities. But it is said that the South has refused to accept or listen to any terms whatever. How do you know that? Has it been tried? Now, gentlemen, I know very well what the papers in support of the administration at Richmond say. I know what men in the Senate and House of Representatives at Richmond declare on this subject; I have read it all. We are indebted to the Abolition papers for the republication of all that. But I do hope that no man who has ever known me in person or by speech supposed for one moment that I expected that the children of that revolution, the men who sprang from it, the men who are dependent upon it, or even the men holding power now under it would, while this war lasted, listen to any terms of settlement. I

would as soon expect Abraham Lincoln and his cabinet to propose such terms on the basis of the Union of fifty years ago as Jefferson Davis or any man in Richmond.

Now I am not, perhaps, the most sensitive man in the world, and yet I have a reasonable degree of sensitiveness and, I hope, some common sense with it; but I do not feel, as I am afraid some of our friends do feel, personally slighted, because, while I have advocated a peaceable settlement of our difficulties — conciliation and compromise for the restoration of the Union of these states — I have met with opposition and with hostility from the papers in Richmond. I did not look for it, gentlemen, although I have a better right to it than some of your friends here from my former relation to the Democratic Party of the South, when they were acknowledging obedience to the Constitution and were still in the Union; but I did not expect that Jefferson Davis, and Benjamin, and Hunter, or any of them would, when I opened my arms and said, "Return, prodigal sons," rush with tears to my embrace — and I do not feel hurt. I am not the least "miffed" by it; and I certainly shall not therefore advocate a vigorous prosecution of the war to punish them.

I am afraid some gentlemen imagined, when they gave out this invitation, that it would be, of course, accepted at once; although one of those who first proclaimed it had even less power than I have, certainly not more — and was very much in the condition of that distinguished personage who, from the top of a certain high mountain, promised all the kingdoms of the world. I do not think that he or I, or any other man while this administration is in place, has the power to conciliate and compromise now.

Take the theory for what it is worth, and let men of intelligence judge; let history attest it hereafter. My theory upon that subject, then, is this — stop this war.

95.

The Question of Continuing the War

Early in 1863 a set of peace resolutions that were to be presented to the New Jersey legislature when it convened on March 13 were published in several local newspapers. The resolutions stirred up Union sentiment in New Jersey and prompted on March 10 the following protest from the Eleventh New Jersey Volunteers who were camped below Falmouth, Virginia. The resolutions were introduced on the opening day of the session and on March 17 or 18 — authorities differ — were passed.

Source: Moore, I, Supplement, Document 97.

I.

New Jersey Peace Resolutions

1. *Be it resolved by the Senate and General Assembly of the state of New Jersey,* that this state, in promptly answering the calls made by the President of the United States, at and since the inauguration of the war, for troops and means to assist in maintaining the power and dignity of the Federal government, believed and confided in the professions and declarations of the President of the United States, in his inaugural address, and in the resolutions passed by Congress on the 25th day of July, 1861, in which, among other things, it was declared "that the war is not waged for conquest or subjugation, or interfering with the rights or established institutions of the states but to maintain and defend the supremacy of the Constitution, with the rights and equality under it unimpaired, and that as soon as these objects shall be accomplished the war ought to cease"; and that, relying upon these assurances, given under the sanctity of official oaths, this state freely, fully, and without delay or conditions contributed to the assistance of the Federal government her sons and her means.

2. *And be it resolved,* that this state, having waited for the redemption of the sacred pledges of the President and Congress with a patience and forbearance only equaled in degree by the unfaltering and unswerving bravery and fidelity of her sons, conceives it to be her solemn duty, as it is her unquestioned right, to urge upon the President and Congress, in the most respectful but decided manner, the redemption of the pledges under which the troops of this state entered upon, and to this moment have continued in, the contest.

And inasmuch as no conditions have delayed nor hesitation marked her zeal in behalf of the Federal government, even at times when party dogmas were dangerously usurping the place of broad national principles and executive and congressional faith; and as the devotion of this state to the sacred cause of perpetuating the Union and maintaining the Constitution has been untainted in any degree by infidelity, bigotry, sectionalism, or partisanship, she now, in view of the faith originally plighted, of the disasters and disgrace that have marked the steps of a changed and changing policy, and of the imminent dangers that threaten our national existence, urges upon the President and Congress a return and adherence to the original policy of the administration as the only means, under the blessing of God, by which the adhering states can be reunited in action, the Union restored, and the nation saved.

3. *And be it resolved,* that it is the deliberate sense of the people of this state that the war power within the limits of the Constitution is ample for any and all emergencies, and that all assumption of power, under whatever plea, beyond that conferred by the Constitution is without warrant or authority, and if permitted to continue without remonstrance will finally encompass the destruction of the liberties of the people and the death of the republic; and therefore, to the end that in any event the matured and deliberate sense of the people of New Jersey may be known and declared, we their representatives in Senate and General Assembly convened, do, in their name and in their behalf, make unto the Federal government this our solemn protest:

Against a war waged with the insurgent states for the accomplishment of unconstitutional or partisan purposes;

Against a war which has for its object the subjugation of any of the states, with a view to their reduction to territorial condition;

Against proclamations from any source by which, under the plea of "military necessity," persons in states and territories sustaining the Federal government, and beyond necessary military lines, are held liable to the rigor and severity of military laws;

Against the domination of the military over the civil law in states, territories, or districts not in a state of insurrection;

Against all arrests without warrant; against the suspension of the writ of habeas corpus in states and territories sustaining the Federal government, "where the public safety does not require it"; and against the assumption of power by any person to suspend such writ, except under the express authority of Congress;

Against the creation of new states by the division of existing ones, or in any other manner not clearly authorized by the Constitution; and against the right of secession as practically admitted by the action of Congress in admitting as a new state a portion of the state of Virginia;

Against the power assumed in the proclamation of the President made January 1, 1863, by which all the slaves in certain states and parts of states are forever set free; and against the expenditures of the public moneys for the emancipation of slaves or their support at any time, under any pretense whatever;

Against any and every exercise of power upon the part of the Federal government that is not clearly given and expressed in the Federal Constitution — reasserting that "the powers not delegated to the United States by the Constitution, nor prohibited by it to the states, are reserved to the states respectively, or to the people."

4. *And be it resolved,* that the unequaled promptness with which New Jersey has responded to every call made by the President and Congress for men and means has been occasioned by no lurking animosity to the states of the South or the rights of her people; no disposition to wrest from them any of their rights, privileges, or property, but simply to assist in maintaining, as she has ever believed and now believes it to be her duty to do, the supremacy of the Federal Constitution; and while abating naught in her devotion to the Union of the states and the dignity and power of the Federal government, at no time since the commencement of the present war has this state been other than willing to terminate, peacefully and honorably to all, a war unnecessary in its origin, fraught with horror and suffering in its prosecution and necessarily dangerous to the liberties of all in its continuance.

5. *And be it resolved,* that the legislature of the state of New Jersey believes that the appointment of commissioners upon the

part of the Federal government to meet commissioners similarly appointed by the insurgent states, to convene in some suitable place for the purpose of considering whether any and, if any, what plan may be adopted, consistent with the honor and dignity of the national government, by which the present civil war may be brought to a close, is not inconsistent with the integrity, honor, and dignity of the Federal government, but as an indication of the spirit which animates the adhering states, would in any event tend to strengthen us in the opinion of other nations; and hoping, as we sincerely do, that the Southern states would reciprocate the peaceful indications thus evinced, and believing, as we do, that under the blessing of God, great benefits would arise from such a conference, we most earnestly recommend the subject to the consideration of the government of the United States and request its cooperation therein.

6. *And be it resolved,* that His Excellency the Governor be requested to forward copies of these resolutions to the government of the United States, our senators and representatives in Congress, and to the governors and legislatures of our sister states, with the request that they give the subject proposed their serious and immediate attention.

7. *And be it resolved,* that the state of New Jersey pledges itself to such prompt action upon the subject of these resolutions as will give them practical effect, immediately upon the concurrence or cooperation of the government and legislatures of sister states.

II.

Protest of the New Jersey Soldiers

Whereas, the legislature of our native state, a state hallowed by the remembrance of the battles of Princeton, Trenton, and Monmouth, fields stained by the blood of our forefathers in the establishment of our government, has sought to tarnish its high honor and bring upon it disgrace by the passage of resolutions tending to a dishonorable peace with armed rebels seeking to destroy our great and beneficent government, the best ever designed for the happiness of the many; and

Whereas, we, her sons, members of the Eleventh Regiment, New Jersey Volunteers, citizens representing every section of the state, have left our homes to endure the fatigues, privations, and dangers incident to a soldier's life, in order to maintain our republic in its integrity, willing to sacrifice our lives to that object; fully recognizing the impropriety of a soldier's discussion of the legislative functions of the state, yet deeming it due to ourselves that the voice of those who offer their all in their country's cause be heard when weak and wicked men seek its dishonor.

Therefore,

Resolved, that the Union of the states is the only guarantee for the preservation of our liberty and independence, and that the war for the maintainance of that Union commands *now,* as it ever has done, our best efforts and our heartfelt sympathy.

Resolved, that we consider the passage or even the introduction of the so-called Peace Resolutions as wicked, weak, and cowardly, tending to aid by their sympathy the rebels seeking to destroy the republic.

Resolved, that we regard as traitors alike the foe in arms and the secret enemies of our government who, at home, foment disaffection and strive to destroy confidence in our legally chosen rulers.

Resolved, that the reports spread broadcast throughout the North, by secession sympathizers, prints, and voices, that the army of which we esteem it a high honor to form a part is demoralized and clamorous for peace on any terms are the lying utterances of traitorous tongues and do base injustice to our noble comrades who have never faltered in the great work, and are now not only willing but anxious to follow their gallant and chivalric leader against the strongholds of the enemy.

Resolved, that we put forth every effort, endure every fatigue, and shrink from no danger, until, under the gracious guidance of a kind Providence, every armed rebel shall be conquered, and traitors at home shall quake with fear, as the proud emblem of our national independence shall assert its power from North to South, and crush beneath its powerful folds all who dared to assail its honor, doubly hallowed by the memory of the patriot dead.

96.

Government Seizure of Property in the Confederacy

The Confederate Army was faced with a serious problem of obtaining supplies. The coast was blockaded; money became vastly inflated; goods were hoarded and profiteering was rampant. Early in the war the Army resorted to impressment of goods for military use. This policy produced widespread abuses, and on March 26, 1863, the Congress of the Confederacy passed the following law regulating impressment, hoping also to stabilize the economy.

Source: *The Statutes at Large of the Provisional Government of the Confederate States of America, etc., etc.,* James M. Matthews, ed., Richmond, Va., 1864, pp. 102-104.

The Congress of the Confederate States of America do enact, that whenever the exigencies of any army in the field are such as to make impressments of forage, articles of subsistence, or other property absolutely necessary, then such impressments may be made by the officer or officers whose duty it is to furnish such forage, articles of subsistence, or other property for such army. In cases where the owner of such property and the impressing officer cannot agree upon the value thereof, it shall be the duty of such impressing officer, upon an affidavit in writing of the owner of such property, or his agent, that such property was grown, raised, or produced by said owner, or is held or has been purchased by him, not for sale or speculation but for his own use or consumption, to cause the same to be ascertained and determined by the judgment of two loyal and disinterested citizens of the city, county, or parish in which such impressments may be made; one to be selected by the owner; one by the impressing officer; and in the event of their disagreement, these two shall choose an umpire of like qualifications, whose decision shall be final. The persons thus selected, after an oath to appraise the property impressed, fairly and impartially . . . shall proceed to assess just compensation for the property so impressed, whether the absolute ownership, or the temporary use thereof, only is required.

Section 2. That the officer or person impressing property, as aforesaid, shall, at the time of said taking, pay to the owner, his agent, or attorney, the compensation fixed by said appraisers; and shall also give to the owner, or person controlling said property, a certificate, over his official signature, specifying the battalion, regiment, brigade, division, or corps to which he belongs, that said property is essential for use of the army, could not be otherwise procured, and was taken through absolute necessity, setting forth the time and place, when and where taken, the amount of compensation fixed by said appraisers, and the sum, if any, paid for the same. Said certificate shall be evidence for the owner, as well of the taking of said property for the public use, as the right of the owner to the amount of compensation fixed as aforesaid. And in case said officer or person taking said property shall have failed to pay the owner or his agent said compensation as hereinbefore required, then said owner shall be entitled to the speedy payment of the same by the proper disbursing officer; which, when so paid, shall be in full satisfaction of all claims against the government of the Confederate States.

Section 3. Whenever the appraisement . . . be impracticable at the time of said impressment, then and in that case the value of the property impressed shall be assessed as soon as possible by two loyal and disinterested citizens of the city, county, or parish wherein the property was taken. . . .

Section 4. That whenever the secretary of war shall be of opinion that it is necessary to take private property for public use, by reason of the impracticability of procuring the same by purchase, so as to accumulate necessary supplies for the army, or the good of the service, in any locality, he may, by general order, through the proper subordinate officers, authorize such property to be taken for the public use; the compensation due the owner for the same to be determined, and the value fixed. . . .

Section 5. That it shall be the duty of the president, as early as practicable after the passage of this act, to appoint a commissioner in each state where property shall be taken for the public use and request the governor of such of the states in which the president shall appoint said commissioner to appoint another commissioner to act in conjunction with the commissioner appointed by the president, who shall receive the compensation of $8 per day, and 10 cents per mile as mileage, to be paid by the Confederate government. Said commissioners shall constitute a board, whose duty it shall be to fix upon the prices to be paid by the government for all property impressed or taken for the public use as aforesaid, so as to afford just compensation to the owners thereof. Said commissioners shall agree upon and publish a schedule of prices every two months, or oftener if they shall deem it proper. . . .

Section 6. That all property impressed or taken for the public use, as aforesaid, in the hands of any person other than the persons who have raised, grown, or produced the same, or persons holding the same for their own use or consumption, and who shall make the affidavit as hereinbefore required, shall be paid for according to the schedule of prices fixed by the commissioners as aforesaid. But if the officer impressing or taking for the public use such property and the owner shall differ as to the quality of the article or property impressed or taken, as aforesaid, thereby making it fall within a higher or lower price named in the schedule, then the owner or agent and the officer impressing or taking, as aforesaid, may select each a loyal and disinterested citizen . . . to determine the quality of said article or property, who shall, in case of disagreement, appoint an umpire of like qualifications, and his decision, if approved by the officer impressing, shall be final; but if not approved, the impressing officer shall send the award to the commissioners of the state where the property is impressed, with his reasons for disapproving the same, and said commissioners may hear such proofs as the parties may respectively adduce, and their decision shall be final: *Provided,* that the owner may receive the price offered by the impressing officer, without prejudice to his claim to receive the higher compensation.

Section 7. That the property necessary for the support of the owner and his family, and to carry on his ordinary agricultural and mechanical business, to be ascertained by the appraisers . . . under oath, shall not be taken or impressed for the public use; and when the impressing officer and the owner cannot agree as to the quantity necessary, as aforesaid, then the decision of the said appraisers shall be binding on the officer and all other persons.

Section 8. Where property has been impressed for temporary use and is lost or destroyed without the default of the owner, the government of the Confederate States shall pay a just compensation therefor; to be ascertained by appraisers appointed and qualified as provided in the 1st Section of this act. If such property, when returned, has, in the opinion of the owner, been injured while in the public use, the amount of damage thereby sustained shall be determined in the manner described in the 3rd Section of this act. . . .

Section 9. Where slaves are impressed by the Confederate government to labor on fortifications or other public works, the impressment shall be made by said government according to the rules and regulations provided in the laws of the state wherein they are impressed; and in the absence of such law, in accordance with such rules and regulations not inconsistent with the provisions of this act as the secretary of war shall from time to time prescribe: *Provided,* that no impressment of slaves shall be made when they can be hired or procured by the consent of the owner or agent.

Section 10. That previous to the 1st day of December next, no slave laboring on a farm or plantation exclusively devoted to the production of grain and provisions shall be taken for the public use without the consent of the owner, except in case of urgent necessity.

Section 11. That any commissioned or noncommissioned officer or private who shall violate the provisions of this act shall be tried before the military court of the corps to which he is attached, on complaint made by the owner or other person, and on conviction, if an officer, he shall be cashiered and put into the ranks as a private; and if a noncommissioned officer or private, he shall suffer such punishment, not inconsistent with military law, as the court may direct.

If General Lee had Grant's resources he would soon end the war; but Old Jack can do it without resources.

GENERAL GEORGE E. PICKETT, letter to his fiancée, Oct. 11, 1862, of "Stonewall" Jackson

97.

WILLIAM H. SEWARD: Our Policy of Nonintervention

The threat of European intervention in the Civil War, particularly Emperor Napoleon's mediation offer in 1862-1863, posed a serious diplomatic problem to Secretary of State William Seward. In a letter to William Dayton, the American minister to France, written on February 6, 1863, Seward replied to the French offer: "I think he [the French foreign minister] can hardly fail to perceive that it amounts to nothing less than a proposition that, while this government is engaged in suppressing an armed insurrection, with the purpose of maintaining the constitutional national authority . . . it shall enter into diplomatic discussion with the insurgents upon the questions whether that authority shall not be renounced, and whether the country shall not be delivered over to disunion."
On May 11, Seward wrote the following letter to Dayton aimed at reminding the French of the traditional American policy of nonintervention in European affairs.

Source: *The Diplomatic History of the War for the Union Being the Fifth Volume of the Works of William H. Seward*, George E. Baker, ed., Boston, 1890, pp. 382-384.

THIS GOVERNMENT IS PROFOUNDLY and agreeably impressed with the consideration which the emperor has manifested toward the United States by inviting their concurrence in a proceeding having for its object the double interests of public order and humanity. Nor is it less favorably impressed with the sentiments and the prudential considerations which the emperor has in so becoming a manner expressed to the court of St. Petersburg. They are such only as appeal to the just emotions and best sympathies of mankind. The enlightened and humane character of the emperor of Russia, so recently illustrated by the enfranchisement of a large mass of the Russian people from inherited bondage, and the establishment of an impartial and effective administration of justice throughout his dominions, warrant a belief that the appeal will be received and responded to by him with all the favor that is consistent with the general welfare of the

great state over which he presides with such eminent wisdom and moderation.

Notwithstanding, however, the favor with which we thus regard the suggestion of the emperor of the French, this government finds an insurmountable difficulty in the way of any active cooperation with the governments of France, Austria, and Great Britain to which it is thus invited.

Founding our institutions upon the basis of the rights of man, the builders of our republic came all at once to be regarded as political reformers, and it soon became manifest that revolutionists in every country hailed them in that character, and looked to the United States for effective sympathy, if not for active support and patronage. Our invaluable Constitution had hardly been established when it became necessary for the government of the United States to consider to what extent we could, with propriety, safety, and beneficence, intervene, either by alliance or concerted action with friendly powers or otherwise, in the political affairs of foreign states. An urgent appeal for such aid and sympathy was made in behalf of France, and the appeal was sanctioned and enforced by the treaty then existing of mutual alliance and defense, a treaty without which, it may even now be confessed, to the honor of France, our own sovereignty and independence could not have been so early secured.

So deeply did this appeal touch the heart of the American people that only the deference they cherished to the counsels of the father of our country, who then was at the fullness of his unapproachable moral greatness, reconciled them to the stern decision that, in view of the location of this republic, the characters, habits, and sentiments of its constituent parts, and especially its complex yet unique and very popular Constitution, the American people must be content to recommend the cause of human progress by the wisdom with which they should exercise the powers of self-government, forbearing at all times and in every way from foreign alliances, intervention and interference.

It is true that Washington thought a time might come when, our institutions being firmly consolidated and working with complete success, we might safely and perhaps beneficially take part in the consultations held by foreign states for the common advantage of the nations. Since that period, occasions have frequently happened which presented seductions to a departure from what, superficially viewed, seemed a course of isolation and indifference. It is scarcely necessary to recur to them. One was an invitation to a congress of newly emancipated Spanish American states; another, an urgent appeal to aid Hungary in a revolution aiming at the restoration of her ancient and illustrious independence; another, the project of a joint guarantee of Cuba to Spain in concurrence with France and Great Britain; and, more recently, an invitation to a cooperative demonstration with Spain, France, and Great Britain in Mexico; and, later still, suggestions by some of the Spanish American states for a common council of the republican states situated upon the American continent. These suggestions were successively disallowed by the government, and its decision was approved in each case by the deliberate judgment of the American people.

Our policy of nonintervention, straight, absolute, and peculiar as it may seem to other nations, has thus become a traditional one, which could not be abandoned without the most urgent occasion, amounting to a manifest necessity. Certainly it could not be wisely departed from at this moment, when the existence of a local, although as we trust only a transient, disturbance deprives the government of the council of a portion of the American people, to whom so wide a departure from the settled policy of the country must in any case be deeply interesting.

The President will not allow himself to think for a single moment that the emperor of the French will see anything but respect and friendship for himself and the people of France, with good wishes for the preservation of peace and order, and the progress of humanity in Europe, in the adherence of the United States on this occasion to the policy which they have thus far pursued with safety, and not without advantage, as they think, to the interests of mankind.

98.

Abraham Lincoln: Habeas Corpus in Time of Rebellion

The arrest and conviction for treason in May 1863 of Clement Vallandigham, an Ohio congressman and leader of the "Copperheads," sparked violent protests among Democrats. At a meeting in New York, the Albany Democratic Convention on May 16 passed resolutions denouncing Lincoln for permitting the arrest. The resolutions were sent to the President, who gave his reply in a letter of June 12, 1863, to Erastus Corning, an influential New York Democrat.

Source: Nicolay-Hay, VIII, pp. 298-314.

THE RESOLUTIONS, as I understand them, are resolvable into two propositions: first, the expression of a purpose to sustain the cause of the Union, to secure peace through victory, and to support the administration in every constitutional and lawful measure to suppress the rebellion; and, second, a declaration of censure upon the administration for supposed unconstitutional action, such as the making of military arrests. And from the two propositions a third is deduced, which is that the gentlemen composing the meeting are resolved on doing their part to maintain our common government and country, despite the folly or wickedness, as they may conceive, of any administration. This position is eminently patriotic, and as such I thank the meeting and congratulate the nation for it. My own purpose is the same; so that the meeting and myself have a common object and can have no difference, except in the choice of means or measures for effecting that object.

And here I ought to close this paper, and would close it if there were no apprehension that more injurious consequences than any merely personal to myself might follow the censures systematically cast upon me for

doing what, in my view of duty, I could not forbear.

The resolutions promise to support me in every constitutional and lawful measure to suppress the rebellion; and I have not knowingly employed, nor shall knowingly employ, any other. But the meeting by their resolutions assert and argue that certain military arrests and proceedings following them, for which I am ultimately responsible, are unconstitutional. I think they are not. The resolutions quote from the Constitution the definition of treason, and also the limiting safeguards and guarantees therein provided for the citizen on trials for treason, and on his being held to answer for capital or otherwise infamous crimes, and in criminal prosecutions his right to a speedy and public trial by an impartial jury.

They proceed to resolve "that these safeguards of the rights of the citizen against the pretensions of arbitrary power were intended more especially for his protection in times of civil commotion." And, apparently to demonstrate the proposition, the resolutions proceed: "They were secured substantially to the English people after years of protracted civil war, and were adopted into our Constitution at the close of the Revolution." Would not the demonstration have been better if it could have been truly said that these safeguards had been adopted and applied during the civil wars and during our Revolution instead of after the one and at the close of the other? I, too, am devotedly for them after civil war and before civil war, and at all times, "except when, in cases of rebellion or invasion, the public safety may require" their suspension.

The resolutions proceed to tell us that these safeguards "have stood the test of seventy-six years of trial under our republican system under circumstances which show that, while they constitute the foundation of all free government, they are the elements of the enduring stability of the republic." No one denies that they have so stood the test up to the beginning of the present rebellion . . . nor does anyone question that they will stand the same test much longer after the rebellion closes.

But these provisions of the Constitution have no application to the case we have in hand, because the arrests complained of were not made for treason — that is, not for the treason defined in the Constitution, and upon the conviction of which the punishment is death — nor yet were they made to hold persons to answer for any capital or otherwise infamous crimes; nor were the proceedings following, in any constitutional or legal sense, "criminal prosecutions." The arrests were made on totally different grounds, and the proceedings following accorded with the grounds of the arrests. Let us consider the real case with which we are dealing, and apply to it the parts of the Constitution plainly made for such cases.

Prior to my installation here it had been inculcated that any state had a lawful right to secede from the national Union, and that it would be expedient to exercise the right whenever the devotees of the doctrine should fail to elect a President to their own liking. I was elected contrary to their liking;

and, accordingly, so far as it was legally possible, they had taken seven states out of the Union, had seized many of the United States forts, and had fired upon the United States flag, all before I was inaugurated, and, of course, before I had done any official act whatever. The rebellion thus begun soon ran into the present civil war and, in certain respects, it began on very unequal terms between the parties. The insurgents had been preparing for it more than thirty years, while the government had taken no steps to resist them. The former had carefully considered all the means which could be turned to their account.

It undoubtedly was a well-pondered reliance with them that in their own unrestricted effort to destroy Union, Constitution, and law, all together, the government would, in great degree, be restrained by the same Constitution and law from arresting their progress. Their sympathizers pervaded all departments of the government and nearly all communities of the people. From this material, under cover of "liberty of speech," "liberty of the press," and "habeas corpus," they hoped to keep on foot among us a most efficient corps of spies, informers, suppliers, and aiders and abettors of their cause in a thousand ways. They knew that in times such as they were inaugurating, by the Constitution itself the "habeas corpus" might be suspended; but they also knew they had friends who would make a question as to who was to suspend it; meanwhile their spies and others might remain at large to help on their cause.

Or if, as has happened, the executive should suspend the writ without ruinous waste of time, instances of arresting innocent persons might occur, as are always likely to occur in such cases; and then a clamor could be raised in regard to this, which might be at least of some service to the insurgent cause. It needed no very keen perception to discover this part of the enemy's program, so soon as by open hostilities their machinery was fairly put in motion. Yet, thoroughly imbued with a reverence for the guaranteed rights of individuals, I was slow to adopt the strong measures which by degrees I have been forced to regard as being within the exceptions of the Constitution and as indispensable to the public safety. Nothing is better known to history than that courts of justice are utterly incompetent to such cases. Civil courts are organized chiefly for trials of individuals, or, at most, a few individuals acting in concert — and this in quiet times and on charges of crimes well-defined in the law. Even in times of peace, bands of horse thieves and robbers frequently grow too numerous and powerful for the ordinary courts of justice.

But what comparison, in numbers, have such bands ever borne to the insurgent sympathizers, even in many of the loyal states? Again, a jury too frequently has at least one member more ready to hang the panel than to hang the traitor. And yet again, he who dissuades one man from volunteering or induces one soldier to desert weakens the Union cause as much as he who kills a Union soldier in battle. Yet this dissuasion or inducement may be so conducted as to be no defined crime of which any civil court would take cognizance.

Ours is a case of rebellion — so called by the resolutions before me — in fact, a clear, flagrant, and gigantic case of rebellion; and the provision of the Constitution that "the privilege of the writ of habeas corpus shall not be suspended unless when, in cases of rebellion or invasion, the public safety may require it" is the provision which specially applies to our present case. This provision plainly attests the understanding of those who made the Constitution, that ordinary courts of justice are inadequate to "cases of rebellion" — attests their purpose that, in such cases, men may be held in custody whom the courts, acting on ordinary rules, would discharge. Habeas corpus does not discharge men who are proved to be guilty

of defined crime; and its suspension is allowed by the Constitution on the purpose that men may be arrested and held who cannot be proved to be guilty of defined crime, "when, in cases of rebellion or invasion, the public safety may require it."

This is precisely our present case — a case of rebellion wherein the public safety does require the suspension. Indeed, arrests by process of courts and arrests in cases of rebellion do not proceed altogether upon the same basis. The former is directed at the small percentage of ordinary and continuous perpetration of crime, while the latter is directed at sudden and extensive uprisings against the government which, at most, will succeed or fail in no great length of time. In the latter case, arrests are made not so much for what has been done as for what probably would be done. The latter is more for the preventive and less for the vindictive than the former. In such cases the purposes of men are much more easily understood than in cases of ordinary crime. The man who stands by and says nothing when the peril of his government is discussed cannot be misunderstood. If not hindered, he is sure to help the enemy; much more if he talks ambiguously — talks for his country with "buts" and "ifs" and "ands."

Of how little value the constitutional provision I have quoted will be rendered, if arrests shall never be made until defined crimes shall have been committed, may be illustrated by a few notable examples: Gen. John C. Breckinridge, Gen. Robert E. Lee, Gen. Joseph E. Johnston, Gen. John B. Magruder, Gen. William B. Preston, Gen. Simon B. Buckner, and Commodore Franklin Buchanan, now occupying the very highest places in the Rebel war service, were all within the power of the government since the rebellion began, and were nearly as well known to be traitors then as now. Unquestionably, if we had seized and held them, the insurgent cause would be much weaker. But no one of them had then committed any crime defined in the law. Every one of them, if arrested, would have been discharged on habeas corpus were the writ allowed to operate. In view of these and similar cases, I think the time not unlikely to come when I shall be blamed for having made too few arrests rather than too many.

By the third resolution the meeting indicate their opinion that military arrests may be constitutional in localities where rebellion actually exists, but that such arrests are unconstitutional in localities where rebellion or insurrection does not actually exist. They insist that such arrests shall not be made "outside of the lines of necessary military occupation and the scenes of insurrection." Inasmuch, however, as the Constitution itself makes no such distinction, I am unable to believe that there is any such constitutional distinction. I concede that the class of arrests complained of can be constitutional only when, in cases of rebellion or invasion, the public safety may require them; and I insist that in such cases they are constitutional wherever the public safety does require them, as well in places to which they may prevent the rebellion extending, as in those where it may be already prevailing; as well where they may restrain mischievous interference with the raising and supplying of armies to suppress the rebellion, as where the rebellion may actually be; as well where they may restrain the enticing men out of the army, as where they would prevent mutiny in the army; equally constitutional at all places where they will conduce to the public safety, as against the dangers of rebellion or invasion.

Take the particular case mentioned by the meeting. It is asserted in substance that Mr. Vallandigham was, by a military commander, seized and tried "for no other reason than words addressed to a public meeting in criticism of the course of the administration and in condemnation of the military orders of the general." Now, if there be no mistake about this, if this assertion is the truth and the whole truth, if there was no other reason for the arrest, then I concede that the arrest was wrong. But the arrest, as I understand, was made for a very different reason. Mr. Vallandigham avows his hostility to the war on the part of the Union; and his arrest was made because he was laboring, with some effect, to prevent the raising of troops, to encourage desertions from the army, and to leave the rebellion without an adequate military force to suppress it.

He was not arrested because he was damaging the political prospects of the administration or the personal interests of the commanding general but because he was damaging the army, upon the existence and vigor of which the life of the nation depends. He was warring upon the military and this gave the military constitutional jurisdiction to lay hands upon him. If Mr. Vallandigham was not damaging the military power of the country, then his arrest was made on mistake of fact, which I would be glad to correct on reasonably satisfactory evidence.

I understand the meeting, whose resolutions I am considering, to be in favor of suppressing the rebellion by military force, by armies. Long experience has shown that armies cannot be maintained unless desertion shall be punished by the severe penalty of death. The case requires, and the law and the Constitution sanction, this punishment. Must I shoot a simpleminded soldier boy who deserts, while I must not touch a hair of a wily agitator who induces him to desert? This is none the less injurious when effected by getting a father, or brother, or friend into a public meeting, and there working upon his feelings till he is persuaded to write the soldier boy that he is fighting in a bad cause, for a wicked administration of a contemptible government, too weak to arrest and punish him if he shall desert. I think that, in such a case, to silence the agitator and save the boy is not only constitutional but withal a great mercy.

If I be wrong on this question of constitutional power, my error lies in believing that certain proceedings are constitutional when, in cases of rebellion or invasion, the public safety requires them, which would not be constitutional when, in absence of rebellion or invasion, the public safety does not require them; in other words, that the Constitution is not in its application in all respects the same in cases of rebellion or invasion involving the public safety as it is in times of profound peace and public security. The Constitution itself makes the distinction, and I can no more be persuaded that the government can constitutionally take no strong measures in time of rebellion, because it can be shown that the same could not be lawfully taken in time of peace, than I can be persuaded that a particular drug is not good medicine for a sick man because it can be shown not to be good food for a well one.

Nor am I able to appreciate the danger apprehended by the meeting that the American people will by means of military arrests during the rebellion lose the right of public discussion, the liberty of speech and the press, the law of evidence, trial by jury, and habeas corpus throughout the indefinite peaceful future which I trust lies before them, anymore than I am able to believe that a man could contract so strong an appetite for emetics during temporary illness as to persist in feeding upon them during the remainder of his healthful life. . . .

And yet, let me say that, in my own discretion, I do not know whether I would have ordered the arrest of Mr. Vallandigham. While I cannot shift the responsibility from myself, I hold that, as a general rule, the commander in the field is the better judge of the necessity in any particular case. Of course, I must practise a general directory and revisory power in the matter.

One of the resolutions expresses the opinion of the meeting that arbitrary arrests will have the effect to divide and distract those who should be united in suppressing the rebellion, and I am specifically called on to discharge Mr. Vallandigham. I regard this as, at least, a fair appeal to me on the expediency of exercising a constitutional power which I think exists. In response to such appeal, I have to say it gave me pain when I learned that Mr. Vallandigham had been arrested (that is, I was pained that there should have seemed to be a necessity for arresting him), and that it will afford me great pleasure to discharge him so soon as I can by any means believe the public safety will not suffer by it.

You are better off than I am, for while you have lost your left, *I have lost my* right *arm*.

ROBERT E. LEE, letter to "Stonewall" Jackson, May 4, 1863. Jackson was wounded at Chancellorsville, May 2, and his arm was amputated on May 3. Lee lost his "right arm" for good when Jackson died a week later.

99.

GEORGE E. PICKETT: Reflections on the Charge at Gettysburg

On the final day of the Battle of Gettysburg, July 3, 1863, General George Pickett led three brigades of 4,300 Confederate troops against the Union line in an heroic attack that became immortalized as "Pickett's Charge." The attack was disastrous and Pickett was forced to retreat, leaving three-fourths of his men behind as casualties. Many historians regard the South's defeat at Gettysburg as the turning point of the war. On July 6, Pickett wrote the following letter about that fateful day to the woman who later became his wife.

Source: *Soldier of the South, General Pickett's War Letters to His Wife,* Arthur C. Inman, ed., Boston, 1928.

ON THE FOURTH — far from a glorious Fourth to us or to any with love for his fellowmen — I wrote you just a line of heartbreak. The sacrifice of life on that bloodsoaked field on the fatal 3rd was too awful for the heralding of victory, even for our victorious foe, who, I think, believe as we do, that it decided the fate of our cause. No words can picture the anguish of that roll call — the breathless waits between the responses. The "Here" of those who, by God's mercy, had miraculously escaped the awful rain of shot and shell was a sob — a gasp — a knell — for the unanswered name of his comrade called before his. There was no tone of thankfulness for having been spared to answer to their names, but rather a toll and an unvoiced wish that they, too, had been among the missing.

But for the blight to your sweet young life, but for you, only you, my darling, your soldier would rather by far be out there, too, with his brave Virginians — dead.

Even now I can hear them cheering as I gave the order, "Forward"! I can feel their faith and trust in me and their love for our cause. I can feel the thrill of their joyous voices as they called out all along the line, "We'll follow you, Marse George. We'll follow you, we'll follow you." Oh, how faithfully they kept their word, following me on, on to their death, and I, believing in the promised support, led them on, on, on. Oh, God!

I can't write you a love letter today, my Sallie, for, with my great love for you and my gratitude to God for sparing my life to devote to you, comes the overpowering thought of those whose lives were sacrificed — of the brokenhearted widows and mothers and orphans. The moans of my wounded boys, the sight of the dead, upturned faces flood my soul with grief; and here am I, whom they trusted, whom they followed, leaving them on that field of carnage, leaving them to the mercy of —— and guarding 4,000 prisoners across the river back to Winchester. Such a duty for men who a few hours ago covered themselves with glory eternal.

Well, my darling, I put the prisoners all on their honor and gave them equal liberties with my own soldier boys. My first command to them was to go and enjoy themselves the best they could, and they have obeyed my order. Today, a Dutchman and two of his comrades came up and told me that they were lost and besought me to help them find their commands. They had been with my men and had gotten separated from their own comrades. So I sent old Floyd off on St. Paul to find out where they belonged and deliver them.

This is too gloomy and too poor a letter for so beautiful a sweetheart, but it seems sacrilegious, almost, to say I love you, with the hearts that are stilled to love on the field of battle.

100.

Braxton Bragg et al.: Conscription Problems in the South

The Confederate Congress passed the first national conscription act in American history on April 16, 1862. The act aroused bitter resistance among Southern politicians, who questioned its constitutionality and argued that it would create a serious labor shortage. Responding to this criticism, the Confederate Congress later passed an act exempting various classes of people from military service. The exemption act aroused opposition in the army because it allowed thousands of men to evade service by finding employment in the exempted classes and led to a reduction of men called into service. In the summer of 1863 General Bragg and other officers of the Army of Tennessee urgently needed fresh troops. On July 25 they sent the following message to General Samuel Cooper, adjutant and inspector general of the Confederate Army.

Source: Ainsworth, Additions and Corrections to 4th Series, II, pp. 670-671.

We, the undersigned officers of the Confederate Army, being deeply impressed with the belief that unless the ranks are speedily replenished our cause will be lost, and being thoroughly satisfied that there are enough able-bodied young men out of the service to accomplish that object, would earnestly implore the president of the Confederate States to take prompt measures to recruit our wasted armies by fresh levies from home. The wisdom of the executive must decide whether this can better be done by calling upon the respective states for enlarged quotas of troops or by assembling the Congress of the nation so to modify the exemption provision in the conscript bill as to increase the Army without interfering materially with the great interests of the country.

The whole system of exemption is based upon a false assumption. It is assumed that none of the machinery of society necessary for its comfort and convenience in a state of peace is to be disturbed amidst the mighty upheaval of a great revolution. Thus, for example, we find multiplied rather than diminished rural post offices and printing presses, which add doubtless to the comfort and convenience of the people, but contribute nothing to our success in arms. In like manner, there is an enormous disproportion between the absolute wants of the people and the number of "shoemakers, blacksmiths, tanners, wagonmakers, millers and their engineers, millwrights, skilled and actually employed at their regular vocation in said trades," the agents and employees of the different bureaus, departments, railroad and telegraph companies, etc.

We have been pained to notice that all those vocations are crowded which afford exemption, while the ranks of the Army are daily becoming thinner. To their lasting reproach upon their manhood, hearty, vigorous young men, rather than take the field, eagerly seek fancy duty which could be performed by women or disabled soldiers.

But we especially deplore that unfortunate provision of the exemption bill which has allowed more than 150,000 soldiers to employ substitutes, and we express our honest conviction that not 1 in 100 of these substitutes is now in the service. In numerous instances, fraudulent papers were employed; in others, diseased men were presented and accepted but to be discharged; in still more cases, vicious and unprincipled substitutes were brought up but to desert at the first favorable moment.

Another heavy source of depletion to the Army cannot be passed over. The friends of timid and effeminate young men are constantly besieging the War Department, through congressional and other agents, to get soldiers in the Army placed upon details or transferred to safe places. The aggregate loss to the Army from this cause alone is most enormous.

We do know certainly that the detailed and exempted men under 45 exceed 250,000 men; and, we think that the Army can be increased 250,000 without more suffering and inconvenience to the country than is to be expected in such a life and death struggle as we are engaged in. Certainly there should be no choice between temporary discomfort to society and the loss of battles, territory, posts, garrisons, and even independence itself.

Certainly the sum total of misery would be less if we even resorted to a levy *en masse* and thus could drive back the invader, than by allowing ourselves to be beaten in detail and our soil everywhere to be overrun. In the vain hope of saving the people at home from transient annoyances and privations, we are endangering the liberties of the country.

Lastly, we would respectfully but earnestly urge prompt action. With every inch of territory lost, there is a corresponding loss of men and the resources of war. Conscripts cannot be got from the region held by the Yankees, and soldiers will desert back to their homes in possession of the enemy. Some do so from disaffection, some from weariness with the war, and some to protect their families against a brutal foe. From these combined causes the occupation of our soil weakens us in men as well as in the means to feed and clothe our troops.

Early and vigorous measures to recruit our wasted ranks may save us further loss of men and resources, and possibly the existence of the Southern Confederacy itself.

A Rich Man's War and a Poor Man's Fight.
    Slogan of the draft rioters in New York, July 1863. The draft
    exempted anyone able to pay $300 for a substitute.

101.

William Tecumseh Sherman: The Executive and the Caprice of the People

One of the ablest Union generals during the Civil War, William T. Sherman has been called the first modern general because of his "total war" tactics in his march through Georgia in 1864. Believing that the war could be won only if the Confederacy's will to continue was completely destroyed, he encouraged his soldiers to destroy all property within reach, although he forbade them to harm civilians. Throughout the war his military conduct was attacked in both the Northern and the Southern press, and he was generally opposed by public opinion. Though he never became involved in politics, his letters to his brother, Senator John Sherman of Ohio, openly expressed his strong political convictions. He wrote the following letter to his brother on August 3, 1863, a month after helping to lead the Union Army to victory in the Battle of Vicksburg.

Source: *The Sherman Letters*, Rachel Sherman Thorndike, ed., New York, 1894, pp. 211-213.

You AND I MAY DIFFER in our premises, but will agree in our conclusions. A government resting immediately on the caprice of a people is too unstable to last. The will of the people is the ultimate appeal, but the Constitution, laws of Congress, and regulations of the executive departments subject to the decisions of the Supreme Court are the laws which all must obey without stopping to inquire why. All *must* obey. Government, that is, the executive, having no discretion but to execute the law, must be to that extent despotic. If this be our government, it is the "best on earth"; but if the people of localities can bias and twist the law or execution of it to suit their local prejudices, then our government is the worst on earth.

If you look back only two years, you will see the application. There are about 6 million men in this country, all thinking themselves sovereign and qualified to govern, some 34 governors of states who feel like petty kings, and about 10,000 editors who presume to dictate to generals, presidents, and cabinets. I treat all these as nothing, but when a case arises I simply ask: Where is the law? Supposing the pilot of a ship should steer his vessel according to the opinion of every fellow who watched the clouds above or the currents below, where would his ship land? No, the pilot has before him a little needle; he watches that, and he never errs. So if we make that our simple code, the law of the land must and shall be executed; no matter what the consequences, we cannot err. Hundreds and thousands may honestly differ as to what the law should be, but it is rarely the case; but all men of ordinary understanding can tell what the law is.

We have for years been drifting toward an unadulterated democracy or demagogism, and its signs were manifest in "mob" laws and vigilance committees all over our country. And states and towns and mere squads of men took upon themselves to set aside the Constitution and laws of Congress and substitute therefor their own opinions. I saw it and tried to resist it in California, but always the general government yielded to the pressure. I say that our government, judged by its conduct as a whole, paved the way for rebellion.

The South that lived on slavery saw the United States yield to Abolition pressure at the North, to pro-slavery pressure at the South, to the miners of California, the rowdies of Baltimore, and to the people everywhere. They paved the way to this rebellion. The people of the South were assured that, so far from resisting an attempt to set up an independent government of homogeneous interests, the United States would give in and yield. They appealed to precedents, and proved it, and I confess I had seen so much of it that I doubted whether our government would not yield to the pressure and die a natural death.

But I confess my agreeable surprise. Though full of corruption and base materials, our country is a majestic one, full of natural wealth and good people. They have risen not in full majesty but enough to give all hopes of vitality. Our progress has been as rapid as any philosopher could ask. The resources of the land in money, in men, in provisions, in forage, and in intelligence has surprised us all, and we have had as much success as could be hoped for.

The Mississippi is now ours, not by commission but by right, by the right of manly power. . . . No great interest in our land has risen superior to government, and I deem it fortunate that no man has risen to dictate terms to all. Better as it is. Lincoln is but the last of the old school presidents, the index (mathematically) of one stage of our national existence. . . . Our government should become a machine, self-regulating, independent of the man. . . .

As to the press of America, it is a shame and a reproach to a civilized people. . . . I begin to feel a high opinion of myself that I am their butt; I shall begin to suspect myself of being in a decline when a compliment appears in type. I know in what estimation I am held by my press — those who have been with me all the time — and they are capable to judge, from private to major generals. I saw a move to bring Grant and myself East. No, they don't. . . .

We will be in Mobile in October and Georgia by Christmas if required. . . .

I see much of the people here — men of heretofore high repute. The fall of Vicksburg has had a powerful effect. They are subjugated. I even am amazed at the effect; we are actually feeding the people. . . .

Grant and wife visited me in camp yesterday. I have the handsomest camp I ever saw, and should really be glad to have visitors come down. I don't think a shot will be fired at a boat till Jeff Davis can call his friends about him and agree upon the next campaign. I want recruits and conscripts and shall be all ready in October.

◆

Vox populi, vox humbug *(The voice of the people is the voice of humbug)*.
WILLIAM T. SHERMAN, letter to his wife, June 2, 1863

102.

Louis Agassiz: The Future of the Free Negro

The Swiss naturalist Louis Agassiz emigrated to America in 1846 and later became a professor of zoology at Harvard. One of the leading natural scientists of his time, he turned his attention in the 1860s to the problem of race and especially to the question of the Negro's role in American life. Initially, he believed strongly that all races were "endowed with one common nature, intellectual and physical." Later, he confessed privately that his first acquaintance with Negroes had left him struck by their racial difference and had led him to assert that the two races should remain separated. When Dr. Samuel Howe, a noted Boston Abolitionist, requested his views on the position of the Negro in America, Agassiz wrote the following letter of August 9, 1863.

Source: *Louis Agassiz, His Life and Correspondence,* Elizabeth C. Agassiz, ed., Boston, 1885, Vol. II, pp. 594-600.

My Dear Doctor:

When I acknowledged a few days ago the receipt of your invitation to put in writing my views upon the management of the Negro race as part of the free population of the United States, I stated to you that there was a preliminary question of the utmost importance to be examined first, since whatever convictions may be formed upon that point must necessarily influence everything else relating to the subject. The question is simply this: Is there to be a permanent black population upon the continent after slavery is everywhere abolished and no inducement remains to foster its increase?

Should this question be answered in the negative, it is evident that a wise policy would look to the best mode of removing that race from these states by the encouragement and acceleration of emigration. Should the question be answered, on the contrary, in the affirmative, then it is plain that we have before us one of the most difficult problems, upon the solution of which the welfare of our own race may in a measure depend, namely, the combination in one social organization of two races more widely different from one another than all the other races. In effecting this combination it becomes our duty to avoid the recurrence of great evils, one of which is already foreshadowed in the advantage which unscrupulous managers are taking of the freedmen, whenever the latter are brought into contact with new social relations.

I will, for the present, consider only the case of the unmixed Negroes of the Southern states, the number of which I suppose to be about 2 million. It is certainly not less — it may be a little more. From whatever point of view you look upon these people you must come to the conclusion that, left to themselves, they will perpetuate their race *ad infinitum* where they are. According to the prevalent theory of the unity of mankind it is assumed that the different races have become what they are in consequence of their settlement in different parts of the world, and that the whole globe is everywhere a fit abode for human beings who adapt themselves to the conditions under which they live. According to the theory of a multiple origin of mankind the different races have first appeared in various parts of the globe, each with the peculiarities best suited to their primitive home. Aside from these theoretical views the fact is that some races inhabit very extensive tracts of the earth's surface and are now found upon separate continents, while others are very limited in their range.

This distribution is such that there is no reason for supposing that the Negro is less fitted permanently to occupy at least the warmer parts of North and South America than is the white race to retain possession of their more temperate portions. Assuming our pure black race to be only 2 million, it is yet larger than the whole number of several races that have held uninterrupted possession of different parts of the globe ever since they have been known to the white race. Thus the Hottentots and the Abyssinians have maintained themselves in their respective homes without change ever since their existence has been known to us, even though their number is less than that of our pure black population. The same, also, is the case with the population of Australia and of the Pacific islands. The Papuan race, the Negrillo race, the Australian race proper, distinct from one another as well as from all other inhabitants of the earth, number each fewer inhabitants than already exist of the Negro race in the United States alone, not to speak of Central and South America.

This being the case, there is, it seems to me, no more reason to expect a disappearance of the Negro race from the continent of America without violent interference than to expect a disappearance of the races inhabiting respectively the South Sea Islands, Australia, the Cape of Good Hope, or any other part of the globe tenanted by the less populous races. The case of the American Indians, who gradually disappear before the white race, should not mislead us, as it is readily accounted for by the peculiar character of that race. The Negro exhibits by nature a pliability, a readiness to accommodate himself to circumstances, a

Louis Agassiz; engraving by C. H. Jeans

proneness to imitate those among whom he lives — characteristics which are entirely foreign to the Indian, while they facilitate in every way the increase of the Negro. I infer, therefore, from all these circumstances that the Negro race must be considered as permanently settled upon this continent, no less firmly than the white race, and that it is our duty to look upon them as cotenants in the possession of this part of the world.

Remember that I have thus far presented the case only with reference to the Southern states, where the climate is particularly favorable to the maintenance and multiplication of the Negro race. Before drawing any inference, however, from my first assertion that the Negro will easily and without foreign assistance maintain himself and multiply in the warmer parts of this continent, let us consider a few other features of this momentous question of race. Whites and blacks may multiply together, but their offspring is never either white or black; it is always mulatto. It is a half-breed, and shares all the peculiarities of half-breeds, among whose most important characteristics is their sterility, or at least their reduced fecundity. This shows the connection to be contrary to the normal state of the races, as it is contrary to the preservation of species in the animal kingdom. . . .

Far from presenting to me a natural solution of our difficulties, the idea of amalgamation is most repugnant to my feelings. It is now the foundation of some of the most ill-advised schemes. But wherever it is practised, amalgamation among different races produces shades of population, the social position of which can never be regular and settled. From a physiological point of view, it is sound policy to put every possible obstacle to the crossing of the races and the increase of half-breeds. It is unnatural, as shown by their very constitution, their sickly physique, and their impaired fecundity. It is immoral and destructive of social equality as it creates unnatural relations and multiplies the differences among members of the same community in a wrong direction.

From all this it is plain that the policy to be adopted toward the miscellaneous colored population with reference to a more or less distant future should be totally different from that which applies to the pure black; for while I believe that a wise social economy will foster the progress of every pure race according to its natural dispositions and abilities and aim at securing for it a proper field for the fullest development of all its capabilities, I am convinced also that no efforts should be spared to check that which is inconsistent with the progress of a higher civilization and a purer morality. I hope and trust that as soon as the condition of the Negro in the warmer parts of our states has been regulated according to the laws of freedom, the colored population in the more northern parts of the country will diminish. By a natural consequence of unconquerable affinities, the colored people in whom the Negro nature prevails will tend toward the South, while the weaker and lighter ones will remain and die out among us.

103.

Abraham Lincoln: Emancipation as a Military Measure

In June 1863 "Copperhead" Democrats, feeding on the war-weariness in the North, held a huge rally in Springfield, Illinois, to protest Lincoln's policies. Republican leaders, heartened by the victories of Gettysburg and Vicksburg, decided to hold a counter-rally in support of the administration. They asked Lincoln to attend, but the President was unable to leave Washington and instead sent the following letter to James C. Conkling, an old friend, on August 26, 1863, asking him to read the letter at the rally.

Source: Nicolay-Hay, IX, pp. 95-102.

My Dear Sir:

Your letter inviting me to attend a mass meeting of unconditional Union men, to be held at the capital of Illinois on the 3rd day of September has been received. It would be very agreeable to me to thus meet my old friends at my own home, but I cannot just now be absent from here so long as a visit there would require.

The meeting is to be of all those who maintain unconditional devotion to the Union; and I am sure my old political friends will thank me for tendering, as I do, the nation's gratitude to those and other noble men whom no partisan malice or partisan hope can make false to the nation's life.

There are those who are dissatisfied with me. To such I would say: "You desire peace; and you blame me that we do not have it." But how can we attain it? There are but three conceivable ways. First, to suppress the rebellion by force of arms. This I am trying to do. Are you for it? If you are, so far we are agreed. If you are not for it, a second way is to give up the Union. I am against this. Are you for it? If you are, you should say so plainly. If you are not for force nor yet for dissolution, there only remains some imaginable compromise. I do not believe any compromise embracing the maintenance of the Union is now possible. All I learn leads to a directly opposite belief.

The strength of the rebellion is its military — its army. That army dominates all the country and all the people within its range. Any offer of terms made by any man or men within that range in opposition to that army is simply nothing for the present; because such man or men have no power whatever to enforce their side of a compromise if one were made with them.

To illustrate, suppose refugees from the South and peace men of the North get together in convention and frame and proclaim a compromise embracing a restoration of the Union. In what way can that compromise be used to keep Lee's army out of Pennsylvania? Meade's army can keep Lee's army out of Pennsylvania and, I think, can ultimately drive it out of existence. But no paper compromise to which the controllers of Lee's army are not agreed can at all affect that army. In an effort at such compromise we should waste time, which the enemy would improve to our disadvantage; and that would be all. A compromise to be effective must be made either with those who control the Rebel army or with the people first liberated from the domination of that army by the success of our own army.

Now, allow me to assure you that no word or intimation from that Rebel army, or from any of the men controlling it, in relation to any peace compromise has ever come to my knowledge or belief. All charges and insinuations to the contrary are deceptive and groundless. And I promise you that if any such proposition shall hereafter come, it shall not be rejected and kept a secret from you. I freely acknowledge myself the servant of the people according to the bond of service — the United States Constitution — and that, as such, I am responsible to them.

But to be plain, you are dissatisfied with me about the Negro. Quite likely there is a difference of opinion between you and myself upon that subject. I certainly wish that all men could be free, while I suppose you do not. Yet I have neither adopted nor proposed any measure which is not consistent with even your view, provided you are for the Union. I suggested compensated emancipation; to which you replied you wished not to be taxed to buy Negroes. But I had not asked you to be taxed to buy Negroes, except in such way as to save you from greater taxation to save the Union exclusively by other means.

You dislike the Emancipation Proclamation and, perhaps, would have it retracted. You say it is unconstitutional — I think differently. I think the Constitution invests its commander in chief with the law of war in time of war. The most that can be said, if so much, is that slaves are property. Is there — has there ever been — any question that by the law of war, property, both of enemies and friends, may be taken when needed? And is it not needed whenever taking it helps us or hurts the enemy? Armies the world over destroy the enemy's property when they cannot use it and even destroy their own to keep it from the enemy. Civilized belligerents do all in their power to help themselves or hurt the enemy, except a few things regarded as barbarous or cruel. Among the exceptions are the massacre of vanquished foes and noncombatants, male and female.

But the proclamation, as law, either is valid or is not valid. If it is not valid, it needs no retraction. If it is valid, it cannot be retracted, any more than the dead can be brought to life. Some of you profess to think its retraction would operate favorably for the Union. Why better after the retraction than before the issue? There was more than a year and a half of trial to suppress the rebellion before the proclamation issued, the last 100 days of which passed under an explicit notice that it was coming unless averted by those in revolt returning to their allegiance. The war has certainly progressed as favorably for us since the issue of the proclamation as before.

[I know, as fully as one can know the opinions of others, that some of the commanders of our armies in the field who have given us our most important successes believe the emancipation policy and the use of the colored troops constitute the heaviest blow yet dealt to the rebellion, and that at least one of these important successes could not have been achieved when it was but for the aid of black soldiers. Among the commanders holding these views are some who have never had any affinity with what is called Abolitionism or with the Republican Party politics, but who hold them purely as military opinions. I submit these opinions as being entitled to some weight against the objections often urged that emancipation and arming the blacks are unwise as military measures and were not adopted as such in good faith.][1]

1. This paragraph, which has been placed between brackets to distinguish it, was not included in the letter as first sent but was forwarded in a separate letter with instructions on Aug. 31, 1863.

You say you will not fight to free Negroes. Some of them seem willing to fight for you; but, no matter. Fight you, then, exclusively to save the Union. I issued the proclamation on purpose to aid you in saving the Union. Whenever you shall have conquered all resistance to the Union, if I shall urge you to continue fighting, it will be an apt time, then, for you to declare you will not fight to free Negroes.

I thought that in your struggle for the Union, to whatever extent the Negroes should cease helping the enemy, to that extent it weakened the enemy in his resistance to you. Do you think differently? I thought that whatever Negroes can be got to do as soldiers leaves just so much less for white soldiers to do in saving the Union. Does it appear otherwise to you? But Negroes, like other people, act upon motives. Why should they do anything for us if we will do nothing for them? If they stake their lives for us, they must be prompted by the strongest motive — even the promise of freedom. And the promise, being made, must be kept.

The signs look better. The Father of Waters again goes unvexed to the sea. Thanks to the great Northwest for it. Nor yet wholly to them. Three hundred miles up, they met New England, Empire, Keystone, and Jersey, hewing their way right and left. The sunny South, too, in more colors than one, also lent a hand. On the spot, their part of the history was jotted down in black and white. The job was a great national one; and let none be banned who bore an honorable part in it. And while those who have cleared the great river may well be proud, even that is not all. It is hard to say that anything has been more bravely and well done than at Antietam, Murfreesboro, Gettysburg, and on many fields of lesser note. Nor must Uncle Sam's webfeet be forgotten. At all the watery margins they have been present. Not only on the deep sea, the broad bay, and the rapid river, but also up the narrow, muddy bayou, and wherever the ground was a little damp, they have been and made their tracks. Thanks to all — for the great republic; for the principle it lives by and keeps alive; for man's vast future — thanks to all.

Peace does not appear so distant as it did. I hope it will come soon, and come to stay; and so come as to be worth the keeping in all future time. It will then have been proved that among freemen there can be no successful appeal from the ballot to the bullet; and that they who take such appeal are sure to lose their case and pay the cost. And then there will be some black men who can remember that with silent tongue, and clenched teeth, and steady eye, and well-poised bayonet, they have helped mankind on to this great consummation; while, I fear, there will be some white ones unable to forget that with malignant heart and deceitful speech they strove to hinder it.

Still, let us not be oversanguine of a speedy final triumph. Let us be quite sober. Let us diligently apply the means, never doubting that a just God, in His own good time, will give us the rightful result.

104.

Anonymous: Canals and Railroads

Canal building in America began in the later eighteenth century as a device for opening Eastern markets to Western produce, mainly agricultural staples. Low cost transportation between the East Coast and the newly settled areas of the old Northwest Territory became available with the completion of the Erie Canal in 1825. Inspired by the financial success of this canal, other states embarked on similar projects, and 3,000 miles of canals had been constructed by 1844. By the 1860s, however, it had become clear that the railroad offered a much superior form of transportation, for it saved both time and money. The following article from a New York trade magazine, emphasizing the need for a new railroad connection with the West, was signed J. E. B.

Source: *Merchants' Magazine and Commercial Review*, August 1863.

It is, we believe, more than twenty-five years since, in making a comparison between canals and railways, we took the ground, in *Hunt's Magazine* and other New York papers, "that railways were the better improvement of the age, and destined eventually to supersede canals, except in the case of the unique Erie." We were then advocating the construction of a railway from the Harlem Railroad to Albany, and were ridiculed for our pains, particularly in a lengthy report now before us, which emanated from a committee appointed by the Chamber of Commerce of New York, composed of those eminent and intelligent merchants in their days — Messrs. James G. King, N. Weed, and Simeon Baldwin. This report is now a curiosity and, reduced to short meter, arrives at the conclusion "that as we had the Housatonic Railroad — through Connecticut and Massachusetts to Albany — for *winter* travel, and the noble Hudson for *summer* travel, we did not want a railway from New York to Albany." A *freight railway*, or one to carry freight, was not thought of. It was only a few years after, however, that the completion of the Western Railroad from Boston to Albany awoke our Rip Van Winkles and led New York to project the Hudson River Road, on the margin of the river, and the Harlem Railroad to Albany — two roads, where we were ridiculed for proposing one a short time previous.

In the July number of *Hunt's Merchants' Magazine* it is clearly shown by facts and figures, well applied, that our canals, as we predicted would be the case, are being superseded by our railroads, and that we do not now want a ship canal from the Mississippi to New York, by Lakes Michigan, Erie, and Ontario, either for commerce or for defense. Such an undertaking might give some politicians fat jobs, but it will damage us greatly by breaking up our Erie and Oswego canals just as we have got them finished, and are preparing with large boats for a navigation of seven feet by seventy, although we think a depth of even six feet (which it now is) will about use up all the water we can get into the canal on the *long level* at Rome in dry times.

But our object in writing at the present time was mainly to call the attention of New Yorkers — and, we will admit, to crow a little over the fulfillment of our former predictions — to the necessity of another railroad connection with the West, our present routes being overworked. For instance, look at the business done over the Pennsylvania Railroad (their Central), as appears by facts given in June number, page 499. This road is 365 miles long (of which 318 miles is a double track), cost $21,806,852, on which they took in gross receipts from business done over it last year, $10,143,738, being nearly 50 percent of its cost! This immense business was done at a total expense of $3,833,345 for operating

the road, or say 38 percent of its gross receipts. These receipts were about double the tolls the state of New York received during the year 1862 on all her canals. This is a startling exhibit of what railroads can do, and shows what powerful industrial machines they are when well located and well managed. The P. and Reading Railroad took, from 1843 to 1859, $36,935,188, and the expenses were $15,792,911. Net receipts in 15 years, $21,142,277. Now the Pennsylvania Railroad has, we believe, forty-feet grades, and yet has done this immense business.

The receipts over the New York and Erie were about half this sum; so were the receipts of the New York Central, if we recollect rightly. The Erie has grades of sixty-five feet to the mile, the measure of its capacity, and the Central has seventy-five feet at its eastern terminus. The Rome and Watertown Railroad has forty-two feet to the mile. It will soon be impossible for the Central Railroad to carry its freight. When the Oswego branch is finished it will have more than it can do. Under these circumstances, it is the duty of the merchants of New York, as well as those of the West, to look round them for another cheaper and shorter, if possible, channel than by Pennsylvania, or by the roads named, to convey the tonnage from the West to the seaboard. As we have stated above, and as the article in your last number proved, no proposed ship canal can do it. We must look elsewhere for the route that will command the trade.

Chicago and the Western grain states already have the natural waters of Lakes Michigan, Erie, and Ontario, and the admirable port at Oswego. We have now lines of railways from the West to Buffalo, and we can have a level and descending grade and line from that place to the county of Oswego. Here, the waters of Little Salmon Creek, from its summit in Amboy, New Jersey, flow westward; and the Little River, heading in the same town and same farm, drains eastward over a summit that is only 250 feet above the mills at Oswego; and the road may thus strike Rome in a direct line, from which point we have the descending valley of the Mohawk from Little Falls to the Hudson. In this way, for this crowded part of the line, we can thus have a quadruple track that can defy competition by any state in the Union. It is a line which New York must see is for her interest to take immediate steps to have examined and constructed.

It has been a favorite project with the writer for many years. Now, as the Erie and Central railroads have nearly all the business they can do, and so must be the case with the Pennsylvania Railroad, the merchants of Chicago, Milwaukee, and the West, according to the doctrine of the *Merchants' Magazine* for this month, should hold *a railroad convention* instead of a ship canal convention to perfect a line of railways from Buffalo, Rochester, and Troy as the best and *most profitable* project of the day.

105.

Manufacturers' Objection to an Income Tax

In order to raise revenues during the Civil War, the government had to raise tariffs and levy an income tax as well as general excise taxes. A convention of manufacturers met in Chicago in June 1863 to protest against what was considered unfair taxation. The author of the following editorial, which appeared in a trade journal in August, argued that manufacturers were already favored by the high tariffs and should accept the taxes levied upon them.

Source: *Merchants' Magazine and Commercial Review*, August 1863:
"Manufacturers' Opposition to the Income Tax."

WHY IS IT THAT ALL THE WORLD goes to Chicago to hold conventions? The manufacturers, feeling themselves aggrieved by the income tax, have lately been there, held a convention, passed resolutions, and gone home. Western members of the craft were not very largely represented, as they are probably but slightly affected by the provisions of the Internal Revenue Law.

As to the resolutions passed, they are certainly plain spoken and to the point. The secretary of the treasury is by them politely requested to suspend the operation of the objectionable provision till the assembling of the next Congress. Such a request as this must be based, we suppose, upon the assumption that the imposition of the tax is purely a mistake made through the inadvertence of the last Congress, which its successor will hasten to rectify — that the framers of the law could not, in their superabundant wisdom and well-known regard for this branch of our national industry, have intended to tax the *profits* of manufacturers after having heavily taxed the manufactures themselves; but, through carelessness, left the statute open to such a construction.

The following is the decided answer that the department returns to the resolutions:

Treasury Department,
Office of Internal Revenue,
Washington, June 15, 1863.

Sir:

Yours of the 11th instant, addressed to the Honorable Secretary of the Treasury, with accompanying note from Hon. Mr. Chandler, your own letter to the Manufacturers' Convention, and the resolutions of said convention, have been received and forwarded to this office. In reply, allow me to express my profound gratification at the lucid manner in which you demonstrate the justice of the law.

Rest assured that the law is not considered by this office in the light either of a mistake or an accident, and that its provisions will be neither explained away nor its operations suspended.

Very respectfully,
EDWARD McPHERSON

E. B. Ward, Esq., *Detroit.*

We think another convention will now be in order, and would suggest that all taxpayers be let in, for we apprehend that manufacturers have less reason to complain than falls to the lot of many classes of businessmen under this tax-reduplicating dispensation. Indeed, the farther removed from the point of consumption any class may be, the lighter its burdens, as a general thing, under the practical workings of the system; so that those who stand at the source of supply, whence the stream of taxation swells and gathers strength in its downward course, are really least affected by it. Like importers under the tariff system whose individual contributions to the public revenue seem to be enormous only at first sight, the manufacturers are really the most disinterested persons in the community so far as the tax upon their products is concerned. There is not even a division of this tax between the producer and consumer; but the whole of it, both specific and *ad valorem*, is invariably added to the prime cost of the manufactured article and ultimately falls either wholly upon the consumer or is partially shared by the retailer — who of all others should be exempt from any portion of it since he stands in the gap between the government and his customers and guarantees to them that the former has no lien upon his goods, and that all excise duties accruing upon them have been honestly paid.

The income tax complained of is really the only government charge in any shape which touches the pockets of manufacturers; and the public treasury will undoubtedly derive a considerable revenue from this source, as their profits have been enormous during the year past. With a tariff which shuts out foreign competition and gives them a virtual monopoly of the home market — such as this great interest has always sought for and at last obtained — it seems to us so long as the government must needs rely in a great measure upon the productive industry of the country for support, that a class so peculiarly favored, in the abundance of their prosperity, will not generally object to rendering this simple *quid pro quo* in the present emergency of our national affairs. If they seek to evade it, it is to be feared their example may have a bad influence upon other classes, less interested, perhaps, in sustaining the government.

◆

Every man over forty is responsible for his face.

ABRAHAM LINCOLN, to a Cabinet member when the President was taken to account for turning down a job applicant because "I don't like his face"

George Eastman House

Confederates on Fredericksburg end of railroad during burial truce, 1862; photo by Brady

A SLOW DEATH

Rifles were grounded and cannons unfired during the frequent burial truces of the war. Both sides consumed manpower with devastating carnage: the North counted nearly 360,000 dead, the South nearly 260,000. On both sides death from disease or other causes was far more common than in battle, and the battle dead consistently outnumbered the wounded.

In 1864 Grant used up men at an appalling rate in a desperate effort to defeat Lee and conquer Virginia. The Wilderness, Spotsylvania, Cold Harbor, Petersburg: these are names of battles and sieges, but they are also records of unparallelled Union ca-

sualties — over 70,000. Grant lost 60,000 men in a single month, nearly as many dead and wounded as Lee could count in his entire defending force. Protests at the bloodshed inundated Washington.

The slaughter appeared to be endless as well as senseless, for the North had far greater reserves on than did the South, and by late 1864 the ultimate issue was so little in doubt that Southern troops were deserting en masse. Two events of late 1864 symbolize the South's impossible position: Jefferson Davis proposed to arm the slaves, and South Carolina nullified a war measure of the Confederate government.

Union outer line at Nashville, Tenn., December 1864

(Above) Confederate generals John B. Hood and Joseph Johnston, who made two attempts to halt Sherman's march to Atlanta. Hood succeeded Johnston and suffered severe defeat in the battle of Nashville, late 1864; (below) members of a Colored Infantry with the Union forces at Nashville

Kennesaw Mountain, Georgia; photo by George Barnard

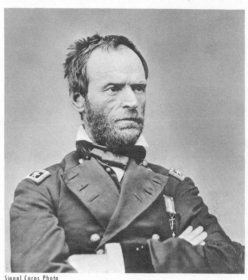

The Atlanta campaign was a classic on both sides. On the defensive, Johnston fought a slow, costly retreat, hoping both to delay and weary the Northern advance. Sherman, with a larger force, moved nonetheless carefully, and on Sept. 1, 1864, took Atlanta with small losses. Atlanta was a small city but an important railhead and supply center for the South; beyond its military importance, its capture assured Lincoln's reelection. In November Sherman left Atlanta, now little more than a smoking ruin, and began his 300-mile march to Savannah, destroying all possible military resources in his path, and laying waste the "garden of the South."

(Right) Gen. William Sherman of the Union Army, photographed in 1865; (below) view of Atlanta, Ga.; photograph by George Barnard

(Above) Union soldiers ripping up railroad tracks in Atlanta, Ga.; (below) ruins of rolling mill and Hood's ordnance train on the Georgia Central following the evacuation of Atlanta in 1864

(Below) View of the river front in Savannah, Ga., 1865; photo by Barnard

Andersonville Prison in Georgia in 1865. Soldiers in foreground gathering roots to make coffee

Andersonville, the infamous Confederate prison camp, was built to relieve the danger of large numbers of Union prisoners in Richmond. Pressure in Richmond forced the use of the camp before its facilities were completed, and its reputation as a virtual death sentence began. Although the conditions in the camp were at first unintentional, Andersonville became an issue in the North, first for immediate reprisals against Southern prisoners, and later in the "bloody shirt" campaigns.

(Right) Confederate prisoners at Gettysburg, Pa., (below) Confederate prisoners at Camp Douglas in Illinois

Non-commissioned officers in Company D of the 93rd New York Infantry at mess

Soldiers off duty: (Above left) boxing match; (above right) group of Negro laborers; (below) cock fighting outside the headquarters of Gen. O. E. Wilcox, Petersburg, Va., 1864

(Above) Sailors and Marines on the deck of U.S.S. "Mendota," about 1864; (left) group of Confederate cavalrymen in Mosby's Rangers

(Below left) Pvt. Edwin Francis Jennison, member of a Georgia regiment in the Confederate Army; (below right) ferrotype of an unidentified Negro soldier

Field hospital set up after the battle of Savage Station, Va., 1862; photo by Gibson

(Above) Ambulance corps in the Union Army; (right) a Civil War nurse

Carver Hospital in Washington, D.C., 1864; photo by Brady

(Above) Barnside Wharf, on the Rappahannock River, located below Acquia Creek Landing and connected with the Fredericksburg Railroad (controlled by the Union forces); photo by Russell

Bridge at Germania ford on the Rappahannock used during Grant's 1864 campaign against Richmond

"Council of War" in Virginia; Grant (left foreground) examines map held by Meade

(Above left) Jubal A. Early, CSA, and (above right) Philip Sheridan, USA, opposing generals in the Shenandoah campaign; (below) troops on Petersburg battlefield, winter 1864-65

(Above) Bomb-proof quarters during battle at Petersburg, Va., (left) Gen. U. S. Grant

Petersburg, controlling the southern approaches to Richmond, was under siege for ten months. Grant, bloodily repulsed in an effort to storm Lee's defenses, simply sat down and waited until Lee was starved out. The long siege lasted from June of 1864 until April 2, 1865. Lee was not cut off from retreat, but was caught between the impossibility of advance and the fall of Richmond should he retreat. Lee's lack of men and supplies to break the dilemma led directly to Appomattox.

(Below) First Union wagon train entering Petersburg, Va., in 1865

(Above) McLean House in Appomattox, Va., scene of the surrender of General Lee

(Right) Robert E. Lee seated on the porch of his Richmond home with Major General George Washington Custis Lee and Col. Walter Taylor, April 1865; (below) Union troops at Appomattox

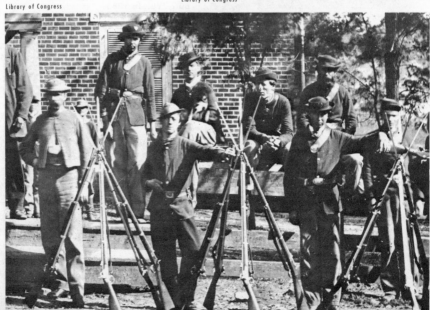

106.

Opposition to the Rise of Labor Unions

In 1863 and 1864, the sudden rise of labor unions caused employers to form associations
for their mutual protection. The iron molders' aggressive labor union practices were
the subject of an address on September 3, 1863, to an employers' association known as
the Iron Founders' and Machine Builders' Association of the Falls of the Ohio.

Source: *Fincher's Trades' Review*, October 3, 1863 [Commons, IX, pp. 89-97].

IT IS A WELL-KNOWN FACT that there has been in existence for more than two years in the city of Louisville, and almost every other city of the United States, an association called the "Iron Molders' Union," which has now gained such strength that it is making its power felt, and in a manner very injurious to the interest of the public, as also to that of the worthier members of the union itself. Its ostensible purpose, according to the published constitution, is "to elevate the moral, social, and intellectual condition of every molder in the country." This is, no doubt, a very laudable object — one which commands the sympathy of all right-thinking men, and no one would aid the association in obtaining such an end more willingly than the employers of the members of the union themselves.

In examining, however, the constitution and practical workings of the Iron Molders' Union, it becomes at once apparent that this is not the real or only object in view, for it will be seen that Section 3, Article IX, of their constitution provides: "No employer can become a member of this union, nor shall any member, becoming an employer, remain a member thereof." And Section 2 of the same article does not even permit a foreman, when he has in any way

become interested in the profits of an establishment, to remain in the Molders' Union. Thus it will be seen that instead of calling upon the employers to cooperate with their union in advancing the "moral, social, and intellectual condition of every molder," which self-evidently is a matter of common interest, the Molders' Union even goes so far as to expel a member as soon as he has, by his superior skill and industry, succeeded in establishing himself independently in business, and thus accomplished one of the avowed objects of the union. This fact alone indicates, if other proofs were wanting, that the Molders' Union look upon their employers as their enemies. Their arbitrary interference with the business management of their employers proves this to be the leading principle of the association.

The Molders' Union has made an attempt, and thus far a successful one, to dictate to and extort the most unreasonable terms from their employers all over the country — terms which, if submitted to, must eventually prove ruinous to the molders themselves, since it would destroy our whole business. They have undertaken to arbitrarily decide not only as to what wages must be paid but even as to the number of apprentices each shop is to employ, the kind and amount of work the laborers in our foundries may or may not be allowed to do, and to prevent any molder from working in a shop who is not a member of their union.

These and numerous other equally unreasonable and inadmissible interferences of the Iron Molders' Union cannot be submitted to any longer without losing not only our business but our self-respect.

Now, therefore, in order to protect ourselves against the injurious interferences of the Iron Molders' Union, or any other similar association now existing or that may hereafter be formed, we, the undersigned foundrymen and machine builders and employers of other ironworkers of Louisville, New Albany, and Jeffersonville, have formed a regularly organized association to be entitled the "Iron Founders' and Machine Builders' Association of the Falls of the Ohio," and do therefore adopt the following as the principle of our organization:

1. We deny the right of the Iron Molders' Union, or any other union, to arbitrarily determine the wages of our employees, regardless of their merits and the value of their services to us, and we are opposed to every combination which has for its object the regulation of wages, whether it be among the employers for the purpose of keeping down wages, or among employees for the purpose of forcing up wages. We desire the utmost individual liberty both for employers and employees. The demand for and the supply of labor, the merits of each individual workman, and the cost of living are the natural causes which should regulate wages. Under the free operation of these causes, the skillful and industrious workman can always feel secure of obtaining the highest wages.

2. We deny the right of the Iron Molders' Union to determine for us how many apprentices we should employ. According to Article VII, Section 7, of their constitution, they dictate to their employers that not more than one apprentice shall be employed

in each machine foundry, and one to every fifteen molders in each stove foundry. This arbitrary interference in our business cannot be defended upon any grounds of right and justice. It is an assault upon the individual liberty of the citizen; it is an act against the laws of society and trade, according to which the expansion or profitableness of any branch of business should determine the number of persons that shall engage in it, and each citizen ought to be left free to choose for himself.

The interests of the whole country may require today double the number of molders that it required a year ago, but the Iron Molders' Union, constituting themselves legislators, determine for the whole country how many molders there shall be, independent of the requirements of this branch of industry, and thus sacrifice to their own selfishness the best interests of the whole community.

3. We shall resist by all legal means, at every sacrifice of time and money, all attempts of any set of men arbitrarily to regulate the supply of labor in any department of trade and business. While we protest against the attempt of the Molders' Union to determine the number of apprentices that shall be employed in each foundry, we shall cheerfully cooperate with them in their efforts to thoroughly educate all apprentices and make them masters of their business; and we further protest against every attempt on the part of the Iron Molders' Union to prescribe to our employees what kind of work they shall or shall not perform. Section 8 of Article VII of their constitution provides: "No member of this union shall permit any helper to ram his flasks." This clause exhibits a disposition on the part of the molders to prevent the laboring man from acquiring knowledge and bettering his condition. While it is of little consequence to us if a molder insists upon doing laboring work which can be performed as well by less skillful hands, yet we protest against the spirit of such enactments,

which we consider alike degrading to those who originate them as to those on whom they are to be enforced.

Course of Action.

1. The corresponding secretary of the Iron Founders' and Machine Builders' Association of the Falls of the Ohio shall put himself into communication with all the parties of the principal cities of the United States engaged in similar business to that of the members of this association and suffering under the same grievances. He shall take the necessary steps to secure their cooperation in all the measures to be taken in our and their own defense. He shall endeavor to cause the interested parties in other cities to form similar associations to ours, and in case he succeeds in doing so, he shall transact all business through the officers of said associations. But in case no associations can be formed, or before they can be organized, the corresponding secretary shall correspond with the individual firms of other cities.

2. To those of our employees who see that we ask nothing but what is reasonable, and who desire to withdraw from the Iron Molders' Union, or who may be in favor of changing the constitution of their society in those particulars to which we take exception, we promise and guarantee full protection to their persons and their property. Should any personal violence be offered to those of our employees who prefer to obey the dictates of reason, right, and liberty in preference to those of the Molders' Union, or should any threats be made to them directly or indirectly by any member of the said union, we will use all our influence and means to see that the laws of the land shall be fully enforced against such conspirators against the individual rights of the citizens and the peace of the community.

3. Should the employees in any of our establishments stop work in order to force their employers to submit to unreasonable demands, the members of the Iron Founders' and Machine Builders' Association of the Falls of the Ohio, and the members of the associations of other cities, or the establishments who have agreed to act in concert with these associations, shall not employ any men engaged in such strike. The names of the parties engaged in any attempt to force their employers to submit to unreasonable demands shall be sent in a circular at the expense of this association to all the other associations or establishments with which we are in correspondence in order that they may be prevented from getting employment until they either withdraw from the Molders' Union or cease to attempt the enforcing of their unjust demands. Similar circulars received from the associations or establishments in other cities shall be respected by this association in like manner.

Finally, the object of all the measures which the Iron Founders' and Machine Builders' Association of the Falls of the Ohio propose to take is self-protection. We have not united for the purpose of oppressing our employees; we only desire not to be oppressed ourselves. We have not united for the purpose of encroaching upon the rights of workmen, but we also possess rights as employers which we do not wish to see encroached upon. We desire that every workman should be paid liberally for the work he performs, and we shall comply with every just demand that may be made upon us. We also desire to cultivate a feeling of friendship and confidence between the employee and employers, and will resist every attempt of those who wish to create a feeling of hostility and hatred between us.

107.

ABRAHAM LINCOLN: The Beginning of Reconstruction

By the middle of 1863 the Union Army had occupied several seceded states, among them Tennessee. The following letter, written by President Lincoln on September 11, 1863, to Andrew Johnson, military governor of Tennessee, is significant in that it provides an early hint of the President's thoughts about postwar Reconstruction of the South. Under Johnson, Tennessee became a laboratory for Reconstruction experiments, and Johnson, who succeeded Lincoln in 1865, adhered to the basic guidelines laid down in this and other early Lincoln statements.

Source: Nicolay-Hay, IX, pp. 116-117.

ALL TENNESSEE IS NOW CLEAR of armed insurrectionists. You need not to be reminded that it is the nick of time for reinaugurating a loyal state government. Not a moment should be lost. You and the cooperating friends there can better judge of the ways and means than can be judged by any here. I only offer a few suggestions. The reinauguration must not be such as to give control of the state and its representation in Congress to the enemies of the Union, driving its friends there into political exile. The whole struggle for Tennessee will have been profitless to both state and nation if it so ends that Governor Johnson is put down and Governor Harris is put up. It must not be so. You must have it otherwise.

Let the reconstruction be the work of such men only as can be trusted for the Union. Exclude all others, and trust that your government so organized will be recognized here as being the one of republican form to be guaranteed to the state, and to be protected against invasion and domestic violence. It is something on the question of time to remember that it cannot be known who is next to occupy the position I now hold, nor what he will do.

I see that you have declared in favor of emancipation in Tennessee, for which may God bless you. Get emancipation into your new state government — constitution — and there will be no such word as fail for your case. The raising of colored troops, I think, will greatly help every way.

I would be very happy to oblige you, if my passes were respected. But the fact is, sir, I have, within the last two years, given passes to two hundred and fifty thousand men to go to Richmond, and not one has got there yet.

ABRAHAM LINCOLN, reply to a man who asked for a "safe conduct" to Richmond, 1863

108.

James Henry Gooding: A Soldier's Plea for Equal Pay

In July 1862, the War Department ruled that Negro soldiers would receive $7 a month, plus $3 for clothing, as compared to white soldiers' pay of $13 a month, plus $3.50 for clothing. On September 28, 1863, Corporal James Gooding, a soldier of the 54th Massachusetts Regiment, all of whom were Negro volunteers, wrote the following letter to President Lincoln asking for equal pay. The Massachusetts 54th had been refusing any pay as a protest against this inequality. According to the opinion of Attorney General Edward Bates in July 1864, "all volunteers competent and qualified to be members of the national forces, are entitled respectively to receive like amounts of pay, bounty, and clothing from the Government." In the same month, Congress equalized the pay scale for Negro and white soldiers, and in September, the soldiers of the 54th Regiment received all their back pay.

Source: National Archives, Record Group 94, Office of the Adjutant General, Colored Troops Division, H133 CT 1863.

Your Excellency, Abraham Lincoln:

Your Excellency will pardon the presumption of a humble individual like myself in addressing you, but the earnest solicitation of my comrades in arms, besides the genuine interest felt by myself in the matter, is my excuse for placing before the executive head of the nation our common grievance.

On the 6th of the last month, the paymaster of the department informed us that if we would decide to receive the sum of $10 (ten dollars) per month, he would come and pay us that sum, but that, on the sitting of Congress, the regiment would, in his opinion, be allowed the other $3 (three). He did not give us any guarantee that this would be as he hoped; certainly *he* had no authority for making any such guarantee, and we cannot suppose him acting in any way interested.

Now the main question is, are we *soldiers* or are we *laborers?* We are fully armed and equipped; have done all the various duties pertaining to a soldier's life; have conducted ourselves to the complete satisfaction of general officers who were, if any, prejudiced *against* us, but who now accord us all the encouragement and honor due us; have shared the perils and labor of reducing the first stronghold that flaunted a traitor flag; and more, Mr. President, today the Anglo-Saxon mother, wife, or sister are not alone in tears for departed sons, husbands, and brothers. The patient, trusting descendants of Afric's clime have dyed the ground with blood in defense of the Union and democracy. Men, too, Your Excellency, who know in a measure the cruelties of the iron heel of oppression, which, in years gone by, the very power their blood is now being spilled to maintain, ever ground them to the dust.

But when the war trumpet sounded o'er the land, when men knew not the friend

Robert G. Shaw, commander of 54th Massachusetts Regiment, a Negro unit which served for a year without pay to protest the policy of lower pay for Negroes

from the traitor, the black man laid his life at the altar of the nation — and he was refused. When the arms of the Union were beaten, in the first year of the war, and the executive called for more food for its ravaging maw, again the black man begged the privilege of aiding his country in her need — to be again refused.

And now he is in the war, and how has he conducted himself? Let their dusky forms rise up out the mires of James Island and give the answer. Let the rich mold around Wagner's parapets be upturned, and there will be found an eloquent answer. Obedient and patient and solid as a wall are they. All we lack is a paler hue and a better acquaintance with the alphabet.

Now, Your Excellency, we have done a soldier's duty. Why can't we have a soldier's pay? You caution the Rebel chieftain that the United States knows no distinction in her soldiers. She insists on having all her soldiers of whatever creed or color to be treated according to the usages of war. Now, if the United States exacts uniformity of treatment of her soldiers from the insurgents, would it not be well and consistent to set the example herself by paying all her *soldiers* alike?

We of this regiment were not enlisted under any "contraband" act. But we do not wish to be understood as rating our service of more value to the government than the service of the ex-slave. Their service *is* undoubtedly worth much to the nation, but Congress made express provision touching their case, as slaves freed by military necessity, and assuming the government to be their temporary guardian. Not so with us. Freemen by birth and consequently having the advantage of *thinking* and acting for ourselves so far as the laws would allow us, we do not consider ourselves fit subjects for the contraband act.

We appeal to you, sir, as the executive of the nation, to have us justly dealt with. The regiment do pray that they be assured their service will be fairly appreciated by paying them as American *soldiers,* not as menial hirelings. Black men, you may well know, are poor; $3 per month, for a year, will supply their needy wives and little ones with fuel. If you, as chief magistrate of the nation, will assure us of our whole pay, we are content. Our patriotism, our enthusiasm will have a new impetus to exert our energy more and more to aid our country. Not that our hearts ever flagged in devotion, spite the evident apathy displayed in our behalf, but we feel as though our country spurned us, now we are sworn to serve her. Please give this a moment's attention.

109.

Patrick Gilmore: "When Johnny Comes Marching Home"

In 1863 Patrick Gilmore, the Irish bandmaster of the Union Army, wrote the words for "When Johnny Comes Marching Home" to a tune he had heard sung in New Orleans. The melody was an old one, belonging to an old Irish street song, "Johnny I Hardly Knew Ye." Gilmore wrote the song for a peace jubilee that was not, in fact, held until 1869. The song was popular during the Civil War and was revived in 1898, when it became a national favorite — the song, indeed, of the Spanish-American War.

Source: *Heart Songs*, Cleveland, 1909.

WHEN JOHNNY COMES MARCHING HOME

When Johnny comes marching home again,
    Hurrah, hurrah!
We'll give him a hearty welcome then,
    Hurrah, hurrah!
The men will cheer and the boys will shout,
The ladies they will all turn out,
And we'll all feel gay when Johnny comes marching home.

The old church bell will peal with joy,
    Hurrah, hurrah!
To welcome home our darling boy,
    Hurrah, hurrah!
The village lads and lassies say,
With roses they will strew the way,
And we'll all feel gay when Johnny comes marching home.

Get ready for the Jubilee,
    Hurrah, hurrah!
We'll give the hero three times three,
    Hurrah, hurrah!
The laurel wreath is ready now
To place upon his loyal brow,
And we'll all feel gay when Johnny comes marching home.

Let love and friendship on that day,
    Hurrah, hurrah!
Their choicest treasures then display,
    Hurrah, hurrah!
And let each one perform some part,
To fill with joy the warrior's heart,
And we'll all feel gay when Johnny comes marching home.

110.

Abraham Lincoln: The Gettysburg Address

After the Union victory at Gettysburg on July 1-3, 1863, a national commission was established to create the National Soldiers' Cemetery at Gettysburg for the several thousand soldiers, of both sides, who gave their lives in the battle. The dedication ceremony was planned for November 19. Edward Everett, former senator, former governor of Massachusetts, former president of Harvard, and a leading orator of the day, was chosen to give the major address. On November 2, President Lincoln was sent an invitation to attend and was requested to make "a few appropriate remarks" after Everett's speech. Lincoln accepted, though many other matters weighed on his mind. He was in the midst of preparing his annual message to Congress, and the events of the war required his constant attention. Having prepared a first draft of the speech he would make, Lincoln left Washington for Gettysburg on November 18 at a time when his son Tad lay sick in bed. During the late afternoon train ride, the President seemed exceptionally weary. That night in his room Lincoln wrote the final draft of his speech, showing it only to Secretary of State Seward. Some 15,000 people were on Cemetery Hill for the ceremony when the President arrived. Everett spoke nearly two hours; then the Baltimore Glee Club sang an ode; finally Ward Hill Lamon, Lincoln's military attaché, presented the President. Lincoln delivered the Gettysburg Address in three minutes and afterward leaned over to Lamon and said: "Lamon, that speech won't scour. It is a flat failure [and] the people won't like it." The following day Everett wrote Lincoln: "I should be glad if I could flatter myself that I came as near to the central idea of the occasion in two hours as you did in two minutes." Lincoln replied: "In our respective parts yesterday, you could not have been excused to make a short address, nor I a long one. I am pleased to know that, in your judgment, the little I did say was not entirely a failure."

Source: Nicolay-Hay, IX, pp. 209-210.

Four score and seven years ago our fathers brought forth on this continent a new nation, conceived in liberty and dedicated to the proposition that all men are created equal.

Now we are engaged in a great civil war, testing whether that nation or any nation so conceived and so dedicated can long endure. We are met on a great battlefield of that war. We have come to dedicate a portion of that field as a final resting place for those who here gave their lives that that nation might live. It is altogether fitting and proper that we should do this.

But, in a larger sense, we cannot dedicate — we cannot consecrate — we cannot hallow — this ground. The brave men, living and dead, who struggled here have consecrated it far above our poor power to add or detract. The world will little note nor long remember what we say here, but it can never forget what they did here. It is for us, the living, rather, to be dedicated here to the unfinished work which they who fought here have thus far so nobly advanced.

It is rather for us to be here dedicated to the great task remaining before us — that from these honored dead we take increased devotion to that cause for which they gave the last full measure of devotion; that we here highly resolve that these dead shall not have died in vain; that this nation, under God, shall have a new birth of freedom; and that government of the people, by the people, for the people shall not perish from the earth.

111.

JAMES ALEXANDER SEDDON: Economic Problems of the Confederacy

The impressment of food and ammunition for the Confederate forces was regulated by a law of the Confederate Congress in March 1863. Difficulties in supplying the troops and various economic problems that the law sought to solve still existed six months later. On November 26, 1863, the Confederate secretary of war, James Seddon, wrote to President Davis. The portions of his letter concerned with supply problems are reprinted here.

Source: Ainsworth, Additions and Corrections to 4th Series, II, pp. 990-1018.

THE QUARTERMASTER and commissary generals, in the administration of their respective departments, have had during the past year extraordinary difficulties and embarrassments to encounter. The manufacturing operations of the former, as in the other bureaus, have indeed been conducted on a large scale, with more economy of material and with greater skill and energy than at past periods, and have made more nearly the supplies for the army from internal resources, but still for some essential articles, such as shoes, blankets, and woolen cloths, partial dependence on importations could not be avoided. In these articles it can scarcely be expected that domestic production can be increased, for, under the wasting consumption of war, the production of the raw material is more likely to be diminished than increased. But the difficulties of both the quartermaster and commissary generals have been most grave in the large necessary purchases and transportation of forage and subsistence.

The abstraction of so much male labor from culture, and the barbarous ravages of the enemy, pursued with a systematic view to curtail our resources by spoliation and destruction, combined with unfavorable seasons to limit, almost beyond precedent, the production of these essential articles. The scarcity, too, was greatest in one or two of the states nearest to our large armies, and the necessity for months of sustaining almost entirely the armies of Northern Virginia from supplies of corn drawn from South Carolina and Georgia will strikingly illustrate both the dearth and the difficulty of supplying it. At one time it was thought necessary to make appeal direct to the feelings and patriotism of the people for the prompt rendition of all surplus of supplies for subsistence, and it is a grateful duty to acknowledge that they who have never failed to recognize as their own the cause of the Confederacy, with zeal and emulation met the exigencies of the case, and in very many instances stinted themselves and their dependents to supply the army. It is most creditable to these departments that they have been able, amid the real deficiencies existing and the many hindrances from distance, defective transportation and other causes, to keep the armies at all times moderately supplied, and even able to make all the movements in the field which the exigencies of the campaign demanded. How long their exertion will avail to assure such results, it must be confessed, is now a matter of grave anxiety.

The consumption of all animal life in the war has been very great, and, in addition, during the past few months, destructive and widespread disease has prevailed among the swine, which constitute the most serviceable as well as largest resource for meat. Bacon and beef must, in view of the needs of the army and the people, be scarce during the coming year. It is confidently believed, indeed, that there is a sufficiency of meat in the Confederacy to afford a reasonable supply to the army and yet sustain the people likewise, but to attain such result it must be husbanded with care and used with more economy than our people have been accustomed to practise.

The supplies of hay and long forage generally are likewise undoubtedly scant, for these articles are not habitually produced in superabundance in the Confederacy, and the season has been decidedly unfavorable. Many substitutes for the better kind of long forage may be readily found on plantations, and it is hoped the people recognize the necessity of parting with the best of their stores for the use of the animals exposed to the much harder toils and labors of the service. This is the more necessary as another of our immediate needs is the due supply of horses for cavalry and artillery, indispensable arms of the service. Our safety demands that we preserve our horses during the rigors of the winter and in a condition to resume efficient service in the spring, as it would then be next to impossible to replace them.

But the gravest difficulty encountered by the Purchasing Department is that the only mode of obtaining supplies available to them is impressment. The inflation of the currency and the insatiable thirst for gain and speculation induced by it have caused inordinate enhancement of the prices of all products and a yet continuing advance, stimulated in part by the increasing volume of the currency and in part by the sordid calculation of large gains from hoarding by holders or speculators. To this has likewise contributed some distrust, not of the cause of the Confederacy but of its future ability, however earnest its desire to preserve its credit and good faith, to redeem the large issues which such enhancements of price rendered inevitable. The consequences have been an almost universal repugnance on the part of producers and holders to sell at any price, except under compulsion. This evil had begun to manifest itself before the close of the last Congress to such a degree that some legislative remedy was recognized to be indispensable. To buy at current prices was seen to be suicidal to the credit of the government, to swell its indebtedness, in a brief period, beyond its utmost capacities for redemption, and at the same time to raise by daily accessions the advancing scale of extravagant prices, until both the fears and interest of the holders would forbid sales at all.

Under these circumstances, Congress devised and authorized a system of impressment of all property required "for the good of the service," or the accumulation of adequate supplies for the army, at the same time recognizing that under the exceptional circumstances of the country and the disturbance of the ordinary laws of trade regulating supply and demand, current prices constituted no criterion of just compensation required by the Constitution to be allowed for the appropriation of private property to public uses. Congress provided for the ascertainment of such just compensation by reference, in the first instance, in part to local appraisers, and then to two commissioners to be appointed for each state, one by the governor and the other by the president of the Confederacy. These officers, combining by their appointment the sanction of the state and Confederate authorities, were not only to entertain appeals from local appraisements but, from time to time, to ascertain and prescribe fair rates of valuation to govern in impressments.

As there seems no other alternative, this was, perhaps, as judicious an arrangement on this delicate and difficult subject as was practicable; and on it the government has been compelled to rely almost exclusively during the past year. This resource, operating with increasing stringency and strain, is at this time its only reliance. The evils attending it are, however, very great, and only less than the failure or deficiency of supplies, which, so far, it has managed to avert. Impressment is evidently a harsh, unequal, and odious mode of supply. With the utmost forbearance and consideration even its occasional exercise is harassing and irritating; but when it has to prevail as a general practice, to be exercised inquisitorially and summarily in almost every private do-

James A. Seddon, Confederate secretary of war

main, by a multitude of subordinate officers, it becomes, beyond measure, offensive and repugnant to the sense of justice and prevalent sentiment of our people.

It has been, perhaps, the sorest test of their patriotism and self-sacrificing spirit afforded by the war; and no other people, it is believed, would have endured it without undue manifestations of discontent and resistance. It has caused much murmuring and dissatisfaction, but a knowledge of the necessities which alone justified it has caused the outcry to be directed rather to the mode and, as alleged, occasional excesses of its exercise than against the system itself. Casual irregularities and abuses in the use of such a power by numerous agents in so many quarters may not be wholly avoidable, but every effort to obtain information respecting them and to afford prompt correctives has been earnestly made by the department.

As to the mode of action, great misapprehension has prevailed. It has been supposed that it was the system of the department to attempt to regulate the prices for the public according to the schedule rates prescribed by the state appraisers, by impressing the products held by all who sold at higher rates, and in like spirit to keep supplies from being enhanced in price by the competition of consumers in the large cities by the impressment of all supplies in transit to market, unless the holders would agree to sell at schedule prices. To this supposed policy was ascribed the great enhancement of prices in the markets of the cities, and the gravest apprehensions of want were entertained by many from the alleged exclusion of free supplies to the cities. The orders and instructions of the department had been, in fact, against such policy, and the republication and reiteration of the regulations on the subject, which had been made soon after the initiation of the system, have, it is hoped, removed such injurious impressions.

At the same time it is found, as throughout it had been feared by the department, that the scarcity and high prices of supplies in the markets of the country have not been due to the law of impressment or to the supposed policy under it. The impressment law applies only to the surplus of producers, and expressly exempts to them and others the reasonable supplies they may have or obtain for the consumption of themselves, their families, or dependents. Thus all consumers are privileged freely to supply themselves. All supplies, too, it is now at least fully known, are exempt in transit to market and for a reasonable time afterward. Yet it is found that all prices have only the more rapidly advanced and are still advancing, and that neither are the markets of the city adequately supplied, nor can consumers, by purchase at current rates, without the utmost difficulty, supply themselves.

The truth is that the explanation, as the cause, is to be found outside of the impressment law, or the action under it. The real difficulty is that the price advancing from day to day with an accelerated ratio and a steady depreciation of the currency, the holders, unless required by positive necessity, prefer to retain their supplies and will not sell for any temptation of present price.

The impressment law is, in fact, almost the only corrective of this feeling, which would else be well-nigh universal. It favors the supply of the market and of consumers. The apprehension that surplus products, if retained, may be impressed by the government at the rates prescribed by the state appraisers constitutes the strongest, as it is nearly the only, inducement to holders to sell at market rates. Setting aside feelings of humanity and patriotism, which, to a creditable degree, may induce sales, and testing the matter by the general motive of self-interest alone, this is a plain matter of calculation — who would sell, unless forced by a present necessity for the money, when constant advance in the price of the product is sure, and the money, if received at once, is no less certain of its depreciation before the occasion of its future use? The difficulty, therefore, with the consumer as with the government, is the redundancy of the currency and the consequent steady inflation of prices. This in its direct, and even more in its indirect, influences, not merely on the market and on the property of citizens but on their instincts of selfishness, on their sentiments, tastes, and aspirations, is a fearful evil, and more demoralizing to our people than the more dire calamities of war.

It pertains to another branch of the government and to an abler mind to portray this subject in its true colors and to propose correctives; but as the mischief weighs as a paralysis on the energies of this department, I may be excused for saying that in my judgment the sole effective remedy is prompt reduction of the existing issues to the amount needed for currency by the people of the Confederacy, and the inflexible determination and pledge never to exceed it. No mode of utilizing the credit of the Confederacy can be so wasteful as the enhancement of all prices by a constantly increasing ratio, or so mischievous as the subversion of the standard of values, tempting all into the wild whirl of speculation, and corroding, by the vile greed of gain, all the nobler elements of character. If the present system be continued, prices, already many hundred percent above true values, must be indefinitely enhanced, the credit of the government must be wrecked utterly, and no alternative left for the continuance of our patriotic struggle and the preservation of our lives and liberties but grinding taxation and the systematized seizure, without present compensation, of all supplies needed for the employees as well as the armies of the Confederacy.

112.

THOMAS BUCKNER: Anti-Negro Rioting in Detroit

Riots against minority groups in America have a long history. In the early 1830s there were a number of anti-Abolitionist riots in Northern cities, especially in New York, when Negroes were beaten and slain and their property destroyed. In the 1840s there were anti-Catholic riots. Between 1840 and 1860 "Native Americans" attacked immigrant groups in the slums of Northern cities. In 1863 anti-Negro riots broke out in several Northern cities, the first occurring in Detroit, on March 6. Thomas Buckner, a Negro, published in the same year, at his own expense, a collection of eyewitness accounts.

Source: [Thomas Buckner] *A Thrilling Narrative from the Lips of the Sufferers of the Late Detroit Riot . . . Detroit, 1863* [Facsimile Edition, The Book Farm, Hattiesburg, Miss., 1945].

PREFACE BY THOMAS BUCKNER

THE PRESENT STATE OF AFFAIRS in relation to the colored people is one of great perplexity, and is not only so on account of the South but also in the North.

There certainly is something mysterious about them. On the one hand, they are being mobbed, and everything that is sacred to a people to make a country or home dear are denied them in many of the large Northern cities. And, on the other hand, they are marching off to the call of the government as if they were sharing all the blessings of the most favored citizens! And it is equally mysterious to see the bitter opposition that a class of men professing loyalty to the government of the United States should have against the colored soldier going out and facing the cannon's mouth in defense of a government that appears to be unable to give them any protection from the rage of the Rebels in the South or their enemies in the North.

But one thing the colored man knows, that the class of men of the same politics as those South are doing the mobbing North; so they are not only ready to suffer but to die in the cause that promises over 3 million of their race liberty.

Whatever, therefore, our treatment may be so far as the rage of the enemies of freedom may be; whatever, through cowardice, a ruthless mob of such men may inflict upon our people, they will not be deterred from the duty they owe to their God, themselves, and posterity, to do all they possibly can to undo the heavy burdens and let the oppressed go free! At the first blast the clarion of emancipation may give to call them forth in the irrepressible conflict, though their houses be sacked, their wives and children turned out-of-doors naked and destitute, they too well know that the way to glory is the way of suffering; therefore they desire rather to bear a good part in the battlefield rather than to be always exposed to such outrages as slavery entails on any class it has in its dominion.

REPORT BY MARCUS DALE

THOMAS FAULKNER, charged of committing the outrages upon Ellen Hover, a colored girl, and also a white girl, was to all intents a white man. This is beyond doubt, for he was a regular voter, and the journals of the city that understood his politics state that he voted the Democratic ticket. And an old veteran of over one hundred years of age declares that in conversing with F., he said, if he thought he had one drop of colored blood in his veins, if he could, he would let it out. And this was the man that caused the mob on colored men!

On the 6th of March an organized mob made their way from the jail down Beaubien Street. They were yelling like demons and crying "Kill all the d — d niggers." In the cooper shop, just below Lafayette Street, were five men working, namely: Robert Bennette, Joshua Boyd, Solomon Houston, Lewis Houston, Marcus Dale. These men were busy at work in the shop until the mob made an attack upon the shop. The windows were soon broken and the doors forced open. The men in the cooper shop were determined to resist any that might attempt to come in. The mob discovered this and did not attempt to come in but stood off and threw stones and bricks into the windows, a perfect shower. There happened to be one old shotgun in the shop, a couple of discharges from which drove the mob back from the shop. The dwelling house was attached to the shop, in which were three women and four children, namely: Mrs. Reynolds, Mrs. Bonn and one child, Mrs. Dale and three children.

Some ten minutes after the mob had fallen back from the shop, they made a rush upon the house in which were the women and children. The men in the shop, seeing this, rushed out of the shop into the house to protect the women and children. The windows of the house were soon all broken in; stones and bricks came into the house like hail. The women and children were dodging from one room to another to escape the stones. The men frequently stood before the women and children to shield them from the stones. Very soon after the men went from the shop into the house, the shop was set on fire by the mob. There were plenty of shavings in the shop, which facilitated the burning. The flames soon reached the house in which were the women and children.

The mob, by this time, had completely surrounded the building. Mrs. Reynolds attempted to go out at the back door but could not get out, for hundreds of stones were flying at that part of the building. Mr. Dale, in shielding his wife, got a blow in the face with a stone, which his wife might have gotten had he not stood before her. Some person outside was heard to say, "The women will be protected — no protection for the men." Hearing this, Mr. Dale told the women to go out at the front door.

Mrs. Dale, seeing the blood running from her husband's face, said, "My dear you are bleeding — you will be killed." Said he to her, "Go out with your children; they say there is protection for the women, but none for the men. I will look out for myself." Mrs. Bonn started for the door, with her child in her arms, followed by Mrs. Dale, with one child in her arms and two children hanging to her. Mrs. Reynolds next followed. When the women approached the door, some fiend in human shape drew back a large club to strike them, but some spectators, having within them a spark of humanity, rushed to the women and rescued them — drawn probably by the screams of Mrs. Bonn.

After the women had got out, the men, one by one, made their way out — were knocked down with stones when they came out and beaten. Father Clark happened to be in the house, was beaten after he came out. The last one who came out was Mr. Dale. When he came out into the backyard, the heat was so intense that he came near being overcome by it — he had his face badly burned. When he came out of the door, some twenty dirty looking Irishmen rushed at him with clubs, crying, "Kill the nager." But being thoughtful enough to come out with something in his hands and having a good deal of physical strength, he made them get back, and he got out without receiving further injuries.

Three families living in the building near the cooper shop lost all they had; namely, Mr. Reynolds, Mr. Dale, and Mr. Bonn.

The mob, not satisfied with burning the cooper shop and building adjacent, proceeded up Fort and Lafayette streets, robbing and burning some fifteen houses belonging to colored people.

Of the men who were in the cooper shop, one has died from wounds received; namely, Joshua Boyd.

REPORT BY THOMAS BUCKNER

The mob, in its first appearance to me, was a parcel of fellows running up Lafayette Street after two or three colored men. They then returned back, and in a short time I saw a tremendous crowd coming up Croghan Street on drays, wagons, and foot, with kegs of beer on their wagons, and rushed for the prison. Here they crowded thick and heavy. After this, while I was standing on the corner with half a dozen other gentlemen, a rifle ball came whistling over our heads, after which we heard several shots, but only one ball passing us. In a short time after this there came one fellow down, saying, "I am shot in the thigh." And another came with his finger partly shot off. A few minutes after that another ruffian came down, saying: "If we are got to be killed up for niggers then we will kill every nigger in this town."

A very little while after this we could hear them speaking up near the jail, and appeared to be drinking, but I was unable to hear what they said. This done, they gave a most fiendish yell and started down Beaubien Street. On reaching Croghan Street, a couple of houses west on Beaubien Street, they commenced throwing, and before they reached my residence, clubs, brick, and missiles of every description flew like hail. Myself and several others were standing on the sidewalk but were compelled to hasten in and close our doors, while the mob passed my house with their clubs and bricks flying into my windows and doors, sweeping out light and sash!

They then approached my door in large numbers, where I stood with my gun and another friend with an axe, but on seeing us, they fell back. They approached four times determined to enter my door, but I raised my gun at each time and they fell back. In the meantime, part of the mob passed on down Beaubien Street. After the principal part had passed, I rushed up my stairs looking to see what they were doing and heard the shattering of windows and slashing of boards. In a few moments I saw them at Whitney Reynolds', a few doors below Lafayette Street. Mr. R. is a cooper; had his shop and residence on the same lot and was the largest colored coopering establishment in the city, employing a number of hands regular.

I could see from the windows men striking with axe, spade, clubs, etc., just as you could see men thrashing wheat. A sight the most revolting, to see innocent men, women, and children, all without respect to age or sex, being pounded in the most brutal manner.

Sickened with the sight, I sat down in deep solicitude in relation to what the night would bring forth; for to human appearance it seemed as if Satan was loose, and his children were free to do whatever he might direct without fear of the city authority.

REPORT BY LOUISA BONN

I HAD GOTTEN HOME from a funeral of a young woman, and, after changing my apparel, commenced to get supper. I heard a yelling up Beaubien Street, and, looking out, saw a crowd of men and boys throwing at Mr. Buckner's house. My husband told me I had better go into my mother's, and he would shut up the house so that they would not think anyone was home. I went in, and in a few moments they were down to my father's house. They then commenced breaking in the front-room windows and the door and windows of the cooper shop.

Myself and child, mother, and Mrs. Dale and her three children and brother kept in the back part of the house while they were throwing stones, and then someone broke the front door open with an axe. Then the dining room caught fire. I started to go out the front door with my babe in my arms, thinking that, as I had not done anything at all to those fiends in human form, they would let me pass. On going to the door, a man met me with a large boulder in his hand and would have knocked me in the head had his hand not been caught by another man!

I then returned in the house, the sheets of flames approaching me and my babe. I then went to the front door and found it locked, but the top panel of the door was all knocked out. Finding I could not get out, I commenced screaming! At this a crowd rushed across the street to me; and I feared it was some of the mob and ran back into the house again. Two gentlemen ran to me and kicked the lower part of the door open — one taking hold of me and the other caught my child and told me I should not be hurt. I could not then tell whether mother was burned up or not.

So I commenced screaming for my mother. Dr. Calhoun told the gentlemen to take me on up street, and he would go in and get my mother out. A Dutchman went in with the doctor and got Mrs. Dale out and took her to Mr. McCutchen's, and I went on up the street.

Before the house was fired, heard them say: "Let us surround the house and burn the niggers up." So I thought my mother was burned up! No tongue can describe the feelings of my mind on that occasion; everything that we had were in burning sheets of flame! My husband, mother, and other friends were all exposed to murderous assaults from those fiends; and to all human appearance there was not a friend in all the thousands that thronged and gazed upon our ruins. Who can form an idea of a female's distress under such circumstances?

After I escaped the mob, I went up to Mrs. R. Clark's, Lafayette Street. I thought, of course, my mother was dead and was gazing intensely to see if I could discover anyone coming up from there, and while thus watching, I saw my dear mother coming up the street all wet, with a trunk in her hands. I ran out to meet her. I then took the trunk from her and went into Mr. C.'s, and told her to come after me.

When we got in, I told her she had better break the trunk open and get out father's money. Mrs. Clark handed her a hammer, and just at that moment a rush of the mob approached and hailed in a shower of bricks and other missiles, smashing in the doors and window. Mrs. Clark and all of us were frightened to desperation. She attempted to run upstairs, but Ma told her not to do that but go out of the house. At this, Ma opened the back door and went down the yard and jumped the fence, leaving the trunk and all its contents sitting behind the stove. My mother knew that the trunk had all my father's money in it; that he was then just preparing to lay in a large stock of cooper stuff. She had dragged it several squares from our dwelling, that the mob had destroyed, to be compelled to leave it in the house of Mrs. Clark to be seized by those vile fiends. The amount of money in the trunk was $1,200, besides a large lot of valuable clothes.

We then proceeded from there up the alley to St. Antoine Street, and from thence on to Clinton Street — as poor wanderers, not knowing where to go to seek an asylum from the coldness of the approaching night. My babe was entirely naked, with the exception of a little dress and skirt, having lost all his clothes, even to his bonnet, in the fire and trying to escape the mob.

Wandering up and down about 8 o'clock at night, we got on Mullett Street and found Mr. E. Harberd was not burned out. We went there and found a shelter from the mob and cold.

During all this time, myself and mother was out-of-doors, without bonnet or shawl. My distress was indescribable on account of the absence of my husband and father. The former I saw last when the dining room fell in. He advised me to stand aside as much as possible out of the flames, as he heard the bell ringing and thought the guards would soon come and I could get out. From this time I never saw him any more till 3 o'clock on Saturday morning, when he and Mr. Dale came to Father Harberd's. Mr. Dale was much wounded in the flames.

My father had gone to the country to see about lumber and told us that if he was not back by 5 o'clock, we need not feel uneasy about him as he would not be back till morning. But still I had the grief and burden of mind for him; for we did not know but what he had come in and fallen into the hands of the mob; and this suspense of mind we had till about 9 o'clock the next morning, when he came home.

REPORT OF MRS. REYNOLDS

I FOUND, on my daughter going to the front door, she had to hasten back to save her life from the mob; so I returned into the room and gave up to be burned up; for I saw from all appearances that if I went out in such a shower of stones, I should be certainly killed, and I just gave myself up to the mercy of God.

I remained in this position and heard my daughter scream again, and then soon it was over. I could not tell whether herself and babe had fallen speechless at the foot of the bloody assassin or fell in the flames!

Not long after this, a couple of gentlemen came in and helped me and Mrs. Dale and children out of the flames.

I had taken care of the trunk.

REPORT OF WHITNEY REYNOLDS

I WAS OUT AT OAKLAND THAT DAY, and, on coming, heard that my wife, daughter, and her husband and child were all burned up, with all my property. This struck me with such force that when I came home and found my family all safe, it filled me with such satisfaction that I did not feel the loss of the property scarcely at all.

I have lost in cash $1,200, and in property over $4,000, and all swept away in an hour for no cause, only the wickedness of a class of men who hate the colored man.

113.

LINDLEY MILLER: "Marching Song of the First Arkansas"

Sung to the tune of "John Brown's Body," the "Marching Song of the First Arkansas"
was the fighting song of the First Arkansas Colored Regiment of the Union Army. It
was written in 1863 by Captain Lindley Miller, a member of a New York regiment and
later commander of this Negro regiment. He called it "a good song to fight with." The
song was widely popular among Negro troops during the war.

❦ MARCHING SONG OF THE FIRST ARKANSAS

Oh, we're the bully soldiers of the "First of Arkansas,"
We are fighting for the Union, we are fighting for the law,
We can hit a Rebel further than a white man ever saw,
    As we go marching on.

Chorus:
Glory, glory, hallelujah,
Glory, glory, hallelujah,
Glory, glory, hallelujah,
    As we go marching on.

See, there above the center, where the flag is waving bright,
We are going out of slavery; we're bound for freedom's light;
We mean to show Jeff Davis how the Africans can fight,
    As we go marching on!

We have done with hoeing cotton, we have done with hoeing corn,
We are colored Yankee soldiers, now, as sure as you are born;
When the masters hear us yelling, they'll think it's Gabriel's horn,
    As we go marching on.

They will have to pay us wages, the wages of their sin,
They will have to bow their foreheads to their colored kith and kin,
They will have to give us house-room, or the roof shall tumble in!
    As we go marching on.

They said, "Now colored brethren, you shall be forever free,
From the first of January, eighteen hundred sixty-three."
We heard it in the river going rushing to the sea,
    As it went sounding on.

Father Abraham has spoken and the message has been sent,
The prison doors he opened, and out the prisoners went,
To join the sable army of the "African descent,"
    As we go marching on.

Then fall in, colored brethren, you'd better do it soon,
Don't you hear the drum a-beating the Yankee Doodle tune?
We are with you now this morning, we'll be far away at noon,
    As we go marching on.

114.

ABRAHAM LINCOLN: A Program for Reconstruction

In his third annual message to Congress on December 8, 1863, Lincoln for the first time presented a program for Reconstruction, a plan marked by considerable leniency. The message was preceded on the same day by a presidential proclamation that laid down the conditions for Reconstruction. Lincoln's plan was based on three assumptions: that the Southern states had never legally been out of the Union; that they could be restored as soon as their political institutions were properly reordered; and that Reconstruction was largely an executive function. The plan aroused bitter resentment among the Radical Republicans. Lincoln's plan was carried out during his lifetime in the restored states, but Congress never recognized "Lincoln governments" in the South. The Proclamation and portions of Lincoln's message are reprinted below.

Source: Richardson, VI, pp. 179-191, 213-215.

I.

Proclamation of Amnesty

Whereas in and by the Constitution of the United States it is provided that the President "shall have power to grant reprieves and pardons for offenses against the United States, except in cases of impeachment"; and

Whereas a rebellion now exists whereby the loyal state governments of several states have for a long time been subverted, and many persons have committed and are now guilty of treason against the United States; and

Whereas, with reference to said rebellion and treason, laws have been enacted by Congress declaring forfeitures and confiscation of property and liberation of slaves, all upon terms and conditions therein stated, and also declaring that the President was thereby authorized at any time thereafter, by proclamation, to extend to persons who may have participated in the existing rebellion in any state or part thereof pardon and amnesty, with such exceptions and at such times and on such conditions as he may

Abraham Lincoln in 1863

and which oath shall be registered for permanent preservation and shall be of the tenor and effect following, to wit:

I, ———, do solemnly swear, in presence of Almighty God, that I will henceforth faithfully support, protect, and defend the Constitution of the United States and the Union of the states thereunder; and that I will in like manner abide by and faithfully support all acts of Congress passed during the existing rebellion with reference to slaves, so long and so far as not repealed, modified, or held void by Congress or by decision of the Supreme Court; and that I will in like manner abide by and faithfully support all proclamations of the President made during the existing rebellion having reference to slaves, so long and so far as not modified or declared void by decision of the Supreme Court. So help me God.

deem expedient for the public welfare; and

Whereas the congressional declaration for limited and conditional pardon accords with well-established judicial exposition of the pardoning power; and

Whereas, with reference to said rebellion, the President of the United States has issued several proclamations with provisions in regard to the liberation of slaves; and

Whereas it is now desired by some persons heretofore engaged in said rebellion to resume their allegiance to the United States and to reinaugurate loyal state governments within and for their respective states:

Therefore, I, Abraham Lincoln, President of the United States, do proclaim, declare, and make known to all persons who have, directly or by implication, participated in the existing rebellion, except as hereinafter excepted, that a full pardon is hereby granted to them and each of them, with restoration of all rights of property, except as to slaves and in property cases where rights of third parties shall have intervened, and upon the condition that every such person shall take and subscribe an oath and thenceforward keep and maintain said oath inviolate,

The persons excepted from the benefits of the foregoing provisions are all who are or shall have been civil or diplomatic officers or agents of the so-called Confederate government; all who have left judicial stations under the United States to aid the rebellion; all who are or shall have been military or naval officers of said so-called Confederate government above the rank of colonel in the Army or of lieutenant in the Navy; all who left seats in the United States Congress to aid the rebellion; all who resigned commissions in the Army or Navy of the United States and afterward aided the rebellion; and all who have engaged in any way in treating colored persons, or white persons in charge of such, otherwise than lawfully as prisoners of war, and which persons may have been found in the United States service as soldiers, seamen, or in any other capacity.

And I do further proclaim, declare, and make known that whenever, in any of the states of Arkansas, Texas, Louisiana, Mississippi, Tennessee, Alabama, Georgia, Florida, South Carolina, and North Carolina, a number of persons, not less than one-tenth in number of the votes cast in such state at the presidential election of the year A.D. 1860, each having taken oath aforesaid, and not having since violated it, and being a qualified voter by the election law of the state existing immediately before the so-called act of secession, and excluding all others, shall reestablish a state government which shall be republican and in nowise contravening said oath, such shall be recognized as the true government of the state, and the state shall receive thereunder the benefits of the constitutional provision which declares that "the United States shall guarantee to every state in this Union a republican form of government and shall protect each of them against invasion, and, on application of the legislature, or the executive (when the legislature cannot be convened), against domestic violence."

And I do further proclaim, declare, and make known that any provision which may be adopted by such state government in relation to the freed people of such state which shall recognize and declare their permanent freedom, provide for their education, and which may yet be consistent as a temporary arrangement with their present condition as a laboring, landless, and homeless class will not be objected to by the national executive.

And it is suggested as not improper that in constructing a loyal state government in any state the name of the state, the boundary, the subdivisions, the constitution, and the general code of laws as before the rebellion be maintained, subject only to the modifications made necessary by the conditions hereinbefore stated, and such others, if any, not contravening said conditions and which may be deemed expedient by those framing the new state government.

To avoid misunderstanding, it may be proper to say that this proclamation, so far as it relates to state governments, has no reference to states wherein loyal state governments have all the while been main-

tained. And for the same reason it may be proper to further say that whether members sent to Congress from any state shall be admitted to seats constitutionally rests exclusively with the respective houses and not to any extent with the executive. And, still further, that this proclamation is intended to present the people of the states wherein the national authority has been suspended and loyal state governments have been subverted a mode in and by which the national authority and loyal state governments may be reestablished within said states or in any of them; and while the mode presented is the best the executive can suggest, with his present impressions, it must not be understood that no other possible mode would be acceptable.

II.

Annual Message to Congress

WHEN CONGRESS ASSEMBLED a year ago, the war had already lasted nearly twenty months, and there had been many conflicts on both land and sea, with varying results. The rebellion had been pressed back into reduced limits; yet the tone of public feeling and opinion, at home and abroad, was not satisfactory.

With other signs, the popular elections, then just past, indicated uneasiness among ourselves, while, amid much that was cold and menacing, the kindest words coming from Europe were uttered in accents of pity, that we were too blind to surrender a hopeless cause. Our commerce was suffering greatly by a few armed vessels built upon and furnished from foreign shores, and we were threatened with such additions from the same quarter as would sweep our trade from the sea and raise our blockade. We had failed to elicit from European governments anything hopeful upon this subject.

The preliminary Emancipation Proclamation, issued in September, was running its assigned period to the beginning of the new year. A month later the final proclamation came, including the announcement that colored men of suitable condi ion would be received into the war service. The policy of emancipation and of employing black soldiers gave to the future a new aspect, about which hope, and fear, and doubt contended in uncertain conflict. According to our political system, as a matter of civil administration, the general government had no lawful power to effect emancipation in any state, and for a long time it had been hoped that the rebellion could be suppressed without resorting to it as a military measure. It was all the while deemed possible that the necessity for it might come, and that if it should, the crisis of the contest would then be presented. It came, and, as was anticipated, it was followed by dark and doubtful days.

Eleven months having now passed, we are permitted to take another review. The Rebel borders are pressed still farther back, and by the complete opening of the Mississippi the country dominated by the rebellion is divided into distinct parts, with no practical communication between them. Tennessee and Arkansas have been substantially cleared of insurgent control, and influential citizens in each, owners of slaves and advocates of slavery at the beginning of the rebellion, now declare openly for emancipation in their respective states. Of those states not included in the Emancipation Proclamation, Maryland and Missouri, neither of which three years ago would tolerate any restraint upon the extension of slavery into new territories, only dispute now as to the best mode of removing it within their own limits.

Of those who were slaves at the beginning of the rebellion, full 100,000 are now in the United States military service, about one-half of which number actually bear arms in the ranks; thus giving the double advantage of taking so much labor from the insurgent cause and supplying the places which otherwise must be filled with so many white men. So far as tested, it is difficult to say they are not as good soldiers as any. No servile insurrection or tendency to violence or cruelty has marked the measures of emancipation and arming the blacks. These measures have been much discussed in foreign countries, and, contemporary with such discussion, the tone of public sentiment there is much improved. At home the same measures have been fully discussed, supported, criticized, and denounced, and the annual elections following are highly encouraging to those whose official duty it is to bear the country through this great trial. Thus we have the new reckoning. The crisis which threatened to divide the friends of the Union is past.

Looking now to the present and future, and with reference to a resumption of the national authority within the states wherein that authority has been suspended, I have thought fit to issue a proclamation, a copy of which is herewith transmitted. On examination of this proclamation it will appear, as is believed, that nothing will be attempted beyond what is amply justified by the Constitution. True, the form of an oath is given, but no man is coerced to take it. The man is only promised a pardon in case he voluntarily takes the oath. The Constitution authorizes the executive to grant or withhold the pardon at his own absolute discretion; and this includes the power to grant on terms, as is fully established by judicial and other authorities.

It is also proffered that if, in any of the states named, a state government shall be, in the mode prescribed, set up, such government shall be recognized and guaranteed by the United States, and that under it the state shall, on the constitutional conditions, be protected against invasion and domestic violence. The constitutional obligation of the United States to guarantee to every state in the Union a republican form of government and to protect the state in the cases stated is explicit and full. But why tender the benefits of this provision only to a state government set up in this particular way? This section of the Constitution contemplates a case wherein the element within a state favorable to republican government in the Union may be too feeble for an opposite and hostile element external to, or even within, the state; and such are precisely the cases with which we are now dealing.

An attempt to guarantee and protect a revived state government constructed in whole or in preponderating part from the very element against whose hostility and violence it is to be protected is simply absurd. There must be a test by which to separate the opposing elements, so as to build only from the sound; and that test is a sufficiently liberal one which accepts as sound whoever will make a sworn recantation of his former unsoundness.

But if it be proper to require as a test of admission to the political body an oath of allegiance to the Constitution of the United States and to the Union under it, why also to the laws and proclamations in regard to slavery? Those laws and proclamations were enacted and put forth for the purpose of aiding in the suppression of the rebellion. To give them their fullest effect, there had to be a pledge for their maintenance. In my judgment they have aided and will further aid the cause for which they were intended. To now abandon them would be not only to relinquish a lever of power but would also be a cruel and an astounding breach of faith.

I may add at this point, that while I remain in my present position I shall not attempt to retract or modify the Emancipation Proclamation; nor shall I return to slavery any person who is free by the terms of that proclamation or by any of the acts of Congress. For these and other reasons it is thought best that support of these measures shall be included in the oath; and it is believed the executive may lawfully claim it in return for pardon and restoration of forfeited rights, which he has clear constitutional power to withhold altogether, or grant upon the terms which he shall deem wisest for the public interest. It should be observed, also, that this part of the oath is subject to the modifying and abrogating power of legislation and supreme judicial decision.

The proposed acquiescence of the national executive in any reasonable temporary state arrangement for the freed people is made with the view of possibly modifying the confusion and destitution which must, at best, attend all classes by a total revolution of labor throughout whole states. It is hoped that the already deeply afflicted people in those states may be somewhat more ready to give up the cause of their affliction, if to this extent this vital matter be left to themselves; while no power of the national executive to prevent an abuse is abridged by the proposition.

The suggestion in the proclamation as to maintaining the political framework of the states on what is called reconstruction is made in the hope that it may do good without danger of harm. It will save labor and avoid great confusion.

But why any proclamation now upon this subject? This question is beset with the conflicting views that the step might be delayed too long or be taken too soon. In some states the elements for resumption seem ready for action, but remain inactive, apparently for want of a rallying point — a plan of action. Why shall A adopt the plan of B, rather than B that of A? And if A and B should agree, how can they know but that the general government here will reject their plan? By the proclamation a plan is presented which may be accepted by them as a rallying point, and which they are assured in advance will not be rejected here. This may bring them to act sooner than they otherwise would.

The objections to a premature presentation of a plan by the national executive consist in the danger of committals on points which could be more safely left to further developments. Care has been taken to so shape the document as to avoid embarrassments from this source. Saying that on certain terms certain classes will be pardoned, with rights restored, it is not said that other classes, or other terms, will never be included. Saying that reconstruction will be accepted if presented in a specified way, it is not said it will never be accepted in any other way.

The movements, by state action, for emancipation in several of the states not included in the Emancipation Proclamation are matters of profound gratulation. And while I do not repeat in detail what I have heretofore so earnestly urged upon this subject, my general views and feelings remain unchanged; and I trust that Congress will omit no fair opportunity of aiding these important steps to a great consummation.

In the midst of other cares, however important, we must not lose sight of the fact that the war power is still our main reliance. To that power alone can we look yet for a time to give confidence to the people in the contested regions, that the insurgent power will not again overrun them. Until that confidence shall be established, little can be done anywhere for what is called reconstruction. Hence our chiefest care must still be directed to the Army and Navy, who have thus far borne their harder part so nobly and well. And it may be esteemed fortunate that in giving the greatest efficiency to these indispensable arms, we do also honorably recognize the gallant men, from commander to sentinel, who compose them, and to whom, more than to others, the world must stand indebted for the home of freedom disenthralled, regenerated, enlarged, and perpetuated.

115.

EDWARD DICEY: Money and Manners in the North

Most Europeans who visited America during the Civil War could not view the conflict dispassionately. Edward Dicey, a noted British journalist and the editor of the Observer, *spent six months in America as a special correspondent for the* Daily Telegraph *in 1862. His report,* Six Months in the Federal States, *from which the chapter "American Society" follows, was one of the few commentaries that achieved objectivity. Unlike many in the upper-class British society to which he belonged, he was sympathetic to the Union, and his writings were read with pleasure by Northerners.*

Source: *Six Months in the Federal States*, London, 1863, Vol. I, pp. 299-310.

I MAY SAY WITHOUT VANITY that during my sojourn in the States I had considerable advantages in entering Society. I was amply provided with letters of introduction: I came at a time when foreign travelers were rare; and also, from an impression that my

sympathies were more Northern than those of the bulk of my fellow countrymen, I was received with, perhaps, undeserved kindness. Still, my great passport to Society consisted in the fact that I was an Englishman. That this should have been so is a fact which throws a good deal of light on American Society.

An American once said to me: "I always envy you to whom England is a home; but, then, I think you ought to envy us for our feelings when we visit England. To you, after all, it is only a country, more or less interesting, where you make and spend your money; to us it is a sort of enchanted land, where everything that is old to you is new to us. You look upon England as a husband looks on his wife; we see her as a lover sees his mistress." The words were spoken half-jestingly, but there was still a good deal of truth in them. The average of educated Americans know as much about English literature, and more, perhaps, about English history, than the average of educated Englishmen. Their language, their history, their literature are those of England. There are few who cannot remember relatives that have come from the Old Country — who do not know of some town or village in the United Kingdom in which they have something of a personal interest.

A visit to Europe and, above all, to England, is the great dream of all Americans who have not crossed the Atlantic — the holiday time, as it were, of life to those who have performed the journey. I always found there was no subject on which Americans talked so willingly as about the recollections of their foreign travels. No doubt this sentimental feeling about England grows weaker with each succeeding generation, and, like all sentimental feelings, it gives place to the action of interests and passions. I often fancied that those Americans who entertained the feeling most strongly were the most hostile to England. Indeed, my chief fear of a war with America arises from the fact that Americans care too much, not too little, about England. The existence, however, of this national feeling is strong enough to create a very kindly sentiment toward individual Englishmen; and probably there is no country in the world where an English traveler meets with so much kindness and so much cordiality, in virtue of his nationality, as he does in America.

Certainly, I found it so in my own case. I know that other English travelers tell a different story. Fellow countrymen of mine have related anecdotes to me of rude speeches and offensive remarks made to them purposely in the States because they were Englishmen. I suspect, in most of such instances, the narrators were to blame. If you are offended because a waiter offers to shake hands with you, or a barkeeper asks you to drink with him, or a laboringman speaks to you without your speaking first to him — well, you had better not travel in America; but if you are willing to take people as you find them, you will get along very pleasantly. Speaking for myself, I can say that, during all my travels, I had never once an offensive or impolite remark made to me. The only occasion on which I ever met with anything like impoliteness was in the smoking room of a fashionable hotel in New York. A number of old gentlemen sitting round the fire were talking politics and abusing England; I was smoking silently, and it struck me they were talking at me. Now, I am by no means an enthusiastic believer in our English doctrine, that whatever England does is right; and, also, I made a rule to be a listener to, not a partaker in, political discussions. But still there is a limit to patience, at any rate to my patience; and at some remark about the mingled folly and knavery of English policy, I spoke out strongly and, I fear, somewhat rudely. At once I was answered by a polite expression of sincere regret that anything should have been said in my presence that could have given offense; and, thereupon, the subject was dropped at once. The incident was trivial in the extreme, and the only reason why I remember it is because it was the sole instance of anything approaching to incivility I met with in the States.

To a stranger there is something wonderfully pleasant about the first blush of American Society: the manners of your hosts appear to an Englishman so frank and cordial; people seem so glad to see you and so anxious to make you feel at home. And I believe that the appearance is not assumed. Life, hitherto, has flowed very easily for the American people. The country is so large that there is room for all and to spare; the battle of life is not an arduous one, compared to what it is in older countries. The morbid dread of poverty, which is the curse of English middle-class existence, is almost unknown in the New World. If the worst comes to the worst, and an American is ruined, the world lies open to him, and in a new state he can start afresh, with as fair prospects as when he set out in life. The desire to provide for one's children, and to secure them a similar position in life to that which the parent occupies himself, is almost unknown. Public opinion does not require the father of a family to do more than give his children a good education. As a rule, the daughters can always marry, and the sons can make their own way. Equal division of property among the children of a family is enforced by custom, though not by law.

In the New England states it has become very common for any wealthy citizen to leave a considerable sum toward some public object; and anyone who fails to comply with this custom is hardly considered to have acted correctly. The result of this state of things is that saving is very uncommon among the middle classes in America. Everybody, as a rule, spends the full amount of his income, and, in consequence, there is much greater luxury in Northern households than would be seen in English families of the same amount of wealth. Hospitality, therefore, is given very readily, and the wheels of life run more easily than they do with us. I was struck constantly with the extreme good nature of the Americans in their private and social relations. I attribute it not so much to the national character —

which, owing to the climate, is a somewhat irritable one — but to the comparative absence of the sordid cares and petty considerations which the fierceness of our struggle for existence, and the exorbitant value attached by us to the respectability of wealth, give rise to perpetually in a densely peopled country like our own.

Paradoxical as the statement may seem, I think I have never known a country where money was less valued than in America. "The worship of the almighty dollar," which we are so apt to consider a characteristic of the Americans, cannot justly be charged to them in the sense in which we understand the phrase. The absence of all social distinctions, and the fact that there are no established positions to which birth and rank and station give an acknowledged entrance, render wealth the chief standard of distinction. In consequence, the natural ambition of every American is to acquire wealth and thus distinguish himself in the only career which is practically open to the vast majority.

Anybody who has known anything of Quakers will understand the working of the causes that I have attempted to describe. There is no body of men more liberal than the Society of Friends, and yet there is none more eager in the pursuit of moneymaking. So it is with the Yankee race. Moneymaking is the chief object of the nation; but they value the possession of the "almighty dollar" rather as a proof of success in life than as an end of existence. The mere ownership of wealth is less valued there than with us. The man who has made his own money is infinitely more respected than the man who has inherited it. Millionaires are rare in the second generation; and the bare fact of wealth gives a man fewer advantages in the North than in any Old World country.

I doubt, too, whether the accusation of extravagance, which is brought so frequently against the Northerners, is a just one. Money is spent freely, just as it is made; but, with the exception of New York, I was never in any American city where the style of living could compare for extravagance with that of the wealthy classes in the Old World. Americans in Europe are not, in this respect, fair specimens of their nation. They come over here for a holiday, and their expenditure is regulated on a holiday scale. But at home, the mode of living is, in most respects, remarkably simple. This is due, partly, to the extreme difficulty of getting servants and the impossibility of keeping a large household of domestics, but still more, I think, to a certain inherent simplicity of taste.

Hours are much earlier than with us, equipages are few in number; and dwelling houses, though eminently comfortable, very seldom possess any claim to splendor or magnificence. In the article of dress, and also in the dainties of the table, Americans will go to an expense that English families of the same rank in life never think of indulging in. In New York, especially, the ladies must spend what we should consider an extravagant amount on Parisian toilettes. I hardly ever remember to have been present at a dinner party in America where champagne was not distributed almost as plentifully as malt liquor would be with us; but in other respects, there is but little ostentatious expense visible to a stranger.

In a moral as opposed to a material point of view, the most striking feature about American Society is its uniformity. Everybody, as a rule, holds the same opinions about everything, and expresses his views, more or less, in the same language. These views are often correct, almost invariably intelligent and creditable to the holders. But still, even at the risk of hearing paradoxes defended, you cannot help wishing, at times, for a little more of originality.

I believe that this monotony in the tone of American talk and opinion arises from the universal diffusion of education. Everybody is educated up to a certain point, and very few are educated above it. They have all learned the same lessons under the same teachers, and, in consequence, share the same sentiments to a degree which it is difficult to an Englishman to appreciate beforehand. This monotony is infinitely more striking in the men than in the women. Ninety-nine American lads in a hundred go through exactly the same system of training. Up to eighteen or nineteen, they are carefully, if not very deeply, grounded in all the branches of a good, ordinary English education. Then they go into business, and from that time their intellectual self-culture ceases. Unless they happen to travel, they have very little time for reading anything except the newspapers.

The women pursue their education even after marriage, and are, in consequence, better read and more intellectual in their tastes than English ladies. In the long run, however, the national tone of mind is always derived from the male sex, and, therefore, the prevalent tone of America is not that of a highly educated society. I do not mean to say, for one moment, that there are not hundreds and thousands of men of really first-class education in the Northern states. On the contrary, some of the most thoroughly educated men it has been my lot to meet with have been Americans. I am speaking of the mass, not of individuals.

This opinion of mine, if it is correct, explains a fact which otherwise would seem discouraging: I mean the small share taken by educated men — in our sense of the word — in American politics. The truth is that if America were governed to any great extent by politicians of classical education, the country would not be fairly represented by its rulers. It is not the case that the fact of a gentleman having received a refined culture is any disqualification to him in the eyes of the constituencies. On the other hand, it is a very small recommendation. I do not deny that this is, in itself, an evil; but the true nature of the evil is not that men of education are disqualified from entering a political career in America but that they form so small a class that they possess no political influence.

Just in the same way, there is no doubt that, relatively to the period, there were more highly educated men in the Union half a century ago than there are now. The early settlers in any new country bring with them a higher degree of individual culture than they can impart to their children. In the same ratio, however, that the education of the individual decreases, the average education of the mass increases, and, on the whole, the general tone of the nation gains in consequence. My friend Mr. Holmes once said to me: "We should find it very hard to match 5,000 American gentlemen with 5,000 English; but we could match 5,000,000 ordinary Americans against the same number of your countrymen without fear of the result." This explanation I believe to be the correct one with regard to the intellectual development of America.

The truth is, the great mistake that we English make in judging of America is the assumption that the New World ought to be the reproduction of the Old Country. We expect our social system, our hierarchy of castes and rank, our forms of thought and feeling to be repeated among a people growing up under conditions totally different from that in which we have been trained for hundreds of generations. Every departure from our own standard we consider to indicate moral degeneracy, while in reality it is only a symptom of development. No one who has lived in America can avoid coming to the conclusion that the Anglo-Saxon frame is gradually modifying itself to a form suited to the new conditions of climate and temperature under which it is called on to exist.

What is true in the physical is true also in the moral world. By degrees, the imported civilization and culture of the Old World are developing themselves into new forms and aspects. What will be the ultimate social system of America it is impossible to say. Never yet in history has a nation grown up under circumstances where all men have started equal, and where want and poverty have been practically unknown. That the product of these conditions will be a remarkable one, we are beginning to see already. I recollect a common Irishwoman I once traveled alongside of in the States saying to me, when talking about her experience of her new home, "This is a blessed country, sir; I think God made it for the poor." And I have often fancied that this saying might be the clue to the future history of America.

I have been asked frequently whether I should like to live in America; and to this question my answer has always been that that depends entirely upon circumstances. Men of highly educated tastes, used to the social pleasures of the Old World, will not find their wants gratified as easily and as fully in a new state of society as in an old. In fact, in plain English, if your tastes and your habits are those of men whose income is counted by hundreds, you had better stop where you are. But the man who has his living to earn is better off, in almost every respect, in America than he is in England. The very circumstances that render the United States unattractive as a residence for the man of wealth and refinement are a positive boon to those who possess neither of the attributes; and I am afraid that in this world the latter class is larger and more important than the former.

These reflections on American Society would be imperfect if I said nothing as to the great charm which surrounds all family relations in the North. Compared with Europe, domestic scandals are unknown; and between parents and their grown-up children, there exists a degree of familiarity and intimacy which one seldom witnesses in this country. If family life is the foundation of all permanent good in the social system, then, in spite of its present defects and shortcomings, the outlook for the American Society of the future is a very bright one.

116.

HENRY WADSWORTH LONGFELLOW: "Paul Revere's Ride"

In the critical year 1863, when it seemed that the Southern cause might succeed, Henry Wadsworth Longfellow published a collection of story-poems, Tales of a Wayside Inn, *modeled after Chaucer's* Canterbury Tales. *The first poem in the collection, "Paul Revere's Ride," became a national favorite. Though Paul Revere's ride was, of course, almost ancient history by this time, the last stanza of the poem sounded the same alarm in the Union's present hour of darkness. The crisis that Revere had faced was now faced, in Longfellow's opinion, by everyone in the nation.*

Source: *Complete Poetical Works,* Cambridge Edition, Boston, 1893.

PAUL REVERE'S RIDE

Listen, my children, and you shall hear
Of the midnight ride of Paul Revere,
On the eighteenth of April, in seventy-five;
Hardly a man is now alive
Who remembers that famous day and year.

He said to his friend, "If the British march
By land or sea from the town tonight,
Hang a lantern aloft in the belfry arch
Of the North Church tower as a signal
      light —
One, if by land, and two, if by sea;
And I on the opposite shore will be,
Ready to ride and spread the alarm
Through every Middlesex village and farm,
For the country folk to be up and to arm."

Then he said, "Good-night!" and with
      muffled oar
Silently rowed to the Charlestown shore,
Just as the moon rose over the bay,
Where swinging wide at her moorings lay
The *Somerset,* British man-of-war;
A phantom ship, with each mast and spar
Across the moon like a prison bar,
And a huge black hulk, that was magnified
By its own reflection in the tide.

Meanwhile, his friend, through alley and
      street,
Wanders and watches with eager ears,
Till in the silence around him he hears

The muster of men at the barrack door,
The sound of arms, and the tramp of feet,
And the measured tread of the grenadiers,
Marching down to their boats on the shore.

Then he climbed the tower of the
      Old North Church,
By the wooden stairs, with stealthy tread,
To the belfry chamber overhead,
And startled the pigeons from their perch
On the somber rafters, that round him
      made
Masses and moving shapes of shade —
By the trembling ladder, steep and tall,
To the highest window in the wall,
Where he paused to listen and look down
A moment on the roofs of the town,
And the moonlight flowing over all.

Beneath, in the churchyard, lay the dead,
In their night encampment on the hill,
Wrapped in silence so deep and still
That he could hear, like a sentinel's tread,
The watchful night wind, as it went
Creeping along from tent to tent,
And seeming to whisper, "All is well!"
A moment only he feels the spell
Of the place and the hour, and the secret
      dread
Of the lonely belfry and the dead;
For suddenly all his thoughts are bent
On a shadowy something far away,
Where the river widens to meet the bay —

A line of black that bends and floats
On the rising tide, like a bridge of boats.

Meanwhile, impatient to mount and ride,
Booted and spurred, with a heavy stride
On the opposite shore walked Paul Revere.

Now he patted his horse's side,
Now gazed at the landscape far and near,
Then, impetuous, stamped the earth,
And turned and tightened his
    saddle-girth;
But mostly he watched with eager search
The belfry tower of the Old North Church,
As it rose above the graves on the hill,
Lonely and spectral and somber and still.
And lo! as he looks, on the belfry's height
A glimmer, and then a gleam of light!
He springs to the saddle, the bridle he
    turns,
But lingers and gazes, till full on his sight
A second lamp in the belfry burns!

A hurry of hoofs in a village street,
A shape in the moonlight, a bulk in the
    dark,
And beneath, from the pebbles, in passing,
    a spark
Struck out by a steed flying fearless and
    fleet:
That was all! And yet, through the gloom
    and the light,
The fate of a nation was riding that night;
And the spark struck out by that steed,
    in his flight,
Kindled the land into flame with its heat.

He has left the village and mounted the
    steep,
And beneath him, tranquil and broad and
    deep,
Is the Mystic, meeting the ocean tides;
And under the alders that skirt its edge,
Now soft on the sand, now loud on the
    ledge,
Is heard the tramp of his steed as he rides.

It was twelve by the village clock
When he crossed the bridge into
    Medford town.
He heard the crowing of the cock,

And the barking of the farmer's dog,
And felt the damp of the river fog
That rises after the sun goes down.

It was one by the village clock
When he galloped into Lexington.
He saw the gilded weathercock
Swim in the moonlight as he passed,
And the meetinghouse windows, blank
    and bare,
Gaze at him with a spectral glare,
As if they already stood aghast
At the bloody work they would look upon

It was two by the village clock
When he came to the bridge in Concord
    town.
He heard the bleating of the flock,
And the twitter of birds among the trees,
And felt the breath of the morning breeze
Blowing over the meadows brown.
And one was safe and asleep in his bed
Who at the bridge would be first to fall,
Who that day would be lying dead,
Pierced by a British musket ball.

You know the rest. In the books you
    have read
How the British regulars fired and
    fled —
How the farmers gave them ball for ball,
From behind each fence and farmyard wall,
Chasing the redcoats down the lane,
Then crossing the fields to emerge again
Under the trees at the turn of the road,
And only pausing to fire and load.

So through the night rode Paul Revere;
And so through the night went his cry of
    alarm
To every Middlesex village and farm —
A cry of defiance and not of fear,
A voice in the darkness, a knock at the
    door,
And a word that shall echo forevermore!
For, borne on the night wind of the past,
Through all our history, to the last,
In the hour of darkness and peril and need,
The people will waken and listen to hear
The hurrying hoofbeats of that steed,
And the midnight message of Paul Revere.

1864

117.

JAMES JACKSON JARVES: The Conditions and Prospects for Art in America

James Jackson Jarves, a noted art critic and collector, had as his major aim in life "the diffusion of artistic knowledge and aesthetic taste in America." He resided in Europe during the 1850s and there began to acquire the works of early Italian masters, which he brought back to the United States. By 1860 he had formed the largest and most important art collection in America. His collection evoked little enthusiasm, and it was only in 1871 that he was able to find a home for it at Yale University. The Art Idea, a portion of which is reprinted here, sought to inspire among his countrymen an appreciation for art.

Source: *The Art Idea,* 5th edition, Boston, 1864, Ch. 13.

AMERICAN SOIL, BUT HALF RESCUED from the wild embrace of the wilderness, is a virgin field of art. By America we mean that agglomerate of European civilizations welded by Anglo-Saxon institutions into the Federal Union. The other portions of the continent are simply offshoots of their parent countries, without national life in art or literature. Consequently, our inquiries belong to that people which, in virtue of their power and progress, have taken to themselves the designation of Americans, sanctioned by the tacit consent of the world, prophetically foreshadowing a period in their destiny, when, by the noble conquest of ideas, the entire continent shall of right be theirs.

An inquiry of this nature, under the circumstances of newness and inexperience which everywhere present themselves, is, in many respects, embarrassing. At the same time, it is interesting, involving as it does, not only the previous points of our investigations, whether by inheritance, transmission, or imitation, but new forms, rooted in novel conditions of national being; in short, the future of the art of the intermingling races of a new world fused into a democracy which is now passing through its gravest struggle for existence, to reissue, as we believe, the most powerful because the most enlightened, the most peaceful because the most free, and the most influential people of the globe because having sacrificed the most for justice and liberty. . . .

For the present, America, like England,

prefers the knowledge which makes her rich and strong to the art that implies cultivation as well as feeling rightly to enjoy it. In either country, climate, race, and religion are adverse, as compared with southern lands, to its spontaneous and general growth. Americans calculate, interrogate, accumulate, debate. They yet find their chief success in getting rather than enjoying; in having rather than being: hence, material wealth is the great prize of life. Their character tends to thrift, comfort, and means rather than final aims. It clings earthward from faith in the substantial advantages of things of sense. We are laying up a capital for great achievements, by and by. Our world is still of the flesh, with bounteous loyalty to the devil. Religion, on the side either of heaven or hell, has but little of the fervid, poetical, affectionate sentiment of the Roman creed and ritual.

In divorcing it from the supersensuous and superstitious, Protestantism has gone to the other extreme, making it too much a dogma. Franklin most rules the common mind. He was eminently great and wise. But his greatness and wisdom was unspiritual, exhibiting the advantages that spring from intellectual foresight and homely virtue; in short, the practical craft of the scientist, politician, and merchant. His maxims have fallen upon understandings but too well disposed by will and temperament to go beyond his meaning, so that we need the counteracting element which is to be found in the art sentiment.

What progress has it made in America?

To get at this, there are three points of view: the individual, national, and universal. American art must be submitted to each to get a correct idea of it as a whole. Yet it can scarcely be said to have fairly begun its existence, because, in addition to the disadvantages art is subjected to in America in common with England, it has others more distinctly its own.

The popular faith is more rigidly puritan-ical in tone. This not only deprives art of the lofty stimulus of religious feeling but subjects it to suspicion, as of doubtful morality. Art also is choked by the stern cares and homely necessities of an incipient civilization. Men must work to live before they can live to enjoy the beautiful.

It has no antecedent art: no abbeys in picturesque ruins; no stately cathedrals, the legacies of another faith and generation; no medieval architecture, rich in crimson and gold, eloquent with sculpture and color, and venerable with age; no aristocratic mansions in which art enshrines itself in a selfish and unappreciating era, to come forth to the people in more auspicious times; no state collections to guide a growing taste; no caste of persons of whom fashion demands encouragement to art growth; no ancestral homes replete with a storied portraiture of the past; no legendary lore more dignified than forest or savage life; no history more poetical or fabulous than the deeds of men almost of our own generation, too like ourselves in virtues and vices to seem heroic — men noble, good, and wise, but not yet arrived to be gods; and, the greatest loss of all, no lofty and sublime poetry. . . .

To this loss of what may be termed a floating aesthetic capital must be added the almost equal destitution of institutions for instruction in the science of art, except in a crude and elementary way. Academies and schools of design are few, and but imperfectly established. Public galleries exist only in idea. Private collections are limited in range, destitute of masterpieces, inaccessible to the multitude. Studios would effect much for the development of taste and knowledge were they freely visited, by bringing our public into more cordial relations with artists, who do not yet exercise their legitimate influence. In a nation of lyceums and lecturers, every topic except art is heard. Indeed, outside of occasional didactic teaching and a few works not much read, we are without other resources of aesthetic education on a public scale than meager exhibitions of pictures on private speculation in some of the chief cities.

This leads us to enlarge on the special disadvantages to American art arising from false criticism. The ordinary productions of men who handle brush or chisel are spoken of in public prints as "works of consummate taste and ability," "perfect gems," proofs of "astonishing genius," and with similar puffery. These vague, swelling words would be received at their real value did not so many of our people, just awakening to aesthetic sensations, have such a mistaken estimate of art. They view it as an undefined something above and apart from themselves and their daily lives, an Eleusinian mystery of a sacred priesthood, to be seen only through the veil of the imagination, not amenable to the laws of science or the results of experience, nor to be spoken of except in high-sounding phrases and wanton praise.

Feeding artists on this diet is like cramming children with colored candies. Every true artist shrinks from it and yearns for a remedy. This will appear as soon as the public comprehend that it is as feasible to teach the young to draw, paint, and model, presupposing average intellectual faculties, as much else they are required to learn; and that the result would equal much that now passes for fine art. We can educate clever external artists as readily as clever artisans; a certain knack of hand and development of taste and of the perceptive faculties being sufficient. When the public see this, they will cast aside their nonsense and mummery about art and judge its mechanical qualities with the same intelligent freedom and decision that they do the manual arts with which they are acquainted. In fact, design and the science of color should be made an elementary branch of instruction in our system of common education, precisely as we are now training the ear to music and the muscles to strength and suppleness.

Genius is not essential to mere painting and modeling, certainly not to a knowledge of principles and a respectable degree of skill or dexterity in their manifestation. These qualities can be acquired by study and application. Genius is the exception, talent the rule of art and literature. It is as fatal an error to postpone the acquisition of knowledge or the development of a faculty, from the want of genius, as to fancy that genius exists because we have a facility of doing certain things. Unless we conform our language to truth, we shall lose sight of the right distinction of words. An artisan who makes a good coat is more useful and respectable than a painter who makes bad pictures. Even a child would laugh at the absurdity of calling "dime novels" or "Rollo storybooks" works of astonishing genius, or of applying to them any of the hyperbolical expressions of admiration which are so lavishly showered by excited friendship or an indiscriminating press upon almost every effort of an American artist. Yet the larger portion of productions are no more matchless or divine than the common run of books, nor imply any more intellect to produce them.

If we should begin with exhausting the capacity for praise of our tongue on penny-a-line writers, what would be left for Irving, Emerson, Hawthorne, Bryant, or Poe? And could we invent words suitable to their merits, which would be doubtful on the scale applied to art, imagination would utterly fail us in coining terms to measure the genius of the absolutely great lights of literature — the Dantes, Homers, Goethes, and Shakespeares. Common sense must stop this debasing flattery by exposing its fallacy. It will be a fortunate day when our public and our artists meet understandingly, face to face, having put out of sight the present pernicious system of befogging and befooling. The reform lies more with the artists than the public, for they are its teachers. Eschewing claptrap, let them recognize only that sort of criticism which justifies its faith by reason and honest likings.

The daily journal of New York most devoted to art thus sums up a notice of the last Artist Fund Exhibition: "All the pictures possess more or less merits and defects. Perhaps the merits preponderate." Sagacious on-the-fence critic! At the opening of this exhibition, at which the elite of the artists and literati of the city were present, they listened complacently to the following nonsense, which we find in the *Evening Post:* "He [the speaker] referred to Cole's picture, hanging before him, as embodying the *chief requirement of art, namely, shadows.*" We will not pursue this ungracious portion of our subject further. Enough has been said to indicate the disadvantage of American art in lacking a discriminating public, and in the present habit of senseless praise; the poorer the art, the more words used to inflate public opinion relative to it.

Before the establishment of the *Round Table* of New York, there was scarcely a newspaper or journal in America sufficiently independent to admit a free discussion of artists and art. An article calculated to provoke discussion was tabooed for fear of wounding the sensibilities or harming the interests of someone. Few writers ventured to assert the cause of art itself because of the artists or their friends. This false system has fostered a deceitful ambition in numbers who might usefully fill other positions; so that we are inundated with bad, mechanical work, exulted over by the press at large as proof of American genius, when in reality it is so much sad evidence of pretense and folly. . . .

In viewing art new to him, one should not abandon himself to first impressions without investigating their soundness. If he does so too hastily, he often finds upon further experience that his wisdom was foolishness. Art may seem obscure or unintelligible, and the fault lie not in it but in us. We can comprehend no work until we have raised ourselves to the level of the author's meaning and feeling. All partial or one-sided comprehension is a mutual loss. Yet the best beginning of any intercourse is frank expression; for the basis of misconception being exposed, an understanding is more than half accomplished.

We sympathize with the visitor who said before us of some early Italian paintings, "I should as soon think of enjoying bad health or bruises as them," because it needs a few hints only entirely to change the point of view. There is, indeed, a wide gulf between the extremes of cultivation and sympathy and stolid apathy or ignorance. Each can be sincere and genuine. The visitor who exclaimed on seeing for the first time gold-background pictures, as he passed from one room into another, "More of these d — d ridiculous Chinese paintings!" was as much a representative of one class of critics among us — such an exclamation would not have occurred in Europe out of England — as the person whom we saw seated, moved to tears, before one of the very works thus profanely condemned was a representative of another.

The rough, uncultivated class is a more hopeful one to elevate to higher perceptions in art than that which looks upon the work of the hands that designed the Spina Church at Pisa, adorned the Cathedral of Orvieto, or wrote Bible stories in fresco at Assisi, covering the walls of its Duomo with spiritual allegory, as but the scrawls of children in comparison with the portfolio of the modern drawing master. The latter class seeks results not sought by the old master. It overlooks the fact that the men whose works it superciliously condemns have received for centuries the unanimous suffrage of the cultivated judges of all nations. There is much technical failure in their work. But it often serves to make more conspicuous their spiritual feeling and depth of earnestness. Chaucer and Shakespeare do not spell as we do; but do these differences of form between the literature of our ancestors and our own prove theirs to be the scrawls and ideas of children? Why should it be held different with art? Giotto was worthy in all respects to be the friend of Dante, and Martini of Petrarch; so the poets themselves tell us. Painting and poetry are but different phases of speech. It becomes us to throw off all conceit of actual superiority in intellect over our predecessors, and, before judging them, to inquire in what circumstances they differed from us, and whether what we do is as well done, and from as exalted inspiration, as what they did. . . .

We are to enjoy both the material and spiritual aspects of art, but each at its relative value. It is an error to suppose there can be no attractiveness in painting without perfect design. Supernal beings can only be suggested by art, just as they are to our imagination. That artist is most successful in this who best impresses the spectator with the *idea* of a spiritual being, avoiding all intrusion of technical artifice or display of anatomical dexterity. . . .

To return from particular to general aspects of the question. Our haste to be rich extends itself in the direction of premature effort and ambition. There is too eager desire of immediate realization. We declare ourselves to be men before attaining the full experience and knowledge of childhood. Premature greatness and newspaper-fed reputations thus become the national foible. It is not manual labor that is shirked but intellectual self-discipline — the patient reflection and slow mental growth, modestly inquiring of the past and studying deeply and earnestly the signs of the present in order to build up a secure future, as have done all great masters, not in the littleness of Dutch broom painting but with the devout and steady inspiration which led an Angelo and a Turner to take no heed of time in their struggle for lasting success. We think we have not leisure to allow the feeling for art its legitimate rights, and so crowd it aside, or talk business to it.

It is an affair of idle moments, a phase of fashion, or the curiosity of a traveler who brings the trick of bargaining into his new-born love of beauty, and fails to appreciate an object of art except as it is cheap or dear, a pretty something to complete the furniture of a house, on a par with upholstery as ornament, to be shut up, like dress coats and best chambers, for occasional use — an article to be ashamed of for its cost, yet to be proud of, in being able to own, a necessity of gentility, a presumptive evidence of cultivation or refinement, a competitive display of art riches — in fact, anything but *itself* — such is the loose, fluctuating, mercenary, and vain sentiment too many dignify as the love of art, but which, in sober truth, is a selfish vanity of possession.

These are some of the general disadvantages art has intrinsically to contend with in America. On the other hand, what it lacks of inspiration from the past is compensated for in the bright horizon of the future.

First, it has freedom of development, and a growing national knowledge, refinement, and taste to stimulate it and strengthen the common instinct of beauty which never wholly deserts human nature even in the most untoward conditions. It has, also, a few earnest hearts to cherish its feeling and promote its spread, with the enthusiasm of sincerity and conviction of its importance to moral welfare and complete education.

Second, it is not overborne by the weight of a glorious past, disheartening the weak of the present, and rendering many, even of the strong, servile, and mind-ridden. True, it has not the compensating virtue of lofty example and noble standard; but the creative faculty is freer and more ready to shape itself to the spirit of its age. Especially is our country free from those weighty intellectual authorities and conventional conditions which powerfully tend to hedge in the student to prescribed paths, undermine his originality, and warp his native individualism.

Third, art is in no sense a monopoly of government, religion, or social caste. It is not even under permanent bondage to fashion. It rather leads or misleads it than is led by it. For its sustenance it appeals directly to the people. Borne along on the vast ocean of democracy, art being a vital principle of life, it will eventually spread everywhere and promote the happiness of all.

Fourth, it possesses a fresh, vigorous, broad continent for its field: in the natural world, grand, wild, and inspiriting; in man, enterprising, energetic, and ambitious, hesitating at no difficulties, outspoken, hardy of limb, and quick of action; thought that acknowledges no limits; mind that dares to solve all questions affecting humanity to their remotest consequences, daring, doubting, believing, and hoping, giving birth to new ideas which are ever passing on to new forms.

But the favorable conditions named are more negative than positive in character. Indeed, in this respect the art of America is on the same footing as the remaining branches of her civilization. Their specific advantages of growth over the Old World are simply greater latitude of choice and few obstacles to overcome in the way of timeworn ideas and effete institutions. In one word, art is free here; as free to surpass all previous art as it is free to remain, if it so inclines, low and common. But if America elects to develop her art wholly out of herself, without reference to the accumulated experience of older civilizations, she will make a mistake and protract her improvement.

There is a set of men among us who talk loftily of the independent, indigenous growth of American art; of its freedom of obligation to the rest of the world; of its inborn capacity to originate, invent, create, and make anew; of the spoiling of those minds whose instincts prompt them to study art where it is best understood and most worthily followed. Perhaps so! Nevertheless, it would be a great waste of time to adopt such a system, and possibly it might fail. This sort of art-know-nothingism is as impracticable and as contrary to our national life as its foolish political brother which perished stillborn.

We have not time to invent and study everything anew. The fast-flying 19th century would laugh us to scorn should we attempt it. No one dreams of it in science, ethics, or physics. Why then propose it in art? We are a composite people. Our knowledge is eclectic. The progress we make is due rather to our free choice and action than to any innate superiority of mind over other nations. We buy, borrow, adopt, and adapt. With a seven-league boot on each leg, our pace is too rapid for profound study and creative thought. For some time to come, Europe must do for us all that we are in too much of a hurry to do for ourselves. It remains, then, for us to be as eclectic in our art as in the rest of our civilization. To get artistic riches by virtue of assimilated examples, knowledge, and ideas, drawn from all sources, and made national and homogeneous by a solidarity of our own, is our right pathway to consummate art.

No invidious nationalism should enter into art competition or criticism. The true and beautiful cannot be permanently monopolized by race, class, or sect. God has left them as free and universal as the air we breathe. We should, therefore, copy His liberality and invite art to our shores, generously providing for it without other motive than its merits. From whatever source it may come — Greek, Italian, French, English, or German, nay, Chinese, Hindu, and African — welcome it and make it our own. Let every public work, as are our institutions, be free to the genius of all men. Let us even compete with other nations in inviting to our shores the best art of the world.

As soon as it reaches our territory, it becomes part of our flesh and blood. Whither the greatest attraction tends, thither will genius go and make its home. Titian was not a Venetian by birth, but his name now stands for the highest excellence of that school, as Raphael does for that of Rome and Leonardo for the Milanese. In adopting genius, a country profits not the artist so much as itself. Both are thereby honored.

Foreign governments set a wise example in throwing open the designs for their public edifices to the artistic competition of the world. Least of all should America be behind in this sound policy, for no country stands in sorer need of artistic aid.

118.

FRANK H. ALFRIEND: A Southern National Literature

Most literary critics in the South prior to the Civil War complained about the lack of Southern literary output. As an editorial in the New Orleans Delta *put it in 1861, "The development of the South up to this time has been almost purely economical and political. Her statesmanship has been almost entirely unsupported by literature. Certainly such literature as she was able to claim for her own . . . was woefully inadequate to cope with the literature arrayed against her." The war, however, brought about considerable development of Southern literature. Poets like Henry Timrod and Paul Hayne wrote distinguished verse. In May 1864 Frank H. Alfriend, editor of the* Southern Literary Messenger, *surveyed the literary scene with greater optimism. Portions of his editorial follow.*

Source: *Southern Literary Messenger,* May 1864, pp. 313-317.

LET US CONSIDER BRIEFLY the *status* of literature in the South, supposing that it will not materially vary before the advent of peace, and in view of the probably early termination of the war.

In the opinion of the world at large, we should be guilty of not a little arrogance in making any pretension to a national literature, notwithstanding the evidence of intellectual activity which the war has evoked and the number of publications which it has called into being. That would be an exceedingly superficial view of the matter which could suppose the mere temporary efflorescence of the popular mind, a certain indication of well-grounded seed promising a permanent and luxuriant growth of healthful and enduring fruits. Nor will the achievement of our independence alone constitute a great millennium of literary regeneration. Just as in the establishment of our political and commercial interests upon a wise and safe basis, we shall need a careful circumspection, we shall have still greater occasion to employ all our energies and all our sagacity in the embarkation of the delicate interests of literature upon the uncertain tide of the future.

Having no history except the tragic present, of whose scenes and events we are the interested spectators and therefore disqualified by our passions and prejudices for impartial judgment, a long time will elapse before we have our Humes, Robertsons,

Guizots, and Gibbons to trace our national progress; the inspiration will not be wanting to create poets. Indeed, in Hope, Thompson, Timrod, Hayne, and others, we have them already; but centuries perhaps will elapse before we can distinguish between our "Schools" of the "Transition" and the "Lake," between our Chaucers and Spensers, Miltons and Cowpers, Burns', Byrons, and Wordsworths. Having virtually no history and, *par consequence*, comparatively few of those great landmarks of thought and reflection in the shape of grand events teaching the significance of historic order in the majestic march of centuries, we shall necessarily find the earlier exhibitions of Southern genius imitative of others rather than creative of a type of our own.

We do not ignore the national individuality of the South, which is quite as palpable and impressive in its features as those of any other mold of nationality. But beyond the expression of the more distinctly pronounced features of this national individuality, for some time to come, our most marked successes in literature will constitute simply approximations to the numerous models before us. The selection of these models of style for themselves and of thought for their readers will constitute one of the most important and delicate duties of Southern writers and journalists. It is to be hoped that no occasion exists for admonition of the propriety of avoiding imitation of Yankee composition, while in the various departments of English literature we shall look for the safest and most attractive examples.

The literary men of the South will receive a salutary lesson, both for themselves and for those whom they wish to be their readers, when they shall appreciate the necessity of avoiding models of a too exclusive or elevated caste. If we wish the people to read, we must make our offerings suitable to their capacity and taste. That capacity and taste can be educated and developed, but not suddenly or by violent remedies. The popular taste can be elevated gradually and even rapidly if it shall receive wholesome food agreeably administered. The people will inexorably demand of those who claim their support information and discussion of those things which concern their personal and national interests, and are agreeable to their individual tastes and fancies. If Southern writers cannot furnish this, the people will inevitably, as heretofore, seek it from those who will with alacrity — Yankees and foreigners.

To thus meet the popular requirements, and at the same time exalt the popular taste, it is not necessary to write down to a level of ignorance and vulgarity, from which education and decency should ever shrink with disgust. The capacity to depict popular subjects in their true traits and colors, so that all classes of society may recognize their fidelity, and yet avoid offense to the refinements of cultivated taste, is the culmination of literary distinction as realized, for example, by Dickens, or Thackeray, or Fielding.

Like all people much given to talking, Southerners, as a people, are little given to reading. Our education, like that of an old Greek, is derived chiefly from conversation and verbal discussion; and though from this cause our opinions and perceptions are always ready and generally clever in subtlety, they are too often characterized by the sophistry of superficiality. We can never become profound in either thought or education until this superficial habit of education shall be supplied by some more durable form of instruction; indeed, not until we shall become more of a reading and less of a talking people, which latter result cannot be consummated until such reading is placed in the hands of the people as will arrest their interested attention.

The mass of men cannot be transformed in an instant into philosophers and savants; and until the dream of Utopia is realized, when all men shall occupy one common footing of blissful equality, some concession must be made to degrees of intellectual advancement as well as to degrees in cultivation of taste. Let our literary men remember this; otherwise those who embrace the profession of letters will do little more than save themselves from starvation while the people look to others for the entertainment which they cannot find at home.

There is nothing whatever in the prospective condition of the Confederacy, either political, commercial, or social, which forbids the sanguine expectation of a permanent advancement of the literary profession. All the theories which can be urged, such as the incompatibility of the predominance of agricultural interests and an advanced state of letters, the indifference of the Southern mind to its literary interests, and the numerous other suggestions of insuperable obstacles to the growth of literature, should be but so many additional incentives to exertion with those who have the matter in hand.

119.

.

ALEXANDER H. STEPHENS: Civil Rights in the Confederacy

The conditions of war in the Confederacy soon led to a centralization of power in the hands of Jefferson Davis. Treasonable activity in parts of the country induced Davis to ask for the power to suspend the writ of habeas corpus, which the Confederate Congress granted him in 1862 for a limited period and again in 1864. Alexander Stephens, the Confederate vice-president and a strict constitutionalist, bitterly opposed Davis' expanded authority. From 1862 Stephens was, in fact, the leader of the opposition to the Davis administration. Throughout 1863 he exiled himself in Georgia, warning the people against the drift toward dictatorship. The Georgia legislature invited him to present his views on the affairs of state. An excerpt from his speech of March 16, 1864, follows.

Source: *Richmond Whig*, April 14, 1864.

I COME, NOW, TO THE LAST of these acts of Congress — the suspension of the writ of habeas corpus in certain cases. This is the most exciting, as it is by far the most important question before you. Upon this depends the question, whether the courts shall be permitted to decide upon the constitutionality of the late conscript act, should you submit that question to their decision; and upon it also depends other great essential rights enjoyed by us as freemen. This act, upon its face, confers upon the president, the secretary of war, and the general commanding in the Trans-Mississippi Department (the two latter acting under the control and authority of the president) the power to arrest and imprison any person who may be simply charged with certain acts, not all of them even crimes under any law. And this is to be done without any oath or affirmation alleging probable cause as to the guilt of the party. This is attempted to be done under that clause of the constitution which authorizes Congress to suspend the privilege of the writ of habeas corpus in certain cases.

In my judgment this is not only unwise, impolitic, and unconstitutional but exceedingly dangerous to public liberty. Its unconstitutionality does not rest upon the idea that Congress has not the power to suspend the privilege of this writ, nor upon the idea that the power to suspend it is an implied one, or that clearly implied powers are weaker, as a class, and subordinate to others positively and directly delegated.

I do not understand the executive of this state to put his argument against this act upon any such grounds. He simply states a fact, as it most clearly is, that the power to suspend at all is an implied power. There is no positive, direct power delegated to do it. The power, however, is clear, and clear only by implication. The language of the constitution, that "the privilege of the writ of habeas corpus shall not be suspended, unless when, in cases of rebellion or invasion, the public safety may require it," clearly expresses the intention that the power may be exercised in the cases stated; but it does so by implication only, just as if a mother should say to her daughter, "You shall not go unless you ride." Here the permission and authority to go is clearly given, though by inference, and implication only. It is not positively and directly given.

This, and this only, I understand the governor to mean when he speaks of the power being an implied one. He raises no question as to the existence of the power, or its validity when rightfully exercised, but he maintains, as I do, that its exercise must be controlled by all other restrictions in the constitution bearing upon its exercise. Two of these are to be found in the words accompanying the delegation. It can never be exercised except in rebellion or invasion.

Other restrictions are to be found in other parts of the constitution — in the amendments to the constitution adopted after the ratification of the words as above quoted. These amendments were made, as is expressly declared in the preamble to them, to add "further declaratory and restrictive clauses," to prevent misconstruction or abuse of the powers previously delegated. To understand all the restrictions, therefore, thrown around the exercise of this power in the constitution, these additional "restrictive clauses" must be read in conjunction with the original grant, whether that was made positively and directly, or by implication only. . . .

The attempted exercise of the power to suspend the privilege of the writ of habeas corpus in this act is in utter disregard, in the very face and teeth of these restrictions, as much so as a like attempt in time of profound peace would be in disregard of the restrictions to cases of rebellion and invasion, as the constitution was originally adopted.

It attempts to provide for depriving persons of "liberty without the process of law." It attempts to annul and set at naught the great constitutional "right" of the people to be secure in their persons against "unreasonable seizures." It attempts to destroy and annihilate the bulwark of personal liberty, secured in our great chart to the humblest as well as the highest, that "no warrants shall issue but upon probable cause, supported by oath or affirmation," and "particularly describing the person to be seized." Nay, more, it attempts to change and transform the distribution of powers in our system of government. It attempts to deprive the judiciary department of its appropriate and legitimate functions, and to confer them upon the president, the secretary of war, and the general commanding the Trans-Mississippi Department, or rather to confer them entirely upon the president, for those subordinates named in the act hold their places at his will, and in arrests under this act are to be governed by his orders. . . .

This act, therefore, is unconstitutional,

not because Congress has not power to suspend the privilege of the writ of habeas corpus but because they have no power to do the thing aimed at in this attempted exercise of it. Congress can suspend the privilege of the writ — the power is clear and unquestioned — neither is the power, as it stands, objectionable. Georgia, in the convention, voted against the clause conferring it in the constitution as originally adopted — that, perhaps, was a wise and prudent vote. But, with the restrictions subsequently adopted, there can be no well-grounded objection to it. It is, under existing restrictions, a wise power. In time of war, in cases of rebellion or invasion, it may often be necessary to exercise it — the public safety may require it. I am not prepared to say that the public safety may not require it now.

I am not informed of the reasons which induced the President to ask the suspension of the privilege of the writ at this time, or Congress to undertake its suspension as provided in this act. I, however, know of no reason that required it and have heard of none. But in the exercise of an undisputed power, they have attempted to do just what cannot be done — to authorize illegal and unconstitutional arrests. There can be no suspension allowing, or with a view to permit and authorize, the seizure of persons without warrant issued by a judicial officer upon probable cause, supported by oath or affirmation — the whole constitution must be read together, and so read and construed as that every part and clause shall stand and have its proper effect under the restrictions of other clauses. . . .

A few thoughts more upon the subject in another view. These relate to the object and workings of the act, if it be sustained and carried out. You have been told that it affects none but the disloyal; none but traitors, or those who are no better than traitors, spies, bridge burners and the like, and you have been appealed to and asked if such are entitled to your sympathies. I af-

firm, and shall maintain before the world, that this act affects and may wrongfully oppress as loyal and as good citizens, and as true to our cause, as ever trod the soil or breathed the air of the South. This I shall make so plain to you that no man will ever venture to gainsay or deny it.

This long list of offenses set forth in such array in the thirteen specifications are, as I view them, but rubbish and verbiage, which tend to cover and hide what in its workings will be found to be the whole gist of the act. Whether such was the real object and intention of its framers and advocates, I know not. Against their motives or patriotism I have nothing to say. I take the act as I find it. The whole gist of it lies, so far as appears upon its face, covered up in the fifth specification, near the middle of the act — "and attempts to avoid military service."

Here is a plain, indisputable attempt to deny to every citizen in this broad land the right, if ordered into service, to have the question whether he is liable to military duty under the laws tried and adjudicated by the courts. Whether this was the real object and intention of those who voted for the bill, I know not, but such would be its undeniable effect if sustained and enforced. . . .

Tell me not to put confidence in the president! That he will never abuse the power attempted to be lodged in his hands! The abuses may not be by the president. He will not execute the military orders that will be given. This will necessarily devolve upon subordinates, scattered all over the country, from the Potomac to the Rio Grande. He would have to possess two superhuman attributes to prevent abuses — omniscience and omnipresence. . . .

You have also seen that there is and can be no necessity for the passage of such an act, even if it were constitutional, in the case of spies, traitors, or conspirators; for, if there be a traitor in the Confederacy — if such a monster exist — if any well-grounded suspicion is entertained that any such exists, why not have him legally arrested by judicial warrant, upon oath or affirmation, setting forth probable cause, and then he can be held under a constitutional suspension of the privileges of the writ — he can be tried and, if found guilty, punished. What more can the public safety by possibility require? Why dispense with the oath? Why dispense with judicial warrants? Why put it in the power of any man on earth to order the arrest of another on a simple charge to which nobody will swear?

Who is safe under such a law? Who knows when he goes forth when or whether he shall ever return? The president, according to the act, is to have power to arrest and imprison whomever he pleases upon a bare charge made, perhaps by an enemy, of disloyalty — the party making the charge not being required to swear it! Who, I repeat, is safe, or would be, under such a law? What were the real objects of the act, in these clauses, as to treason, disloyalty, and the others, I do not know. To me it seems to be unreasonable to suppose that it was to reach real traitors and persons guilty of the offenses stated; for that object could have been easily accomplished without any such extraordinary power. . . . I have heard that one object was to control certain elections and expected assemblages in North Carolina, to put a muzzle upon certain presses and a bit in the mouth of certain speakers in that state. If this be so, I regard it the more dangerous to public liberty. . . .

One other view only that relates to the particularly dangerous tendency of this act in the present state of the country and the policy indicated by Congress — conscription has been extended to embrace all between seventeen and fifty years of age. It cannot be possible that the intention and object of that measure was really to call and keep in the field all between these ages. The folly and ruinous consequences of such a policy are too apparent. Details are to be made, and must be made, to a large extent. The effect and the object of this measure, therefore, was not to raise armies and procure soldiers but to put all the population of the country between those ages under military law. Whatever the object was, the effect is to put much the larger portion of the labor of the country, both white and slave, under the complete control of the president.

Under this system almost all the useful and necessary occupations of life will be completely under the control of one man. No one between the ages of seventeen and fifty can tan your leather, make your shoes, grind your grain, shoe your horse, lay your plow, make your wagon, repair your harness, superintend your farm, procure your salt, or perform any other of the necessary vocations of life (except teachers, preachers, and physicians, and a very few others) without permission from the president. This is certainly an extraordinary and a dangerous power. . . . Could the whole country be more completely under the power and control of one man, except as to life and limb? Could dictatorial powers be more complete? . . .

In any and every view, therefore, I look upon this habeas corpus suspension act as unwise, impolitic, unconstitutional, and dangerous to public liberty.

But you have been asked, what can you do? Do? You can do much. If you believe the act to be unconstitutional, you can and ought so to declare your judgment to be. . . . Our government is composed of Executive, Legislative, and Judicial departments, under the constitution. He most truly and faithfully supports the government who supports and defends the constitution.

120.

Henry Clay Work: "Come Home, Father"

Between 1846 and 1855 thirteen states passed prohibition laws. Henry Clay Work, though best known as an Abolitionist songwriter, also wrote much in behalf of the temperance movement. His most famous temperance song is "Come Home, Father," written in 1864. For years it was sung in the play Ten Nights in a Barroom, *a popular temperance drama.*

Source: *Heart Songs,* Cleveland, 1909.

COME HOME, FATHER

Father, dear father, come home with me
    now!
The clock in the steeple strikes one.
You said you were coming right home
    from the shop,
As soon as your day's work was done.
Our fire has gone out, our house is all
    dark,
And mother's been watching since tea,
With poor brother Benny so sick in her
    arms,
And no one to help her but me.
Come home! come home! come home!
Please, father, dear father, come home.

    Chorus:
    Hear the sweet voice of the child
    Which the night winds repeat as they
      roam!
    Oh, who could resist this most plain-
      tive of prayers?
    "Please, father, dear father, come
      home!
    Come home! come home! come home!
    Please, father, dear father, come home."

Father, dear father, come home with me
    now!
The clock in the steeple strikes two.
The night has grown colder and Benny is
    worse,
But he has been calling for you.
Indeed he is worse, Ma says he will die,
Perhaps before morning shall dawn;
And this is the message she sent me to
    bring:
"Come quickly, or he will be gone."
Come home! come home! come home!
Please, father, dear father, come home.

Father, dear father, come home with me
    now!
The clock in the steeple strikes three.
The house is so lonely, the hours are so
    long,
For poor weeping mother and me.
Yes, we are alone, poor Benny is dead,
And gone with the angels of light;
And these were the very last words that
    he said:
"I want to kiss Papa good night."
Come home! come home! come home!
Please, father, dear father, come home.

121.

Frank Wilkeson: How Americans Die in Battle

While there is no lack of written accounts about the Civil War, few ordinary soldiers in the war wrote extensively of their own personal experiences. Frank Wilkeson was an exception. As a private and later an officer in the Union Army, he wrote a brutally honest account of his war experiences, which he later published in Recollections of a Private Soldier in the Army of the Potomac. *The excerpt reprinted here deals with events of the war in May 1864.*

Source: *Recollections of a Private Soldier in the Army of the Potomac,*
New York, 1887: "How Men Die in Battle."

ALMOST EVERY DEATH on the battlefield is different. And the manner of the death depends on the wound and on the man, whether he is cowardly or brave, whether his vitality is large or small, whether he is a man of active imagination or is dull of intellect, whether he is of nervous or lymphatic temperament. I instance deaths and wounds that I saw in Grant's last campaign.

On the second day of the Battle of the Wilderness, where I fought as an infantry soldier, I saw more men killed and wounded than I did before or after in the same time. I knew but few of the men in the regiment in whose ranks I stood; but I learned the Christian names of some of them.

The man who stood next to me on my right was called Will. He was cool, brave, and intelligent. In the morning, when Corps II was advancing and driving Hill's soldiers slowly back, I was flurried. He noticed it and steadied my nerves by saying, kindly: "Don't fire so fast. This fight will last all day. Don't hurry. Cover your man before you pull the trigger. Take it easy, my boy, take it easy, and your cartridges will last the longer." This man fought effectively. During the day I had learned to look up to this excellent soldier and lean on him.

Toward evening, as we were being slowly driven back to the Brock Road by Longstreet's men, we made a stand. I was behind a tree firing, with my rifle barrel resting on the stub of a limb. Will was standing by my side, but in the open. He, with a groan, doubled up and dropped on the ground at my feet. He looked up at me. His face was pale. He gasped for breath a few times, and then said faintly: "That ends me. I am shot through the bowels." I said: "Crawl to the rear. We are not far from the entrenchments along the Brock Road." I saw him sit up and indistinctly saw him reach for his rifle, which had fallen from his hands as he fell. Again I spoke to him, urging him to go to the rear. He looked at me and said impatiently: "I tell you that I am as good as dead. There is no use in fooling with me. I shall stay here." Then he pitched forward dead, shot again and through the head. We fell back before Longstreet's soldiers and left Will lying in a windrow of dead men.

When we got into the Brock Road entrenchments, a man a few files to my left dropped dead, shot just above the right eye. He did not groan, or sigh, or make the slightest physical movement, except that his chest heaved a few times. The life went out of his face instantly, leaving it without a particle of expression. It was plastic and, as the facial muscles contracted, it took many shapes. When this man's body became cold and his face hardened, it was horribly distorted, as though he had suffered intensely. Any person who had not seen him killed would have said that he had endured supreme agony before death released him. A few minutes after he fell, another man, a little farther to the left, fell with apparently a precisely similar wound. He was straightened out and lived for over an hour. He did not speak, simply lay on his back, and his broad chest rose and fell, slowly at first, and then faster and faster, and more and more feebly, until he was dead. And his face hardened, and it was almost terrifying in its painful distortion. I have seen dead soldiers' faces which were wreathed in smiles and heard their comrades say that they had died happy.

I do not believe that the face of a dead soldier, lying on a battlefield, ever truthfully indicates the mental or physical anguish, or peacefulness of mind, which he suffered or enjoyed before his death. The face is plastic after death, and as the facial muscles cool and contract, they draw the face into many shapes. Sometimes the dead smile, again they stare with glassy eyes, and lolling tongues, and dreadfully distorted visages at you. It goes for nothing. One death was as painless as the other.

After Longstreet's soldiers had driven Corps II into their entrenchments along the Brock Road, a battle-exhausted infantryman stood behind a large oak tree. His back rested against it. He was very tired and held his rifle loosely in his hand. The Confederates were directly in our front. This soldier was apparently in perfect safety. A solid shot from a Confederate gun struck the oak tree squarely about four feet from the ground; but it did not have sufficient force to tear through the tough wood. The soldier fell dead. There was not a scratch on him. He was killed by concussion.

While we were fighting savagely over these entrenchments, the woods in our front caught fire, and I saw many of our wounded burned to death. Must they not have suffered horribly? I am not at all sure of that. The smoke rolled heavily and slowly before the fire. It enveloped the wounded, and I think that by far the larger portion of the men who were roasted were suffocated before the flames curled round them. The spectacle was courage-sapping and pitiful, and it appealed strongly to the imagination of the spectators; but I do not believe that the wounded soldiers, who were being burned, suffered greatly, if they suffered at all.

Wounded soldiers, it mattered not how slight the wounds, generally hastened away from the battle lines. A wound entitled a man to go to the rear and to a hospital. Of course there were many exceptions to this rule, as there would necessarily be in battles where from 20,000 to 30,000 men were wounded. I frequently saw slightly wounded men who were marching with their colors. I personally saw but two men wounded who continued to fight.

During the first day's fighting in the Wilderness, I saw a youth of about twenty years skip and yell, stung by a bullet through the thigh. He turned to limp to the rear. After he had gone a few steps he stopped, then he kicked out his leg once or twice to see if it would work. Then he tore the clothing away from his leg so as to see the wound. He looked at it attentively for an instant, then kicked out his leg again, then turned and took his place in the ranks and resumed firing. There was considerable

Dead soldiers on the battlefield at Gettysburg at the end of the first day's fighting

disorder in the line, and the soldiers moved to and fro — now a few feet to the right, now a few feet to the left. One of these movements brought me directly behind this wounded soldier. I could see plainly from that position, and I pushed into the gaping line and began firing. In a minute or two the wounded soldier dropped his rifle and, clasping his left arm, exclaimed: "I am hit again!" He sat down behind the battle ranks and tore off the sleeve of his shirt. The wound was very slight — not much more than skin-deep. He tied his handkerchief around it, picked up his rifle, and took position alongside of me. I said: "You are fighting in bad luck today. You had better get away from here." He turned his head to answer me. His head jerked, he staggered, then fell, then regained his feet. A tiny fountain of blood and teeth and bone and bits of tongue burst out of his mouth. He had been shot through the jaws; the lower one was broken and hung down. I looked directly into his open mouth, which was ragged and bloody and tongueless. He cast his rifle furiously on the ground and staggered off.

The next day, just before Longstreet's sol-

diers made their first charge on Corps II, I heard the peculiar cry a stricken man utters as the bullet tears through his flesh. I turned my head, as I loaded my rifle, to see who was hit. I saw a bearded Irishman pull up his shirt. He had been wounded in the left side just below the floating ribs. His face was gray with fear. The wound looked as though it were mortal. He looked at it for an instant, then poked it gently with his index finger. He flushed redly and smiled with satisfaction. He tucked his shirt into his trousers and was fighting in the ranks again before I had capped my rifle. The ball had cut a groove in his skin only. The play of this Irishman's face was so expressive, his emotions changed so quickly, that I could not keep from laughing.

Near Spotsylvania I saw, as my battery was moving into action, a group of wounded men lying in the shade cast by some large oak trees. All of these men's faces were gray. They silently looked at us as we marched past them. One wounded man, a blond giant of about forty years, was smoking a short briarwood pipe. He had a firm grip on the pipestem. I asked him what he was doing. "Having my last smoke, young fellow," he replied. His dauntless blue eyes met mine, and he bravely tried to smile. I saw that he was dying fast. Another of these wounded men was trying to read a letter. He was too weak to hold it, or maybe his sight was clouded. He thrust it unread into the breast pocket of his blouse and lay back with a moan.

This group of wounded men numbered fifteen or twenty. At the time, I thought that all of them were fatally wounded and that there was no use in the surgeons wasting time on them, when men who could be saved were clamoring for their skillful attention. None of these soldiers cried aloud, none called on wife, or mother, or father. They lay on the ground, palefaced, and with set jaws, waiting for their end. They moaned and groaned as they suffered, but none of them flunked. When my battery returned from the front, five or six hours afterward, almost all of these men were dead. Long before the campaign was over I concluded that dying soldiers seldom called on those who were dearest to them, seldom conjured their Northern or Southern homes, until they became delirious. Then, when their minds wandered and fluttered at the approach of freedom, they babbled of their homes. Some were boys again and were fishing in Northern trout streams. Some were generals leading their men to victory. Some were with their wives and children. Some wandered over their family's homestead; but all, with rare exceptions, were delirious.

At the North Anna River, my battery being in action, an infantry soldier, one of our supports, who was lying face downward close behind the gun I served on, and in a place where he thought he was safe, was struck on the thighs by a large jagged piece of a shell. The wound made by this fragment of iron was as horrible as any I saw in the army. The flesh of both thighs was torn off, exposing the bones. The soldier bled to death in a few minutes, and before he died he conjured his Northern home, and murmured of his wife and children.

In the same battle, but on the south side of the river, a man who carried a rifle was passing between the guns and caissons of the battery. A solid shot, intended for us, struck him on the side. His entire bowels were torn out and slung in ribbons and shreds on the ground. He fell dead, but his arms and legs jerked convulsively a few times. It was a sickening spectacle. During this battle I saw a Union picket knocked down, probably by a rifle ball striking his head and glancing from it. He lay as though dead. Presently, he struggled to his feet, and, with blood streaming from his head, he staggered aimlessly round and round in a circle, as sheep afflicted with grubs in the brain do. Instantly, the Confederate sharpshooters opened fire on him and speedily killed him as he circled.

Wounded soldiers almost always tore their clothing away from their wounds so as to see them and to judge of their character. Many of them would smile and their faces would brighten as they realized that they were not hard hit and that they could go home for a few months. Others would give a quick glance at their wounds and then shrink back as from a blow, and turn pale as they realized the truth that they were mortally wounded. The enlisted men were exceedingly accurate judges of the probable result which would ensue from any wound they saw. They had seen hundreds of soldiers wounded, and they had noticed that certain wounds always resulted fatally. They knew when they were fatally wounded, and after the shock of discovery had passed, they generally braced themselves and died in a manly manner. It was seldom that an American or Irish volunteer flunked in the presence of death.

122.

Walter Kittredge: "Tenting on the Old Camp Ground"

This popular Civil War song was written by Walter Kittredge in 1862, shortly after he entered the Union Army; but Kittredge could not get it published for two years, and so it did not start to be sung until 1864. Then it was sung by everybody — by soldiers on both sides, and by the folks at home, with the result that the sheet music sale ran into many thousands.

Source: *Famous Songs and Those Who Made Them*, Helen K. Johnson and
   Frederic Dean, eds., New York, 1895, pp. 32-34.

TENTING ON THE OLD CAMP GROUND

We're tenting tonight on the old camp
   ground,
Give us a song to cheer
Our weary hearts, a song of home,
And friends we love so dear.

Chorus:
Many are the hearts that are weary
   tonight,
Wishing for the war to cease;
Many are the hearts looking for the
   right,
To see the dawn of peace.
Tenting tonight, tenting tonight,
Tenting on the old camp ground.

We've been tenting tonight on the old camp
   ground,
Thinking of days gone by,
Of the loved ones at home that gave us the
   hand,
And the tear that said, "Good-bye!"

We are tired of war on the old camp
   ground,
Many are dead and gone,
Of the brave and true who've left their
   homes,
Others been wounded long.

We've been fighting today on the old camp
   ground,
Many are lying near;
Some are dead and some are dying,
Many are in tears.

Last chorus:
Many are the hearts that are weary
   tonight
Wishing for the war to cease;
Many are the hearts looking for the
   right,
To see the dawn of peace.
Dying tonight, dying tonight,
Dying on the old camp ground.

President Lincoln and Gen. John A. McClernand at Antietam, October 1862

WARTIME POLITICS

Lincoln was President of the United States as well as commander in chief of the armed forces; he had to remember the voters as well as the conduct of the war. Under constant fire from the regular Democrats, the "peace Democrats," the Copperheads, and the Radical Republicans as well as the Confederate propagandists, he had to stay in power. This meant appearing at battlefields, haggling with politically powerful generals and legislators, cajoling governors, keeping uneasy peace with border states, and maintaining diplomatic negotiations with foreign countries to stave off intervention. Through it all he had to face the inevitable problem of what to do about slavery.

Abolitionists kept demanding immediate emancipation, but many Northerners who were willing to fight for preservation of the Union cared nothing about the slavery issue.

The President finally decided that a carefully circumscribed emancipation of slaves would be expedient, but he needed a military victory to remove any appearance of desperation. Antietam gave him this opportunity, and he drafted a preliminary Emancipation Proclamation to take effect Jan. 1, 1863, in only those states actively engaged in war against the Union. Emancipation was put into effect as Northern troops occupied Southern territory.

(Above) Gen. Winfield Scott, commanding general of the U.S. Army at the start of the war; (below) Gen. George McClellan, commander of the Union Army until April 1862

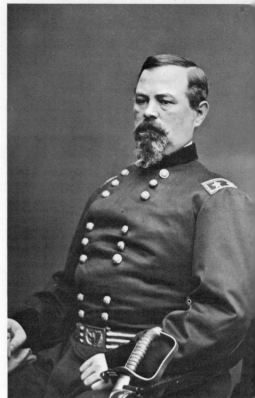

Maj. Gen. Irwin McDowell, first commander of the Army of the Potomac

One of the severest problems Lincoln had to face in the early days of the war was the incompetence or extreme caution of his generals in the Eastern theater. While Jefferson Davis, himself a military man, had the cream of West Point at his disposal, Lincoln's generals were generally long on talk, short on action. Unwarranted delays and costly mistakes dogged the Union armies. Lincoln's first secretary of war, Simon Cameron, allowed intrigue to dominate his department, and little effective work was done until January 1862, when Edwin Stanton replaced him. Lincoln, often under pressure, regularly replaced his commanders when they failed to take the initiative, but Union leadership continued to be ineffective until General Meade took command in the East in 1863.

(Above) "Great News: First citizen: 'The Army of the Potomac has crossed the Rappahannock again.' Second citizen: 'Which way?' "

(Above) Gen. Henry Halleck, whose success in the Western campaign led to his being given the command of the Union Army in July 1862; (below left) Maj. Gen. A. E. Burnside with two staff members near Richmond, Va. He held several commands without success; (below right) "Lincoln's Midnight Think" by C. W. Reed

(Above) Grand review of Sherman's Army in Washington, D.C., May 1865

From Lincoln's inauguration in 1861 to the final Grand Review of the Army in 1865, Washington was an armed camp. At the outbreak of war, the unfinished Capitol was taken over by the Army as a barracks and storehouse. The city was ringed with forts and encampments against the constant danger of invasion. Though many major battles were fought near Washington, the only direct threat was the raid by Gen. Jubal Early in July of 1864 which was finally turned back at Fort Stevens, within sight of the Capitol.

(Left) Civil War sergeant; (below) view of Washington at the end of the war, 1865

(Left) Entrenchments of the Massachusetts Battery along the B&O Railroad in Maryland; (center) guard on Chain Bridge over the Potomac River outside Washington; (bottom) Camp Northumberland, base for the 96th Pennsylvania Infantry outside Washington

Hannibal Hamlin, Lincoln's first vice-president

William Seward, secretary of state

The administration was in poor condition to conduct a war in 1861. Few officers, even in the Cabinet, respected Lincoln; Seward was considered by many, including himself, to be the leader of the Republican Party and of the government. The split in the country and in Congress was reflected in the Cabinet — some welcomed secession; some, notably Seward, sought for conciliation and compromise; others, the radicals, demanded punitive action. Lincoln's problem was to maintain a middle course without weakness; to gain control of policy without resort to radical means.

(Left) Lincoln with his son, Tad; (below left) Salmon P. Chase, secretary of the treasury; (below right) Secretary of War Edwin Stanton

Office-seekers at Washington during the inauguration, 1861

(Left) Lincoln receives an elkhorn chair from California hunter Seth Kinman, 1861; sketch by Waud; (below) Lincoln, hatless, is seated left of center in this photo of the dedication ceremonies for a cemetery at Gettysburg Battlefield, November 1863

"Emancipation Proclamation," painted by A. A. Lamb about 1865

Emancipation was originally the aim only of the Abolitionists and Radical Republicans. Lincoln, determined to retain the loyal slave states and border areas, declared as his sole aim the preservation of the Union. Slaves liberated by Union advances were declared contraband and organized into labor divisions. The Confiscation Act of 1862 freed them and opened the way for the recruiting of Negroes into the army. Slavery was abolished in the District of Columbia in June of 1862 and general emancipation followed in January 1863.

(Left) Negro troops liberating slaves in North Carolina, 1864; (below) the 26th Infantry in formation; Negro enlistments began in 1863

A group of fugitive Negroes crossing the Rappahannock River in Virginia, 1862

A group of "contrabands" at Cumberland Landing, Va. in 1862; (below) Union troops in front of the "slave pen" in Alexandria, Virginia

Prison camp on "Belle Isle" with Richmond visible in the background

(Above) Jefferson Davis and Judah P. Benjamin, who served as attorney general, secretary of war, and secretary of state in the Confederate government; (below) Confederate White House

The Confederate political climate, though not formally divided by parties and organized factions, was nonetheless far from unified. Behind the seemingly solid front of anti-Northern feeling and defensive unity, dissention was constant. Vice-president Stephens and several state governors refused to comply with orders abridging personal liberties and state sovereignty. Martial law was imposed by military commanders without authorization, and often remained in effect even when revoked by Davis.

Cartoons by Adalbert Volck: (Top) Northern officials worship the Negro altar made up of numerous sins, all grounded on Puritanism; (right) devil holds Lincoln's inkpot as he signs Emancipation Proclamation; (below) "Free Negroes" shows a scene of murder and debauchery in which an Abolitionist is handing a beggar a pamphlet

(Above) James Murray Mason and John Slidell, Confederate diplomats to England and France; (right) cartoon showing England's anger at the Union seizure of the "Trent" carrying the diplomats to Europe in 1861

Probably the South's greatest error was to expect heavy financial and military aid from France and England. France contributed some money, but withheld recognition. England granted virtual recognition to the Confederacy, rattled a sword over the Trent affair, and built five ships for the South, two of which were undelivered. But their aid consisted mainly of diplomatic harassment of the Union — the threat of England to break diplomatic relations as a result of the seizure of Mason and Slidell was almost redundant.

(Below) Battle between the English blockade runner "Alabama" and the Union's "Kearsarge" in harbor of Cherbourg, France; painted by Manet

Blockade runner, "Old Dominion" docked at Bristol, England

(Above) "John Bull's Neutrality — the Guardian of Civilization in Full Play"; anti-British cartoon in "Harper's Weekly," 1862; (below) wreck of a blockade runner

THE CHICAGO PLATFORM AND CANDIDATE.

Currier and Ives lithograph satirizing McClellan's campaign platform, 1864

The election of 1864 was almost melodramatic. Secretary of Treasury Salmon Chase split with Lincoln and vied for Radical support; a failure as a general, Fremont sought the western Radical bloc's nomination. Both were lost in the maneuvers of an unexpectedly adept Lincoln, who was renominated by a National-Union Convention in Baltimore. The Democratic convention produced an amazing ticket — on a peace and defeat platform of Copperhead origin, it ran war hero Gen. George McClellan.

(Above) Torchlight procession for McClellan in New York; (left) "The Copperhead plan for subjugating the South"; (below) Clement Vallandigham (center) with leaders of the "Copperheads"

123.

John L. Ransom: Andersonville Diary

The largest Confederate military prison was at Andersonville, Georgia. Early in 1864, the first Northern soldiers were imprisoned there, in a log stockade covering sixteen and one-half acres. By summer, there were over 30,000 prisoners. Andersonville became notorious for its lack of adequate sanitation, water supply, medical care, and food. Nearly 13,000 prisoners died there; Northerners viewed it as a deliberate effort to murder the captives. Many prisoners wrote accounts of their sufferings, the most famous being the diary of John Ransom, excerpts from which are reprinted here. Andersonville was commanded by Captain Henry Wirz, who was tried, convicted, and executed as a war criminal in 1865.

Source: *Andersonville Diary, etc., etc.*, Auburn, N.Y., 1881, pp. 75-95.

July 3. Three hundred and fifty new men from West Virginia were turned into this summer resort this morning. They brought good news as to successful termination of the war, and they also caused war after coming among us. As usual, the raiders proceeded to rob them of their valuables, and a fight occurred in which hundreds were engaged. The cutthroats came out ahead. Complaints were made to Captain Wirtz [Henry Wirz] that this thing would be tolerated no longer; that these raiders must be put down, or the men would rise in their might and break away if assistance was not given with which to preserve order.

Wirtz flew around as if he had never thought of it before, issued an order to the effect that no more food would be given us until the leaders were arrested and taken outside for trial. The greatest possible excitement — hundreds that have before been neutral and noncommital are now joining a police force; captains are appointed to take charge of the squads, which have been furnished with clubs by Wirtz. As I write, this middle of the afternoon, the battle rages.

The police go right to raider headquarters, knock right and left, and make their arrests. Sometimes the police are whipped and have to retreat, but they rally their forces and again make a charge in which they are successful.

Can lay in our shade and see the trouble go on. Must be killing some by the shouting. The raiders fight for their very life and are only taken after being thoroughly whipped. The stockade is loaded with guards who are fearful of a break. I wish I could describe the scene today. A number killed. After each arrest a great cheering takes place.

Night. Thirty or forty have been taken outside of the worst characters in camp, and still the good work goes on. No food today and don't want any. A big strapping fellow called "Limber Jim" heads the police. Grand old Michael Hoare is at the front and goes for a raider as quick as he would a Rebel. Patrol the camp all the time and gradually quieting down. The orderly prisoners are feeling jolly.

July 4. The men taken outside yesterday

are under Rebel guard and will be punished. The men are thoroughly aroused, and now that the matter has been taken in hand, it will be followed up to the letter. Other arrests are being made today, and occasionally a big fight. Little Terry, whom they could not find yesterday, was today taken. Had been hiding in an old well, or hole in the ground. Fought like a little tiger, but had to go. "Limber Jim" is a brick and should be made a major general if he ever reaches our lines. Mike Hoare is right up in rank, and true blue. William B. Rowe also makes a good policeman, as does "Dad" Sanders. Battese says he "no time to fight, must wash." Jimmy Devers regrets that he cannot take a hand in, as he likes to fight, and especially with a club. The writer hereof does no fighting, being on the sick list. The excitement of looking on is most too much for me. Can hardly arrest the big graybacks crawling around.

Captain Moseby is one of the arrested ones. His right name is Collins and he has been in our hundred all the time since leaving Richmond. Has got a good long neck to stretch. Another man whom I have seen a good deal of, one Curtiss, is also arrested. I haven't mentioned poor little Bullock for months, seems to me. He was most dead when we first came to Andersonville, and is still alive and tottering around. Has lost his voice entirely and is nothing but a skeleton. Hardly enough of him for disease to get hold of. Would be one of the surprising things on record if he lives through it, and he seems no worse than months ago. It is said that a court will be formed of our own men to try the raiders. Anyway, so they are punished. All have killed men, and they themselves should be killed. When arrested, the police had hard work to prevent their being lynched. Police more thoroughly organizing all the time.

An extra amount of food this P.M., and police get extra rations, and three out of

our mess is doing pretty well, as they are all willing to divide. They tell us all the encounters they have, and much interesting talk. Mike has some queer experiences. Rebel flags at half-mast for some of their great men. Just heard that the trial of raiders will begin tomorrow.

July 5. Court is in session outside and raiders being tried by our own men. Wirtz has done one good thing, but it's a question whether he is entitled to any credit, as he had to be threatened with a break before he would assist us. Rations again today. I am quite bad off with my diseases, but still there are so many thousands so much worse off that I do not complain much, or try not to however.

July 6. Boiling hot, camp reeking with filth, and no sanitary privileges; men dying off over 140 per day. Stockade enlarged, taking in eight or ten more acres, giving us more room, and stumps to dig up for wood to cook with. Mike Hoare is in good health; not so Jimmy Devers. Jimmy has now been a prisoner over a year and, poor boy, will probably die soon. Have more mementos than I can carry, from those who have died, to be given to their friends at home. At least a dozen have given me letters, pictures, etc., to take North. Hope I shan't have to turn them over to someone else.

July 7. The court was gotten up by our own men and from our own men; judge, jury, counsel, etc. Had a fair trial and were even defended, but to no purpose. It is reported that six have been sentenced to be hung, while a good many others are condemned to lighter punishment, such as setting in the stocks, strung up by the thumbs, thumbscrews, head hanging, etc. The court has been severe, but just. Mike goes out tomorrow to take some part in the court proceedings.

The prison seems a different place altogether; still, dread disease is here and mowing down good and true men. Would seem to me that 300 or 400 died each day, though officially but 140 odd is told. About 27,000, I believe, are here now in all. No new ones for a few days. Rebel visitors, who look at us from a distance. It is said the stench keeps all away who have no business here and can keep away. Washing business good. Am negotiating for a pair of pants. Dislike fearfully to wear dead men's clothes and haven't to any great extent.

July 8. Oh, how hot, and oh, how miserable. The news that six have been sentenced to be hanged is true, and one of them is Moseby. The camp is thoroughly under control of the police now, and it is a heavenly boon. Of course, there is some stealing and robbery, but not as before. Swan, of our mess, is sick with scurvy. I am gradually swelling up and growing weaker. But a few more pages in my diary. Over 150 dying per day now, and 26,000 in camp. Guards shoot now very often. Boys, as guards, are the most cruel. It is said that if they kill a Yankee they are given a thirty-day furlough. Guess they need them as soldiers too much to allow of this. The swamp now is fearful, water perfectly reeking with prison offal and poison. Still men drink it and die. Rumors that the six will be hung inside. Bread today and it is so coarse as to do more hurt than good to a majority of the prisoners. The place still gets worse.

Tunneling is over with; no one engages in it now that I know of. The prison is a success as regards safety; no escape except by death, and very many take advantage of that way. A man who has preached to us (or tried to) is dead. Was a good man, I verily believe, and from Pennsylvania. It's almost impossible for me to get correct names to note down; the last-named man was called "the preacher," and I can find no other name for him. Our quartette of singers a few rods away is disbanded. One died, one nearly dead, one a policeman, and

the other cannot sing alone, and so where we used to hear and enjoy good music evenings, there is nothing to attract us from the groans of the dying.

Having formed a habit of going to sleep as soon as the air got cooled off and before fairly dark, I wake up at 2 or 3 o'clock and stay awake. I then take in all the horrors of the situation. Thousands are groaning, moaning, and crying, with no bustle of the daytime to drown it. Guards every half hour call out the time and post, and there is often a shot to make one shiver as if with the ague. Must arrange my sleeping hours to miss getting owly in the morning. Have taken to building air castles of late, on being exchanged. Getting loony, I guess, same as all the rest.

July 9. Battese brought me some onions, and if they ain't good, then no matter; also a sweet potato. One-half the men here would get well if they only had something in the vegetable line to eat, or acids. Scurvy is about the most loathsome disease, and when dropsy takes hold with the scurvy, it is terrible. I have both diseases but keep them in check, and it only grows worse slowly. My legs are swollen, but the cords are not contracted much, and I can still walk very well. Our mess all keep clean, in fact are obliged to or else turned adrift. We want none of the dirty sort in our mess. Sanders and Rowe enforce the rules, which is not much work, as all hands are composed of men who prefer to keep clean. I still do a little washing, but more particularly haircutting, which is easier work. You should see one of my haircuts. Nobby! Old prisoners have hair a foot long or more, and my business is to cut it off, which I do without regard to anything except get it off.

I should judge that there are 1,000 Rebel soldiers guarding us, and perhaps a few more, with the usual number of officers. A guard told me today that the Yanks were "gittin licked," and they didn't want us exchanged; just as soon as we should die here as not; a Yank asked him if he knew what exchange meant; said he knew what shootin' meant, and as he began to swing around his old shooting iron, we retreated in among the crowd. Heard that there were some new men belonging to my regiment in another part of the prison; have just returned from looking after them and am all tired out. Instead of belonging to the 9th Michigan Cavalry, they belong to the 9th Michigan Infantry. Had a good visit and quite cheered with their accounts of the war news.

Someone stole Battese's washboard and he is mad; is looking for it — may bust up the business. Think Hub Dakin will give me a board to make another one. Sanders owns the jacknife of this mess, and he don't like to lend it either; borrow it to carve on roots for pipes. Actually take solid comfort "building castles in the air," a thing I have never been addicted to before. Better than getting blue and worrying myself to death. After all, we may get out of this dod-rotted hole. Always an end of some sort to such things.

July 10. Have bought of a new prisoner quite a large (thick, I mean) blank book so as to continue my diary. Although it's a tedious and tiresome task, am determined to keep it up. Don't know of another man in prison who is doing likewise. Wish I had the gift of description that I might describe this place. Know that I am not good at such things, and have more particularly kept track of the mess which was the "Astor House Mess" on Belle Isle and is still called so here. Thought that Belle Isle was a very bad place, and used about the worst language I knew how to use in describing it, and so find myself at fault in depicting matters here as they are. At Belle Isle we had good water and plenty of it, and I believe it depends more upon water than food as regards health. We also had good pure air from up the James River. Here we have the very worst kind of water. Nothing can be worse or nastier than the stream drizzling its way through this camp. And for air to breathe, it is what arises from this foul place. On all four sides of us are high walls and tall trees, and there is apparently no wind or breeze to blow away the stench, and we are obliged to breathe and live in it. Dead bodies lay around all day in the broiling sun, by the dozen and even hundreds, and we must suffer and live in this atmosphere. It's too horrible for me to describe in fitting language.

There was once a very profane man driving a team of horses attached to a wagon in which there were forty to fifty bushels of potatoes. It was a big load and there was a long hill to go up. The very profane man got off the load of potatoes to lighten the weight, and started the team up the hill. It was hard work, but they finally reached the top and stopped to rest. The profane man looked behind him and saw that the end board of the wagon had slipped out just as he had started, and there the potatoes were, scattered all the way along up the hill. Did the man make the very air blue with profanity? No, he sat down on a log, feeling that he couldn't do the subject justice and so he remarked: "No! it's no use, I can't do it justice." While I have no reason or desire to swear, I certainly cannot do this prison justice. It's too stupendous an undertaking Only those who are here will ever know what Andersonville is.

July 11. This morning, lumber was brought into the prison by the Rebels, and near the gate a *gallows* erected for the purpose of executing the six condemned Yankees. At about 10 o'clock they were brought inside by Captain Wirtz and some guards, and delivered over to the police force. Captain Wirtz then said a few words about their having been tried by our own men and for us to do as we choose with them, that he washed his hands of the whole matter, or words to that effect. I could not catch the exact language, being some little distance away. I have learned by inquiry their names, which are as follows: John Sarsfield, 144th New York; William Collins, alias Moseby, Co. D, 88th Pennsylvania; Charles Curtiss, Battery A, 5th Rhode Island Artillery; Pat Delaney, Co. E, 83d Pennsylvania; A. Munn, U.S. Navy; and W. R. Rickson of the U.S. Navy.

After Wirtz made his speech he withdrew his guards, leaving the condemned at the mercy of 28,000 enraged prisoners, who had all been more or less wronged by these men. Their hands were tied behind them, and one by one they mounted the scaffold. Curtiss, who was last, a big stout fellow, managed to get his hands loose and broke away and ran through the crowd and down toward the swamp. It was yelled out that he had a knife in his hand, and so a path was made for him. He reached the swamp and plunged in, trying to get over on the other side, presumably among his friends. It being very warm he overexerted himself, and when in the middle or thereabouts, collapsed and could go no farther. The police started after him, waded in and helped him out. He pleaded for water and it was given him. Then led back to the scaffold and helped to mount up.

All were given a chance to talk. Munn, a good-looking fellow in Marine dress, said he came into the prison four months before, perfectly honest and as innocent of crime as any fellow in it. Starvation, with evil companions, had made him what he was. He spoke of his mother and sisters in New York, that he cared nothing as far as he himself was concerned, but the news that would be carried home to his people made him want to curse God he had ever been born. Delaney said he would rather be hung than live here as the most of them lived, on their allowance of rations. If al-

lowed to steal could get enough to eat, but as that was stopped had rather hang. Bid all good-bye. Said his name was not Delaney and that no one knew who he really was, therefore his friends would never know his fate, his Andersonville history dying with him. Curtiss said he didn't care a ——, only hurry up and not be talking about it all day; making too much fuss over a very small matter. William Collins, alias Moseby, said he was innocent of murder and ought not to be hung; he had stolen blankets and rations to preserve his own life, and begged the crowd not to see him hung as he had a wife and child at home, and for their sake to let him live.

The excited crowd began to be impatient for the "show" to commence as they termed it. Sarsfield made quite a speech; he had studied for a lawyer; at the outbreak of the rebellion he had enlisted and served three years in the army, been wounded in battle, furloughed home, wound healed up, promoted to first sergeant and also commissioned; his commission as a lieutenant had arrived but had not been mustered in when he was taken prisoner; began by stealing parts of rations, gradually becoming hardened as he became familiar with the crimes practised; evil associates had helped him to go downhill, and here he was. The other did not care to say anything. While the men were talking, were interrupted by all kinds of questions and charges made by the crowd, such as "don't lay it on too thick, you villain," "get ready to jump off," "cut it short," "you was the cause of so and so's death," "less talk and more hanging," etc., etc.

At about 11 o'clock, they were all blindfolded, hands and feet tied, told to get ready, nooses adjusted, and the plank knocked from under. Moseby's rope broke and he fell to the ground, with blood spurting from his ears, mouth, and nose. As they was lifting him back to the swinging-off place, he revived and begged for his life, but no use, was soon dangling with the rest, and died very hard. Munn died easily, as also did Delaney; all the rest died hard, and particularly Sarsfield, who drew his knees nearly to his chin and then straightened them out with a jerk, the veins in his neck swelling out as if they would burst. It was an awful sight to see, still a necessity. Moseby, although he said he had never killed anyone, and I don't believe he ever did deliberately kill a man, such as stabbing or pounding a victim to death, yet he has walked up to a poor sick prisoner on a cold night and robbed him of blanket, or perhaps his rations, and if necessary using all the force necessary to do it. These things were the same as life to the sick man, for he would invariably die. The result has been that many have died from his robbing propensities. It was right that he should hang, and he did hang most beautifully, and Andersonville is the better off for it. None of the rest denied that they had killed men, and probably some had murdered dozens. It has been a good lesson; there are still bad ones in camp, but we have the strong arm of the law to keep them in check.

All during the hanging scene the stockade was covered with Rebels, who were fearful a break would be made if the raiders should try and rescue them. Many citizens, too, were congregated on the outside in favorable positions for seeing. Artillery was pointed at us from all directions ready to blow us all into eternity in short order; Wirtz stood on a high platform in plain sight of the execution and says we are a hard crowd to kill our own men. After hanging for half an hour or so, the six bodies were taken down and carried outside. In noting down the speeches made by the condemned men, have used my own language; in substance it is the same as told by them. I occupied a near position to the hanging and saw it all from first to last, and

stood there until they were taken down and carried away. Was a strange sight to see, and the first hanging I ever witnessed. The raiders had many friends who crowded around and denounced the whole affair, and, but for the police, there would have been a riot; many both for and against the execution were knocked down. Some will talk and get into trouble thereby; as long as it does no good there is no use in loud talk and exciting arguments; is dangerous to advance any argument, men are so ready to quarrel.

Have got back to my quarters, thoroughly prostrated and worn out with fatigue and excitement, and only hope that today's lesson will right matters as regards raiding. Battese suspended washing long enough to look on and see them hang and grunted his approval. Have omitted to say that the good Catholic priest attended the condemned. Rebel Negroes came inside and began to take down the scaffold; prisoners took hold to help them and resulted in its all being carried off to different parts of the prison to be used for kindling wood, and the Rebels get none of it back and are mad. The ropes even have been gobbled up, and I suppose sometime may be exhibited at the North as mementos of today's proceedings. Mike Hoare assisted at the hanging. Some fears are entertained that those who officiated will get killed by the friends of those hanged. The person who manipulated the "drop" has been taken outside on parole of honor, as his life would be in danger in here.

Jimmy thanks God that he has lived to see justice done the raiders; he is about gone — nothing but skin and bone and can hardly move hand or foot; rest of the mess moderately well. The extra rations derived from our three messmates as policemen helps wonderfully to prolong life. Once in a while some of them gets a chance to go outside on some duty and buy onions or sweet potatoes, which is a great luxury.

July 12. Good order has prevailed since the hanging. The men have settled right down to the business of dying, with no interruption. I keep thinking our situation can get no worse, but it does get worse every day, and not less than 160 die each twenty-four hours. Probably one-fourth or one-third of these die inside the stockade, the balance in the hospital outside. All day and up to 4 o'clock P.M., the dead are being gathered up and carried to the south gate and placed in a row inside the dead line. As the bodies are stripped of their clothing, in most cases as soon as the breath leaves and in some cases before, the row of dead presents a sickening appearance. Legs drawn up and in all shapes. They are black from pitch-pine smoke and laying in the sun. Some of them lay there for twenty hours or more, and by that time are in a horrible condition.

At 4 o'clock, a four- or six-mule wagon comes up to the gate, and twenty or thirty bodies are loaded onto the wagon and they are carted off to be put in trenches, one hundred in each trench, in the cemetery, which is eighty or a hundred rods away. There must necessarily be a great many whose names are not taken. It is the orders to attach the name, company, and regiment to each body, but it is not always done. I was invited today to dig in a tunnel but had to decline. My digging days are over. Must dig now to keep out of the ground, I guess. It is with difficulty now that I can walk, and only with the help of two canes.

July 13. Can see in the distance the cars go poking along by this station, with wheezing old engines, snorting along. As soon as night comes a great many are blind, caused by sleeping in the open air, with moon shining in the face. Many holes are dug and excavations made in camp. Near our quarters is a well about five or six feet deep, and the poor blind fellows fall into

this pit hole. None seriously hurt, but must be quite shaken up. Half of the prisoners have no settled place for sleeping, wander and lay down wherever they can find room.

Have two small gold rings on my finger, worn ever since I left home. Have also a small photograph album with eight photographs in. Relics of civilization. Should I get these things through to our lines they will have quite a history. When I am among the Rebels, I wind a rag around my finger to cover up the rings, or else take them and put in my pocket. Bad off as I have been, have never seen the time yet that I would part with them. Were presents to me, and the photographs have looked at about one-fourth of the time since imprisonment. One prisoner made some buttons here for his little boy at home, and gave them to me to deliver, as he was about to die. Have them sewed onto my pants for safekeeping.

July 14. We have been too busy with the raiders of late to manufacture any exchange news, and now all hands are at work trying to see who can tell the biggest yarns. The weak are feeling well tonight over the story that we are all to be sent North this month, before the 20th. Have not learned that the news came from any reliable source. Rumors of midsummer battles with Union troops victorious. It's "bite dog, bite bear" with most of us prisoners; we don't care which licks, what we want is to get out of this pen. Of course, we all care and want our side to win, but it's tough on patriotism. A court is now held every day and offenders punished principally by buck and gagging, for misdemeanors. The hanging has done worlds of goods, still there is much stealing going on yet, but in a sly way, not openly. Hold my own as regards health. The dreaded month of July is half gone, almost, and a good many over 150 die each day, but I do not know how many. Hardly anyone cares enough about it to help me any in my inquiries. It is all self with the most of them. A guard by accident shot himself. Have often said they didn't know enough to hold a gun. Bury a Rebel guard every few days within sight of the prison. Saw some women in the distance. Quite a sight. Are feeling quite jolly tonight since the sun went down.

Was visited by my new acquaintances of the 9th Michigan Infantry, who are comparatively new prisoners. Am learning them the way to live here. They are very hopeful fellows and declare the war will be over this coming fall, and tell their reasons very well for thinking so. We gird up our loins and decide that we will try to live it through. Rowe, although often given to despondency, is feeling good and cheerful. There are some noble fellows here. A man shows exactly what he is in Andersonville. No occasion to be any different from what you really are. Very often see a great big fellow in size, in reality a baby in action, actually sniveling and crying, and then again you will see some little runt, "not bigger than a pint of cider," tell the big fellow to "brace up" and be a man. Stature has nothing to do as regards nerve, still there are noble big fellows as well as noble little ones. A Sergeant Hill is judge and jury now, and dispenses justice to evildoers with impartiality. A farce is made of defending some of the arrested ones. Hill inquires all of the particulars of each case, and sometimes lets the offenders go as more sinned against than sinning. Four receiving punishment.

July 15. Blank cartridges were this morning fired over the camp by the artillery, and immediately the greatest commotion outside. It seems that the signal in case a break is made is cannon firing. And this was to show us how quick they could rally and get into shape. In less time than it takes for me to write it, all were at their posts and in condition to open up and kill nine-tenths of all here. Sweltering hot. Dying off 155 each day. There are 28,000 confined here now.

July 16. Well, who ever supposed that it could be any hotter; but today is more so than yesterday, and yesterday more than the day before. My coverlid has been rained on so much and burned in the sun, first one and then the other, that it is getting the worse for wear. It was originally a very nice one, and homemade. Sun goes right through it now, and reaches down for us. Just like a bake oven. The rabbit mules that draw in the rations look as if they didn't get much more to eat than we do. Driven with one rope line, and harness patched up with ropes, strings, etc. Fit representation of the Confederacy. Not much like U.S. Army teams. A joke on the Rebel adjutant has happened. Someone broke into the shanty and tied the two or three sleeping there, and carried off all the goods. Tennessee Bill (a fellow captured with me) had charge of the affair and is in disgrace with the adjutant on account of it. Everyone is glad of the robbery. Probably there was not $10 worth of things in there, but they asked outrageous prices for everything. Adjutant very mad, but no good. Is a small, sputtering sort of fellow.

July 17. Cords contracting in my legs and very difficult for me to walk — after going a little ways have to stop and rest and am faint. Am urged by some to go to the hospital but don't like to do it; mess say had better stay where I am, and Battese says shall not go, and that settles it. Jimmy Devers anxious to be taken to the hospital but is persuaded to give it up. Tom McGill, another Irish friend, is past all recovery; is in another part of the prison. Many old prisoners are dropping off now this fearful hot weather; knew that July and August would thin us out; cannot keep track of them in my disabled condition. A fellow named Hubbard, with whom I have conversed a good deal, is dead; a few days ago was in very good health, and it's only a question of a few days now with any of us.

Succeeded in getting four small onions about as large as hickory nuts, tops and all, for two dollars Confederate money. Battese furnished the money but won't eat an onion; ask him if he is afraid it will make his breath smell? It is said that two or three onions or a sweet potato eaten raw daily will cure the scurvy. What a shame that such things are denied us, being so plenty the world over. Never appreciated such things before but shall hereafter. Am talking as if I expected to get home again. I do.

July 18. Time slowly dragging itself along. Cut some wretch's hair most every day. Have a sign out "Haircutting," as well as "Washing"; and, by the way, Battese has a new washboard made from a piece of the scaffold lumber. About half the time do the work for nothing, in fact not more than one in three or four pays anything — expenses not much though, don't have to pay any rent. All the mess keeps their hair cut short, which is a very good advertisement. My eyes getting weak with other troubles. Can just hobble around. Death rate more than ever, reported 165 per day; said by some to be more than that, but 165 is about the figure. Bad enough without making any worse than it really is. Jimmy Devers most dead and begs us to take him to the hospital and guess will have to. Every morning the sick are carried to the gate in blankets and on stretchers, and the worst cases admitted to the hospital. Probably out of 500 or 600, half are admitted. Do not think any lives after being taken there; are past all human aid. Four out of every five prefer to stay inside and die with their friends rather than go to the hospital. Hard stories reach us of the treatment of the sick out there, and I am sorry to say the cruelty emanates from our own men who act as nurses. These deadbeats and bummer nurses are the same bounty jumpers the U.S. authorities

have had so much trouble with. Do not mean to say that all the nurses are of that class, but a great many of them are.

July 19. There is no such thing as delicacy here. Nine out of ten would as soon eat with a corpse for a table as any other way. In the middle of last night I was awakened by being kicked by a dying man. He was soon dead. In his struggles he had floundered clear into our bed. Got up and moved the body off a few feet, and again went to sleep to dream of the hideous sights. I can never get used to it as some do. Often wake most scared to death, and shuddering from head to foot. Almost dread to go to sleep on this account. I am getting worse and worse, and prison ditto.

July 20. Am troubled with poor sight, together with scurvy and dropsy. My teeth are all loose and it is with difficulty I can eat. Jimmy Devers was taken out to die today. I hear that McGill is also dead. John McGuire died last night; both were Jackson men and old acquaintances. Mike Hoare is still policeman and is sorry for me. Does what he can. And so we have seen the last of Jimmy. A prisoner of war one year and eighteen days. Struggled hard to live through it, if ever anyone did. Ever since I can remember have known him. John Maguire, also, I have always known. Everybody in Jackson, Michigan, will remember him, as living on the east side of the river near the wintergreen patch, and his father before him. They were one of the first families who settled that country. His people are well-to-do, with much property. Leaves a wife and one boy. Tom McGill is also a Jackson boy and a member of my own company. Thus you will see that three of my acquaintances died the same day, for Jimmy cannot live until night, I don't think. Not a person in the world but would have thought either one of them would kill me a dozen times enduring hardships. Pretty hard to tell about such things. Small squad of poor deluded Yanks turned inside with us, captured at Petersburg. It is said they talk of winning recent battles. Battese has traded for an old watch and Mike will try to procure vegetables for it from the guard. That is what will save us, if anything.

July 21. And Rebels are still fortifying. Battese has his hands full. Takes care of me like a father. Hear that Kilpatrick is making a raid for this place. Troops (Rebel) are arriving here by every train to defend it. Nothing but cornbread issued now, and I cannot eat it any more.

July 22. A petition is gotten up signed by all the sergeants in the prison, to be sent to Washington, D.C., *begging* to be released. Captain Wirtz has consented to let three representatives go for that purpose. Rough that it should be necessary for us to *beg* to be protected by our government.

July 23. Reports of an exchange in August. Can't stand it till that time. Will soon go up the spout.

July 24. Have been trying to get into the hospital, but Battese won't let me go. George W. Hutchins, brother of Charlie Hutchins of Jackson, Michigan, died today — from our mess. Jimmy Devers is dead.

July 25. Rowe getting very bad. Sanders ditto. Am myself much worse, and cannot walk, and with difficulty stand up. Legs drawn up like a triangle, mouth in terrible shape, and dropsy worse than all. A few more days. At my earnest solicitation was carried to the gate this morning to be admitted to the hospital. Lay in the sun for some hours to be examined, and finally my turn came, and I tried to stand up, but was so excited I fainted away. When I came to myself I lay along with the row of dead on the outside. Raised up and asked a Rebel for a drink of water, and he said: "Here, you Yank, if you ain't dead, get inside there!" And with his help was put inside again. Told a man to go to our mess and tell them to come to the gate, and pretty soon Battese and Sanders came and carried

me back to our quarters; and here I am, completely played out. Battese flying around to buy me something good to eat. Can't write much more. Exchange rumors.

July 26. Ain't dead yet. Actually laugh when I think of the Rebel who thought if I wasn't dead I had better get inside. Can't walk a step now. Shall try for the hospital no more. Had an onion.

July 27. Sweltering hot. No worse than yesterday. Said that 200 die now each day. Rowe very bad and Sanders getting so. Swan dead, Gordon dead, Jack Withers dead, Scotty dead, a large Irishman who has been near us a long time is dead. These and scores of others died yesterday and day before. Hub Dakin came to see me and brought an onion. He is just able to crawl around himself.

July 28. Taken a step forward toward the trenches since yesterday and am worse. Had a wash all over this morning. Battese took me to the creek; carries me without any trouble.

July 29. Alive and kicking. Drank some soured water made from meal and water.

July 30. Hang on well, and no worse.

Aug. 1. Just about the same. My Indian friend says: "We all get away."

Aug. 2. Two hundred and twenty die each day. No more news of exchange. . . .

Aug. 13. A nice spring of cold water has broken out in camp, enough to furnish nearly all here with drinking water. God has not forgotten us. Battese brings it to me to drink. . . .

Aug. 20. Some say 300 now die each day. No more new men coming. . . .

Aug. 26. Still am writing. The letter from my brother has done good and cheered me up. Eyesight very poor and writing tires me. Battese sticks by; such disinterested friendship is rare. Prison at its worst.

Aug. 27. Have now written nearly through three large books, and still at it. The diary, am confident, will reach my people if I don't. There are many here who are interested and will see that it goes North. . . .

Sept. 6. Hurrah! Hurrah!! Hurrah!!! Can't holler except on paper. Good news. Seven detachments ordered to be ready to go at a moment's notice.

Later. All who cannot walk must stay behind. If left behind, shall die in twenty-four hours. Battese says *I shall go.*

Later. Seven detachments are going out of the gate; all the sick are left behind. Ours is the tenth detachment and will go tomorrow, so said. The greatest excitement; men wild with joy. Am worried fearful that I cannot go, but Battese says I shall.

Sept. 7. Anxiously waiting the expected summons. Rebels say as soon as transportation comes, and so a car whistle is music to our ears. Hope is a good medicine and am sitting up and have been trying to stand up but can't do it; legs too crooked and with every attempt get faint. Men laugh at the idea of my going, as the Rebels are very particular not to let any sick go, still Battese says I am going.

Most Dark. Rebels say we go during the night when transportation comes. Battese grinned when this news come and can't get his face straightened out again.

Marine Hospital, Savannah, Ga., Sept. 15, 1864. A great change has taken place since I last wrote in my diary. Am in heaven now compared with the past. At about midnight, September 7, our detachment was ordered outside at Andersonville, and Battese picked me up and carried me to the gate. The men were being let outside in ranks of four, and counted as they went out. They were very strict about letting none go but the well ones, or those who could walk. The Rebel adjutant stood upon a box by the gate, watching very close. Pitch-pine knots were burning in the near vicinity to give light. As it came our turn to go, Battese got me in the middle of the rank, stood me up as well as I could stand, and, with himself on one side and Sergeant

Rowe on the other, began pushing our way through the gate. Could not help myself a particle, and was so faint that I hardly knew what was going on. As we were going through the gate the adjutant yells out: "Here, here! hold on there, that man can't go, hold on there!" and Battese crowding right along outside. The adjutant struck over the heads of the men and tried to stop us, but my noble Indian friend kept straight ahead, hallooing: "He all right, he well, he go!" And so I got outside, and adjutant having too much to look after to follow me. After we were outside, I was carried to the railroad in the same coverlid which I fooled the Rebel out of when captured, and which I presume has saved my life a dozen times. We were crowded very thick into boxcars. I was nearly dead and hardly knew where we were or what was going on.

We were two days in getting to Savannah. Arrived early in the morning. The railroads here run in the middle of very wide, handsome streets. We were unloaded, I should judge, near the middle of the city. The men, as they were unloaded, fell into line and were marched away. Battese got me out of the car and laid me on the pavement. They then obliged him to go with the rest, leaving me; would not let him take me. I lay there until noon with four or five others, without any guard. Three or four times, Negro servants came to us from houses nearby and gave us water, milk, and food. With much difficulty I could set up but was completely helpless. A little after noon a wagon came and *toted* us to a temporary hospital in the outskirts of the city, and near a prison pen they had just built for the well ones. Where I was taken it was merely an open piece of ground, having wall tents erected and a line of guards around it. I was put into a tent and lay on the coverlid. That night some gruel was given to me, and a nurse whom I had seen in Andersonville looked in, and my name was taken.

The next morning, September 10, I woke up and went to move my hands, and could not do it; could not move either limb so much as an inch. Could move my head with difficulty. Seemed to be paralyzed, but in no pain whatever. After a few hours a physician came to my tent, examined and gave me medicine, also left medicine, and one of the nurses fed me some soup or gruel. By night I could move my hands. Lay awake considerable through the night thinking. Was happy as a clam in high tide. Seemed so nice to be under a nice clean tent, and there was such cool, pure air. The surroundings were so much better that I thought now would be a good time to die, and I didn't care one way or the other.

Next morning the doctor came, and with him Sergeant Winn. Sergeant Winn I had had a little acquaintance with at Andersonville. Doctor said I was terribly reduced, but he thought I would improve. Told them to wash me. A nurse came and washed me, and Winn brought me a white cotton shirt and an old but clean pair of pants; my old clothing, which was in rags, was taken away. Two or three times during the day I had gruel of some kind, I don't know what. Medicine was given me by the nurses. By night I could move my feet and legs a little. The cords in my feet and legs were contracted so, of course, that I couldn't straighten myself out. Kept thinking to myself, "Am I really away from that place Andersonville?" It seemed too good to be true.

124.

Henry Timrod: "Charleston"

Located at the mouth of the harbor of Charleston, South Carolina, Fort Sumter was a fortification of masonry and brick that rose sixty feet above the water line. Originally Federal property, it had been the first Confederate prize of the war; it was natural that the Union would want it back. The siege of Charleston — so-called, although the city was never actually besieged from the land — began July 10, 1863, and continued for 567 days of more or less continuous bombardment. Henry Timrod, "the laureate of the Confederacy," wrote this poem about the city in 1864.

Source: *Poems*. Memorial Edition, Richmond, Va., 1901.

CHARLESTON

Calm as that second summer which precedes
   The first fall of the snow,
In the broad sunlight of heroic deeds,
   The city bides the foe.

As yet, behind their ramparts stern and proud,
   Her bolted thunders sleep —
Dark Sumter, like a battlemented cloud,
   Looms o'er the solemn deep.

No Calpe frowns from lofty cliff or scar
  To guard the holy strand;
But Moultrie holds in leash her dogs of war
  Above the level sand.

And down the dunes a thousand guns lie couched,
  Unseen, beside the flood —
Like tigers in some Orient jungle crouched
  That wait and watch for blood.

Meanwhile, through streets still echoing with trade,
  Walk grave and thoughtful men,
Whose hands may one day wield the patriot's blade
  As lightly as the pen.

And maidens, with such eyes as would grow dim
  Over a bleeding hound,
Seem each one to have caught the strength of him
  Whose sword she sadly bound.

Thus girt without and garrisoned at home,
  Day patient following day,
Old Charleston looks from roof, and spire, and dome,
  Across her tranquil bay.

Ships, through a hundred foes, from Saxon lands
  And spicy Indian ports,
Bring Saxon steel and iron to her hands,
  And summer to her courts.

But still, along yon dim Atlantic line,
  The only hostile smoke
Creeps like a harmless mist above the brine,
  From some frail, floating oak.

Shall the spring dawn, and she still clad in smiles,
  And with an unscathed brow,
Rest in the strong arms of her palm-crowned isles,
  As fair and free as now?

We know not; in the temple of the Fates
  God has inscribed her doom;
And, all untroubled in her faith, she waits
  The triumph or the tomb.

125.

An Act to Encourage Immigration

The continuing labor shortage in Eastern factories was the main reason behind a plank in the Republican platform of 1860 that declared that the party was "opposed to any change in our naturalization laws or any state legislation by which the rights of citizenship hitherto accorded to immigrants from foreign lands shall be abridged or impaired." The Republican-controlled Congress fulfilled its pledge on July 4, 1864, by passing an Act to Encourage Immigration. The Act angered the American working class because it encouraged the importation of cheap labor.

Source: *Statutes*, XIII, pp. 385-387.

Be it enacted, by the Senate and House of Representatives of the United States of America, in Congress assembled, that the President of the United States is hereby authorized, by and with the advice and consent of the Senate, to appoint a commissioner of immigration, who shall be subject to the direction of the Department of State, shall hold his office for four years, and shall receive a salary at the rate of $2,500 a year. The said commissioner may employ not more than three clerks, of such grade as the secretary of state shall designate, to be appointed by him, with the approval of the secretary of state, and to hold their offices at his pleasure.

Section 2. *And be it further enacted,* that all contracts that shall be made by emigrants to the United States in foreign countries, in conformity to regulations that may be established by the said commissioner, whereby emigrants shall pledge the wages of their labor for a term not exceeding twelve months, to repay the expenses of their emigration, shall be held to be valid in law, and may be enforced in the courts of

the United States, or of the several states and territories; and such advances, if so stipulated in the contract, and the contract be recorded in the recorder's office in the county where the emigrant shall settle, shall operate as a lien upon any land thereafter acquired by the emigrant, whether under the Homestead Law when the title is consummated or on property otherwise acquired until liquidated by the emigrant; but nothing herein contained shall be deemed to authorize any contract contravening the Constitution of the United States or creating in any way the relation of slavery or servitude.

Section 3. *And be it further enacted,* that no emigrant to the United States who shall arrive after the passage of this act shall be compulsively enrolled for military service during the existing insurrection, unless such emigrant shall voluntarily renounce under oath his allegiance to the country of his birth and declare his intention to become a citizen of the United States.

Section 4. *And be it further enacted,* that there shall be established in the city of New

York an office to be known as the United States Emigrant Office; and there shall be appointed, by and with the advice and consent of the Senate, an officer for said city, to be known as superintendent of immigration, at an annual salary of $2,000; and the said superintendent may employ a clerk of the first class; and such superintendent shall, under the direction of the commissioner of immigration, make contracts with the different railroads and transportation companies of the United States for transportation tickets, to be furnished to such immigrants and to be paid for by them, and shall, under such rules as may be prescribed by the commissioner of immigration, protect such immigrants from imposition and fraud, and shall furnish them such information and facilities as will enable them to proceed in the cheapest and most expeditious manner to the place of their destination. And such superintendent of immigration shall perform such other duties as may be prescribed by the commissioner of immigration:

Provided, that the duties hereby imposed upon the superintendent in the city of New York shall not be held to affect the powers and duties of the commissioner of immigration of the state of New York; and it shall be the duty of said superintendent in the city of New York to see that the provisions of the act commonly known as the Passenger Act are strictly complied with, and all breaches thereof punished according to law.

Section 5. *And be it further enacted,* that no person shall be qualified to fill any office under this act who shall be directly or indirectly interested in any corporation having lands for sale to immigrants, or in the carrying or transportation of immigrants, either from foreign countries to the United States and its territories or to any part thereof, or who shall receive any fee or reward, or the promise thereof, for any service performed or any benefit rendered to any person or persons in the line of his duty under this act. And if any officer provided for by this act shall receive from any person or company any fee or reward, or promise thereof, for any services performed or any benefit rendered to any person or persons in the line of his duty under this act, he shall, upon conviction, be fined $1,000 or be imprisoned, not to exceed three years, at the discretion of a court of competent jurisdiction, and forever after be ineligible to hold any office of honor, trust, or profit in the United States.

Section 7. *And be it further enacted,* that said commissioner of immigration shall, at the commencement of each annual meeting of Congress, submit a detailed report of the foreign immigration during the preceding year, and a detailed account of all expenditures under this act.

Section 8. *And be it further enacted,* that the sum of $25,000, or so much thereof as may be necessary in the judgment of the President, is hereby appropriated out of any money in the Treasury not otherwise appropriated, for the purpose of carrying the provisions of this act into effect.

I never knew a man who wished himself to be a slave. Consider if you know any good thing that no man desires for himself.

ABRAHAM LINCOLN, written in an album at a Sanitary Commission Fair, 1864

126.

A Call for an International Trades' Assembly

Labor unionism declined during the early years of the Civil War, but a strong revival occurred by the end of 1863, when every major industrial center in the East had trades' assemblies whose purpose was to promote labor organization. In April 1864 the Trades' Assembly and League of Friendship of Louisville, Kentucky, took the initiative to build a national organization of trades' assemblies and circulated a letter throughout America and Canada proposing a national convention. The effort was initially unsuccessful, but Robert Gilchrist, the president of the Louisville Assembly, persisted and published the following open letter in a trade magazine on August 13. A month later a small convention took place out of which grew the International Industrial Assembly of North America.

Source: *Fincher's Trades' Review,* August 13, 1864 [Commons, IX, pp. 118-120].

To the officers and members of the trades' assemblies that are now organized on the continent of America, or that may be organized before the 21st of September:

Gentlemen:

As our notice, which has been inserted in *Fincher's Trades' Review* for the last three months, has failed to elicit a correspondence from all the trades' assemblies that are now organized, we are forced to adopt this method of communicating with you in regard to calling an international convention of the trades' assemblies of the United States and Canada.

We think great results would be produced by organizing ourselves into an international body. Are not capitalists and employers of almost every city organizing themselves into unions, and is it not patent to everyone that their object is the overthrow of our organizations? Are we to shrink with fear when we behold this spectacle? We answer, no; but it should stimulate us to powerful exertion; we ought to work with renewed energy and labor zeal-

ously to organize the mechanics of every branch, and if necessary, laboring men, into protective unions, and draw these unions into international bodies, the same as the molders, machinists and blacksmiths, printers, etc. In a word, the trades' assemblies ought to be the agents through which the mechanics of the different branches will be organized into local unions, and from local unions to international unions.

Suppose that we should be successful in organizing the mechanics of America as above stated: according to our views, the result would be this, viz.: Should the employers by combination attempt to overthrow any one branch of the trades, the other branches or organizations of mechanics would make the cause of the trade or branch struck at their cause and would lend their aid and sympathy to the trade; for if one branch was overthrown, we as a body would be weakened by it, knowing that the next blow struck might be at our branch; hence we are bound to protect each other.

There are many other benefits to be derived by combinations, but we have not the time nor space to mention but one more, and we think that it is sufficient of itself to stir you to action; it is this. Combination will do away with strikes, for by combination we will become so powerful that the capitalists or employers will cease to refuse us our just demands and will, if we make any unreasonable demands, condescend to come down on a level with us, and by argument and positive proof show to us that our demands are unjust; but this would have to be explained to the satisfaction of the trades' assembly of the city in which the demand was made.

We believe there are over 200,000 mechanics now represented in protective unions in the United States and Canada, and that they could be brought under the jurisdiction of the International Trades' Assembly in less than six months.

Gentlemen, we exhort you to send delegates to the convention; it will not cost much, and if you do not think that you will be benefited by it, you can instruct your delegates to withdraw.

We would suggest that Wednesday, the 21st of September, be named as the day of assembling, and that Louisville be the place; we name Louisville for the reason that if we have to correspond with each other for the purpose of selecting a place, it would take six months to come to an understanding.

We expect that the first convention will adjourn to meet about the 1st of May, 1865; by this date we expect to see a trades' assembly in nearly every city of the United States and Canada.

Hoping that you will take immediate action on the subject, and that you will proceed to elect one or two delegates to represent you, and immediately notify us of your determination, we remain, fraternally yours.

127.

WILLIAM H. SEWARD: Trade with Japan

The first American diplomatic mission to the Far East had been dispatched in 1832, but it was not until March 1854 that Commodore Matthew C. Perry concluded a treaty with the Japanese that paved the way for American commerce with their country. Adhering to the traditional American policy of encouraging trade and diplomacy in the East, Secretary of State William Seward sent the following instructions on August 20, 1864, to Robert H. Pruyn, the American minister to Japan.

Source: PRFA, 1864, III, p. 594.

LORD LYONS HAS, by direction of Earl Russell, Her Britannic Majesty's principal secretary of state for foreign affairs, submitted to me, for my perusal, in confidence, a copy of the earl's instructions of July 26 to Sir Rutherford Alcock, in relation to the course to be pursued by him at the present moment in regard to the existing troubles in Japan.

The instructions are based on a voluminous correspondence between Sir Rutherford Alcock and his government, in which he has included a note, addressed by you to him on the 13th of May last, in which you fully discussed the Japanese relations toward the Western powers.

The sum of Earl Russell's note is that his policy concurs with the views which are expressed in your aforementioned note. It may be stated as follows:

1. To give every encouragement and support to such of the tycoon's ministers and to such of the daimios as are favorable to foreign trade, and thus lead to the ultimate revoking of the feudal system and of the exclusive theory of Japan.

2. To make arrangements with the Japanese government for the protection of the foreign settlements at Yokohama.

3. To keep for the present a strong squadron in the Japanese seas.

4. To endeavor to establish an understanding with the government of France, the Netherlands, and the United States, with a view to our common interest in Japan.

I have now to inform you that the President approves of the policy thus defined.

In the present condition of our affairs, we shall probably find it inconvenient to keep constantly a naval force in the Japanese seas, but we shall endeavor to have some one vessel appear there so often as to make a suitable impression upon the Japanese government.

The substance of this instruction will be made known to Her Britannic Majesty's government.

128.

Abraham Lincoln: Opposition to the Congressional Plan for Reconstruction

After Lincoln presented his plan for Reconstruction to Congress on December 8, 1863, the Radical Republicans, led by Representative Henry Davis and Senator Benjamin Wade, attacked it on the grounds that it was too lenient and also that it usurped Congress' prerogative to establish Reconstruction policy. On July 2, 1864, Congress proposed its own Reconstruction program, the Wade-Davis Bill, which laid down stricter requirements for seceded states to rejoin the Union. Lincoln pocket-vetoed the bill and on July 8 issued the following statement explaining his action. This provoked Davis and Wade to issue a bitter manifesto on August 5, declaring that "a more studied outrage on the legislative authority of the people has never been perpetrated."

Source: Richardson, VI, pp. 222-223.

Whereas, at the late session Congress passed a bill "to guarantee to certain states whose governments have been usurped or overthrown a republican form of government," a copy of which is hereunto annexed; and

Whereas, the said bill was presented to the President of the United States for his approval less than one hour before the *sine die* adjournment of said session, and was not signed by him; and

Whereas, the said bill contains, among other things, a plan for restoring the states in rebellion to their proper practical relation in the Union, which plan expresses the sense of Congress upon that subject, and which plan it is now thought fit to lay before the people for their consideration:

Now, therefore, I, Abraham Lincoln, President of the United States, do proclaim, declare, and make known that while I am (as I was in December last, when, by proclamation, I propounded a plan for restoration) unprepared by a formal approval of this bill to be inflexibly committed to any single plan of restoration, and while I am also unprepared to declare that the free state constitutions and governments already adopted and installed in Arkansas and Louisiana shall be set aside and held for naught, thereby repelling and discouraging the loyal citizens who have set up the same as to further effort, or to declare a constitutional competency in Congress to abolish slavery in states, but am at the same time sincerely hoping and expecting that a constitutional amendment abolishing slavery throughout the nation may be adopted, nevertheless I am fully satisfied with the system for restoration contained in the bill as one very proper plan for the loyal people of any state choosing to adopt it, and that I am and at all times shall be prepared to give the executive aid and assistance to any such people so soon as the military resistance to the United States shall have been suppressed in any such state and the people thereof shall have sufficiently returned to their obedience to the Constitution and laws of the United States, in which cases military governors will be appointed with directions to proceed according to the bill.

129.

GEORGE PERKINS MARSH: The Instability of American Life

George Perkins Marsh, a New England lawyer and diplomat, in 1864 wrote Man and Nature, *reissued in 1874 under the title* The Earth as Modified by Human Action. *The work resulted from Marsh's observations made during extensive travels as the minister to Turkey and Italy. Called "the fountainhead of the conservation movement" by Lewis Mumford, the book suggested ways by which man could restore the natural environment that he had exhausted and wasted. An excerpt from the book is reprinted here.*

Source: *The Earth as Modified by Human Action,* New York, 1907, pp. 385-386.

ALL HUMAN INSTITUTIONS, associate arrangements, modes of life have their characteristic imperfections. The natural, perhaps the necessary, defect of ours is their instability, their want of fixedness, not in form only but even in spirit. The face of physical nature in the United States shares this incessant fluctuation, and the landscape is as variable as the habits of the population. It is time for some abatement in the restless love of change which characterizes us and makes us almost a nomad rather than a sedentary people.

It is rare that a middle-aged American dies in the house where he was born, or an old man even in that which he has built; and this is scarcely less true of the rural districts, where every man owns his habitation,

George Perkins Marsh, first minister to the Kingdom of Italy, appointed in 1860

than of the city, where the majority lived in hired houses. This life of incessant flitting is unfavorable for the execution of permanent improvements of every sort, and especially of those which, like the forest, are slow in repaying any part of the capital expended in them. It requires a very generous spirit in a landholder to plant a wood on a farm he expects to sell, or which he knows will pass out of the hands of his descendants at his death. But the very fact of having begun a plantation would attach the proprietor more strongly to the soil for which he had made such a sacrifice; and the paternal acres would have a greater value in the eyes of a succeeding generation if thus improved and

beautified by the labors of those from whom they were inherited. Landed property, therefore, the transfer of which is happily free from every legal impediment or restriction in the United States, would find, in the feelings thus prompted, a moral check against a too frequent change of owners, and would tend to remain long enough in one proprietor, or one family, to admit of gradual improvements which would increase its value both to the possessor and to the state.

We have now felled forest enough everywhere, in many districts far too much. Let us restore this one element of material life to its normal proportions, and devise means of maintaining the permanence of its relations to the fields, the meadows, and the pastures, to the rain and the dews of heaven, to the springs and rivulets with which it waters the earth.

The establishment of an approximately fixed ratio between the two most broadly characterized distinctions of rural surface — woodland and plowland — would involve a certain persistence of character in all the branches of industry, all the occupations and habits of life which depend upon or are immediately connected with either, without implying a rigidity that should exclude flexibility of accommodation to the many changes of external circumstance which human wisdom can neither prevent nor foresee, and would thus help us to become, more emphatically, a well-ordered and stable commonwealth, and, not less conspicuously, a people of progress.

When Grant once gets possession of a place, he holds on to it as if he had inherited it.

ABRAHAM LINCOLN, to Benjamin F. Butler, June 22, 1864

130.

THOMAS LOW NICHOLS: Work and Play in America

Thomas Low Nichols was a utopian crusader for hydrotherapy, vegetarianism,
spiritualism, and women's rights. He established a short-lived "School of Life"
at Yellow Springs, Ohio, in 1856, where he tried to practise the ideas he advocated.
When the Civil War came, he and his wife moved to England, regarding the war as
an evil and the government as a "military despotism." In 1864 he published
Forty Years of American Life, *a vivid and highly readable social and cultural*
history of America. A portion of the book is reprinted here.

Source: *Forty Years of American Life,* 2nd edition, London, 1874:
"Recreations and Amusements."

THE PUBLIC AMUSEMENTS in the United States are not very different from those in England. There are no fairs, but there are every year state and county agricultural exhibitions, with trotting matches for horses and prizes for the best female equestrianism. Hunting, as practised in England, with horse and hound, scarcely exists out of Maryland and Virginia, where English customs are best preserved, but there is no lack of game or sportsmen. There are, however, no game laws, except the prohibition to kill in certain seasons. The[r]e are no preserves or licenses, and everyone shoots or fishes where he likes. Warnings against trespass are unheard of. Racing is a custom of the middle states and the larger cities. There are racecourses near New York, Philadelphia, Baltimore, and New Orleans, and in many places in Tennessee and Kentucky. In New England and most of the North, horse racing is supposed to have been prohibited in the decalogue, and the few races that take place are not very reputably attended. Circuses traverse the country and diffuse a taste for gymnastics, and there is no lack of menageries of wild beasts, performing ponies, and monkeys.

There are a few cricket clubs, mostly made up of "British residents," but the American game of baseball is played by hundreds of clubs. There are bowling alleys in every village, and in the larger towns some are kept expressly for ladies, who also play with gentlemen at the watering places. Billiards everywhere. There are a few yacht clubs, and rowing clubs are more numerous. Nearly all Americans ride well and are fond of driving. Morphy made chess fashionable. The Germans excel in gymnastics, and hold Turner festivals with abundance of waltzing, and more abundant *lager bier,* which Americans are also learning to drink instead of whiskey.

New York has an opera house larger, I think, and certainly more splendid, than any in London, and a dozen or more handsome theaters. There are theaters in every considerable town, and plenty of wandering stars, but scarcely any strolling companies; and they have an abundance of music halls, Negro minstrels, German concert gardens, and a sort of theaters called varieties with a rapid succession of songs, dramatic scenes, gymnastics, etc.

America can boast of some novelties in the way of amusements never seen in Europe — floating theaters and circuses, propelled by steam, going from town to town on the great Western rivers, and carrying not only stage, auditorium, scenery, etc., but lodging and accommodations for the company, and, in the case of circuses, stabling and forage for the horses. The bills are posted weeks in advance. On the appointed day the floating theater comes in sight, flags flying, band playing, or a steam organ [calliope] filling the whole region with its obstreperous harmonies.

The huge floating monster steams round, with its head upstream, moors to the bank, and throws out its gangways. A crowd of idlers, black and white, gathers on the shore to stare at it and get glimpses of the actors and actresses, or riders and tumblers, low-comedy man or clown, as the case may be. The hour of performance arrives at last, and a procession of gaily dressed people issues from the broad streets of the town and boards the floating show, which has been "floating down the river, the O-hi-o," and the Mississippi, Missouri, Red River, and Arkansas, and their tributaries. White people fill the boxes and parquet, while every Negro within five miles who can raise the indispensable shilling is packed into the gallery. Orchestra strikes up, curtain rises, tragic sensations, screaming farces, roars of laughter, rounds of applause, and under all the great current sweeping onward to the Gulf.

Since my remembrance, nearly every dramatic or operatic star of any magnitude has made the American tour, which extends from Boston and New York along the Atlantic coast to Charleston and Savannah, then west to Mobile and New Orleans, sometimes by way of Havana, in Cuba, then up the Mississippi, across the continent to Utah and California, and back by the lakes — a tour of 4,000 or 5,000 miles; or, once on the Pacific, they go to Japan, China, and Australia. We have had singers from Malibran to Patti, both of whom, by the way, made their first successes in New York; actors from the elder Kean and Kemble to the younger Kean and Mathews; actresses from Fanny Kemble to Lydia Thompson; Celeste, Fanny Ellsler — how can I remember all the dancers? We had a visit from Rachel, and later from her rival Ristori. Then we have had stars of our own — Booth, Hackett, Forrest, Jefferson, Miss Cushman, Miss Bateman, and many more whose names may not have been heard of on this side of the Atlantic.

For many years all our actors and actresses were from England. In the first companies I knew, scarcely any were born in America. Now, probably two-thirds are Americans. Still, our best actors have been, and perhaps still are, English. Some have preferred Booth to Kean, and Forrest to Macready, but I do not think we ever had American actors like Dowton, who delighted us when past seventy. It seems impossible that America should ever produce such a low, such a *very* low comedian as Jack Reeve — scarcely such a comedian as Power. We have done better in tragedy and eccentric drama. It should be observed that many reputed American actors are of English birth, and have taken their first lessons on the English stage. Nearly all the so-called American actors I have seen in London were born in England or Ireland.

Music is more cultivated in America, up to a certain point, than in any country in the world, except Germany. I am sure there are ten pianofortes in every American town or village to one in England. Singing is taught in the public schools, and the number of bands and amateurs is very great. As to a national music, I can say little. The Negro melodies are nearly all we have to boast of. These have a charm that has made them popular everywhere. Are they really Negro? Yes, in their origin, undoubtedly. The Negroes have plaintive, simple airs, which they sing to the rude accompaniment of the banjo. The instrument is native African; so, in its rudiments, is the music; but both have been improved upon. The Negro melodies are the product of a cross between African paganism and American Methodism. Then the airs, as composed by the Negroes, have been refined by white performers, and others have been composed in the same spirit. These last constitute the greater number.

Some of these airs have a very singular character. There is "Dixie's Land," for example. I do not know its origin, but have no doubt that its germ, at least, was Negro and that it came from the South. When it was first played in St. Louis, the effect was very remarkable. It was at the theater. The leader had got hold of the air and arranged it for the orchestra. It was played between the acts. The audience listened in breathless silence, and then, waking from their astonishment, suddenly burst into one simultaneous yell of delight and made the band play it over eleven times before they would be satisfied. It was one of the last tunes I heard in America and the first I heard in London; the next, I believe, was also an Africo-American air, the "Prairie Flower."

There are American composers of operatic music, but they have the same difficulties in obtaining recognition as American authors. Why should a manager risk the production of an American opera, and pay for it, when the *chefs d'oeuvre* of Mozart and Rossini, Verdi and Gounod, Hervé, Lecocq, and Offenbach are ready to his hand? There are not many original dramatists or composers in England; it is a wonder that there should be any in America.

In art we are a little better. There are several clever American sculptors, and more painters. I see no better English landscapes than I have seen in America. Cole and Du-

rand of the older landscape artists, and Church, Kensett, and Cropsey of the younger may place their works by the side of most I have seen in the Royal Academy.

American summer resorts ought to be reckoned among their recreations and amusements. Once, thousands of Southerners, planters and merchants, used to come North in the summertime. The more patriotic came no farther than the Virginia Springs, but the more fashionable were seen at Saratoga and Niagara, Atlantic City and Newport. The New Yorkers leave town by the 4th of July. They scatter along the seacoast or make the tour of Lake Champlain, Montreal, and Niagara. They camp out among the Adirondacks, or visit the wonderful scenery of the Yosemite in California.

One of our favorite summer resorts was the Catskill Mountain House. Take the day boat at New York, one of those magnificent twenty-knot steamers, and glide past the palisades and through the highlands, until the Catskills rise like a cloud before you. At 3 o'clock, P.M., you land at a sleepy village and get into a stagecoach, which, after a picturesque ride of two hours, sets you down at a great hotel, standing on the brow of an overhanging precipice, 2,000 feet high, while the peaks of the mountains rise 1,000 or 1,500 feet more. You dine, and then take a chair out on the naked rock, as close to the edge of the cliff as you like, and have a view over an expanse of 3,000 square miles — a view bounded by the mountains on the horizon. The Hudson, from 12 to 30 miles away, is like a thread of silver at your feet. Next morning, you go back to the Catskill Falls; the day after, you ascend the mountain peaks — that is, if you like the roughest sort of climbing.

The next place to do is Saratoga. It is a nice village of white houses with green blinds, wide streets, shaded by the American elms, those broad, stately, and graceful trees that throw out their branches like the pillars of a Gothic cathedral, and hotels

— hotels which accommodate, in the aggregate, eight or ten thousand people. As we go to Saratoga for health, we rise early, go to the bubbling springs, and drink from six to twelve tumblers of Congress water. Then breakfast; then a drive to the lake, or the bowling alley, or billiards, or mere lounging, with the necessary mint juleps or sherry cobblers, until an early dinner, gregariously eaten in the American fashion. After dinner, the band plays under the trees, and we saunter or lounge and read the New York journals. An American gets all possible chairs and makes himself comfortable. Then tea; and after tea a dance — a hop they call it — just a little gentle exercise, such as the Schottische, the waltz and the polka can give, and so, with more or less of flirtations, ice creams, mint juleps, or other cooling beverages, the day gets through. The next is the same, ditto repeated, and so on, *ad libitum, ad infinitum.*

I think I will not describe Niagara. No one describes it; they only tell how they felt when they saw it. The tailor's exclamation — "Gods! what a place to sponge a coat!" — is as good as another. So the painters have tried to give an idea of it. The pictures of Cropsey and Church remind you of Niagara, if you have seen it. They give little idea otherwise. It is too big a thing to put into words or on canvas. . . .

Newport is the nicest of seaside and bathing places, but Atlantic City is, perhaps, the most popular. At each there is a beautiful seabeach, with the Atlantic surf rolling upon it and with no shingles to cut the feet. Americans have no bathing machines but long ranges of dressing rooms on shore. Ladies and gentlemen put on their bathing dresses in these rooms and then go into the surf together, let the waves roll over them if they cannot swim — if they can, they plunge through and swim outside. Many of the ladies are excellent swimmers. At New York there are lady teachers of swimming, who give public exhibitions when their pupils swim for prizes. The Newport season begins after the Saratoga season has ended. A grand ball closes each.

We talk in America of our great, our enlightened, our free, and, above all, our happy country! I never thought America *was* a happy country — only that it ought to be. In all the years of peace and plenty we were not happy. In no country are the faces of the people furrowed with harder lines of care. In no country that I know of is there so much hard, toilsome, unremitting labor; in none so little of recreation and enjoyment of life. Work and worry eat out the hearts of the people, and they die before their time. It is a hard story, but it is a true one.

The scarcity and high price of labor compel the small proprietors, called farmers, to do their own work. They raise large crops with heavy and continuous labor. The owner of a hundred acres is a slave to his land, a slave to his cattle, a slave to the necessities of his position. His family must live as well and dress as well as their neighbors. The harvests press upon the reapers.

It is seldom that an American retires from business to enjoy his fortune in comfort. Moneymaking becomes a habit. He works because he always has worked and knows no other way. Of the few who retire, many become hypochondriacs, and some commit suicide. An American millionaire, on being congratulated on his immense possessions, said: "Would you take care of all my property for your board and clothes?"

"No — certainly not!" was the answer.

"Well," said the Yankee Croesus, "that is all I get."

It is all that most wealthy Americans get. Whatever the amount of their fortunes, they get board and clothes — no better, often not so good, as others.

Then why the universal and everlasting struggle for wealth? Because it is the one thing needful; the only secure power, the only real distinction. Americans speak of a man being *worth* so many thousands or millions. Nowhere is money sought so eagerly; nowhere is it so much valued; and in no civilized country does it bring so little to its possessor.

The real work of America is to make money for the sake of making it. It is an end, and not a means. The value of a dollar consists in its power to make dollars. "Get money, honestly if you can, but get it." To the preacher, "a loud call" means the offer of a large salary. To the politician, a good office is one which offers the highest pay or the richest perquisites. In politics and business, and, I am afraid, in many other matters, money is the great object, and scruples are thrown to the wind.

Certain conventional notions of morality are regarded. There are few men of position in America who would like to have it known that they had made their money by gambling at cards, but they would have no scruple against the most odious cheating, the most gigantic frauds on the Stock Exchange. One may be a "bull" or "bear" in Wall Street; but it will not be so respectable to keep a faro bank in Broadway; though I have known one professional gambler to go to Congress and another to hold an important office under the Federal government.

Nearly all Americans trade and speculate. They are ready to swap horses, swap watches, swap farms; and to buy and sell anything. Talleyrand said America was a detestable country, where a man was ready to sell a favorite dog. I think the habit of fixing a price to everything may have misled the diplomatist. A man might be very unwilling to sell his dog; but he would be very likely to describe him as worth so many dollars. A mockingbird that fills a house with the songs of a hundred birds, besides the barkings of dogs, the mewing of cats, the filings of saws, and the noises of

the knife grinder, is declared, in addition to all his accomplishments, to have cost $25. Everything, whether for sale or not, has a money value. Money is the habitual measure of all things. I believe the American husband unconsciously values his wife in the Federal currency; and a pretty child is associated with some such idea as $1,000.

The first element of happiness, or the enjoyment of life, is contentment. There is no such thing in America as being contented with one's position or condition. The poor struggle to be rich, the rich to be richer. Everyone is tugging, trying, scheming to advance — to get ahead. It is a great scramble in which all are troubled and none are satisfied. In Europe, the poor man, as a rule, knows that he must remain poor, and he submits to his lot and tries to make the best of it. In England, the peasant does not expect to become a noble. Most men live and die in the position to which they are born. The exceptions are too rare to excite much effort or discontent. Not so in America. Every other little ragged boy dreams of being President or [a] millionaire. The dream may be a pleasant one while it lasts, but what of the disappointing reality? What of the excited, restless, feverish life spent in the pursuit of phantoms? What of the widespread demoralization, with its Tweeds and Fiskes, its cormorants and "carpetbaggers"?

The chief source of human happiness is the enjoyment of the domestic affections. In the countries of the Old World the loves of parents and children for each other — the family affections — make up a large portion of the enjoyment of life. America is strangely destitute of these affections. Whatever may be the causes, there is no doubt about the fact. Travelers have observed and natives have deplored it. It would be too much to say that Americans were without natural affection; but it is strange how little they appear to have.

Our Puritan ancestors had much to do

with it. The settlers of New England were a cold, hard race. They conscientiously suppressed the expression of their natural affections until they starved them out. A faculty unused is lost. The Puritans lost the power of loving, as the fishes in the dark river of the Mammoth Cave have lost their eyes. The Blue Laws of Connecticut punished a man for kissing his wife or child on the Sabbath day. What was forbidden on Sunday was considered a mark of human frailty on all other days.

Then the grim Pilgrims were Calvinists of the most rigid type. I do not wish to enter upon the thorny paths of religious controversy, but few men can doubt the tendency of a belief in the doctrine of eternal reprobation to harden the heart. Why should the father or mother love the child possibly doomed before its birth to endless perdition? I am certain that the early creed of New England made the people hard, harsh, and inhuman. The effect has lasted beyond the cause.

In the Northern states, especially, the ties of family are so often broken that they are loosely held. New England, for a hundred years, has been the hive that poured its swarms of emigrants over the new regions of the West. Families are scattered far and wide. One son settles in Wisconsin, another goes to Texas, a third to Oregon. One daughter marries an Alabamian, another settles in California. This separation of families, which was the infrequent and exceptional hardship of slavery, is the habitual lot of the Northern people.

Whatever the causes, the fact of an absence of family affection must greatly lessen the sum of human enjoyment. The more people are isolated, the less they have to love, the less are their sources of earthly happiness. They tend more to the Ishmaelism of competition and the fierce struggle for worldly wealth.

Socialism, in America, in its various forms, has been a protest and reaction against Mammonism and a growing and almost universal selfishness. As families were scattered, as society scarcely pretended to exist, as politics became more and more debased and despicable, as wealth failed to satisfy and could not purchase what was not in the market for sale, men naturally inquired if there were not some other form of social life less exhausting and fuller of enjoyment. A few tried Owenism or Fourierism. The former was generally repugnant because the Americans, holding to equality in theory, all the more resolutely reject it in practice. Fourierism they could not understand, and, at the period of its introduction, were unprepared for. Fourierism has a religion and morality of its own, and Americans twenty years ago were not quite ready to abandon the religion and morals which they had all professed, if they did not all practise.

Instead, therefore, of rushing into communities and phalansteries, they emigrated. As fast as they were disgusted with the older communities they founded new ones. There were far-spreading lands of promise in the West. There were broad prairies ready for the plow. Great states were building up beyond the Mississippi. The lawyer who could not get clients in New York could be a member of Congress from Minnesota. I knew a little infidel spouter in New York who became a United States senator from Oregon. Men seemed to expand as they increased their distance from the older states, as balloons grow larger when rising into the rarer heights of the atmosphere. Sometimes, in the one case as in the other, they burst and collapsed in the process. America is a great country; it has been, and for a long time to come can scarcely fail to be, a prosperous country; but I fear no one can, without a sad mental reservation, conscientiously sing —

Hail Columbia, happy land!

1865

131.

The First International to Abraham Lincoln

When Lincoln issued the Emancipation Proclamation, it was received with tremendous enthusiasm by English laboring men. They heartily endorsed Lincoln's antislavery policy in a series of meetings, despite the fact that his policy of blockading the South cut off the shipment of cotton to England and created unemployment among the English textile workers. Realizing that his war policy had created misfortune for them and appreciating their sentiments, Lincoln wrote the workers of Manchester in January 1863: "I cannot but regard your decisive utterances upon the question [of slavery] as an instance of sublime Christian heroism." When Lincoln was reelected in 1864, the International Workingmen's Association, of which Karl Marx was president, sent him a copy of an address in his honor.

Source: *The Bee-Hive*, London, January 7, 1865 [Karl Marx and Frederick Engels, *Letters to Americans 1848-1895*, New York, 1953].

WE CONGRATULATE THE AMERICAN PEOPLE upon your reelection by a large majority. If resistance to the slave power was the reserved watchword of your first election, the triumphant war cry of your reelection is "Death to slavery."

From the commencement of the titanic American strife, the workingmen of Europe felt instinctively that the star-spangled banner carried the destiny of their class. The contest for the territories which opened the dire epopee, was it not to decide whether the virgin soil of immense tracts should be wedded to the labor of the emigrant or prostituted by the tramp of the slave driver?

When an oligarchy of 300,000 slaveholders dared to inscribe for the first time in the annals of the world "slavery" on the banner of armed revolt; when on the very spots where hardly a century ago the idea of one great democratic republic had first sprung up, whence the first declaration of the Rights of Man was issued, and the first impulse given to the European revolution of the eighteenth century; when on those very spots counterrevolution, with systematic thoroughness, gloried in rescinding "the ideas entertained at the time of the formation of the old Constitution," and maintained "slavery to be a beneficent institution, indeed the only solution of the great problem of the relation of labor to capital," and cynically proclaimed property in man "the cornerstone of the new edifice"; then the working classes of Europe understood at once, even before the fanatic partisanship of the upper classes for the Confederate gentry had given its dismal warning, that the slaveholders' rebellion was to sound the tocsin for a general holy crusade of property against labor, and that for the men of labor with their hopes for the future, even their past conquests were at stake in that tremendous conflict on the other side of the Atlantic. Everywhere they bore therefore patiently the hardships imposed upon them by the cotton crisis, opposed enthusiastically the pro-slavery intervention, importunities of their "betters," and from most parts of Europe contributed their quota of blood to the good cause.

While the workingmen, the true political power of the North, allowed slavery to defile their own republic; while before the Negro, mastered and sold without his concurrence, they boasted it the highest prerogative of the white-skinned laborer to sell himself and choose his own master. They were unable to attain the true freedom of labor or to support their European brethren in their struggle for emancipation, but this barrier to progress has been swept off by the red sea of civil war.

The workingmen of Europe feel sure that as the American War of Independence initiated a new era of ascendancy for the middle class, so the American antislavery war will do for the working classes. They consider it an earnest of the epoch to come that it fell to the lot of Abraham Lincoln, the single-minded son of the working class, to lead his country through the matchless struggle for the rescue of an enchained race and the reconstruction of a social world.

132.

James D. Burn: American Laborers and Immigrants

James Burn, an English journalist, visited America during the Civil War and studied the social and economic conditions of the North. By the summer of 1862 the war had stimulated the Northern economy, giving rise to full employment, increased labor activity, and immigration. In 1865 Burn published an account of his travels, a discerning but critical view of American society that compared it with British society. The fact that he had come to America to "make his fortune" and failed may account for the frequent flashes of hostility in his account. Selections from his book are reprinted below.

Source: *Three Years Among the Working-Classes in the United States During the War,* London, 1865, pp. 182-189, 300-303.

For the benefit of those of my countrymen who are engaged in the hat manufacturing business, I will endeavor to lay before them such information as may be of interest, but more particularly to those among them who may think of emigrating.

In 1852, when Kossuth, the Hungarian exile, visited the United States, he wore a stuff felt hat, without any other stiffening than a little in the brim; that very unassuming chapeau was the means of revolutionizing the whole trade of the country by producing an entire change in both the form and character of the hat. Since that period, soft felt hats have held both the market and the heads of all the lords of creation in the country, with very few exceptions. During the change of styles, the demand for soft hats was very considerable, and as the process of *bowing,* or forming the bodies by hand, was found too slow for the fast men, some ingenious member of the trade made a forming machine, by which means both the bows and hurdles, which had been wedded to the trade beyond the ken of history, were kicked about their business.

Like nearly all other new mechanical productions, I presume, the first forming machine was anything but perfect; it was only a short time in operation (though guarded with a miser's care against the inspection of strangers) when several others were introduced into the trade, in which the imperfections of the first were avoided. During the last seven or eight years, few stuff bodies have been formed by the hand except in the far West; machines are now scattered over the whole of the hat manufacturing districts, namely, Newark in the state of New Jersey; Danbury, Connecticut, Brooklyn, and Philadelphia. The principal seats of the trades are, however, in Newark and Brooklyn, and I fancy I am not far wrong in stating that, in time of brisk trade, Newark, Orange, and the adjacent villages will contain from 600 to 800 men.

Mr. Prentice, in Brooklyn, is the largest manufacturer in the States. This gentleman's method of disposing of his goods is peculiar to himself. Instead of selling his hats to the merchants in the ordinary way of business, he disposes of them by auction, twice a year, on his own premises in New York. In Newark, there are several large employers; among these Messrs. Yates and Wharton, Vail, Jaques and Gillham, Moore and Selia — and the French company; the business of this latter firm may be looked

upon as of an exceptional character, being wholly confined to the manufacture of "brush hats." This class of goods is only known to the trade in Great Britain by name. I believe it is of German origin.

The method of making these hats is as follows: The bodies are formed of fine Russian hare's wool, pretty strongly carroted and sized into within about an inch and a half of the size required when they leave the hands of the brushers. After the bodies are dried they are carded until a thick flowing nap is produced; they are then taken to the plank and brushed in water with a weak solution of vitriolic acid. The brushes are made especially for the purpose; the hair is close and short, and the backs are made to be handled with freedom.

Brushing is exceedingly laborious work; every hat must be brushed on the plank, and during the operation the kettle must be kept boiling. A hat in the hands of an ordinary workman will take an hour's constant labor before the stuff (or, as it is called, the stock) will become ripe; the operator will know when his hat has had sufficient work by the yellow color of the nap and the free-flowing character which it assumes. After these hats are brushed the first time, they are dried and the nap cut quite short by a machine; after this, they are brushed a second time, blocked, and sent to the color shop.

I may mention that there are few men whose hands can stand blocking brush hats for any great length of time. The most of this work is done by Germans, Frenchmen, and Italians; and those accustomed to it can make from $14 to $20 a week, according to their readiness at the business.

Since the price of hatters' materials has undergone such a great advance in consequence of the war tariff, sizing hats has become a very variable process. Much of the refuse of hat shops which heretofore was looked upon as useless rubbish is now mixed up with new stock and made into hats. The quantity of this worn-out material used in some lots of bodies is so dispropor-tioned to the new stock that the men have often much difficulty in making their work sound.

Generally speaking, where the stock is not overlaid, the men can make very fair wages, but a stranger would scarcely credit the very great difference there is both be-tween the character of the work and the prices paid for it in shops, not only in the same district but within a few doors of each other. Mr. Joseph Gillham, in whose shop I worked, pays on a higher scale than any man in the trade within my knowledge; his goods, however, as a general rule, are of better quality than those made by other houses, and as his bodies are laid a large size, they require much diligence and well-applied labor before they are fit to pass through the hands of the foreman.

When business is in anything like a healthy condition, an ordinary good sizer can make from $12 to $15 a week. It may be noted that the British workmen who learned their trade when they had to form their own bodies, as a general rule, make a very poor figure in competing with men who have obtained a knowledge of their business in the States. Many of these men will size two hats for one with some of the best English workmen. The old system of operating upon a single hat at the plank has been superseded by the American workmen who size three and occasionally four bodies together in a cloth. The whole secret in get-ting through the work quickly lies in keep-ing a loose roll until the bodies are nearly into the required size. While some men who were ordinary fair sizers labored over a dozen of bodies in a day, I have seen oth-ers, without any apparent effort, do from two to three dozen. I have frequently had occasion to observe a good deal of disparity between workmen at home, but never any-thing like that which I have witnessed in America.

It will scarcely be credited by the old journeymen in England that some of the fire-eaters among the Yankee hatters have been known to make as much as $50 in one week at certain kinds of work. I know several men within my own sphere of ob-servation who, when in full employment, made from $20 to $35 a week. These people, however, belong to the class who labor like horses with the lash continually held over them, and many of them drink like savages. So far as my own experience is in question, I have rarely ever known one of these extremely fast workmen who could make it convenient to save a cent. As they made their money, they spent it, and in a manner which showed that they were thor-oughly regardless of the contingencies of health or continued employment.

If the hat business could be relied upon as a steady source of industry, I daresay it would be one of the best trades in the country. I am sorry to say, however, that there is no manufacturing business of which I have a knowledge so decidedly spasmodic in its character. This is accounted for by the amazing power of production which the "Forming Machine" gives the manufactur-ers. An order for 1,000 dozen hats in a dis-trict only lasts a short time. In the phraseol-ogy of the trade, the "squirts" quickly gob-ble up the work. These fast men have such ravenous appetites for labor that they can scarcely spare time to eat their victuals for fear they should not get their full share.

In most of the shops the men get the work out of hand as quickly as they can do it, and the fast men have all the chances of monopolizing more than an equal share of the hats, which is certainly not using the slower class of workmen fairly. In the Old Country I have never witnessed anything so disgustingly disagreeable as this selfishness of the American hat makers. No doubt it arises in part from the unsteady nature of the business and from their wants being in-creased by their highly artificial state of ex-istence.

When the business is in a prosperous condition, there is a constant struggle between the men and their employers about prices. I have seen as many as four shop calls (meetings) in the course of a day upon as many different kinds of work. It may be mentioned that each shop regulates its own prices. It is a rule with the employers, in giving out a new lot of hats, to leave a margin of from 4 to 10 cents, according to the nature of the stock and weight upon each hat; if the work is accepted by the men at the price on the tickets, nothing is said; but if the work should prove to be underpaid, the shop is called and a higher rate demanded. In consequence of this state of things, the men and their employers are continually watching each other.

I have observed that the turnouts which have occurred in the trade in the localities in which I have been situated have been caused by a set of headstrong young men who acted from the mere impulse of feeling; and by far the worst feature in these matters is that men of prudence and experience dare not open their mouths or use their influence at the public meetings for fear of being blackballed. As a general thing, the men have little regard for the feelings or interests of each other, and respect of persons is a matter quite out of the question. Should any man with a proper sense of right and wrong attempt to defend an employer in a disputed case, he would be sure to be branded as a traitor as well as being made a butt of ridicule by every fool in the shop who chose to raise a laugh at his expense or to gratify his own evil disposition.

I have no hesitation in saying that the most vulgar, the most ignorant, self-conceited, and headstrong class of men either in my own trade or any other are to be found among those who belong to one or other of the three divisions of the United Kingdom. This probably arises from an endeavor on the part of the newcomers to imitate the worst features in the character of the natives, and in attempting this they out-Herod Herod in Yankee swagger and arrogance.

The men in America, like the same class in Great Britain, who are the most loud-mouthed bawlers for trade rights and manly independence are, with few exceptions, the meanest Jerry Sneaks and subservient tools in the trade when they come to be tested by even a small pressure of want. In seasons of dull trade the employers have matters all their own way and, of course, are not slow to ring the changes upon the men. On these occasions the "all or none" gentlemen have no alternative but to accept a half loaf as being better than no bread.

Before the commencement of the war, a man in the trade, with economy and ordinary prudence, if employed even two-thirds of his time, might have saved money, as he could have supported a moderate family with $6 a week. That time in the United States, like a dream of the past, is gone and I fear never to return. From the open nature of both the hat trade and many other branches of skilled industry in America, a few years will thoroughly overstock them with hands, the immediate consequence of which will be a corresponding depreciation in the value of labor. In the meantime, from the loose system of apprenticeship which prevails, journeymen are being turned out as if by steam. I think the time is not far distant on this continent when the exclusive system of the European guilds will be introduced into the various branches of skilled industry.

As long as trades offer inducements to young men to join them, few will be content to spend their lives in the drudgery of the fields or in what is looked upon as the meaner occupations of civilized life. The working classes in America will be more impatient under a severe commercial pressure than any other people when their government ceases to spend $1 billion annually, as they are doing while I am writing. They will find that four years of feverish prosperity have swelled their ranks and narrowed the field of their labor at the same time. This will not only be the case; but when the whole trade of the nation is made to collapse like an empty bladder and the overstocked labor market supplemented by return volunteers who have escaped death in the field or by disease, the struggle to live in many cases will be one of life and death.

One of the worse features in the hat trade in America for the journeyman is the constant liability to be moved about from one establishment to another. When an employer finds his business begin to slacken, he immediately discharges a number of his men. This uncertainty prevails throughout the whole trade. It is therefore a matter of indifference where a man removes to; he is never safe from being shuttlecocked from one place to another. I have known twenty men shopped who were all on the road again in less than a fortnight. No fault can be found with the employers for thus sending the journeymen about their business when it may suit either their taste or convenience, inasmuch as the men are in the habit of playing the same game when their end of the beam is up.

If a journeyman hatter in any part of the United Kingdom can earn from 25 to 30s. a week, I would certainly advise him to remain where he is, nor do I know any class of tradesmen under the altered circumstances of the country who are likely to better their condition. As I have said before, the only people likely to improve their social condition by removing to the United States are the strong, healthy, unskilled laborers who now crowd the labor markets at home. How long the country may even suit this class I cannot presume to say. . . .

Many emigrants, after settling in America, feel disappointed as to the manners and habits of the people, and those who possess the means often return home. Afterward, when comparing the value of labor in their own country and their humble daily fare with the superior wages and excellent food they had in America, the original discontent with their old homes is revived, and they again cross the Atlantic. This is more especially the case with unskilled laborers to whom the difference of fare is much greater than to artisans. Another class of people, though they remain in America, never feel reconciled to their adopted country, but continually yearn for the land of their birth, which seems to them the only possible abode of happiness.

These, perhaps, are prevented from obeying the impulse of their feelings in consequence of their families having got anchored to the soil by marriage, so that they are bound to the country by paternal affection, or they cannot raise the means of transport. Or again — and these are much the larger number — they have been so long absent from their own country, that though it is the warmest wish of their hearts to return, they are prevented from doing so from the knowledge that all their relations and old friends are either removed by death or gone into the wide world far from the places of their birth. When any of the members of this latter class return to the homes of their youth, they are placed in much the same condition as if they were again beginning life in a new country among strangers. For these there can be no better advice than that they should cheerfully accept the facts of their existence, instead of indulging in vain regrets.

The first-named class may, with more practical benefit, be warned to reflect well before they throw away their time and money on a return trip to England, which, in the majority of cases, can only end in disappointment. In a word, I may say to both classes, life is too short to be wasted in vain regrets. . . .

Three classes of people are most likely to better their condition by removing to the United States. In the first place, I would name unskilled laborers who have been accustomed to a low standard of wages, poor food, and miserable dwellings. The second class consists of those whose social and political rights and liberties are in the keeping of their lords and masters, as in several of the German states. The third class is made up of men from the various grades of society in the Old World who have managed their business of appropriation in such a bungling manner as to make them forfeit the good opinion of their neighbors and cause the administrators of the law to be solicitous for their personal safety!

All these will find a ready market for labor and enterprise in the United States, and with health, strength, and a willing mind, it is a man's own fault if he does not make himself a useful member of society and secure many of the comforts and conveniences of civilized life to which he was a stranger at home. One condition, perhaps, ought to be named as essential to the success of workingmen; they should bring with them youth and good health so that they may be enabled to battle with the seasons until they become acclimatized.

133.

Advertisement to Supply Immigrant Contract Labor

The Contract Labor Law of July 4, 1864, encouraged the importation of laborers from abroad. Employers advanced passage money to their prospective employees in Europe, who, in return, worked under contract for one year upon arrival in the United States. Following the passage of the law, the American Emigrant Company was established in New York to act as a middleman between the American employer and the foreign laborer. An agent for this company in Missouri, one Thomas Souper, placed the following advertisement in the Daily Missouri Democrat *on May 15, 1865, offering his services to employers.*

Source: *Daily Missouri Democrat*, May 15, 1865.

HAVING RESIGNED MY SITUATION as secretary of the Excelsior Insurance Company . . . I am about to enter upon the great enterprise of inducing labor and capital to Missouri. I have been honored with an appointment from Governor Fletcher as a commissioner on the Board of Immigration. Already my duties have led to an extensive correspondence with leading parties in England and Scotland, and consequent upon this appointment, the American Emigrant Company of New York have designated me their agent for Missouri.

This company has been formed under the auspices of leading members of our government, of the Immigration Bureau at Washington, and of leading merchants, bankers, senators, and representatives, chiefly in the Eastern states. It has been "chartered for the purpose of procuring and assisting emigrants from foreign countries to settle in the United States." The company has a paid-up capital of $540,000. The direct advantages are these:

First, it secures a supply of diversified labor necessary to develop the varied resources of the country and to prosecute every branch of industry.

Second, it offers facilities to large corporations or special industrial interests to import in sufficient quantity the special kind of labor which they require.

Third, it gives each individual employer the opportunity of supplying himself with the exact number and description of operatives he needs.

Fourth, it will tend to equalize the value of labor in Europe and America, and thus, by raising the rate of wages in the Old World, undermine and finally destroy its manufacturing supremacy.

Fifth, it opens, by its agencies, new sources of immigration and aims at the introduction in large numbers of a superior class of men from northern Europe, Belgium, France, Switzerland, as well as Germany, England, Scotland, and Wales.

My books of registry are now open for inspection, and according to instructions I shall make free use of our daily press, with all communications bearing upon the material and moral interests of my adopted state.

To railroad companies, mining companies, manufacturers of iron and steel, machinists, boilermakers, ship and house builders, manufacturers of all kinds, as well as to the farming interests generally, I now tender my best services and shall be happy to meet all my old friends in my new position.

134.

E. W. Wynkoop: Army Atrocities Against the Indians

The Cheyenne Indians in Colorado and South Dakota were among the fiercest enemies of the white settlers. Along with the Sioux and Apaches, they did more than any other Indian tribes to block white settlement of the West. From 1857 to 1879 these tribes were engaged in wars with the federal government. On November 28, 1864, a Union Army detachment brutally attacked one of their villages at Sand Creek, Colorado, and slew several hundred innocent villagers. A congressional committee held an investigation of the incident, which many regarded as an outrage. The following testimony by Major Wynkoop was sent to the committee on January 16, 1865.

Source: 39 Congress, 2 Session, Senate Document No. 156, pp. 62-64.

Sir:

In pursuance of Special Order No. 43, Headquarters District of the Upper Arkansas, directing me to assume command of Fort Lyon, Colorado Territory, as well as to investigate and immediately report in regard to late Indian proceedings in this vicinity. I have the honor to state that I arrived at this post on the evening of the 14th of January, 1865, assumed command on the morning of the 15th, and the result of my investigation is as follows, viz.:

As explanatory, I beg respectfully to state that, while formerly in command of this post, on the 4th day of September, 1864, and after certain hostilities on the part of

the Cheyenne and Arapaho Indians, induced, as I have had ample proof, by the
overt acts of white men, three Indians,
Cheyenne, were brought as prisoners to
myself, who had been found coming toward
the post and who had in their possession a
letter written, as I ascertained afterwards,
by a half-breed in the Cheyenne camp, as
coming from Black Kettle and other prominent chiefs of the Cheyenne and Arapaho
nation, the purport of which was that they
desired peace, had never desired war with
the whites, and as well as stating they had
in their possession some white prisoners,
women and children, whom they were willing to deliver up, providing that peace was
granted them.

Knowing that it was not in my power to
insure and offer them peace for which they
sued, and at the same time anxious, if possible, to accomplish the rescue of the white
persons in their possession, I finally concluded to risk an expedition, with a small
command I could raise, numbering 127
men, to the rendezvous, where I was informed they were congregated to the number of 2,000, and endeavor by some means
to procure the aforesaid white persons, and
to be governed in my course of accom-
plishing the same entirely by circumstances. . . .

In my expedition I have but to say that I
succeeded, procuring four white captives
from the hands of these Indians, simply giving them, in return, a pledge that I would
endeavor to procure for them the peace for
which they so anxiously sued; feeling that
under the proclamation issued by John Evans, governor of Colorado and superintendent of Indian affairs, a copy of which becomes a portion of this report, by virtue of
my position as a United States officer,
highest in authority in the country included
within the bounds prescribed as the country
of the Arapaho and Cheyenne nations, I
could offer them protection until such time
as some measures might be taken by those

higher in authority than myself in regard to
them.

I took with me seven of the principal
chiefs, including Black Kettle, to Denver
City for the purpose of allowing them an
interview with the governor of Colorado,
by that means making a mistake of which I
have since become painfully aware, that of
proceeding with these chiefs to the governor of Colorado Territory instead of to the
headquarters of my district to my commanding officer. In the consultation with
Governor Evans the matter was referred entirely to the military authorities. Col. J. M.
Chivington, at that time commander of the
District of Colorado, was present at the
council held with these Indian chiefs and
told them that the whole matter was referred to myself, who would act toward
them according to the best of my judgment,
until such time as I could receive instructions from the proper authority.

Returning to Fort Lyon, Colorado Territory, I allowed the Indians to bring their
villages to the vicinity of the fort, including
their squaws and papooses, and in such a
position that I could at any moment, with
the garrison, have annihilated them had
they given any evidence of hostility of any
kind in any quarter. I then immediately dispatched my adjutant, Lieut. W. W. Dennison, with a full statement, to the commanding general of the department asking for instructions; but in the meanwhile various
false rumors having reached district headquarters in regard to my course, I was relieved from the command of Fort Lyon,
Colorado Territory, and ordered to report
to district headquarters.

Maj. Scott J. Anthony, 1st Cavalry of
Colorado, who had been ordered to assume
command of Fort Lyon, Colorado Territory, previous to my departure, held a consultation with the chiefs in my presence and
told them that though acting under strict
orders, under the circumstances, could not
materially differ from the course which I

had adopted, and allowed them to remain in the vicinity of the post with their families, assuring them of perfect safety until such time as positive orders should be received from headquarters in regard to them.

I left the fort on the 26th of November, 1864, for the purpose of reporting to district headquarters. On the second day after leaving Fort Lyon, while on the Plains, I was approached by three Indians, one of whom stated to me that he had been sent by Black Kettle to warn me that about 200 Sioux warriors had proceeded down the road between where I was and Fort Larned to make war, and desired that I should be careful — another evidence of these Indians' good faith; all of his statement proved afterwards to be correct. Having an escort of twenty-eight men, I proceeded on my way, but did not happen to fall in with them.

From evidence of officers at this post, I understand that on the 28th day of November, 1864, Col. J. M. Chivington, with the 3rd Regiment of Colorado Cavalry (one hundred-days men) and a battalion of the 1st Colorado Cavalry, arrived at this post, ordered a portion of the garrison to join him, under the command of Maj. Scott J. Anthony, against the remonstrances of the officers of the post, who stated circumstances of which he was well aware, attacked the camp of friendly Indians, the major portion of which were composed of women and children. The affidavits which become a portion of this report will show more particulars of that massacre; anyone whom I have spoken to whether officers or soldiers, agree in the relation that the most fearful atrocities were committed that were ever heard of: women and children were killed and scalped, children shot at their mother's breast, and all the bodies mutilated in the most horrible manner.

Numerous eyewitnesses have described scenes to me, coming under the notice of Colonel Chivington, of the most disgusting

and horrible character, the dead bodies of females profaned in such a manner that the recital is sickening. Col. J. M. Chivington all the time inciting his troops to these diabolical outrages previous to the slaughter. Commencing, he addressed his command, arousing in them, by his language, all their worst passions, urging them on to the work of committing all these diabolical outrages, knowing himself all the circumstances of these Indians resting on the assurances of protection from the government given them by myself and Maj. S. J. Anthony. He kept his command in entire ignorance of the same, and when it was suggested that such might be the case, he denied it positively, stating that they were still continuing their depredations and lay there threatening the fort.

I beg leave to draw the attention of the colonel commanding to the fact, established by the enclosed affidavits, that two-thirds or more of that Indian village were women and children. I desire also to state that Col. J. M. Chivington is not my superior officer but is a citizen mustered out of the United States service, and also to the time this inhuman monster committed this unprecedented atrocity he was a citizen by reason of his term of service having expired, he having lost his regulation command some months previous.

Colonel Chivington reports officially that between 500 and 600 Indians were left dead upon the field. I have been informed by Captain Booth, district inspector, that he visited the field and counted but 69 bodies, and by others who were present, but that few, if any, over that number were killed, and that two-thirds of them were women and children.

I beg leave to further state, for the information of the colonel commanding, that I talked to every officer in Fort Lyon, and many enlisted men, and that they unanimously agree that all the statements I have made in this report are correct. In conclusion, allow me to say that from the time I held the consultation with the Indian chiefs, on the headwaters of Smoky Hill, up to the date of the massacre by Colonel Chivington, not one single depredation had been committed by the Cheyenne and Arapaho Indians; the settlers of the Arkansas Valley had returned to their camps and had been resting in perfect security, under assurances from myself that they would be in no danger for the present, by that means saving the country from what must inevitably become a famine were they to lose their crops; the lines of communication to the states were opened, and travel across the plains rendered perfectly safe through the Cheyenne and Arapaho country.

Since this last horrible murder by Chivington the country presents a scene of desolation: all communication is cut off with the states, except by sending large bodies of troops, and already over 100 whites have fallen as victims to the fearful vengeance of these betrayed Indians. All this country is ruined; there can be no such thing as peace in the future but by the total annihilation of all these Indians on the Plains. I have most reliable information to the effect that the Cheyenne and Arapaho have allied themselves with the Kiowa, Comanche, and Sioux, and are congregated to the number of ——— thousand on the Smoky Hill.

Let me also draw the attention of the colonel commanding to the fact stated by the affidavits, that John Smith, United States interpreter, a soldier, and citizen, were presented in the Indian camp by permission of the commanding officer of this camp, another evidence to the fact of these same Indians being regarded as friendly Indians; also, that Colonel Chivington states in his official report that he fought from 900 to 1,000 Indians, and left from 500 to 600 dead upon the field, the sworn evidence being that there were but 500 souls in the village, two-thirds of them being women and children, and that there were but from 60 to 70 killed, the major portion of whom were women and children.

It will take many more troops to give security to the travelers and settlers in this country and to make any kind of successful warfare against the Indians. I am at work placing Fort Lyon in a state of defense, having all, both citizens and soldiers, located here, employed upon the works, and expect to have them soon completed and of such a nature that a comparatively small garrison can hold the fort against any attack by Indians. Hoping that my report may receive the particular attention of the colonel commanding, I respectfully submit the same.

135.

Henry Clay Work: "Marching Through Georgia"

In November 1864 General William T. Sherman began the famous march from Atlanta to the sea that was to embitter Southern feelings toward the North perhaps more than any other event of the war. The purpose of the march was to destroy everything the South might be able to use to carry on the war: factories, railroads, food supplies. To the city council of Atlanta, Sherman wrote: "You cannot qualify war in harsher terms than I will," and he kept his word by leaving a wide path of devastation from Atlanta to Savannah. To commemorate this act of "total war," Henry Clay Work wrote the spirited song "Marching Through Georgia." Though written too late to be sung much in the Civil War, it has since become an international favorite.

Source: *Marching Through Georgia*, Boston, 1889.

MARCHING THROUGH GEORGIA

Bring the good old bugle, boys! we'll sing another song,
Sing it with a spirit that will start the world along —
Sing it as we used to sing it, fifty thousand strong,
    While we were marching through Georgia.
Chorus:
    "Hurrah! hurrah! we bring the Jubilee!
    Hurrah! hurrah! the flag that makes you free!"
    So we sang the chorus from Atlanta to the sea,
        While we were marching through Georgia.

How the darkeys shouted when they heard the joyful sound!
How the turkeys gobbled which our commisary found!
How the sweet potatoes even started from the ground,
    While we were marching through Georgia.

Yes, and there were Union men who wept with joyful tears,
When they saw the honored flag they had not seen for years;
Hardly could they be restrained from breaking forth in cheers,
    While we were marching through Georgia.

"Sherman's dashing Yankee boys will never reach the coast!"
So the saucy Rebels said, and 'twas a handsome boast;
Had they not forgot, alas! to reckon with the host,
    While we were marching through Georgia.

So we made a thoroughfare for freedom and her train,
Sixty miles in latitude, three hundred to the main;
Treason fled before us, for resistance was in vain,
    While we were marching through Georgia.

136.

Abraham Lincoln: Second Inaugural Address

As Lincoln prepared for his second inauguration, there could be little doubt that the Confederacy would soon collapse. Lee's army was besieged at Petersburg; Union forces were pushing on to Richmond; and General Sherman had devastated Georgia and South Carolina. In the four years since he had assumed the presidency, Lincoln had greatly broadened his war aims. No longer were victory and political reunification his only objectives. He now set his sights on the greater task of the moral reconstruction of the nation. A year before, in 1864, he had expressed his vision in a letter to a Southern critic of his policy: "Now, at the end of three years' struggle, the nation's condition is not what either party, or any man devised, or expected. God alone can claim it. . . . If God now wills the removal of a great wrong [slavery], and wills also that we of the North as well as you of the South, shall pay fairly for our complicity in that wrong, impartial history will find therein new cause to attest and revere the justice and goodness of God." On March 4, 1865, Lincoln delivered his Second Inaugural Address, with the realization that victory for the Union would pose even greater problems for the nation than the political schism preceding it. When Thurlow Weed, the New York journalist, complimented Lincoln on his speech, the President replied: "I expect the latter [Second Inaugural] to wear as well as — perhaps better than — anything I have produced; but I believe it is not immediately popular. Men are not flattered by being shown that there has been a difference of purpose between the Almighty and them. . . . It is truth which I thought needed to be told." Charles Francis Adams, Jr., recognized the significance of Lincoln's address better than most. "What do you think of the inaugural?" he asked. "That rail-splitting lawyer is one of the wonders of the day. . . . This inaugural strikes me . . . as being for all time the historical keynote of this war. . . . Not a prince or minister in all Europe could have risen to such an equality with the occasion."

Source: Nicolay-Hay, XI, pp. 44-47.

At this second appearing to take the oath of the presidential office, there is less occasion for an extended address than there was at the first. Then, a statement, somewhat in detail, of a course to be pursued seemed fitting and proper. Now, at the expiration of four years, during which public declarations have been constantly called forth on every point and phase of the great contest which still absorbs the attention and engrosses the energies of the nation, little that is new could be presented. The progress of our arms, upon which all else chiefly depends, is as well known to the public as to myself, and it is, I trust, reasonably satisfactory and encouraging to all. With high hope for the future, no prediction in regard to it is ventured.

On the occasion corresponding to this four years ago, all thoughts were anxiously directed to an impending civil war. All dreaded it, all sought to avert it. While the inaugural address was being delivered from this place, devoted altogether to saving the

Union without war, insurgent agents were in the city seeking to destroy it without war — seeking to dissolve the Union and divide effects by negotiation. Both parties deprecated war, but one of them would make war rather than let the nation survive, and the other would accept war rather than let it perish. And the war came.

One-eighth of the whole population were colored slaves, not distributed generally over the Union but localized in the southern part of it. These slaves constituted a peculiar and powerful interest. All knew that this interest was somehow the cause of the war. To strengthen, perpetuate, and extend this interest was the object for which the insurgents would rend the Union, even by war, while the government claimed no right to do more than to restrict the territorial enlargement of it.

Neither party expected for the war the magnitude or the duration which it has already attained. Neither anticipated that the cause of the conflict might cease with or even before the conflict itself should cease. Each looked for an easier triumph and a result less fundamental and astounding. Both read the same Bible and pray to the same God, and each invokes His aid against the other.

It may seem strange that any men should dare to ask a just God's assistance in wringing their bread from the sweat of other men's faces, but let us judge not that we be not judged. The prayers of both could not be answered. That of neither has been answered fully. The Almighty has His own purposes. "Woe unto the world because of offenses! for it must needs be that offenses come; but woe to that man by whom the offense cometh."

If we shall suppose that American slavery is one of those offenses which, in the providence of God, must needs come, but which, having continued through His appointed time, He now wills to remove, and that He gives to both North and South this terrible war as the woe due to those by whom the offense came, shall we discern therein any departure from those divine attributes which the believers in a living God always ascribe to Him? Fondly do we hope, fervently do we pray, that this mighty scourge of war may speedily pass away.

Yet, if God wills that it continue until all the wealth piled by the bondsman's 250 years of unrequited toil shall be sunk, and until every drop of blood drawn with the lash shall be paid by another drawn with the sword, as was said 3,000 years ago, so still it must be said, "The judgments of the Lord are true and righteous altogether."

With malice toward none, with charity for all, with firmness in the right as God gives us to see the right, let us strive on to finish the work we are in, to bind up the nation's wounds, to care for him who shall have borne the battle and for his widow and his orphan — to do all which may achieve and cherish a just and lasting peace among ourselves and with all nations.

In this temple as in the hearts of the people for whom he saved the Union the memory of Abraham Lincoln is enshrined forever.
ANON., (Daniel Chester French, sculptor?), inscription in Lincoln Memorial, Washington

137.

Jefferson Davis: A Final Exhortation to the Confederate People

During the winter of 1864-1865 the military might of the Confederacy was crumbling. Yet President Davis still was deluded by his power and blindly optimistic that the tide of war would turn. Even during the siege of Petersburg, when Lee's army was immobilized and starving, Davis asserted to an audience in Richmond on February 6: "Let us then unite our hands and our hearts. . . . We may well believe that before another summer solstice falls upon us, it will be the enemy who will be asking us for conferences." On April 3 the Union Army took Richmond, forcing Davis to move the government to Danville. In the desperate hope that Lee and Johnston would unite their forces to defeat Sherman, Davis delivered this last address to the Confederacy on April 4. A month later he was captured in Georgia.

Source: *Jefferson Davis, Constitutionalist, His Letters, Papers and Speeches,*
Dunbar Rowland, ed., Jackson, Miss., 1923, Vol. VI, pp. 529-531.

To the People of the Confederate States of America:

The general in chief of our army has found it necessary to make such movements of the troops as to uncover the capital and thus involve the withdrawal of the government from the city of Richmond.

It would be unwise, even were it possible, to conceal the great moral as well as material injury to our cause that must result from the occupation of Richmond by the enemy. It is equally unwise and unworthy of us, as patriots engaged in a most sacred cause, to allow our energies to falter, our spirits to grow faint, or our efforts to become relaxed under reverses, however calamitous. While it has been to us a source of national pride that for four years of unequaled warfare we have been able, in close proximity to the center of the enemy's power, to maintain the seat of our chosen government free from the pollution of his presence; while the memories of the heroic dead who have freely given their lives to its defense must ever remain enshrined in our hearts; while the preservation of the capital, which is usually regarded as the evidence to mankind of separate existence, was an object very dear to us, it is also true, and should not be forgotten, that the loss which we have suffered is not without compensation.

For many months the largest and finest army of the Confederacy, under the command of a leader whose presence inspires equal confidence in the troops and the people, has been greatly trammeled by the necessity of keeping constant watch over the approaches to the capital, and has thus been forced to forego more than one opportunity for promising enterprises.

The hopes and confidence of the enemy have been constantly excited by the belief that their possession of Richmond would be the signal for our submission to their rule and relieve them from the burden of war which, as their failing resources admonish them, must be abandoned if not speedily brought to a successful close.

It is for us, my countrymen, to show by our bearing under reverses how wretched has been the self-deception of those who have believed us less able to endure misfortune with fortitude than to encounter danger with courage.

We have now entered upon a new phase of a struggle the memory of which is to endure for all ages and to shed ever increasing luster upon our country. Relieved from the necessity of guarding cities and particular points, important but not vital to our defense, with our army free to move from point to point and strike in detail the detachments and garrisons of the enemy; operating in the interior of our own country, where supplies are more accessible and where the foe will be far removed from his own base and cut off from all succor in case of reverse, nothing is now needed to render our triumph certain but the exhibition of our own unquenchable resolve. Let us but will it, and we are free; and who, in the light of the past, dare doubt your purpose in the future?

Animated by that confidence in your spir-it and fortitude, which never yet has failed me, I announce to you, fellow countrymen, that it is my purpose to maintain your cause with my whole heart and soul; that I will never consent to abandon to the enemy one foot of the soil of any one of the states of the Confederacy; that Virginia, noble state, whose ancient renown has [been] eclipsed by her still more glorious recent history; whose bosom has been bared to receive the main shock of this war; whose sons and daughters have exhibited heroism so sublime as to render her illustrious in all time to come; that Virginia, with the help of the people and by the blessing of Providence, shall be held and defended, and no peace ever be made with the infamous invaders of her homes by the sacrifice of any of her rights or territory.

If by stress of numbers we should ever be compelled to a temporary withdrawal from her limits, or those of any other border state, again and again will we return, until the baffled and exhausted enemy shall abandon in despair his endless and impossible task of making slaves of a people resolved to be free.

Let us not then [d]espond, my countrymen, but, relying on the never failing mercies and protecting care of our God, let us meet the foe with fresh defiance, with unconquered and unconquerable hearts.

Let us summon from the shades the immortal soul of James Harlan, born in 1820, entered into rest in 1899. In the year 1865 this Harlan resigned from the United States Senate to enter the cabinet of Abraham Lincoln as Secretary of the Interior. One of the clerks in that department, at $600 a year, was Walt Whitman, lately emerged from three years of service as an army nurse during the Civil War. One day, discovering that Whitman was the author of a book called "Leaves of Grass," Harlan ordered him incontinently kicked out, and it was done forthwith. Let us remember this event and this man; he is too precious to die. Let us repair, once a year, to our accustomed houses of worship and there give thanks to God that one day in 1865 brought together the greatest poet that America has ever produced and the damndest ass.

H. L. MENCKEN, first printed in the *Smart Set*, June 1919, and thereafter every year; *American Mercury*, April 1924

138.

WALT WHITMAN: "Come Up From the Fields Father"

The Civil War had a great impact on Walt Whitman's life. He moved to Washington in 1863 and, after volunteering as a wound dresser in Washington hospitals, determined to devote his life to war service. His experiences during the war inspired many poems, a collection of which, Drum-Taps, *was published in 1865. "Come Up From the Fields Father," which appears to be based on a real incident, is one of his few attempts at characterization and dramatic presentation of a scene. The* New York Times, *in reviewing* Drum-Taps, *commented: "Mr. Whitman has fortunately better claims on the gratitude of his countrymen than any he will ever derive from his vocation as a poet. . . . His devotion to the most painful duties in the hospitals . . . will confer honor on his memory when . . .* Drum-Taps *have ceased to vibrate."*

Source: *Leaves of Grass*, New York, 1867.

COME UP FROM THE FIELDS FATHER

Come up from the fields father, here's a letter from our Pete,
And come to the front door mother, here's a letter from thy dear son.

Lo, 'tis autumn,
Lo, where the trees, deeper green, yellower and redder,
Cool and sweeten Ohio's villages with leaves fluttering in the moderate wind,
Where apples ripe in the orchards hang and grapes on the trellised vines,
(Smell you the smell of the grapes on the vines?
Smell you the buckwheat where the bees were lately buzzing?)

Above all, lo, the sky so calm, so transparent after the rain, and with wondrous clouds,
Below too, all calm, all vital and beautiful, and the farm prospers well.

Down in the fields all prospers well,
But now from the fields come father, come at the daughter's call,
And come to the entry mother, to the front door come right away.

Fast as she can she hurries, something ominous, her steps trembling,
She does not tarry to smooth her hair nor adjust her cap.

Open the envelope quickly,
O this is not our son's writing, yet his name is signed,
O a strange hand writes for our dear son, O stricken mother's soul!
All swims before her eyes, flashes with black, she catches the main words only,
Sentences broken, *gunshot wound in the breast, cavalry skirmish, taken to hospital,*
At present low, but will soon be better.

Ah now the single figure to me,
Amid all teeming and wealthy Ohio with all its cities and farms,
Sickly white in the face and dull in the head, very faint,
By the jamb of a door leans.

Grieve not so, dear mother (the just grown daughter speaks through her sobs,
The little sisters huddle around speechless and dismayed),
See, dearest mother, the letter says Pete will soon be better.

Alas poor boy, he will never be better (nor maybe needs to be better, that brave
    and simple soul),
While they stand at home at the door he is dead already,
The only son is dead.

But the mother needs to be better,
She with thin form presently dressed in black,
By day her meals untouched, then at night fitfully sleeping, often waking,
In the midnight waking, weeping, longing with one deep longing,
O that she might withdraw unnoticed, silent from life escape and withdraw,
To follow, to seek, to be with her dear dead son.

139.

George E. Pickett: The Night Before Appomattox

In the spring offensive of 1865, the Union armies repeatedly forced the Confederate armies to retreat and regroup. On March 31 and April 1, the division of Confederate General George Pickett suffered heavy losses at Five Forks, west of Petersburg. Pickett took the fight to the enemy on the first day but was turned back; the counterattack on April 1 caught Pickett unprepared and the battle ended in a rout by the Union forces led by General Philip Sheridan. Pickett himself narrowly escaped capture, and with the remainder of his command joined Lee's forces near Appomattox. In the following letter to his wife, Pickett recorded his own and the Confederate Army's desperate situation. The letter is dated "Appomattox — Midnight — the night of the 8th and the dawn of the 9th," just prior to Lee's surrender.

Source: *Soldier of the South, General Pickett's War Letters to His Wife,*
    Arthur C. Inman, ed., Boston, 1928, pp. 134-137.

I would have your life, my darling, all sunshine, all brightness. I would have no sorrow, no pain, no fear come to you but all

    To be as cloudless, save with rare and
        roseate shadows
    As I would thy fate.

And yet the very thoughts of me that come to you must bring all that I would spare you.

Tomorrow may see our flag furled, forever.

Jackerie, our faithful old mail carrier, sobs behind me as I write. He bears tonight this

— his last — message from me to you. He is commissioned with three orders, which I know you will obey as fearlessly as the bravest of your brother soldiers. Keep up a stout heart. Believe that I shall come back to you. Know that God reigns. After tonight, you will be my whole command — staff, field officers, men — all.

Lee's surrender is imminent. It is finished. Through the suggestion of their commanding officers as many of the men as desire are permitted to cut through and join Johnston's army. The cloud of despair settled over all on the 3rd, when the tidings came to us of the evacuation of Richmond and its partial loss by fire. The homes and families of many of my men were there, and all knew too well that with the fall of our capital, the last hope of success was over. And yet, my beloved, these men as resolutely obeyed the orders of their commanding officers as if we had just captured and burned the Federal capitol.

The horrors of the march from Five Forks to Amelia Court House, and thence to Sailor's Creek, beggar all description. For forty-eight hours the man or officer who had a handful of parched corn in his pocket was most fortunate. We reached Sailor's Creek on the morning of the 6th — weary, starving, despairing.

Sheridan was in our front, delaying us with his cavalry, according to his custom, until the infantry should come up. Mahone was on our right; Ewell on our left. Mahone was ordered to move on, and we were ordered to stand still. The movement of Mahone left a gap which increased as he went on. Huger's battalion of artillery, in attempting to cross the gap, was being swept away, when I pushed on with two of my brigades across Sailor's Creek.

We formed line of battle across an open field, holding it against repeated charges of Sheridan's dismounted cavalry. At about 3 o'clock, the infantry which Sheridan had been looking for came up, completely hemming us in. Anderson ordered me to draw off my brigades to the rear and to cut our way out in any possible manner that we could. Wise's brigade was deployed in the rear to assist us but was charged upon on all sides by the enemy, and, though fighting manfully to the last, was forced to yield. Two of my brigadiers, Corse and Hunton, were taken prisoners. The other two barely escaped, and my life, by some miracle, was spared. And by another miracle, greater still, I escaped capture.

A squadron of the enemy's cavalry was riding down upon us, two of my staff and myself, when a small squad of my men recognized me and, risking their own lives, rallied to our assistance and suddenly delivered a last volley into the faces of the pursuing horsemen, checking them for a moment. But in that one moment we, by the speed of our horses, made our escape. Ah, my darling, the sacrifice of that little band of men was like unto that which was made at Calvary.

It is finished! Ah, my beloved division! Thousands of them have gone to their eternal home, having given up their lives for the cause they knew to be just. The others, alas, heartbroken, crushed in spirit, are left to mourn its loss. Well, it is practically all over now. We have poured out our blood, and suffered untold hardships and privations, all in vain. And now, well — *I* must not forget, either, that God reigns.

◆

Blackguard and buffoon as [Lincoln] is, he has pursued his end with an energy as untiring as an Indian and a singleness of purpose that might almost be called patriotic.

ANON., in the *Charleston Mercury*, Jan. 10, 1865

140.

HORACE PORTER: The Meeting at Appomattox Court House

General Robert E. Lee's army, retreating from Richmond and Petersburg, bivouacked near Appomattox Court House on the evening of April 8, 1865. Planning to push on to Lynchburg, Lee found the roads blocked by Union troops. General Grant, viewing the Confederate situation as hopeless, sent Lee a proposal for the surrender of his army. On April 9, Lee met with Grant and accepted the terms of surrender. In his Personal Memoirs *(1885), Grant described the interview: "What General Lee's feelings were I do not know. As he was a man of much dignity, with an impassive face, it was impossible to say whether he felt inwardly glad that the end had finally come, or felt sad over the result, and was too manly to show it. . . . But my own feelings, which had been quite jubilant . . . were sad and depressed. I felt like anything rather than rejoicing at the downfall of a foe who had fought so long and valiantly, and had suffered so much for a cause." The following account of the meeting was written by Brigadier General Horace Porter, Grant's aide-de-camp.*

Source: *Battles and Leaders of the Civil War*, New York, 1887 [1956, Vol. IV, pp. 729-746].

THE ROAD WAS FILLED WITH MEN, animals, and wagons, and to avoid these and shorten the distance we turned slightly to the right and began to "cut across lots"; but before going far we spied men conspicuous in gray, and it was seen that we were moving toward the enemy's left flank, and that a short ride farther would take us into his lines. It looked for a moment as if a very awkward condition of things might possibly arise and Grant become a prisoner in Lee's lines instead of Lee in his. Such a circumstance would have given rise to an important cross-entry in the system of campaign bookkeeping. There was only one remedy — to retrace our steps and strike the right road, which was done without serious discussion.

About 1 o'clock the little village of Appomattox Court House, with its half dozen houses, came in sight, and soon we were entering its single street. It is situated on some rising ground, and beyond the country slopes down into a broad valley. The enemy was seen with his columns and wagon trains covering the low ground. Our cavalry, the V Corps, and part of Ord's command were occupying the high ground to the south and west of the enemy, heading him off completely. Generals Sheridan and Ord, with a group of officers around them, were seen in the road, and, as our party came up, General Grant said: "How are you, Sheridan?" "First-rate, thank you; how are you?" cried Sheridan, with a voice and look that seemed to indicate that on his part he was having things all his own way. "Is Lee over there?" asked General Grant, pointing up the street, having heard a rumor that Lee was in that vicinity. "Yes, he is in that brick house," answered Sheridan. "Well, then, we'll go over," said Grant.

The general in chief now rode on, accompanied by Sheridan, Ord, and some others, and soon Colonel Babcock's orderly was seen sitting on his horse in the street in front of a two-story brick house, better in appearance than the rest of the houses. He said General Lee and Colonel Babcock had gone into this house a short time before, and he was ordered to post himself in the street and keep a lookout for General Grant so as to let him know where General Lee was. Babcock told me afterward that in carrying General Grant's last letter he passed through the enemy's lines and found General Lee a little more than half a mile beyond Appomattox Court House. He was lying down by the roadside on a blanket which had been spread over a few fence rails on the ground under an apple tree, which was part of an orchard. This circumstance furnished the only ground for the widespread report that the surrender occurred under an apple tree. Babcock dismounted upon coming near, and, as he approached on foot, Lee sat up, with his feet hanging over the roadside embankment. The wheels of the wagons in passing along the road had cut away the earth of this embankment and left the roots of the tree projecting. Lee's feet were partly resting on these roots. One of his staff officers came forward, took the dispatch which Babcock handed him, and gave it to General Lee.

After reading it, the general rose and said he would ride forward on the road on which Babcock had come but was apprehensive that hostilities might begin in the meantime, upon the termination of the temporary truce, and asked Babcock to write a line to Meade informing him of the situation. Babcock wrote accordingly, requesting Meade to maintain the truce until positive orders from General Grant could be received. To save time it was arranged that a Union officer, accompanied by one of Lee's officers, should carry this letter through the enemy's lines. This route made the distance to Meade nearly ten miles shorter than by the roundabout way of the Union lines. Lee now mounted his horse and directed Col. Charles Marshall, his military secretary, to accompany him.

They started for Appomattox Court House in company with Babcock and followed by a mounted orderly. When the party reached the village, they met one of its residents, named Wilmer McLean, who was told that General Lee wanted to occupy a convenient room in some house in the town. McLean ushered them into the sitting room of one of the first houses he came to, but upon looking about and finding it quite small and meagerly furnished, Lee proposed finding something more commodious and better fitted for the occasion. McLean then conducted the party to his own house, about the best one in the town, where they awaited General Grant's arrival.

The house had a comfortable wooden porch with seven steps leading up to it. A hall ran through the middle from front to back, and on each side was a room having two windows, one in front and one in rear. Each room had two doors opening into the hall. The building stood a little distance back from the street, with a yard in front, and to the left was a gate for carriages and a roadway running to a stable in rear. We entered the grounds by this gate and dismounted. In the yard were seen a fine large gray horse, which proved to be General Lee's, and a good-looking mare belonging to Colonel Marshall. An orderly in gray was in charge of them and had taken off their bridles to let them nibble the grass.

General Grant mounted the steps and entered the house. As he stepped into the hall, Colonel Babcock, who had seen his approach from the window, opened the door of the room on the left, in which he had been sitting with General Lee and Colonel Marshall awaiting General Grant's arrival. The general passed in, while the members of the staff, Generals Sheridan and Ord, and some general officers who had gathered in the front yard, remained outside, feeling that he would probably want his first interview with General Lee to be, in a measure, private. In a few minutes Colonel Babcock came to the front door and, making a motion with his hat toward the sitting room, said: "The general says, come in." It was then about half-past one of Sunday, the 9th of April. We entered, and found General Grant sitting at a marble-topped table in the center of the room, and Lee sitting beside a small oval table near the front window, in the corner opposite to the door by which we entered and facing General Grant. Colonel Marshall, his military secretary, was standing at his left. We walked in softly and ranged ourselves quietly about the sides of the room, very much as people enter a sick chamber when they expect to find the patient dangerously ill. Some found seats on the sofa and the few chairs which constituted the furniture, but most of the party stood.

The contrast between the two commanders was striking and could not fail to attract marked attention as they sat ten feet apart facing each other. General Grant, then nearly forty-three years of age, was five feet eight inches in height, with shoulders slightly stooped. His hair and full beard were a nutbrown, without a trace of gray in them. He had on a single-breasted blouse, made of dark-blue flannel, unbuttoned in front, and showing a waistcoat underneath. He wore an ordinary pair of top boots, with his trousers inside, and was without spurs. The boots and portions of his clothes were spattered with mud. He had had on a pair of thread gloves, of a dark-yellow color, which he had taken off on entering the room. His felt, "sugarloaf," stiff-brimmed hat was thrown on the table beside him. He had no sword, and a pair of shoulder straps was all there was about him to designate his rank. In fact, aside from these, his uniform was that of a private soldier.

Lee, on the other hand, was fully six feet in height and quite erect for one of his age, for he was Grant's senior by sixteen years. His hair and full beard were a silver-gray, and quite thick, except that the hair had become a little thin in front. He wore a new uniform of Confederate gray, buttoned up to the throat, and at his side he carried a long sword of exceedingly fine workmanship, the hilt studded with jewels. It was said to be the sword that had been presented to him by the state of Virginia. His top boots were comparatively new and seemed to have on them some ornamental stitching of red silk. Like his uniform, they were singularly clean and but little travel stained. On the boots were handsome spurs, with large rowels. A felt hat, which in color matched pretty closely that of his uniform, and a pair of long buckskin gauntlets lay beside him on the table. We asked Colonel Marshall afterward how it was that both he and his chief wore such fine toggery and looked so much as if they had turned out to go to church, while with us our outward garb scarcely rose to the dignity even of the "shabby genteel." He enlightened us regarding the contrast by explaining that when their headquarters wagons had been pressed so closely by our cavalry a few days before and it was found they would have to destroy all their baggage except the clothes they carried on their backs, each one, naturally, selected the newest suit he had, and sought to propitiate the god of destruction by a sacrifice of his second-best.

General Grant began the conversation by saying: "I met you once before, General Lee, while we were serving in Mexico, when you came over from General Scott's headquarters to visit Garland's brigade, to which I then belonged. I have always remembered your appearance, and I think I should have recognized you anywhere." "Yes," replied General Lee, "I know I met you on that occasion, and I have often thought of it and tried to recollect how you looked, but I have never been able to recall a single feature."

After some further mention of Mexico, General Lee said: "I suppose, General Grant, that the object of our present meeting is fully understood. I asked to see you to ascertain upon what terms you would receive the surrender of my army." General Grant replied: "The terms I propose are those stated substantially in my letter of yesterday — that is, the officers and men surrendered to be paroled and disqualified from taking up arms again until properly exchanged, and all arms, ammunition, and supplies to be delivered up as captured property." Lee nodded an assent and said: "Those are about the conditions which I expected would be proposed." General Grant then continued: "Yes, I think our correspondence indicated pretty clearly the action that would be taken at our meeting; and I hope it may lead to a general suspension of hostilities and be the means of preventing any further loss of life."

Lee inclined his head as indicating his accord with this wish, and General Grant then went on to talk at some length in a very pleasant vein about the prospects of peace. Lee was evidently anxious to proceed to the formal work of the surrender, and he brought the subject up again by saying: "I presume, General Grant, we have both carefully considered the proper steps to be taken, and I would suggest that you commit to writing the terms you have proposed, so that they may be formally acted upon."

"Very well," replied General Grant, "I will write them out." And calling for his manifold order book, he opened it on the table before him and proceeded to write the terms. The leaves had been so prepared that three impressions of the writing were made. He wrote very rapidly and did not pause until he had finished the sentence ending with "officers appointed by me to receive them." Then he looked toward Lee, and his eyes seemed to be resting on the handsome sword that hung at that officer's side. He said afterward that this set him to thinking that it would be an unnecessary humiliation to require the officers to surrender their swords, and a great hardship to deprive them of their personal baggage and horses, and after a short pause he wrote the sentence: "This will not embrace the side arms of the officers, nor their private horses or baggage." When he had finished the letter he called Col. (afterward General) Ely S. Parker, one of the military secretaries on the staff, to his side and looked it over with him and directed him as they went along to interline six or seven words and to strike out the word "their," which had been repeated. When this had been done, he handed the book to General Lee and asked him to read over the letter. It was as follows:

Appomattox Ct. H, Va.,
April 9, 1865

General R. E. Lee,
Commanding C. S. A.

General: In accordance with the substance of my letter to you on the 8th inst., I propose to receive the surrender of the Army of Northern Virginia on the following terms, to wit: Rolls of all the officers and men to be made in duplicate, one copy to be given to an officer to be designated by me, the other to be retained by such officer or officers as you may designate. The officers to give their individual paroles not to take up arms against the government of the United States until properly exchanged, and each company or regimental commander to sign a like parole for the men of their commands. The arms, artillery, and public property to be parked, and stacked, and turned over to the officers appointed by me to receive them. This will not embrace the side arms of the officers, nor their private horses or baggage. This done, each officer and man will be allowed to return to his home, not to be disturbed by the United States authorities so long as they observe their paroles and the laws in force where they may reside.

Very respectfully,
U. S. Grant, Lieutenant General

Lee took it and laid it on the table beside him while he drew from his pocket a pair of steel-rimmed spectacles and wiped the glasses carefully with his handkerchief. Then he crossed his legs, adjusted the spectacles very slowly and deliberately, took up the draft of the letter, and proceeded to read it attentively. It consisted of two pages. When he reached the top line of the second page, he looked up and said to General Grant: "After the words 'until properly,' the word 'exchanged' seems to be omitted. You doubtless intended to use that word."

"Why, yes," said Grant; "I thought I had put in the word 'exchanged.'"

"I presumed it had been omitted inadvertently," continued Lee, "and with your permission I will mark where it should be inserted."

"Certainly," Grant replied.

Lee felt in his pocket as if searching for a pencil, but did not seem to be able to find one. Seeing this and happening to be standing close to him, I handed him my pencil. He took it and, laying the paper on the table, noted the interlineation. During the rest of the interview he kept twirling this pencil in his fingers and occasionally tapping the top of the table with it. When he handed it back it was carefully treasured by me as a memento of the occasion. When Lee came to the sentence about the officers' side arms, private horses, and baggage, he showed for the first time during the reading of the letter a slight change of countenance and was evidently touched by this act of generosity. It was doubtless the condition mentioned to which he particularly alluded when he looked toward General Grant as he finished reading and said with some degree of warmth in his manner: "This will have a very happy effect upon my army."

General Grant then said: "Unless you have some suggestions to make in regard to the form in which I have stated the terms, I will have a copy of the letter made in ink and sign it."

"There is one thing I would like to mention," Lee replied after a short pause. "The cavalrymen and artillerists own their own horses in our army. Its organization in this respect differs from that of the United States." This expression attracted the notice of our officers present, as showing how firmly the conviction was grounded in his mind that we were two distinct countries. He continued: "I would like to understand whether these men will be permitted to retain their horses?"

"You will find that the terms as written do not allow this," General Grant replied; "only the officers are permitted to take their private property."

Lee read over the second page of the letter again, and then said: "No, I see the terms do not allow it; that is clear." His face showed plainly that he was quite anxious to have this concession made, and Grant said very promptly and without giving Lee time to make a direct request:

"Well, the subject is quite new to me. Of course I did not know that any private soldiers owned their animals, but I think this will be the last battle of the war — I sincerely hope so — and that the surrender of this army will be followed soon by that of all the others, and I take it that most of the men in the ranks are small farmers, and as the country has been so raided by the two armies, it is doubtful whether they will be able to put in a crop to carry themselves and their families through the next winter without the aid of the horses they are now riding, and I will arrange it in this way: I will not change the terms as now written, but I will instruct the officers I shall appoint to receive the paroles to let all the men who claim to own a horse or mule take the animals home with them to work their little farms." (This expression has been quoted in various forms and has been the subject of some dispute. I give the exact words used.)

Lee now looked greatly relieved, and though anything but a demonstrative man, he gave every evidence of his appreciation of this concession, and said, "This will have the best possible effect upon the men. It will be very gratifying and will do much toward conciliating our people." He handed the draft of the terms back to General Grant, who called Col. T. S. Bowers of the staff to him and directed him to make a copy in ink. Bowers was a little nervous, and he turned the matter over to Colonel (afterward General) Parker, whose handwriting presented a better appearance than that of anyone else on the staff. Parker sat down to write at the table which stood against the rear side of the room. Wilmer McLean's domestic resources in the way of ink now became the subject of a searching investigation, but it was found that the contents of the conical-shaped stoneware inkstand which he produced appeared to be participating in the general breaking up and had disappeared. Colonel Marshall now came to the rescue and pulled out of his pocket a small boxwood inkstand, which was put at Parker's service, so that, after all, we had to fall back upon the resources of the enemy in furnishing the stage "properties" for the final scene in the memorable military drama.

Lee, in the meantime, had directed Colonel Marshall to draw up for his signature a letter of acceptance of the terms of surrender. Colonel Marshall wrote out a draft of such a letter, making it quite formal, beginning with "I have the honor to reply to your communication," etc. General Lee took it, and, after reading it over very carefully, directed that these formal expressions be stricken out and that the letter be otherwise shortened. He afterward went over it again and seemed to change some words, and then told the colonel to make a final

copy in ink. When it came to providing the paper, it was found we had the only supply of that important ingredient in the recipe for surrendering an army, so we gave a few pages to the colonel. The letter when completed read as follows:

Headquarters, Army of Northern Virginia,
April 9, 1865

General: I received your letter of this date containing the terms of the surrender of the Army of Northern Virginia as proposed by you. As they are substantially the same as those expressed in your letter of the 8th inst., they are accepted. I will proceed to designate the proper officers to carry the stipulations into effect.

R. E. Lee, General

Lieutenant General U. S. Grant.

While the letters were being copied, General Grant introduced the general officers who had entered and each member of the staff to General Lee. The General shook hands with Gen. Seth Williams, who had been his adjutant when Lee was superintendent at West Point some years before the war, and gave his hand to some of the other officers who had extended theirs, but to most of those who were introduced he merely bowed in a dignified and formal manner. He did not exhibit the slightest change of features during this ceremony until Colonel Parker of our staff was presented to him. Parker was a full-blooded Indian, and the reigning chief of the Six Nations. When Lee saw his swarthy features, he looked at him with evident surprise, and his eyes rested on him for several seconds. What was passing in his mind probably no one ever knew, but the natural surmise was that he at first mistook Parker for a Negro and was struck with astonishment to find that the commander of the Union armies had one of that race on his personal staff.

Lee did not utter a word while the introductions were going on, except to Seth Williams, with whom he talked quite cordially. Williams at one time referred in rather jocose a manner to a circumstance which occurred during their former service together, as if he wanted to say something in a good-natured way to break up the frigidity of the conversation, but Lee was in no mood for pleasantries, and he did not unbend, or even relax the fixed sternness of his features. His only response to the allusion was a slight inclination of the head. General Lee now took the initiative again in leading the conversation back into business channels. He said:

"I have 1,000 or more of your men as prisoners, General Grant, a number of them officers whom we have required to march along with us for several days. I shall be glad to send them into your lines as soon as it can be arranged, for I have no provisions for them. I have, indeed, nothing for my own men. They have been living for the last few days principally upon parched corn, and we are badly in need of both rations and forage. I telegraphed to Lynchburg, directing several trainloads of rations to be sent on by rail from there, and when they arrive I should be glad to have the present wants of my men supplied from them."

At this remark all eyes turned toward Sheridan, for he had captured these trains with his cavalry the night before, near Appomattox Station. General Grant replied: "I should like to have our men sent within our lines as soon as possible. I will take steps at once to have your army supplied with rations, but I am sorry we have no forage for the animals. We have had to depend upon the country for our supply of forage. Of about how many men does your present force consist?"

"Indeed, I am not able to say," Lee answered after a slight pause. "My losses in killed and wounded have been exceedingly heavy, and, besides, there have been many stragglers and some deserters. All my reports and public papers, and indeed my own private letters, had to be destroyed on the march to prevent them from falling into the hands of your people. Many companies are entirely without officers, and I have not seen any returns for several days; so that I have no means of ascertaining our present strength."

General Grant had taken great pains to have a daily estimate made of the enemy's forces from all the data that could be obtained, and, judging it to be about 25,000 at this time, he said: "Suppose I send over 25,000 rations, do you think that will be a sufficient supply?" "I think it will be ample," remarked Lee, and added with considerable earnestness of manner, "and it will be a great relief, I assure you."

General Grant now turned to his chief commissary, Col. (now General) M. R. Morgan, who was present, and directed him to arrange for issuing the rations. The number of officers and men surrendered was over 28,000. As to General Grant's supplies, he had ordered the army on starting out to carry twelve days' rations. This was the twelfth and last day of the campaign.

Grant's eye now fell upon Lee's sword again, and it seemed to remind him of the absence of his own, and by way of explanation he said to Lee: "I started out from my camp several days ago without my sword, and as I have not seen my headquarters baggage since, I have been riding about without any side arms. I have generally worn a sword, however, as little as possible, only during the actual operations of a campaign."

"I am in the habit of wearing mine most of the time," remarked Lee; "I wear it invariably when I am among my troops, moving about through the army."

General Sheridan now stepped up to General Lee and said that when he discovered some of the Confederate troops in motion during the morning, which seemed to be a violation of the truce, he had sent him (Lee) a couple of notes protesting against this act, and as he had not had time to copy them he would like to have them long enough to make copies. Lee took the notes out of the breast pocket of his coat and handed them to Sheridan with a few words expressive of regret that the circumstance had occurred, and intimating that it must have been the result of some misunderstanding.

After a little general conversation had been indulged in by those present, the two letters were signed and delivered, and the parties prepared to separate. Lee before parting asked Grant to notify Meade of the surrender, fearing that fighting might break out on that front and lives be uselessly lost. This request was complied with, and two Union officers were sent through the enemy's lines as the shortest route to Meade — some of Lee's officers accompanying them to prevent their being interfered with. At a little before 4 o'clock General Lee shook hands with General Grant, bowed to the other officers, and with Colonel Marshall left the room. One after another we followed, and passed out to the porch. Lee signaled to his orderly to bring up his horse, and while the animal was being bridled, the general stood on the lowest step and gazed sadly in the direction of the valley beyond where his army lay — now an army of prisoners.

He smote his hands together a number of times in an absent sort of a way; seemed not to see the group of Union officers in the yard who rose respectfully at his approach; and appeared unconscious of everything about him. All appreciated the sadness that overwhelmed him, and he had the personal sympathy of everyone who beheld him at this supreme moment of trial. The approach of his horse seemed to recall him from his reverie, and he at once mounted.

General Grant now stepped down from the porch and, moving toward him, saluted

him by raising his hat. He was followed in this act of courtesy by all our officers present; Lee raised his hat respectfully and rode off to break the sad news to the brave fellows whom he had so long commanded.

General Grant and his staff then mounted and started for the headquarters camp, which in the meantime had been pitched nearby. The news of the surrender had reached the Union lines, and the firing of salutes began at several points, but the general sent orders at once to have them stopped, and used these words in referring to the occurrence: "The war is over, the Rebels are our countrymen again, and the best sign of rejoicing after the victory will be to abstain from all demonstrations in the field."

Mr. McLean had been charging about in a manner which indicated that the excitement was shaking his system to its nervous center, but his real trials did not begin until the departure of the chief actors in the surrender. Then the relic hunters charged down upon the manor house and made various attempts to jump Mr. McLean's claims to his own furniture. Sheridan set a good example, however, by paying the proprietor $20 in gold for the table at which Lee sat, for the purpose of presenting it to Mrs. Custer, and handed it over to her dashing husband, who started off for camp bearing it upon his shoulder. Ord paid $40 for the table at which Grant sat, and afterward presented it to Mrs. Grant, who modestly declined it and insisted that Mrs. Ord should become its possessor. Bargains were at once struck for all the articles in the room, and it is even said that some mementos were carried off for which no coin of the realm was ever exchanged.

Before General Grant had proceeded far toward camp, he was reminded that he had not yet announced the important event to the government. He dismounted by the roadside, sat down on a large stone, and called for pencil and paper. Colonel (afterward General) Badeau handed his order book to the general, who wrote on one of the leaves the following message, a copy of which was sent to the nearest telegraph station. It was dated 4:30 P.M.:

Hon. E. M. Stanton,
Secretary of War,
Washington

General Lee surrendered the Army of Northern Virginia this afternoon on terms proposed by myself. The accompanying additional correspondence will show the conditions fully.

U. S. Grant, Lieut. General

Upon reaching camp he seated himself in front of his tent, and we all gathered around him, curious to hear what his first comments would be upon the crowning event of his life. But our expectations were doomed to disappointment, for he appeared to have already dismissed the whole subject from his mind, and turning to Gen. Rufus Ingalls, his first words were: "Ingalls, do you remember that old white mule that so-and-so used to ride when we were in the city of Mexico?" "Why, perfectly," said Ingalls, who was just then in a mood to remember the exact number of hairs in the mule's tail if it would have helped to make matters agreeable. And then the general in chief went on to recall the antics played by that animal during an excursion to Popocatepetl. It was not until after supper that he said much about the surrender, when he talked freely of his entire belief that the rest of the Rebel commanders would follow Lee's example, and that we would have but little more fighting, even of a partisan nature.

He then surprised us by announcing his intention of starting to Washington early the next morning. We were disappointed at this, for we wanted to see something of the opposing army, now that it had become civil enough for the first time in its existence to let us get near it and meet some of the officers who had been acquaintances in

former years. The general, however, had no desire to look at the conquered and but little curiosity in his nature, and he was anxious above all things to begin the reduction of the military establishment and diminish the enormous expense attending it, which at this time amounted to about $4 million a day. When he considered, however, that the railroad was being rapidly put in condition and that he would lose no time by waiting till noon of the next day, he made up his mind to delay his departure.

That evening I made full notes of the occurrences which took place during the surrender, and from these the above account has been written.

There were present at McLean's house, besides Sheridan, Ord, Merritt, Custer, and the officers of Grant's staff, a number of other officers and one or two citizens who entered the room at different times during the interview.

About 9 o'clock on the morning of the 10th, General Grant with his staff rode out toward the enemy's lines, but it was found upon attempting to pass through that the force of habit is hard to overcome, and that the practice which had so long been inculcated in Lee's army of keeping Grant out of his lines was not to be overturned in a day, and he was politely requested at the picket lines to wait till a message could be sent to headquarters asking for instructions. As soon as Lee heard that his distinguished opponent was approaching, he was prompt to correct the misunderstanding at the picket line and rode out at a gallop to receive him. They met on a knoll that overlooked the lines of the two armies, and saluted respectfully by each raising his hat. The officers present gave a similar salute and then grouped themselves around the two chieftains in a semicircle, but withdrew out of earshot. General Grant repeated to us that evening the substance of the conversation, which was as follows:

Grant began by expressing a hope that

the war would soon be over; and Lee replied by stating that he had for some time been anxious to stop the further effusion of blood, and he trusted that everything would now be done to restore harmony and conciliate the people of the South. He said the emancipation of the Negroes would be no hindrance to the restoring of relations between the two sections of the country, as it would probably not be the desire of the majority of the Southern people to restore slavery then, even if the question were left open to them. He could not tell what the other armies would do or what course Mr. Davis would now take, but he believed it would be best for their other armies to follow his example, as nothing could be gained by further resistance in the field.

Finding that he entertained these sentiments, General Grant told him that no one's influence in the South was so great as his and suggested to him that he should advise the surrender of the remaining armies and thus exert his influence in favor of immediate peace. Lee said he could not take such a course without consulting President Davis first. Grant then proposed to Lee that he should do so and urge the hastening of a result which was admitted to be inevitable. Lee, however, was averse to stepping beyond his duties as a soldier and said the authorities would doubtless soon arrive at the same conclusion without his interference. . . .

After the conversation had lasted a little more than half an hour and Lee had requested that such instructions be given to the officers left in charge to carry out the details of the surrender that there might be no misunderstanding as to the form of paroles, the manner of turning over the property, etc., the conference ended. The two

commanders lifted their hats and said goodbye. Lee rode back to his camp to take a final farewell of his army, and Grant returned to McLean's house, where he seated himself on the porch until it was time to take his final departure.

During the conference Ingalls, Sheridan, and Williams had asked permission to visit the enemy's lines and renew their acquaintance with some old friends, classmates, and former comrades in arms who were serving in Lee's army. They now returned, bringing with them Cadmus M. Wilcox, who had been General Grant's groomsman when he was married; Longstreet, who had also been at his wedding; Heth, who had been a subaltern with him in Mexico, besides Gordon, Pickett, and a number of others. They all stepped up to pay their respects to General Grant, who received them very cordially and talked with them until it was time to leave.

The hour of noon had now arrived, and General Grant, after shaking hands with all present who were not to accompany him, mounted his horse, and started with his staff for Washington without having entered the enemy's lines. Lee set out for Richmond, and it was felt by all that peace had at last dawned upon the land. The charges were now withdrawn from the guns, the campfires were left to smolder in their ashes, the flags were tenderly furled — those historic banners, battle-stained, bullet-riddled, many of them but remnants of their former selves, with scarcely enough left of them on which to imprint the names of the battles they had seen — and the Army of the Union and the Army of Northern Virginia turned their backs upon each other for the first time in four long, bloody years.

141.

Robert E. Lee: General Order Number Nine

On the morning of April 9, 1865, General Robert E. Lee surrendered the Army of
Northern Virginia to General Ulysses S. Grant, thereby effectually ending the Civil War.
Lee's surrender was marked by dignity and goodwill. Grant in a magnanimous gesture
had made important concessions to Lee in allowing the Confederate officers to retain
their side arms and all soldiers to keep their horses. The day after the surrender,
Lee composed the following farewell to his army. Colonel Charles Marshall read the
order to the soldiers.

Source: *Memoirs of Robert E. Lee, etc., etc.,* A. L. Long, ed., New York, 1886, pp. 692-693.

AFTER FOUR YEARS of arduous service, marked by unsurpassed courage and fortitude, the Army of Northern Virginia has been compelled to yield to overwhelming numbers and resources. I need not tell the survivors of so many hard-fought battles, who have remained steadfast to the last, that I have consented to this result from no distrust of them; but, feeling that valor and devotion could accomplish nothing that could compensate for the loss that would have attended the continuation of the contest, I have determined to avoid the useless sacrifice of those whose past services have endeared them to their countrymen.

By the terms of the agreement, officers and men can return to their homes and remain there until exchanged. You will take with you the satisfaction that proceeds from the consciousness of duty faithfully performed; and I earnestly pray that a merciful God will extend to you His blessing and protection.

With an increasing admiration of your constancy and devotion to your country, and a grateful remembrance of your kind and generous consideration of myself, I bid you an affectionate farewell.

Duty then is the sublimest word in our language. Do your duty in all things.
You cannot do more. You should never wish to do less.
ROBERT E. LEE, inscribed beneath his bust in Hall of Fame

142.

ABRAHAM LINCOLN: Last Public Address

*On the evening of April 11, two days after the surrender of Lee's army, Lincoln
delivered a speech from the balcony of the White House outlining his plans for
Reconstruction. Congress would not meet until December. The President was
well aware that the Radicals would press for a harsh and vindictive policy against
the South and appeal to the desire for revenge that had welled up in the North.
He decided to avert this by persuading the people to support his own policy.
The immense and boisterous crowd that heard him misunderstood his intentions.
They had come to celebrate a victory and vent their emotions. They expected the
President to deliver a brief triumphant victory speech commemorating the end of
the terrible struggle. Instead, Lincoln, without passion or eloquence, delivered
the following statesmanlike plea for the reacceptance of Louisiana into the Union
to mark the beginning of a new era. Three nights later he was assassinated.*

Source: Nicolay-Hay, VI, pp. 84-92.

WE MEET THIS EVENING not in sorrow but in gladness of heart. The evacuation of Petersburg and Richmond and the surrender of the principal insurgent army give hope of a righteous and speedy peace, whose joyous expression cannot be restrained. In the midst of this, however, He from whom all blessings flow must not be forgotten.

A call for a national thanksgiving is being prepared and will be duly promulgated. Nor must those whose harder part give us the cause of rejoicing be overlooked. Their honors must not be parceled out with others. I myself was near the front and had the high pleasure of transmitting much of the good news to you; but no part of the honor for plan or execution is mine. To General Grant, his skillful officers and brave men, all belongs. The gallant Navy stood ready but was not in reach to take active part.

By these recent successes, the reinauguration of the national authority — reconstruc-
tion — which has had a large share of thought from the first, is pressed much more closely upon our attention. It is fraught with great difficulty. Unlike a case of war between independent nations, there is no authorized organ for us to treat with — no one man has authority to give up the rebellion for any other man. We simply must begin with and mold from disorganized and discordant elements. Nor is it a small additional embarrassment that we, the loyal people, differ among ourselves as to the mode, manner, and measure of reconstruction.

As a general rule, I abstain from reading the reports of attacks upon myself, wishing not to be provoked by that to which I cannot properly offer an answer. In spite of this precaution, however, it comes to my knowledge that I am much censured for some supposed agency in setting up and seeking to sustain the new state government of Louisiana. In this I have done just so much and no more than the public knows.

In the annual message of December 1863, and the accompanying proclamation, I presented a plan of reconstruction, as the phrase goes, which I promised, if adopted by any state, should be acceptable to and sustained by the executive government of the nation. I distinctly stated that this was not the only plan which might possibly be acceptable, and I also distinctly protested that the executive claimed no right to say when or whether members should be admitted to seats in Congress from such states. This plan was, in advance, submitted to the then Cabinet and distinctly approved by every member of it. One of them suggested that I should then and in that connection apply the Emancipation Proclamation to the theretofore excepted parts of Virginia and Louisiana; that I should drop the suggestion about apprenticeship for freed people; and that I should omit the protest against my own power in regard to the admission of members to Congress. But even he approved every part and parcel of the plan which has since been employed or touched by the action of Louisiana.

The new constitution of Louisiana, declaring emancipation for the whole state, practically applies the proclamation to the part previously excepted. It does not adopt apprenticeship for freed people, and it is silent, as it could not well be otherwise, about the admission of members to Congress. So that, as it applies to Louisiana, every member of the Cabinet fully approved the plan. The message went to Congress, and I received many commendations of the plan, written and verbal, and not a single objection to it from any professed emancipationist came to my knowledge until after the news reached Washington that the people of Louisiana had begun to move in accordance with it. From about July 1862, I had corresponded with different persons supposed to be interested in seeking a re-construction of a state government for Louisiana. When the message of 1863, with the plan before mentioned, reached New Orleans, General Banks wrote me that he was confident that the people, with his military cooperation, would reconstruct substantially on that plan. I wrote to him and some of them to try it. They tried it, and the result is known. Such has been my only agency in setting up the Louisiana government.

As to sustaining it, my promise is out, as before stated. But, as bad promises are better broken than kept, I shall treat this as a bad promise and break it whenever I shall be convinced that keeping it is adverse to the public interest; but I have not yet been so convinced. I have been shown a letter on this subject, supposed to be an able one, in which the writer expresses regret that my mind has not seemed to be definitely fixed on the question whether the seceded states, so called, are in the Union or out of it. It would perhaps add astonishment to his regret were he to learn that since I have found professed Union men endeavoring to make that question, I have purposely forborne any public expression upon it. As appears to me, that question has not been nor yet is a practically material one, and that any discussion of it, while it thus remains practically immaterial, could have no effect other than the mischievous one of dividing our friends. As yet, whatever it may hereafter become, that question is bad as the basis of a controversy, and good for nothing at all — a merely pernicious abstraction.

We all agree that the seceded states, so called, are out of their proper practical relation with the Union, and that the sole object of the government, civil and military, in regard to those states is to again get them into that proper practical relation. I believe that it is not only possible but in fact easier to do this without deciding or even considering whether those states have ever been out of the Union than with it. Finding themselves safely at home, it would be utterly immaterial whether they had been abroad.

Let us all join in doing the acts necessary to restore the proper practical relations between these states and the Union, and each forever after innocently indulge his own opinion whether, in doing the acts, he brought the states from without into the Union, or only gave them proper assistance, they never having been out of it. The amount of constituency, so to speak, on which the Louisiana government rests would be more satisfactory to all if it contained 50,000, or 30,000, or even 20,000, instead of only about 12,000, as it does. It is also unsatisfactory to some that the elective franchise is not given to the colored man. I would myself prefer that it were now conferred on the very intelligent, and on those who serve our cause as soldiers.

Still, the question is not whether the Louisiana government, as it stands, is quite all that is desirable. The question is, Will it be wiser to take it as it is and help to improve it, or to reject and disperse? Can Louisiana be brought into proper practical relation with the Union sooner by sustaining or by discarding her new state government? Some 12,000 voters in the heretofore slave state of Louisiana have sworn allegiance to the Union, assumed to be the rightful political power of the state; held elections; organized a state government; adopted a free-state constitution, giving the benefit of public schools equally to black and white, and empowering the legislature to confer the elective franchise upon the colored man. Their legislature has already voted to ratify the constitutional amendment recently passed by Congress abolishing slavery throughout the nation. These 12,000 persons are thus fully committed to the Union and to perpetuate freedom in the state — committed to the very things, and nearly all the things, the nation wants — and they ask the nation's recognition and its assistance to make good their committal.

Now, if we reject and spurn them, we do our utmost to disorganize and disperse them. We, in fact, say to the white man: You are worthless or worse; we will neither help you nor be helped by you. To the blacks we say: This cup of liberty which these, your old masters, hold to your lips, we will dash from you and leave you to the chances of gathering the spilled and scattered contents in some vague and undefined when, where, and how. If this course, discouraging and paralyzing both white and black, has any tendency to bring Louisiana into proper practical relations with the Union, I have so far been unable to perceive it. If, on the contrary, we recognize and sustain the new government of Louisiana, the converse of all this is made true. We encourage the hearts and nerve the arms of the 12,000 to adhere to their work, and argue for it, and proselyte for it, and fight for it, and feed it, and grow it, and ripen it to a complete success. The colored man, too, in seeing all united for him, is inspired with vigilance, and energy, and daring to the same end. Grant that he desires the elective franchise, will he not attain it sooner by saving the already advanced steps toward it than by running backward over them? Concede that the new government of Louisiana is only what it should be as the egg is to the fowl, we shall sooner have the fowl by hatching the egg than by smashing it.

Again, if we reject Louisiana, we also reject one vote in favor of the proposed amendment to the national Constitution. To meet this proposition, it has been argued that no more than three-fourths of those states which have not attempted secession are necessary to validly ratify the amendment. I do not commit myself against this further than to say that such a ratification would be questionable and sure to be persistently questioned, while a ratification by three-fourths of all the states would be unquestioned and unquestionable.

I repeat the question: Can Louisiana be brought into proper practical relation with the Union sooner by sustaining or by discarding her new state·government? What has been said of Louisiana will apply generally to other states. And yet so great peculiarities pertain to each state, and such important and sudden changes occur in the same state, and withal so new and unprecedented is the whole case, that no exclusive and inflexible plan can safely be prescribed as to details and collaterals. Such exclusive and inflexible plan would surely become a new entanglement. Important principles may and must be inflexible.

In the present situation, as the phrase goes, it may be my duty to make some new announcement to the people of the South. I am considering, and shall not fail to act, when satisfied that action will be proper.

143.

GIDEON WELLES: The Death of President Lincoln

On the evening of April 14, 1865 — Good Friday — President Lincoln, exhausted by the events of the past weeks, went to Ford's Theatre in Washington for a few hours of relaxation. At 10:15 P.M., as he was sitting in a box watching an otherwise forgotten play, Our American Cousin, *he was shot in the back of the head by the actor John Wilkes Booth. Lincoln was carried to a nearby house where he died the next morning. At about the same time Secretary of State Seward was attacked by an associate of Booth and badly beaten. Booth was captured in a barn near Bowling Green, Virginia, on April 26, where he (probably) shot himself. Of the nine other persons implicated in the assassination, four were hanged on July 7, four were imprisoned, and the ninth was acquitted. Gideon Welles, Lincoln's effective secretary of the navy throughout the war, was present when the President died and described the event in his diary — as well as its consequences for the new President, for the Cabinet, and especially for the grief-stricken Negroes of both North and South. The following selection comprises entries from Welles's diary for the period from April 15 to May 12.*

Source: *Diary of Gideon Welles*, Boston, 1911, Vol. II, pp. 287-293, 300-305.

April 15. A door which opened upon a porch or gallery and also the windows, were kept open for fresh air. The night was dark, cloudy, and damp, and about six it began to rain. I remained in the room until then without sitting or leaving it, when, there being a vacant chair which someone left at the foot of the bed, I occupied it for nearly two hours, listening to the heavy groans and witnessing the wasting life of the good and great man who was expiring before me.

About 6 A.M. I experienced a feeling of faintness and, for the first time after entering the room, a little past eleven, I left it and the house, and took a short walk in the open air. It was a dark and gloomy morning, and rain set in before I returned to the house, some fifteen minutes later. Large groups of people were gathered every few rods, all anxious and solicitous. Some one or more from each group stepped forward as I passed to inquire into the condition of the President and to ask if there was no hope. Intense grief was on every countenance when I replied that the President could survive but a short time. The colored people especially — and there were at this time more of them, perhaps, than of whites — were overwhelmed with grief.

Returning to the house, I seated myself in the back parlor, where the attorney general and others had been engaged in taking evidence concerning the assassination. Stanton and Speed and Usher were there, the latter asleep on the bed. — There were three or four others also in the room. While I did not feel inclined to sleep, as many did, I was somewhat indisposed. I had been so for several days. — The excitement and bad atmosphere from the crowded rooms oppressed me physically.

A little before seven, I went into the room where the dying President was rapidly drawing near the closing moments. His wife soon after made her last visit to him. The death struggle had begun. Robert, his son, stood with several others at the head of the bed. He bore himself well, but on two occasions gave way to overpowering grief and sobbed aloud, turning his head and leaning on the shoulder of Senator Sumner. The respiration of the President became suspended at intervals and at last entirely ceased at twenty-two minutes past seven.

A prayer followed from Dr. Gurley; and the cabinet, with the exception of Mr. Seward and Mr. McCulloch, immediately thereafter assembled in the back parlor, from which all other persons were excluded, and there signed a letter which was prepared by Attorney General Speed to the vice-president informing him of the event and that the government devolved upon him.

Mr. Stanton proposed that Mr. Speed, as the law officer, should communicate the letter to Mr. Johnson with some other member of the cabinet. Mr. Dennison named me. I saw that, though all assented, it disconcerted Stanton, who had expected and intended to be the man and to have Speed associated with him. I was disinclined personally to disturb an obvious arrangement and therefore named Mr. McCulloch as the first in order after the secretary of state.

I arranged with Speed, with whom I rode home, for a cabinet meeting at twelve meridian at the room of the secretary of the treasury, in order that the government should experience no detriment, and that prompt and necessary action might be taken to assist the new chief magistrate in preserving and promoting the public tranquillity. We accordingly met at noon. Mr. Speed reported that the President had taken the oath, which was administered by the chief justice, and had expressed a desire that the affairs of the government should proceed without interruption. Some discussion took place as to the propriety of an inaugural address, but the general impression was that it would be inexpedient. I was most decidedly of that opinion.

President Johnson, who was invited to be present, deported himself admirably, and on the subject of an inaugural said his acts would best disclose his policy. In all essentials it would, he said, be the same as that of the late President. He desired the members of the cabinet to go forward with their duties without any change. Mr. Hunter, chief clerk of the State Department, was designated to act ad interim as secretary of state. I suggested Mr. Speed, but I saw it was not acceptable in certain quarters. Stanton especially expressed a hope that Hunter should be assigned to the duty.

A room for the President as an office was proposed until he could occupy the Executive Mansion, and Mr. McCulloch offered the room adjoining his own in the Treasury Building. I named the State Department as

Gideon Welles, Lincoln's secretary of the navy

appropriate and proper, at least until the secretary of state recovered, or so long as the President wished, but objections arose at once. The papers of Mr. Seward would, Stanton said, be disturbed; it would be better he should be here, etc., etc. Stanton, I saw, had a purpose, among other things, feared papers would fall under Mr. Johnson's eye which he did not wish to be seen.

On returning to my house this morning, Saturday, I found Mrs. Welles, who had been ill and confined to the house from indisposition for a week, had been twice sent for by Mrs. Lincoln to come to her at Peterson's. The housekeeper, knowing the state of Mrs. W.'s health, had without consultation turned away the messenger, Major French; but Mrs. Welles, on learning the facts when he came the second time, had yielded and imprudently gone, although the weather was inclement. She remained at the Executive Mansion through the day. For myself, wearied, shocked, exhausted, but not inclined to sleep, the day, when not actually and officially engaged, passed off strangely.

I went after breakfast to the Executive Mansion. There was a cheerless cold rain and everything seemed gloomy. On the Avenue in front of the White House were several hundred colored people, mostly women and children, weeping and wailing their loss. This crowd did not appear to diminish through the whole of that cold, wet day; they seemed not to know what was to be their fate since their great benefactor was dead, and their hopeless grief affected me more than almost anything else, though strong and brave men wept when I met them.

At the White House all was silent and sad. Mrs. W. was with Mrs. L. and came to meet me in the library. Speed came in, and we soon left together. As we were descending the stairs, "Tad," who was looking from the window at the foot, turned and, seeing us, cried aloud in his tears, "Oh, Mr. Welles, who killed my father?" Neither Speed nor myself could restrain our tears nor give the poor boy any satisfactory answer.

April 16. Sunday, the 16th, the President and cabinet met by agreement at 10 A.M. at the Treasury. The President was half an hour behind time. Stanton was more than an hour late. He brought with him papers and had many suggestions relative to the measure before the cabinet at our last meeting with President Lincoln. The general policy of the treatment of the Rebels and the Rebel states was discussed. President Johnson is not disposed to treat treason lightly, and the chief Rebels he would punish with exemplary severity.

Stanton has divided his original plan and made the reestablishing of state government applicable to North Carolina, leaving Virginia, which has a loyal government and governor, to arrange that matter of election to which I had excepted but elaborating it for North Carolina and the other states.

Being at the War Department Sunday evening, I was detained conversing with Stanton. Finally, Senator Sumner came in. He was soon followed by Gooch and

Dawes of Massachusetts and some two or three others. One or more general officers also came in. Stanton took from his table, in answer to an inquiry from Sumner, his document which had been submitted to the cabinet and which was still a cabinet measure.

It was evident the gentlemen were there by appointment, and I considered myself an intruder or out of place. If so, Stanton did not know how to get rid of me, and it seemed awkward for me to leave. The others doubtless supposed I was there by arrangement; perhaps I was, but I felt embarrassed and was very glad, after he had read to them his first program for Virginia and had got about half through with the other, when Sumner demanded to know what provision was made for the colored man to vote. A line was brought me at this time by the messenger, which gave me an opportunity to leave.

April 17. On Monday, the 17th, I was actively engaged in bringing forward business which had been interrupted and suspended, issuing orders, and in arranging for the funeral solemnities of President Lincoln. Secretary Seward and his son continue in a low condition, and Mr. Fred Seward's life is precarious.

April 18, Tuesday. Details in regard to the funeral, which takes place on the 19th, occupied general attention and little else than preliminary arrangements and conversation was done at the cabinet meeting. From every part of the country comes lamentation. Every house, almost, has some drapery, especially the homes of the poor. Profuse exhibition is displayed on the public buildings and the dwellings of the wealthy, but the little black ribbon or strip of black cloth from the hovel of the poor Negro or the impoverished white is more touching.

I have tried to write something consecutively since the horrid transactions of Friday night, but I have no heart for it, and the jottings down are mere mementos of a period, which I will try to fill up when more composed and I have leisure or time for the task.

Sad and painful, wearied and irksome, the few preceding incoherent pages have been written for future use, for the incidents are fresh in my mind and may pass away with me but cannot ever be by me forgotten.

April 19. The funeral on Wednesday, the 19th, was imposing, sad, and sorrowful. All felt the solemnity and sorrowed as if they had lost one of their own household. By voluntary action, business was everywhere suspended, and the people crowded the streets.

The cabinet met by arrangement in the room occupied by the President at the Treasury. We left a few minutes before meridian so as to be in the East Room at precisely 12 o'clock, being the last to enter. Others will give the details.

I rode with Stanton in the procession to the Capitol. The attendance was immense. The front of the procession reached the Capitol, it was said, before we started, and there were as many, or more, who followed us. A brief prayer was made by Mr. Gurley in the Rotunda, where we left the remains of the good and great man we loved so well. Returning, I left Stanton, who was nervous and full of orders, and took in my carriage President Johnson and Preston King, their carriage having been crowded out of place. Coming down Pennsylvania Avenue after this long detention, we met the marching procession in broad platoons all the way to the Kirkwood House on Twelfth Street.

There were no truer mourners, when all were sad, than the poor colored people who crowded the streets, joined the procession, and exhibited their woe, bewailing the loss of him whom they regarded as a benefactor and father. Women, as well as men, with their little children, thronged the streets; sorrow, trouble, and distress depicted on their countenances and in their bearing. The vacant holiday expression had given way to real grief. Seward, I am told, sat up in bed and viewed the procession and hearse of the President, and I know his emotion. Stanton, who rode with me, was uneasy and left the carriage four or five times.

May. The calls upon the President by associations claiming to represent states and municipalities are becoming less. To some extent they may have been useful in the peculiar condition of public affairs by inspiring confidence, and in giving the President an opportunity to enunciate his opinions in the absence of any inaugural, but they have been annoying at times, obstructions to business, and were becoming irksome. The President was not displeased with these manifestations and has borne himself well through a period which has been trying and arduous and is gathering to himself the good wishes of the country.

I called up the subject of free communication through the coast to all vessels having regular clearance, but was told the President and secretary of the treasury were endeavoring to make a satisfactory arrangement which should be in conformity with the act of July 2, 1864. It is obvious that the intention of that act was to place the treasury above, or independent of, the President — one of Chase's demonstrations, and his hand is in this movement.

A proclamation, or order, that those who were taken plundering our commerce should be punished, and that forbearance to put in execution the proclamation of the 19th of April, 1861, would not longer be exercised, was opposed by Stanton and Speed. Others failed to sustain me, except McCulloch, who gave me partial support. Stanton considers it his special province to guard Seward's policy as it has been, not being aware that Seward has changed.

The subject of reestablishing the Federal authority and of a reorganization of the state governments in the insurrectionary region was discussed. The secretary of war was requested to send copies of the modified plan to each head of department, and a special cabinet meeting was ordered on Monday, the 8th, to consider the subject.

At the cabinet meeting the plan of asserting the Federal authority and of establishing the state government in Virginia was fully considered. Stanton's project, with several radical amendments presented by me, was adopted. I was surprised and gratified with the alacrity and cheerfulness he exhibited, and the readiness with which he adopted and assented to most of my amendments. In one instance he became a little pugnacious, Speed and Dennison having dissented. Two of my recommendations were not adopted, and as no other one presented amendments, I cared not to appear fastidious but am nevertheless satisfied I was right. The session was long, over four hours.

May 9, Tuesday. A proclamation of amnesty proposed by Speed was considered and, with some changes, agreed to.

The condition of North Carolina was taken up, and a general plan of organization intended for all the Rebel states was submitted and debated. No great difference of opinion was expressed except on the matter of suffrage. Stanton, Dennison, and Speed were for Negro suffrage; McCulloch, Usher, and myself were opposed. It was agreed, on request of Stanton, we would not discuss the question, but each express his opinion without preliminary debate. After our opinions had been given, I stated I was for adhering to the rule prescribed in President Lincoln's proclamation, which had been fully considered and matured, and besides, in all these matters, I am for no further subversion of the laws, institutions, and usages of the states respectively, nor for Federal intermeddling in local matters, than is absolutely necessary in order to rid them of the radical error which has caused our national trouble. All laws, not inconsistent with those of the conquerors, remain until changed to the conquered, is an old rule.

This question of Negro suffrage is beset with difficulties growing out of the conflict through which we have passed and the current of sympathy for the colored race. The demagogues will make use of it, regardless of what is best for the country and without regard for the organic law, the rights of the state, or the troubles of our government. There is a fanaticism on the subject with some who persuade themselves that the cause of liberty and the Union is with the Negro and not the white man. White men, and especially Southern white men, are tyrants. Senator Sumner is riding this one idea at top speed. There are others, less sincere than Sumner, who are pressing the question for party purposes.

On the other hand, there may be unjust prejudices against permitting colored persons to enjoy the elective franchise, under any circumstances; but this is not, and should not be, a Federal question. No one can claim that the blacks, in the slave states especially, can exercise the elective franchise intelligently. In most of the free states they are not permitted to vote. Is it politic and wise, or right even, when trying to restore peace and reconcile differences, to make so radical a change, provided we have the authority, which I deny, to elevate the ignorant Negro, who has been enslaved mentally as well as physically, to the discharge of the highest duties of citizenship, especially when our free states will not permit the few free Negroes to vote?

The Federal government has no right and has not attempted to dictate on the matter of suffrage to any state, and I apprehend it will not conduce to harmony to arrogate and exercise arbitrary power over the states which have been in rebellion. It was never intended by the founders of the Union that the Federal government should prescribe suffrage to the states. We shall get rid of slavery by constitutional means. But confer-

ring on the black civil rights is another matter. I know not the authority. The President, in the exercise of the pardoning power, may limit or make conditions, and, while granting life and liberty to traitors, deny them the right of holding office or of voting. While, however, he can exclude traitors, can he legitimately confer on the blacks of North Carolina the right to vote? I do not see how this can be done by him or by Congress.

This whole question of suffrage is much abused. The Negro can take upon himself the duty about as intelligently and as well for the public interest as a considerable portion of the foreign element which comes among us. Each will be the tool of demagogues. If the Negro is to vote and exercise the duties of a citizen, let him be educated to it. The measure should not, even if the government were empowered to act, be precipitated when he is stolidly ignorant and wholly unprepared. It is proposed to do it against what have been and still are the constitutions, laws, usages, and practices of the states which we wish to restore to fellowship.

Stanton has changed his position, has been converted, is now for Negro suffrage. These were not his views a short time since. But aspiring politicians will, as the current now sets, generally take that road.

The trial of the assassins is not so promptly carried into effect as Stanton declared it should be. He said it was his intention the criminals should be tried and executed before President Lincoln was buried. But the President was buried last Thursday, the 4th, and the trial has not, I believe, commenced.

I regret they are not tried by the civil court, and so expressed myself, as did McCulloch; but Stanton, who says the proof is clear and positive, was emphatic; and Speed advised a military commission, though at first, I thought, otherwise inclined. It is now rumored the trial is to be secret, which is another objectionable feature and will be likely to meet condemnation after the event and excitement have passed off.

The rash, impulsive, and arbitrary measures of Stanton are exceedingly repugnant to my notions, and I am pained to witness the acquiescence they receive. He carries others with him, sometimes against their convictions as expressed to me.

The President and cabinet called on Mr. Seward at his house after the close of the council. He came down to meet us in his parlor. I was glad to see him so well and animated, yet a few weeks have done the work of years, apparently, with his system. Perhaps, when his wounds have healed and the fractured jaw is restored, he may recover in some degree his former looks, but I apprehend not. His head was covered with a close-fitting cap, and the appliances to his jaw entered his mouth and prevented him from articulating clearly. Still, he was disposed to talk, and we to listen. Once or twice, allusions to the night of the great calamity affected him more deeply than I have ever seen him.

May 10, Wednesday. Senator Sumner called on me. We had a long conversation on matters pertaining to the affairs of Fort Sumter. He has been selected to deliver an oration on Mr. Lincoln's death to the citizens of Boston and desired to post himself in some respects. I told him the influence of the Blairs, and especially of the elder, had done much to strengthen Mr. Lincoln in that matter, while Seward and General Scott had opposed.

Sumner assures me Chase has gone into Rebeldom to promote Negro suffrage. I have no doubt that Chase has that and other schemes for presidential preferment in hand in this voyage. S. says that President Johnson is aware of his (Chase's) object in behalf of the Negroes and favors the idea of their voting. On this point I am skeptical. He would not oppose any such movement

were any state to make it. I so expressed myself to Sumner, and he assented but intended to say the Negroes were the people.

May 11. The papers, and especially those of New York, are complaining of the court which is to try the assassins, and their assault is the more severe because it is alleged that the session is to be secret. This subject is pretty much given over to the management of the War Department, since Attorney General Speed and Judge Advocate General Holt affirm that to be legal, and a military court the only real method of eliciting the whole truth. It would be impolitic and, I think, unwise and injudicious to shut off all spectators and make a "Council of Ten" of this commission. The press will greatly aggravate the objections, and do already.

May 12, Friday. The President does not yet sufficiently generalize but goes too much into unimportant details and personal appeals. He will, however, correct this with a little experience, I have no doubt.

I inquired of the secretary of war if there is any foundation for the assertion that the trial of the assassins is to be in secret. He says it will not be secret, although the doors will not be open to the whole public immediately. Full and minute reports of all the testimony and proceedings will be taken and in due time published; and trusty and reliable persons, in limited numbers, will have permission to attend. This will relieve the proceeding of some of its objectionable features.

Stanton has undertaken to get the projected amnesty proclamation (as last altered, amended, corrected, and improved) printed; also the form of government for North Carolina as last shaped, and as far as anything decisive had taken place. Dennison inquired when he might have copies, and he promises to send immediately. The truth is, it is still in the hands of the President, who will shape it right. King has been of service in this matter.

Mourning women among the ruins in a burned section of Richmond, Va., April 1865

THE UNION RESTORED

General Grant's Army of the Potomac relentlessly pressed for final victory over the Southern forces. Lee sought to keep his Army intact by evasion, but when his attempt proved futile, he surrendered at Appomattox. The Civil War was over. The Union had been preserved — but in what form? Were the states of the Confederacy to be received back into the Union with full political rights? Were the Confederate leaders to retain their political power? Did the federal government have a responsibility to the former Negro slaves? Such questions were to occupy the center of the political stage in the decade following the war. But

for most Southerners the pressing question immediately after Appomattox was one of sheer physical survival. The major cities of the South lay in ruins. Transportation was at a standstill: railroads had been torn up, rolling stock destroyed. Savings had been wiped out, for Confederate currency or bonds were never to be repaid. There was still the farmland, to be sure, but the labor force to work the fields had been freed.

The North had experienced an economic boom as a result of the war. But it was not free of suffering. Over half of the more than 600,000 Americans killed in the war had been Northerners.

(Above) Lincoln at his second inauguration; all the assassination conspirators stand directly below Lincoln; (left) four days before the assassination

Lincoln had hoped to "bind up the nation's wounds" in the calm of peace, but six weeks after his second inauguration he lay dead — shot by an extremist Southern sympathizer. Unfortunately, few men of politics understood as well as he had the fundamental issue of the times — the survival of American political institutions. Although Lincoln had been vilified and ridiculed by many, his death was a profound shock to the American people, and their mourning for him was genuine.

(Below left) John Wilkes, Edwin, and Junius Brutus Booth in "Julius Caesar"; (below right) John Wilkes Booth, Lincoln's assassin

(Above) Lincoln's funeral procession in Chicago; (below) funeral parade in New York City passing the flag-draped Roosevelt mansion on the left, from which young Theodore watched

Two views of the Confederate capital, Richmond, in ruins. The city was set afire by the Davis government fleeing before the on-coming Union Army in April 1865. (Above) Burnt district seen from the canal basin; (left) ruined Gallego flour mills on the James River

(Left) Ruins of the Pinckney Mansion in Charleston, S.C.; photograph by G. N. Barnard, 1865

(Right) Charleston, S.C., following the bombardment by the Union forces under General Sherman, 1865

(Right) Nashville, Tenn., in 1864; railroad yard and depot are in the foreground and the Capitol in the upper right. Union forces under George Thomas routed Hood's army and captured the city in December. (Below) View of Fredericksburg, Va., in May 1864

View of the south side of Buffalo Street during the 1865 flood in Rochester, N.Y.

(Left) Tintype of a storefront by an unknown photographer; (right) view of the Old South Church in Boston, Mass.; from a stereograph by John P. Soule

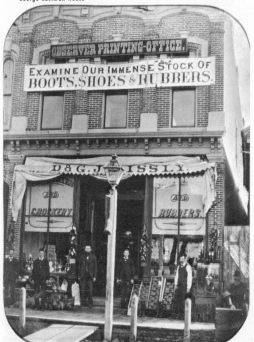

Plymouth, N.H.; from a stereograph by Charles Bierstadt

George Eastman House

Alexandria, Va.; view from the Pioneer Mill, looking up the wharf on the Potomac River, 1865

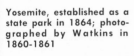

Library of Congress

Yosemite, established as a state park in 1864; photographed by Watkins in 1860-1861

View of the horse-drawn buses along Broadway in New York City, c. 1863; (below) Negro orphans' home in New York City, 1862

The Northern victory ended secession but did not automatically restore the Union. Lincoln had wanted to return the Confederate states to full political rights as speedily as possible. However, many Republicans who feared Southern opposition to high tariffs and pro-business legislation wanted to delay Southern reintegration into national politics. Other Republicans feared that Southerners were devising new ways to maintain slavery and urged the military occupation of the South. For the federal government, the problem of restoring Southern political rights eventually centered on the question, "How much social and political change shall be required of the Confederate states?"

(Above) Raising the American flag over Fort Sumter during ceremonies held April 14, 1865; (right) grand review of the Army in Washington, D.C., May 1865; photo by Brady

(Above) "The Union Christmas Dinner"; published in "Harper's Weekly" in 1864. It depicts Lincoln's invitation to the South to rejoin the Union on an equal basis with the other states. (Right) Publishing the first issue of the "Loyal Georgian" following the entry of Union troops into Savannah, December 1864; (below) Freedman's Village in Arlington, Va.

144.

Andrew Johnson: Proclamation of Amnesty and Pardon for the Confederate States

On May 29, 1865, President Johnson issued a proclamation of amnesty and pardon for the citizens of those Confederate states that had not been restored under Lincoln's Reconstruction policy. Generally in accord with Lincoln's amnesty proclamation of December 8, 1863, Johnson's proclamation differed on one major point. A lifelong supporter of small farmers and the lower classes in general, he specifically excluded the wealthy classes from the benefits of the proclamation.

Source: Richardson, VI, pp. 310-312.

Whereas, the President of the United States, on the 8th day of December, A.D. 1863, and on the 26th day of March, A.D. 1864, did, with the object to suppress the existing rebellion, to induce all persons to return to their loyalty, and to restore the authority of the United States, issue proclamations offering amnesty and pardon to certain persons who had, directly or by implication, participated in the said rebellion; and

Whereas, many persons who had so engaged in said rebellion have, since the issuance of said proclamations, failed or neglected to take the benefits offered thereby; and

Whereas, many persons who have been justly deprived of all claim to amnesty and pardon thereunder by reason of their participation, directly or by implication, in said rebellion and continued hostility to the government of the United States since the date of said proclamations, now desire to apply for and obtain amnesty and pardon.

To the end, therefore, that the authority of the government of the United States may be restored and that peace, order, and freedom may be established, I, Andrew Johnson, President of the United States, do proclaim and declare that I hereby grant to all persons who have, directly or indirectly, participated in the existing rebellion, except as hereinafter excepted, amnesty and pardon, with restoration of all rights of property, except as to slaves and except in cases where legal proceedings under the laws of the United States providing for the confiscation of property of persons engaged in rebellion have been instituted; but upon the condition, nevertheless, that every such person shall take and subscribe the following oath (or affirmation) and thenceforward keep and maintain said oath inviolate, and which oath shall be registered for permanent preservation and shall be of the tenor and effect following, to wit:

I, ———— ————, do solemnly swear (or affirm), in presence of Almighty God, that I will henceforth faithfully support, protect, and defend the Constitution of the United States and the Union of the States thereunder, and that I will in like manner abide by and faithfully support all laws and proclamations which have been made during the existing rebellion with reference to the emancipation of slaves. So help me God.

The following classes of persons are excepted from the benefits of this proclamation:

Andrew Johnson, photographed by Brady

First, all who are or shall have been pretended civil or diplomatic officers or otherwise domestic or foreign agents of the pretended Confederate government.

Second, all who left judicial stations under the United States to aid the rebellion.

Third, all who shall have been military or naval officers of said pretended Confederate government above the rank of colonel in the army or lieutenant in the navy.

Fourth, all who left seats in the Congress of the United States to aid the rebellion.

Fifth, all who resigned or tendered resignations of their commissions in the Army or Navy of the United States to evade duty in resisting the rebellion.

Sixth, all who have engaged in any way in treating otherwise than lawfully as prisoners of war persons found in the United States service as officers, soldiers, seamen, or in other capacities.

Seventh, all persons who have been or are absentees from the United States for the purpose of aiding the rebellion.

Eighth, all military and naval officers in the Rebel service who were educated by the government in the Military Academy at West Point or the United States Naval Academy.

Ninth, all persons who held the pretended offices of governors of states in insurrection against the United States.

Tenth, all persons who left their homes within the jurisdiction and protection of the United States and passed beyond the Federal military lines into the pretended Confederate States for the purpose of aiding the rebellion.

Eleventh, all persons who have been engaged in the destruction of the commerce of the United States upon the high seas and all persons who have made raids into the United States from Canada or been engaged in destroying the commerce of the United States upon the lakes and rivers that separate the British Provinces from the United States.

Twelfth, all persons who, at the time when they seek to obtain the benefits hereof by taking the oath herein prescribed, are in military, naval, or civil confinement or custody, or under bonds of the civil, military, or naval authorities, or agents of the United States as prisoners of war, or persons detained for offenses of any kind, either before or after conviction.

Thirteenth, all persons who have voluntarily participated in said rebellion and the estimated value of whose taxable property is over $20,000.

Fourteenth, all persons who have taken the oath of amnesty as prescribed in the President's proclamation of December 8, A.D. 1863, or an oath of allegiance to the government of the United States since the date of said proclamation and who have not thenceforward kept and maintained the same inviolate.

Provided, that special application may be made to the President for pardon by any person belonging to the excepted classes, and such clemency will be liberally extended as may be consistent with the facts of the case and the peace and dignity of the United States.

The secretary of state will establish rules and regulations for administering and recording the said amnesty oath, so as to insure its benefit to the people and guard the government against fraud.

145.

Andrew Johnson: Provisional Government in North Carolina

Under Lincoln's Reconstruction program, Louisiana, Tennessee, Arkansas, and Virginia were restored to the Union under provisional governments. Radical Republicans, remembering Johnson's fiery pronouncements on reconstruction immediately after he assumed the presidency, believed Johnson would accede to their demands for a radical program. After a month in office, however, Johnson changed his position and largely adopted Lincoln's moderate Reconstruction program. On May 29, 1865, Johnson issued the following proclamation establishing a provisional government for North Carolina. When Congress convened in December, all the Confederate states, except Texas, had been reorganized under Johnson's policy.

Source: Richardson, VI, pp. 312-314.

Whereas, the 4th Section of the 4th Article of the Constitution of the United States declares that the United States shall guarantee to every state in the Union a republican form of government and shall protect each of them against invasion and domestic violence; and

Whereas, the President of the United States is by the Constitution made commander in chief of the Army and Navy, as well as chief civil executive officer of the United States, and is bound by solemn oath faithfully to execute the office of President of the United States and to take care that the laws be faithfully executed; and

Whereas, the rebellion, which has been waged by a portion of the people of the United States against the properly constituted authorities of the government thereof in the most violent and revolting form, but whose organized and armed forces have now been almost entirely overcome, has in its revolutionary progress deprived the people of the state of North Carolina of all civil government; and

Whereas, it becomes necessary and proper to carry out and enforce the obligations of the United States to the people of North Carolina in securing them in the enjoyment of a republican form of government:

Now, therefore, in obedience to the high and solemn duties imposed upon me by the Constitution of the United States and for the purpose of enabling the loyal people of said state to organize a state government whereby justice may be established, domestic tranquillity insured, and loyal citizens protected in all their rights of life, liberty, and property, I, Andrew Johnson, President of the United States and commander in chief of the Army and Navy of the United States, do hereby appoint William W. Holden provisional governor of the state of North Carolina, whose duty it shall be, at the earliest practicable period, to prescribe such rules and regulations as may be necessary and proper for convening a convention composed of delegates to be chosen by that portion of the people of said state who are loyal to the United States, and no others, for the purpose of altering or amending the constitution thereof, and with authority to exercise within the limits of said state all the powers necessary and proper to enable such loyal people of the state of North Carolina to restore said state to its constitutional relations to the Federal government and to present such a republican form of state government as will entitle the state to the guarantee of the United States therefor and its people to protection by the United States against invasion, insurrection, and domestic violence:

Provided, that in any election that may be hereafter held for choosing delegates to any state convention as aforesaid no person shall be qualified as an elector or shall be eligible as a member of such convention unless he shall have previously taken and subscribed the oath of amnesty as set forth in the President's proclamation of May 29, A.D. 1865, and is a voter qualified as prescribed by the constitution and laws of the state of North Carolina in force immediately before the 20th day of May, A.D. 1861, the date of the so-called ordinance of secession; and the said convention, when convened, or the legislature that may be thereafter assembled, will prescribe the qualification of electors and the eligibility of persons to hold office under the constitution and laws of the state — a power the people of the several states composing the Federal Union have rightfully exercised from the origin of the government to the present time.

And I do hereby direct:

First, that the military commander of the department and all officers and persons in the military and naval service aid and assist the said provisional governor in carrying into effect this proclamation; and they are enjoined to abstain from in any way hindering, impeding, or discouraging the loyal people from the organization of a state government as herein authorized.

Second, that the secretary of state proceed to put in force all laws of the United States the administration whereof belongs to the State Department applicable to the geographical limits aforesaid.

Third, that the secretary of the treasury proceed to nominate for appointment assessors of taxes and collectors of customs and internal revenue, and such other officers of the Treasury Department as are authorized by law, and put in execution the revenue laws of the United States within the geographical limits aforesaid. In making appointments the preference shall be given to qualified loyal persons residing within the districts where their respective duties are to be performed; but if suitable residents of the districts shall not be found, then persons residing in other states or districts shall be appointed.

Fourth, that the postmaster general proceed to establish post offices and post routes and put into execution the postal laws of the United States within the said state, giving to loyal residents the preference of appointment; but if suitable residents are not found, then to appoint agents, etc., from other states.

Fifth, that the district judge for the judicial district in which North Carolina is included proceed to hold courts within said state in accordance with the provisions of the act of Congress. The attorney general will instruct the proper officers to libel and bring to judgment, confiscation, and sale property subject to confiscation and enforce the administration of justice within said state in all matters within the cognizance and jurisdiction of the Federal courts.

Sixth, that the secretary of the navy take possession of all public property belonging to the Navy Department within said geographical limits and put in operation all acts of Congress in relation to naval affairs having application to the said state.

Seventh, that the secretary of the interior put in force the laws relating to the Interior Department applicable to the geographical limits aforesaid.

146.

DAVID ROSS LOCKE ("PETROLEUM V. NASBY"): A Platform for Northern Democrats

David Ross Locke, who achieved fame as a political satirist under the pseudonym Petroleum V. Nasby, published his first Nasby letter in March 1861. The letters, which purportedly were written in support of the South, appeared in the Findlay Jeffersonian *and the* Toledo Blade, *Ohio papers that Locke edited. Nasby was humorously portrayed as an ignorant and often corrupt "Copperhead" whose appalling logic defeated his cause without need of rebuttal. The following letter proposing a postwar platform for the Northern Democrats, in fact ridiculed the Democrats' attitude toward public policy, particularly on the question of the Negro's position in society.*

Source: *The Struggles Social, Financial and Political of Petroleum V. Nasby, etc., etc.,* Boston, 1888: "Lays Down a Platform for the Coming Campaign."

Saint's Rest (wich is in the Stait uv Noo Jersey), June the 23d, 1865

These is the dark days uv the dimokrasy. The misforchoons that befell our armies in front uv Richmond, the fall uv our capital, follered by the surrender uv our armies to Grant and Sherman, hez hurt us. Our leaders are either pinin in loathsome dunguns, incarseratid by the hevin-defyin, man-destroyin, tyrannical edix uv our late lamented President, or are baskin in the free air uv Italy and Canady. We hev no way uv keepin our voters together. Opposin the war won't do no good, for before the next elecshun the heft uv our voters will hev diskiverd that the war is over. The fear uv drafts may do suthin in some parts uv Pennsylvany and suthern Illinoy, for sum time yit, but that can't be depended on.

But we hev wun resource for a ishoo — ther will alluz be a dimokrasy so long as ther's a nigger.

Ther is a uncompromisin dislike to the nigger in the mind uv a ginooine dimekrat. The Spanish bullfighter, when he wants to inflame the bull to extra cavortin, waves a red flag afore him. When yoo desire a dimekrat to froth at the mouth, yoo will find a black face will anser the purpose. Therefore, the nigger is, today, our best and only holt. Let us use him.

For the guidance uv the faithful. I shel lay down a few plain rools to be observed, in order to make the most uv the capital we hev:

1. Alluz assert that the nigger will never be able to take care uv hisself, but will alluz be a public burden. He may, possibly, give us the lie by goin to work. In sich a emergency, the dooty uv every dimekrat is plane. He must not be allowed to work. Associashens must be organized, pledged to neither give him employment, to work with him, to work for anyone who will give him

work, or patronize any wun who duz. (I wood sejest that sich uv us ez hev bin forchoonit enuff to git credit, pay a trifle on account, so ez to make our patronage worth suthin.) This course, rigidly and persistently follered, will drive the best uv em to stealin, and the balance to the poorhouses, provin wat we hev alluz claimed, that they are a idle and vishus race. Think, my brethren, wat a inspirin effeck our poorhouses and jails full uv niggers wood hev on the people! My sole expands ez I contemplate the deliteful vision.

2. Likewise assert that the nigger will come North, and take all the good places, throwin all our skilled mechanics out uv work by underbiddin uv em. This mite be open to two objecshuns, to-wit: It crosses slitely rool the 1, and white men mite say, ef there's jist enuff labor for wat's here, why not perhibit furriners frum comin? I anser: It's the biznis uv the voter to reconsile the contradicshun — he may beleeve either or both. Ez to the second objeckshun, wher is the Dimekrat who coodent be underbid, and stand it even to starvashen, ef the underbiddin wuz dun by a man uv the proud Caukashen race? And wher is the Dimekrat so lost to manhood ez not to drink blood, ef the same underbiddin is dun by a nigger? The starvin for work ain't the question — it's the color uv the cause uv the starvashen that makes the difference.

Nigger equality may be worked agin to advantage. All men, without distincshun uv sex, are fond uv flatrin theirselves that somebody's lower down in the scale uv humanity than they is. Ef 'twan't for niggers, what wood the dimokrasy do for sumbody to look down upon? It's also shoor to enlist wun style uv wimmen on our side. In times gone by, I've notist gushin virgins uv forty-five, full sixteen hands high and tough ez wire, holdin aloft banners onto which wuz inscribd — "Save us frum Nigger Equality." Yoo see it soothed em to hev a chanse uv advertisin, 1st, That they wuz frail, helplis critters; and, 2d, That, anshent and tough ez they wuz, some wun wuz still goin for em.

Ef ther ain't no niggers, central commities must furnish em. A half dozen will do for a ordinary county, ef they're hustled along with energy. Ef they won't steal, the central commities must do it theirselves. Show yer niggers in a township in the mornin, an the same nite rob the clothes-lines and henroosts. Ever willin to sacrifice myself for the cause, I volunteer to do this latter dooty in six populous counties.

These ijees, ef follered, will, no doubt, keep us together until our enemies split, when we will reap the reward uv our constancy and fidelity. May the Lord hasten the day.

PETROLEUM V. NASBY
Lait Paster uv the Church uv
the Noo Dispensashun

Looking upon African slavery from the same standpoint held by the noble framers of our Constitution, I have ever considered it one of the greatest blessings (both for themselves and us) that God ever bestowed upon a favorite nation.

JOHN WILKES BOOTH, letter left with his sister Asia before his assassination of Lincoln, April 14, 1865

147.

Sheep in the Midst of Wolves

*Four million Negroes gained their freedom after the Civil War. Even before passage
of the Fourteenth Amendment (1868), Southern legislatures, fearing Negro aspirations,
enacted "Black Codes" restricting Negro freedom. When Congress in March 1865
established a Freedmen's Bureau to protect Negroes against restrictive legislation
and to improve their economic conditions, Negroes began to cherish the hope that they
would soon acquire economic and political power, but the former slaveholders were
able to thwart Negro demands. Realizing their plight, Negroes began to organize,
and in 1865 and 1866 they held conventions in major Southern cities to discuss their
problems. The following statement, adopted by a convention held in Alexandria,
Virginia, in August 1865, was typical of Southern Negro opinion.*

Source: *Proceedings of the Convention of the Colored People of Virginia,
Held in the City of Alexandria, August 2, 3, 4, 5, 1865,
Alexandria, 1865, pp. 21-22 [Great Issues in American History,
Richard Hofstadter, ed., New York, 1958, Vol. II, pp. 21-22].*

WE, THE UNDERSIGNED MEMBERS of a convention of colored citizens of the state of Virginia, would respectfully represent that, although we have been held as slaves and denied all recognition as a constituent of your nationality for almost the entire period of the duration of your government, and that by *your permission* we have been denied either home or country and deprived of the dearest rights of human nature; yet when you and our immediate oppressors met in deadly conflict upon the field of battle — the one to destroy and the other to save your government and nationality — we, with scarce an exception, in our inmost souls espoused your cause, and watched, and prayed, and waited, and labored for your success. . . .

When the contest waxed long and the result hung doubtfully, you appealed to us for help, and how well we answered is written in the rosters of the 200,000 colored troops now enrolled in your service; and as to our undying devotion to your cause, let the uniform acclamation of escaped prisoners, "whenever we saw a black face we felt sure of a friend," answer.

Well, the war is over, the rebellion is "put down," and we are *declared* free! Four-fifths of our enemies are paroled or amnestied, and the other fifth are being pardoned, and the President has, in his efforts at the reconstruction of the civil government of the states late in rebellion, left us entirely at the mercy of these subjugated but unconverted Rebels, in *everything* save the privilege of bringing us, our wives, and little ones to the auction block. . . . We *know* these men — know them *well* — and we assure you that, with the majority of them, loyalty is only "lip deep," and that their professions of loyalty are used as a cover to the cherished design of getting restored to their former relations with the Federal government, and then, by all sorts of "unfriendly legislation," to render the freedom you have given us more intolerable than the slavery they intended for us.

We warn you in time that our only safety is in keeping them under governors of the *military persuasion* until you have so amended the Federal Constitution that it will prohibit the states from making any distinction between citizens on account of race or color. In one word, the only salvation for us besides the power of the government is in *the possession of the ballot.* Give us this, and we will protect ourselves. . . . But, 'tis said we are ignorant. Admit it. Yet who denies we know a traitor from a loyal man, a gentleman from a rowdy, a friend from an enemy? The 12,000 colored votes of the state of New York sent Governor Seymour home and Reuben E. Fenton to Albany. Did not they know who to vote for? . . . All we ask is an *equal chance* with the white traitors varnished and japanned

with the oath of amnesty. Can you deny us this and still keep faith with us? . . .

We are "sheep in the midst of wolves," and nothing but the military arm of the government prevents us and all the *truly* loyal white men from being driven from the land of our birth. Do not then, we beseech you, give to one of these "wayward sisters" the rights they abandoned and forfeited when they rebelled until you have secured *our* rights by the aforementioned amendment to the Constitution. . . .

Trusting that you will not be deaf to the appeal herein made, nor unmindful of the warnings which the malignity of the Rebels are constantly giving you, and that you will rise to the height of being just for the sake of justice, we remain yours for our flag, our country, and humanity.

148.

John H. Reagan: An Open Letter to the People of Texas

John Reagan, the Confederate postmaster general, remained loyal to President Davis until the end, but became a Southern moderate advocating reconciliation with the North after the war. A prisoner at Fort Warren in Boston Harbor, Reagan, in May 1865, sent a letter to President Johnson urging a lenient policy of Reconstruction. His letter had a great impact on the President. After Reagan addressed the following open letter to his fellow Texans on August 11, pleading for acceptance of the presidential Reconstruction policy, Johnson and Secretary of State Seward urged him to return to Texas to lead the fight in defense of his views. However, most Texans condemned his ideas.

Source: *Memoirs with Special Reference to Secession and the Civil War,*
       Walter F. McCaleb, ed., New York, 1906, Appendix C.

THE CONDITION OF THE COUNTRY is such as to awaken the anxious solicitude of every citizen. Portions of you have honored me with your confidence on many occasions. I have tried to repay that confidence by sincere efforts for your good, and by faithful service. Though now a prisoner, in solitary confinement, and far from you, without

knowing when, if ever, I shall be permitted to mingle with you again, and my children and relatives and friends among you, my anxiety for their and your welfare induces me to ask the permission of the government to send you this communication.

I have tried to form a correct estimate of the condition of affairs, and send you the result of my reflections. The times demand the exercise of thought and reason, and the free expression of opinions. I hope mine may be the least suggestive. As our condition forces unwelcome thoughts and actions on us, and as, in my judgment, your best interests require you to assent to facts and conclusions, and to adopt measures conforming to the new order of things, which must be repugnant to your past experience and to your reason and prejudices, I take the liberty of suggesting to you frankly that line of action which seems to me best calculated to promote your welfare. I need not assure you of my sympathy with you, and I trust I need not doubt your confidence that I would advise you to no course which I did not think best for you.

I see that General Hamilton, who has been appointed provisional governor by the President, has entered on the discharge of his duties. He will have advised you of the policy of the government, and of what will be expected of you, and will no doubt call a convention to organize the state government, as is being done in other states similarly situated.

Your condition as a people is one of novelty and experiment, involving the necessity of political, social, and industrial reconstruction, after a sweeping and thorough revolution in all these respects; and this is to be accomplished in opposition to your education, traditional policy, and prejudices.

I do not propose to discuss either what belongs to the past or the policy of what is now required of you, but to accept the present condition of things as the result of the war and of inevitable necessity, and from this, as a starting point, to inquire what policy our people should adopt for the future.

You must, in the first place, recognize the necessity of making the most you can of your present condition, without the hope of doing all you might desire. This is required both by reason and necessity.

The state occupies the condition of a conquered nation. State government and state sovereignty are in abeyance, and will be so held until you adopt a government and policy acceptable to the conquerors. A refusal to accede to these conditions would only result in a prolongation of the time during which you will be deprived of a civil government of your own choice.

And it would do more than this — it would keep questions of the gravest character open for discussion and agitation, and by degrees accustom the whole country to a sort of military government, which, if greatly protracted, must necessarily subvert the civil government and result in the establishment of a military despotism, without bringing you any nearer to the attainment of your wishes than you are at present. In order to secure to yourselves again the blessings of local self-government and to avoid military rule and the danger of running into military despotism, you must agree:

First, to recognize the supreme authority of the government of the United States, within the sphere of its powers, and its right to protect itself against disintegration by the secession of the states.

And, second, you must recognize the abolition of slavery, and the rights of those who have been slaves to the privileges and protection of the laws of the land.

From what I can see, this much will be required as the least that would likely satisfy the government and secure to you the benefits of civil government and the admission of your members into the Congress of the United States.

But even this may fail of the attainment of those ends unless provision shall be made, by the new state government, for conferring the elective franchise on the former slaves. And present appearances indicate that this will be required by Northern public opinion and by Congress. And our people are in no condition to disregard that opinion or power with safety. But I am persuaded that you may satisfy both without further injury to yourselves than has already occurred. If you can do this, and secure to yourselves liberty, the protection of the Constitution and laws of the United States, and the right of local self-government, you will be more fortunate than many conquered peoples have been. The government and the people of the Northern states will, I have no doubt, recognize the necessity of your securing these blessings, as important to the whole country, as a means of preserving to it constitutional liberty and the present form of republican government.

This is new language to employ in addressing you and will be as unwelcome to you as it is sorrowful to me. But it would be more than folly, it would be a great crime for you and me and those who may be charged with the duty of reorganizing and restoring the state to the Union, to refuse to recognize the facts of your situation, however disagreeable, and to speak of and deal with them with candor and directness.

While the government offers its terms for the restoration of the state to the Union, it demands no other sacrifices than those already made by the result of the war, of renouncing the right of secession and recognizing the abolition of slavery, with its necessary consequences. These demands being complied with, the civil governments will be organized, the military government withdrawn, your members will be admitted to their seats in Congress, and the state will be in the Union on an equality in all respects with other states; with no further disabilities save only such as may attach to individuals. While the government prescribes the conditions of this return, it authorizes the people of the state, through representatives of their own choice, to execute them. It seems to be the object of the government, in pursuing this course, to secure what it regards as the fruits of the victory it has won and at the same time to preserve our form of government and the liberties of the people.

I know that those who look to the past only, with its sacrifices and losses of principles believed to be true, of property possessed, of national independence sought, and of the heroic dead, may say why talk of liberty now and of equality in the Union? The answer is, that having attempted to secure and preserve these by an appeal to the God of battles, we failed, and they now, so far as it relates to our political restoration, belong to the dead past, where it is the policy of the conquerors to leave them, and we are required to look to the living present and to the future. If it be thought hard to surrender so much, it must be remembered that such is the fate of war, and we must not forget that by the appeal to arms, whether willingly made or not, we staked not only what the government exacts but all our rights and property on the result. That we are not required to surrender all is due, not to the laws of war but to the enlightened and Christian age and country in which we live, to the liberality of the government, and to the spirit and genius of our institutions.

The questions as to which party to the contest was right or wrong, or as to whether both were partly right and partly wrong, and as to whether we did right or wrong in staking all on the fate of battle, were discussed before the war was commenced, and were decided by each party for itself, and, failing to agree, they made their appeal to the dread arbitrament of arms. It was precisely because the parties could not agree as to the issues between them that they went to war, to settle them in that way. Why should we now think of reopening the discussion of these questions? What good would come of doing so? Wisdom requires us to accept the decision of battle upon the issues involved and to be thankful that no more has been demanded by the conquerors, and to unite frankly and as cheerfully as we can with the government in carrying out the policy it has propounded.

Some of our people seem to still think

they can retain their property in slaves under the authority of the Constitution and laws of the United States. If the question had been originally submitted to the courts of the country instead of to the trial of battle this might have been the case. But we are not now permitted to claim the protection of the government which we repudiated and fought against, unless by its consent. It says to the great mass of our people, you may retain your property except your slaves. They are now free. And unless you agree to this you can neither get back into the government as a citizen nor into its courts to assert your claims to slaves or any other species of property.

The only wise and safe course for you to pursue is to accept promptly, unreservedly, and in good faith the terms and policy offered, and to go forward in the work of reorganization and restoration to the Union. This requires your assent to great pecuniary sacrifices, momentous changes in your social and industrial system, and a surrender of your opinions and prejudices on most important questions. It is humbling to our self-esteem, humiliating to our pride, and cannot be more unwelcome to you than it is painful to me to feel that duty requires me to give and you to accept this advice. It is not that sort of advice which persons sometimes give but do not accept for themselves. It is for me and mine as well as for you and yours. . . .

I have no doubt that you can adopt a plan which will fully meet the demands of justice and fairness, and satisfy the Northern mind and the requirements of the government, without endangering good government and repose of society. This can be done by:

First, extending the privileges and protection of the laws over the Negroes as they are over the whites, and allowing them to testify in the courts on the same conditions, leaving their testimony subject to the rules relating to its credibility, but not objecting to its admissibility. And in this you will

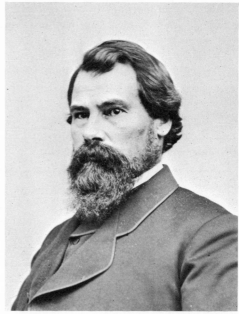

Library of Congress

John H. Reagan, active in government of the Confederacy, who urged Texans to accept outcome of war and work for effective peace in the state

conform with the wise current of modern legislation and the tendency of judicial decisions in all enlightened countries.

And, second, by fixing an intellectual and moral, and, if thought advisable, a property test for the admission of all persons to the exercise of the elective franchise, without reference to race or color, which would secure its intelligent exercise.

My own views would be: First, that no person now entitled to the privilege of voting should be deprived of it by any new test. I would recognize in this the difference between taking away a right heretofore enjoyed and the conferring of a right not heretofore exercised. Second, that to authorize the admission of persons hereafter to the exercise of the elective franchise they should be, (1) males; (2) twenty-one years of age; (3) citizens of the United States; (4) should have resided in the state one year, and in the district, county, or precinct six months next preceding any election at which they proposed to vote; (5) should be able to read in the English language understandingly; and (6) must have paid taxes for the last year preceding for which such taxes were due and payable, subject to any disqualification for crime of which the person may have been duly convicted, which may be prescribed by law.

The adoption of these measures, in addition to those before mentioned, would, in my judgment, meet the ends of justice and fairness, secure the reestablishment of the state government, the admission of her senators and representatives in Congress, the suspension of military rule, and the restoration of civil, constitutional, and local self-government. And it would do more. It would secure your protection against other great and pending evils, and is, I am persuaded, of the greatest consequence to your future peace, prosperity, and happiness.

149.

Charles H. Smith ("Bill Arp"): Open Letter to Artemus Ward

Under the pseudonym "Bill Arp," Charles Smith was to the South what David Locke's "Petroleum V. Nasby" was to the North. Employing the illiterate homespun style of American humorists of his day, Smith initially created Arp as a caricature of a ludicrous Southern Yankee sympathizer. When the war ended, he transformed Arp into a humorous, but wise, rustic philosopher who voiced the needs and feelings of the Southern people in a vernacular style but with greater honesty. The letters of Arp were immensely popular in the South. The following letter of September 1, 1865, to "Artemus Ward," the pseudonym of the brilliant literary pundit of the North, Charles Farrar Browne, was the most touching of all the Arp letters.

Source: *Bill Arp, So Called. A Side Show of the Southern Side of the War,* New York, 1866, pp. 132-138.

Mr. Artemus Ward, *Showman* —
Sir:

The reason I write to you in perticler, is becaus you are about the only man I know in all God's country, *so-called.* For some several weeks I hav been wantin to say sumthin. For some several years we rebs, *so-called,* but now late of said county deceased, have been tryin mighty hard to do somethin. We didn't quite do it, and now it's very painful, I assure you, to dry up all of a sudden, and make out like we wasn't there.

My friend, I want to say somethin. I suppose there is no law agin thinkin, but thinkin don't help me. It don't let down my thermometer. I must explode myself generally so as to feel better. You see I'm tryin to harmonize. I'm tryin to soften down my feelin's. I'm endeavoring to subjugate myself to the level of surroundin circumstances, *so-called.* But I can't do it until I am allowed to say somethin. I want to quarrel with somebody and then make friends. I ain't no giant-killer. I ain't no Norwegian bar. I ain't no boar-constricter, but I'll be hornswaggled if the talkin and writin and slanderin has got to be all done on one side any longer. Sum of you folks have got to dry up or turn our folks loose. It's a blamed outrage, *so-called.*

Ain't your editors got nothin else to do but peck at us, and squib at us, and crow over us? Is every man what kan write a paragraph to consider us bars in a cage, and be always a-jabbin at us to hear us growl? Now you see, my friend, that's what's disharmonious, and do you jest tell 'em, one and all, e pluribus unum, *so-called*, that if they don't stop it at once or turn us loose to say what we please, why we rebs, *so-called*, have unanimously and jointly and severally resolved to — to — to — think very hard of it — if not harder.

That's the way to talk it. I ain't agoin to commit myself. I know when to put on the brakes. I ain't agoin to say *all* I think, like Mr. Etheridge, or *Mr. Adderrig, so-called.* Nary time. No, sir. But I'll jest tell you, Artemus, and you may tell it to your show: If we ain't allowd to express our sentiments, we can take it out in *hatin;* and hatin runs heavy in my family, shure. I hated a man once so bad that all the hair cum off my head, and the man drownd himself in a hog-waller that night. I could do it agin, but you see I'm tryin to harmonize, to acquiesce, to becum calm and sereen.

Now, I suppose that, poetically speakin,
In Dixie's fall,
We sinned all.

But talkin the way I see it, a big feller and a little feller, *so-called*, got into a fite, and they fout and fout a long time, and everybody all round kep hollerin hands off, but kep helpin the big feller, until finally the little feller caved in and hollered enuf. He made a bully fite I tell you, Selah. Well, what did the big feller do? Take him by the hand and help him up, and brush the dirt off his clothes? Nary time! No, sur! But he kicked him arter he was down, and throwd mud on him, and drug him about and rubbed sand in his eyes, and now he's gwine about hunting up his poor little property. Wants to confiscate it, *so-called*. Blame my jacket if it ain't enuf to make your head swim.

But *I'm* a good Union man, *so-called.* I ain't agwine to fight no more. *I* shan't vote for the next war. *I* ain't no gurilla. I've done tuk the oath, and I'm gwine to keep it, but as for my being subjugated, and humilyated, and amalgamated, and enervated, as Mr. Chase says, it ain't so — nary time. I ain't ashamed of nuthin neither — ain't repentin — ain't axin for no one-horse, short-winded pardon. Nobody needn't be playin priest around me. I ain't got no twenty thousand dollars. Wish I had; I'd give it to these poor widders and orfins. I'd fatten my own numerous and interestin offspring in about two minits and a half. They shouldn't eat roots and drink branch-water no longer. Poor, unfortunate things! to cum into this subloonary world at sich a time. There's four or five of 'em that never saw a sirkis nor a monkey-show — never had a pocket-knife, nor a piece of chees, nor a reesin. There's Bull Run Arp, and Harper's Ferry Arp, and Chikahominy Arp, that never saw the pikters in a spellin book.

I tell you, my friend, we are the poorest people on the face of the earth — but we are poor and proud. We made a bully fite, Selah, and the whole American nation ought to feel proud of it. It shows what Americans can do when they think they are imposed on — *"so-called."* Didn't our four fathers fight, bleed, and die about a little tax on tea, when not one in a thousand drunk it? Bekaus they succeeded, wasn't it glory? But if they hadn't, I suppose it would have been treason, and they would have been bowin and scrapin round King George for pardon. So it goes, Artemus, and to my mind, if the whole thing was stewed down it would make about half pint of humbug. We had good men, great men, Christian men, who thought we was right, and many of 'em have gone to the undiscovered country, and have got a pardon as is a pardon. When I die I am mighty willing to risk myself under the shadow of their wings, whether the climate be hot or cold. So mote it be. Selah!

Well, maybe I've said enough. But I

don't feel easy yet. I'm a good Union man, certain and sure. I've had my breeches died *blue*, and I've bot a *blue* bucket, and I very often feel *blue*, and about twice in a while I go to the doggery and git *blue*, and then I look up at the *blue* serulean heavens and sing the melancholy chorus of the *Blue-tailed Fly*. I'm doin my durndest to harmonize, and think I could sucseed if it wasn't for sum things.

When I see a black-guard goin around the streets with a gun on his shoulder, why right then, for a few minutes, I hate the whole Yanky nation. Jerusalem! how my blood biles! The institution what was handed down to us by the heavenly kingdom of Massachusetts, now put over us with powder and ball! Harmonize the devil! Ain't we human beings? Ain't we got eyes and ears and feelin and thinkin? Why, the whole of Africa has come to town, women and children and babies and baboons and all. A man can tell how fur it is to the city by the smell better than the milepost. They won't work for us, and they won't work for themselves, and they'll perish to death this winter as shure as the devil is a hog, *so-called*. They are now basking in the summer's sun, livin on roasting ears and freedom, with nary idee that the winter will come agin, or that castor-oil and salts costs money. Sum of 'em, a hundred years old, are whining around about goin to kawlidge.

The truth is, my friend, sombody's badly fooled about this bizness. Sombody has drawd the elefant in the lottery, and don't know what to do with him. He's jest throwing his snout loose, and by and by he'll hurt sumbody. These niggers will have to go back to the plantations and work. I ain't agoing to support nary one of 'em, and when you hear anybody say so, you tell 'em it's a lie, *so-called*. I golly, I ain't got nuthin to support myself on. We fought ourselves out of every thing excepting children and land, and I suppose the land are to be turned over to the niggers for grave-yards.

Well, my friend, I don't want much. I ain't ambitious, as I used to was. You all have got your shows and monkeys and sir-cusses and brass band and orgins, and can play on the petrolyum and the harp of a thousand strings, and so on, but I've only got one favor to ax of you. I want enough powder to kill a big yaller stump-tail dog that prowls around my premises at night. Pon honor, I won't shoot at any thing blue or black or mullater. Will you send it? Are you and your folks so skeered of me and my folks that you won't let us have any ammunition? Are the squirrels and crows and black racoons to eat up our poor little corn-patches? Are the wild turkeys to gobble all around with impunity? If a mad dog takes the hiderphoby, is the whole community to run itself to death to get out of the way? I golly! It looks like your people had all took the rebelfoby for good, and was never gwine to get over it. See here, my friend, you must send me a little powder and a ticket to your show, and me and you will harmonize sertin.

With these few remarks I think I feel better, and I hope I hain't made nobody fitin mad, for I'm not on that line at this time.

I am truly your friend, all present or accounted for.

BILL ARP, *so-called*

P. S. — Old man Harris wanted to buy my fiddle the other day with Confederit money. *He* sed it would be good agin. *He* says that Jim Funderbuk told him that Warren's Jack seen a man who had jest come from Virginny, and *he* said a man had told his cousin Mandy that Lee had whipped 'em *agin*. Old Harris says that a feller by the name of Mack C. Million is coming over with a million of men. But nevertheless, notwithstandin, somehow or somehow else, I'm dubus about the money. If you was me, Artemus, would you make the fiddle-trade?

B. A.

150.

Robert E. Lee: The Restoration of the Union

After the Civil War General Robert E. Lee's supreme aim was the restoration of the South. Though he shunned politics, he patiently counseled his countrymen to bury their memories of the war and redirect their attention to reconstructing their own society. Lee's sentiments were expressed in the following letter of September 7, 1865, to Josiah Tattnall, who had been a captain in the Confederate Navy. Lee's example of obedience to civil authority was an inspiration to many Southerners. However, despite his request for amnesty, he never received official "forgiveness" for his role in the Civil War.

Source: *Personal Reminiscences, Anecdotes, and Letters of Gen. Robert E. Lee,* J. William Jones, ed., New York, 1875, pp. 205-206.

I HAVE RECEIVED YOUR LETTER . . . and in reply will state the course I have pursued under circumstances similar to your own, and will leave you to judge of its propriety. Like yourself, I have, since the cessation of hostilities, advised all with whom I have conversed on the subject, who come within the terms of the President's proclamations, to take the oath of allegiance and accept in good faith the amnesty offered. But I have gone further and have recommended to those who were excluded from their benefits to make application, under the *proviso* of the proclamation of the 29th of May, to be embraced in its provisions. Both classes, in order to be restored to their former rights and privileges, were required to perform a certain act, and I do not see that an acknowledgement of fault is expressed in one more than the other.

The war being at an end, the Southern states having laid down their arms and the questions at issue between them and the Northern states having been decided, I believe it to be the duty of everyone to unite in the restoration of the country and the reestablishment of peace and harmony. These considerations governed me in the counsels I gave to others and induced me on the 13th of June to make application to be included in the terms of the amnesty proclamation. I have not received an answer and cannot inform you what has been the decision of the President. But whatever that may be, I do not see how the course I have recommended and practised can prove detrimental to the former president of the Confederate States.

It appears to me that the allayment of passion, the dissipation of prejudice, and the restoration of reason will alone enable the people of the country to acquire a true knowledge and form a correct judgment of the events of the past four years. It will, I think, be admitted that Mr. Davis has done nothing more than all the citizens of the Southern states and should not be held accountable for acts performed by them in the exercise of what had been considered by them unquestionably right. I have too exalted an opinion of the American people to believe that they will consent to injustice; and it is only necessary, in my opinion, that truth should be known for the rights of everyone to be secured. I know of no surer way of eliciting the truth than by burying contention with the war.

I enclose a copy of my letter to President Johnson, and feel assured that, however imperfectly I may have given you my views on the subject of your letter, your own high sense of honor and right will lead you to a satisfactory conclusion as to the proper course to be pursued in your own case.

151.

THADDEUS STEVENS: The Rights of the Conqueror

Thaddeus Stevens' bitter hatred for slavery and Southern institutions in general motivated him to press for a harsh Reconstruction policy. As the leader of the Republican Party of Pennsylvania and the dominant member of the Joint Congressional Committee on Reconstruction, Stevens urged Congress to enact a policy of military rule in the South. Calling the South the "conquered province," he advocated the immediate arming of Negroes, confiscation of Confederate property, and severe punishment of Confederate leaders. In the following address of September 6, 1865, delivered at Lancaster, Pennsylvania, Stevens summarized his Reconstruction program. The decisive Radical Republican victory in the congressional elections of 1866 gave Stevens the means to carry out his policies.

Source: *New York Herald*, Supplement, December 13, 1865.

FOUR YEARS of bloody and expensive war waged against the United States by eleven states, under a government called the "Confederate States of America" to which they acknowledged allegiance, have overthrown all governments within those states which could be acknowledged as legitimate by the Union. The armies of the Confederate States having been conquered and subdued, and their territory possessed by the United States, it becomes necessary to establish governments therein which shall be republican in form and principles, and form a "more perfect union" with the parent government. It is desirable that such a course should be pursued as to exclude from those

governments every vestige of human bondage and render the same forever impossible in this nation, and to take care that no principles of self-destruction shall be incorporated therein.

In effecting this, it is to be hoped that no provision of the Constitution will be infringed and no principle of the law of nations disregarded. Especially must we take care that in rebuking this unjust and treasonable war, the authorities of the Union shall indulge in no acts of usurpation which may tend to impair the stability and permanency of the nation. Within these limitations we hold it to be the duty of the government to inflict condign punishment on the Rebel belligerents, and so weaken their hands that they can never again endanger the Union; and so reform their municipal institutions as to make them republican in spirit as well as in name.

We especially insist that the property of the chief Rebels should be seized and appropriated to the payment of the national debt caused by the unjust and wicked war which they instigated.

How can such punishments be inflicted and such forfeitures produced without doing violence to established principles? Two positions have been suggested:

First, to treat those states as never having been out of the Union, because the Constitution forbids secession, and, therefore, a fact forbidden by law could not exist.

Second, to accept the position in which they placed themselves as severed from the Union — an independent government *de facto* and an alien enemy to be dealt with according to the laws of war.

The crime of treason can be committed only where the person is actually or potentially present. Jefferson Davis sitting in Richmond, counseling or advising or commanding an inroad into Pennsylvania, has committed no overt act in this state, and can be tried, if anywhere, only in the Richmond district. The doctrine of constructive presence and constructive treason will never, I hope, pollute our statutes or judicial decisions. Select an impartial jury from Virginia and it is obvious no conviction could ever be had. Possibly a jury might be packed to convict; but that would not be an "impartial" jury. It would be judicial murder. . . .

What right has anyone to direct a convention to be held in a sovereign state of this Union to amend its constitution and prescribe the qualifications of voters? The sovereign power of the nation is lodged in Congress. Yet where is the warrant in the Constitution for such sovereign power, much less the executive, to intermeddle with the domestic institutions of a state, mold its laws, and regulate the elective franchise? It would be rank, dangerous, and deplorable usurpation. *In reconstruction, therefore, no reform can be effected in the Southern states if they have never left the Union.*

But reformation must be effected; the foundation of their institutions — political, municipal, and social — must be broken up and relaid, or all our blood and treasure have been spent in vain. This can only be done by treating and holding them as a conquered people. Then all things which we can desire to do follow with logical and legitimate authority. As conquered territory, Congress would have full power to legislate for them; for the territories are not under the Constitution except so far as the express power to govern them is given to Congress. They would be held in a territorial condition until they are fit to form state constitutions, republican in fact, not in form only, and ask admission into the Union as new states.

If Congress approve of their constitutions and think they have done works meet for repentance, they would be admitted as new states. If their constitutions are not approved of, they would be sent back until they had become wise enough so to purge their old laws as to eradicate every despotic and revolutionary principle — until they shall have learned to venerate the Declaration of Independence.

I do not touch on the question of Negro suffrage. If in the Union, the states have long ago regulated that, and for the central government to interfere with it would be mischievous impertinence. If they are to be admitted as new states, they must form their own constitution, and no enabling act could dictate its terms. Congress could prescribe the qualifications of voters while a territory or when proceeding to call a convention to form a state government. This is the extent of the power of Congress over the elective franchise, whether in a territorial or state condition.

Thaddeus Stevens, photo by Brady

The President has not even this or any other power to meddle in the subject except by advice to Congress — and they on territories. Congress, to be sure, has some sort of compulsory power by refusing the states admission until they shall have complied with its wishes upon this subject. Whether those who have fought our battles should all be allowed to vote, or only those of a paler hue, I leave to be discussed in the future when Congress can take legitimate cognizance of it. . . .

There are about 6 million freemen in the South. The number of acres of land is 465 million. Of this, those who own above 200 acres each number about 70,000 persons, holding in the aggregate — together with the states — about 394 million acres, leaving for all the others, below 200 each, about 71 million acres. By thus forfeiting the estates of the leading Rebels, the government would have 394 million acres besides their town property, and yet nine-tenths of the people would remain untouched. Divide this land into convenient farms. Give, if you please, 40 acres to each adult male freedman. Suppose there are 1 million of them. That would require 40 million acres, which deducted from 394 million leaves 354 million acres for sale. Divide it into suitable farms and sell it to the highest bidders. I think it, including town property, would average at least $10 per acre. That would produce $3,540,000,000.

Let that be applied as follows, to wit:

1. Invest $300 million in 6 percent government bonds, and add the interest semi-annually to the pensions of those who have become entitled by this villainous war.

2. Appropriate $200 million to pay the damage done to loyal men, North and South, by the rebellion.

3. Pay the residue, being $3,040,000,000, toward the payment of the national debt.

Our war debt is estimated at from $3 billion to $4 billion . . . $470 million to be raised by taxation! Our present heavy taxes will in ordinary years produce but little more than half that sum. Can our people bear double their present taxation? He who unnecessarily causes it will be accursed from generation to generation. It is fashionable to belittle our public debt lest the people should become alarmed and political parties should suffer. I have never found it wise to deceive the people. They can always be trusted with the truth. Capitalists will not be affected for they cannot be deceived. Confide in the people and you will avoid repudiation. Deceive them, and lead them into false measures, and you may produce it. . . . The plan we have proposed would pay at least three-fourths of our debt. The balance could be managed with our present taxation.

While I hear it said everywhere that slavery is dead, I cannot learn who killed it. No thoughtful man has pretended that Lincoln's proclamation, so noble in sentiment, liberated a single slave. It expressly excluded from its operation all those within our lines. No slave within any part of the Rebel states in our possession or in Tennessee, but only those beyond our limits and beyond our power, were declared free. . . . The President did not pretend to abrogate the slave laws of any of the states. "Restoration," therefore, will leave "the Union as it was" a hideous idea. . . .

The President says to the Rebel states, "Before you can participate in the government you must abolish slavery and reform your election laws." That is the command of a conqueror. That is reconstruction, not restoration — reconstruction, too, by assuming the powers of Congress. This theory will lead to melancholy results. Nor can the constitutional amendment abolishing slavery ever be ratified by three-fourths of the states, if they are states to be counted. Bogus conventions of those states may vote for it; but no convention honestly and fairly elected will ever do it. The frauds will not permanently avail. The cause of liberty must rest on a firmer basis. Counterfeit governments, like the Virginia, Louisiana, Tennessee, Mississippi, and Arkansas pretenses, will be disregarded by the sober sense of the people, by future law, and by the courts. "Restoration" is replanting the seeds of rebellion, which within the next quarter of a century will germinate and produce the same bloody strife which has just ended.

If the South is ever to be made a safe republic, let her lands be cultivated by the toil of the owners or the free labor of intelligent citizens. This must be done even though it drive her nobility into exile. If they go, all the better.

It will be hard to persuade the owner of 10,000 acres of land, who drives a coach and four, that he is not degraded by sitting at the same table, or in the same pew, with the embrowned and hard-handed farmer who has himself cultivated his own thriving homestead of 150 acres. This subdivision of the lands will yield ten bales of cotton to one that is made now, and he who produced it will own it and feel himself a man.

It is far easier and more beneficial to exile 70,000 proud, bloated, and defiant Rebels than to expatriate 4 million laborers, natives to the soil and loyal to the government. This latter scheme was a favorite plan of the Blairs, with which they had for a while inoculated our late sainted President. But a single experiment made him discard it and his advisers.

Since I have mentioned the Blairs, I may say a word more of these persistent apologists of the South; for, when the virus of slavery has once entered the veins of the slaveholder, no subsequent effort seems capable of wholly eradicating it. They are a family of considerable power, some merit, of admirable audacity and execrable selfishness. With impetuous alacrity they seize the White House and hold possession of it, as in the late administration, until shaken off by the overpowering force of public indignation. Their pernicious counsel had wellnigh defeated the reelection of Abraham Lincoln; and if it should prevail with the present administration, pure and patriotic as President Johnson is admitted to be, it will render him the most unpopular executive — save one — that ever occupied the presidential chair. But there is no fear of that. He will soon say, as Mr. Lincoln did, "Your time has come."

Is this great conquest to be in vain? That will depend upon the virtue and intelligence of the next Congress. *To Congress alone belongs the power of reconstruction — of giving law to the vanquished.* . . . But we know how difficult it is for a majority of Congress to overcome preconceived opinions. Besides, before Congress meets, things will be so inaugurated — precipitated — it will still be more difficult to correct. *If a majority of Congress can be found wise and firm enough to declare the Confederate States a conquered enemy, reconstruction will be easy and legitimate; and the friends of freedom will long rule in the councils of the nation.*

If restoration prevails, the prospect is gloomy, and "new lords will make new laws." The Union Party will be overwhelmed. The "Copperhead" Party has become extinct with secession. But with secession it will revive. Under "restoration" every Rebel state will send Rebels to Congress; and they, with their allies in the North, will control Congress and will occupy the White House. Then restoration of laws and ancient constitutions will be sure to follow; our public debt will be repudiated or the Rebel national debt will be added to ours; and the people be crushed beneath heavy burdens.

Let us forget all parties and build on the broad platform of "reconstructing" the government out of the conquered territory converted into new and free states and admitted into the Union by the sovereign power of Congress, with another plank — "The property of the Rebels shall pay our national debt, and indemnify freedmen and loyal sufferers; and that under no circumstances will we suffer the national debt to be repudiated or the interest scaled below the contract rates; nor permit any part of the Rebel debt to be assumed by the nation."

Let all who approve of these principles rally with us. Let all others go with "Copperheads" and Rebels. Those will be the opposing parties. Young men, this duty devolves on you. Would to God, if only for that, that I were still in the prime of life that I might aid you to fight through this last, greatest battle of freedom.

152.

Opposing Views on the Restoration of the Union

President Johnson issued the first of his Reconstruction orders, the North Carolina Proclamation, on May 29, 1865; additional ones for other states followed during the summer and fall. Republicans and Democrats interpreted them differently, according to their own wishes. The Republicans viewed the President's plan as an experiment in reorganizing a Confederate state that would yield evidence upon the basis of which Congress, when it met that winter, could fashion a reconstruction policy. The Democrats, on the other hand, regarded the moderate proclamations as the final word on Reconstruction. Thus both parties supported the President's program during this period, though for different reasons. The following editorials, the first published in the Republican Harper's Weekly *and the second in the Democratic* Indianapolis Daily State Sentinel, *reflected the views of both parties.*

Source: *Harper's Weekly*, September 30, 1865.
       Indianapolis Daily State Sentinel, October 6, 1865.

I.

A Republican Editorial

WE ELSEWHERE CALL ATTENTION to a remarkable speech of General John A. Logan's in Jacksonville, Illinois. The general says that the policy of reconstruction adopted by the administration is an experiment, and that it is the duty of all good citizens to stand heartily by the President until it is proved a failure.

That is precisely the ground which a true conservatism now occupies. The Democratic conventions, in breathless haste to eat their own words of the last few years, vociferate their adherence to the President's policy, and amiable poets of the morning press behold vast hosts of Jacobins marshaling under blood-red banners to oppose it. But as the President is merely trying an experiment, it is rather premature vehemently to support or rancorously to oppose his policy; nor is any country in a very "parlous state" when its Jacobins are the most intelligent, conservative, and substantial part of its population.

The President, acting from the necessity of the case and for the public safety, has set aside the civil officers elected in various states under their constitutions and has appointed provisional governors of his own. He has further prohibited thirteen certain classes of voters under the constitutions of those states from exercising the right of suffrage, and has authorized a certain number, who are also qualified by the state constitutions, to vote for members of a convention. This convention is to remodel the existing state constitutions and to proceed, under them, to elect state officers and representatives in Congress. The constitutions and, by consequence, the validity of the officers elected, are to be submitted to the government for approval. In the President's words, the convention is "to present such a republican form of state government as will entitle the state to the guaranty of the United States therefor and the people to protection by the United States against invasion, insurrection, and domestic violence."

This is all that the President has done. This is his whole policy thus far. It is, as General Logan says, "an experiment." The President virtually says to certain persons in the states, "See what you can do. Suggest your plan." But he does not say that the plan shall be adopted. He does not promise that the constitution shall be approved and the elections under it legitimated. The very object he has in view is to try the temper of the class of the population which he selects

to prove whether the local political power of the states may be safely confided to them. Nor does he assume finally to decide so vital a question. He leaves it where it belongs — to the nation itself, to the representatives of the people.

The Democratic resolutions and the amiable chatter about opposition assume that it is not an experiment; that the President has declared the constitution framed by the voters he has selected, and the elections held under it, to be the law without further process or approval. This is exactly what he has not done and could have no pretense of authority for doing. If he had done it, if he had said that a certain class of persons in the states named by him should elect a convention, that that convention should frame a constitution, that the elections should be held under the constitution, and that thereupon the state should be recognized as having resumed all its relations in the Union, and its representatives and senators should be admitted to Congress as a matter of course, then, indeed, he would have laid down a policy, and the whole country would have crackled in opposition to it. . . .

Thus far, the President is merely trying an experiment, and whether we think the principles upon which it proceeds promise success or failure, we ought loyally and patiently to await the event. So says General Logan; so says Maine; so says Vermont; so says California; so say we all.

II.

A Democratic Editorial

THE ABOLITION PRESS are consoling themselves and their leaders with the idea that the restoration policy of President Johnson is only an experiment. There is no foundation for such a representation of his views. Neither is it in character with his whole course in life. Firmness even to obstinacy has marked his career. And more than this, he has repeatedly stated that his plan of restoration was the policy of his administration, and upon it he would stand or fall. Certainly such expressions give no color to the contrary representations of the Abolition papers. Governor Morton endeavors to show, in his Richmond [Ind.] speech, that the policy of the late and the present presidents are identical. This view only accumulates the evidence that the President's policy of restoration is fixed, not an experiment liable to change as the listless wind.

There is no doubt that if Mr. Lincoln had lived that his terms of amnesty to the Southern people would have been far more liberal than any his successor has yet proposed. Even Jefferson Davis and the leaders of the rebellion who are now incarcerated would have been permitted to escape the country. "With malice toward none and charity for all" was the spirit which would have animated Mr. Lincoln in his treatment of the rebellion after its military power had been crushed and the whole people subjugated.

If, then, President Johnson intends to follow in the footsteps of his predecessor, as Governor Morton insists that he does, there is nothing whatever upon which to base the statement that his plan of restoration is only an experiment. Upon all questions of political economy, President Johnson avows himself to be as thorough a Democrat now as he ever was. Slavery is no longer an issue, and Governor Morton declares that all fear of secession or resistance to the national authority is forever extinguished, hence there is no reason why the President should not guide the policy of his administration by the old Democratic landmarks. This he avows he intends to do; and the declaration is having a marked effect all over the country.

Everywhere we find men who left the Democratic Party on account of their opposition to African slavery returning to the old banner; and conservative Republicans are rallying under the same standard. President Johnson looks to this class for his support and not to the men who, with honeyed words, endorse his administration but still adhere to the political organization which is guided by radical Abolitionists. In language unmistakable, the President declares that this is a white man's government, and such he intends it shall be so far as his influence can maintain it. And this is the growing sentiment of the country.

From Idaho the voice first came for a white man's government, and old Connecticut, at her recent election, took position in the same line. Nothing but fraud, corruption, and prejudice will prevent New York, Pennsylvania, Ohio, Wisconsin, Minnesota, and even Iowa swelling the column for a white man's government. Never was there a greater delusion than that President Johnson looks upon his restoration policy as an experiment.

———◆———

God reigns and the government at Washington still lives.
JAMES A. GARFIELD, reassuring crowd in Wall Street, New York, on the news of the assassination of Lincoln, April 15, 1865. Garfield was himself assassinated sixteen years later.

153.

Ira Steward: Shorter Hours and Higher Wages

Ira Steward, who began his career as a machinist's apprentice under the twelve-hour system, became an intellectual leader of the labor movement during the 1860s. In 1863 he started to agitate for an eight-hour working day to replace the customary ten-hour, sometimes still twelve-hour, day. Believing that labor union pressure on political parties would be more effective than purely economic action, he lobbied incessantly before the Massachusetts legislature and made union influence felt within the major parties. In September 1865 the Massachusetts Republican State Convention put an eight-hour plank into its platform. By 1867 six state legislatures had adopted eight-hour laws, but these proved unenforceable. Steward's argument for an eight-hour working day was best expressed in a pamphlet published by the Boston Labor Reform Association in 1865, portions of which appear below.

Source: *Fincher's Trades' Review*, October 14, 1865 [Commons, IX, pp. 284-301].

"Well," says a workingman, "I should certainly be very glad to work less hours, but I can scarcely earn enough by working ten to make myself and family comfortable."

Sir, as strange as it may seem to you at first blush, it is a fact that your wages will never be permanently increased until the hours of labor are reduced. Have you never observed that those who work the hardest and longest are paid the least, especially if the employment is very disagreeable, while those whose employment is more agreeable usually receive more, and many who do nothing receive more than either?

You are receiving your scanty pay precisely because you work so many hours in a day, and my point now is to show why this is true, and why reducing the hours for the masses will eventually increase their wages. . . .

The truth is, as a rule, that men who labor excessively are robbed of all ambition to ask for anything more than will satisfy their bodily necessities, while those who labor moderately have time to cultivate tastes and create wants in addition to mere physical comforts. How can men be stimulated to demand higher wages when they have little or no time or strength to use the advantages which higher wages can buy or procure?

Take an extreme case for illustration of this — that of an average operative or mechanic employed by a corporation fourteen hours a day. His labor commences at half-past four in the morning, and does not cease until half-past seven P.M. How many newspapers or books can he read? What time has he to visit or receive visits? to take baths? to write letters? to cultivate flowers? to walk with his family? Will he not be quite as likely to vote in opposition to his real interest as in favor? What is his opinion good for? Will anyone ask his advice? Which will he most enjoy, works of art or rum? Will he go to meeting on Sunday? Does society care whether he is happy or miserable? sick or well? dead or alive? How often are his eyes tempted by the works of art? His home means to him his food and his bed. His life is work with the apparition, however, of sometime being without, for his work means bread! "Only that and nothing more." He is debased by excessive toil! He is almost without hope!

Think how monotonous that path leading from house to factory, and from factory to house again: the same sidewalk every day, rain or shine, summer or winter, leading by the same low houses, inhabited by beings walking the same social treadmill as himself. Half-past seven comes at last, and as the wheel stops he catches his coat and, half staggering with fatigue, hurries homeward in the darkness, thinking of nothing but food and rest. What are his motives?

From the fourteen-hour system let us turn to that of eight hours for a day's work and see if the real secret of low and high wages does not lie in the vast difference which the two systems make in the daily habits and ways of living of the masses. In the eight-hour system labor commences at 7 o'clock A.M. and, as an hour and a half is allowed for dinner, the labor of the day ends at half-past four in the afternoon instead of half-past seven in the evening. Think carefully of the difference between the operative and mechanic leaving his work at half-past seven (after dark, the most of the year), and that of the more leisurely walk home at half-past four P.M., or three hours earlier. Remember also that there is a vast difference in the strength and feelings of those who commence labor at half-past four in the morning and those who commence two hours and a half later, or at 7 o'clock. It is the hard, practical, necessary differences between the two systems which control the daily habits and thoughts of all who are living under them.

You can hardly dwell too long upon this point, for upon it turns this whole question of social science: poverty and wealth, vice and virtue, ignorance and knowledge. The follies, burdens, and crimes of our later civilization are hanging upon this question, and the temptation to leave the simple and comparatively unimportant fact that reducing the hours will increase the wages and launch out upon broader and more sublime results is almost irresistible. The simple increase of wages is the first step on that long road which ends at last in a more equal distribution of the fruits of toil; for wages will continue to increase until the capitalist and laborer are one. But we must confine ourselves to the first simple fact that a reduction of hours is an increase of wages; and when we are perfectly satisfied of its soundness, we can build upon it until the consequences grow to the extent of our comprehension or imagination.

Think then of the difference which will soon be observed in a man or woman emancipated by the eight-hour system from excessive toil! Not the first day nor the first week, perhaps, but in a very little while. The first feeling may be one merely of simple relief; and the time for a while may be spent, as are many of the Sabbaths, by the overworked in sleeping and eating, and frequently in the most debasing amusements. The use which a man makes of his leisure depends largely upon the use which has been made of him. If he has been abused, he will be pretty sure to abuse his first opportunities. An hour in the hands of John Quincy Adams meant a golden opportunity, in the hands of a Newcastle collier it means debauchery, and in the hands of a New England operative, an hour extra will mean the difference balanced or divided between the two.

Many make the mistake of supposing that leisure will be abused by workingmen, as if leisure of itself were necessarily corrupting. Leisure, however, is neither positively good or bad. Leisure or time is a blank — a negative — a piece of white paper upon which we stamp, picture, or write our past characters. If we have been soured and disappointed by a life of poverty and drudgery, if opportunities have been few and far between, if education has been neglected and habits of thought and observation have not been cultivated, if we have inherited qualities which are ever leading us into temptation, we shall be sure to stamp this humiliating record upon the first leisure hour in the eight-hour system. The most of men will make a clumsy use of anything which they have not become familiar with. Progress in the arts and sciences is marked by a line of accidents, burnings, explosions, losses, and deaths, to which we may liken the abuse of the laborer's first opportunities. But the remedy is not in depriving him of his chance to experiment. . . .

Mankind will be virtuous and happy when they have full power to choose between good and evil with plenty of motives for deciding right. Men will not abuse power when they are made responsible for its abuse. While therefore giving the masses more time will give them increased power to do wrong, the motives to do right will increase very much faster.

Assuming that the leisure we propose is not so positively debasing, let us return to the main question. My theory is, first, that more leisure will create motives and temptations for the common people to ask for more wages.

Second, that where all ask for more wages, there will be no motive for refusing, since employers will all fare alike.

Third, that where all demand more wages, the demand cannot be resisted.

Fourth, that resistance would amount to the folly of a "strike" by employers themselves against the strongest power in the world, viz., the habits, customs, and opinions of the masses.

Fifth, that the change in the habits and opinions of the people through more leisure

will be too gradual to disturb or jar the commerce and enterprise of capital.

Sixth, that the increase in wages will fall upon the wastes of society in its crimes, idleness, fashions, and monopolies, as well as the more legitimate and honorable profits of capital in the production and distribution of wealth.

Seventh, in the mechanical fact that the cost of making an article depends almost entirely upon the number manufactured is a practical increase of wages by tempting the workers through their new leisure to unite in buying luxuries now confined to the wealthy, and which are costly because bought only by the wealthy.

The first point in this theory is the vital one "that more leisure will create motives and temptations for the most ordinary laborer to insist upon higher wages." A few, comparatively, insist upon more pay now, but they are in competition with the great body of laborers who do not and who never will until, in the language of John Stuart Mill, "a change has been wrought in their ideas and requirements."

There is a law or two in this case which proves on examination to be a blessing in disguise. The law is, first, that if one employer pays for the same quality and quantity of labor enough more than another that his business will be ruined and his workmen finally thrown out of employment; and, second, that if a workman of superior tendencies to the majority of his fellows is not paid more than they for performing the same kind of labor his general influence and his opportunities for usefulness will be cramped and limited accordingly. The blessing in disguise is this — the necessity created by these two laws of elevating all who labor!

Every laborer in rags is a walking admonition to those who are not; for he says, unconsciously, of course, "I must continue to labor for what my rags cost until I am placed in a position where I am ashamed to wear them; and as long as I am paid only enough to buy rags, you cannot be paid much more; so please help me up!" Every laborer who saves rent by living in crowded tenement houses, narrow alleys, and unhealthy localities can underbid the few who will not live in them. Parents who do not educate their children but send them into factories and shops can underbid those who do. Men who do not marry can underbid those who do. The charm of the eight-hour system is that it gives time and opportunity for the ragged, the unwashed, the ignorant and ill-mannered to become ashamed of themselves and their standing in society. . . .

The eight-hour system will make a coalition between ignorant labor and selfish capital on election day impossible.

When an intelligent workingman applies for employment, he doesn't want to meet a fellow laborer offering to do about the same thing for 50 or 75 cents less per day; yet he will be there "every time" until allowed the leisure necessary to be reached through his low pride or envy, if nothing higher, by wife, children, neighbors, and society generally. Give the masses time to come together and they cannot be kept apart; for man is a social being; and when they come together expenses multiply because the inferior will struggle to imitate the superior in many things which cost. To see is to desire, from babyhood to old age; to desire is to struggle; and to struggle is to succeed, sooner or later.

Imagine operatives or laborers of average capacity leaving work at half-past four; they are liable to meet those whose good opinion is worth everything to them, and they think that a neat personal appearance is positively necessary; and it must be confessed that while fine clothes do not make a man, we all look at them as a certain sort of index to his character.

Men who are governed only by their pride are low indeed; but those who have no pride at all are very much lower. We must take human nature as we find it, hoping and believing that the era of personal display will be succeeded by one of mental and moral accomplishment. A valuable point has been gained in pushing the man into a position where he is made to feel the imperative necessity of dress, and for this he will struggle. An operative running from the shop in the evening, tired, hungry, and unwashed, has not time to be ashamed of his personal appearance; and our modern laborer passing through the streets at 6 has not time and strength enough; but the improvement which has been made in the personal appearance of ten-hour laborers over those of the twelve- and fourteen-hour system is suggestive of what two hours more of leisure may soon accomplish.

A man who is satisfied with his personal appearance will be likely to go abroad and take his wife and children, and they must have "something to wear." If he visits, he must receive visits, and what will visitors say if his house and its surroundings do not look as respectable as other folks'?

Many things can be done for self, family, and domicile which cost nothing but time and labor; but when done are sure to suggest one or two things more costing money. There is time after eight hours' labor to attend an evening concert, which adds a little to the expense but much to the enjoyment of the family. The Smiths and Jones "and everybody" are going, "and who wants to be so different from everybody else?" If these are trivial considerations to intelligent minds, they are the only ones which can be brought to bear upon the masses to tempt them to bid for higher wages. The great majority of men and women must "act like other folks." "What will people think?" or "What will people say?" is the most terrible question which they can be asked. There are not many in society who have the courage to stand up alone and be very much different from their neighbors or acquaintances. . . .

Some children drop their playthings sooner than others, and the amusements of later years last certain minds longer than others; but so thoroughly aroused am I to the necessity of something for every human being to enjoy that I cry out reverently, "God bless every baby pleased with a rattle." Tempt every producer of wealth, then, by theaters, concerts, fine clothes, stories; and the leisure to enjoy and the higher wages necessary to support them will, by wiser fellows, be used to study political economy, social science, the sanitary condition of the people, the prevention of crime, woman's wages, war, and the 10,000 schemes with which our age teems for the amelioration of the condition of man. In other words, intelligent workers, if you want $10 to invest in some scientific, reformatory, religious, or literary scheme, you must see to it that everyone who performs your kind of labor wants something which will cost as much! And those who are tempted to leave their own occupation because they are underpaid, and to learn yours, must have the temptation removed by a rise in their wages.

An extra hod carrier may become a poor mason, and his wages, higher than those paid to hod carriers, may still be the means of bringing down the price of skillful masons. An extra striker may raise his wages by attempting the trade of blacksmithing and yet be the means of bringing down the price of those who have never done anything else but forge. It pays employers to teach the trade or the business to the uninitiated as soon as the wages of the skillful run up to a certain point. It may be urged that a hod carrier or a striker is not worth as much as a mason or a blacksmith, but who shall decide how much this labor is really worth? Building houses and forging iron would come to an end if there were no hod carriers or strikers, and what more can be said for the trade of the mason or blacksmith? You say there are a plenty who are glad to carry the hod or wait upon the blacksmith. There is a plenty of water, gravel, iron; but none the less valuable are they.

Without attempting to settle, definitely, how much common labor is worth — for it is a broad question — I will make the claim that no man's compensation should be so low that it will not secure for himself and family a comfortable home, education for his children, and all of the influence to which he is entitled by his capacity, virtue, and industry. As the present system of labor does not pay a majority of workers enough, we may conclude that something is wrong; and whatever our speculations upon the system, it must be clear that the masses will not insist upon more pay without additional motives and temptations; and that all who do the work of the masses must receive their pay. . . .

With 365 days of opportunities created by the eight-hour system, we can say to the laborer, "Your industry helps to support that monopoly or abuse, and the man you voted for at the last election helped to make that abuse possible." He has time to listen, digest, and plan.

If our eight-hour friends in Boston, New York, and Philadelphia would make this the issue at their next city elections — that no laborer employed by those cities shall work longer than eight hours per day and that they shall have the usual wages — they would discover its immense importance by observing the tenacity with which the moneyed interests would oppose the movement. The establishment of the eight-hour system in those three cities would be an eight-hour "Sermon on the Mount."

Twelve hundred common laboring men, agitating the eight-hour question and carrying it into cellars or byplaces never reached by any sound but a trumpet blast from capital on election day! This terrible reservoir of cheap labor must be run off, and the motives which prompt us to its accomplishment are not unlike those which we shall present to a certain class above us socially — to those whose wealth is invested in untaxed government bonds. We shall say to them: "Gentlemen, the repudiation of the national debt is threatened by the unprincipled and the ignorant. Emancipate the great industrial classes of America from excessive toil and you create a bulwark of popular intelligence against which the threats of repudiation will dash in vain forever. The overworked and underpaid are dangerous enough in any country, but especially so in America where they have votes. A word to the wise is sufficient. . . ."

In the eight-hour system a dollar will be worth more than a dollar in the long-hour system; not immediately, of course, but in a comparatively short time. The reason of this lies in the fact, which every good mechanic understands, that the cost of making an article depends almost entirely on the number manufactured. It pays to build elaborate machinery to manufacture something which everyone will buy; while those who make the manufacture a study will improve upon their machinery and reduce the cost continually, especially if in competition with others equally anxious to produce something which everybody wants. One of the reasons why a calendar clock, for instance, or an oval picture frame, or a law book costs so much is because so few buy; while a common clock, excursion tickets, water pails, and Bibles are wanted by everybody and are cheapened accordingly; and when everybody can be made to feel that they must have certain luxuries now confined to the wealthy, they will be cheapened accordingly.

How much do you imagine a single copy of the *Atlantic Monthly* or of *Our Young*

Folks would cost if bought by ten times their present number of subscribers? One could spend hours in describing the saving which this patronage would make in the manufacture of those publications alone. Meantime, you who will buy the *Atlantic* or *Our Young Folks* are paying the present prices because there are so many who will not buy at all. Your loss is doubled; they keep your wages down because they do without these publications, and keep the prices of these publications up because they do without them.

Here, then, is an increase of wages, practically, at the expense of no one; and the general fact that much of the increase is to fall upon the wastes of society, caused by its idleness, crimes, fashions, and accidents at last, and that the increase will be very gradual, ought to disarm all opposition. Meantime, the temptation to fraud and idleness will be measurably lessened by the removal, through the reduction of hours and the increase of wages, of the burdens upon labor.

I put the question to any man who thinks: "Is labor honored and respected? Is Henry Wilson respected because he did make shoes or because he does not? Are Abraham Lincoln, Andrew Johnson, and N.P. Banks honored because they once toiled with their hands or because they were fortunate enough to lift themselves into a position where it was no longer necessary?" Is labor in the shop or on the farm, ten and twelve hours a day, the place for a man anxious to exert an influence upon the questions of the hour? When labor is honored, idleness will be dishonored. The courts of justice and state prisons of our land are less feared and dreaded as possible contingencies than are its farms and workshops by the more intelligent class. Can we wonder then that crimes in legislation are increasing; that 10,000 applications are on file in the Treasury Department, at Washington, for clerkships; that there are 6 applications for every situation in the Boston customhouse; that every fourth year there is a grand national scramble for the post offices of the United States?

This system, however, falls the most crushingly upon woman by lowering her wages to the starvation point and sending her onto the streets of all our large cities and towns for bread! The horrors of the middle passage, which an advancing civilization has consigned to eternal infamy, are here repeated and magnified on a large scale in the present labor system. Women elbowing women; aggravating each other's difficulties and creating a system of abominations which cannot be described. Small compensation, however, explains all this.

Because fathers are paid low wages they send their children — who ought to be at school — into factories and shops to do cheaply what women ought to be fairly paid for doing. Because husbands are underpaid, they consent that their wives may crowd the labor market in competition with maidens who have no husbands to make up for their low wages. And because single men are not paid enough for their daily labor, they do not marry; and thus the maidens who ought to be married, and the wives who ought to be out of the labor market and attending to themselves and families, and the children who ought to be at school, are bringing down woman's wages until her cry of want and despair is splitting the ears of the nation! It is fashionable to sympathize with the "poor sewing girl," but when will men dare to go to the root of the difficulty?

Presenting the foregoing as a mere fragment of the argument, proving that a reduction of hours is an increase of wages, I submit, in conclusion, that the "increase" does not mean an increase of the price of the article produced as do the "strikes" for higher wages, when successful. In a reduction of hours the producer and the consumer will come together more frequently and stay longer, and the knowledge they will exchange will commence melting and dividing between them the profits of capital. The capitalist, as we now understand him, is to pass away with the kings and royalties of the past. In America every man is king in theory and will be in practice eventually, and in the good time coming every man will be a capitalist. The capitalist of today, however, is as necessary as was the king once, to preserve order. Nothing but a higher standard of popular intelligence can supersede the necessity of the one-man power.

The eight-hour system will put the man who made the shoes and the man who bought them together; and they will compare the prices paid for the labor and the sale of the shoes; and observing the great difference, will begin to think! This thought and its consequences melt back into the hands which produced it, the wealth of the world. It means anti-pauperism, anti-aristocracy, anti-monopoly, anti-slavery, anti-prostitution, anti-crime, want, waste, and idleness; and the vast moral and material consequences flowing from such a conference justify the legislation necessary to secure the time.

154.

John Sherman: On Postwar Industrial Expansion

The Civil War had produced a considerable economic boom in the North. The rise in economic activity was reflected in the increased production of raw materials and manufactured goods, the growth of transportation facilities, and the expansion of trade and commerce. Senator John Sherman of Ohio devoted most of his public life to economic matters. As chairman of the Senate Committee on Finance after 1867, he exerted a tremendous impact on fiscal policy and ten years later he became secretary of the treasury under President Hayes. In the following letter to his brother, General William T. Sherman, dated November 10, 1865, he expressed his glowing view of the nation's economic prosperity.

Source: *The Sherman Letters*, Rachel Sherman Thorndike, ed., New York, 1894, pp. 258-259.

I AM GLAD TO HEAR YOU ARE SETTLED, and, from all accounts, delightfully. You deserve quiet and repose after five years of change and labor. When in New York the other day, I found that party of English capitalists were delighted with their visit with you and seemed especially polite to me on that account. I got for two of them Bowman and Nichol's works [*Lives of General Sherman*], which they wanted to take home.

But for my political employment, I could have received from them very lucrative employment in the prosecution of their vast railroad schemes. Even as it is, if they, within six months, show their ability to execute their plans, I will identify myself much more with them.

The truth is, the close of the war with our resources unimpaired gives an elevation, a scope to the ideas of leading capitalists far higher than anything ever undertaken in this country before. They talk of millions as confidently as formerly of thousands. No doubt the contraction that must soon come will explode merely visionary schemes, but many vast undertakings will be executed. Among them will be the Pacific R.R. and extensive ironworks, like some in England. Our manufactures are yet in their infancy, but soon I expect to see, under the stimulus of a great demand and the protection of our tariff, locomotive and machine shops worthy of the name.

I do not fear, whatever may be the result of the senatorial election, but I can find enough to do and without lowering the position I have occupied. As for the chances, from all the information I can gather, there is but little doubt a majority of the legislature is for me. Still I know enough of the shifts and dangers in a new body of men like a legislature not to be oversanguine. Since I am in the contest I will do all I can for success and hope my friends will do likewise but if defeated will bear it patiently. In a short time I will send you a list of the members who are from the military service, in the hope that you may know some of them well enough to influence them. You can feel perfectly easy in doing this, as my opponents use to the uttermost against me any prejudice or feeling against you.

This election over, I think I shall be very willing to say good-by to politics and will then seek to settle myself comfortably in some part of Ohio where I can engage in railroads, banking, or manufacturing. The law in this country is now only useful as the pathway to other pursuits. . . .

I have seen Johnson several times. He seems kind and patient with all his terrible responsibility. I think he feels what everyone must have observed, that the people will not trust the party or men who, during the war, sided with the Rebels. The Democratic Party is doomed forever as a disloyal organization, and no promises, or pledges, or platform they can make will redeem them from the odium they justly gained.

155.

Horace Greeley: The First Fruits of Reconstruction

Horace Greeley, editor of the New York Tribune, *was an uncompromising advocate of Negro suffrage and generally favored a firm policy toward the South. But in the early days of Reconstruction he came to support President Johnson's moderate policy with the hope that it would produce a swift reconciliation between North and South. His motto for Reconstruction was "Universal Amnesty and Impartial Suffrage." By the end of 1865, however, events began to indicate to him that Johnson's lenient policy was ineffective. Negroes were denied their rights by the "Black Codes." Unreconstructed Southern politicians resumed control of their state legislatures. Greeley became increasingly frustrated by Southern behavior. He expressed his disillusionment in the following* Tribune *editorial of November 15, 1865.*

Source: *New-York Daily Tribune*, November 15, 1865.

WE CAN BEST UNDERSTAND the success of the experiment of Reconstruction by looking at the results in many of the Southern states. It is six months since the President threw open the doors of the Union to the defeated Rebels and invited all who were willing to become good citizens and obedient to the laws to enter and resume their seats at the old family board. History does not present an example of similar magnanimity. Men speak of the merciful revolution of William III, forgetting that William sent Fenwick to the scaffold and bestowed the choicest estates of the Jacobites upon his supporters and favorites. We have punished no one for treason. Jefferson Davis was arrested for conspiring to commit murder; and, as that charge has never been abandoned, we presume it is as a "murderer" he is now at Fortress Monroe. Clement C. Clay was imprisoned on the same charge. The men executed were executed as murderers. Wirz died as one guilty of murder. All the confiscated lands have not quite

Horace Greeley, daguerreotype dated 1855

been restored, but the pardon that embraces Tredegar Anderson will soon envelop in its consoling folds every remaining Rebel.

Those who have criticized that policy certainly admit that the President's motives were kind and charitable. Perhaps we can no better illustrate that kindness than by remembering that to gratify the South he was willing to postpone justice to the Negro. Those who know how deeply and earnestly the honest Northern heart felt on this subject will appreciate the sacrifice that the President was willing to make to propitiate the South. If any statesman commanded their gratitude, their support, their undeviating kindness, it was the President. They made protestations. They were the President's most sincere friends. They would show him the true devotion of a Southern heart. He was their bulwark against Radicalism. He would stand between them and "Abolition ghouls." They, on their part, would be his most devoted supporters. They would take up arms for him as they took up arms against him, and under the fostering care of Andrew Johnson, poor white, but now President of all these states, they would assist in building up a republic that would rival in imperial grandeur the proudest days of the Commonwealth of Rome.

Well, we have tried them, and what? Let us go down to Louisiana. Here is a state rich in resources — her great metropolis overflowing with the good things that commerce can bring. This, peace gave its people, and how have they answered it? In the first place, we have a governor like Wells, an accident of the war, who took advantage of the peace to hold his place by pandering to the worst Rebel feelings. We find the Negro downtrodden. Men are imprisoned for speaking their opinions about Negro suffrage. The worst features of the slave laws are revived, and a large party is, with difficulty, dissuaded — dissuaded, let us own it — by such men as Beauregard and Hays from going to Mexico and bringing the runaway Rebel Allen back as governor. The good results of former administrations are wiped away in an instant, and the Rebels, headed by military popinjays like Fullerton, are rapidly rushing their state back to the terror and gloom of the ante-rebellion period.

If we go into Mississippi, we find not only a refusal to allow the Negroes the rights of jurors but even the rights of witnesses. In South Carolina, the Rebels almost force Wade Hampton into the gubernatorial chair, merely because such action would be a defiance to the President. As for the Rebel debt, she will pay her share, this rebellious Carolina, dollar for dollar. As for the constitutional amendment, it comes by compulsion. South Carolina will vote for it now that she may kick open the doors of Congress and stand before the speaker's chair with six electoral votes in her hand — six votes, to our shame be it spoken, that represent a power as great as Connecticut with 80,000 white men less. Then we come to North Carolina and find Jonathan Worth elected governor because Holden was the choice of the President. Not one word about the constitutional amendment.

As with these states it is everywhere throughout the South. What one state has come back frankly and accepted all the issues of the war, even the issues of the President? For the temporary purpose of an argument, we will lay aside manhood suffrage. What Southern state has accepted all the presidential propositions? Not one; and for this reason only that the Rebels will not concede one jot or tittle toward reconstructing a Union that does not eternalize slavery and strengthen the power of the slaveholders. They know full well that if we leave the Negro in their hands a freedman and allow them to group around him laws as degrading as those of South Carolina, they will have little trouble in perpetuating a system more degrading than slavery — in this, that it gives the master power over the Negro and, at the same time, releases him from any pecuniary or personal responsibility.

Let us emphasize these two points. The Rebels play for a winning game. "Let us," they say, "kick open the doors of Congress, and what then? We have our apportionment increased; for, the Negro being free, he must be counted man for man. At home, we have Negro labor at slave prices and no responsibility. We may turn the Negro out to the commons when he is seventy, just as we turn out horses. Our laws compel him to work for us — we may do as we please with him. The government has released us from our obligation to the Negro and placed an obligation upon him. Altogether, we have made a jolly exchange and

trumped the Yankees nicely in their own game."

These gentlemen of the South mean to win. They meant it in 1861 when they opened fire on Sumter. They meant it in 1865 when they sent a bullet through the brain of Abraham Lincoln. They mean it now. The moment we remove the iron hand from the Rebels' throats they will rise and attempt the mastery. If South Carolina adopts the amendment, she does it under compulsion — the compulsion of a dispatch from Washington. South Carolina can well afford to adopt the amendment when she is permitted to reenact the slave code. The power that compels this action on her part is the power that could have compelled her to grant manhood suffrage six months ago.

The danger of our Reconstruction is that we trifle with our own power — that, instead of waiting until the prodigal really comes home, we send the fatted calf to him. We do not give the true men of the South a chance. If with all our power we permit such men as Durant in Louisiana, Hamilton of Texas, and even the conservative Holden in North Carolina to be overslaughed and beaten by returned Rebels, how can we expect Durants and Hamiltons and Holdens to rise up in the South? When Union men find they can only rise by eating Rebel dirt, we shall have a crop of Wells politicians over the South living on this unsavory diet. Therefore, we not only break faith with the Negro but with the true Union men — with those who went into the caves with Andrew Johnson and with him suffered for their principles. The first fruits of Reconstruction promise a most deplorable harvest, and the sooner we gather the tares, plow the ground again, and sow new seed, the better.

156.

BENJAMIN G. HUMPHREYS: Justice but Not Equality for the Negro

Benjamin Humphreys was the first elected governor of Mississippi after the Civil War. The federal authorities had favored another candidate, and at the time of his election Humphreys had not yet received a federal pardon despite his having taken the oath of amnesty. However, three days before the Mississippi legislature convened, he was provisionally recognized by President Johnson. On November 20, 1865, Humphreys delivered the following address to the legislature. In his career as governor he temporized on most issues, at times obstructing federal laws, at other times cooperating with federal authorities. He was eventually removed from his position on June 15, 1868, by federal military authorities.

Source: *Report of the Joint Committee on Reconstruction*, 39 Congress, 1 Session, Washington, 1866, Pt. 3, pp. 182-183.

BY THE SUDDEN EMANCIPATION of over 300,000 slaves, Mississippi has imposed upon her a problem of vast magnitude, upon the proper solution of which depend the hopes and future prosperity and welfare of ourselves and of our children.

Under the pressure of federal bayonets, urged on by the misdirected sympathies of the world in behalf of the enslaved African, the people of Mississippi have abolished the institution of slavery and have solemnly declared in their state constitution that "the legislature should provide by law for the protection and security of person and property of the freedmen of the state and guard them and the state against any evils that may arise from the sudden emancipation." How this important provision and requirement of the constitution is to be carried into effect is the question presented for our solution.

We must now meet the question as it is and not as we would like to have it. The rule must be justice. The Negro is free, whether we like it or not; we must realize that fact now and forever. *To be free, however, does not make him a citizen or entitle him to social or political equality with the white man.* But the constitution and justice do entitle him to protection and security in his person and property, both real and personal.

In my humble judgment, no person, bond or free, under any form of government can be assured of protection or security in either person or property except through an independent and enlightened judiciary. The courts, then, should be open to the Negro. But of what avail is it to open the courts and invite the Negro to "sue and be sued" if he is not permitted to testify himself and introduce such testimony as he or his attorney may deem essential to establish the truth and justice of his case? Whether the witness be white or black, it is the denial of the most common privilege of freedom, an unmeaning delusion, the merest mockery.

[As] a measure of domestic policy, whether for the protection of the person or the property of the freedman, or for the protection of society, the Negro should be allowed and required to testify for or against the white and black according to the truth. There are few men living in the South who have not known many white criminals to go "unwhipped of justice" because Negro testimony was not permitted in the courts. And now that the Negro is no longer under the restraints and protection of his master, he will become the dupe and the "cat's-paw" of the vile and vicious white man, who seeks his association and will plunder our lands with entire security from punishment unless he can be reached through Negro testimony. It is an insult to the intelligence and virtue of our courts and juries of white men to say or suspect that they cannot or will not protect the innocent, whether white or black, against the falsehood and perjury of black witnesses.

The question of admitting Negro testimony for the protection of their person and property sinks into insignificance by the side of the other great question of *guarding them and the state* against the evils that may arise from their sudden emancipation. What are the evils that have already arisen against which we are to guard the Negro and the state? The answer is patent to all — vagrancy and pauperism, and their inevitable concomitant, crime and misery, hang like a dark pall over a once prosperous and happy but now desolated land.

To the guardian care of the Freedmen's Bureau have been entrusted the emancipated slaves. The civil law and the white man outside of the bureau have been deprived of all jurisdiction over them. Look around you and see the result. Idleness and vagrancy have been the result. Our rich and productive fields have been deserted for the filthy garrets and sickly cellars of our towns and cities. From producers they are converted into consumers, and, as winter approach-

Library of Congress

Benjamin G. Humphreys, Confederate general from Mississippi; first elected postwar governor of that state

es, their only salvation from starvation and want is Federal rations, plunder, and pillage. *Four years of cruel war, conducted on principles of vandalism disgraceful to the civilization of the age, were scarcely more blighting and destructive to the homes of the white man, and impoverishing and degrading to the Negro, than has resulted in the last six or eight months from the administration of this black incubus.* Many of the officers connected with that bureau are gentlemen of honor and integrity, *but they seem incapable of protecting the rights and property of the white man against the villainies of the vile and villainous with whom they are associated.*

How long this *hideous curse,* permitted of heaven, is to be allowed to rule and ruin our unhappy people, I regret it is not in my power to give any assurance further than can be gathered from the public and private declarations of President Johnson, that "the troops will all be withdrawn from Mississippi when, in the opinion of the government, the peace and order and civil authority have been restored and can be maintained without them." In this uncertainty as to what will satisfy the government of our loyalty and ability to maintain order and peace and civil government, our duty, under the constitution, to guard the Negro and the state from the evils arising from sudden emancipation must not be neglected.

Our duty to the state and to the freedmen seems to me to be clear, and I respectfully recommend, first, that Negro testimony should be admitted in our courts, not only for the protection of the person and property of the freedmen but for the protection of society against the crimes of both races.

Second, that the freedman be encouraged at once to engage in some pursuit of industry for the support of his family and the education of his children by laws assuring him of friendship and protection. Tax the freedman for the support of the indigent and helpless freedmen, and *then with an iron will and the strong hand of power take hold of the idler and the vagrant and force him to some profitable employment.*

Third, pass a militia law that will enable the militia to protect our people against the insurrection, or any possible combination of vicious white men and Negroes.

I deem the passage of these measures, before you take recess, of vital importance. By them we may secure the withdrawal of the Federal troops and thus again inspire our people with hope and confidence in the future and encourage them to engage again in agricultural pursuits, upon which our all depends. If we fail to pass them, the future is all uncertainty, doom, and despondency.

157.

Mississippi Black Code

The status of the Negro was the focal problem of Reconstruction. Slavery had been abolished by the Thirteenth Amendment, but the white people of the South were determined to keep the Negro in his place, socially, politically, and economically. This was done by means of the notorious "Black Codes," passed by several of the state legislatures. Northerners regarded these codes as a revival of slavery in disguise. The first such body of statutes, and probably the harshest, was passed in Mississippi in November 1865. Four of the statutes that made up the code are reprinted below.

Source: *Laws of the State of Mississippi, Passed at a Regular Session of the Mississippi Legislature, held in . . . Jackson, October, November, and December, 1865,* Jackson, 1866, pp. 82-93, 165-167.

I.

Apprentice Law

Section 1. *Be it enacted by the legislature of the state of Mississippi,* that it shall be the duty of all sheriffs, justices of the peace, and other civil officers of the several counties in this state to report to the Probate courts of their respective counties semiannually, at the January and July terms of said courts, all freedmen, free Negroes, and mulattoes under the age of eighteen within their respective counties, beats, or districts who are orphans, or whose parent or parents have not the means, or who refuse to provide for and support said minors; and thereupon it shall be the duty of said Probate Court to order the clerk of said court to apprentice said minors to some competent and suitable person, on such terms as the court may direct, having a particular care to the interest of said minors:

Provided, that the former owner of said minors shall have the preference when, in the opinion of the court, he or she shall be a suitable person for that purpose.

Section 2. *Be it further enacted,* that the said court shall be fully satisfied that the person or persons to whom said minor shall be apprenticed shall be a suitable person to have the charge and care of said minor and fully to protect the interest of said minor. The said court shall require the said master or mistress to execute bond and security, payable to the state of Mississippi, conditioned that he or she shall furnish said minor with sufficient food and clothing; to treat said minor humanely; furnish medical attention in case of sickness; teach or cause to be taught him or her to read and write, if under fifteen years old; and will conform to any law that may be hereafter passed for the regulation of the duties and relation of master and apprentice:

Provided, that said apprentice shall be bound by indenture, in case of males until they are twenty-one years old, and in case of females until they are eighteen years old.

Section 3. *Be it further enacted,* that in the management and control of said apprentices, said master or mistress shall have power to inflict such moderate corporeal chastisement as a father or guardian is allowed to inflict on his or her child or ward at common law:

Provided, that in no case shall cruel or inhuman punishment be inflicted.

Section 4. *Be it further enacted,* that if any apprentice shall leave the employment of his or her master or mistress without his or her consent, said master or mistress may pursue and recapture said apprentice and bring him or her before any justice of the peace of the county, whose duty it shall be to remand said apprentice to the service of his or her master or mistress; and in the event of a refusal on the part of said apprentice so to return, then said justice shall commit said apprentice to the jail of said county, on failure to give bond, until the next term of the county court; and it shall be the duty of said court, at the first term thereafter, to investigate said case; and if the court shall be of opinion that said apprentice left the employment of his or her master or mistress without good cause, to order him or her to be punished, as provided for the punishment of hired freedmen, as may be from time to time provided for by law, for desertion, until he or she shall agree to return to his or her master or mistress:

Provided, that the court may grant continuances, as in other cases; and *provided,* further, that if the court shall believe that said apprentice had good cause to quit his said master or mistress, the court shall discharge said apprentice from said indenture and also enter a judgment against the master or mistress for not more than $100, for the use and benefit of said apprentice, to be collected on execution, as in other cases.

Section 5. *Be it further enacted,* that if any person entice away any apprentice from his or her master or mistress, or shall knowingly employ an apprentice, or furnish him or her food or clothing, without the written consent of his or her master or mistress, or shall sell or give said apprentice ardent spirits, without such consent, said person so offending shall be deemed guilty of a high misdemeanor, and shall, on conviction thereof before the county court, be punished as provided for the punishment of persons enticing from their employer hired freedmen, free Negroes, or mulattoes.

Section 6. *Be it further enacted,* that it shall be the duty of all civil officers of their respective counties to report any minors within their respective counties to said Probate Court who are subject to be apprenticed under the provisions of this act, from time to time, as the facts may come to their knowledge; and it shall be the duty of said court, from time to time, as said minors shall be reported to them or otherwise come to their knowledge, to apprentice said minors as hereinbefore provided.

Section 7. *Be it further enacted*, that in case the master or mistress of any apprentice shall desire, he or she shall have the privilege to summon his or her said apprentice to the Probate Court, and thereupon, with the approval of the court, he or she shall be released from all liability as master of said apprentice, and his said bond shall be canceled, and it shall be the duty of the court forthwith to reapprentice said minor; and in the event any master of an apprentice shall die before the close of the term of service of said apprentice, it shall be the duty of the court to give the preference in reapprenticing said minor to the widow, or other member of said master's family:

Provided, that said widow or other member of said family shall be a suitable person for that purpose.

Section 8. *Be it further enacted*, that in case any master or mistress of any apprentice, bound to him or her under this act shall be about to remove or shall have removed to any other state of the United States by the laws of which such apprentice may be an inhabitant thereof, the Probate Court of the proper county may authorize the removal of such apprentice to such state upon the said master or mistress entering into bond, with security, in a penalty to be fixed by the judge, conditioned that said master or mistress will, upon such removal, comply with the laws of such state in such cases:

Provided, that said master shall be cited to attend the court at which such order is proposed to be made and shall have a right to resist the same by next friend, or otherwise.

Section 9. *Be it further enacted*, that it shall be lawful for any freedman, free Negro, or mulatto having a minor child or children to apprentice the said minor child or children as provided for by this act.

Section 10. *Be it further enacted*, that in all cases where the age of the freedman, free Negro, or mulatto cannot be ascertained by record testimony, the judge of the county court shall fix the age.

II.

Vagrancy Law

Section 1. *Be it enacted by the legislature of the state of Mississippi*, that all rogues and vagabonds, idle and dissipated persons, beggars, jugglers, or persons practising unlawful games or plays, runaways, common drunkards, common nightwalkers, pilferers, lewd, wanton, or lascivious persons, in speech or behavior, common railers and brawlers, persons who neglect their calling or employment, misspend what they earn, or do not provide for the support of themselves or their families or dependents, and all other idle and disorderly persons, including all who neglect all lawful business, or habitually misspend their time by frequenting houses of ill-fame, gaming houses, or tippling shops, shall be deemed and considered vagrants under the provisions of this act; and, on conviction thereof, shall be fined not exceeding $100, with all accruing costs, and be imprisoned at the discretion of the court not exceeding ten days.

Section 2. *Be it further enacted*, that all freedmen, free Negroes, and mulattoes in this state over the age of eighteen years found on the second Monday in January 1866, or thereafter, with no lawful employment or business, or found unlawfully assembling themselves together either in the day- or nighttime, and all white persons so assembling with freedmen, free Negroes, or mulattoes, or usually associating with freedmen, free Negroes, or mulattoes on terms of equality, or living in adultery or fornication with a freedwoman, free Negro, or mulatto, shall be deemed vagrants; and, on conviction thereof, shall be fined in the sum of not exceeding, in the case of a freedman, free Negro, or mulatto, $50, and a white man, $200, and imprisoned at the discretion of the court, the free Negro not exceeding ten days, and the white man not exceeding six months.

Section 3. *Be it further enacted,* that all justices of the peace, mayors, and aldermen of incorporated towns and cities of the several counties in this state shall have jurisdiction to try all questions of vagrancy in their respective towns, counties, and cities; and it is hereby made their duty, whenever they shall ascertain that any person or persons in their respective towns, counties, and cities are violating any of the provisions of this act, to have said party or parties arrested and brought before them and immediately investigate said charge; and, on conviction, punish said party or parties as provided for herein. And it is hereby made the duty of all sheriffs, constables, town constables, city marshals, and all like officers to report to some officer having jurisdiction all violations of any of the provisions of this act; and it shall be the duty of the county courts to inquire if any officers have neglected any of the duties required by this act; and in case any officer shall fail or neglect any duty herein, it shall be the duty of the county court to fine said officer, upon conviction, not exceeding $100, to be paid into the county treasury for county purposes.

Section 4. *Be it further enacted,* that keepers of gaming houses, houses of prostitution, all prostitutes, public or private, and all persons who derive their chief support in employments that militate against good morals or against laws shall be deemed and held to be vagrants.

Section 5. *Be it further enacted,* that all fines and forfeitures collected under the provisions of this act shall be paid into the county treasury for general county purposes; and in case any freedman, free Negro, or mulatto shall fail for five days after the imposition of any fine or forfeiture upon him or her for violation of any of the provisions of this act to pay the same, that it shall be, and is hereby made, the duty of the sheriff of the proper county to hire out said freedman, free Negro, or mulatto to any person who will, for the shortest period of service, pay said fine or forfeiture and all costs:

Provided, a preference shall be given to the employer, if there be one, in which case the employer shall be entitled to deduct and retain the amount so paid from the wages of such freedman, free Negro, or mulatto then due or to become due; and in case such freedman, free Negro, or mulatto cannot be hired out, he or she may be dealt with as a pauper.

Section 6. *Be it further enacted,* that the same duties and liabilities existing among white persons of this state shall attach to freedmen, free Negroes, and mulattoes to support their indigent families and all colored paupers; and that, in order to secure a support for such indigent freedmen, free Negroes, and mulattoes, it shall be lawful, and it is hereby made the duty of the boards of county police of each county in this state, to levy a poll or capitation tax on each and every freedman, free Negro, or mulatto, between the ages of eighteen and sixty years, not to exceed the sum of $1 annually, to each person so taxed, which tax, when collected, shall be paid into the county treasurer's hands and constitute a fund to be called the Freedman's Pauper Fund, which shall be applied by the commissioners of the poor for the maintenance of the poor of the freedmen, free Negroes, and mulattoes of this state, under such regulations as may be established by the boards of county police, in the respective counties of this state.

Section 7. *Be it further enacted*, that if any freedman, free Negro, or mulatto shall fail or refuse to pay any tax levied according to the provisions of the 6th Section of this act, it shall be prima facie evidence of vagrancy, and it shall be the duty of the sheriff to arrest such freedman, free Negro, or mulatto, or such person refusing or neglecting to pay such tax, and proceed at once to hire, for the shortest time, such delinquent taxpayer to anyone who will pay the said tax, with accruing costs, giving preference to the employer, if there be one.

Section 8. *Be it further enacted*, that any person feeling himself or herself aggrieved by the judgment of any justice of the peace, mayor, or alderman in cases arising under this act may, within five days, appeal to the next term of the county court of the proper county, upon giving bond and security in a sum not less than $25 nor more than $150, conditioned to appear and prosecute said appeal, and abide by the judgment of the county court, and said appeal shall be tried *de novo* in the county court, and the decision of said court shall be final.

III.

Civil Rights of Freedmen

Section 1. *Be it enacted by the legislature of the state of Mississippi*, that all freedmen, free Negroes, and mulattoes may sue and be sued, implead and be impleaded in all the courts of law and equity of this state, and may acquire personal property and choses in action, by descent or purchase, and may dispose of the same in the same manner and to the same extent that white persons may:

Provided, that the provisions of this section shall not be construed as to allow any freedman, free Negro, or mulatto to rent or lease any lands or tenements, except in incorporated towns or cities, in which places the corporate authorities shall control the same.

Section 2. *Be it further enacted*, that all freedmen, free Negroes, and mulattoes may intermarry with each other, in the same manner and under the same regulations that are provided by law for white persons:

Provided, that the clerk of probate shall keep separate records of the same.

Section 3. *Be it further enacted*, that all freedmen, free Negroes, and mulattoes who do now and have heretofore lived and cohabited together as husband and wife shall be taken and held in law as legally married, and the issue shall be taken and held as legitimate for all purposes. That it shall not be lawful for any freedman, free Negro, or mulatto to intermarry with any white person; nor for any white person to intermarry with any freedman, free Negro, or mulatto; and any person who shall so intermarry shall be deemed guilty of felony and, on conviction thereof, shall be confined in the state penitentiary for life; and those shall be deemed freedmen, free Negroes, and mulattoes who are of pure Negro blood; and those descended from a Negro to the third generation inclusive, though one ancestor of each generation may have been a white person.

Section 4. *Be it further enacted*, that in addition to cases in which freedmen, free Negroes, and mulattoes are now by law competent witnesses, freedmen, free Negroes, or mulattoes shall be competent in civil cases when a party or parties to the suit, either plaintiff or plaintiffs, defendant or defendants, also in cases where freedmen, free Negroes, and mulattoes is or are either plaintiff or plaintiffs, defendant or defendants, and a white person or white persons is or are the opposing party or parties, plaintiff or plaintiffs, defendant or defendants. They shall also be competent witnesses in all criminal prosecutions where the crime charged is alleged to have been committed by a white person upon or against the person or property of a freedman, free Negro, or mulatto:

Provided, that in all cases said witnesses

shall be examined in open court on the stand, except, however, they may be examined before the grand jury, and shall in all cases be subject to the rules and tests of the common law as to competency and credibility.

Section 5. *Be it further enacted,* that every freedman, free Negro, and mulatto shall, on the second Monday of January 1866, and annually thereafter, have a lawful home or employment, and shall have a written evidence thereof, as follows, to wit: if living in any incorporated city, town, or village, a license from the mayor thereof; and if living outside of any incorporated city, town, or village, from the member of the board of police of his beat, authorizing him or her to do irregular and job work, or a written contract, as provided in Section 6 of this act, which licenses may be revoked for cause, at any time, by the authority granting the same.

Section 6. *Be it further enacted,* that all contracts for labor made with freedmen, free Negroes, and mulattoes for a longer period than one month shall be in writing and in duplicate, attested and read to said freedman, free Negro, or mulatto by a beat, city, or county officer, or two disinterested white persons of the county in which the labor is to be performed, of which each party shall have one; and said contracts shall be taken and held as entire contracts; and if the laborer shall quit the service of the employer before expiration of his term of service without good cause, he shall forfeit his wages for that year, up to the time of quitting.

Section 7. *Be it further enacted,* that every civil officer shall, and every person may, arrest and carry back to his or her legal employer any freedman, free Negro, or mulatto who shall have quit the service of his or her employer before the expiration of his or her term of service without good cause, and said officer and person shall be entitled to receive for arresting and carrying back every deserting employee aforesaid, the sum of

$5, and 10 cents per mile from the place of arrest to the place of delivery, and the same shall be paid by the employer, and held as a setoff for so much against the wages of said deserting employee:

Provided, that said arrested party, after being so returned, may appeal to a justice of the peace or member of the board of police of the county, who, on notice to the alleged employer, shall try summarily whether said appellant is legally employed by the alleged employer and has good cause to quit said employer; either party shall have the right of appeal to the county court, pending which the alleged deserter shall be remanded to the alleged employer or otherwise disposed of as shall be right and just, and the decision of the county court shall be final.

Section 8. *Be it further enacted,* that upon affidavit made by the employer of any freedman, free Negro, or mulatto, or other credible person before any justice of the peace or member of the board of police, that any freedman, free Negro, or mulatto, legally employed by said employer, has illegally deserted said employment, such justice of the peace or member of the board of police shall issue his warrant or warrants, returnable before himself, or other such officer, directed to any sheriff, constable, or special deputy, commanding him to arrest said deserter and return him or her to said employer, and the like proceedings shall be had as provided in the preceding section; and it shall be lawful for any officer to whom such warrant shall be directed to execute said warrant in any county of this state, and that said warrant may be transmitted without endorsement to any like officer of another county, to be executed and returned as aforesaid, and the said employer shall pay the cost of said warrants and arrest and return, which shall be set off for so much against the wages of said deserter.

Section 9. *Be it further enacted,* that if any person shall persuade or attempt to persuade, entice, or cause any freedman, free Negro, or mulatto to desert from the legal employment of any person before the expiration of his or her term of service, or shall knowingly employ any such deserting freedman, free Negro, or mulatto, or shall knowingly give or sell to any such deserting freedman, free Negro, or mulatto any food, raiment, or other thing, he or she shall be guilty of a misdemeanor; and, upon conviction, shall be fined not less than $25 and not more than $200 and the costs; and, if said fine and costs shall not be immediately paid, the court shall sentence said convict to not exceeding two months' imprisonment in the county jail, and he or she shall moreover be liable to the party injured in damages:

Provided, if any person shall, or shall attempt to, persuade, entice, or cause any freedman, free Negro, or mulatto to desert from any legal employment of any person with the view to employ said freedman, free Negro, or mulatto without the limits of this state, such person, on conviction, shall be fined not less than $50 and not more than $500 and costs; and, if said fine and costs shall not be immediately paid, the court shall sentence said convict to not exceeding six months' imprisonment in the county jail.

Section 10. *Be it further enacted,* that it shall be lawful for any freedman, free Negro, or mulatto to charge any white person, freedman, free Negro, or mulatto, by affidavit, with any criminal offense against his or her person or property; and, upon such affidavit, the proper process shall be issued and executed as if said affidavit was made by a white person; and it shall be lawful for any freedman, free Negro, or mulatto, in any action, suit, or controversy pending or about to be instituted, in any court of law or equity of this state, to make all needful and lawful affidavits, as shall be necessary for the institution, prosecution, or defense of such suit or controversy.

Section 11. *Be it further enacted,* that the penal laws of this state, in all cases not otherwise specially provided for, shall apply and extend to all freedmen, free Negroes, and mulattoes.

IV.

Penal Code

Section 1. *Be it enacted by the legislature of the state of Mississippi,* that no freedman, free Negro, or mulatto not in the military service of the United States government, and not licensed so to do by the board of police of his or her county, shall keep or carry firearms of any kind, or any ammunition, dirk, or Bowie knife; and, on conviction thereof in the county court, shall be punished by fine, not exceeding $10, and pay the costs of such proceedings, and all such arms or ammunition shall be forfeited to the informer; and it shall be the duty of every civil and military officer to arrest any freedman, free Negro, or mulatto found with any such arms or ammunition, and cause him or her to be committed for trial in default of bail.

Section 2. *Be it further enacted,* that any freedman, free Negro, or mulatto committing riots, routs, affrays, trespasses, malicious mischief, cruel treatment to animals, seditious speeches, insulting gestures, language, or acts, or assaults on any person, disturbance of the peace, exercising the function of a minister of the Gospel without a license from some regularly organized church, vending spirituous or intoxicating liquors, or committing any other misdemeanor the punishment of which is not specifically provided for by law shall, upon conviction thereof in the county court, be fined not less than $10 and not more than $100, and may be imprisoned, at the discretion of the court, not exceeding thirty days.

Section 3. *Be it further enacted,* that if any white person shall sell, lend, or give to any freedman, free Negro, or mulatto any firearms, dirk, or Bowie knife, or ammunition, or any spirituous or intoxicating liquors, such person or persons so offending, upon conviction thereof in the county court of his or her county, shall be fined not exceeding $50, and may be imprisoned, at the discretion of the court, not exceeding thirty days:

Provided, that any master, mistress, or employer of any freedman, free Negro, or mulatto may give to any freedman, free Negro, or mulatto apprenticed to or employed by such master, mistress, or employer spirituous or intoxicating liquors, but not in sufficient quantities to produce intoxication.

Section 4. *Be it further enacted,* that all the penal and criminal laws now in force in this state defining offenses and prescribing the mode of punishment for crimes and misdemeanors committed by slaves, free Negroes, or mulattoes be and the same are hereby reenacted and declared to be in full force and effect against freedmen, free Negroes, and mulattoes, except so far as the mode and manner of trial and punishment have been changed or altered by law.

Section 5. *Be it further enacted,* that if any freedman, free Negro, or mulatto convicted of any of the misdemeanors provided against in this act shall fail or refuse, for the space of five days after conviction, to pay the fine and costs imposed, such person shall be hired out by the sheriff or other officer, at public outcry, to any white person who will pay said fine and all costs and take such convict for the shortest time.

158.

ULYSSES S. GRANT: Report on Conditions in the South

In the fall of 1865 President Andrew Johnson sent several prominent men, including Carl Schurz, Harvey Watterson, and General Grant, to tour the South and report to him on the conditions they observed. Schurz's report dwelt on Southern intransigence and urged a harsher Reconstruction policy in line with the recommendations of Congress. Watterson and Grant, on the other hand, pointed out that the South was conciliatory and upheld the President's policy. Grant, who left Washington on November 29 and visited major cities in North and South Carolina, and Georgia, sent the following report to the President on December 18.

Source: 39 Congress, 1 Session, Senate Executive Document No. 2, pp. 106-108.

Sir:

In reply to your note of the 16th instant requesting a report from me giving such information as I may be possessed of coming within the scope of the inquiries made by the Senate of the United States in their resolution of the 12th instant, I have the honor to submit the following:

With your approval, and also that of the honorable secretary of war, I left Washington city on the 27th of last month for the purpose of making a tour of inspection through some of the Southern states, or states lately in rebellion, and to see what changes were necessary to be made in the disposition of the military forces of the country; how these forces could be reduced and expenses curtailed, etc.; and to learn, as far as possible, the feelings and intentions of the citizens of those states toward the general government.

The state of Virginia, being so accessible to Washington city, and information from this quarter, therefore, being readily obtained, I hastened through the state without conversing or meeting with any of its citizens. In Raleigh, North Carolina, I spent one day; in Charleston, South Carolina, two days; Savannah and Augusta, Georgia, each one day. Both in traveling and while stopping, I saw much and conversed freely with the citizens of those states, as well as with officers of the Army who have been stationed among them. The following are the conclusions come to by me.

I am satisfied that the mass of thinking men of the South accept the present situation of affairs in good faith. The questions which have heretofore divided the sentiment of the people of the two sections — slavery and state's rights, or the right of a state to secede from the Union — they regard as having been settled forever by the highest tribunal — arms — that man can resort to. I was pleased to learn from the leading men whom I met that they not only accepted the decision arrived at as final but, now that the smoke of battle has cleared away and time has been given for reflection, that this decision has been a fortunate one for the whole country, they receiving like benefits from it with those who opposed them in the field and in council.

Four years of war, during which law was executed only at the point of the bayonet throughout the states in rebellion, have left the people possibly in a condition not to yield that ready obedience to civil authority the American people have generally been in the habit of yielding. This would render the presence of small garrisons throughout those states necessary until such time as labor returns to its proper channel and civil

authority is fully established. I did not meet anyone, either those holding places under the government or citizens of the Southern states, who think it practicable to withdraw the military from the South at present. The white and the black mutually require the protection of the general government.

There is such universal acquiescence in the authority of the general government throughout the portions of country visited by me that the mere presence of a military force, without regard to numbers, is sufficient to maintain order. The good of the country and economy require that the force kept in the interior, where there are many freedmen (elsewhere in the Southern states than at forts upon the seacoast no force is necessary), should all be white troops. The reasons for this are obvious without mentioning many of them. The presence of black troops, lately slaves, demoralizes labor, both by their advice and by furnishing in their camps a resort for the freedmen for long distances around. White troops generally excite no opposition, and therefore a small number of them can maintain order in a given district. Colored troops must be kept in bodies sufficient to defend themselves. It is not the thinking men who would use violence toward any class of troops sent among them by the general government, but the ignorant in some places might; and the late slave seems to be imbued with the idea that the property of his late master should, by right, belong to him, or at least should have no protection from the colored soldier. There is danger of collisions being brought on by such causes.

My observations lead me to the conclusion that the citizens of the Southern states are anxious to return to self-government within the Union as soon as possible; that while reconstructing they want and require protection from the government; that they are in earnest in wishing to do what they think is required by the government, not humiliating to them as citizens, and that if such a course were pointed out they would pursue it in good faith. It is to be regretted that there cannot be a greater commingling, at this time, between the citizens of the two sections, and particularly of those entrusted with the lawmaking power.

I did not give the operations of the Freedmen's Bureau that attention I would have done if more time had been at my disposal. Conversations on the subject, however, with officers connected with the bureau lead me to think that in some of the states its affairs have not been conducted with good judgment or economy, and that the belief widely spread among the freedmen of the Southern states that the lands of their former owners will, at least in part, be divided among them has come from the agents of this bureau. This belief is seriously interfering with the willingness of the freedmen to make contracts for the coming year. In some form the Freedmen's Bureau is an absolute necessity until civil law is established and enforced, securing to the freedmen their rights and full protection. At present, however, it is independent of the military establishment of the country and seems to be operated by the different agents of the bureau according to their individual notions. Everywhere General Howard, the able head of the bureau, made friends by the just and fair instructions and advice he gave; but the complaint in South Carolina was that when he left, things went on as before.

Many, perhaps the majority, of the agents of the Freedmen's Bureau advise the freedmen that by their own industry they must expect to live. To this end they endeavor to secure employment for them and to see that both contracting parties comply with their engagements. In some instances, I am sorry to say, the freedman's mind does not seem to be disabused of the idea that a freedman has the right to live without care or provision for the future. The effect of the belief in division of lands is idleness and accumulation in camps, towns, and cities. In such cases I think it will be found that vice and disease will tend to the extermination or great reduction of the colored race. It cannot be expected that the opinions held by men at the South for years can be changed in a day, and therefore the freedmen require, for a few years, not only laws to protect them but the fostering care of those who will give them good counsel and on whom they rely.

The Freedmen's Bureau, being separated from the military establishment of the country requires all the expenses of a separate organization. One does not necessarily know what the other is doing or what orders they are acting under. It seems to me this could be corrected by regarding every officer on duty with troops in the Southern states as an agent of the Freedmen's Bureau, and then have all orders, from the head of the bureau sent through department commanders. This would create a responsibility that would secure uniformity of action throughout all the South; would insure the orders and instructions from the head of the bureau being carried out, and would relieve from duty and pay a large number of employees of the government.

159.

John Greenleaf Whittier: "Laus Deo!"

The Thirteenth Amendment to the Constitution was passed by Congress on February 1, 1865, and the last of the necessary number of states ratified it on December 18 of the same year, thus making it a part of the supreme law of the land that henceforth neither slavery nor involuntary servitude should exist within the United States. The Amendment was the concrete fulfillment of the moral purpose of the North throughout the Civil War, and was hailed by "clang of bell and roar of gun" in the towns of Massachusetts and other Union states. Inspired by the news, John Greenleaf Whittier sat down on Christmas Day of 1865, as tradition has it, to put into words his own joyous reaction. The result was "Laus Deo!" ("Praise Be to God!"). The poem was published shortly after the new year.

Source: *Complete Poetical Works*, Cambridge Edition, Boston, 1894.

LAUS DEO!

It is done!
Clang of bell and roar of gun
Send the tidings up and down.
How the belfries rock and reel!
How the great guns, peal on peal,
Fling the joy from town to town!

Ring, O bells!
Every stroke exulting tells
Of the burial hour of crime.
Loud and long, that all may hear,
Ring for every listening ear
Of Eternity and Time!

Let us kneel:
God's own voice is in that peal,
And this spot is holy ground.
Lord, forgive us! What are we,
That our eyes this glory see,
That our ears have heard the sound!

For the Lord
On the whirlwind is abroad;
In the earthquake He has spoken;
He has smitten with His thunder
The iron walls asunder,
And the gates of brass are broken!

Loud and long
Lift the old exulting song;
Sing with Miriam by the sea;
He has cast the mighty down;
Horse and rider sink and drown;
"He hath triumphed gloriously!"

Did we dare,
In our agony of prayer,
Ask for more than He has done?
When was ever His right hand
Over any time or land
Stretched as now beneath the sun?

How they pale,
Ancient myth and song and tale,
In this wonder of our days,
When the cruel rod of war
Blossoms white with righteous law,
And the wrath of man is praise!

Blotted out!
All within and all about
Shall a fresher life begin;
Freer breathe the universe
As it rolls its heavy curse
On the dead and buried sin!

It is done!
In the circuit of the sun
Shall the sound thereof go forth.
It shall bid the sad rejoice,
It shall give the dumb a voice,
It shall belt with joy the earth!

Ring and swing,
Bells of joy! On morning's wing
Send the song of praise abroad!
With a sound of broken chains
Tell the nations that He reigns,
Who alone is Lord and God!

HE RETURNS NO MORE.

Index of Authors

The numbers in brackets
indicate selection numbers
in this volume

AGASSIZ, LOUIS (May 28, 1807-Dec. 12, 1873), naturalist, geologist, and teacher. Born Switzerland; professor of zoology (1848-73) at Lawrence Scientific School, Harvard; established (1859) the collections now in Harvard Museum of Comparative Zoology; founded (1873) Anderson School of Natural History; wrote *Contributions to the Natural History of the United States* (4 vols., 1857-63). **[102]**

ALFRIEND, FRANK H. (fl. 1864), editor of the *Southern Literary Messenger.* **[118]**

BEERS, ETHEL LYNN (Jan. 13, 1827-Oct. 11, 1879), poetess. Wrote "All Quiet Along the Potomac To-Night" (1861) and *General Frankie: a Story for Little Folks* (1863). **[54]**

BENJAMIN, ISRAEL (1818-1864), Rumanian traveler and writer. Toured North Africa, the Near East, China, and America; described his travels in U.S. in *Three Years in America 1859-1862* (1862). **[84]**

BRAGG, BRAXTON (March 22, 1817-Sept. 27, 1876), Confederate soldier. Major general, then general (1862) commanding the 2nd Corps in Kentucky and Tennessee during the Civil War. **[100]**

BROWN, JOHN (May 9, 1800-Dec. 2, 1859), Abolitionist. Proposed (from 1856) abolishing slavery by force; involved in Kan-

sas unrest (1856); with financial aid of Massachusetts Abolitionists, seized federal arsenal at Harpers Ferry, Va. (Oct. 16-17, 1859), as a base of operations for freeing slaves; apprehended, convicted, and hanged (Dec. 2, 1859); became a martyr to Northern Abolitionists and was commemorated in marching song "John Brown's Body." **[24]**

BROWN, JOSEPH EMERSON (April 15, 1821-Nov. 30, 1894), lawyer and public official. Governor of Georgia (1857-65); chief justice (1868-70) of the Georgia Supreme Court; U.S. senator (1880-91). **[81]**

BROWNSON, ORESTES A. (Sept. 16, 1803-April 17, 1876), clergyman and writer. Universalist minister (1826-29); Unitarian minister (1832-44); converted to Roman Catholicism (1844); published *Brownson's Quarterly* (1844-65, 1872-75) as a journal of personal opinion. **[86]** See also Author Index, Vol. 6.

BUCHANAN, JAMES (April 23, 1791-June 1, 1868), lawyer and statesman. Fifteenth President of the United States (1857-61); U.S. representative from Pennsylvania (1821-31); minister to Russia (1832-33); U.S. senator (1834-45); secretary of state under Polk; minister to Great Britain (1853-56). **[39]**

BUCKNER, THOMAS (fl. 1863), journalist. Author of *A Thrilling Narrative from the Lips of the Sufferers of the Late Detroit Riot* (1863). [112]

BURN, JAMES D. (fl. 1865), English writer. Author of *Three Years Among the Working-Classes in the United States During the War* (1865) and *The Autobiography of a Begger-Boy*. [132]

BURROWS, JOHN LANSING (fl. 1863), clergyman. Pastor (*c*. 1863) of the First Baptist Church of Richmond, Va. [91]

BUTLER, BENJAMIN F. (Nov. 5, 1818-Jan. 11, 1893), Union soldier, lawyer, and public official. Military governor of New Orleans (1862); U.S. representative from Massachusetts (1867-75, 1877-79); governor (1882-84). [55]

CHESNUT, MARY BOYKIN (1823-*c*. 1885), diarist. Daughter of Gov. Stephen Miller of South Carolina; wife of James Chesnut, a former U.S. senator and military aide to Jefferson Davis; author of a journal published (1905) as *A Diary From Dixie*. [62]

CHOATE, RUFUS (Oct. 1, 1799-July 13, 1859), lawyer and public official. U.S. representative from Massachusetts (1831-34); U.S. senator (1841-45); attorney general of Massachusetts (1853-54); leader of the Massachusetts bar. [7] See also Author Index, Vol. 7.

COOPER, PETER (Feb. 12, 1791-April 4, 1883), manufacturer and inventor. Manufactured the first steam locomotive built in America (1830); developed the first structural iron for fireproof buildings (1854); founded (1857-59) Cooper Union in New York City for the advancement of science and art. [21]

CRITTENDEN, JOHN J. (Sept. 10, 1787-July 26, 1863), lawyer and public official. U.S. senator from Kentucky (1817-19, 1835-41, 42-48, 55-61); U.S. district attorney for Kentucky (1827-29); U.S. attorney general (1840-41) under W. H. Harrison and Tyler and (1850-53) under Fillmore. [40, 48]

DAVIS, JEFFERSON (June 3, 1808-Dec. 6, 1889), soldier and statesman. Served with the army on the frontier (1828-35) and in the Mexican War (1846-47); U.S. representative from Mississippi (1845-46); U.S. senator (1847-51, 1857-61); secretary of war under Pierce; president of the Confederate States of America (1861-65); captured by the Union Army and imprisoned (1865); released (May 14, 1867); wrote *The Rise and Fall of the Confederate Government* (1881). [45, 52, 137]

DICEY, EDWARD (1832-1911), English journalist. Special correspondent (1862-69) for the *London Daily Telegraph* and editor (1870-89) of the *London Observer*. [115]

DICKINSON, EMILY (Dec. 10, 1830-May 15, 1886), poetess. Born, lived, and died at Amherst, Mass.; spent later years (from 1860) in seclusion; wrote the major portion of her poetry between 1858 and 1866, some of it in response to a frustrated romantic attachment, possibly for the Rev. Charles Wadsworth of Philadelphia; seven volumes (1890, 1891, 1896, 1914, 1929, 1932, 1945) of poetry published after her death. [85]

DOUGLAS, STEPHEN A. (April 23, 1813-June 3, 1861), lawyer, orator, and political leader. Justice (1841-43) of the Illinois Supreme Court; U.S. representative (1843-47); U.S. senator (1847-61); drafted the Kansas-Nebraska Bill (1854); engaged in the famed series of debates with Abraham Lincoln (1858). [1, 2] See also Author Index, Vol. 8.

EMERSON, RALPH WALDO (May 25, 1803-April 27, 1882), poet, essayist, and philosopher. Wrote *Nature* (1836) and *Essays* (1841, 1844) on his transcendentalist philosophy, and for many years kept his *Journals;* edited (1842-44) the *Dial;* lectured in England and in the U.S. on a variety of subjects, such as self-reliance, individual freedom, and abolition of slavery. [12] See also Author Index, Vols. 6, 7, 8.

EMMETT, DANIEL DECATUR (Oct. 29, 1815-June 28, 1904), minstrel singer and composer. Wrote both words and music for "Dixie" (1859), which became the unofficial national anthem of the South. [26] See also Author Index, Vol. 6.

FIELD, STEPHEN J. (Nov. 4, 1816-April 9, 1899), jurist. Justice (1857-63) of the California Supreme Court; associate justice (1863-97) of the U.S. Supreme Court. [15] See also Author Index, Vol. 10.

GIBBONS, JAMES SLOAN (July 1, 1810-Oct. 17, 1892), Abolitionist, banker, and financial writer. Wrote *The Public Debt of the United States* (1867); gave financial support to the *National Anti-Slavery Standard;* wrote the popular Civil War song "We Are Coming, Father Abraham, Three Hundred Thousand More" (1862). [80]

GILMORE, PATRICK S. (Dec. 25, 1829-Sept. 24, 1892), bandmaster and organizer of music festivals. Served as bandmaster with the 24th Massachusetts Regiment during the Civil War and composed the lyric to the marching tune "When Johnny Comes Marching Home." [109]

GODEY, LOUIS ANTOINE (June 6, 1804-Nov. 29, 1878), publisher. Established (1836) the *Philadelphia Saturday News and Literary Gazette* and (1842) the *Lady's Musical Library;* published (1830-77) *Godey's Lady's Book,* which attained a circulation of 150,000 (1858) and was the most widely read women's magazine of its time. [19]

GOODING, JAMES HENRY (1835-?), Union soldier. Served with the all-Negro 54th Massachusetts Infantry Regiment during the Civil War. [108]

GRANT, ULYSSES S. (April 27, 1822-July 23, 1885), soldier and statesman. Eighteenth President of the United States (1869-77); served in U.S. Army during Mexican War; commanded Department of the Tennessee (1862-63); promoted to lieutenant general and commander of all U.S. armies (1863-65); received Lee's surrender at Appomattox Court House (April 9, 1865); promoted to general (1866); wrote *Personal Memoirs* (1885). [158] See also Author Index, Vol. 10.

GRAY, SYLVESTER (fl. 1860), pioneer. Defended the right of Negro settlers to stake land claims in the West. [34]

GREELEY, HORACE (Feb. 3, 1811-Nov. 29, 1872), editor and political leader. Founded (1834) the *New Yorker* and merged it (1841) with the *New York Tribune;* under his editorship (1841-72) the *Tribune* supported the Free Soil movement, abolition of slavery, and the Lincoln administra-

tion's conduct of the Civil War. [22, 75, 155] See also Author Index, Vol. 8.

GREENHOW, ROSE O'NEAL (?-1864), Confederate spy. Wife of physician and historian Robert Greenhow; arrested and tried (March 25, 1862) for spying and treason; returned to South. Drowned off the Carolina coast while attempting to smuggle gold through the Union naval blockade. [68]

HAWTHORNE, NATHANIEL (July 4, 1804-May 19, 1864), novelist. Gathered material for his writing during residences in Salem, Mass. (1804-37), at Boston Customhouse (1839-40), at Brook Farm (1841), as U.S. consul in Great Britain (1853-57), and in Italy (1858-59); wrote *Twice-Told Tales* (1837, 1842), *The Scarlet Letter* (1850), *The House of the Seven Gables* (1851), *The Blithedale Romance* (1852), *The Marble Faun* (1860). [87] See also Author Index, Vol. 7.

HOLMES, OLIVER WENDELL (Aug. 29, 1809-Oct. 7, 1894), physician, poet, and humorist. Professor of anatomy (1838-40) at Dartmouth College and (1847-82) at Harvard Medical School, wrote humorous works (*The Autocrat of the Breakfast-Table,* 1857), poetry ("Old Ironsides," "The Chambered Nautilus," "The Wonderful One-Hoss Shay"), biographies (*Ralph Waldo Emerson,* 1885), and hymns ("Lord of all being! throned afar"). [6, 27] See also Author Index, Vols. 8, 11.

HOWE, JULIA WARD (May 27, 1819-Oct. 17, 1910), author and social reformer. With her husband, Samuel Gridley Howe, edited *The Commonwealth;* composed "The Battle Hymn of the Republic" (1862); led woman suffrage movement (from 1868) and international peace movement (from 1870); wrote poetry, biographies, and travel sketches. [64]

HUMPHREYS, BENJAMIN G. (Aug. 24 or 26, 1808-Dec. 20, 1882), Confederate soldier, planter, and public official. First post-Civil War governor of Mississippi (1865-68); removed from the governorship (June 1868) by federal troops during Radical Reconstruction. [156]

JARVES, JAMES JACKSON (Aug. 20, 1818-June 28, 1888), editor, author, critic, and pioneer art collector. Founded (1840) and edited the *Polynesian,* one of the first newspapers in the Hawaiian Islands; U.S. vice-consul at Florence, Italy (1880-82); wrote numerous histories, travel and art books. [117]

JOHNSON, ANDREW (Dec. 29, 1808-July 31, 1875), soldier, legislator, and statesman. Seventeenth President of the United States (1865-69); U.S. representative from Tennessee (1843-53); governor (1853-57); U.S. senator (1857-62, 1875); brigadier general, U.S. Army, and military governor of Tennessee (1862-64); Vice-President of the United States (March 4-April 15, 1865) under Lincoln; impeached and acquitted (1868) by Congress for his Reconstruction policies. [144, 145] See also Author Index, Vol. 10.

KITTREDGE, WALTER (fl. 1862-1864), New Hampshire ballad singer. Wrote "Tenting on the Old Camp Ground" (1862) shortly after he was drafted into the Army during the Civil War. [122]

LEE, ROBERT E. (Jan. 19, 1807-Oct. 12, 1870), soldier. Superintendent (1852-55) of the U.S. Military Academy at West Point; commanded U.S. troops at Harpers Ferry (1859); at outbreak of Civil War, resigned from U.S. Army to join Confederate cause; commanded the Army of Northern Virginia; appointed general in chief of all Confederate armies (Feb. 6, 1865); surrendered to Grant at Appomattox Court House (April 9, 1865); president (1865-70) of Washington College (renamed Washington and Lee University). [51, 141, 150]

LEWIS, ELLIS (May 16, 1798-March 19, 1871), jurist. President judge (1833-51) of U.S. District Courts in Pennsylvania; justice (1851-54) and chief justice (1854-58) of the Pennsylvania Supreme Court; wrote An Abridgment of the Criminal Law of the United States (1848). [8]

LINCOLN, ABRAHAM (Feb. 12, 1809-April 15, 1865), lawyer and statesman. Sixteenth President of the United States (1861-65); U.S. representative from Illinois (1847-49); defeated in senatorial campaign (1858) by Stephen A. Douglas; issued the Emancipation Proclamation (Jan. 1, 1863); delivered dedicatory address at Gettysburg National Cemetery (Nov. 19, 1863); assassinated by John Wilkes

Booth, a fanatical actor, only five days after Lee's surrender to Grant at Appomattox Court House. [1, 2, 20, 30, 49, 50, 53, 58, 67, 75, 88, 90, 98, 103, 107, 110, 114, 128, 136, 142] See also Author Index, Vols. 6, 8.

LOCKE, DAVID ROSS, "Petroleum V. Nasby" (Sept. 20, 1833-Feb. 15, 1888), journalist and political satirist. Founded (1852) the Plymouth (Ohio) Advertiser; edited (c. 1854-64) the Findley (Ohio) Jeffersonian and (1865-71) the Toledo Blade; the Nasby political satires appeared first (March 21, 1861) in the Jeffersonian and later (1865-87) in the Blade. [69, 146]

LONGFELLOW, HENRY WADSWORTH (Feb. 27, 1807-March 24, 1882), poet. Professor of modern languages (1829-35) at Bowdoin College and (1835-54) at Harvard College; wrote Ballads and Other Poems (1841), Evangeline (1847), The Song of Hiawatha (1855), The Courtship of Miles Standish (1858), Tales of a Wayside Inn (1863); translated The Divine Comedy of Dante Alighieri (3 vols., 1865-67). [29, 116] See also Author Index, Vol. 7.

LOWELL, JAMES RUSSELL (Feb. 22, 1819-Aug. 12, 1891), poet, literary critic, and diplomat. Professor of modern languages (1855-86) at Harvard College; edited (1857-61) the Atlantic Monthly and (1864-72) the North American Review; minister to Spain (1877-80); minister to Great Britain (1880-85); wrote Poems (1844), A Fable for Critics, The Biglow Papers, and The Vision of Sir Launfal (1848), Three Memorial Poems (1877), Democracy and Other Addresses (1887), Political Essays (1888). [42] See also Author Index, Vol. 7.

McCARTY, HARRY (fl. 1861), composer and singer of songs of the Confederacy. [60]

McCLELLAN, GEORGE B. (Dec. 3, 1826-Oct. 29, 1885), soldier and public official. Served in Mexican War; recommended new type of saddle used in U.S. Army cavalry; commissioned major general at outbreak of Civil War; commanded Department of the Ohio and Department of the Potomac (1861); general in chief of all U.S. armies (1861-62); Democratic candidate for President (1864), defeated by Lincoln; governor of New Jersey (1878-81). [74]

SHAW, HENRY WHEELER, "Josh Billings" (April 21, 1818-Oct. 14, 1885), humorist. Wrote *Josh Billings, His Sayings* (1865), *Josh Billings' Farmers' Allminax* (annual editions, 1870-79), *Josh Billings Struggling With Things* (1881). [32]

SHERMAN, JOHN (May 10, 1823-Oct. 22, 1900), lawyer and public official. Brother of William Tecumseh Sherman; U.S. representative from Ohio (1855-61); U.S. senator (1861-77, 1881-97) and chairman (1867-77) of the Senate Finance Committee; author of the Sherman Anti-Trust Act (1890) and the Sherman Silver Purchase Act (1890); secretary of the treasury under Hayes; secretary of state (1897-98) under McKinley. [41, 154]

SHERMAN, WILLIAM TECUMSEH (Feb. 8, 1820-Feb. 14, 1891), soldier. Brother of John Sherman; served in the first Battle of Bull Run (July 21, 1861); major general in command of the Army of the Tennessee (1863) and the military division of the Mississippi (1864); led the "March to the Sea" that ended at Savannah, Ga. (Dec. 21, 1864); received Gen. J. E. Johnston's surrender (April 26, 1865). [92, 101] See also Author Index, Vol. 10.

SMITH, CHARLES H., "Bill Arp" (June 15, 1826-Aug. 24, 1903), journalist and humorist. Wrote humorous social and political commentary for the *Atlanta* (Ga.) *Constitution*; author of *Bill Arp, So Called* (1866), *Bill Arp: From the Uncivil War to Date* (1903). [149]

STANTON, ELIZABETH CADY (Nov. 12, 1815-Oct. 26, 1902), social reformer. Organized the first women's rights convention, Seneca Falls, N.Y. (July 19-20, 1848), from which the woman suffrage movement was launched; first president (1869-90) of the National Woman Suffrage Association. [28]

STEPHENS, ALEXANDER H. (Feb. 11, 1812-March 4, 1883), author and politician. U.S. representative from Georgia (1843-59, 1873-82); Vice-President of the Confederacy (1861-65); U.S. senator-elect, but was refused his seat (1866); governor (1882-83); wrote *A Constitutional View of the Late War Between the States* (1868-70). [37, 119] See also Author Index, Vol. 10.

STEVENS, THADDEUS (April 4, 1792-Aug. 11, 1868), lawyer and public official. U.S. representative from Pennsylvania (1849-53, 1859-68); leader of the Radical Republicans in Congress after the Civil War; proposed and managed the impeachment trial of Andrew Johnson. [70, 151] See also Author Index, Vol. 6.

STEWARD, IRA (March 10, 1831-March 13, 1883), labor leader. At the convention of the International Union of Machinists and Blacksmiths, Boston, Mass. (1863), he secured passage of the first demand for an eight-hour labor law; president of the Boston Eight-Hour League and of the National Ten-Hour League. [153]

STRONG, GEORGE TEMPLETON (1801-?), diarist. [9] See also Author Index, Vol. 6.

SUMNER, CHARLES (Jan. 6, 1811-March 11, 1874), Abolitionist and statesman. U.S. senator from Massachusetts (1851-74); leader of the antislavery faction in Congress and the first prominent official to urge emancipation (Oct. 1861); severely injured when attacked in the Senate (May 22, 1856) by Rep. Preston Brooks of South Carolina for his remarks on slavery. [65] See also Author Index, Vols. 7, 8, 10.

TAPPAN, HENRY P. (April 18, 1805-Nov. 15, 1881), educator, clergyman, and philosopher. Professor of moral and intellectual philosophy (1832-37) at University of the City of New York (New York University); first president (1852-63) of the University of Michigan; wrote *Elements of Logic* (1844), *University Education* (1851). [14]

TERRY, DAVID SMITH (March 8, 1823-Aug. 14, 1889), soldier, lawyer, jurist, and political leader. Served in the War for Texan Independence and the Mexican War; justice (1855-57) and chief justice (1857-59) of the California Supreme Court; shot and killed while attacking U.S. Supreme Court Justice Stephen J. Field for rendering a verdict unfavorable to him in a court case. [15]

THOREAU, HENRY DAVID (July 12, 1817-May 6, 1862), writer, poet, and philosopher. Schoolteacher (1839-41) in Concord, Mass.; resided (1841-43, 1847-48) with Ralph Waldo Emerson and associated with the New England Transcendentalists; moved to a cabin at Walden Pond (1845-47) to write and to study nature; wrote *A Week on the Concord and Merrimack Rivers* (1849), *Walden; or, Life in the Woods* (1854), and his *Journals* (20 vols., 1906). [23] See also Author Index, Vols. 7, 8.

TIMROD, HENRY (Dec. 8, 1828-Oct. 6, 1867), poet. Earned recognition as the "laureate of the Confederacy" for his poems inspired by the Civil War, among them "Charleston," "The Cotton Boll," "Katie," "A Cry to Arms," "Carolina," and "Magnolia Cemetery." [46, 124]

TOOMBS, ROBERT (July 2, 1810-Dec. 15, 1885), lawyer and public official. U.S. representative from Georgia (1845-53); U.S. senator (1853-61); secretary of state of the Confederacy (1861); brigadier general, Confederate Army. [37]

TROLLOPE, ANTHONY (April 24, 1815-Dec. 6, 1882), English novelist. Author of more than fifty novels, including the "Barsetshire Chronicles" and the "Parliamentary series"; traveled in U.S. on a mission for the British Post Office and wrote *North America* (1862) to describe his impressions. [83]

VALLANDIGHAM, CLEMENT L. (July 29, 1820-June 17, 1871), lawyer and political leader. U.S. representative from Ohio (1857-63); as leader of the "peace Democrats" (Copperheads), defied Gen. Burnside's order banning declarations of sympathy with the Southern cause; arrested (May 5, 1863), tried, and convicted of expressing treasonable sympathy; banished to the Confederacy. [94]

WADE, BENJAMIN F. (Oct. 27, 1800-March 2, 1878), lawyer and political leader. U.S. senator from Ohio (1851-69); a leader of the antislavery group in the Senate; joint author of Wade-Davis Bill (Aug. 5, 1864) declaring Congress the supreme authority on Reconstruction policy. [40]

WALKER, ALEXANDER (Oct. 13, 1818-Jan. 24, 1893), journalist and author. Manager (c. 1840-46) of the *New Orleans Jeffersonian*; editor (1855-57) of the *Cincinnati Enquirer* and (1861-65) of the *New Orleans Delta*; wrote *The Life of Andrew Jackson* (1860). [77]

WELLES, GIDEON (July 1, 1802-Feb. 11, 1878), public official and political leader. Co-owner and editor (1826-36) of the *Hartford Times*; helped organize the Republican Party, and founded (1856) a Republican newspaper, the *Hartford Evening Press*; secretary of the navy under Lincoln and Johnson. [143]

WHITMAN, WALT (May 31, 1819-March 26, 1892), poet, schoolteacher, and journalist. Edited (1846-48) the *Brooklyn Eagle* and wrote (1848) for the *New Orleans Crescent*; hospital nurse (1862-64) in Washington D.C.; clerk in U.S. Department of the Interior (1865), but dismissed by the secretary of the interior because of the "licentiousness" of his poetry; wrote *Leaves of Grass* (1855 and nine later revisions), *Drum-Taps* (1865), *Democratic Vistas* (1871). [31, 138] See also Author Index, Vols. 7, 8, 10, 11.

WHITTIER, JOHN GREENLEAF (Dec. 17, 1807-Sept. 7, 1892), poet, journalist, Abolitionist, and humanitarian. Editor (1830-32) of the *New England Weekly Review;* wrote *Justice and Expediency* and poems in behalf of the Abolitionist cause; also wrote religious works and poems of New England, including "Snow-Bound" (1866). [78, 159] See also Author Index, Vols. 6, 7, 8.

WILKESON, FRANK (fl. 1864), soldier and writer. Private, later an officer, Union Army; wrote account of his war experiences, published in 1887. [121]

WOOD, FERNANDO (June 14, 1812-Feb. 14, 1881), public official and political leader. U.S. representative from New York (1841-43, 1863-65, 1867-81); leader of Tammany Hall; mayor of New York City (1855-58, 1860-62). [43]

WORK, HENRY CLAY (Oct. 1, 1832-June 8, 1884), songwriter. Wrote the famous temperance song "Come Home, Father" (1864), and songs for the Union cause, including "Kingdom Coming" (1861), "Babylon is Fallen!" (1863), and "Marching Through Georgia" (1865). [89, 120, 135]

WYNKOOP, E. W. (fl. 1864), officer, Union Army, assigned to Colorado Territory. [134]